Czempiel Greg.
July 65.

Gregor W. Czempiel
Ottawa Ont. Canada

An Introduction to the Principles of Psychology

Albert H. Hastorf, *Consulting Editor*

Gardner Lindzey and Others
Assessment of Human Motives

Theodore R. Sarbin and Others
Clinical Inference and Cognitive Theory

William C. Schutz
FIRO: A Three-Dimensional Theory of Interpersonal Behavior

B. R. Bugelski

PROFESSOR OF PSYCHOLOGY
UNIVERSITY OF BUFFALO

AN INTRODUCTION TO THE PRINCIPLES OF PSYCHOLOGY

Holt, Rinehart and Winston ***New York***

May, 1961

Printed in the United States of America
Library of Congress Catalog Card Number: 60-6487
21149-0310

for my father and mother

PREFACE

Psychology is frequently described as a "young" science. As a science it may be young, but its problems are as ancient as man. Many of these problems are very complex, and as psychologists struggle with them they discover new problems with ramifications into other areas. The breadth and scope of psychology can be bewildering and a college course in psychology can be a chaotic experience if the student tries to learn "everything." The field of psychology is much too broad to present in any great detail in one course. What has been attempted here is to develop a systematic orientation for the student, a concentration on essentials, the basic principles underlying the superstructure of psychology, the philosophical and logical foundations of psychology as a scientific enterprise.

This text has been prepared for qualified and serious college students. It is not written "up" or "down." Some topics or concepts are difficult to appreciate and require more attention than others. Students looking for "snap" courses should not choose psychology over any other science course. The book is biased, as is any text. Students should know that the bias here is in favor of a biological or physiological orientation. The present writer draws no distinction between "natural" or "physical" and "social" sciences. They are all science if they follow the same assumptions and use objective methods to gather their data. The emphasis in this text is not on physiology as such, but rather on the working principles of psychologists as they approach age-old problems—thinking, feeling, and choosing—and more modern questions in the areas of perception, learning, and cultural interactions. The approach is very general. More specific treatment must be obtained in subsequent courses. No distinction is made in this text between those who plan to "major" in psychology and those who have other goals. Such distinctions are made by those who believe they can break up psychology successfully to suit the consumer. It is doubtful that a smattering of ignorance should be presented to the nonmajor. He is required to make the same effort if he is to be introduced to psychology as a science.

It should be appreciated that this text contains no great parade of facts. The "facts" the author used to teach his students twenty years ago do not appear to be so important or so factual any more. Nor does this text attempt to teach students how to become better adjusted or more effective in social or business affairs. What the student will find will be a great many questions and points of view, differences of opinion, and controversial issues. He should expect his instructor to take issue with the text and expose its inadequacies, for that is education.

While the author takes sole responsibility for the errors and weaknesses of this book it should not be inferred from the number of such inadequacies that he has no friends, that no one tried to save him. On the contrary, many colleagues did their best to improve the working papers the writer imposed upon them. He is greatly indebted to Dr. W. Leslie Barnette for a meticulous and critical analysis of the manuscript. Dr. Herbert Lansdell and Dr. Ira Cohen were especially helpful in their comments. Dr. Walter Cohen, Dr. Raymond Hunt, and Mr. Walter Flakus helped considerably in orienting the writing toward the needs of instructors.

The writer attempted the ancient test or "proof of the pudding" with two classes of beginning students. To do so required copies of the text prior to formal publication. Dr. Olive P. Lester made it possible to provide a multilith edition at the University of Buffalo and in every way encouraged the writer in this work. She also arranged for special classes to try out the text. It is on the basis of work with these classes that the writer has the temerity to offer this book for others to consider.

A professor of philosophy once told the writer that "Books are like babies. You have one; then you have another." The philosopher may or may not have had the author's wife in mind. In this instance, the author's wife was very much involved and the present effort is very much a joint product. She provided many of the illustrations and criticized the manuscript from the point of view of communication, in addition to assisting in the labor of the physical birth of the text.

A special note of appreciation is owed to the broad array of professional critics assembled by the publisher, particularly Professors Elliot Aaronson of Stanford University, Albert H. Hastorf of Dartmouth College, Robert Leeper of the University of Oregon, and Stanley B. Williams of the College of William and Mary. The degree of "ego-involvement" shown in their criticisms suggests that the book will be "provocative." If the students find it so, the writer will be satisfied.

B. R. B.

Buffalo, New York
January, 1960

CONTENTS

LIST OF FIGURES

LIST OF TABLES

PART I

The Modifiable Aspects of Man

CHAPTER 1

Introduction

Popular views of psychology · Scientific views · Obstacles to a definition of psychology · Areas related to psychology · Psychology, a science and a profession · Philosophical origins · Faculty psychology · Schools of psychology · A preliminary definition of psychology · The nature of science · Science and common sense · Parapsychology · Prediction and control · The aims and assumptions of science

Man has lived through the Stone Age, the Iron Age, and the Bronze Age. More recently he has been living in an Electronic or Atomic Age. Now, according to some enthusiasts, he lives in the Age of Psychology.[1] The way psychology is depicted in popular magazines and other mass media might lead to the impression that modern man has arrived at the stage where human affairs and problems are being nicely handled by psychologists using specialized techniques, or, at least, that we are on the brink of such an era. We are told how psychologists test children and adults, how they plan educational and vocational careers, how they handle disordered personalities, how they assist advertisers in controlling our buying habits and patterns of living, how they design our automobiles, airplanes, and even our homes. Business executives are analyzed by psychologists and business trends and cycles are attributed to psychological influences; the conduct of international affairs is, to some extent, based on "psychological warfare." Our novels, TV dramas, movies, even our comic strips as well as serious art, are talked about as "psychological." No walk of life, apparently, is untouched by psychology.

POPULAR VIEWS OF PSYCHOLOGY

Newspapers, magazines, and novels, to say nothing of television and the movies, are devoted to psychological themes, plots, and items of

[1] The expression "Age of Psychology" is the title of a short book by Ernest Havemann. It presents a fair account of the widespread activities of modern psychologists. A full reference to this book will be found in the bibliography at the end of the text. In general, when psychological writers are cited, their names will be followed by the date of publication of the work under consideration.

many kinds. Even "western" stories have become "psychological." Hardly a Sunday supplement can be found in the land which does not discuss the psychology of child rearing, delinquency, sex and divorce, hypnotism, extrasensory perception, or neuroses and psychoses. Every year a new problem is exploited, especially in the summer months (a form of summer madness?), which agitates the public to the point where congressional committees are formed to conduct investigations. One year it is a Bridey Murphy, an eighteenth-century Irish lass, who is discovered by a hypnotist to be wandering around in the body of a twentieth-century woman; another year Johnny can't read, and the next year he reads too many comic books; another year finds us stewing over our horrible educational system compared to that of the Soviets; still another has us pondering the three or four faces of Eve, houses where furniture moves about by itself, tranquilizing drugs, the sex life of the American male, the American female, and who knows what next.

Some writers are gaily optimistic about the benefits mankind is to derive from scientific "human engineering." They foretell our enjoying a carefree Utopia scientifically planned by psychologists who will see that we even marry mates with appropriate brain wave patterns. Others view with alarm the horrible prospects of a world where psychologists will assist advertisers in "the hidden sell"[2] by exciting our unconscious minds with messages that we cannot see on our television and motion picture screens, or exploit other unconscious mechanisms through "hidden persuaders." Some novelists, like George Orwell, picture a *1984* where the human mind has become completely enslaved by "brain-washing" procedures. Aldous Huxley (1958) is still fighting the *Brave New World* he conjured up in 1932, and is now looking for solace in exotic drugs which provide beautiful visions and searching for new powers of the human mind by which the race can be saved.

SCIENTIFIC VIEWS

In all of the talk about psychology and psychological influences, it is rarely that a psychologist is doing the talking. For the most part, psychologists are quiet workers in academic surroundings who publish their findings in professional journals that are read only by other psychologists. They take little part in public debate and most of them are inclined to dismiss nine-tenths of what appears in popular media as sheer rubbish. Some would argue that ten-tenths would be a more appropriate figure. It may be an Age of Psychology, but if it is, most psy-

[2] "Motivation Research" or MR has been described for the popular reader by Vance Packard (1957).

chologists are not quite ready to welcome it. The citizen, still, is going to be assaulted daily by claims based on alleged findings of modern psychology. It behooves him to learn something about the actual findings, methods, and beliefs of psychologists as they work about in their laboratories and clinics so that he will be in a better position to avoid erroneous arguments and influences and consequent ill-advised action. In view of the scope and power of the daily assault, there appears to be "a clear and present danger." It is the purpose of this text to help mitigate this danger to some degree.

It was just remarked that psychologists rarely speak to the public about what psychology can do or cannot do. Some do speak to a psychological public, that is, to a scientific body, and it might be worth our while to consider what they say on this issue when they give it some thought. We can take as a sample the remarks of an outstanding and outspoken American psychologist, B. F. Skinner, of Harvard University, who engaged in a debate before the American Psychological Association with Carl Rogers, an equally prominent psychologist, in the summer of 1956.[3] We shall have occasion to talk about the work of these psychologists again, and it is well to learn their names and views.

In his remarks, Skinner argued that psychology as a science of behavior had arrived at the state where it could, when applied by men of good will, result in developing people to the point where they could all be "truly happy, secure, productive, creative, and forward looking." The principles and techniques by which this could be done we will leave for later except to note that they involve controlling the environment and learning history. The promises or goals that Skinner described are all that concern us now. Skinner claimed that by the proper use of psychological science people can be educated, trained, or reared to far greater standards of performance than any we dream of now. In other places, Skinner has remarked that all students can, in effect, earn A grades, if they are properly taught. Delinquency, disorderliness, and undesired modes of behavior can be eliminated, and a happy, adjusted, creative race can be developed. If psychology is really at this stage, it is certainly a subject to be studied avidly, and the student should waste no time getting himself thoroughly involved.

What did Rogers reply to Skinner in his part of the debate? Did he deny Skinner's confident claims? Not at all. He reacted primarily with a mild horror at the prospect of controlling humanity to the extent required to achieve the goals and then he questioned the capacity of scientists to establish such goals in the first place. Is it good for everyone to be happy, adjusted, creative, healthy, productive? How do we know?

[3] A verbatim account of the debate was published in *Science*. See Skinner (1956).

It is not the business of scientists, said Rogers, to establish *values*. Their job is to discover facts and principles.[4] Skinner, in rebuttal, asked, Who is better qualified to establish values? Are not values being established all the time by people who are unqualified, incompetent, and far from admirable? Are psychologists to stand aside and merely serve the wishes of the next tyrant or dictator who chooses to use the human race for his own value system? Both Skinner and Rogers agreed that psychological principles can be used both by men of evil will and by men of good will. If this is so, then mankind had better look into the matter, and quickly.

At no time in the debate did Rogers challenge Skinner's claims that psychology is an extremely "potent" science. This might be interpreted then as agreement with the basic proposition that it is possible through control of the environment and training practices so to manipulate the human organism as to create pretty much what is desired by the trainer.

It is interesting to observe that the same kind of claim was made by John B. Watson in 1930. Watson is considered by some to have been the most important American psychologist (see Bergman, 1957). In 1912 he launched Behaviorism, a movement which strongly affected the development of psychology in the United States. In the thirties Watson's influence began to wane and his approach to psychological problems was modified in a somewhat more sophisticated Neo-Behaviorism. We shall consider these movements in greater detail later. For the moment we are concerned only with making the point that most American psychologists today are, to one degree or another, "behavioristic," i.e., concerned with an objective study of the activities or "behavior" of organisms as they live in and respond to influences in their environments. In many respects Skinner's views parallel Watson's, particularly in connection with the possibilities of controlling behavior through the manipulation of environmental influences.

Returning now to Watson's claim, we note that he offered to take any normal child and make him a "rich man, poor man, beggar man, thief, doctor, lawyer," or any of the rest of the nursery jingle, if he were given sufficient help and full control of the environment. No one ever offered Watson the control of the children he wanted and his claim was never brought to a test. Even with his own children, a psychologist can excuse failure to produce the ideal results because he has not been given sufficient control over the environment. Children, for example, have to be entrusted to the schools, be exposed to neighbors that are not of one's choice, and in thousands of ways come in contact with social factors over which psychologists have no control. One cannot even argue

[4] As a matter of fact, Rogers (1956) is quite convinced that psychologists are able to arrange conditions that will seriously modify behavior, for good or evil.

that, given all of the limitations, psychologist's children should be, somehow, a better adjusted lot, on the whole, than the children of chemists or other kinds of educators. The psychologist can claim that given the world as it is, children have to accommodate themselves to it and any effort to "improve" the child along any special lines would result in a greater maladjustment. However the argument may run, the claims of Skinner and Watson have not been put to a test and until they are the argument is fruitless. In this text we will examine the principles Watson and Skinner indicate they might employ, and considering some of the factors involved in determining behavior, we can try to arrive at an evaluation of their claims, at least in principle.

Lest the student come to the conclusion that all psychologists are ready to take over and guide the human race to happier days, it is important to note that while they might wish that this were possible, the great majority probably is far less confident of the outcome of practical applications of psychology to human affairs. Most writers prefer to emphasize the infancy of psychology; comparatively speaking, they point out, psychology is really the latest science to appear on the historical stage. While laboratory methods were introduced in the study of human sense capacities in the 1850's, and a formal laboratory established in Leipzig in 1879 by Wilhelm Wundt, much of what was studied was only superficially interesting from the viewpoint of the control of behavior. Many American psychologists have written about the past in terms of erroneous orientations, false starts, and blind-alley approaches; some even feel that psychology did not really begin until they began to devote some attention to the subject. We might argue, for example, that everything written before 1935 or 1950 is only of historical interest and that psychology started with the work of this or that currently important theorist. Everything that came before was analogous to the days of alchemy in relation to chemistry. Since we are never likely to be in a position to evaluate our own efforts historically, it is impossible to say what the judgment of current psychology will be in 2058. The evaluators of that time might regard the 1950's as the Age of Fable instead of the Age of Psychology.

One psychologist, Kenneth Spence, of Iowa, should be heard from in the light of the above remarks. Spence (1956) believes, perhaps more strongly than most, that psychology is just beginning to become a science, that it is just learning how to think about the analysis of behavior, and that it is just starting to develop some preliminary orientations about the simplest kinds of organisms. Spence argues that psychology is just now developing "low order laws" involving "specific response variables in the several specific experimental situations" which are yet to be integrated or unified with "higher generalizations (i.e., theories)." To "the question as to whether the theories developed from these laboratory experiments, when sufficiently elaborated, will ever provide for the explanation and control of behavior in real life situations," Spence states: "No definitive answer, of course, can be given at the present time, for as yet none of them is sufficiently abstract or complete to account even for all the laboratory findings. One can only point to the success that such types of theory have had in the physical sciences and assume that the same developments will occur in psychology."

OBSTACLES TO A DEFINITION OF PSYCHOLOGY

We have been talking about psychology conversationally. The term is a familiar one; everyone uses it. However, like many other scientific terms—"atom," "fusion," or "gravity"—its meaning is far from clearly appreciated by the people who use it. This may be especially so with the term "psychology" because, whatever else psychology may involve, it refers somehow to people. Everyone has experience with people and thinks he knows something about them. In some vague way people regard psychology as having something to do with what "makes you tick," with the "mind," with influencing people, usually through devious and indirect, if not occult, means. When the average person meets a psychologist he may become wary lest he give himself away, fearful that the psychologist will "read" his mind or otherwise control him. The fact that none of this is true cannot be impressed upon such people; they even take the protest as a sly psychological trick. Much of the confusion about the nature of psychology has been created by motion picture portrayals of psychologists as bald-domed, mysterious characters with heavy lenses over piercing eyes and by the popular press in its depictions of psychological issues and practices including such matters as brain washing, mental testing, juvenile delinquency, and crime detection. Detectives in popular fiction search for the "motive" and consider the workings of the "criminal mind," using their "little gray cells" to bring the culprit to book. Actually, psychologists are quite ordinary people who have specialized in one line of study just as have geologists, physicists, or mathematicians. They lead the same kinds of lives as other scientists—they marry, have children, mow their lawns, and worry over death and taxes. It is impossible to use "appearance" to pick out psychologists from any assortment of people.

Because "we are all psychologists in our own little ways" and we have all had experiences in dealing with people and appreciating their ways and motives, we get impatient with the problem of definition. Yet most of what the average person regards as psychology is just about so much fiction and before any intelligent start can be made in dealing with the subject, a lot of rubbishy thinking about psychology has to be swept away. Other scientists do not have this onerous task to perform. Physicists do not waste time defining their subject. They can assume that their students do not pretend to know anything about the subject and they can go right to work. Psychologists have to begin by clearing away the mess of superstition, "common sense," and general misinformation about their subject.

Areas related to psychology

To cut out a scientific area for specialized study is a difficult task, particularly so when we are dealing with a new science which is intruding upon ancient and established disciplines as well as other new ones. It is especially difficult when some problems adopted as their own by psychologists have already been examined to some degree by older sciences and when there is considerable overlap of interest and methods. We shall have to treat this problem at length later. For the present we will have done enough if we differentiate psychology from some closely allied approaches like psychiatry, psychoanalysis, physiology, anthropology, and sociology.

We can best start with psychiatry. This is a medical specialty requiring a medical degree and a residency in a "mental" hospital. The work of psychiatrists is to diagnose and give therapy to mental patients. They do this on the basis of clinical experience and medical studies. They are licensed to use drugs, electrical shock, diet control, and surgery. Psychologists without medical degrees are not allowed by law to do any of these things. Sometimes psychiatrists use therapeutic methods consisting primarily of listening and talking. Psychologists are allowed to do this and some psychologists do participate in therapy involving no physical treatment of the patients. The services of "clinical psychologists" frequently include the administration of tests which are used for diagnostic purposes or counseling clients. When psychologists do therapy, it is usually in connection with less severe cases (neurotics compared with psychotics), and often in co-operation with psychiatrists or other physicians.

Psychoanalysis is a very specialized technique of psychotherapy which is practiced by some psychiatrists, perhaps in some degree by a majority of psychiatrists. Again, a medical degree is virtually a necessity. There are some psychoanalysts who do not have medical degrees, but they are extremely rare. Psychoanalysts must first be analyzed themselves and attend special schools to learn the techniques and theory. You do not walk up to a psychologist and say "Psychoanalyze me." It is most unlikely that the psychologist would be qualified to do so. Most psychologists know something about psychoanalysis, to be sure, but they do not practice it. This is basically a medical specialty (which has practically nothing to do with medicine). Psychologists might do research in psychoanalytic as well as in psychiatric areas but they do not regard themselves as psychoanalysts. Incidentally, you should not ask for a psychoanalysis as if it were but a moment's work. It takes about three years.

In contrast to psychiatrists and psychoanalysts who are medical men, psychologists are most reasonably defined as people who have had graduate school training in psychology, usually up to the level of the Ph.D. Usually they are members of the American Psychological Association. They work in academic situations, laboratories, or clinics and sometimes are associated with various social agencies (family, child welfare) or educational systems as "school psychologists." Sometimes psychologists set up "private practice" and may work at diagnosis or therapy. Some psychologists work in industry helping to design machinery or various kinds of equipment for efficient use. The government also employs some psychologists in various departments where their work is chiefly of an educational or psychometric nature (psychometrics includes mental and personality testing or "measurement"). Some psychologists are concerned mainly with testing children and adults for various aptitudes and frequently function as counselors or vocational guides. Many states have legal definitions of psychologists and will certify or license properly qualified individuals. In the absence of such laws anyone can call himself a psychologist and hang out a shingle offering his services to anyone who cares to employ him. In most large cities a number of quacks mulct an innocent public by offering to improve personality, memory, or whatever is desired by the customer. Psychology is rapidly becoming a highly specialized profession involving years of preparation and adherence to a rigid code of ethics. At present there are about 16,000 recognized psychologists in the United States in contrast to about 250,000 medical doctors.

Before we continue with the description of psychology and psychologists it might be useful to point out the difference between physiologists and sociologists and psychologists. Physiologists are primarily concerned with specific organs of the body or organ systems like digestion, circulation, the kidney, the ear, and so on. Psychologists, while also interested in the physiology of the body, are far more concerned with the complete, organized, more or less intact body as a whole. Some specialists are working so close to a hypothetical borderline that it is difficult to do anything except call them "physiological psychologists." Such workers might be primarily concerned with some small section of the brain as far as their working day is concerned. If they are psychologists, however, they are concerned with how this small part affects the whole or some general activity like learning, and not with the part per se. Other psychologists are interested in activities of groups of people, how individuals make up and interact in groups, how an individual affects a group and vice versa. It is difficult to distinguish these from sociologists and anthropologists who are primarily concerned with groups and the role of culture in group behavior.

Though psychologists divide themselves into some eighteen divisions in the American Psychological Association, and though their interests run from infancy to old age and crisscross over various other areas, they do have a more or less common bond in their basic education as well as fundamental interests in the behavior of human beings, some more practically, others more abstractly. They are all interested in "human nature" or "man."

Psychology, a science and a profession

We can return now to the problem of defining psychology. It is not a simple matter of putting together a number of words that form a sentence. In fact, books have been written about the definition of psychology, and even these have not proved adequate as the growth and complexity of psychology quickly exceed the definitions so elaborately worked out. One of the troubles with defining psychology is that it is not a single thing nor a static one. What was psychology in 1879 is no longer regarded as even a serious part of psychology today. What is psychology in England or France is not regarded with much concern in the United States and vice versa. In the United States, particularly, psychology must be thought of in at least two different senses. On the one hand it is an academic discipline, a division of science, and on the other, it is a profession or technology. As a profession it has primary aims and interests that are quite in contrast to those held by academic scientists. The practitioners are interested in advising, counseling, helping people. They are concerned with individuals, with cases, with clients, patients, or customers; their aims are practical. As scientists, psychologists have no more concern about people than do physicists or mathematicians; many of them never work with people at all, confining their efforts to rats, pigeons, monkeys, dogs, and cats. When they do study people, they are interested in them only as "subjects" in an experiment, and not as personalities. As a science, psychology has very little to do with people, at least in the flesh. Scientific psychologists are interested in people *in the abstract,* in "man," not men. It is important to emphasize this point as many students are drawn to psychology because they want to work with people, they are interested in human problems, they want to help. Such students might eventually work out as clinicians or other kinds of professional workers. They might find it difficult, however, to undergo the scientific training that is usually a prerequisite because so little of what they would study would have any bearing on their interests or future practices. They might do better to enter some field of social work.

The above remarks are not meant to draw a black and white distinction between academic psychologists and practitioners. Many practitioners are engaged full time in research of many kinds (evaluating therapy, conducting and evaluating experimental programs in education, counseling, rehabilitation, etc.). Other practitioners, singly or in teams, devote at least part of their time to research activities. At the same time, many academic psychologists confine themselves to administrative or teaching activities and may do little or no research. At the present time, psychologists receive pretty much the same kinds of training regardless of their eventual employment. The training usually involves a heavy emphasis on research methodology, and most psychologists apply such training to the extent that their employment makes research possible.

We are almost ready to begin our definition of psychology. So far we have been emphasizing what psychology is not. We will have to continue in this vein for a while as we develop the definition because part of the function of a definition is to differentiate, that is, to discriminate some one thing from others that might be mistaken for it or related to it in some fashion. Although the student might be getting impatient by now and be asking for a plain statement of the score, it is improper for anyone to state categorically that psychology is this or that without taking into account the long history of psychology with its many changes of emphasis. A historical perspective is the best antidote for fixed ideas the student may have brought with him.

PHILOSOPHICAL ORIGINS

The term "psyche" is of Greek origin and referred to some presumed nonphysical aspects of the body variously referred to over the centuries as "spirit," "soul," "form," and sometimes "function." The English word "mind" is the most popular current equivalent. The term "ology" refers to study, and consequently, "psychology" for centuries past was identified as the study of the mind.

The term "mind" is very useful in common conversation—it is used in many ways, and some degree of communication is obviously established or the term would die out. In talking with our friends we might use the term in such contexts as "Make up your mind," "Are you losing your mind?," "I see it in my mind's eye," "That *reminds* me." "He's got a fine mind" (or a feeble one, or a keen one), "My mind tells me one thing; my heart tells me another," "It's all in your mind," "He has the mind of a criminal" (or a two-year-old, or a woman), "His mind is far away," or "He can put his mind to it," and so on and on. Now, obviously, people who say these things intend to convey some information, and they do. Equally obviously other words could be used to convey the same information and the term "mind" could be dropped if we decided to drop it. There is no quarrel with popular usage of the term. The trouble comes in at a much higher level when we try to study the mind. To study something we must be able to apply some technique or methodology to it. In studying physical things, we can weigh, measure, touch or feel, or look at the object in direct or indirect ways. When we have to deal indirectly with something, as with atoms, for example, we have to measure some indirect *indicators* of the behavior or function of the atom. We have some prejudice in favor of more direct observations if these are possible and rely on indicators only when we have to.

How can we go about studying the mind? It would be necessary to define it in some way and agree upon indicators of the mind's activities. What is it? Can we rely on popular usage and describe the mind as something that can be weak or strong, dull or keen, something that can be made up, that can be changed, that can be lost, that contains things, that even has eyes or perhaps other senses, that tells us what to do, that is different in children and women? This catalogue is not very helpful. When we forsake popular usage and turn to philosophers, we get little comfort. Philosophers have pretty generally endorsed the proposition that human beings, at least, have in addition to a physical body, some kind of nonphysical equipment or apparatus referred to as the mind. For some philosophers the mind was a kind of an entity, that is, a structure, or thing of no physical substance. The mind's functions were thought of as "mental" in contrast to physical functions of the body. A host of theological and philosophical questions have been considered in the course of time, all of them arising from the assumption of some nonphysical agency which presumably inhabits the body. The basic question, however, has always been: What is the relationship between the mind and the body?

The French philosopher Descartes (see Hampshire, 1956) is perhaps as responsible as anyone for the trends in thinking about this "mind-body problem" which have continued from his time and before. Descartes firmly declared that man had a dual nature, a mental and physical nature (this position is philosophically identified as "dualism" in contrast to "monism" which is a position that only one kind of substance exists—it may be only physical substance, in which case the position is one of physical monism, or only mental substance, or mentalistic monism). Descartes re-examined the ancient problem of how the mind and body are related. He started, he reports, with no convictions of any kind. He began by *doubting* everything, even that he himself existed. In what is commonly regarded as a flash of genius, it occurred to him that the very process of doubting was proof of his existence, because how could there be any doubting if there were no doubter? He expressed this in a now famous phrase, *"Cogito, ergo sum."* This is usually translated to read: "I think, therefore I am." Some interpreters favor the view that it should read: "I doubt, therefore I am." But, Descartes assumed, doubting is a mental function, an operation of a mind, and therefore a mind exists.

The method of Descartes is called a rational method. It depends on reasoning and not on observation (observation and measurement are called "empirical" operations) and no suggestions were offered about how to go about to develop some other, independent way of establishing the existence of the mind or of its functions. Descartes was free to go on and develop his reasoning about the nature and characteristics of the mind wherever his reasoning process took him. It should be pointed out, of course, that anyone else is equally free to reason out his own views, starting from whatever assumptions he regards as useful. The fact that reasoning is employed, however, is no guarantee that the results are correct when considered empirically. The logic may be flawless, but the whole effort empirically meaningless. To the extent that one can secure support from others, to that extent a doctrine can be established as powerful or influential whether the doctrine is right or wrong by any other test.

To the question of how the mind is related to the body, Descartes developed an answer known as "interactionism." The mind is presumed to affect the body and vice versa. The interaction for Descartes took place in the pineal gland, a small gland more or less in the lower center of the brain which had no other known function. Through the pineal gland the mind, with its functions of reasoning and willing, influenced the body to perform its various functions. We should note that some philosophers adopted a position that the mind and body were independent of each other, but mirrored each other's functions in a parallelistic manner—this view is known as "parallelism." According to this view, whatever happens to the body is reflected in the mind, and vice versa, but neither causes the other to happen or function in any way.

The interacting dualism of Descartes is the most popular philosophical orientation today. Most people in Western civilization profess to have minds which reason and make decisions to be carried out by the body and also that the behavior of the body is felt or known by or influences the mind.

Faculty psychology

In the course of time various attempts were made to describe the functions of the mind. These functions were defined as independent "faculties." Such activities or characteristics as thinking, loving, hating, jealousy, generosity, pugnacity, and a great many others were localized in the mind. Any aspect of behavior could be "explained" by ascribing it to the operation of some "faculty." Since by more or less common agreement, the mind was located in the head, some earnest scientists like Gall and Spurzheim in the early 1800's attempted to get at an analysis of the mind's functions by examining the conformations of human skulls. The basic assumption was that a person with a prominent faculty, as observed in his behavior, would also have a prominence or unusually large development in the skull, presumably located just above the locus of that mental function. Gall and Spurzheim were serious scientists who established what was then the science of phrenology. Because of their ignorance of brain anatomy they failed to consider that the soft tissue of the brain would not affect the external structure of the skull, nor its internal structure, for that matter, and all of their painstaking searches and measurements went for naught. Their procedure was to find someone quite famous for, say, inventiveness; they would then examine his skull and if he happened to have an unusual bump on some part of his head, they would label that section as the "inventiveness" region of the mind. Today we find phrenologists only at amusement parks or circuses and no longer take them seriously. In the nineteenth century, however, they were regarded as serious scientists, a point we should not lose sight of in considering today's scientists in whatever field.

Schools of psychology

By 1850 other attempts were being made to determine the relationship of mind to body. Experimental techniques were being devised to measure "subjective" (i.e., mental) reactions to physical stimuli. The experimenter would ask a subject to heft two small weights in succession and tell which was heavier. The amount of difference in weight (physical world) needed to "register" a difference in the "mental" world was noted and various "psychophysical functions" were plotted showing the relationships between physical stimulus strength and "strength of sensation." These experiments provoked great interest and by 1879, in Germany, scientists with backgrounds in physiology, physics, and philosophy began to turn to the analysis of mental phenomena. One such scientist, Wilhelm Wundt, considered the analysis of the mind to be important enough to call for special preparation and training, and he prevailed upon German university authorities to establish a new academic "chair" or discipline which would be concerned with primarily psychological problems. Wundt became the first professor of psychology and opened a laboratory for psychological studies at the University of Leipzig.

Wundt felt the need for a new methodology to study the mind and devised a technique which he called "introspection." When introspecting, the scientist would observe mental processes as they occurred and thereby get at the *structure* of the mind. Wundt *assumed* that mental life consisted of the flow of three basic kinds of processes or elements, which he labeled sensations, images, and feelings. The complex mental life we "experience" (are conscious of) consists of combinations of sensations, images, and feelings. The task of psychology is to analyze these basic components or atoms of mental life into their various dimensions and characteristics just as chemists analyze complex substances into their atomic components. By adding just the right components in the right combinations, a mental experience could presumably be synthetized. Psychology was to be a kind of mental chemistry. By assuming that sensations and images had various dimensions and qualities or attributes (such as duration, intensity, clarity) and that feelings similarly had attributes (of unpleasantness-pleasantness, excitement-calm, tension-relaxation), Wundt called on his introspecting subjects to describe their experiences as they looked at a patch of red light, listened to a tone, smelled an odor, et cetera. The experiences were spoken of as "existences" and Wundtian psychology was variously called Structuralism, Introspectionism, or Existentialism.[5]

Wundtian psychology at first was very popular and students came to Wundt from all over Europe and the United States. One of the most important of Wundt's students was Edward B. Titchener, an Englishman

[5] The current French philosophical movement called Existentialism concerns itself with metaphysical problems dealing with the reasons for man's existence and purposes in life. It is not to be confused with Wundt's Existentialism which dealt with mental phenomena called "existences."

who came to America and introduced Wundtian psychology at Cornell University. When introduced into the United States, however, Structuralism did not take root. It appeared sterile, unreal, and impractical and did not suit the American temper. It seemed to American psychologists that Wundt was getting out of the mind only what he chose to put into it by training his subjects to use a particular kind of language. It was argued that introspection amounted to a contradiction in terms—how can anyone see himself seeing? Who is doing the seeing and with what? Wundt and his students actually made many great contributions to our knowledge of sense organ functions—but contributed very little beyond that.

American psychologists, strongly influenced by practical considerations in an expanding American economy and impelled by an individualistic philosophy stemming from American political philosophy and Darwinian evolutionary theory, looked for a more vital approach. They reacted against "structuralism" with what was thought of as a "functional" approach, an approach concerning itself with adaptive processes, with adjustment to the environment, with survival, with individual differences. John Dewey, whom most of us identify with progressive education and pragmatism which he inherited from William James, was a leader of the Functional "school." The Functionalists retained the subjective, introspective methods of Wundt but began to find them quite unprofitable in relation to their needs and gradually began to give them up in favor of more "objective" methods like "testing" and observation of subjects. The final blow to Structuralism was given by John B. Watson, a student of Dewey, who challenged the very basis of Structuralism by denying that conscious processes were of any consequence at all for a proper psychology. The only important subject matter for Watson was *behavior*. Behavior, argued Watson, could be observed objectively, it could be recorded, there would be *social* agreement (that is, by numerous observers) on what occurred, and only by objective methods could we hope to establish a science. Like Wundt, Watson was forced to select something to observe (you cannot observe "behavior"—this is a collective, abstract, general term), and Watson hit upon reflexes as his units. Psychologists would observe reflexes and note their combinations and interactions out of which all behavior could be synthesized. Watson, like Wundt, was an elementarist; he thought of reflexes as basic structural units which could be modified by learning (conditioned reflexes) and which served as building blocks for more and more complex patterns. Watson's movement was known as Behaviorism. It aroused considerable opposition because of its denial of the importance of the mind or consciousness. Behaviorists were accused of brutalizing man, making a machine, a soulless, mindless machine, of man. Most American psychologists were attracted to Behaviorism in one degree or another because of its emphasis on objectivity. Objectivity was at that time equated with science and the prestige value of science was as strong in the twenties as it is today. Many regarded Watson's views as too radical, that he had "thrown out the baby with the bath." Some felt that he had retained the bath water. For all of the criticism, Watson did exert the most significant influence on American psychology that it has yet enjoyed. His systematic thinking on many psychological problems became a point of departure for succeeding generations of psychologists, many of whom today regard themselves as Behaviorists or Neo-Behaviorists, that is, behaviorists with one kind or another of reservation or modification of Watson's views.

It should have been noted that both Wundt and Watson based their approaches on the proposition that psychology consists of *analysis,* breaking down complex processes into more unitary functions. In Germany, about 1912, a group of psychologists came together under the leadership of Max Wertheimer and condemned the notion of analysis as of any value in psychology because they saw in psychological functions a totality or pattern, a wholeness, or "Gestalt" (the German word for "pattern" or "form"). They argued that to analyze a psychological process was to destroy it and they denounced both Wundt and Watson with equal vigor. The "Gestalt" psychologists, as they came to be known, emphasized the essential unity of behavior and of mental experience and argued for attention to "integration," to viewing behavior as "a whole." Their arguments won many adherents and American educators began to apply or misapply Gestalt thinking in their attempts at "educating the whole child," emphasizing "whole" methods, replacing traditional drill exercises with techniques calculated to enable the child to "see relationships," to "organize the whole," to react to patterns instead of more unitary structures. Much of the confusion that reigns in the field of reading instruction comes from poorly assimilated and too hastily advanced principles about how learning to read comes about. Some argue that a child should be exposed to a whole world at a time, so that he recognizes its shape and form, and comes to use it as a "whole" rather than a phonetic pattern approach where the child learns to pronounce segmentary noises. Some distorters even criticize what they call the "look and say" method as being basically some undesirable form of conditioning (which, we are warned, Communists practice) and consider their own phonetic techniques which *are* based on conditioning principles as employing Gestalt principles. Gestalt views have enjoyed a considerable favor among American educators and most American psychologists have incorporated much of what they offered into their own thinking. (Consult Woodworth, 1931.)

A PRELIMINARY DEFINITION OF PSYCHOLOGY

We have described these various "schools" of psychology not only out of a sense of historical obligation but to illustrate the point that a definition of psychology strongly depends upon the times and places in which it is developed. There would be no agreement among Structuralists, Functionalists, Behaviorists, and Gestaltists as to a definition. Because American psychologists have borrowed heavily from each of these developments to the point where most of what seemed reasonable has been accepted from whatever source, it should be expected that any definition of psychology as thought of in current American views will be a clumsy combination of an eclectic nature. Actually, as far as definitions go, there appears to be a reasonable degree of unanimity among textbook writers in their definitions of psychology. Most writers recognize that psychology is a division of science, i.e., it is a *study,* first of all, a study of behavior, and here too we have general agreement. If we stopped there and defined psychology as the study of behavior, we would achieve general agreement except for those psychologists who want to add either or both of the following amendments. The first is to include along with behavior, as a necessary and basic area, the study of *experience,* not perhaps in the Wundtian sense, but at least to recognize that much of what is important in human behavior occurs *privately,* inside the person, that it may or may not be reportable by the person and yet be so important as not to be ignored. Some psychologists object to this inclusion of experience as quite unnecessary because, regardless of what goes on inside a person, it can only have its effects externally and appropriate observation of externals will be sufficient for the formulation of psychological laws. Other psychologists tend to identify such "inner experience" with operations of the nervous system and believe that the understanding of the structure and function of the brain will either account for such experience or at least help to explain it, as well as a great deal of externally observable behavior. Both of these views represent scientific biases or prejudices which sometimes result in rather extreme statements. One psychologist might claim that he could not care less if the skull was stuffed with cotton while another insists that psychologists should devote themselves to the study of the brain. Because of the subjective connotations of "experience" we shall not include it in our definition but will make room for "internal" behavior and will amend the definition to include both external and internal responses and response mechanisms. The other amendment that would be desired by some is to recognize that man is a mammal and that much of his behavior is similar to the behavior of other mammals, and that a proper science of behavior might well include the behavior of all mammals, if not all living creatures. Some psychologists would want the definition to state that psychology is the study of the behavior of living organisms. This would provide for the psychologists who study the behavior of ants, spiders, bees, and other insects, for those who study fish, reptiles, and birds, as well as for the more commonly studied rats, dogs, cats, monkeys, and chimpanzees.

The inclusion of all organisms in a science of psychology disturbs some people who tend to regard mankind as the only important residents of the earth, and who are concerned with practical applications to human problems instead of with a comprehensive scientific orientation. Such a viewpoint might limit the work of astronomers to observations of the moon and the navigational stars since outside of these there might be little of an immediately practical nature in astronomy. From a scientific viewpoint, the behavior of a mosquito or elephant is just as interesting as that of the human and to the extent that some principles might be important at many evolutionary levels, we cannot afford to exclude organisms by arbitrary edicts. We do not know where interesting leads may develop and must follow them all. In this text we will not have time to indulge in much comparative psychology, but it is well to note that behavior is not the exclusive property of man. The psychologist who is now investigating the activity of the brain of a carp may provide the clue that will open whole new areas of investigation and change fundamental approaches.

With the several amendments, we are ready to describe psychology as the scientific study of the behavior (internal and external) of organisms. In this definition we have included an undefined term, namely, "scientific." [6] Because we cannot assume that the term is uniformly understood in all of its implications, and because of the relevance of these implications for an appreciation of psychology, we will have to examine it with some care.

The nature of science

It is not easy to describe science. As in the case of defining psychology, controversial books have been written on the philosophy and

[6] The term "behavior" has also been left undefined. This term requires extensive consideration and will be treated in the next chapter. For the present the reader might translate it as referring to actions or responses like walking, talking, moving about, grasping and releasing things, and so on.

nature of science. And again, there is not complete agreement among the writers. In our considerations, we shall not endeavor to cover all of the problems of scientific work and thinking, but shall restrict ourselves to implications for psychology. We will have to look at the aims of science and the methods of science as they relate to our subject and distinguish scientific approaches and attitudes from nonscientific ones.

Science and common sense

Psychologists must spend more time considering the nature of science than do other scientists because so much *unscientific* misinformation has become the common property of the population. All people have experience with others and draw their own conclusions about how people behave. Unless their observations have been obtained under appropriate (scientific) standards, their conclusions may be worthless, if not actually harmful. Ordinary, everyday observations are made under rather casual circumstances with no special preparation. Things happen and we report what we think we saw or heard. The reliability of such observations is notoriously poor as has been established in hundreds of courtrooms and classrooms. People tend to generalize on the basis of single instances and overlook the many factors or conditions that may have been present. Frequently they see what they want to see or what they expect to see and ignore negative instances. Scientific observation, on the other hand, makes use of trained observers who work under controlled conditions (controlled, in effect, means that only one factor can operate at a time, all others being held constant) called experiments. The observers are ready to make the observations when they occur, they do not simply happen upon them, and they record the events under observation, both positive and negative instances being accepted with equal grace and importance. Only after a considerable body of data has been accumulated which meets carefully planned statistical tests are the scientists willing to venture tentative conclusions about tendencies, trends, probabilities. Such careful restraint is not the common characteristic of the general public and yet many serious issues are decided upon unreliable conclusions about "human nature." Sometimes a situation exists which demands action and there is not time to go about the orderly collection of data under controlled conditions; at such times people operate under their best "guesses" and these guesses then become principles controlling the lives of thousands or millions of others even though they may be basically incorrect. They become "prejudices" which in some instances even prevent a scientific examination of the problem because the issue has been closed. Some races may be denied the privilege of education or certain kinds of employment because somebody has decided that this group of people is incompetent or impossible "as anyone with any sense can tell."

Sometimes hard facts are difficult to live with. Easy ways out are much more attractive and many fallacious beliefs have been adopted by the public in its effort to solve the multitudinous problems of mankind. The chief concerns of people are about their own futures, the inevitability of death and the hope of some kind of survival after death, and the desire to control events or other people. Such concerns have allowed numerous quacks and frauds to prey upon the public by offering information about the future, the possibility of communicating with the dead, and easy solutions to difficult problems. We shall not waste time about such obvious frauds as palmistry and tea leaf reading. Irresponsible newspapers carry daily horoscopes which may beguile simple-minded old ladies and movie starlets or devotees of the sport of kings. Even moderately stupid people know enough to waste no time on tea leaves or stars; the others we might tolerate unless they become dictators. When charlatans offer to put you in contact with dear departed grandma, however, it is a more serious issue and bears watching.

Parapsychology

There is one area, on the fringe of psychology, where numerous scientifically oriented persons work seriously at determining the possibility that some people, some time, can influence the action of material objects or be aware of events without the use of any of the normal channels of sensory contact or physical manipulation. In connection with so-called "extrasensory perception" for example, it is alleged that some individuals can report more accurately than chance would presumably allow what someone else is doing or looking at. It is also argued that some subjects, by strongly wishing for certain faces to appear on dice, can actually cause the dice to roll in such a way that these faces come up more frequently than chance expectancy. Such "mind over matter" control is called "psychokinesis." There is no objection to anyone investigating anything he wants to, of course, but sometimes the investigators become carried away by their findings and make claims like: There is no question but that extrasensory perception is a genuine phenomenon. There may be no such question for the person who makes the statement, but there is still considerable question about the reality of any such phenomenon as extrasensory perception or psychokinesis (ESP and PK). There have been many critical evaluations of the data accumulated by such researchers and the majority of psychologists have little or no use for the claims made in connection with extrasensory perception, clairvoyance, psychokinesis, and similar ventures. There is no need to repeat such criticisms here. What we are concerned to point out, however, is that in their effort to be scientific and experimental, such researchers develop certain routines and procedures which result in the accumulation of data of a sort. What these data mean, however, is the important issue. The interpretation seized upon by the experimenters who *want* to find that such capacities exist may not be the only conclusion to be drawn. In fact it may be the only conclusion *not* to be drawn. Let us examine the dice-throwing experiment as an illustration.

A group of people are given dice cups, each with a fixed number of dice, say six, and are told to wish for "aces" or "fives" or whatever number is selected by the experimenter. They then shake the cups, toss the dice onto a table, and count the number of desired faces. By chance there should be only one of such a wished-for face. The dice are thrown many times and a count is kept of the total of the "hits." At the end of a series of throws, the "hits" are compared with the chance expectancy and there may or may not be a discrepancy. There may be exactly one-sixth (this is unlikely unless there were a great many tosses), there may be fewer, or there may be more. Those people who report more hits may be asked to try again, or they may be, perhaps tentatively, labeled as possessing "psychokinesis" capacities. All that we have to go on is the discrepancy between the hypothetical chance expectancy and the actual scores. What do such discrepancies mean? To a gambler they might mean "a run of luck," to the believer they mean "psychokinesis," to the experimental psychologist they might mean that there are factors at work which resulted in such a discrepancy, factors that need investigation and control. One such factor might be the simple question of whether the chance expectancy has actually been violated. Another might be the validity of the reports (it has been shown that believers report falsely inflated scores, and nonbelievers falsely deflated scores). Still another factor might be the quality of the dice. Gambling houses are very careful to procure finely machined dice which roll true. When such dice bump each other, as they inevitably must in a dice cup, they become less true and are quickly disposed of in the casino. One student of gambling reports that no self-respecting casino would use the dice that "parapsychologists"[7] use; they are not "loaded," to be sure, but they may be very biased and certain faces may very well turn up more frequently than expected.

If the experimental psychologist cannot make the dice rolls match mathematical expectancy (gambling casino managers have been manag-

[7] An interesting account of psychokinesis and other "parapsychological" research can be found in Gardner (1957) and an autobiographical book by Scarnes (1957).

ing to do this for generations in spite of the strongest-wishing clientele imaginable), he is still not forced to assume positively that a conclusion like that drawn by parapsychologists is the logical necessity. He can admit ignorance and temporarily consider the problem unsolved. The point is that results of an experiment do not necessarily prescribe the conclusion to be drawn. While we point this moral at the parapsychologist it is equally pointed at all experimental science. The conclusions drawn may be fallacious even though logically tight. Future investigators may discover the operation of factors undreamed of by the original experimenters. This has happened time and again in science and will undoubtedly happen in the future. We are well warned to regard data or observations as suspect, as problematical. The very nature of an experiment involves the accumulation of data which are *designed* to *indicate* something about a *hypothetical* process or entity. They may actually indicate something quite different when we continue our investigations.

Prediction and control

We shall have more to say about science and psychology in the next chapter when we observe psychologists at work. It is necessary now to examine the aims and assumptions of a scientific psychology. It might be better to start with the aims because the assumptions might be found to hinge on the aims. Many writers, imbued by an enthusiasm for remaking the human race or by other practical ambitions, argue that the aims of psychology are to predict and control behavior. It appears that they are confusing the purpose of an experiment with the purpose of science. In an experiment which is based on some theoretical derivation, it is necessary for the scientist to commit himself to a prediction. He is, in effect, saying: If this is so, and that is so, then this must follow. His experiment is a demonstration of a prediction. Prediction is vital to science, but only in the testing of hypotheses. As far as making practical predictions is concerned, scientists could hardly be less interested. Weather forecasts are made by weathermen, not meteorologists. The latter study weather and do not care if it rains, snows, or freezes so long as it rains, snows, or freezes when their studies tell them that it should as a test of their principles. Similarly scientists are not especially concerned with practical applications of their findings. Technologists are; part of their business is the making of predictions. The technological interests of practical people, however, are not the basis for assessing the aims of science. As far as controlling people, most scientists are horrified at the thought and would shrink from any association with such an ambition. They are concerned about controlling the outcomes of experiments, and control here means, simply, keeping conditions constant and allowing only one factor to vary at a time. This is a far cry from wanting to control human behavior.

It is inevitable that at times scientists get involved with practical affairs. Physicists made the atom bomb, for example, and some then came to regret their success. While making the bomb, however, the physicists were still testing a theory and they were much concerned with prediction. Once the theory had been tested and bombs became practical affairs, the physicists lost interest in them as such, if they did not come to have negative interests. It is still true that no man can be all scientist at all times. As a citizen or consumer or parent he may have personal needs for controlling one feature or another in his environment, but such desires for control are part of his citizen, consumer, or parent "roles" and not part of his role as scientist. Scientists aim at understanding. This is a sufficiently engaging ambition to fill their needs as scientists.

It is not intended in the above remarks to suggest that practical affairs or applied science is in some way unworthy of a scientist's attention. When scientists turn to applied problems they behave in exactly the same way as they do ordinarily with more "pure" research. Applied problems, when they are new, can be just as challenging and interesting as any other kind. In fact, the solution to a fresh applied problem only comes about through additional "pure" research. Most of what we now know as science came about because people have had problems, problems of survival, of getting enough food, or housing, clothing, shelter. (See Hogben, 1938.) Until the laws of nature are learned there can be only accidental "inventions" or discoveries of useful applications. The automobile depended upon a long history of scientific discoveries involving gases, combustion, and electricity, to say nothing of mechanics. The discovery of "useful" drugs for medical purposes presupposes a knowledge of chemistry, anatomy, and physiology; more useful drugs await a more thorough knowledge of these basic sciences. It is hypothetically possible that some child might stumble on some mixture of leaves and grasses that will cure cancer, but the probability is so remote that we need not even consider it.

Scientists who are engaged in the study of problems that seem remote from human affairs are sometimes called upon to defend their activity. Faraday, for example, demonstrated to Disraeli an elementary form of dynamo. Disraeli asked: "What good is it?" Faraday retorted: "Some day you may tax it." While this remark is charming and now an honored classic, it was out of order as far as a scientist's philosophy is concerned. So is the other common reply: "What good is a new baby?"

Scientists need not offer any bribes or promises to defend their work. It should be sufficient to say: I find it interesting. It might help explain some other problem we have not come across yet.

While we recognize that some psychologists are interested in controlling other people, we can insist that such interests are not part of their necessary equipment to function as scientists and that the alleged aim of "predict and control" is a practical need for experimental work, but not of the theoretical structure the experiment is designed to support.

The aims and assumptions of science

Scientists who cope with problems that arise in a material world and who work with material methods are bound to assume that such a real, material world, does in fact exist. This might appear a strange assertion but there are philosophers who have challenged the very existence of a real world. They are the "idealists." Idealists are not necessarily people who have "ideals." The term refers to "ideas" rather than to ideals. Idealists prefer to picture the world itself as a construction of ideas and emphasize the proposition that only ideas exist. Things like wagons, horses, airplanes, and watermelons are only ideas in our minds. If we could not see, hear, taste, or feel, such things would not exist for us. It is only our sensory reactions that give them whatever reality they possess and sensory reactions are, according to idealists, simply mental experiences. This position is rejected by scientists who assume that a real, material world exists whether we are around to "experience" it or not. The famous paradox of the tree falling in the forest when there is no one around to hear it might help illustrate the difference. Is there a sound when the tree falls? The idealist says "no," because he defines sound as a reaction of the human mind. The materialist says "yes" because he defines sound as a matter of wave energy. For the materialist events are independent of their observers. When there are observers, the materialist expects general agreement on what was observed; he further expects that a repetition of the event will bring about the same observations in the case of future observers.

A second assumption of science is that of orderliness or regularity or repeatability. This means that given the same conditions, the same events will be observed to take place. If the same event does not occur, it is presumed that some change in the conditions must have taken place. The phenomena of nature are not the results of some chaotic or capricious whims and fancies of unknowable agencies. In other words, events are predictable. Given A, then B follows, is the general formula. It should be plain that without this assumption the scientist would be unable to work. If he should be unable to predict what will happen the next time (in terms of what he witnessed on earlier occasions), his efforts would be of no interest to him or to anyone else.

A third assumption is that the world is knowable. This follows from the above assumption. If the world is not knowable, if laws or principles cannot be discovered, then, again, the scientist's work is an absurd waste of time. It is well to recognize this assumption explicitly in spite of its obviousness. Sometimes it is argued that everything in the universe is related to everything else and that it is, in principle, impossible to describe all the conditions for controlling and predicting an event. The scientist argues for a *finite* or limited number of factors being related to any particular condition or event and that with sufficient and careful work, all the factors of consequence can be recognized and taken into account. If the price of cotton on the stock exchange were to depend upon the fact that someone in Australia has just lost a Siamese postage stamp, or, if Mr. A is divorcing Mrs. A in Reno because a coconut has just fallen on the head of a Polynesian in Samoa, then scientists would be unable to make much, if any progress. Scientists assume that however complicated the event under examination, it is possible to systematically unravel the interactions among the relevant antecedent conditions, note their relative significance or contributions, and reduce them to an orderly array of principles. Again, we note without the assumption of a limited or definite number of factors related to any phenomenon, scientific work could not be attempted.

Implied above is another basic assumption, that of determinism. We shall consider this assumption again in considering the problem of motivation (see p. 331), but for the present, we can note that for psychological science, assuming determinism amounts to assuming that whatever happens was bound to happen and could not have happened in any other way. This is not the same predeterminism as believed by some religious groups like the Mohammedans who believe that prior to their births, they have an appointed day to die and that their lives are merely the unfolding of a plan. Determinism, as applied to science, or behavior, means no more than what we have described as orderliness and predictability. Given a certain set of conditions a certain kind of consequence can be expected. For the psychologist, the past history of an organism determines its future behavior. For the Mohammedan, the future determines his present activity. Sometimes the assumption of determinism is viewed with alarm as a violation of the "freedom of the will." Psychologists are not concerned with freedom of the will. They are unable to work with such a concept in an empirical, experimental science. The concept of "will" is a *rational* concept, just as is the concept of the "mind" or the "intellect." The study of such concepts belongs to a different frame of reference, that of theology, philosophy, or "rational psychology." Experimental psychologists have no way of handling or working with such concepts and are forced to exclude them from their work. To the extent that these concepts are significant in behavior, to just that extent, psychology as an experimental science must suffer whatever limitations its assumptions necessitate. For the most part, the psychologist in his daily work presumes that a rat in a maze is following the dictates of its habit history and present stimulation. The college student memorizing some poetry is also following the dictates of his habit history and present stimulation. To the extent that the psychologist can make correct predictions of such behavior he can afford to ignore factors he is unable to control. Should it turn out that a scientific psychology is handicapped in predicting behavior because it has ignored the will or some other rational principle, then so much the worse for psychology.

The interlocking assumptions we have described above—materialism, orderliness, knowability, and determinism—reveal the psychologist as approaching his problems with a philosophical orientation that can be summarized as "physical monism." Organisms are regarded as "machines," behaving or responding to conditions in ways that can be described in terms of general principles or laws which reflect an orderly relationship between conditions and behavior. Lest anyone become disturbed or excited by this "crass, materialistic" view, it should be pointed out that these are "working" assumptions. Without them, no work is possible in this area. If they turn out to be foolish, they must be abandoned. So far there has been enough progress to justify the assumptions and no reason for modifying or abandoning them. Occasionally it is argued that such assumptions are contrary to some religious orientation and, therefore, wrong. Most religious orientations today have adopted positions which make science reasonably compatible with their views. They take the position that there is only one truth and that there can be no real conflict with science. If some truth which is attained by scientific methods is at variance with religious views, most religious organizations adjust their views to accommodate the new findings as soon as they are reasonably fully established. Some move slowly in determining when something has been established, as well they might. Frequently enough what is the science of one day proves to be the superstition or the erroneous approach of another day. Scientists themselves are not too ready to accept every new claim that is advanced without careful scrutiny and repeated verification.

In scientific psychology then, we go along with certain working assumptions that are quite explicitly made. These assumptions limit us to certain kinds of operations and exclude others. We will not make reference to or use of nonmaterialist constructs like "minds" or "ideas," unless we first translate these into materialist terms. Because of the confusion that is likely to result if such terms are used at all, it might be best to avoid them entirely in scientific discourse even though they appear to be useful in ordinary conversations. From time to time it might be necessary to use some nonscientific expression to delineate a problem area. When this is the case, we shall have to be watchful. With the aims, assumptions, and definitions involved now explicitly before us, we are ready to begin our study of psychology as an empirical science.

CHAPTER 2

The Science of Psychology

The methods of science · The nature of theory · Psychology and science · Psychological theory construction · The S ⟶ R view · Stimulus and response variables · The definition of behavior · The data of psychology · Interaction with the environment · "Internal" and "external" behavior · Implicit behavior · Traditional psychological problem areas · The task of psychology · The analysis of behavior · Organismic variables · Intervening variables · Operational definitions · Hypothetical constructs · Hypothetical constructs and intervening variables · The problems of an S ⟶ R psychology · Psychology and physiology · One-stage and multiple-stage theories · A "response" psychology orientation · Summary of S ⟶ R views · Continuity and noncontinuity · Molar and molecular approaches · Reductionism

In the preceding chapter we indicated the great concern of psychologists with the nature and concepts of science. To put psychology on a scientific foundation, psychologists have examined the methods of science and tried to emulate the work of scientists in other areas. The methods of science, however, are not simple patterns of procedure. You do not look them up in a book. There is no such thing, for example, as *the* scientific method.[1] While there are some steps or stages where the activity of one scientist might look like the behavior of another, there is no simple formula to follow in attacking a problem. What characterizes scientists more than their methods is their interest in arriving at an orderly account of phenomena in terms of abstract laws. This is a kind of goal or end-product of a scientific endeavor. A good example of what scientists might like to achieve in their own interest areas is Euclidean geometry. Conant points out that Euclidean geometry is a completely closed abstract system which can handle any kind of concrete or specific problem pertinent to the system. The three angles of a triangle always add to 180 degrees, for example. This is true of any

[1] James B. Conant (1953) has written a most challenging little book, *Modern Science and Modern Man.* It is of special interest for those students who might think of themselves as "social" scientists.

triangle that can be drawn. Such a statement amounts to a law of triangles. It applies to right triangles, scalene triangles, equilateral triangles, isosceles triangles, little triangles and big ones, triangles drawn on paper with ink, or in the sand with your toes.

In the world of physics we have similar abstractions. We have, for example, the pressure-volume law. $PV = K$, or pressure times volume, is a constant quantity. The law applies to all kinds of gases in all kinds of containers and while it is necessary to add "corrections" like that of holding temperature constant, the law itself is an abstraction. It applies not only to the particular situation in which it was first observed but to all possible instances. Einstein's law of $E = mc^2$ is a similar abstraction, as is "the law of gravity" or any other law, like $F = MA$.

THE METHODS OF SCIENCE

It should be recognized that such laws as we have listed did not result from the application of any fixed pattern of investigation. In some cases scientists worked for thousands of years laying the foundation for a law through the slow accumulation of experience. In other cases, like that of Archimedes, for example, a law was "discovered" more or less accidentally and recognized through the ingenuity of its discoverer. (Actually, laws are not discovered. They do not exist in some undiscovered state awaiting an investigator. Laws are man-made descriptions of observations.) Perhaps all laws in science require such ingenuity, but ingenuity by itself does not appear to be enough. There must be, first of all, a problem which interests the scientist, a problem about which a certain amount of information is available. In some instances, the information may be the accumulation of hundreds of years of observations; in others the actual observations may be fragmentary and isolated. What the scientist does is to try to describe these observations in terms of a general statement (a law) which will "organize" (make sense of) these observations and hold for observations still to be made in the future. If the scientist is successful, the law becomes an accepted part of the science. If he fails, he starts all over again, correcting, modifying, gathering more observations.

Some scientists are at a stage in the solution of some problems where the "facts" or observations are scanty and they work at getting more and more observations. When they have made enough observations, they attempt to "induce," that is, formulate a generalization or principle which will cover the observations—this might be called the procedure of "induction." It is unlikely however, that anyone patiently accumulates observations without making tentative generalizations, anticipating the data, extrapolating beyond his own observations to future instances (Hebb, 1951). In the early phases of any problem-solving venture, however, some fact gathering is required. Facts are the first order of scientific business.

The nature of theory

Once some inductive generalizations are available, however, the scientist is not content. He has seen how, frequently, one inductive generalization fits in with other inductive generalizations to make a more complete account of observations in some area. When several laws are formulated, each of which applies to some observations in a given problem area, and where these laws are not contradictory, but mutually supportive, a theory has been constructed. A theory consists of a set of laws which mutually support each other in accounting for the observations that can be made in some problem area. Some theories which may be familiar to the student are the Copernican theory, the kinetic theory, the evolutionary theory, the Mendelian theory in heredity, and the atomic theory. Sometimes a theory makes use of definitions and axioms as in Euclid's geometry, which is also a theory, a theory of spatial relationships in plane surfaces. One of the advantages of a theory, besides its obvious virtue of bringing together a large number of observations, is that a theory may generate new information. On a simple level, a syllogism can represent this function of a theory. We are all familiar with the classical syllogism about Socrates:

All men are mortal.	(an inductive generalization or law)
Socrates is a man.	(also an inductive generalization)
Therefore, Socrates is mortal.	(a prediction, or "new" information)

It is unlikely that anyone will be startled by the conclusion that is *deduced* from the premises of the syllogism. You might even wish to argue that the minor premise about Socrates being a man includes the characteristic of mortality referred to in the major premise. The point is, however, that unless the two propositions are juxtaposed in some such fashion, it might not occur to anyone to draw the conclusion. In more involved syllogisms, the conclusion may not be so clearly evident and the information contained in it is, for all practical purposes, essentially new. It may not occur to the high-school student as he works out the "proofs" in geometry that he is actually following a deductive process and that each theorem is the deduced conclusion from a collection of "postulates." Now the postulates of Euclid are no different in essence from the laws of science. The high-school student works backwards. The theorems have already been deduced, and these "theorems" are given as conclusions for which justification must be found. In science, one first has to find and assemble the postulates and then work forwards to see what can be deduced from the postulates.

The task of psychology is to accumulate the postulates which will make sense out of observations about behavior. The procedure for accumulating such postulates we have already described as the inductive process. This can be the hard, grubbing, slow, and painstaking business of observing and tabulating, or it can be done, as hinted above, by risking guesses about what the postulate might be like if the painstaking labor had already been done by someone else. Some psychologists are content to follow the difficult road to patient fact collection. Others feel that such a process will take far too long, certainly more than their lifetimes, and prefer the more venturesome process of guessing at laws and then testing such laws. And again we note, even the most careful and patient fact seeker is probably venturing guesses as to the outcomes of his labors, so that there is not too much of a real difference between the two approaches.

When some tentative postulates (guesses) or laws have been decided upon, the scientist proceeds to deduce consequences of his premises, not always in a rigorously logical fashion. He develops "hypotheses." Hypotheses are lower-level generalizations derived or deduced from theories (collections of laws). Hypotheses are necessarily rather general statements. We might call them theorems, the offspring of theories. The term "hypothesis" is frequently misused or misrepresented in ordinary conversation. We are always saying, "take a hypothetical case"—we mean an imaginary case in most instances as it is unlikely that we have arrived at a theorem by a deductive process from carefully stated first principles. The hypothesis will be a verbal statement, in general terms, about some observations that might be made if someone went to the trouble of making them. Thus, a theorem in Euclid states that the sum of the squares on the sides of a right triangle will equal the square of the hypotenuse. This is a general kind of prediction. It does not refer to any particular right triangle; the prediction is a *logical action*. If one is to set about proving this theorem or hypothesis practically, it is necessary to translate it into some real situation. An actual right triangle must be constructed, the sides measured and squared and checked against the square of the measured hypotenuse. When we have done this we have performed an experiment. An experiment is a practical or "empirical" test of a prediction or hypothesis. It is in the universality of the reliance upon an experimental check that scientists show their greatest agreement in methodology.

An experiment, as was just indicated, is a test of a prediction. Since the prediction was generated by a theory, the experiment is thus a test of a theory. If the prediction is confirmed, the theory is held to be supported. If the experiment fails, i.e., the prediction is not confirmed, the theory is held to be weakened. Something is wrong with the theory and it is necessary to revise the postulates, assuming the deductive process was correct. In the very nature of the case, it is impossible to prove theories. They can only be supported. Some better theory might be advanced which would permit the same deductions. Similarly, it is virtually impossible to disprove a theory, especially one that does not generate testable hypotheses. When experiments fail to support a theory, the theorist rarely gives up his brain child. He defends it as parents defend children. If the theory frequently fails in its experimental tests it loses supporters who turn to other views. Theories, like old soldiers, never die; "they just fade away." Psychology is replete with theories lingering on from ages past. Many are essentially untestable, and, in a sense, scientifically illegal, but there is nothing one can do about them except disregard them. Many theories are loosely framed and to a considerable extent unverbalized, containing hidden assumptions, improbable postulates which have never been examined. We hear the results or consequences of such theories every day, in the home, in the school, from politicians, businessmen, editorial writers, and barbers, to say nothing of psychologists.

We have gone to such an extent in describing the nature of theories because the student must be careful in dealing with psychological problems to discriminate fact from fancy, hypotheses from facts and from postulates. He must learn to look for hidden postulates and to evaluate postulates, to recognize those that are based on adequate inductive foundations as well as those that amount to mostly guess work. He must be tolerant of "working postulates," recognizing them as such and not as fundamental verities. In psychological thinking there will be a great deal of such speculative postulation. So long as everyone is playing in the same game and observing the same rules, no great harm can result; but, it is important to know the rules and the nature of the game.

PSYCHOLOGY AND SCIENCE

Now we can take a look at the scientific game as played by psychologists. Some we will find spend a great deal of time collecting observations relevant to some specific problem. They might be interested, for example, in whether girls are brighter than boys. The only way to find out is to give tests of "brightness" to a sufficient number of both kinds of subjects and accumulate the scores. Sooner or later enough data will be available to justify some conclusion of an empirical kind. The conclusion might have little or no theoretical value while, at the same time, it might have considerable practical value. If girls are really brighter, perhaps they should not be in the same classes as boys of the same age. Many interesting questions can be attacked by this procedure. Is drill better than learning by "understanding"? Are men more interested in sex activity than women? Is the phonetic method of learning to read superior to the "look and say" method? Is learning a foreign language by the "oral" method better than the traditional approach through grammatical analysis? Is it better to reward a learner every time he does the correct thing than to reward him every other time? Thousands of such questions can be asked and attacked by going to work accumulating observations.

A great many such problems have interested various psychologists at odd times and places and much data have been accumulated, data about IQ's, about learning, and forgetting, about various sensory and neural processes and capacities. It is a "statistical fact," for instance, that girls at the age of 13 find their parents more troublesome than at any other age (Bühler, 1933). This kind of information interests some parents and some psychologists and even some students, but not all of any of these groups. There are psychologists who could not care less. Their lack of interest is due to the relative isolation of such a fact from other facts. Such facts may be connected with others but the nature of the connection has not been described and it is the "laws" of the relationships between facts that interest many psychologists.

Most textbooks in psychology contain a great many such facts, more or less isolated. Facts about learning may indeed be grouped in a chapter on learning and facts about teenagers may be found in another chapter, but there will not necessarily be a connection between the two chapters, nor even among the facts of a given chapter. The student of psychology may finish the course with an accumulation of assorted information, some of a practical nature, some of a little vaguer variety, and fail to achieve any satisfactory sense of unity or even a sense that he has been studying a particular subject matter. If he is also studying physics, biology, and sociology, he may come across the same facts several times in different courses and begin to wonder about which subject deals with what.

Some psychologists, however, believe that the piecemeal approach mentioned above is wasteful of energy and time. They believe that answers to such questions could be obtained much more readily if we had an adequate theory from which we could generate these answers as hypotheses. Accordingly they urge that we consider the alternative attack:

Formulate theories based on as plausible a set of postulates or laws as we can develop and let the information spill out as theorems. If the theorems can be supported by experiment, we are encouraged to continue the use of the postulates responsible; if they are not so supported, we can revise the postulates and try again. In this vein, some psychologists aim at rather comprehensive theoretical formulations taking in all behavior; others, more modestly, hope to create "miniature" systems, taking one problem area at a time, developing a well-knit structure of laws for that kind of behavior, and hoping that one miniature system will correspond with others developed for other behavioral areas, gradually building up a total behavioral system (Spence, 1956).

Psychological theory construction • The S ⟶ R view

Under the influence of the Functionalists and Behaviorists, psychologists came to regard their problem as one of accounting for the behavior of man or other organisms in relation to the ever-present environment. There can be no behavior without an environment, as is obvious, to be sure, but the orientation under which most American psychology has developed is that the behavior is a *result* of environmental forces or circumstances. Behavior cannot occur in a vacuum and it is plausible to start an analysis of behavior in terms of the conditions under which it does occur. Such an orientation gave rise to what has come to be known as the S ⟶ R law or *stimulus-response* law. From this point of view, behavior occurs only when there is a generating condition, called the stimulus (Latin—goad). When a response is observed, it is inferred that some appropriate stimulus must have been present. If some object or activity that might otherwise be considered a stimulus is noted as present but no reaction can be observed, it is presumed that the observer was in error. The object or activity was not really a stimulus. It should already be apparent that we are going to have trouble with these terms, but for the moment we will overlook the difficulties and continue with the general view.

Stimulus and response variables

From the S ⟶ R viewpoint, an adequate theory would enable one to predict the response, given the stimulus, and, given the response, "postdict" the stimulus, i.e., tell what the stimulus conditions must have been like. The basic task for psychology, then, would break down into an analysis of the environment on the one hand and the analysis of behavior on the other to discover the laws under which stimulus conditions lead to behavior in all of its manifestations. The task is indeed a formidable one. On the environmental or stimulus side, we have to consider such things as the nature of the stimulus (a light, a sound, an odor? Is it a simple energy-change affair? Is the background important? Does it arise from some simple physical object or from another human, perhaps a child, an older person, a group of people? Is it a modest energy change or a violent one? A barely noticeable one? Is it repeated?). Psychology would be rather dull if we restricted our interest to single stimuli like lights and sounds, and sometimes complex environmental circumstances are referred to as "stimulus situations." It is obvious that it would be extremely difficult to really describe the details of any complex situation such as a "cocktail party" or even a family dinner table with several people present. Yet such situations are sometimes referred to as the stimulus or stimulus situation. Usually, the psychologist assumes that much of the complexity can be considered as "constant" or unimportant and he pays attention to some selected aspects of the situation or stimulus. Sometimes he is able to take care of one aspect of a complex situation at a time and eventually hopes to take them all into account. Thus we arrive at a concept of "stimulus variables" or situational factors that represent the S side of the S ⟶ R law.

On the other side of the law, we have to deal with behavioral variables. Up to now we have not defined behavior in any real sense. We have mentioned that it is a collective and abstract term presumably covering anything and everything organisms do.

The definition of behavior

But we cannot dismiss the concept of behavior as an abstraction and say no more about it. Abstractions, after all, derive from some kinds of observations of concrete events or phenomena. It is necessary to attempt, at least roughly, to classify the kinds of events or phenomena which occupy the psychologist and differentiate them from those which interest other scientists but not psychologists. We need, as has been pointed out by Waters (1958), some criteria for what the psychologist calls behavior and what he does not.

What kinds of events and phenomena do interest psychologists? Here we can point to some areas of interest by noting what psychologists observe and study. They do not, for example, worry about the stars, mechanical objects, or plants. Living animal organisms seem to be the generators of the only "behavior" of concern. But granted an interest in living animal organisms (from amoeba to elephant) these organisms do many things that no psychologist bothers with except perhaps incidentally. All organisms eat and excrete, for example, but what they eat and how is of little concern to psychologists in any direct sense. It might be necessary to know how much food (and what kind) a paramecium ingests if one is to use food as bait or a reward, but that is about as far as a psychologist's interest might go in the assimilation and digestive processes of an animal. On the positive side we find so many different kinds of animal activities that interest psychologists that any catalogue would prove too extensive for our present purpose. Many such separate activities can be classified as basically related in some more limited number of categories. We can attempt to classify some of the major and minor behavioral groupings of psychological concern. Not all psychologists would agree with any specific set of categories but the general tradition would probably include most of those listed below with some differences in opinion about relative importance.

The data of psychology

Interaction with the environment · "Internal" and "external" behavior

Psychology, historically at least, has concerned itself with two broad classes of events which we can label, to begin with, as externally observable and internal or implicit events. These events, however, occur in situations in which an organism interacts with the environment. Such interaction, by definition, is of a dual aspect in that while the environment affects the organism, the organism, in turn, may affect or change the environment. We can now consider these several categories of events.

When the environment affects the organism we become concerned with the various aspects of environmental characteristics, its features, energies, and so on that are of importance to the organism in any way. We are immediately concerned with the "sensitivity" of the organism to changes in the environment, i.e., with its sensory capacities, the sense organ functions, the limitations of the organism to "receiving" stimulation from one form of energy or another. If the organism is not able to respond in any way to vibrations in the air that occur at a rate of 30,000 cycles per second, such vibrations are of no interest to the psychologist. When a "stimulus energy" is within the capacity or sensitivity range of the organism, we are then concerned with what the organism does when such energy impinges upon it. This involves a concern with the nervous system and the motor or muscle equipment of the organism as we try to trace the effect of the environmental changes on the activity of the organism.

Between the external energy change (ignoring for the moment energy changes that develop within the skin) and some activity that can be observed by an outsider, there will be a more or less complex amount of activity that some organisms, humans, can allude to or describe verbally. Such "private" or "implicit" activity may be described by humans as resulting from the external energy changes or as leading to or "causing" the movements of parts such as the hands, feet, the tongue in speech, the muscles of the face and so on. Such movements are difficult to describe in detail and frequently various kinds of substitutions can be effected. One can use the foot to move an object as well as the hand, and sometimes we can ask someone else to move it, or we can employ a tool to do the job. It is awkward to be restricted to descriptions of bodily movements especially when they involve a great many members or muscles and the term "response" has been adopted generally as a more general label for more or less organized sets of movements that have some effect on the environment. Instead of stating exactly what a rat does when it displaces a metal bar in an experimental compartment, psychologists do not feel uncomfortable when they say the rat "pressed the bar." It should be recognized that pressing involves an environmental effect and is no longer strictly a description of movements. It is possible on occasion to be misled by attending to the environment at the expense of the organism, but it is a risk that is taken for convenience's sake. When an environmental consequence is the result of some movement pattern, we might describe the affair as an "act." In general psychologists try to steer some sort of middle course between becoming absorbed in movements and concentrating on acts. The term "response" is a compromise that is most commonly followed.

The consequences of environmental stimulation take place, then, in terms of responses. The psychologist's ambition is to track the series of such responses from environmental stimulus to environmental act taking cognizance of what goes on in between these two observable events. In order to trace such a course he becomes concerned with sense organ and nervous structures and the immediate consequences of activity therein. When a human subject is reporting on such immediate effects, he might use words like "sensation" and "perception" to describe these internal events. It is important to note that "sensations" and "perception" are here regarded as *events* or activities, and not entities or "things." Additional internal events that might be described by words like "meaning" or "thinking" are also commonly reported by human observers of internal events. These, too, are basic interest areas for psychologists. Sometimes responses occur which involve the elimination of some form of environmental energy or objects which are responsible for this energy. Thus, an organism may move or act in such a way as to take it away from some stimulation or toward some other. It may move toward food for example, and by manipulating its environment in some way, secure and consume the food. When organisms act in such a manner as to consume some object or eliminate it from the field, it is possible to speak of the objects themselves or what happens to the object as a "goal" and to infer the presence of a "purpose." The concepts of goals and purposes are popular with some psychologists who emphasize that most behavior is "goal-directed." Other psychologists reject such interest as imbued with metaphysical orientations of an unsupportable variety and dismiss the concepts as "teleological." A purpose implies that the future affects the present, a working-backwards in time. Such an assumption would be incompatible with the determinism assumption. We note that "goals" and "purposes" are not *events* or activities but somehow represent "things" or "possessions" of the organism, something that the organism *has.* It is perhaps wiser to refrain from inferring unobservable purposes in organisms and adopt a more objective orientation in which such apparently purposive behavior is described in terms of *consummatory* activity. The influence of the stimulus objects on the organism can be described in terms of activities and events in the organism that, in principle, can be observed in some fashion.

Whatever orientation is adopted it will be noted that psychologists are concerned with the effects of the organism's activities on its environment and it should be noted further that this environment will include other organisms of the same and different species. Thus the interactions of one man and another might represent the basic paradigm or model of psychology. Each serves as a stimulus for the other and does things he might otherwise not do in the absence of the other. As they act and interact they systematically eliminate one form of stimulation after another.

Implicit behavior · Traditional psychology problem areas

The interactions of organisms with their environments may be the basic and primary subject matter of psychology, but the tracing of these interactions from beginning to end and on to new beginnings in the endless sequence of behavior involves the appreciation of many mechanisms and processes with which the organism performs its interactions.  The interactions which we can call events, and the internal activities which we can label "phenomena," can only be effected through the various parts of the body, and, from the psychologist's point of view, through subsequently observable explicit behavior. In some instances humans will report activity that is not related to external energy changes and is said to occur "spontaneously" or because of some alleged "faculty" or "force" which is not further described. In either event, psychologists are interested in such implicit behavior assuming that something does take place, reported or not (as in the case of nonspeaking organisms), and this internal behavior is a major concern of many psychologists. In some simple activities or events like a knee jerk, for example, the amount of the internal activity reported is minimal or of a zero amount, yet it is assumed that at least neural activity has taken place and such neural processes are studied by special techniques because it is presumed that in more complex events similar neural activity is also involved.

When different individuals report different internal events or when different organisms display different activity to what can be described as the "same" energy change, the psychologist assumes that, barring abnormal or varied physiological equipment or conditions, something found in the history of the organism is responsible for the varied activity. Because such variability is widespread, psychologists, perforce, are basically concerned with the histories of organisms, that is, with their past experience. It is assumed that such past experience resulted in changes which can be described as resulting from "learning." Consequently psychologists are necessarily concerned with learning and how it takes place. Any events or activities that can be considered to reflect "learning," modifiability, or "docility" are, *ipso facto,* psychological subject matter.

Because activity that shows the effects of learning must, of necessity, be repeated, or "persistent," psychologists can be expected to concern themselves with activity that shows the characteristic of persistence and repetition. By and large, psychologists are not especially interested in single events. The very nature of their studies involves prediction as a test of hypotheses and prediction is more readily attained with events that recur from time to time or can be made to recur upon demand.

The interaction of organism and environment involves some effect upon the environment as well as upon the organism. When the organism does something that creates or results in a change in the environment, that too becomes psychological subject matter. Ordinarily, the kinds of environmental effects psychologists study are those which are reasonably regular, repetitive, and, to a degree, predictable. Sometimes, however, the activities of organisms are not readily predictable or show some extreme characteristics. On some of these occasions, humans will refer to internal events which they describe as "emotions" or "feelings." These are also important interest areas.

In many cases, persons unsophisticated in psychology report such internal events in terms that have only vague or obscure references to anything observable. They might report a pounding heart or a cold sweat, an urge, an impulse, a choice, a feeling of bewilderment, and so on. Our language is full of expressions which are satisfactory enough for conversational use but do not provide exact communication by scientific standards. Most psychologists have come to regard such "psychic" terms as unsatisfactory, unsuitable, and unhelpful, if not directly misleading, and prefer to deal with internal events in more material terms, such as minimal or fractional movements, implicit speech (talking to oneself), or other postulated mechanisms which might some day be observed, measured, and recorded. They argue that there is only one kind of reality, that behavior is behavior whether it occurs within the skin and cannot be observed by outsiders, or whether it is available to public scrutiny. There are not two kinds of events; there are only different locations where they take place. While there is not complete agreement on this matter, with some psychologists preferring an ultraobjective program of studying only what can be observed from the outside in some other organism, there appears to be common agreement that the kinds of interests mentioned above must be taken into account, accounted for, explained, or explained away. We can then describe psychology as follows: it is concerned basically with interactions of the organism with the environment, with a special interest in consummatory "behavior" which is strongly modified by learning, and with concomitant interests both in immediate reactions to sensory stimulation and in internal reactions that over the centuries have come to be termed thinking, meaning, emotion, and choice.

THE TASK OF PSYCHOLOGY

When psychologists actually get down to business, they deal with stimuli and responses. These as we noted are general terms and cover a multitude of complex movements and activities. Some responses, to be sure, are rather simple, for example, those of the nature of limited movements or reactions. Among these would be the various reflexes such as knee jerk, eyelid blink, salivary discharge, and other glandular secretions. Considered anatomically, other responses are more involved. An organism might be said to have responded when it pushed against some object or pulled a string, made a left turn or a right turn, said something, ran away from or toward something, and so on. A response, then, is some more or less complex collection of movements which can be selected from a repertoire of such movements and described with sufficient exactitude so that common agreement among observers can be attained. When psychologists study behavior, then, they actually observe *samples of behavior*. These samples are selected not for themselves. Psychologists do not really care about how a knee jerks, or how a human being makes the sound "yes" (there are other scientists who do make much of these processes). The behavior selected for observation is chosen because it is convenient and serves the real purpose of the psychologist which is to discover the laws relating responses to stimuli.

In dealing with responses, psychologists are not content merely to witness a response. They break it down further into its own general characteristics. If it is repeated, for example, its frequency can be counted. If it involves a direction, that can be noted. It might vary in intensity or amplitude and this can be noted. One important way in which responses vary is in reaction time or latency. This is frequently recorded in experimental sessions.

The analysis of behavior

When a psychologist is finished with his observations he may have accumulated information about a number of stimulus variables (intensity, quality, duration, frequency, complexity, for example) and a number of response variables (intensity, latency, direction, frequency). He can now appraise his findings to see if any reliable relationships can be discovered between stimulus variables and response variables. This is the general task of psychology. We can express it in a formula with a mathematical flavor which might read

$$R = f(S).$$

This formula can be translated to read: Behavior (response variables) is a function of Stimuli (stimulus variables). The f in the formula refers to the mathematical term "function." A function, in turn, refers to some kind of operation such as multiplying, squaring, determining a proportion, a logarithmic ratio, or whatever must be done to the right side of the equation to make it equal to the left hand side. So long as we remain on the general level of $R = f(S)$ we are merely restating the $S \longrightarrow R$ formula. The real business of psychology is to identify the f's, the functions that will make the equation work.

Organismic variables

The general task of psychology has just been described as one of fitting together the environmental variables or stimuli with behavioral variables or responses. For some psychologists this is quite enough of a task and they go about their work attempting to discover such relationships. Other psychologists believe that such an orientation is too naive and that it ignores the most obvious fact of all psychology—between stimulus and response there has to be an organism, an organism which (when considered in relation to other organisms of the same or different species) may vary in its capacities, its sensitivities, its skills, its prior background of experience (its habit history), age, and present physical condition. If one or another of these factors is ignored, any relationship found between stimuli and responses may not hold at another time or with another organism. In terms of a simple illustration, one organism will eat grass while another eats worms. One worm-eater may eat worms now and not later when it has had enough. To accommodate all these additional "organismic" variables into the S side of the formula might be possible, but it is argued, it is foolhardy, cumbersome, and far less efficient an approach than to take into consideration the "organismic" variables directly and analyze their relationships or functions in connection with behavior.

Intervening variables

Organismic variables include all of the possible ways, traits, or characteristics in which individuals and species may vary. They include not only permanent or relatively permanent features like skills, capacities, habits, sex, or size, but also temporary conditions such as physiological states of depletion or satiation and other on-going processes. An organism might be prepared or "set" for some stimulus and not for others, for example, and this would alter the stimulus-response relationship that might otherwise prevail. Because such organismic variables intervene between stimuli and responses, some psychologists refer to them as "intervening variables" (I.V.). The S ⟶ R formula has been expanded by these psychologists to read: R (Behavior) = f(I.V.) *and* S. The *and* is emphasized because of a question which now arises about the nature of the relationship between I.V. and S. Are they simply added to each other, do they multiply each other's effects, or, how *do* they interact with each other? Thus another problem arises for the psychologist.

Some intervening variables can be readily mentioned though what they actually mean or what their relationship to behavior may be is a problem in its own right. It is possible simply to state a subject's age or sex, as, for example, age thirty-seven, sex, male. Other organismic or intervening variables might be more difficult to describe, as, general health, or prior history. Here no convenient numbers or labels are readily available. Other variables, such as how hungry or how thirsty an organism may be, can be described in terms of how long it has not had food or water, i.e., how long it has been "deprived." This may not be quite so satisfactory as the age figure. Not all organisms are equally "hungry" after equal intervals of deprivation. Still such an approach might be fruitful. But "hunger" and "thirst" are only two ways in which an organism might be "deprived." To base a psychology on such specific principles would result in a bulky, unwieldy, and awkward science. It would be convenient if all deprivation conditions could be thought of as representing one general operation or circumstance, one intervening variable. The smaller the number of intervening variables which have to be taken into account, the more manageable would the system become. When it appears feasible to group a number of separate but presumably similar conditions into one general variable this might be done with a special label of some inclusive nature. In the case of deprivation conditions such a label as "drive" might be used. "Drive" or "motivation" might then be terms for intervening variables of one type. Another variable mentioned earlier is prior history or experience. Here we might make use of the term "habit" or "habit strength" to represent such prior experience and treat such experience as an intervening variable of "habit." If some procedure can be devised for assigning a numerical value to such variables, the process of filling out the S ⟶ R formula would be that much further advanced.

Operational definitions

The intervening variables we have been considering so far have been described in terms of potential measurement, as conditions that might be described in terms of such operations as counting the number of hours of deprivation, the years since birth, counting the historical record of frequencies of successes and failures (as a measure of habit strength). When concepts are defined in terms of measurement or some statement of procedural routine, we have defined the concept "operationally." "Operational definitions" are highly regarded in science. When we have defined something operationally, we have spelled out a procedure for producing the event or phenomenon or object. In the case of "hunger," we might not be able to point to much, there might be nothing to see, but *if we all agree* that what we mean by "hunger" is whatever happens to an organism if it is deprived of food for twenty-four hours, then we all know what we are talking about. We may not have defined "hunger" to everyone's satisfaction, but at least there is agreement on what we have done. Similarly if we define an IQ (intelligence quotient) by stating that it is the result of dividing the "mental age" by the chronological age of a person (and where mental age is the numerical score obtained on a particular test), we have defined IQ operationally. Anyone knows how to obtain it and everyone can agree on the "meaning" (see p. 178).

Hypothetical constructs

In the preceding paragraphs we have used such expressions as "age," "drive," "IQ," "habit strength," "skills," and "set." We have emphasized that for scientific purposes, such terms, if they are to be treated as "intervening variables," must be reduced to some kind of measurement. With IQ and age, this is not a difficult matter, as we have indicated. The other terms might be more troublesome. But besides being numbers, what else do age and IQ amount to? Are they anything else? It is difficult to think of age and IQ as being simply numbers. It is almost inevitable that we "associate" additional "meanings" with the numbers. There may be value judgments—a high IQ is "good," a youthful age is more desirable to old people than "old" age, and so on. Such "excess meanings" are almost inevitable accompaniments of numbers; we believe that there must be *something* "behind" the numbers that either produces the numbers themselves or which the numbers merely reflect. When we use the term "hunger" we are not satisfied to have it indicate only 12 or 24 or 48 hours without food—we assume that some kinds of changes have taken place in the body, in the cell structures, in the sugar level of the blood, perhaps in the conditions that we might loosely call the environment of the brain. Similarly with "drive" we believe that there is some physiological condition, some "mechanism" that underlies the "drive." We are not content to think only in numerical terms which is all that we are allowed to insert into a formula. Thus, while, as scientists, we should be concerned with developing numerical values for the formula we have described as

$$R = f(\text{I.V.}) \textit{ and } S$$

our actual thinking about behavior goes on in terms of presumed mechanisms underlying whatever numbers we are able to place in the formula. We tend to populate the organism with devices, mechanisms, processes, agencies, even "faculties" such as "intelligence" (for most of us, it is impossible to think of an IQ as anything but the reflection of something real, inside of us, which is our "intelligence"). Similarly, we endow ourselves with "motives," with "perceptions," with "ideas" or "concepts," with "emotions," with "volitions," "choices," "habits," "wishes," "mind," "ideals," "goals," and as many other devices or processes as we seem to require to account for behavior.

Since no one has ever seen a habit or a drive, a motive, or an idea, or any of the rest of such *imagined* or inferred underlying processes or mechanisms, we must recognize them for what they are, the products of speculation, thinking, theorizing, or hypothesizing. Professor Clark L. Hull [2] gave such products of imagination a name; he called them "hypothetical constructs." They are hypothetical because they are not directly observable and have been "deduced" or "induced" through some kind of rational or reasoning activity. They are "constructs" because they have been "built up" from pieces of presumed evidence and they have taken on the appearance of real *things* or "entities."

Such hypothetical constructs are the stock in trade of everyone who discusses human affairs. They are part of our language and we use them every day. In ordinary discourse they are used as loose, undefined, unmeasured, intervening variables. Thus, "I hit him on the nose because I was mad at him" translated into psychological language says: the behavior (hitting someone) was a function of an intervening variable of anger or some emotional state, in addition to the stimulus variables. If a science prospers in terms of how effectively it can reduce its variables to measurement, then, to the extent that psychology is going to make use of hypothetical constructs as intervening variables, they must also be reduced to measurement. Before the hypothetical constructs can be reduced to measurement, they must be strictly defined (operationally). Hull proposed that a hypothetical construct could be employed in theoretical operations if it could be "firmly anchored at both ends"; i.e., since a hypothetical construct intervenes between stimulus and response, it must be described in terms of its relationship to both stimulus and response. If such a relationship cannot be described, then the construct is inadmissible in a scientific psychology. In the case of a construct like "drive," for example, it must be shown on the stimulus side what conditions, factors, events, or operations would generate or lead to the drive, and on the response side, what the drive has to do with the behavior. The process of systematically defining constructs would strip them of "excess" meaning, provide numerical values, and give them a place in the stimulus-response formula.

As an example of how Hull would proceed in the analysis of behavior we can consider one of his basic statements or principles in a somewhat simplified form. Hull thought of behavior in terms of the probability of a response; that is, given certain conditions, what is the probability that a certain response will occur. The nature of the response under consideration must always be spelled out. Let us, for an illustration, consider the behavior of a white rat placed in a simple maze that consists of a T-shape. The rat is put on the "starting leg," the stem of the T and runs up to the "choice" point where it will turn left or right.

[2] Professor Clark L. Hull was a prominent behavior theorist. His most popular work was *The Principles of Behavior* (1943).

Let us assume that it has previously been fed at the left a number of times. On this particular trial (or we might think in terms of many rats and many trials) the question might be: what is the probability that the rat will turn left? Hull's answer would be stated in terms of a formula; this formula would presuppose the basic formula

$$R = f(\text{I.V.})\ \textit{and}\ S.$$

But in Hull's systematic thinking, and for the special situation involved, the important intervening variables would be the amount of drive (D) and the habit strength (H). These two variables would have been measured in some fashion, perhaps for D we could use number of hours of deprivation and for H we could use the number of times the rat had found food at the left in the past. The probability of behavior would be expressed as what Hull called "excitatory potential," symbolized as "E." This expression would substitute for R in the original formula and the new formula would read

$$E = H \times D$$

or, translated, the probability of a left turn is a function of the habit strength multiplied by the drive strength. We note that the relationship between drive and habit is multiplicative. This is necessary because if either factor were of zero strength then no behavior would result and this is a possibility that must be taken into account. If the relationship were additive, then there would be, for example, some probability of response even if there were no drive, a possibility that Hull's system did not provide.

In the example we have chosen we indicated the rough definitions of the intervening variables of D and H. We did not, however, show how they were "anchored securely at each end." To do so would take us too far afield in terms of our present more general interests. Hull's definitions have been challenged by critics and it is unlikely that in the early stages of a science anyone will hit upon universally accepted definitions for intervening variables that stem from hypothetical constructs laden with ages of excess meaning. The point, however, remains, that unless a hypothetical construct is properly related to both stimulus and response aspects in any situation where it is to be employed, it is subject to criticism and possible rejection. We must note immediately that most of the hypothetical constructs that psychologists have inherited from philosophy, from physiology, and from historical usage are far from being defined in a suitable manner for use in mathematical formulas.

For the most part psychology today consists of an examination of such hypothetical constructs at a very primitive level. In the remainder of this text we shall struggle with many such constructs, try to evaluate them, try to decide whether they add to or detract from a scientific effort, and in fact, introduce some new ones. Lest such newly introduced constructs be uncritically accepted as of genuine scientific value, we have gone to the trouble to examine the nature of such constructs in the preceding pages so that the student can judge the level of "scientific" rigor of the material under discussion. He should be able to recognize whether some argument is on a theoretical level, a hypothetical level, an inductive or deductive level, whether he is dealing with a "proper" intervening variable or with a poorly appreciated hypothetical construct. The student of psychology must be continuously watchful of such matters or he will soon find himself out on a limb, supporting opinions and views that will bring him and the limb crashing down to a painful and realistic earth.

Hypothetical constructs and intervening variables

The notion of hypothetical constructs is not novel in science or peculiar to psychology. In physics, for example, the atom is a hypothetical construct as are all of its presumed components. An unseen planet whose orbit is measured indirectly also is a hypothetical construct and will remain so until it is directly observed. Resistance, current, and voltage are hypothetical constructs. Sometimes in physics, we encounter terms which are hypothetical constructs to some scientists but not to others who are somewhat more sophisticated; thus "force" or "gravity" might be regarded by some naive students as referring to real *its,* but the physicist knows that he is merely speaking of a relationship between measureables. Force is nothing more than mass multiplied by acceleration. Outside this multiplication operation, it has or should have no other meaning. Yet "mass" itself is a hypothetical construct measured indirectly and "acceleration" refers to speed per time as a further function of time when both distance and time are hypothetical *its.* The hypothetical construct is respectable enough, yet there is a danger in its use, a danger that comes from loose thinking and casual associations. By reifying some *term* we may tend to attribute qualities and functions to it that are unnecessary, undesirable, or unreal.

Professor Edward C. Tolman,[3] of the University of California, was particularly careful in considering intervening variables for inclusion in

[3] The late Edward C. Tolman was an outstanding American psychologist. Together with Hull he was responsible for shaping much of the theoretical orientation of American psychology. See his 1938 paper, "The determiners of behavior at a choice point."

his own systematic approach to psychology. He chose to treat intervening variables as a sort of convenient shorthand for a *mathematical* relationship between measureables. He was especially careful to avoid excess meanings that might be attached to such relationships and went to great trouble to invent a new vocabulary to refer to such relationships rather than risk the excess meaning associations. Because words like "drive" and "motivation" have such excess meaning, he proposed the word "demand" to represent a relationship between some performance and time since eating or other deprivation. For past experience he chose the expression "bias." All of the variables he included in his program were given such new names with the strict understanding that they did not refer to any underlying mechanism of any kind whatsoever. They stood for only mathematical relationships between measurables.

The fact that two leading theoretical thinkers in psychology (Hull and Tolman) differed in their emphases on the nature of intervening variables, the former assuming that some kind of physiological mechanism would eventually be found that was the basis for his "hypothetical constructs" and the latter dissociating himself from any implications about the possible mechanisms and emphasizing a strictly mathematical orientation, has led to some confusion about the concepts we have been describing. Most psychologists nowadays tend to think of "intervening variables" as referring to a more general, all inclusive, expression relating external world stimuli or conditions to behavior. The term "hypothetical construct" is usually reserved for "potentially identifiable" mechanisms (MacCorquodale and Meehl, 1948). Some confusion will remain so long as both expressions are retained because those psychologists who think in terms of hypothetical constructs also try to reduce them to measurement in order to use them in their research. When a hypothetical construct has been so reduced to measurement, it is an intervening variable in the more mathematical, Tolman sense.

THE PROBLEMS OF AN S ⟶ R PSYCHOLOGY

By this point the student might be asking himself what the purpose of an analysis of behavior in terms of the S ⟶ R formula might be, with or without intervening variables. If he has arrived at the point of asking this question, he has done well. An analysis of behavior in stimulus-response terms, alone, can have only the function of prediction. The entire emphasis appears to rest on the final outcome of the work of external stimuli and/or organismic conditions in terms of observable responses. The behavioral side is rather restricted to predicting what an organism will do in some situation, perhaps, as Tolman emphasized, in a situation where it is faced with a choice of some kind. Yet behavior might be considered to include more than choices. It can be argued that behavior is always and must be purposive, if purpose is defined broadly enough. Yet there are many aspects or features of behavior of considerable interest within the broad purposive framework. We might be interested per se in such aspects of behavior as thinking or problem solving, for example. Admitting that the organism has some need or purpose to survive or solve a problem, *how* does it go about doing so? Or again, while emotion or conflict may very readily be related to some "purpose," how does emotion or conflict arise and dissipate? And admitting that purposes might be served or somehow involved in education, how does an organism learn, how does it adjust? In other words, an emphasis on intervening variables and on the stimulus-response formula in terms of prediction ignores many questions, or perhaps, the basic scientific question of *how*. The ability to predict behavior in any situation and to be content with predictions would not represent a science of psychology or a science at all. It would be an elaborate calculation enterprise, and only a very complex computational and technological achievement if it were successful. If the system included the possibility of not only predicting perfectly but also of controlling perfectly, it would be only that much more of a technological masterpiece.

The S ——→R approach handles the "how" question only on the surface; it gives it a mathematical answer. "Demand" and "bias," or "drive" and "habit strength," are related perhaps by multiplication. But such multiplication does not refer to bodily processes. It refers to numbers. Bodily processes cannot be multiplied. They occur and interact and the question of "how" remains unanswered in the simple S ——→R predictive approach. How does the organism learn, for example? We cannot say, with much satisfaction, that an organism learns when time is multiplied by some other measureable. The organism learns when something happens inside its skin, presumably in its nervous system, something that may be related, to be sure, to "time-since-eating." But the nature of the relationship inside the skin must be spelled out, not necessarily in physiological terms, but in terms of principles that bring the external world to bear upon the organism and in turn permit the organism to bear upon the external world. To measure behavior in terms of the number of times a counter registers is not psychology. It is, perhaps, a technology, but leaving out the organism in the analysis results in something that may be quite divorced from a science of behavior. Only organisms behave, and the behavior can be described only in terms of processes or events that occur within the organism, and

which are related to external events in an unending sequence. Any other approach is an artificial separation of phenomena which, while perhaps technologically useful, is not satisfactory as a science which seeks a detailed account of the intimate relationships, step by step, of all events in the universe and does not rid itself of problems by skipping intermediates.

Psychology and physiology

Do the remarks above mean that psychology must be physiological, that perhaps psychology is nothing more than physiology? To some extent this is true and a knowledge of physiology would be of extreme value to a psychologist. But it is not necessary if he knows enough not to make erroneous observations and draw erroneous conclusions. The psychologist can only work with his own tools and equipment just as the physiologist works with his. If skilled enough, either could do the other's job. But because of varying interests in aspects of a problem, there is enough for each to do and plenty left over for the chemist, the physicist, and so on. Some questions can be answered with physiological tools and some with psychological tools. It depends upon the question that is asked.

The questions that are asked reflect the interests of the askers and the interests depend upon the previous activities and skills. Psychologists generally are interested in questions involving behavior of an intact organism, an integrated whole. Physiologists appear to be more definite or specific in their interests; they frequently are interested in specific organs, structures, or systems, starting most commonly with a functioning organ. The behavior of the heart, as such, can be of primary interest to a physiologist. The role played by the heart in a more complete cycle relating the external environment to behavior or effectors as these are employed in altering the environment is quite a different matter and more likely to be the psychologist's concern. But the psychologist would find little of interest in the heart as such. Its behavior would be of interest only as it functioned as part of a totality of internal events that translated itself into effector action.

The internal events that interest the psychologist are primarily neural. But here again, interest is in general neural operations and not in specific neural action. In general, the psychologist does not get concerned with which specific neurons "fire" [4] but rather with the fact that

[4] The concept of neural firing refers to the excitation of one neuron by another. The neurons do not really "fire," but because a neural impulse proceeds along a nerve in a manner analogous to the combustion along a burning powder fuse, with one unit or section apparently "setting-off" the next, the term "fire" is commonly used.

they do fire, that nothing else of importance happens unless they do, and that by appreciating the general principles underlying neural action, the nature of the relationship between external events in the environment and externally observable behavior can be understood (see Hebb, 1958).

The position of the psychologist might be, then, one that would require concern over what went on under the skin even if the skin were never opened to reveal the contents. As far as the psychologist is concerned, if he did not know there was a nervous system, he would have invented one and given it characteristics that would do his job for him. Engineers sometimes use the analogy of the *Black Box* to parallel this type of situation. Wires come into and out of the box and the engineer is supposed to decide what goes on in the box on the basis of what he sees happening outside the box. Depending upon his sophistication, the engineer may deduce the essential internal arrangements and structures with varying success. Similarly the psychologist proposes principles concerning internal neural and/or other events to tie together his observations of the external world and behavior.

The extent to which psychologists get involved with their black boxes varies from a standoffish position such as described above in connection with mathematical intervening variables where the psychologist ignores the box entirely and measures only external events, to the opposite extreme where the psychologist takes scalpel in hand and starts examining the contents of the box under a microscope. The latter type is the physiological psychologist, the former is the strict behavior analyst. Between these two extremes we find varying degrees of interest in the specific physiological facts with most psychologists quite content to postulate some kinds of events or structures which will meet their needs. When such events or structures are described quite imaginatively we refer to hypothetical constructs. Such constructs are described as effectively as possible for physiologists to find them or otherwise test for their existence. More frequently than not, physiologists are wrapped up in their own affairs and spend little time looking for psychologists' inventions.

Yet without such invention, psychology remains inadequate, incomplete, a technology or art instead of a science. This is not to gainsay the efforts of those who ignore the box and concentrate on either environmental or behavioral ends of the totality. Excellent analyses have been made on these extreme observables and without them speculation about the workings of the box would be even more weird than sometimes appears. But the box itself is an essential element of the whole and ignoring it prevents us from attacking some of the most significant kinds of behavior, that is, behavior which will take place in the future. With a given environmental event (S) and a given behavioral event (R) we are limited to observations that can be made of the specific features of each. These may never recur in the history of the organism in the same precise form. In any event we are forced to operate on a probability basis which rests upon past observations of frequencies or other relationships. We cannot predict an event without having observed it before. It must have an actuarial status in our data book; otherwise it cannot be forecast. Will a person commit suicide? Will he kill his mother? Such things can be done only once. They are outside the scope of an S ⟶ R psychology's prediction. One might get around it and predict statistically, that a given per cent of people will commit suicide on July 4, for example, but this amounts to the same kind of prediction that Safety Councils make before every holiday. If the figures correspond, the Safety Council can say: "See!" If they do not, they say (if the count is below the prediction): "Our campaigning is working." Nowhere do we find an account of who will have an accident and under what conditions it will take place.

Not only is the simple S ⟶ R view unable to predict novel events until they are no longer novel, but it must predict some kinds of events incorrectly. If, for example, a subject is trained to press a button when he sees candy in front of him, it is difficult and awkward, if not impossible, for the simple S ⟶ R psychologist to account for such a button press when the word *candy* appears in the appropriate place instead of the physical candy itself. Since there is no resemblance between a chocolate bar and an arbitrary jumble of print, there is no basis for a prediction without reference to some process within the organism.

It might be argued that the printed word "candy" has become related to the physical stimuli involving chocolate bars on some basis that could be handled by a strictly S ⟶ R view; i.e., we need not exclude the possibility that words as spoken sounds or written symbols can come to substitute for direct object properties. Indeed, they must. But can they become predictable indicators of behavioral events without involving some intermediate step intimately involving processes inside the skin? When words are used in sequences, in fact when any sequence of events is initiated by some one external event, how does a theory oriented only to external events fare? It appears undeniable that some process of self-stimulation is required to maintain the chain of events. In some cases, the events themselves might be observed and the theory might proceed to handle the situation. More frequently, perhaps, the events are not currently observable and must be postulated. Without such postulation the external-events theorists must postulate more and more extensive prior experience, or engage in circumlocutions that approach the fantastic. In accounting for walking behavior, for example, it seems appropriate to postulate that stimuli from the extensor muscles of one leg simultaneously initiate flexion in the other, and subsequent stimuli from the pressure or stepping or the extension itself initiate extensor movements in the opposite leg. We begin to arrive at some comprehension of stepping behavior when we examine the "crossed-extensor reflex" (see p. 76). The strictly behavioral psychologist must content himself with the observation that moving one leg ("a hollow one") is followed by moving the other.

An even more serious difficulty arises from the preoccupation with external events to the exclusion of internal ones. The difficulty stems from the conception of the nervous system as nothing but a connecting device which can be ignored since it always does the same job of connecting. Recent physiological findings have made us realize more than ever before how wrong this view is. We now recognize that the operations of the brain itself determine what stimuli are going to enter the connecting system and make a connection possible or probable. The observer of external events may observe stimuli at length and get no behavioral event to observe if the nervous system is not at the moment available or "tuned in" on the appropriate channels. What an organism will react to in a receiving sense depends to a considerable degree on what the organism happens to be doing or more correctly, what the brain is doing or has just been doing. Thus a subject who has been looking at a screen and raising his finger when a green light flashes, and has done this thirty times in succession, now fails to raise his finger as rapidly when a red light comes on even though he has been instructed to do so. A subject who has been looking at a series of letters briefly exposed on a screen now fails to see effectively a series of numbers. The child watching television may not hear the call to dinner or even "ice cream."

Such control over the entry of stimulation seems to require a concern with internal processes. Most psychologists are willing to admit an interest in such processes, some almost exclusively so. It has always been the concern of psychology to take account of the organism and will probably remain so. This does not mean, however, that a physiological orientation is required. It does mean a strong interest in generally described physiological propositions relating external events to internal ones and a subsequent relation of internal events to externally observable behavior. The psychologist has found his area of operations in a concern with problems such as thinking, feeling, wishing, deciding, learning, and perception. By and large all these involve considerable speculation about internal events. It is how these events are thought of that has really been the root of troubles in psychology.

One-stage and multiple-stage theories

In the preceding pages we have described a simple or "strict" S ——→R theory and contrasted it with a view that emphasizes intervening events within the organism. The simple S ——→R theory can be called a one-stage theory. Every factor taken into account is on the same level or plane of observation. Numbers can be assigned to stimulus variables and to response variables and observed behavior can be translated into or explained in terms of observed conditions. A simple knee-jerk reflex might be a suitable illustration. The tap on the knee cap is followed by a swinging reaction of the leg.

As soon as hypothetical constructs of any kind are postulated, the theory has become a two-stage or multiple stage view (Osgood, 1953). Now it is held that stimuli lead to conditions, processes, activation of mechanisms, internal responses or what not, that either directly control the response or lead to it by developing additional, internal stimuli. It is still a stimulus-response theory, but in a two-stage or multiple-stage theory, the position is taken that the original external world stimulation (we can label it "S") first initiates some response inside the organism, perhaps only in terms of a simple neural process, or some pattern of movements; this we can label "r." Lower-case type is meant to suggest that this response is not the final one which we will eventually observe. Now, as we will learn in a later chapter, any response made by the organism, say the contraction of some muscles, will result in the activation of sense organs or receptors within the muscles and automatically create new stimuli. These stimuli, like any others, will also initiate a response or pattern of responses, giving rise to new stimuli, and so on. Eventually, the stimuli generated by some responses will lead to a final response, i.e., the response in which we are interested in terms of observing behavior; this response we can label "R." By capitalizing this label, we indicate that it is the end-product, the response of major concern. Some psychologists like to differentiate such final responses by some additional label. Professor Hull, for example, called such responses, Goal Responses and labeled them "R_G." Because the term "goal" has connotations which suggest a purposive aspect to the behavior, and because some final responses may not actually meet the criteria by which we might define a purposive response we will not use the "goal" label in describing the final response. Yet, it is desirable to indicate that there is something special about this response to distinguish it from others and it might be useful to call it a *consummatory* or "end" response. While this term also has some undesirable or undesired connotations, perhaps even including a "goal" connotation, it also suggests a finality about the response, which makes it appropriate. If we think of the final response as terminating a series of responses, as eliminating, in a sense, the original stimulation, getting rid of it, then the term "consummatory" might be a helpful label. We could symbolize it by "R_c." It should be recognized that an R_c will also lead to stimulation and new responses. The chain is never broken until death. However, the behavior in which we are interested can be thought of as stopping with an R_c. We can now represent the pattern of events involved in a two or multiple stage theory as follows:

$$S \longrightarrow r_1 \longrightarrow s_1 \longrightarrow r_2 \longrightarrow s_2 \longrightarrow R_c$$

In this pattern of events, r_1, s_1, r_2, and s_2 are hypothetical events, intervening events which occur between the original S and the consummatory response R_c. Because they do intervene, and because they serve the function of *carrying on* the pattern of activity, they can be labeled "mediators" or "mediating" events. In one form or another, such mediating events are presumed to intervene between stimuli and final responses in many phases or kinds of behavior. They may be very simple in nature, amounting to no more than muscle movements and their consequent stimuli which lead to further muscle movements as in the case of walking. In such behavior where one movement leads to another, via stimuli generated by a previous movement, we might refer to "movement-produced stimuli" as does Professor Guthrie.[5] He has labeled such "movement-produced stimuli" as "MPS," and in his theoretical writings, he has placed a heavy burden of explanation on these MPS mediators. Similarly, at a higher, but vaguer, level of discourse, we might consider the flow of words in a sentence or conversation as "one-word leading to another" in the same sense of $S \longrightarrow r \longrightarrow s \longrightarrow R_c$; in the same way, at a still higher, and still vaguer level, we might talk about one "idea" leading to another, or one "association" leading to another. In these latter frames of reference, we would have to, in some manner, reduce the "idea" or "association" to some kinds of "response" and retain the stimulus-producing nature of the response concept in order to stay within the $S \longrightarrow r \longrightarrow s \longrightarrow r \longrightarrow s \longrightarrow R_c$

[5] E. R. Guthrie was Professor Emeritus of Psychology at the University of Washington. For many years he was a champion of American behavioristic psychology but one with his own highly individualistic stamp. Along with Hull and Tolman he was a central figure in the Neo-Behaviorist movement. His most influential work is *The Psychology of Learning* (1952).

formula. This might become difficult at times, but the basic assumption of physical monism requires such a position and the effort must be made if we are to remain scientific about our subject.

We will have a great deal more to say about such mediation activity in future chapters. In fact, the concept of mediation is perhaps the key principle to have been developed by modern psychology. For the present, our interest lies in pointing out that the mediation principle allows the psychologist to retain an S———→R orientation while at the same time it permits him to go beyond the investigation of simple reflexive behavior into a consideration of sequences of responses such as are characteristic of most behavior patterns. It does not sacrifice the interest in prediction while, at the same time, it requires that the psychologist attend to the nature of "internal" events. From this point of view, the psychologist is forced to concern himself with what goes on in the organism when it is "thinking," "emoting," "desiring," etc.—the traditional problem areas of psychology. The psychologist is also forced to consider the operations of the nervous system as a possible source of mediational activity in order to account for some of the behavior of his organisms, especially behavior that is not readily reducible to muscle contractions.

A "response" psychology orientation

We would be remiss if we did not mention one other point of view in connection with basic scientific orientations toward the analysis of behavior. It is the point of view associated with the work of Professor Skinner, whom we have already introduced to the student. Skinner (1938) early recognized that a simple S———→R view restricted the psychologist to behavior where the S could be identified and controlled. For the most part, as far as laboratory work was concerned, this confined the psychologist to the study of rather simple behavior patterns, reflexes like eyelid blinks and glandular secretions. This kind of behavior, strictly under the control of stimuli, Skinner labeled "Respondent" behavior or "Type S" because it depended so completely on the presence of an identifiable S. Skinner argued that most behavior of any consequence could not be traced so easily to specific stimuli and that psychologists who were interested in anything more significant than reflex responses were shouldering an unnecessary and heavy burden in concerning themselves with stimuli in the first place. What they should do, Skinner asserted, was to concentrate on the response aspects of behavior and discover the laws that governed the occurrence of responses. According to Skinner, any response of consequence to an organism will occur from time to time and can be observed under controlled conditions. A response is considered of consequence if it in some way alters the organism's environment, that is, if it "operates" on the environment and affects it or changes it. A response might, for example, bring the organism to food, or food to the organism. A verbal response might halt another organism or alter its behavior in some way. Skinner called such responses "Operants," or "Type R," because the interest lies in the nature of the response itself and its effects on the environment. In a given period of time, a response will occur with some frequency, perhaps once every five minutes, or twice an hour, or whatever it turns out to be. This normal frequency of occurrence of a response, Skinner called the "operant rate." Such responses as occur with any frequency at all can now be studied to determine how the frequency can be modified, increased or decreased in rate. Skinner's orientation automatically leads to an interest in what happens after a response occurs, since he is concerned with the aftereffects of a response, with what happened to the environment. We can anticipate here a bit and note that if the aftereffects are generally beneficial to the organism, the behavior in question might show an increase in "operant rates"; if they are punitive or inimical, the "operant rate" might decline. Skinner is not committed to any notions of beneficial or harmful aftereffects. He takes a strictly objective position that some consequences of a response are followed by an increase in operant rate, some by decrease. If the response shows an increase in frequency as the consequence of some aftereffect, Skinner says the response was reinforced (actually he says only that the rate increases). The problem for the psychologist, according to Skinner, is to discover what kinds of aftereffects do alter what kinds of operant responses and what kinds of relations hold between response rates and manipulable aspects of aftereffects. The psychologist might control the aftereffects so that some responses are followed by the effect and some are not. How much change would be observed in the response rate if the effect occurred only every other time, or only 10 per cent of the time, or if it were withheld after having occurred a number of times? Such manipulation of aftereffects Skinner labels "schedules of reinforcement" and the job of the psychologist is to discover the laws that describe the relationships that hold between response rates and schedules of reinforcement.

The student might be wondering about what happened to the stimulus in Skinner's views. After all, we do respond to stimuli. We react to people, to telephone bells, to traffic signals, and so on. Skinner is perfectly aware of the fact that stimuli are present, that behavior occurs in an environment, and that things go on in the environment. Even schedules of reinforcement have to be administered in some environment, in some kinds of controlled conditions or situations. The point, however, according to Skinner, is that the stimuli that are present do not force or elicit behavior in the same, immediate sense that a tap on the knee makes the leg jerk. A red traffic signal does not automatically bring about a stopping response in a small child or even an expert driver. In fact, the expert driver may notice the red light, look about the area, and proceed to drive on through the intersection. A color-blind driver once pointed out the absurdity of standing at an intersection waiting for a light to change when there was no traffic about. He followed the expedient (presumably illegally, half the time) of riding on if he saw no cross traffic. When some stimulus is present at the time the organism "emits" some operant response, and this response is followed by a "reinforcer," and, if no reinforcer follows the response in the absence of that stimulus, the organism gradually comes to respond only in its presence. Such a stimulus has acquired a certain amount of control over the behavior, but it does not, according to Skinner, directly elicit or evoke the responses; it merely sets the stage for it. Let us illustrate. Suppose that some small animal is placed in a box which has a chain hanging from the top. The animal has not eaten for some time. It can be observed to move about. Sooner or later, it brushes against the chain and may begin to chew on it or tug at it. If the experimenter wishes, he can arrange for a piece of food to drop into the box whenever a sufficient pull has been exerted on the chain. If this is done, the animal will more or less readily "learn" to pull the chain and supply itself with food. Here we have a simple operant response with reinforcement changing the rate of occurrence of the operant behavior. Now a light can be turned on in the box by the experimenter. When the animal pulls the chain it is fed and the light goes off. If the chain is pulled in the absence of the light, no food follows. Pulling "pays off" only when the light is on. The animal again "learns" to pull when the light is present; when there is no light, the animal will not pull the chain frequently and may merely sit around; as soon as the light comes on, it runs over to the chain and pulls. According to Skinner, the light has become differentiated from other features of the box; it now functions as a *discriminated* stimulus, in Skinner's notation, an "S^{D}." The term "discriminated" refers to the fact that something is done in its presence which is not done in its absence. From Skinner's point of view, most behavior of consequence follows the general pattern described: we emit operants from time to time. Some of these are reinforced (with different kinds of schedules); sooner or later, in most cases, we come to differentiate the situations in which reinforcers will follow the response from those in which they will not; i.e., we begin to discriminate stimuli related to the reinforcement schedule. It is possible, according to this view, to control the operant rate of any response by the process of reinforcement and the use of discriminated stimuli. We will return to considerations of the nature of the learning involved in later chapters.

Summary of S ——→R views

In this chapter we have described how psychologists think when they are wearing their scientist hats. How they think at home, at a football game, a cocktail party, or on a fishing trip is another matter. When working in laboratories or on research problems, they take one form or another of the S ——→R view. We have indicated a number of variations and developments of this view and it may help to review these at this point:

1. The one-stage S ——→R position. This was the original starting point of Behaviorism. Stimuli lead to responses. Presentation of the proper stimuli results in the occurrence of the behavior of interest. The psychologist's job is to identify the stimuli which evoked specific kinds of behavior, and to observe the S ——→R combinations that comprise behavior. Some S ——→R combinations are natural or "innate," others are learned or "conditioned," and these combinations served as the "building blocks" of more complex behavior patterns.

2. As psychology became more sophisticated, it was recognized that the organism had to be taken into account and various organismic variables were taken into consideration. These were thought of as "intervening variables." For some psychologists intervening variables consist only of mathematical relationships between environmental conditions or organismic factors and the behavior under study. Other psychologists are willing to postulate potentially discoverable mechanisms within the organism which also intervene between environment and behavior. They call these mechanisms or processes "hypothetical constructs." When hypothetical constructs are introduced between S and R, we have a two-stage or "multiple" S ——→R theory. The hypothetical constructs, in many instances, are presumed to be internal responses or conditions that generate stimuli or unobserved movements or processes that produce stimuli. Professor Hull, for example, pictured his hypothetical construct of "Drive" as a state or condition that generates "drive stimuli," or S_D. These unobserved stimuli (potentially observable, by assumption) are presumed to lead to responses which can be directly observed and thought of as the behavior under study, or they may simply lead to other unobserved responses which produce more stimuli,

leading to new responses, and so on until some final observable response occurs. Proponents of two-stage S ——→R views are sometimes referred to as Neo-Behaviorists.

3. It is possible to think of the S as having a deciding role, a mechanically forcing role, or merely as playing a stage-setting role. In Skinner's view, S's are considered as serving only the "discriminative" function and not a directly eliciting or evoking function. Skinner's emphasis is on the R side of the S ——→R formula, with the S side given a different interpretation from that held by one-stage or multiple-stage theorists. This orientation still qualifies as a Behaviorism but it must be distinguished from the other views.

Continuity and noncontinuity

Over the years, if not the centuries, psychologists have been divided on an issue that involves the fundamental approaches to behavior study and analysis. Adherents of one approach *assume* that behavior is a *cumulative resultant* of everything that has gone before, that the mass of past experience, both favorable and unfavorable, happiness and unhappiness, good fortune and bad, sum up algebraically to determine present behavior. For example it is assumed by the "continuity" theorists that if two organisms have different past histories in connection with some kind of situation, say in obtaining food by pushing a lever, then their behavior in respect to the lever will be predictably different. If one organism has obtained food 100 times and failed to get food 10 times where the other has obtained food only 50 times and failed only twice, then the first one can be expected to push the lever more frequently than the second in a test situation where neither receives food any longer. This might appear to be reasonable enough, yet there are many factors to take into account in even such a simple situation and the prediction might not always work out. In more complex human affairs we are frequently at a loss to understand some behavior. Parents of delinquents often insist: "But he was such a good boy." The failure of our predictions based on a knowledge of past experience may be due to inadequate knowledge. Not all parents know what their children are up to away from home. If all of the past experience were taken into account the prediction might be more accurate. This leaves us with an insecure position. We might find ourselves arguing for a continuity approach when it works and when it fails we would retreat under the protection of a claim of incomplete information. It is important to emphasize at this point that continuity psychologists operate in terms of a *cumulative* effectiveness of past experience. We restate this point because it is sometimes misunderstood when the position of other psychologists who have been labeled "noncontinuity" theorists is considered. The noncontinuity psychologists have as much respect for past experience as anyone else; they do not ignore it but urge that other principles besides algebraic summation might have to be taken into account in predicting or explaining behavior. Thus they argue that there may be many factors in the present situation that have to be considered along with the previous history of an organism. They call attention to the comparative strength of factors now operating on the organism. On the human level, for example, some people do quit smoking after a long history of enjoying and practicing the habit. The fear of cancer after reading a newspaper report or a promise made to a dying relative may outweigh years of practice for some people. Other people quit smoking every day, never managing to succeed. Such individual differences, however, prompt the continuity theorists to argue even more strongly that the *total* history must be taken into account. Why does one individual fear cancer enough to stop smoking while others do not?

The noncontinuity view must not be regarded as supporting a view of lawlessness in human behavior. Behavior is still regarded as determined, but the emphasis is placed on development, on changes in point of view, on re-evaluations of the past, on new "insights" and reorganized perceptions. Thus the girl who swore that she would never drink or smoke when she was fourteen may be the life of the party at eighteen. All little boys want to become firemen or cowboys but only a few actually do.

We shall run into this problem of noncontinuity or continuity in connection with such topics as learning, problem-solving, motivation, personality, and personality disorders. For the present we can conclude the discussion with some cautions against some loose thinking about behavioral problems that is rather generally enjoyed by the public and even by respected authorities in other fields. It is held, for example, by some thinkers about human problems that a child reaches an "age of reason" at some stage in his life, perhaps at the age of seven. Prior to this his behavior might have been more or less irrational and irresponsible. Now, on his seventh birthday he is supposed to come into himself in some fashion, to recognize the difference between right and wrong or in some other ways manifest some hitherto absent rationality. In a sense, everything that happened prior to the age of seven is forgivable and of no consequence. American society has extended this "age of reason" to some time around the age of sixteen. Juvenile delinquents, for example, are not mentioned by name in newspapers if they are below this age. In other legal situations other age limits are set by society—for driver's licenses, marriage licenses, voting, the privilege of purchasing cigarettes or alcoholic beverages, and so on. The teenager might argue with great vehemence that one day, or one month, or one year will make no difference in his abilities or maturity, but the laws are rigid on such matters, and may well be based on implicit assumptions about the emergence of a sense of responsibility, maturity of judgment, etc., at certain ages or when one passes through some ceremonial ritual.

We should make special note of the common view expressed when some individuals become mentally ill. We hear various remarks which are colorful slang but probably poor psychiatry: "He flipped his lid." "He blew his stack." Generally the victims of mental disorder are described as having been, up to a point, "all right." Then, presumably, "the strain got to be too much for him," "he reached a breaking point" and suddenly "cracked-up." In such cases the continuity or noncontinuity issue is not as clear to the psychologist as it is to the layman. Some psychiatrists do take the the position that mental breakdowns are related to a continuing history of maladjustment stemming from childhood (traumatic experiences in the very early years, rejection by parents, and a host of other possible circumstances). They argue that the surface adjustment reported by friends or family was a superficial façade with, in some cases, the patient himself unaware of his true condition. Others, again, emphasize the present situation and its difficulties and do not look for troubles in the early years as the sole causes of current personality disorders.

No one actually denies some kind of significance for past experience; this is not the issue. The question about which there is debate in psychology is: Can there be abrupt breaks in behavior patterns with organisms now operating as if they had in one degree or another or in some way divorced themselves from past experience? Can individuals make breaks with their pasts, voluntarily or otherwise? Can habits be broken? Can criminals be reformed? Do such changes, if they do take place, occur only through the *cumulative effect* of new experiences added to the prior history, or are there some psychological processes that can be tapped, invoked, or otherwise introduced that appear to negate the totality of past experience and bring about reliable changes in a short time? These are the real issues. We might conclude this preliminary discussion by asking if it is true that "as the twig is bent, so grows the tree," and is the child "father to the man" as the poet tells us?

In the succeeding chapters we shall have a chance to examine the findings, the arguments, and the tentative principles psychologists have developed in their studies and have a chance to evaluate the various viewpoints we have uncovered so far. We shall see that in many problem areas the progress has not been very great or even promising. Psychologists have not yet learned how to think effectively about some problems, many of which, for the student, might represent the *real* problems of psychology. Some of the answers suggested may appear trivial and of no real consequence for present day living. The student should recognize, as Conant (1953) emphasizes, that answers always become trivial as soon as they are obtained. What is interesting is the questions that the just-obtained answer forces us to face. Psychology abounds with interesting questions. That is how a science should be.

Molar and molecular approaches

Reductionism

Another issue concerning approaches to the study of behavior which divides psychologists into occasionally warring camps is the problem of "reductionism." It is generally agreed by scientists that there is a "unity" to science; that when all the facts about the universe are known they will all fit nicely into one grand integrated theoretical view; that the facts and principles discovered by one group, say, biologists, will not contradict the facts and principles discovered by chemists, physicists, geologists, psychologists, and so on. There is also the commonly shared opinion that there will develop a hierarchy of principles from less to greater and greater generality. In the current "politics" of science it is believed that the various disciplines, approaches, techniques, and "facts" can be arranged in a hierarchy of scientific areas, with physics the most general science with the broadest laws or generalizations of all. From the viewpoint of some psychologists, the hierarchy would be something as follows: the laws of chemistry could be deduced as theorems from the laws of physics, the laws of biology could, in turn, be deduced from those of chemistry, from biology, the laws of physiology could be determined, and from physiology those of psychology would develop as theorems. Such an orientation would place psychology at the end of a sequence of "natural" sciences. For those who are concerned with social problems, it might be argued that social sciences must begin with a foundation of psychology from which the laws of social psychology and sociology would be deducible as theorems.

From this point of view, physics is regarded as a sort of master science of the highest degree of generality, and the other sciences become less general and more particular as we descend the hierarchy. The terms "molar" and "molecular" might be used to describe the relative degree of interest in broad principles as contrasted to more and more detailed knowledge. Chemistry would be molecular compared to physics, but molar compared to biology; physiology would be molecular for biology but molar for psychology, and so on.

The whole hierarchy could be reversed, of course, so long as we are merely speculating, and psychology could become the major discipline with broad general principles which would find their detailed explanations in physiology, which in its turn would find its more detailed particulars accounted for in biology, chemistry, and physics. If we took this position, then psychology would be molar and physiology molecular. The principles of one science would be "reduced" to the facts of the next. When a science translates its findings into a more "molecular" account in the facts of another science, the procedure is termed "reductionism."

Regardless of the status of other sciences in the hypothetical hierarchies that might be considered, the close relationship between psychology and physiology is generally acknowledged and the borderline between them is sometimes indistinguishable as far as the work of individuals in the two fields is concerned. Some psychologists would like to be able to spell out the principles of psychology in terms of physiological functions or operations. In this way, it is argued, one science can help another, and advance the "unity of science." Those psychologists who try to spell out the characteristics of their intervening "hypothetical constructs" in physiological terms are considered "reductionists"; their efforts are characterized as "molecular." Other psychologists are less concerned about the unity of science and presume it will come about in its own good time, that there is enough to do on a "molar" level in psychology, and that psychologists should content themselves with observations of the intact organism in its environment, seeking relationships between stimuli and responses. When they find it necessary to postulate hypothetical constructs they prefer to do this in more general terms without special reference to physiological mechanisms. In a two-stage S——→R theory, for example, it might be postulated that some "mediating process" occurs without trying to specify the muscular or neural events that comprise it. Some might, as indicated earlier, even try to get along without reference to the nervous system or other internal structures at all, taking account only of external observables and espousing an "empty organism" point of view. Those psychologists who question the advisability of physiological interests or attempts to reduce psychology to physiology assume that behavior can be studied in its own right and lead to the discovery of purely psychological principles. How they state these principles depends upon their orientations with respect to the S——→R assumptions we have already examined and upon the kinds of positions they adopt with respect to the issues of continuity and intervening variables. Certainly it would be an admirable achievement for psychologists to develop an extensive set of reliable relationships based only on molar observations and their efforts are just as praiseworthy as those of any other workers.

CHAPTER 3

Nature and Nurture

Heredity and environment · Tendencies and talents · Maturation · Walking and talking · The developmental sequence · The development of speech · Instincts · Tropisms · Imprinting · The relative importance of the early years · Early and late learning · The effects of infantile deprivation or enrichment · Adolescent behavior · Maturation and the later years

The psychologist analyzing behavior may be subject to the "specialist's bias." Like the surgeon who may regard the scalpel as the obvious answer to a medical problem or the internist who first considers drugs as a remedy, so the psychologist leans toward an environmental explanation of his observations. It is necessary to caution the student about this bias as well as to account for it. In the preceding chapters we have noted the preoccupation with stimuli and responses. In practical operations these are all the psychologist has to work with. He cannot change organisms by drugs or surgery; indeed, he is not allowed by law to try. All he can manipulate is the environment (stimuli) if he is to do any changing at all. Because he is restricted to such practices, he sometimes acts as if nothing else were of any consequence. To change people, says the psychologist, you must change the world around them. Sometimes the psychologist tries techniques calculated to make the world *look* different to his subjects, but even this he does by changing something in the world itself.

From the work of psychologists one would gather that the present behavior is the resultant of an organism's behavioral history, of how the organism has been reared, and its past experience, especially in its early days or years, taken in conjunction with a present situation. The possible contribution of heredity to behavior is frequently ignored or honored by only nominal lip service. On the other hand, the average citizen tends to offer simple explanations of complex patterns of behavior by referring to "blood is thicker than water," "it was in his blood," a "bad seed," "it runs in the family," "just like his father," and similar uncritical expressions.

When we add to such hereditary behavior patterns that are presumed to be transmitted within families the traits and functions that are supposed to be natural, innate, or unlearned in an entire species, the issue becomes even more thoroughly confused. Editors and novelists are lavish in their references to "instinct," "oriental cunning," "Slavic stolidity," "German industriousness," and similar easy generalizations which clear up all questions of any importance. Sports writers are chronic offenders in this lazy and ill-considered usage of references to native equipment. "A natural switch-hitter," a real "fighting heart," "catlike reflexes," "a born horsewoman," and similar expressions dot the daily sport columns accounting for the proficiency of any performer. The fact that great tennis players like Bill Tilden used to spend hours on a court practicing serves with dozens of balls is rarely cited. Why should it be? Was he not obviously a natural-born tennis player? Even the lovelorn columnists glory in women's intuition, a mother's instinctive knowledge of what is right, and the "all men are alike" routine.

It is obvious that between the psychologist's environment and the behavior we observe there is an organism; an organism that was born of parents, and which was equipped with a particular set of physical characteristics or features. These features, in any particular behavioral example, might or might not be of fundamental importance. Whether we can ascribe to heredity, in the sense of characteristics transmitted through the germ plasm of the parents, any serious role in a particular kind of activity, is a question that demands a factual answer, not an opinion. Such answers we can only obtain through experimentation. The student of behavior is obliged to take heredity into account and appraise its contribution before he proceeds on the basis of an environmental bias. In this chapter, we can only hope to touch on the logical issues involved.

HEREDITY AND ENVIRONMENT

The topic of heredity might be more properly left to the special branch of biology known as "genetics," and, indeed, the nature of hereditary mechanisms will not be discussed here. The student will have had some familiarization with the subject in secondary school and should get more at the college level. What is of concern to the psychologist is that in the realm of behavior so much is thoughtlessly attributed to heredity by those who are either ignorant or biased or both that not much progress can be made toward the study of behavior until the contribution of heredity is properly assessed.

It would not serve our purpose to catalogue every human feature or characteristic that is inherited and every trait that is not. It is quite impossible to make such statements seriously if all details of the hereditary process are rigorously analyzed. In general terms, such catalogues have already been arranged for us [1] and it can be agreed for practical purposes that blue eyes are hereditary and glass ones are not; that hemophilia and color blindness are hereditary but dirty fingernails and crew cuts are not. Hereditary wealth seems obviously a variation in the meaning of the term, and blue-blood or royal strains seem quite fanciful extrapolations of the concept of inheritance.

It is apparent that individuals who are content with their social status and who are threatened in this position might wish to bolster their security by claiming a hereditary right to their positions. To doubly insure their status they might also hope that those members of society who occupy an inferior status might similarly be entitled to none better because of hereditary limitations. Consequently some individuals arbitrarily label certain groups or racial strains inferior while at the same time, they label themselves superior, a Herrenvolk, or master race. Such views are as ancient as history. In the *Republic* Plato stated that some men are born to be slaves. The class or caste societies found throughout the world are the social reflections of such faulty thinking about heredity.

On the other hand, in some societies or among some individuals we have an equally untenable espousal of the view that "all men are born equal," ignoring Orwell's (1946) caustic observation in *Animal Farm* that "some are more equal than others." Equality before the law is a proper ideal of Western civilization, but it can hardly be extended to the realm of biology as it ignores the obvious physical differences with which individuals are born—some with healthy, undamaged tissues, others doomed to feeblemindedness because of undeveloped or damaged brains, or otherwise deformed or malfunctioning organs.

The barest attention to the question should provoke the obvious consideration that men are not born all virtue or all vice, that whatever is provided by nature is worked over by the environment, that neither heredity nor environment can work without each other. We must think of a given behavior pattern as a *product* in a mathematical sense of heredity × environment, and not an *addition* of heredity plus environment. In theory, the question resolves itself into: given this organism or this species (at any particular stage in the life history), to what extent can the behavior be modified by altering the environment? And

[1] The student will enjoy reading *The New You and Heredity* (Scheinfeld, 1950). This popular presentation describes the various traits, good and bad, that appear to be passed on genetically. It is particularly interesting in the discussion of the Dionne quintuplets who had an identical genetic start.

correspondingly, in a stable environment, to what extent can behavior be expected to vary with parenthood? Actually, the possibility of knowing the complete contribution of heredity or the degree of stability of the environment is extremely remote and is not a practical concern in the operations of psychology. To work effectively in this area, psychologists would need a supply of identical twins that exceeds by far their appearance in maternity wards. Since each pair would differ from every other pair, the prospects of getting a sizable population for any particular problem are discouraging. If changes are to be effected in environmental patterns of such twins, a genuine social and human problem arises in the need to rear twins separated from each other (different homes, foster parents, etc.). Such twins are rarely observed.

Controversies in the nature-nurture field (fed as they are by social philosophies) rarely lead to meaningful principles. A few years ago in the Soviet Union, Lysenko created considerable stir with his anti-Mendelian view which, generally speaking, stated that genetics as studied in the West was antisocial (and antisocialist) dogma, that genes and chromosomes could be largely ignored, that great changes could be produced in plants and animals by carefully manipulating the environment, that changes can be made to occur in plant size and characteristics by fertilization, irrigation, and other agricultural techniques. That the changes are "great" is a matter of degree and evaluation. Changes occur in the size of children in the United States from generation to generation with improvements in nutrition. Children of immigrants vary in size depending on whether they are born and raised in Europe or the United States. Such changes, however, do not bear on the Mendelian explanation of hereditary mechanisms. *In a given environment,* certain dependable predictable results can be obtained by manipulating parentage. Hybrid crossings are responsible for more agricultural gains than Lysenko cares to admit.

The basic point is that heredity cannot be separated from environment, and that environment must be recognized as including more than geography and climate. In the animal kingdom, we count the uterine (prenatal) environment and must also reckon with congenital experience. Environmental effects begin long before we are born, operate when we are born, and forever after. Similarly, hereditary functions in a given environment may determine the span of life, the appearance of adolescence (in the time of menstruation, for example), and menopause, of baldness, and various weaknesses and failings of old age.

Every organism is a resultant of a given hereditary contribution in a given environment (Hebb, 1953). There is no way to separate these contributions as neither can operate in the absence of the other. If heredity can be held constant, as in the case of identical twins raised in different environments, whatever *variations* in behavior can be observed can be considered to reflect the influence of those environments on that heredity. The contribution of heredity would still be inseparable from the influence of the environments. With a different heredity, these environments might interact differently, and correspondingly, still different environments might have resulted in different patterns of behavior from those observed. In later chapters we shall have occasion to consider this problem again when we try to appreciate the role of experience and learning in the modification of behavior. There we shall see how important *early* environmental factors are in the development of what is often considered inborn, instinctive, or "innate."

Many of the effects of heredity show up in behavior indirectly. A short boy is called "runt" or "shrimp" and takes offense, reacts against such labels with aggressive patterns or by withdrawal. Obviously, size is significant in social relations, yet size is in many aspects governed by heredity. But not all boys react in the same way and the effects must be thought of as indirect. Aggression is not, so far as we know, a hereditary trait—extralarge adrenal glands might be. There is no point to listing all the ways in which heredity indirectly influences behavior. That much is obvious. It is only important to note that it is the physical characteristics, the structures, the shape of the nose, or the eyebrow, the size of the kidney, and so on that is inherited in a given environment, and not dominance, archness, cupidity, or timidity. It is equally important to note that whatever the shape of the nose or the eyebrow, extremely different kinds of behavior can be found in different individuals with the "same" hereditary structures.

Tendencies and talents

We can turn now to the vague no-man's land of tendencies, susceptibilities, resistances, and potentialities. Here we run into a difficult logical situation which hampers thought and research. If you are exposed to a draft, get your feet wet, and get thoroughly chilled you may find that you did not catch a cold. The reason for this is that your "resistance" was high. If you bask in the warm sun and do get a summer cold, your resistance was low. The supporting logic in such situations is more than exasperating. It is of negative value because the concept of resistance is not defined except in terms of whether you caught the cold. It has no independent status. At no time can we *measure* resistance before you go out into the sun or the rain. Similarly, those who favor the use of tobacco will point to the centenarians who puff away on their one-hundreth anniversaries as proof that tobacco is not only harmless but probably kills germs that might shorten your life. When the nonsmoker, nondrinker reaches one-hundred, he attributes it to "never-touching-the-stuff." In neither case do we know what would have happened if the opposite habits had been characteristic of the individuals. A popular song tells us that you will live until you die. While this lore might help establish a teenager's "philosophy of life," it is as meaningless as a "tendency for a long life." Our days are filled with advice. "If you take care of yourself, you'll live a long time yet," says the heart specialist to the victim of an attack. The victim dies. "He didn't watch himself," says the specialist.

"Blood will tell" says the moralist on either side of the fence. "He'll come to no good end." If he dies before he gets into trouble, he simply did not live long enough. Against such views there is no defense, no answer. One can only repeat the demand for evidence, for independent, operational definitions, for appropriate tests and experimental proofs.

The problem of "talent" is similar. You have talent or you haven't. If you are successful in some line of activity to which the term appears applicable, you have talent. If you fail (even after prior successes), you have no talent. If your parents have talent, they pass it on to you. If you are unsuccessful, you did not take advantage of your hereditary gifts, or they "never developed," or the talent is still there, but it is "latent." Someday it will be revealed. If you have talent but your parents had none (or had not demonstrated it), then it must have been passed on as a recessive trait from grandparents or earlier ancestors. Toscanini's parents, for example, had no musical talent. The spokesman for a hereditary interpretation, then, is faced with a dilemma: either Toscanini had no talent, and this is absurd, or somewhere back up the hereditary chain, there must have been an ancestor who passed on his talent in a recessive form. The fact that proof of such an ancestor is shady at best does not discourage the hereditist. When Toscanini's daughter showed no special musical aptitudes she was endowed by one spokesman with "critical talent." The point of the present discussion is that "talent" is not inherited. The term is an abstract concept and we do not inherit abstract concepts. We inherit good or bad eyes, ears, long fingers or short ones, etc. If a happy combination of structures and environmental experiences works together, we may have a talented individual. Certainly without structure we have nothing. With structure we have something on which to work. The pianist Van Cliburn has hands that span twelve keys on the piano. He also had a mother who was a piano teacher.

In the world of creative arts we have only poor criteria by which to measure talent. Many factors contribute to our judgment or evaluation of the artist, some of which have nothing to do with talent. The just-mentioned Van Cliburn was just as good before he won the Tchaikovsky contest in Moscow as after; yet his appearances in the United States before the contest were only modestly followed even though he had been recognized in musical circles as a brilliant performer. Talent frequently depends on social judgments. Society, not biology, decides whether you have talent. When a chimpanzee can win first prize in a painting exhibition, it is time to look at our standards. The completely lost soul, however, will argue that the chimpanzee deserved the prize because his work, however accomplished or achieved, was "true art." Such people can only be loved. They need not be accepted as contributing to our knowledge.

What has been said of talent applies to intelligence and any other "skill." These are not inherited in any sense other than that of physical structure. Certainly we can be born with a well-formed, healthy brain with no defective features or we can "inherit" one that offers but a poor instrument for interacting with environmental influences. Not only the brain structure itself, but the whole complex machinery which supplies the brain with oxygen and nutrients is inherited. The healthy body includes a healthy brain. Without the structure to work with, there is no intelligence. With the structure, the organism can be modified so that its behavior will be appraised as intelligent or stupid. The basically inferior brain cannot be made to do much, but what it can accomplish rests with the world into which it is born.

MATURATION

The great difficulty with an analysis of the nature-nurture problem is that nurture starts so soon. The moment of conception marks the start of environmental influence, and yet, we cannot test the organism for traits, talents, or what not until it has matured sufficiently. A baby's intelligence cannot be tested. Standard tests cannot be applied until the child is talking, perhaps reading, and going to school. By that time a complex welter of environmental influences has been at work. Nature and nurture are inextricably tangled. Some hereditary traits will not show themselves for years. The pattern of facial hair, body build, or breast structure, for example, can be examined only after adolescence has been reached. We have to take cognizance of this factor of aging, growth, or "maturation."

Maturation refers to ripening, to growth and development, to the unfolding of previously invisible features, which, in a given environment, characteristically appear, usually at predictable stages. The farmer can plan his harvest in the spring. Certain brands of hybrid corn mature in

90 days or 102 days, others in more or less. So with tomatoes, watermelons, and humans. There is some variation, of course, even in corn. No one expects to pick a uniform crop on September 3. Some ears will be ready on the first, some not till September 5. Others will never develop. Too much shade or too little or too much water or worms can delay the ripening or survival. Babies can be expected to lie in a fixed position for a few weeks. The day will come when they will roll off the bed onto their heads. The day will also come when they will climb out of their cribs, when they will stop sucking their thumbs, when they will go to the bathroom by themselves, and when they will become interested in the opposite sex. All of these affairs are dependable and predictable, in general. The fate of the human race depends upon just such reliable development. But even these events depend upon an environment. One cannot roll off a bed without the bed's being there, nor could one be interested in the opposite sex if there were none. The amoeba has no sex life because there are no little boy and girl amoebas.

Walking and talking

To make the matter clear, consider two outstanding human features: an erect posture and walking on two legs, and speech. How do we get around to walking on two legs, and how do we get around to talking? The answers to these questions have interested every parent and many psychologists. Most parents cannot wait for "nature to take its course." Psychologists have long studied these particular illustrations of the course of nature.

Walking erect is supposed to be a rather inefficient pattern for the human structure. We are not built for it, our spines suffer from our erect postures; yet, humans do stand and walk on two legs all over the world. There are reports occasionally of "wolf-children" or other "feral" (wild) children who are alleged to run about on all fours and who live in low caves, but we need not pay serious attention to such reports. If they are not pure fabrications, they may involve the disposal of unwanted or feebleminded children by feebleminded mothers and we have no controlled studies to go by. The more obvious point is that children about nine to twelve months of age get up off the floor and begin to move about, haltingly at first, then with reckless abandon, with narrow escapes from various disasters, and finally master the art of walking.

Now again, we find that nobody just gets up off the floor and walks. The child has been in a walking environment for many months. He has been carried about and held up and supported in standing positions. Proud parents have held the child by the hands and urged the child by voice and hand. They have encouraged picking up the feet and placing them forward, etc. The child is equipped by nature with a neural mechanism that provides for a movement pattern called a "crossed-extensor reflex." What this amounts to is that whenever one leg is forced into a stretched position, the other normally and automatically flexes and vice versa. In other words, there is a built-in system which provides for a necessary co-ordination which will later be employed in walking. It remains to provide a means for stretching or flexing leg muscles, and this occurs automatically when a child stands up. Both sets of leg muscles are stretched. Immediately neural impulses leading to the flexors are excited and contractions of the flexors are initiated; but one cannot get both feet into the air at the same time, and only one leg will be raised. Once this happens it can be replaced on the floor either in the same place or slightly forward or away from the original position. If it is moved away at all, a step has been taken. Replacing the foot excites the extensors of that leg and initiates flexion of the other which has become "fatigued" in the meantime. The other leg will then be raised, and the child is ready for the next step. Picking them up and putting them down in sequence is walking. If this were all there was to it, a child would walk some fine day as soon as it stood erectly. But the child is an ungainly creature, top heavy and un-co-ordinated. He must now "learn" to walk. Many postural modifications involving head, neck, arms, and trunk must be integrated with the crossed-extensor reflexes. Such integration means balance, and balance, while again, innately provided for, can only come about through use of the involved musculature. The learning, such as it is, proceeds automatically (just as all learning does). A child cannot be taught to walk. He can be encouraged to make movements which will become integrated. Such integration depends upon the readiness of the neural structure and the musculature to perform their proper functions. This, in turn, means that a period of growth and development must be spanned (see Dennis and Dennis, 1940).

The developmental sequence

It is interesting that this growth and development follows a pattern. The first movements of an infant are massive and un-co-ordinated. The child rolls over, he picks up his head, he becomes able to sit up, later to crawl, still later to pull himself up to a standing position, and finally to walk. This sequence cannot be violated. No child can walk before he can crawl, for example. This does not mean that any given child must crawl. He simply must pass through a stage when he *is able* to crawl. He may not be permitted to crawl on the floor in fastidious households, but unless he is restrained, he will crawl in his crib. He obviously cannot walk

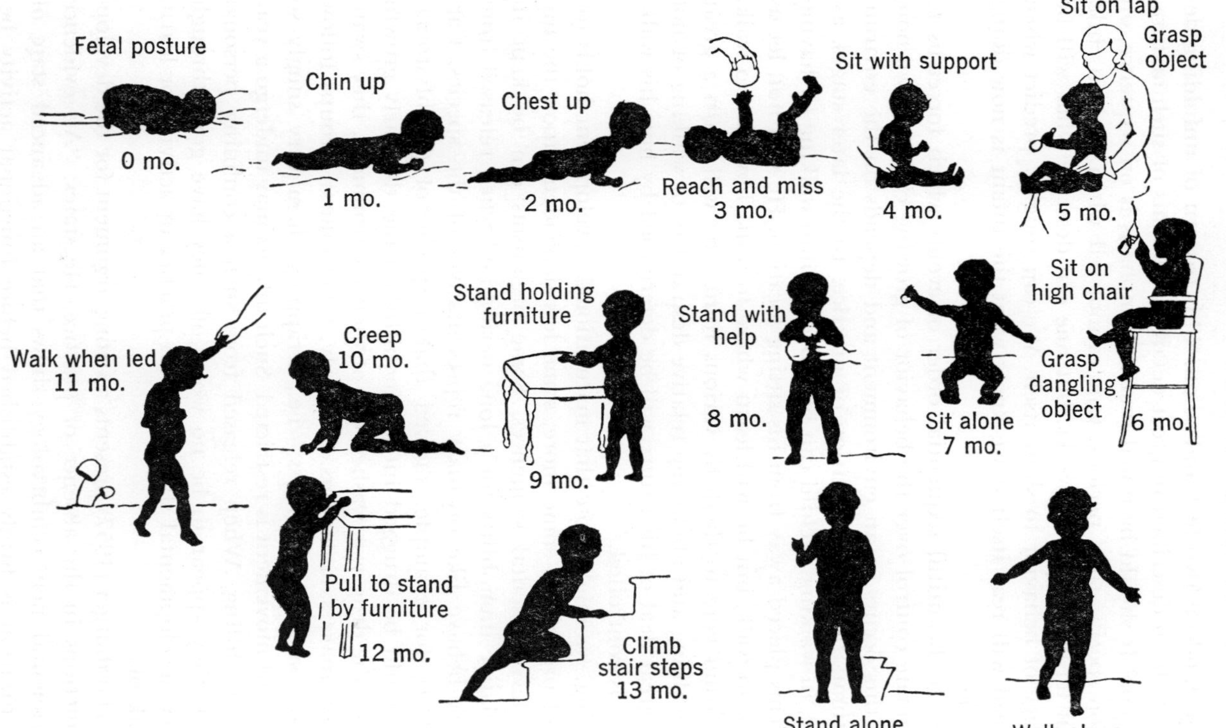

Figure 1 Shirley's developmental sequence. These are median performances of 25 infants. (From M. M. Shirley, 1933.)

until he can stand on two feet and so on. This pattern of unfolding development has been described in great detail by students of such maturational progress.[2] It should be noted that the emphasis is on sequence, on order, not on specific time periods. One cannot tell when a given child will walk in terms of days or weeks, but one can describe what will be the next stage of behavior to show itself. We can roughly predict when the little head will rear itself if we know what the infant is now doing (Shirley, 1937).

Despite the beautiful sequential order of events which forces us to accept an innate control over the behavior of growing children, we note again, that this occurs in an environment and depends on the environment for stimulation and repetition or practice. In the later stages, as, for example, in walking, a child can be provoked into walking by having desirable items placed away from his sitting location. He will *not,* let us repeat, *learn* to walk, but he will learn where to walk, how fast to walk, how to get from here to there by various routes; he will learn a great deal about walking and about the relative desirability of walking or not walking. A great deal of his future will be determined by how his walking behavior is controlled.

In passing, we might note that maturational development holds for all species of organisms, some more, some less dependent upon the unfolding of developmental sequences. Some organisms can be kept in a state of relative immobility for a long period and when released from such control, behave like ordinary representatives of the species. Carmichael (1954), for example, showed that a species of (Amblystoma) salamander could be drugged into immobility during the early growth period. When the drug was washed out of their environment, they swam about like ordinary salamanders. Similarly, some human groups follow a practice of "swaddling infants," i.e., wrapping them very snugly so that virtually all movement is restricted. Such infants may undergo a year or more of swaddling. When released from such a confining personal environment, they appear to be no worse off; they have gone through the necessary developmental stages with no practice or activity, or learning, to speak of.

Victor Hamburger (1957) presents a strong argument for the development of functions in the absence of practice. He states: "All evidence from experimental neuro-embryology shows that an advanced state of neural organization is firmly established before functional activity be-

[2] For studies of maturation and the developmental sequence consult Gesell and Thompson (1941) and McGraw (1935). In their work they employed a technique called "co-twin control." In such studies, one twin is trained to perform in some fashion (climbing stairs, roller skating, etc.), while the other receives no formal training. Later on both twins are tested to evaluate the influence of practice.

gins." After reviewing evidence obtained from fetuses at various ages as well as experiments in which organs and limbs are transplanted from one part of a body to other parts, Hamburger concludes: "The basic machinery for co-ordination is established by maturation processes in prefunctional stages, without the benefit of learning." We should not leave this topic with such a strong conclusion without considering the warning posted by Underwood (1957) who criticizes much maturational research because the experimental design is basically weak. In most maturation experiments, the object of the researcher is to demonstrate that two groups (one given practice and opportunities to learn while the other is not) do not differ in some one respect that is being measured. Such an objective is contrary to that of traditional experimentation which is designed to demonstrate a *difference* between two groups. When no difference is found it might not necessarily prove that the "control" group came to be the same as the trained group without some kind of practice. It might be that the control group benefits through practicing something else which then "transfers" (see Chapter 8) to the test situation. Underwood's argument might not apply too forcefully to observations on fetuses but it should be considered in any comparisons of developing infants and older children.

The development of speech

The most important human feature is that of speech, communication, with its allied art of writing and consequent historical benefits. Man passes on his culture via language and without language we would be little different from the apes. At the moment our concern is with how speech comes into a behavior repertoire and here we find a contrasting parallel to walking. Walking is primarily a maturational phenomenon. Talking is basically a learning phenomenon, but it also depends upon the maturation process, not only for the structural development that is a prerequisite for speech, but also for the vocalization activity out of which speech develops. Although no one knows how language started in man's development, there appears to be universal agreement that babies babble spontaneously, mumbling over and over a large variety of noises or sounds, the basic speech elements out of which any and all languages of the earth might be developed. If the babble of a baby were recorded over any extensive period, it would probably utter at one time or another every sound ever made in human speech. Judicious splicing of a tape could result in the preparation of any kinds of words in any language. A baby could be made to appear to be reciting the "Gettysburg Address" in Russian or the "Ode to Joy" in Japanese. Any normal baby can learn any language which it hears being spoken around it. The fact that French babies learn to speak French, then, is not mysterious even though an American teenager might express some surprise at hearing French children converse. We should note, also, that long before the babbling stage, a baby has cried on varied occasions of pain, hunger, or discomfort, and has already learned the virtues of tears and wails as means of controlling adult behavior. The speech process itself later becomes another technique for such control, but that is another problem. For the present, it is generally assumed that babies learn to talk by babbling, that they tend to repeat any particular babble to some degree, and that some such babbles become the basis for rudimentary words (mama, papa, dada, the French *bébé*). The process which appears to be agreed upon by most observers is something like this: First, for unknown reasons, a baby makes some noise, e.g., *da*. The baby hears itself make this noise. Hearing the noise represents a form of stimulation and initiation of neural activity from the ear to the brain. If the neural activity responsible for initiating the vocal activity in saying *da* occurs at about the same time as the activity involved in hearing *da,* a connection will be formed in the brain between these two neural activities. For the present we shall call such a connection an "association"—you can picture for yourself the association as representing a lowering of barriers between neural elements so that activity in one can initiate activity in the other. If such a connection is actually formed, then whenever the baby hears the sound *da,* it will tend to repeat it. This repetition, being heard, will tend to initiate another repetition, and the baby will start a chain of *da-da-da-da* responses.

If the sound *da* is a useful one in the society in which the baby is being reared, and *da* is one in western English culture, a father may appear on the scene and start the chain going by saying *da* himself. If the baby looks at the father while saying *da,* the neural activity involved in the visual system will become associated with saying *da* so that in the future, the appearance of the father might initiate the sound *da* from the baby. Similarly, the sound can be brought under the control of a picture of the father, or of any visual stimulation that in some degree is similar to the visual effect produced by the father. The baby will say *da* for mother, brother, or the milkman. Most such improper responses will not be repeated frequently, as we shall appreciate when we talk about learning, and other responses will be associated with mother, brother, and the milkman in due course. The sound *da* can be further associated with pointing ("there," or such visual stimuli as emanate from dolls, or the word "down," etc.).

A similar process is involved with many other sound units or "phonemes" that happen to play a role in the child's culture. *Fa, ma, goo, boo,* and all the other potentially useful noises get their share of exercise if parents or other caretakers attend to the child's vocalizing. Almost needless to say, if a child is deaf, it will not learn to talk in this manner; and, if no one pays attention to a child, its speech development will be correspondingly delayed. This does not mean that the development of speech can be controlled in the opposite direction. You can't teach a child to talk before the child is ready to talk in terms of maturation. This usually takes from a year to eighteen months of speechless but noisy growth. Some children develop speech sooner than others for little understood reasons; girls are a little faster than boys. If a child is unusually slow to develop in spite of a reasonably stimulating environment and is not talking to some degree by twenty-four months, there is reason to suspect that something is definitely wrong—this something could be one of a number of things and frequently is a sign of retardation. Hasty conclusions must, of course, be avoided and a thorough check made by properly trained specialists to determine if the difficulty is correctable.

This is as far as we need to go with the speech development process; our concern has been to point up the interrelationship between maturational and the environmental aspects in this activity. There is a great deal of information about how particular parts of speech—nouns, verbs, adjectives, and pronouns, for example—come into the picture in a sequential way and reflect a further dominance by maturational factors, but we can leave that to the interested student to investigate for himself (Trager, 1957).

We have selected walking and talking as examples of maturational influences in behavior. Many other kinds of responses also show the influence of maturation. We grow into and out of certain kinds of behavior with the passage of time. Hardly any response is free of some maturational influence. But maturation too depends upon environment as we have pointed out with our samples. No child will learn the language of its parents if it is brought up in isolation and never hears speech, but hearing speech is not enough in itself. The child must await the maturation of the structures involved in speaking, hearing, and the neural processes involved in learning. It cannot be *forced* to learn before the time is ripe. Much of our behavior depends upon such a "readiness." In some cases the "readiness" appears to be a matter of simple physiological growth; in other cases, the organisms must have certain prior experiences before subsequent experiences can be usefully exploited. The separation of growth from experience becomes a difficult task. Teachers of reading rely heavily on the concept of "reading readiness," for example. Does such readiness naturally arrive at some stage of life or can it be hastened by practice? Some children can play the piano with some skill at the age of three. Are they ready for instruction or have they already had a good deal of it? Can algebra be taught to ten-year-olds or are they too "young"? Can they be *made* old enough by training or must they wait till they are high-school freshmen? It is not always easy to decide, and special cases, geniuses, for example, confuse the picture. One might try to discover in an individual what his state of readiness for anything might be. With groups in schools it is difficult.

The problem of maturation becomes rather involved in the area of emotion. Babies are not afraid of the dark, or rats, or snakes. When they get to be about four or five years old they begin to fear things they never feared before and have no "good reason" for fearing. Does this happen automatically with maturation or have the children, by that time, learned something that makes it possible for them to be frightened? Hebb (1946) argues that learning is indeed the answer to such responses. The children do not learn to fear; that comes naturally. But they have learned a whole series of other responses which they are unable to make in the fear situation. Hebb describes the common fear of corpses on the part of people who have never before seen a corpse and consequently could not have learned to be afraid of one. Why do people fear corpses when these are seen for the first time? Because of the wealth of experience with non-corpse people who move, smile, respond, and, at least, breathe. The corpse does none of these things and we are left nonplussed with a repertoire of reactions that cannot be performed. Such inability to respond to a stimulus because of prior experience with some features or aspects of a situation or stimulus leaves us confused, disoriented, frustrated, and perhaps, "fearful."

When we recognize how maturation becomes inevitably interwoven with experience and learning, we are forced to examine each situation in the light of the total complexity that may be involved. We cannot settle for easy answers: this is inherited; that is the result of maturation; this is learned. All behavior involves maturation, inheritance, and learning. This complicates our problem, but may also keep us from oversimplification and subsequent error. For any particular kind of behavior we have to look into all aspects. We note developmental sequences, opportunities to practice, the learning of related but perhaps contradictory response patterns, and also consider the genetic background; then, and not till then, can we talk about "readiness." Readiness for high heels, for lipstick, for algebra, and readiness for marriage do not come about merely by aging. Some people are never ready for any of these functions.

INSTINCTS

By the time the student comes to concern himself with the study of behavior he has already learned from his parents, novels, and newspapers that much of what we do is by instinct. The pugilist with the "killer instinct" crawls to his knees by instinct, protects himself by instinct, and instinctively finds the "button" of his opponent whom he proceeds to flatten. The opponent, if he does not have the proper instincts, just lies there. In the newspapers, mothers instinctively rush to the defense of their babes in burning buildings, dogs instinctively find their way home from across the country, and Republicans instinctively suspect Democrats. We instinctively protect ourselves against dangers, follow our finer instincts (or our worse), and so on and on. In novels the hero instinctively knows that his true love has entered the crowded room, that he will face death at the end of this mission (after a heroic achievement), and whatever else the novelist is unable to account for in more prosaic language. Mobs come together instinctively, surrender their finer instincts and lynch malefactors (innocent or guilty) who instinctively fight to preserve themselves and the species. What in the world are they talking about?

What is an instinct? The popular view apparently refers to some innate, inborn tendency to behave in some more or less specific manner in some more or less specific situation. The behavior involved is presumably automatic, sometimes irrational, possibly unconscious, probably unlearned (or we would find the users saying "habitually"). It is natural behavior, that which would be expected, presumably of anyone in that situation. It is also an explanation of the behavior because no further explanation is required or needed by the user. It answers the question of how this behavior came into being. Students sometimes mean "impulsive" or thoughtless behavior when they use the term "instinctive."

At one time in psychology, the doctrine of instincts was very popular. There was little or no agreement on how many instincts there were or which ones did exist. William James (1890), for example, listed 127. William McDougall (1915) needed only 7. It was a very easy psychology to practice. If you saw someone behaving in a polite manner, and anyone else expressed a wonder about it, you could easily say that he had a politeness instinct. If acquisitive behavior was under discussion, then an acquisitive instinct was ready at hand to use as an explanation. If aggressive behavior was to be explained, there was a pugnacity instinct, an instinct toward war or peace or minding your own business. The situation was obviously unsatisfactory so long as there was disagreement on number and class. In order to make order, psychologists began to establish criteria for admitting a behavior sample into the category of instincts. Among others which were individually suggested, the following have been accepted as more or less necessary qualifications for classifying behavior as instinctive:

1. The behavior pattern must appear more or less perfectly, the first time; i.e., there must be no gradual practice and learning effect.

2. The behavior must be universal within a species. That is, we cannot tolerate one instinct in one individual and not expect to find the same instinct in another. We would never know, then, if a given behavior pattern exhibited by both individuals was instinctive in one and not in the other. In short, there would be no point to having the instinct in the first place.

3. The behavior must involve the whole organism as a unit, and not be a specific sensory-motor pattern of the nature of a reflex.

Sneezing is not an instinct because it is basically a matter of the lungs and nose. A knee jerk is not an instinct because it is essentially limited to a segment of the body. Mating behavior, on the other hand, in a mammalian species could be an instinct since it does involve the whole organism even though there might be a special concern with certain structures. In general, an instinct would involve the organism in some instrumental way with its environment. That is, the behavior would have to modify the environment in some way, or change the relationship between the organism and the environment. Thus, a spider spinning a web could be thought of as altering its environment; since it moves about in space, the whole body is involved, even though the spinning elements are necessarily involved if there is to be a web. It is conceivable, however, that the spider might initiate some of the spinning movements without the secretions being present. We would have then, a sample of a "blind" instinct. The spider so carefully and fatefully observed by Robert the Bruce went through the necessary motions repeatedly, if fruitlessly at first. Similarly, other species can be tricked experimentally into what is "foolish" behavior. Chickens can be made to hide from nonhawks, fish can be tricked into reproductive behavior by wooden models, etc. (Beach, 1951). The essence of an instinct, then, by general agreement, is that in a given situation, a behavior pattern is displayed, which is more or less useful, which involves the whole organism, which is common to the species, and which appears without any opportunity for learning. Instincts are inborn "habits" and are usually thought of positively, as having survival value.

Tropisms

In contrasts to instincts, we should mention tropisms—automatic reactions to specific types of stimuli which do involve the whole organism but which are not instrumental in changing the environment to any serious degree. The moth that flies into the flame is exhibiting tropistic behavior. It could not help itself. There may be other instances of what are really tropisms masquerading as instincts. The homing pigeon, for example, might be responding in a purely physical way to some types of radiation, magnetic or otherwise, and might be better spoken of as illustrating a tropism rather than an instinct. Perhaps we might restrict the instinct terminology to situations where the organism acts on the environment (including other members of its species or other species) in the form of constructive, survival behavior. Thus nest building, insect activity with respect to providing food for the yet unborn young, etc., might be the prototype by which we might wish to judge other samples.

Defining a sample of behavior as an instinct does not explain it, however. This is the fallacy of which our earlier psychologists were patently guilty. By attaching a label to some activity, they felt that an adequate account had been given of the sources and nature of the behavior. If there is no further interest in the matter, it might suffice to label the business and forget it. However, just as with the general problem of heredity, we found that it was necessary to insist that hereditary effects must be evaluated or judged as pertinent to a given environment —i.e., some things are inherited in one environment and not in another— so with instincts, we must insist that what is instinctive at one time and place may not be instinctive in another environment.

The influence of the environment and early experience is most difficult to evaluate. By the time an organism is old enough to display some "instinct" it has also acquired a history, a history of learning which has modified the nervous system of the organism in one way or another and made it possible or impossible for some "potential instinct" to operate. If the learning has been such as to prevent the instinct from "emerging," then it is not much of an instinct. If the learning, on the other hand, has been such as to facilitate the instinctive activity, then again it is not a purely inherited operation. Later on we shall have occasion to consider animals that are brought up without the use of some senses and will be able to see how early experience modifies an "instinct." It is usually held for example that monkeys and chimpanzees engage in "grooming" themselves and each other "by instinct." If infant chimpanzees have their arms and legs encased in cardboard mailing tubes so that they cannot use their arms and digits, they do not engage in grooming in later life (Nissen,

Chow, and Semmes, 1951). Here we see the dependence of an "instinct" upon a certain kind of normal experience being permitted in the growing-up stage. When some behavior appears to be instinctive we must be careful to insist that it is instinctive only with a given kind of behavior history or a given kind of environment. When the behavior emerges in spite of our best efforts to modify the environment and history, we are forced to accept it as "instinctive," at least until we learn better how the behavior might be altered or controlled.

By altering the environment we learn more intimately what can be subjected to revision and prediction and what cannot. Thus, homing pigeons would be very useful in military matters if they could home in the dark. Unfortunately, they cannot do so. Obviously, vision is involved in homing. How, we might not be able to say, but that much we know. Similarly, periods of migration in some birds at least seem to be governed by the length of the day. When artificial illumination is supplied, migration can be delayed. The migratory instinct, then, is not an inevitable affair. Neither is the migratory behavior of salmon free of environmental influence. It appears that physiological changes in the maturing salmon are of the nature that the ocean currents are too warm for comfort and that the fish swims against the current in the direction of a cooler environment. This does not account for all of the fantastically involved maneuvering of the salmon, but it helps to reveal something more about its nature. To label some behavior "instinctive" is to relegate it to the area of the unknowable and such a practice is harmful to a scientific understanding. Instead of accepting the label, every instance of the use of the label should be recognized as a cover or shield for ignorance and be an open invitation for additional research. If we clearly understand that we are labeling for convenience only, and only until we can attend to the matter in more detail, there may be no harm in the use of the term to indicate that some creatures are endowed with relatively fixed association pathways in their nervous systems by which certain behavior patterns will emerge *under appropriate circumstances.* This may well be true, although, as yet, no one has demonstrated such inherited circuits and related them to the behavior pattern they call for.

In human behavior, we find that the criteria set up for the definition of instincts do not seem to permit any heretofore described behavior pattern to fit. There appears to be no sample of behavior which is universal in the species, is unlearned, involves the whole organism, and is instrumental in survival. Mother love appears to be wanting in certain mothers who drown their young or smother them, suicides obviously eliminate self-preservation, pacifists speak strongly against a war instinct, and atheists deny a religious instinct. Individuals differ so widely in their reactions to almost any situation that universality is difficult to observe. One of the behavior patterns that seems to meet almost universal support is the taboo against incest, but even this occurs sometimes in the most highly civilized cultures.

Since there is little likelihood of finding any human patterns that will meet the criteria, we had best not use the term in connection with human, and perhaps any other animal behavior. At best the label will reveal only a problem, not an answer. There is no harm in looking for basic, elemental patterns; in fact, that we must continue to do. The harm comes in not looking beyond the pattern, into its components, and trying to determine what factors are operating to control the components. When we are able to trace a chain of events, initiate any state that we wish, control and predict, then we might arrive at as close to what amounts to an explanation as we can ever get in science. It might turn out that with each successful step we arrive more and more closely at what amounts to a tropistic explanation, even of the most complex behavior at the highest levels.

Imprinting

In recent years we have been presented by certain naturalists (Lorenz, 1952) with a new concept that demands attention in this nature-nurture controversy. It has been observed, for instance, that certain species of animals, particularly barnyard fowl, will develop rather strong, relatively fixed patterns of behavior, very soon after birth or hatching. It is further noted that such behavior fixations will only occur at certain life stages and if the stage is passed, the fixation will not occur. Thus, a gosling follows the goose down to the pond. If, instead of a goose, the first object fixated upon happens to be a naturalist, then the gosling follows the naturalist as it would the parent. Such an early fixation of a behavior pattern is called "imprinting." It calls our attention to the possibility that in any species, some patterns of behavior might be established and persist for a long time, if at some stage in infancy, a particular form of stimulation is present which calls for an innate reaction of a certain type (see Ramsay and Hess, 1954).

While imprinting might become a principle of some importance in the psychology of the future, we must recognize that the goslings give up following the goose in good time and become geese themselves. Imprinting might prove to be significant only for the early years or months of life and have no serious bearing upon adult behavior. It is possible that during the stage of life when imprinting might have some effect, still other circumstances might come to bear in some manner that will indirectly affect later life. If a human child has been imprinted in some fashion, its parents might develop attitudes toward the child as well as ways of dealing with the child that they might never change. When the imprinting phase is over and done with, the parents might not recognize the change and continue in their acquired patterns, controlling and influencing the life of the child. At the present time we have no good evidence that imprinting is of any subsequent consequence for humans. Young children are notorious for their "one-trial learning" and their ritualistic behavior. Everything has to be done "just so" or the children will not eat, or sleep, or have their baths, and so on. Sometimes this infant tyranny keeps up for months and even years; yet, eventually, changes do take place; the child begins to dress himself, feed himself, and even go to bed by himself. Most of us, when we become men, "put away childish things." Until more research accumulates on the subject, we must think of imprinting as a principle that might have some pertinence for infantile behavior and perhaps the early childhood years, but even this has not been established for humans, although folklore has plenty of examples to offer. The difficulties in the path of investigation are great and we are unlikely to come up with much in this connection for many years, if ever. It is a possibility, however, and one that must be reckoned with especially in considering accounts of early influences on behavior, an area of most serious concern and considerable misrepresentation by practically anyone who has anything to say on the subject.

THE RELATIVE IMPORTANCE OF THE EARLY YEARS

Philosophers, teachers, psychiatrists, theologians, and neighbors have all emphasized the seriousness of the early years of life. It should be obvious that most such emphasis is based on speculation and uncontrolled observation and hence is suspect. We have practically no evidence about how important the early years of the human child may be as viewed from an interest in his later conduct or behavior. How important is a broken home? How important is it to be a member of a large family, a small one, the only child, the child of young or old parents? How important is it to be raised with or by grandparents and other relatives instead of by parents? What about being raised in foster homes, institutions, or in the slums or in palaces? Here we lack the bare facts on which to speculate, yet speculation is rampant and all sorts of consequences are traced, *post hoc,* to the child's early years. Any attempt by anyone to state a time or age when "character is set" or where personality is more or less rigidly determined would be an impossible and unsupportable venture. Psychoanalysts are fond of tracing neurotic origins to the age of three or even younger, to toilet training patterns or to chance observations of the "primal scene." There is, unfortunately, no evidence of a scientific nature to support their hypotheses. There is no evidence that stubborn, nasty, dirty, mean, obnoxious children turn out to be delinquents, neurotic, insane, etc. What the effects of juvenile behavior problems are in some more final analysis are unknown. Senators might have been car thieves, Presidents weaklings, great singers and speakers might have lisped through their early years. In one study of twenty-five children, aged six, who were referred for psychiatric attention as seriously disturbed, all but one turned out to be quite normal by the time they were twenty-six years old. This is better than one could expect from a "normal" group of children. Such studies are exceedingly rare, but for what it is worth, it does not appear to justify any specific conclusions about dire consequences from infantile or even juvenile behavior. It is equally likely that no firm conclusions can be drawn from observations of a group of exemplary children in so far as behavior and personality are concerned. The famous studies of genius by Terman (1947) do testify to the fact that those who were geniuses as adults were also quite brilliant as youngsters. Terman followed the careers of about 1,000 young Americans with high IQ scores. These young people developed into rather successful adults, mostly professionals. The intelligence demonstrated at an early age held up over the years. This, of course, does not bear on the current problem, as we do not have controlled data on behavior patterns then and now, nor do we know the influences brought to bear.

Early and late learning

The effects of infantile deprivation or enrichment

Despite the fact that so much speculation has been indulged in for centuries about the influence and importance of the early years, there is virtually no evidence of a scientific nature on this subject. Here we have the paramount problem of psychology, actually *the* problem of psychology, and very little research. We have a few proverbs: Spare the rod and spoil the child. As the twig is bent, so grows the tree. But that folk wisdom just about sums up the total lore on the subject. It is easy to account for this paucity of research. No scientist can plan on living long enough to follow through an adequate sample of subjects from birth to maturity. His desire to report some findings and arrive at solutions to problems tends to force him into immediately rewarding research. In addition to this, any attempt at controlling variables involved in the rearing of children will not be looked upon kindly by the culture. The S.P.C.A. and antivivisectionists get alarmed when dogs, cats, or monkeys are subjected to treatments that might result in alleviating human suffering. These obstacles may account for the reluctance to engage in the research, but they do not license the outpouring of child guidance advice that floods our press and bewilders successive generations of mothers as they switch faithfully from breast feeding to bottles on demand or fixed schedules, as they punish or become "permissive." We have no facts.

In the post-World War II period, psychologists have become more keenly aware of this basic nature-nurture problem and have begun to attack it in the only feasible way—through research with young animals. The basic approach has been to rear infant rats (Hymovitch, 1952), dogs (Clarke, 1951), or chimpanzees (Riesen, 1950) in different kinds of environments and compare these to control animals which are allowed to grow up in what might be accepted as a "normal" environment. It should be recognized that no one knows what a normal environment for a rat or dog or chimpanzee might be. Certainly not life in a laboratory. Whether a dog raised in a home as a house pet is leading a normal dog's life is also a question. It depends upon the home, other dogs in the neighborhood, etc. But we have no better comparison group, and proceed *faute de mieux*.

There are two general approaches to the problem: a group of animals can be reared under conditions of "enrichment" with all creature comforts amply provided or in a bare minimum of survival conditions. The enriched environment is difficult to define in any meaningful way. What is enrichment for a rat or dog? Plenty of food and drink? Toys? Companions? Do dogs or rats want toys or companions? The term "free" environment is sometimes used as a substitute label. This usually means that there is more room provided for running about. If the usual living cage is two-feet square, the free environment may be four- or six-feet square. Why not fifty-feet square? In the free environment there might be a collection of stove pipes, boxes, tunnels, teeter-totters, exercise wheels, etc. How much does a rat enjoy such items? It is customary to put several animals into such a situation. Does this increase freedom or enrichment or does it decrease it? A dominant, aggressive rat in a free environment might make it a concentration camp for the others.

The impoverished environment is easier to define. Remove everything but the bare essentials for survival on a limited diet. Remove light and heat, restrict movement, and eliminate companions, sound, etc. In most instances so far reported, the basic restriction has been that of vision. Dogs might be reared in boxes where they could see nothing but the ceiling and the walls of the box. They might never see another dog or human. Rats might be reared in complete darkness. At some later period comparable to adolescence or youth in man, the animals are transferred from the restricted environment to a normal routine and tested or compared with graduates of a normal or enriched routine.

What are the findings of such research? While there are some contradictions and perplexities, the general findings appear to be that enriched environments tend to develop better problem solvers and more adjusted animals. Deprived animals appear to suffer in emotional adjustment and learning ability even to the point of being unable to use their sense organs effectively. While rats do not appear to suffer much, if any, from being brought up in the dark, chimpanzees brought up without having the opportunity for using their eyes normally, appear quite blind when exposed to the light and this condition persists for several weeks. It appears that chimpanzees have to learn to use their eyes, or learn to see. Similarly, if chimpanzees are raised with cardboard tubes encasing their arms and hands, they appear to be rather insensitive to stimulation of those members. They are unable to localize points of stimulation. We have noted earlier that they do not engage in the grooming behavior that is a basic behavior pattern in the primate. Dogs brought up in isolation appear insensitive to pain and appear to have to learn to react to painful stimuli in a defensive fashion. We shall return to a consideration of such early experiences in our discussion of transfer of training in a later chapter. For the present we merely note that psychologists are beginning to do controlled studies of the effects of infantile experience. Passing mention should also be made of attempts to compare children brought up in institutions with normally reared children. Such studies, although carefully done, and with the best intentions, can hardly meet the criteria of controlled experimentation. If they did, we would not need to resort to animals. The much longer lifespan of the human makes institutional studies difficult to evaluate. To test institutional graduates in adult years without an adequate measure of the factors operating in the institution and in the intervening period is extremely hazardous. It is similar to the problem of comparing adults who were raised in slums with adults who were residents on the other side of the tracks. The number of variables that would have to be taken into account is prohibitive.

Adolescent behavior

The press and popular magazines, to say nothing of educators and child guidance "experts," are continually bewailing the fact that children no longer behave as they used to in "the good old days." They also point to the many changes in our modern ways of life—the pace of modern living, changes in the form of entertainment, travel, household ways, etc., all of which are from time to time considered bad, even when used. An amusing book (*Where Did You Go? Out. What Did You Do? Nothing.*) is a nostalgic reminiscence about young boyhood in the early 1920's. The author (Smith, 1958) is sorry for his and other modern children—they aren't having any fun—all they do is watch television. He and his friends, now, they used to have fun! Smith, like so many adults, does not appear to realize that his own children might be writing similar books in their adult years, bemoaning the dull lives of their children and looking wistfully back to the day when television was real, when they showed good stuff!

The complaints of adults about their young is as old as time. Plato complained about the younger generation. Newspaper editorials of the last century, viewing with alarm the rising tide of delinquency, vandalism, lack of respect for elders, etc., could be reprinted intact today. When young hoodlums attack teachers in the public schools we wonder what the world is coming to, not knowing perhaps that in the golden days of the nineteenth century, three college presidents were murdered by disgruntled students.

Our educational system is attacked as inadequate—we are no longer doing the job. But what is the job? Is it to prepare students to live in the nineteenth century or to break ground for the twenty-first? Invidious comparisons are made between the student achievement of today and that of an earlier time when only the upper crust of society indulged in education. Nowadays nearly everyone goes to school for a compulsory period of eleven or fourteen years. This includes young people with intellectual limitations whose academic progress might never go beyond the sixth grade level. Something must be done for these students if they are forced into the schools. Pundits sneer at "Personality Improvement" courses, driving courses, etc. It might be better for an academically limited youngster to learn some manners and driving courtesy than be allowed to wander about at his own vague direction, too young to work, too old to play.

The students who have academic aptitude are as productive as, if not more so than, ever. If educational products are to be compared, the comparisons must be made between similar circumstances or populations. This is almost never done. Adults prefer to view with alarm. It is always easier to complain. The basic trouble is a two-pronged difficulty. In the first place, parents watch their children develop slowly from infancy to adolescence. The process is gradual with only nominal milestones, like birthdays. At no time does the child suddenly become a man in the parent's eyes. The basic protective adjustments that are made in the first year of life continue on for as long as the parent lives. Mothers at sixty-eight will caution their forty-five-year-old children to watch out when crossing the streets, to be sure to bolt the door at night, what to eat, and where to go, whom to see, etc. The old codger of eighty-two refers to his sixty-year-old son as "the boy." "The boy" is still, of course, irresponsible, as he always was, and needs supervision. The protective habits of the early years remain unchanged even though the situation no longer calls for such reactions. Young people are obviously irresponsible, careless, sloppy, disrespectful, and every other annoying thing that can be thought of.

On the other side of the family game, the children never feel a confident independent security which would enable them to break with their parents when they reach "maturity." The attitudes of fear or love or whatever relationships developed in the early years prevent the children from behaving rationally in their adulthood. They, of course, will be different parents, but they never are. They begin the protective domineering behavior the moment they become parents and never give it up. While to a twelve-year-old, someone who is eighteen is an adult, a man, a hero, to the twenty-year-old, the same eighteen-year-old is a fresh kid, the forty-year-old regards anyone under thirty-five as a youngster, an adolescent, while he himself is at the prime of life. This prime condition continues forever. At eighty he will still be in the prime of life, denouncing modern youth, the educational system, newfangled ideas, labor saving devices, etc. It would be strange indeed if an objective, scientific appraisal could be made of adolescents by adults. A popular magazine described a fifteen-year-old chess champion as gangly, all arms and legs, flailing about. The picture is colorful but hardly objective. The fifteen-year-old might well be better co-ordinated than the writer of the description, but in our culture, fifteen-year-olds are children who gangle and spill things. Adults are mature, adjusted, dignified people, who spill things because they slipped or were wet or someone got in the way.

MATURATION AND THE LATER YEARS

The concept of maturation is frequently restricted to infancy or the early years in the research treatments. This is almost necessarily so because few scientists can afford to follow through the same children from infancy to death. Yet we must presume that maturation as a matter of growth, development, or bodily change continues until death. We do know that with increasing age various bodily changes occur that directly or indirectly affect our behavior. In our older years we lose our youthful efficiency in seeing, hearing, and probably all our other senses. We deteriorate in learning ability and retention. We dwell on earlier memories and forget what happened yesterday. Gradually we go the full cycle that Shakespeare described in his seven ages. Our concern here, however, is with what will emerge behavior-wise with the passing years which might be mistakenly attributed to environmental influences rather than to the nature of man.

The problem is almost infinitely complicated by cultural influences. In a given culture we might be able to predict that girls will start yearning for high heels and lipsticks in the seventh grade, that they will rebel against baby sitters at thirteen, but the cultural impact is obvious. To know what to expect at any age past the third or fourth year becomes more and more difficult. The studies by Gesell and Ilg and Ames (1943, 1946, 1956) on *The Child from Five to Ten* and *Youth,* while extremely interesting and valuable for a middle-class American culture, do not carry the weight of the *Infant and Child in the Culture of Today* where the child is still pretty largely considered a biological product. Even in infancy, as the Gesell title suggests, culture is of great significance, and it is the rash, not to say bold, psychologist who will say at any age that biology stopped and nurture took over. Biology does not stop till the organism is dead. In the consideration of psychological problems, we will be wise to keep a close watch over the biological factors that must be taken into account in any behavior sample. An unbiological psychology, that is, a psychology which does not take into account the nature of the organism at every moment, is not likely to prove meaningful.

CHAPTER 4

The Basic Equipment 1—Senses and Sensory Processes

Acts and movements · Motor equivalence · Basic mechanisms · The sense organs · Sensation and perception · Phenomenology · Internal events · Perception and learning · Sensory reactions · Imagery · Characteristics of sensory action · Classification of sense organs · Sensory functions · Thresholds · Adaptation · Attention · The concept of optimum stimulation · The measurement of thresholds · The psychophysical methods · Errors in measurement · Constant and variable errors · Weber's Law · The measurement of attitudes · Relative aspects of stimulation: the general problem · Gestalt principles of perception · The figure-ground proposition · Good figures · Relativity in stimulation · Constancy · Closure · Grouping and patterning

The study of behavior may begin with stimuli and end with responses, but it cannot ignore the behaving organism which imposes its own limits on what comes in and what goes out. What is it that does the behaving? Perhaps we can find out by discovering what behavior consists of. We have already considered the dangers in treating behavior abstractly. We are ready to turn from such general considerations to our real work. We can start by reviewing the concepts of acts and movements. Such a review might prove most informative.

ACTS AND MOVEMENTS

In discussing our own or others' behavior we usually skip over the actual behavior involved and talk about the end results of that behavior. Take anyone's account of his day as he might report it in a diary: "Rose, shaved, bathed, broke fast, and so to work. Signed letters, lunched with Harry, conferred with J. G., bawled out Sam—Sam pretty broken up—dinner at the club, danced with the redhead, read a few chapters in Boswell, and so to bed." That gives us a neat little picture of the day's behavior. Or does it? There is not a single word in the passage which described behavior. We know only what was accomplished; we know nothing of what was done or how it was done. We are left only with some data, an empty plate, a dog-ear in a book, a ring in the bathtub, and possibly other physical evidence of prior activity, but what that activity was we must now try to infer. And our inference is usually from such a second order of facts. What should our diarist have written? He started with the business of getting out of bed. There are all kinds of ways of getting out of a bed and of wakening to the day's adventures. One can fall out, roll out, get out of the wrong side, face up, face down, both feet at once, left or right first, one can sit on the edge and stretch and yawn, rumple the hair, and on and on. Each one of these little features of leaving the bed can be described more and more minutely. The point is that getting out of bed is an end-result, an accomplishment, albeit a minor one. We might call it an "act." Guthrie (1952) has been insisting for the last forty years that "acts" cannot be the units of behavior. They represent effects of behavior and since these effects can be brought about in many ways, we immediately lose sight of the behavior as soon as we attend to the end-product. We don't know what happened, what movements the organism made, in what sequence, for what reason, or indeed, anything about the behavior.

Now the illustration chosen above may sound facetious. What difference does it make how you get out of bed so long as you get out? But the same error is committed when we discuss other behavior in these abstract terms, and the errors involved may prevent us from arriving at an understanding of the principles of psychology. Suppose we ask the second-grade child: How much is five and six?, and the child answers "Eleven." We now ask the child: How do you know? The new answer is: "I add them up." Do we know what the child did? How did he "add them up"? Or, in a more involved business, perhaps, we inquire about how a problem is solved, a poem memorized, a decision made, and we get answers like, "I saw the point at once," or "It came to me," or "I memorized it," or "I just made up my mind." We are not even back where we started. We are set even further back because not only have we not been given useful answers; we have been given bad answers which have to be cleared away before we can get a fresh attack organized on the problem.

Guthrie's proposal is that we stop all discussion of acts and start investigating *movements*. If we could catalogue all of the movements in the sequence in which they occurred in any given situation, we would have a description of behavior which might reveal the principles underlying the total pattern of activity. We might be in position to infer the laws that provide an effective description and analysis of behavior if we operated at the first-order level of data, the actual observable actions or movements of the organism. If we stick to the second or higher order of data, we may not develop a psychology at all.

The view just described may appear extreme to the student and not all psychologists are in agreement with Guthrie—it is not so much that they disagree as that they regard it, as the student will already have decided, as too elaborate, too detailed, confining and narrow, all at the same time. They are willing to take a more risky approach and accept certain limited "acts" such as a turn in a maze, or a push against a panel or lever as a more workable unit. They do not feel it is necessary to describe in detail each muscular contraction involved in turning left or right or in pressing a lever. It is enough that a rat turns left or presses the lever. Much of the data accumulated by psychologists is of this latter type, and much of it is useful, to a degree. There is always a danger, however, that you don't really know what you are talking about if you skip or slide over details. Perhaps the penalty or price of science is attention to detail. The broad generalization may be the ultimate ambition, but it is of little value if it does not really work. There are many ways of phrasing generalizations which appear to cover the data. The final test always lies in the details. Whether gravity works by pulling things or pushing them (as Einstein held) may not matter in gross, everyday experience; nor does it matter whether light consists of electromagnetic waves or quanta of energy as far as lighting your living room is concerned. But for a scientific understanding of what goes on, it does matter. An incorrect theory will get its comeuppance sooner or later, and that will come because it does not square with a detail.

It is debatable that we can proceed as Guthrie would like and stick to a description of behavior in minute detail. Guthrie himself does not do this. There are many movements, for example, that are too tiny to observe without fine instrumentation. The situations in which we may be interested might not be amenable to such observations anyhow. Guthrie feels free to assume that certain kinds of movements must be taking place, movements which could be observed if we were in position to and had the means or tools by which to observe and record them. This might be a necessary compromise at the present state of the science. The general working proposition might be that we attempt to scrutinize detail as closely as possible in refined laboratory situations and trust that the observations made there also hold in the more complex situations in which our opportunities for observation are limited. In any case, we can adopt an orientation which will let us recognize when we are dealing with abstract "acts" and when we are observing movements or "responses." We can remind ourselves continually that there will be no final answer until, at the level of psychology, we have traced out the movement sequences involved, and that we have described the situation as nearly as we can for the next stage of reduction, i.e., we have presented the physiologist with a meaningful question. We cannot forget that behavior is a function of a living organism, with a nervous system, an internal environment, that behavior, whatever else it may be, is a complex physiological function. This does not mean that we must now be able to trace the neural correlates of each movement in a sequence or that we cannot concern ourselves with problems where current physiology is extremely vague and undeveloped, but our leaps into the unknown must be carefully prepared in the framework of a potential physiological treatment and not do violence to known biological facts. While the above remarks are sympathetic to a "reductionist" viewpoint, the student must be cautioned against concluding that progress in psychology depends in any way on progress in physiology. The study of behavior is a science in its own right. All that is required is that we attempt to be compatible and not operate with obviously contradictory assumptions.

Motor equivalence

When we present our problems to the physiologist we must not misrepresent a situation. A narrow interpretation of the above emphasis on movements might result in the conclusion that the movements per se are the important elements, perhaps the only elements of interest. We might easily be led into faulty or at least awkward conclusions if we do not permit the proper scope to behavior. Many aspects of behavior do have the appearance or flavor of "acts"; that is, the organism behaves in such a manner as to accomplish an apparent end or purpose and the specific movements are of little or minor interest. One set of movements might be as good as another—that is, equivalent. Traditionally, psychologists identify this matter as that of "motor equivalence." The movements involved in any given end-result might be movements that have never been practiced in that connection, appearing for the first time in a satisfactory manner. The pilot forced down in a snow-blanketed area might write the word "HELP" in 200-foot-long letters by trudging through the snow systematically. The prisoner might write a letter in blood, using the tip of a shoe lace, or if his hands are tied, he might wield a stick with his mouth and leave a message in this unorthodox orthography. Such illustrations provoke the observer to postulate the action of other elements or mechanisms. It might be argued that here is intelligence at work, or a creative mind adapting itself to a situation. Because there is, in fact, more than one way to skin a cat, and new ones will be developed if the market for catskins increases, we must be careful to avoid the narrow view, and be ready to handle "motor equivalence" when it occurs. We shall deal with this problem again (see Mediation, p. 308). At the present time we are concerned with the more elemental aspects of behavior, the machinery of the body, and cannot afford to digress. It is of the highest importance, however, to recognize that views like Guthrie's call for learning each and every kind of movement pattern that is ever used for a second time, and that the facts of behavior make this a tenuous doctrine. It is more likely to expect that behavior will include various novel adjustments which may take advantage of prior learning without specific practice of particular movements in a fixed sequence.

BASIC MECHANISMS

What are the biological facts and limitations with which we must be armed? The great tradition in psychology started with an interest in sense organs and sensory experience. It was not long before an interest in sensory experience required an orientation with respect to the nervous system. A later, but rather a necessary, step called for an interest in the muscular system, the effective agents of behavior. We have already learned about the historical sequence. It is time that we took a closer look at these basic mechanisms of behavior. Before we begin our consideration of this equipment we must observe that the activities of psychologists have spread out in such wondrous detail, into so many areas of interest, that we cannot hope to discuss in anything like beginning adequacy the nature and structure of each sense organ, muscle, and segment of the nervous system. Indeed many books are devoted to fragmentary aspects of single sense organs. A marvelous book on the retina of the eye has appeared recently representing the accumulated wisdom of years of study of this one structure. Rather than spending time on anatomical and physiological detail in this text, we will try to spell out what is important for the psychologist to know about the principles of action involved, and trust that the student will devote time to courses in physiology and biology where he can learn, with proper attention to detail, whatever he has time to digest. Our treatment will be schematic.

The sense organs

Man has been traditionally viewed as being endowed with five senses. Psychologists would not be able to name these particular five, for painstaking study from the last hundred years has suggested that it is quite fruitless to try to enumerate separate structures which can be labeled as sense organs. The eye, for example, may be considered as some unitary globe in the front of the face, and be the "window of the soul" or the mechanism of vision, but vision is a complex set of reactions to radiant energy of certain wavelengths and intensities and may involve a great many additional or subsense organs. It is known, for example, from microscopic studies that the retina is populated with tiny structures called rods and cones, and that these structures are involved in vision at low levels of illumination (rods) and at higher levels (cones). For color vision, cones are required. Different kinds of cones are presumed to exist and to respond to different wavelengths of light, although these have not been specifically identified. Since man can identify perhaps as many as 150 different hues (the aspect of color that is related to differences in wavelength of incident light), the question arises as to whether man has 150 or more different kinds of cones or does some smaller number, perhaps as few as 3, or even 2, handle the job by some complex interaction of a chemical nature such as we have in color photography (see Land, 1959).

Similarly in relation to sound, we can respond to tones ranging from some small number of cycles (vibrations in a medium), say 20, to some high-pitched tones in the 20,000-cycle range. Does this suggest that there are 20,000 receiving sense organ structures or, again, does some smaller number of structures handle the job by complicated interactions?

In the skin we have receptor mechanisms for mediating reactions to heat (and cold), touch, pressures, and pain, as well as complex reactions such as clamminess, tickle, prickle, itch, roughness, smoothness, squishiness, and what not. Are these all provided for by separate structures or again by complex interactions?

Psychology texts of any earlier day spent much time upon the question of the structure and function of sense organs. The interested student will consult these earlier texts as well as modern physiological studies for the fascinating facts that have been acquired over the years. We must content ourselves with a more diagrammatic appreciation at this introductory level.[1]

The sense organs are traditionally thought of as receptors, that is, receiving agents. In engineering terminology, they "handle the inputs." These inputs can be only in the nature of physical energy which takes various forms. We have already mentioned radiant energy which can affect the specialized structures in the eye as light (color, and black and white) or the entire body as heat, if the wavelength is of the appropriate range. Heat waves affect structures in the skin. The actual structures

[1] The student can profitably pursue the subject in Wenger, Jones, and Jones (1956) and Geldard (1953).

for heat reception are not identified unequivocally, but we can think of the body as provided with a means for reacting to temperature changes mostly through blood vessel action (contraction and relaxation) with or without the help of specialized end-organs in the skin. The loss of heat to the environment, and the consequent "cold" reaction also involves its own machinery. This too may be mediated by blood vessel contraction or through the functioning of a specialized structure. We need not be concerned over it for the present. It is sufficient to know that the human reacts to radiant energy of a certain wavelength in terms of a temperature sense and that the organism can lose heat to the external world when there is a lower external temperature than the organism happens to have.

Another form of energy to which we are sensitive is mechanical pressure in audition. This amounts to pressures in the air against our eardrums or vibrations against our skin or bones. When the energy involved is discretely localized so that the skin tissue is damaged as by a needle prick, we talk about a pain stimulation. No specialized organs have ever been discovered for pain and this reaction is ordinarily attributed to fine nerve endings which abound in the skin.

Chemical energy in terms of substances in solution or in volatile action also affect us in terms of taste or smell. Cooling and burning effects as from the evaporation of ether on the skin or inhalation of ammonia or imbibing of alcohol represent a type of sensitivity to chemical energy.

In the long run, perhaps all of this energy will turn out to be electrical in nature and we would be remiss in not considering the fact that the body does comprise a kind of electrochemical system, that perhaps all transformations of external energy change amount to a reduction to electrical or electrochemical effects. In any event, once the sense organ, or specialized receptor for transforming external energy, has been affected, the nervous system conducts such energy to and within itself in terms of electrical-chemical change. We find the sensory structures, then, the agencies by which inputs of various kinds of energy are translated into neural action, regardless of their original nature. A painting by Picasso or DaVinci, a sonata by Beethoven or Mozart, become electrochemical excitations in the nervous system from the point of view of psychologists when they are concerned about psychology and not enjoying the arts.

Sensation and perception

In the Wundtian psychology of the last century, mental experience was presumed to consist of sensations, images, and feelings. In various combinations these atoms or units made up more complex "experiences" like ideas and perceptions. No clear definition was ever given of such phenomena; they were psychological "givens"; primitive elements assumed to exist and serving as the foundation on which the structure of psychology was to be built. In some vague way a "sensation" was thought of as an elemental mental unit directly related to the nature of the impinging stimulation. One psychologist defined it as "the first response of the brain to a stimulus," but this brain response was supposed somehow to generate something unique, some qualitatively different kind of event which itself was left undefined unless we accept the term "mental" as needing no definition. The student was left to wrestle with himself, using whatever procedure he could in attempting to understand sensations and other mental "experiences."

Some negative distinctions were introduced by Wundt in his instructions to introspectors with a warning not to commit the "stimulus error." This meant, for Wundt, not to confuse the basic, elemental experience or sensation with the object or stimulus which produced the sensation. Thus, if the introspector were shown a piece of blackboard chalk and asked to describe his mental content, he must not say: "I see a piece of chalk." He should instead say something like: I have a visual sensation (this indicated the "quality"); it is white and bright and extends more in one direction than in the other; it is clear and well-defined. Such remarks were supposed to characterize the sensory experience in terms of the "attributes of sensation" (see Boring, 1933) which included such "dimensions" as quality, intensity, duration, extensity, and clearness; sometimes volume was considered an attribute of such sensations as were produced by the tones of an organ. These attributes of a mental experience presumably represented the work of the mind as it responded to and took account of a stimulus.

But a naive introspector would still see a piece of chalk. This, argued Wundt, was because the observer was describing a *perception* and not a sensation. A perception was the *second* response of the brain to a stimulus; a complex mental product of sensations, images, and feelings, plus the effects of past experience or learning. Perceptions had "meanings" related to past experience and, as such, could not be accepted as the primary mental content because such past experience had to come *after* the basic sensory process occurred on the first occasion for any observer. The problem of psychology was to discover the laws which described how sensations, images, and feelings combined to produce percepts and ideas, second-order mental products. This could not be done by naively reporting combinations or complex events instead of concentrating on the elements.

Perception was regarded as a mental event, an event involving meaning. The student today is perfectly willing to talk about such events occurring in his own brain but he does so not in the terminology of Wundt, nor yet that of neurology, but in terms of common speech. Our language is unfortunately most misleading when we try to talk about what goes on in our heads, as Wundt insisted all along. The student tells us that he "sees" people, sports cars, that he "digs the beat," that he smells roses, or tastes corn flakes. He has no lack of words to describe his personal, inner, reactions. Others familiar with his language appear to be satisfied that a satisfactory account of what goes on in the reporter's brain has been rendered. Psychologists are not so easily satisfied. Even the student recognizes that what he sees is not always what someone else sees in the same object; it is common enough to hear: What does he see in her? To cite an overworked illustration of the point, the boy scout, the fisherman, the artist, the poet, the engineer, the farmer all see different things when coming upon the running brook or "rippling stream," as the poet might call it. The element of past experience is readily admitted by all. Such "total" private reactions to stimuli involving past experience are called percepts or perceptions. The presumed inner activity is called perceiving. Perceiving has been a major preoccupation of psychologists from the beginning of the science and today represents a problem area in which many researches are being done.

PHENOMENOLOGY

Some modern psychologists who concern themselves primarily with the perception problem have no reluctance about their subjects committing stimulus errors. They, in fact, require their subjects to be as "naive" as possible and report what they see or hear as directly as possible without any screening of their language. Such psychologists are sometimes called "phenomenologists" because they are studying "phenomena" (mental events?) directly as they are reported with no theoretical preconceptions about what an observer should report. Other psychologists, some with Gestalt leanings or backgrounds, worry over the problems of how much of perceiving activity is a basic, natural capacity of man and how much must be ascribed to experience. Later on we shall consider some of the principles advanced by Gestalt psychologists as descriptions of native or natural perceptual activities.

Frequently, psychologists working with problems in perception proceed about their business without worrying about the problem of what a perception is. They ignore the problem of definition as something upon which there will be no agreement for some time and go about the business of studying relationships between stimuli and the reports of observers. They are not concerned about behavior in the sense of movements or observable activities but in the inner responses or events aroused by stimuli. They might, for example, ask a subject to tell them when an illuminated rod in a dark room is tilted and when it is perpendicular to the unseen floor. Or they might ask a subject to look at a large disc for four minutes and then look at a small disc which is centered in the same position as was formerly occupied by the large disc. Another small disc placed somewhat to one side is used as a comparison stimulus. Under such conditions the first small disc might look smaller than the comparison disc. Such a "phenomenon" is called a "figural aftereffect" (Köhler and Wallach, 1944). Many aspects of behavior involve the inner responses of a subject, responses that occur prior to any overt activity, and "perception psychologists" concentrate on such inner events, events that frequently do not lead to any overt activity other than some verbal report and that only when it is asked for. If a subject looks at a red object he may appear, to an external observer, to be doing nothing. Yet he is behaving, internally, and such internal behavior is of major concern, not only for itself alone, but for practically all other psychologically interesting activity. It is no longer popular to keep any distinction between sensations and perceptions and some psychologists would refer to any internal behavior with one term or the other, being indifferent to the historical problem, or regarding it as a great but misguided effort. The emphasis on a "first" or "second" response of the brain was probably unwise. It is doubtful that any such distinction could be established in the brain as the neural activity would be complex and continuous even though a starting point might be located in the sensory activity. It is now solidly established that whatever "experiences" we have do not amount to anything until they have been rather thoroughly "diffused" in the brain and it is more meaningful to think of internal activity as a complex unit than of first or primary steps and subsequent developments (Hebb, 1949).

Internal events

Yet a problem remains. People do report the occurrence of internal events which are strongly and specifically related to certain stimuli, objects, or events. The human observer reports: "I heard a noise," or, "I heard music, apparently a violin." "I saw Henry yesterday." What do such reports indicate? A dog responds to his master's call but not to that of a stranger. What does this indicate as going on inside the dog's head? Perhaps the illustration just cited provides a cue to the nature of perception. On the animal level where no speech is possible and we can get no reports, we recognize that some kinds of "discriminations" occur, i.e., the organism responds selectively to its environment. Not all stimuli evoke the same responses even when the stimuli are quite similar. In order to make such selective responses, the animal must be trained or otherwise learn to react to one form or pattern of energy and not to another which may be somewhat like the first. This kind of learning in turn, depends upon the efficiency of the sense organs and their capacity for providing different kinds of neural excitation and/or different neural pathways which are activated by one form of stimulation but not another, or at least, not to the same degree. When the animal is reacting selectively to some stimulus we can assume (and the student should note that this is an assumption, one that we shall make more explicit in the next chapter) that some neural activity of a specific form occurred prior to the overt response, a neural activity that led to the response. Such neural activity accompanied by slight motor activity or *tendencies* toward such activity is further assumed to represent or *be* the perception.

The overt response may be modest or minimal, and, in a sense, even negative. Thus, the dozing dog that opens one eye slowly when its master enters the room and then goes back to his dozing, must have had a neural process occur which amounted to "discriminating" the master from all other men. The opening of the eye was the only overt activity noted, yet previous experience with the dog might establish quite clearly that no stranger would be so accepted. Similarly on the human level, the citizen sitting on his front porch watches the world go by but does little more than sit, responding, if at all, internally, presumably again neurally, to the cars and passersby. His eyes may follow one object after another, briefly, but he might be unable to report much of what went on—how many cars, what kind, and so on. Occasionally a car or a person might set off a particular more complex neural action which leads to some overt activity. The observer might wave or say "Hello." He has "discriminated" some one stimulus pattern from many others, both preceding and occurring simultaneously from the background which had not generated enough neural activity to lead to any observable overt response. On the human level we can talk about such neural behavior which leads to overt reactions as "identifying" reponses. The identification may be vague and fleeting, or, finely detailed. A traveler in the far north is amazed when he discovers that Eskimos have a dozen or so different terms for various kinds of snow. For the traveler, snow has been that white stuff which does, sometimes, look crisp and other times "mushy," but the Eskimo has much finer identifying responses. Similarly the South Sea islander has dozens of names for coconuts in various stages of ripening. For the traveler a coconut may be green or ripe and that ends it. We respond to one person with a neatly organized or integrated neural pattern, which leads more or less directly to a verbal response: "How are you, John?" To another similar pattern we respond with "the face is familiar but I can't place the name." To still others we say: "I don't know him—never saw him before."

Sometimes overt behavior is a major feature of the perception. When teenagers listen to the latest form of popular music they listen with their entire bodies, swaying, gyrating, clapping hands, and otherwise engaging in various contortions. Children at the Saturday matinee practically tear the theater and each other apart as they "watch" a movie. They are incapable of watching with the eyes alone; their hands and feet have to get into the act. As humans mature they gradually restrict the overt activities to some irreducible minimum, but this minimum may be enough to escape ordinary observation. The audience at a symphony concert sit quietly, not even tapping their feet in time with the music which is an adolescent way of listening to music. One would hardly be able to tell what the audience was doing merely by looking at it if he could not see and hear the orchestra. Actually many of the audience are probably not listening; some of them have so reduced the overt activities that they are asleep or practically so. When overt activity is minimal we must depend upon verbal descriptions from the subjects.

Prior to any such overt verbal responses we assume that a neural activity pattern initiated by the stimulus had to occur. The nature of such a hypothetical pattern will depend upon a host of factors besides the sense organ activity and the initial sensory nerve process that results from stimulation of a sense organ. The first time such a pattern occurs, say in infancy, we can assume that nothing "meaningful" happens. The infant does not "perceive" anything (Riesen, 1947). If the pattern is repeated often enough, it can be further assumed that it will become "channeled" or systematized, i.e., lead to a specific pattern of neural activity which will normally lead to some overt response, perhaps an eye movement or a "negative" response such as doing nothing overt, closing the eyes, or looking elsewhere. Stimulation from the ceiling or walls of the nursery might result in such "negative" responses.

If there is a picture on the wall the stimulation from it might lead to a series or pattern of eye movements of a specific extent and duration. Items in the picture might lead to other specific eye movements, head turning, or reaching behavior. The observer of such a child says: He is looking at the picture. He may be looking, but what he sees or perceives is still unknown. Later on he will learn to talk about the picture while looking at it and begin to use words society provides for such situations. These words will come to serve as descriptions of the inner or neural activity in so far as words can be used when other neural and perhaps motor activity is taking place. Such verbal descriptions are as close as we can come to describing our perceptions. They serve well enough for conversations even though they do not actually approximate describing what is actually going on. We say "There is a green bottle over there" and everyone familiar with the language can now "look over there." If they do, neural processes that have previously occurred in them when green bottles were stimulating their retinas will occur in the new observers. If someone looks in the wrong place no such process will take place and he will say "I don't see any green bottle." If one of the observers is color blind, but has learned, as color blind people do, to call certain neural reactions green, especially if others are saying "green," he too will agree that a green bottle is present, even though his neural activity will not be like that of the others.

We must not presume that when observers agree on what is present all of them have the same neural process occurring. They can only be presumed to have some process occurring for which they have learned a common label. Each observer's patterns are probably quite different. An adult seeing the bottle will have very different neural activities occurring from those in the brain of a small child. These differences are presumably due to learning. Besides the factor of learning, many other conditions can alter our perceptions although some of these processes themselves are modified by learning. Thus, physiological conditions related to hunger, for example, may alter the operations of the brain so that objects are seen in terms of their food potential. Starving people are said to dream of food. Such dreams are perceptions, too, only their overt accompaniments, if any, are not appreciated by an observer because he does not know what stimuli are important to the sleeper. Many experiments have been done demonstrating that "motives" influence perceptions. We shall look into these later but for the present we can accept the hypothesis that such effects are possible.

Perception and learning

A central issue in psychology is the problem of the role of perception in learning. We have already indicated that perceptions themselves have to be learned. It is necessary to recognize also, however, that perceptions will affect future learning. If learning consists of associating one neural pattern with another or with some other kind of neural activity, then the learner must "perceive" the items to be associated, that is, discriminate them or otherwise identify them. If he does not have the necessary neural patterns already available on the basis of past experience and prior learning, he will have to acquire such patterns before he learns the new associations. If he has already built up specific patterns which happen to be incorrect, i.e., inappropriate in the current learning context, he will have further trouble. In the Russian language, for example, the letter H is read as an N. The novice in Russian will have such "interference" patterns holding up his learning. In learning lists of nonsense syllables (three-letter meaningless words like, ken, fap, yev), the subject does better in memorizing after first "familiarizing" himself with the individual syllables, that is, learning the necessary perceptions (Hovland and Kurtz, 1952). Every time we learn the name of a stranger, we must establish new neural patterns involving his appearance in addition to the activity that is associated with the face which leads, eventually, to calling him by name. The initial stages of learning may consist almost entirely of acquiring the "perceptual responses." Before children can learn to read they must learn to see E, F, and L and all the rest of the alphabet as different, that is they must perceive the stimulus objects. This can only mean that the neural pattern initiated by E is different from F. If it is not, the reader is in for a difficult time. When the basic perceptual responses are running off efficiently, the learner is ready to associate other responses with the perceptual patterns.

It might be fruitful to summarize at this point, to establish a position about the nature of perception. We have defined a perception as a neural event (which might include minimal motor reactions), a pattern of activity associated with some specific form of stimulation. Such a pattern may or may not lead to any specific overt activity which can be observed by others. This may be because many patterns are initiated that are only fleetingly active and are rapidly replaced by others as when we scan the sky or a field of hay, a stream of passing cars, or faces in a crowd. Under some conditions, perhaps of a stronger or persistent stimulation some overt activity, e.g., eye movements, might occur from which the inference of a perception might be drawn by an observer. One learns to perceive in that neural activity comes to be "identified" or discriminated from other neural activity in terms of the responses that are made to one pattern and not to another. Humans learn to label this activity that precedes an overt response or that follows some kinds of stimulation but which does not evoke any observable activity. Much of the labeling is done in terms of naming objects or characteristics of stimuli or stimulus objects, that is, in terms of what the early introspectors called the "stimulus error." We still make this error; it is part of our daily lives. It should be appreciated by the student that perceiving reactions, when they lead to some overt activity, belong in the class of events we described in Chapter 2 as *mediators*. When the perception is not followed by any overt activity, nothing has been mediated except in the sense of negative reactions, but even these are important in the continuing process of behavior. As we search through a drawer for some object or for a book on our shelves, we barely "notice" the items we are *not* looking for. The items were "seen," i.e., the neural and minimal motor actions involved did occur but they led to behavior that amounted to a dismissal of these items as the search continued. When the appropriate object is reached, we make a total identifying response. We have perceived.

Sensory reactions

An immediate consequence of the above description of sensory functions and internal responses to stimuli may prove startling if not somewhat dismaying to the student. Once the sense organ has done its job, namely to transfer the external energy to the sensory or afferent nerve endings, there is nothing left but electrochemical action in the nervous system. In modern psychological theory there is no room for pictures being transmitted to the brain or some hypothetical mind or developing room. There are no sounds in the brain, no tunes, no songs running around, no one sees in his "mind's eye," there is only electrical activity. To put the matter as strongly as possible, we do not "see" people or pictures, or scenes—light rays from such objects initiate changes in the rods and cones of the retina; there is a photoelectrical effect which initiates an electrochemical activity in nerve structures, and this is conducted, like an electrical current (although much more slowly), to the brain. From there the current passes out through various substructures of the brain to motor nerves which lead to muscles, glands, and the sense organs themselves, and initiate movements or other kinds of reactions. Among these reactions might be the verbal one of "Say, look at that, would you? Isn't it beautiful?" Among other tasks, the psychologist has chosen for himself the responsibility for accounting for each step of the total pattern involved from the analysis of the light rays emanating from Van Gogh's "Peach Orchard" to the response "Isn't it wonderful!" For some of his steps he calls on the physiologist for help. For the rest, he must reply on working propositions with which the physiologist might not, at the moment, be too concerned.

An interesting sidelight to the above remarks is that, while they represent a wholly mechanistic interpretation of what goes on during a sensory process and its consequences, a somewhat similar analysis led Bishop Berkeley,[2] the best known proponent of philosophical "idealism," to deny the existence of the physical world and proclaim the inde-dependent existence of a nonmaterial psychic universe. According to Berkeley, it was the activity of the mind that generated physical objects as appearances in an *apparent* physical world. Sounds, sights, odors, tastes, etc., were mental experiences which depended upon the mind alone and out of which we constructed alleged items in an alleged external world. It is hypothetically correct, if we could initiate the same neural activity in the optic nerve that follows stimulation from some source, say the reflected light from a particular person or painting, that we would then "see" that painting or person without actual presence of the external stimuli. To a degree, we are always doing this with all of our senses, more effectively with some than with others. Think for a moment of a pan on the stove with a mess of sliced onions sizzling away. It is unlikely that these words have not affected you in some fashion. You are probably willing to say that you can more or less see the pan with the onions, you can hear the sound of the sizzling fat, perhaps you can smell, and even imagine the taste if you should pick up a segment. The behavior involved when people report seeing or hearing, or otherwise experiencing objects in their absence, is called "imagery."

Imagery

At one time psychologists made a great deal of fuss about imagery. It was considered by Wundt one of the three basic psychic processes, an element of mental activity. Galton (1883) studied individual differences in imagery in a celebrated introduction of the questionnaire technique in psychology. He asked several hundred friends to imagine their breakfast table and describe carefully all their reactions as they called it up in their fancy. Other psychologists wondered if thinking went on through the process of imagery and in some cases decided that thinking could go on in the absence of any image content. They became known as the "imageless thought" school. When Watson launched his program of behavioristic psychology he dismissed images from psychology as mystical hangovers from an unscientific day. Watson's debonair dismissal of the image by the simple process of denial disturbed many psychologists who could not so easily dismiss their own images. For many years an uneasy atmosphere prevailed in relation to talking about images in psychology. A strictly behavioristic view denied the

[2] The idealistic philosophy of Berkeley can be examined in a preliminary way in Burtt (1939) and Berlin (1956).

possibility of observing such private experience. There was some concession to an undeniable fact in connection with so-called "afterimages" (if you look persistently at some patch of color for about thirty seconds and then look at a neutral surface you will "see" an apparent color on this surface which will be the color complement of the original, if the original was red, the aftereffect will be blue-green, e.g.). Afterimages were grudgingly admitted by the most extreme behaviorist, but other images were treated as some sort of spiritualistic poltergeist and inadmissible in scientific conversation. We have now become somewhat more sophisticated on this subject and images are again coming into psychological conversations. But now it is held that the image is no different in origin and nature from the original kind of reaction except for whatever support the actual stimulation might provide. If by any means, the neural activity involved in seeing your mother, for example, can be initiated without mama's actually being present, then you will be likely to report that you can see your mother, perhaps a little vaguely, but to some degree. Such neural activity can be aroused, it is argued through the arousal of other neural activity which has been associated with that which occurred during the original stimulation. To use some technical jargon, the image is a "conditioned" neural reaction. If one desired to speak of the basic neural reaction involved in the original stimulation as a "sensation," then an image would be a "conditioned sensation."

The concept of the image as a conditioned sensation has been illustrated by Leuba (1940) in a series of experiments using hypnosis as a technique for isolating the presumed basic processes. A subject is hypnotized (see p. 368) and told that he can only hear a buzzer and the hypnotist's voice, that he can see nothing, and feel nothing except on the back of one hand. The experimenter then sounds the buzzer and at the same time pricks the back of the subject's hand with a needle or pencil point. The subject is then brought back to a normal condition and while he is otherwise occupied, the buzzer is sounded. Immediately the subject starts to rub the back of the hand which had been pricked earlier. When asked why he does this, he replies that he felt an itch. If this hypnotic experimental analogue is taken as a suggestion about how imagery is initiated, we might presume that the occurrence of appropriate stimuli in the external world, or internal reactions which might generate stimuli, might also give rise to neural activity which previously accompanied such stimuli and the subject will have an image. Such imaginal activity, i.e., the neural processes involved, can by a similar process be associated with other imaginal neural surrogates so that a whole chain of imagery can be initiated by some one stimulus. One image can lead to another, just as other sequential activities as in walking, etc., can occur.

CHARACTERISTICS OF SENSORY ACTION

CLASSIFICATION OF SENSE ORGANS

While we are not going to concern ourselves with specialized receptor systems, it is important to note that stimulation has numerous ports of entry into the human nervous system. They are briefly discussed below.

Exteroceptors (*distant*). Some forms of energy can affect the organism even though the source of stimulation is far removed. Thus we can see for great distances, that is, reflected light rays from objects at varying distances can enter the eye. Similarly, sound energy can travel for miles from its original source, if, like thunder, it is intense enough, and reach our ears. Odors from stockyards can travel for several city blocks. Stimulation from objects at some distance from the body is classified as being received by exteroceptors or distance receptors. It might be argued that actual physical contact is made via some medium and this is clearly so in the case of audition where air, water, or some other medium is agitated at the locus of the ear drum, but we might have difficulty with light rays since the physicists have become disenchanted about the concept of a luminiferous ether.

Exteroceptors (*contact*). The various skin senses, and here we have to include the taste buds on the tongue, form another class of receptors. Here actual physical contact must occur although this is a rather vague affair in the temperature discrimination which we make in terms of outdoor weather conditions. Touching hot or cold objects is clearly a contact matter but feeling cold in the winter time calls for a more abstract concept of contact. In order to taste a substance, the material must be dissolved and flow around the taste buds which are somewhat hidden within the papillae on the tongue.

Interoceptors (*organic*). The various internal organs are supplied with sensitive cells which can initiate neural impulses under some conditions such as distention by food or gas. Unusual activity in the heart, lungs, intestine, or the esophageal tract initiates sensory stimulation. Most of these organs are insensitive to stimulation of external origin but are effective sources of impulses from internal pressures and distress conditions, inflammation, etc. Many organs in the viscera appear not to be effective sources of stimulation—we are unable to report activity in the liver, pancreas, and other glands. The lungs and heart, on the other hand, provide a variety of stimulation, including auditory and visual effects.

Proprioceptors. The muscles, tendons, and joints are supplied with sense organ structures which react to movements of flexion or relaxation. These stimuli comprise the kinesthetic sense or sense of movement and are especially important in co-ordinated activities and in balance. Because each muscular contraction and skeletal movement is a rich source of stimulation, movements can be organized in sequences in which one movement leads to another and, through the process of conditioning, a habitual sequence can run off with no visual or other aids. These "movement-produced stimuli" play a great role in Guthrie's systematic psychology and, indeed, one form or another of such internal stimulation is used by most theoretical speculators to account for continuous or prolonged action beyond the reflex level. We shall return to, and rely heavily on, movement-produced stimulation in our later considerations. We will make use of them as "mediators."

The vestibular senses. In the internal ear, along with the cochlear structures which are essential for auditory stimulation there are to be found the semicircular canals, the utricle, and the saccule all of which are concerned with the senses of balance and orientation in space of the head and of the body. The semicircular canals contain a liquid which is displaced whenever the head moves and the flow of this liquid past tiny hair structures provides the stimulation which we learn to associate with head position. In the utricle and saccule we have tiny grains (ear stones or otoliths) which are imbedded in a gelatinous mass. These tiny structures also stimulate the vestibular branch of the auditory nerve through specialized hair cells and provide us with a sense of "gravity" or body weight. Under normal earthly conditions we manage to perambulate effectively because of the so-called pull of gravity on the otoliths. Damage to these structures would deprive us of a sense of weight—we would be weightless, as our space children will be when they take off for Mars in a rocket and are deprived of the gravitational influence on the otoliths.

SENSORY FUNCTIONS

The sense organs can be thought of as specialized endings of the afferent nerves, i.e., the nerves that carry impulses into the central nervous system which consists of the brain and the spinal cord. They are, in effect, part of the nervous system. The eye, for instance, is basically a part of the brain; it develops from the same tissue and is set apart in location, in early development, but remains one with the brain. As specialized endings developed in evolution for the various afferent nerves, they enlarged the scope of energy forms to which the organism could respond. The primitive sponge responds only to actual body contact, to pressure on the muscles; the mammal can react to stimuli of various kinds at some distance. The function of the sense organs, accordingly, is to react to changes in the thermal, chemical, photic, mechanical, or electrical environment of the organism. Such changes are more or less constantly occurring for the living organism and it must, correspondingly, adjust to these changes as they occur. The complex array of incoming impulses is beyond any current capacity of ours to appraise. Even at our most quiescent stages, lying or sitting down, there is a continuous input from the muscles as they stretch and contract or just merely support our weight. One investigator (Strughold, 1953), in what might be thought of as an amusing experiment in some respects, injected novocaine into his buttocks, and then went for an airplane ride in which the pilot engaged in some acrobatics. The passenger, without the benefit of incoming stimuli from his seat, became disturbed, bewildered, and distressingly upset. The "seat of the pants" is of much more than sitting value. The millions of impulses arriving at the central nervous system every second from all parts of our bodies, to say nothing of the skin and exteroceptors, call for a central control station of unimaginable complexity. The brain serves as such a central depot or exchange and we will have a look at it shortly. For the moment, we can look at some factors that make the job of the brain a little easier or that, in some cases, make it more difficult.

Thresholds. Not all energy changes that take place in the internal or external environment will initiate impulses in the nervous system. The sense organs, while extremely "sensitive" to physically measured energies, do have their limitations. Under ideal conditions of relative lack of stimulation from other sources, rather minute amounts of energy can be sensed or detected. The ear, for example, is so sensitive, that if it were any more sensitive, it would pick up the sound generated by the motion of molecules of air in the absence of any vibrating body (Boring, 1945). We are rarely in conditions of complete quiescence, however, and all energy changes must compete for entry against some background or general "noise level." In order to set off a neural impulse, then, the energy change must be of sufficient amplitude or degree. What this degree of change amounts to cannot be stated in fixed terms for any person or at any time. It must be conceived of as an average amount, with sometimes a little more energy change required, sometimes a little less. Whatever the amount is, if it is sufficient, we talk about it figuratively as crossing a "threshold," or "limen," a liminal amount. The threshold varies from time to time because of a number of factors. If the receiving neural element (a neuron) has just been used ("fired"), it cannot be used again for some time (a brief period in the neighborhood of 0.001 sec.). This period during which a neuron cannot be fired is called refractory phase; it is a recovery period.

Adaptation. Neurons will not respond to an energy change if the change is more or less steady, constant (even though intermittent), or prolonged. While the mechanisms involved are not understood, the nervous system does manage to adjust to stimulation sources that are relatively inconsequential for the organism even though under some conditions the same stimulation is adequate for crossing the threshold. We do not hear the ticking of a clock, perhaps, in a reasonably quiet room when we are otherwise preoccupied. If the clock stops we may hear it stop which appears somewhat paradoxical. The energy change represented by the periodic ticking was somehow taken account of as inconsequential to the organism's survival and shunted off into channels that automatically disposed of it. Such a neural adjustment to a constant energy change is called "adaptation" or sometimes, "habituation." In some instances, the habituation is more or less complete and we cannot react to the energy involved even though we deliberately set out to do so. For example, after smelling an odoriferous substance like Limburger cheese for several minutes, we are no longer able to react to the substance, or, when we immerse a hand in water of room temperature, we may not be able to detect any temperature features of the liquid stimulation. The pressure of our clothing disappears almost immediately. We hardly can tell whether we have socks on or not without looking. In other instances, we can react to the energy change by "attending" to it. Thus, the ticking clock can become a source of auditory stimulation if someone asks us to listen to the ticking.

Attention. The just mentioned function of attention, now requires our attention. For the moment we will assume that everyone knows what attention is, even if no one does, and taking advantage of this false security, we can note that many energy changes of more than adequate amplitude or volume to elicit a neural response can occur and gain no entry into the nervous system under certain conditions. A child watching a cartoon on television cannot be "distracted." Parents can call for dinner or even offer ice cream in a loud voice and get no place. The phenomenon is distressing to parents but of great interest to psychologists. Why does a signal of more than adequate strength for normal responding, fail to get into the organism when the organism is otherwise "absorbed"? We do not have a good answer for this question, but we are able to go a step beyond the analysis accepted by the average parent. The parent may be prone to call the child willful, inattentive, or negative, "he hears all right, but he doesn't care." This has been demonstrated recently by some investigators who placed recording electrodes on the neural outlets of the cochlea in a cat's brain.[3] When they generated a sharp clicking sound in the cat's vicinity, a potential drop in the recording system was observed, the impulse was getting through, and the cat responded to the click. Now, when a jar containing live mice was placed in front of the cat and the same click was sounded, no such impulse was observed. The cat did not respond to the click. It never got into the nervous system. What the mechanisms are that block certain inputs and permit others entry is still unknown, but such mechanisms must be constantly at work or we would be continually scratching at all parts of our bodies, shifting and moving about, stretching, grimacing, and otherwise contorting ourselves. Some of us are less inhibited than others and do react on what might be thought of as an unrestricted level. The student who engages in classroom acrobatics might very well have little or no interest in what is going on on the lecture platform or anywhere else for that matter.

Thresholds, then, are relative levels at which energy changes can be transformed into neural action. They are subject to variation from refractory phase, adaptation, and attention to other stimuli, all of which tend to raise the threshold. Thresholds can be lowered to some degree just as they can be raised, primarily through attention and freedom from distracting stimulation although the latter point must be somewhat amended. Before we describe the last point, it should be noted that in the case of some senses it is possible to increase sensitivity through a rest process. Thus if you do not use your eyes but remain in a dark room for a half hour or so, your sensitivity to light will be greatly enhanced and you will be able to detect light sources or illuminated objects which you could not see when you first entered the room. The experience is common to every movie goer. On first entering the darkened theater, you may be "night-blind," unable to see anything except the screen. The usher who has been there for some time leads you confidently to seats some place in the darkened pit and you stumble over previously seated patrons. After a while, if you glance about you can recognize faces, empty seats, even the decorations on the walls and you might even begin to wonder if the theater is dark enough for showing films. The "dark adaptation" process is of great benefit to shipboard watchstanders who

[3] An account of the experiment by Hernandez-Péon is included in *Contributions to Modern Psychology,* edited by D. E. Dulany, *et al.* (1958).

must scan the dark sea for floating objects or distant shores. Nowadays radar might be the more effective method for spotting an enemy vessel, but the human's capacity for effective night vision through adaptation is presumably a hereditary or evolutionary gift from our ancestors who had to see by starlight if they were to survive enemy attack. There appears to be no evidence and perhaps the subject has not been investigated enough to determine whether other senses would improve if they were not used for some time. We cannot hear better after being in a quiet room for some period, or if we can, it might be difficult to prove as it is possible that we rapidly lose whatever gain in sensitivity had accrued. Resting our noses does not necessarily help our sense of smell even though tea tasters and perfume samplers might think so. It is said of Parisian perfume testers that they walk about with their noses covered to keep them pure—the method might help avoid colds and infections, but it is not necessarily effective in detecting fine shades or nuances of musk and roses. While it is true that continued smelling or sniffing of the same substances will "kill" the sense of smell for that odor, it does not appear to do anything to other odors. Still, it may be possible that a period of rest may improve any sense organ's capacity. Watchmakers, for example, have "heavy" days and "light" days, in their work. On light days they repair wrist watches and do other work that calls for extremely fine movements and control; on heavy days they work on alarm clocks. They do not like to switch from one set of sensori-motor adjustments to another. The watchmaker's activity may, of course, represent a number of other kinds of adjustment, but it appears that a certain amount of relief from one kind of stimulation is of benefit for another.

THE CONCEPT OF OPTIMUM STIMULATION

We can return now to the point left unsettled above when we indicated that complete freedom from other stimulation was not necessarily of benefit. It appears that one sense can help another to a considerable degree. In a quiet room, a much lower tone can be heard if just before the onset of the tone, a dim light is illuminated. Possibly the reverse might also be true although it has not been established. It may be that too much quiet makes for inefficiency. Enough of it is certainly conducive to sleep and when we retire we seek to minimize all forms of stimulation. It appears that the waking up process amounts to permitting sufficient stimulation into the nervous system to get it going in an adequate fashion. Not enough stimulation is followed by sleep; too much results in excited agitation, and in abnormal cases, convulsions. Somewhere between the two situations we can presume that there is an optimum level of stimulation (Leuba, 1955, 1958). The student who sits in a comfortable chair in a quiet room may be forcing himself to stay awake. He might better employ outside aids for this purpose—a radio or record player with some appropriately selected program which is not sufficiently interesting in itself to control attention might well provide the necessary help to keep the nervous system going effectively. We must be careful about generalizing excessively about this concept of optimum stimulation. It is not necessarily any goal of mankind to be optimally stimulated, but it may be that the brain does not work effectively in the absence of such a level and an inactive brain at certain times of the day may lead us into states which create trouble and which we might learn to avoid. We might, in effect, learn to be up and doing for no other good reason than that the brain needs stimulation and the condition of not enough stimulation might in some fashion develop its own cues to initiate more action on the part of the organism.

The measurement of thresholds

THE PSYCHOPHYSICAL METHODS

For some purposes it becomes desirable to have a numerical indication of a threshold. One might want to know what is the minimal energy level of some type which must be present to arouse action. This might be measured directly by taking amplified readings of neural action associated with the sensory receptor involved or less directly by having the subject either report that he senses or detects the presence of a stimulus. In experiments with animals, the animal might be trained to respond in a certain way to some stimulus and the strength of this stimulus might be systematically lowered until the responses no longer occurred. This stimulus value is an "absolute threshold." It might also be desirable to discover, at the opposite extreme, how much of some type of energy an organism can stand, e.g., loudness of tones or degree of heat. Such points would be called "terminal thresholds." More often we are not dealing with extremes along some continuum but rather well within some average and tolerable amount of stimulation and our interest might be be in detecting the smallest degree of change that could be discriminated successfully. Since a standard amount would have to be used as a comparison, we would have to change the amount of stimulation in some fashion until the subject reported a difference. We would then be detecting "difference thresholds" or "difference limens" or DL's.

A number of more or less standard techniques have been evolved for measuring the various types of thresholds. They have been described as "psychophysical methods" by their early originators because these investigators believed they were plotting relationships between mental experience and physical world changes. We no longer maintain this view but the methods are quite independent of what anyone wants to attribute to them. They are merely careful experimental procedures based on the logic of measurement. We can describe three of these methods briefly to indicate their general nature (see Thurstone, 1948):

1. *The method of average error.* In using this method, a *subject* manipulates some control by which a comparison stimulus is changed in the direction of the standard. For example, the subject might slowly turn a knob by which the amount of light in one source (the comparison) was gradually dimmed until it appeared equal to a standard. Some physical measurement could then be taken and if an error were found, its amount and direction would be recorded. After a series of such measures, starting sometimes with a dim light and a bright one on the other half of the trials, a tabulation could be made of the errors. These could be averaged and this value would be treated as a DL. The meaning of the DL here would be simply that the subject would not be able to tell the difference between a light with the average error value and the standard. In order to tell a difference, the two lights would have to differ by some amount greater than the average error. This method could be used in many kinds of measurement and is in fact commonly used by everyone who goes about with a ruler and checks his measurements, taking account of the fact that he does not always get the same reading, winding up with the remark "Give or take a little." The "little" is the DL.

2. *The method of limits.* In this method the subject is usually asked to make judgments while someone else manipulates the comparison stimulus. He does not proceed in a smooth and continuous change, however; instead he changes the comparison stimulus by a fixed small amount on each occasion through a series of steps. Sooner or later the subject will have to report that the stimuli are the same or that the relationship between them has altered. The point at which he treats the two as equal is then noted and approached from the other direction. After a number of such determinations, the equal points are averaged and the difference from the standard is again the DL. There are many additional controls to be observed but we have described the gist of this method.

3. *The method of constant stimuli* consists of devising a procedure where a standard or a number of standard stimuli are all judged at once or in some determined order against the comparison stimuli. The essence of the method is to insure that every comparison stimulus is compared with the standard an equal number of times. In judging bathing beauties, for example, one would want to compare every contestant with every

other contestant to be sure that no points were overlooked. If a series of weights that do not differ greatly among themselves is to be judged, one would make certain that each weight was compared with every other weight or with the standard an equal number of times. The percentage of times in which a correct or positive judgment was obtained for each item of comparison would then provide an indication of the *just noticeable differences* or JND's. One could say how often one stimulus was confused with another, judged better or greater than another, etc. Various levels of confidence could then be calculated, as desired. For example, one could ask: How much must the stimuli differ in order to be judged correctly 50 per cent or 95 per cent of the time?

ERRORS IN MEASUREMENT

Constant and variable errors. Whenever we make measurements of any kind, we are likely to make errors in reading or interpreting our scales. The psychophysical methods reveal the range and nature of such errors even in simple tasks such as measuring the length of a line with a ruler. When we read pointer positions on dials we also make errors, particularly when we do not have a direct, head-on view of the dial. The passenger in an automobile might read the gas gauge as "empty," while the driver with a more direct view sees that he still has plenty of gas. Such errors, due to a particular viewing position are called errors of "parallax." In many kinds of observations, similar biases creep in and distort the readings or judgments in one direction or another. If most of the errors are in one direction, the resulting "average error" can be thought of as including some bias or "constant error." When errors are equally distributed around some central reading they are referred to as "variable errors." The combination of variable and constant errors determines the total deviation or variability. It should be noted that a constant error can be corrected if the subject is informed about it and makes allowances. An archer, for example, makes an allowance for wind or other factors that might tend to bring his arrows to the left of the mark. He simply aims to the right of the mark after he discovers such a constant tendency. Variable errors seem to be inherent in the individual or the situation and there is little, if anything, that can be done about them. They may be due to changing standards, practice, or fatigue, lapses of attention, varying adjustments of position, etc. In a long series of judgments they tend to balance out so that the subject errs as often on one side of a standard as on the other. If we average such errors, the subject might appear to have a perfect score. To measure the actual amount of variability we must ignore the sign or direction of error; to measure the constant error we take the sign into account.

The concepts of variable and constant errors have been applied to many other aspects of behavior besides psychophysical judgments. Any kind of behavior we observe involves variability on the part of the subject. The observer's variability might have to be taken into account (scientists are not free from erroneous judgments and biases), but the observed performance of a subject might fluctuate widely in various respects from day to day or trial to trial. As with subjective judgments, objective behavior may involve constant and variable aspects. If we observe how quickly a subject can stop a car by pressing a foot brake or how well he can track a moving target, we find variability in the performance. The subject may be said to "oscillate" around some mean or average performance. In a learning situation, for example, a subject may do well on one trial and poorly on the next, for no reason that is apparent to the experimenter. Such fluctuations have to be taken into account either by eliminating the "sources of error" or by resorting to statistical techniques that call for great numbers of observations over many cases. Variability is one of the prime obstacles to neat predictions of behavior. When we add to any individual's variability the variabilities of other people, we find ourselves forced to talk about the abstract "average man" or about groups of people "in general." Constant and variable errors force the student of psychology to become a student of statistics.

From the description of constant and variable errors, we recognize that any particular judgment, measure, or response may vary from some standard or average value. Whenever we judge something, for example, when we try to adjust one light so that it is just as bright as another, we may be absolutely correct, but more often than not we will be a little off. Because we cannot tell the difference between absolute equality and being "a little off," we finally settle for some acceptable value. The difference between the actual or true value and the one we accept as adequate is a difference that we cannot appreciate for whatever reasons. Any value above or below this difference we do not accept. Consequently, any difference that we will not tolerate or are able to recognize is a noticeable difference. If we only recognize this difference part of the time we might refer to it as a "just noticeable difference" or a JND. For most psychophysical purposes, the JND and the DL or Difference Limen amount to the same thing.

Weber's Law. In the last paragraph we introduced the term "just noticeable difference." This term, commonly abbreviated JND, is a convenient psychological unit of measurement. A great deal was made of this unit in the early speculations about the relationship between the mind and the body.[4] As far back as 1850 the German physicist Weber

[4] An interesting account of the development of psychophysics and the Weber-Fechner laws is available in Garrett (1930).

and the theologian-physicist Fechner believed that they had found a key to the mind-body problem. It was discovered that the JND's normally found in a modest range of stimuli tended to reflect constant relationships between the stimuli; thus, if a light were to be judged brighter, just noticeably, then another light, it would have to be about 2 per cent brighter physically. One hundred and two candles would be judged brighter than one hundred candles and so on. Various statements of this relationship were attempted such as: sensation increases physically as stimulation increases geometrically, etc. One of the more standard statements was made by Weber, who left us a formula or his law, which states that there is a constant relationship between the increment that must be added to or subtracted from a standard stimulus and the standard value, or in formula terms:

$$\frac{\Delta S}{S} = k$$

Weber's Law is hardly a law since it has been discovered that the k is by no means the same throughout the entire range of stimulus values. It varies with the standard. It varies, of course, with the nature of the energy under discussion, for example, the constant reported for light is about 1 or 2 per cent, for sound intensity it is reported as between 20 and 30 per cent; for weight, it is about 3 per cent and so on. It varies with the individual and within the individual and can hardly be said to be an exact figure. It does have a value in correcting the possibly general fallacy that additional stimulation should be reacted to equally. It might also explain why the last straw, which the camel surely did not notice, broke the camel's back. To be serious about it, however, it is wise to recognize the relative nature of judgments with respect to a standard. An inch added to the trunk of an elephant is of little consequence and even the elephant might not notice it; an inch added to the average human nose might prove very distressing. In practical terms, notice of relative reactions at different stages within a continuum must be taken into account in such modern innovations as power steering and power brakes. The engineer must build in a "feel" of control and this feel must correspond in some way with the task in hand. When a driver needs to make an energetic movement, the control should not be so helped mechanically as to give the driver no sense of doing anything. Frictional resistances have to be built in. The pilot of the huge transport could not begin to manipulate the control surfaces with his own strength. A hydraulic or electrical system is introduced to do the actual work. The pilot now must be made to feel that he is controlling the airplane and the "feels" must be real. He must be made to push harder for a greater effect. How much harder must correspond to the JND's involved or the total effect will be most unsatisfactory.

Whether the JND will ever become more than it is now, a convenient reminder of the relative nature of human reactions along different points in an energy spectrum cannot be said. There have been attempts to use it as a purely psychological measure. These cannot be said to have been unqualified successes. The psychophysical methods, however, are commonly used, frequently without being recognized as such, and we can expect them to be around for a long time.

THE MEASUREMENT OF ATTITUDES

One application of psychophysical methods with JND's clearly in mind was that made by Thurstone, (1959) who in the late 1920's began to devise scales for measuring such subjective variables as attitudes and values. Attitudes are abstract affairs; they are not something we can measure in inches or pounds. They refer to how we feel about persons, places, institutions, etc. When we try to describe our attitudes toward something we start out by using terms such as "I like" or "I detest" or "I don't think much of." If we wish to indicate degrees of feeling we include modifiers like "very" or we substitute various synonyms for "like" and "dislike." Thus we might find two people expressing attitudes toward strawberries and cream by statements like: "I just love strawberries and cream" and "I can't stand them." Should both of them say: "I like them very much" we cannot be sure that each actually has the same degree of liking. Many people are very loose with language and expressions like "I simply adore it" or "I loathe it" sprinkle conversations dealing with matters that do not, in fact, generate any serious degree of feeling.

Attitudes toward such institutions as the church, the law and courts, family life, toward such matters as war and peace, industrial relations, or toward various national, racial, or social groups are, of course, of great importance in human life. It would be very helpful if we could obtain suitable estimates of such attitudes. We could, of course, ask any individual what his attitude was toward any particular thing and get some reply which would not convey any numerical or measured information. We could also ask him to fill out a "rating scale" which might consist of a series of steps running from "very much" through "neutral" to "very little." With such a device we could make comparisons between individuals but the comparisons would still leave much to be desired. We would not know, for example, if the *physical* distance on the scale between "very much" and "some" and "some" and "neutral" was equivalent to the *psychological* distance between such scale positions. Nor would we know, in every instance, whether "very much" means the same thing to everyone. What is needed is a scale on which the steps are equal psychological distances apart, just as inches on a ruler are equal physical distances apart.

Thurstone set about creating such psychological scales of "equal-appearing intervals" by attempting to select statements reflecting attitudes that were "just noticeably different" from each other. The just noticeable difference would serve as a unit for the scale. The development of such a scale would permit describing different amounts of attitude in numerical terms. Thus, one person might have an attitude that measured seven JND's on the scale and he would be considered to have a more favorable attitude than someone who measured at five JND's, and a less favorable attitude than someone measuring nine JND's. What is more, we could then say, presumably, that he was just as much more favorable than the one as he was less favorable than the other, two JND's in each case.

How did Thurstone go about this interesting venture? He worked on one scale at a time; a separate scale would be required to measure attitudes toward any particular thing. We can examine the procedure for developing a scale of attitudes "toward capitalism," for an illustration. The first step is to collect a great many verbal expressions (opinions) or statements about capitalism. These can be obtained from speeches, books, newspaper stories, or simply by asking people to say something about capitalism. One person might remark: "It's the greatest economic system that has ever been developed." Another might say: "It's the cause of all our troubles." A third might give: "It's the least efficient system we could have." Hundreds of such statements would be collected. At this stage a group of "judges" would be selected to sort out the statements from "unfavorable" to "favorable." Each judge would try to decide whether a given statement was more or less favorable than a previous statement. With a large number of statements this would be a formidable task and Thurstone simplified the operation for the judges by asking them to form groups of statements that appeared to be just about alike. He decided that 12 groups (providing an 11-point scale) would prove most efficient and be about as refined as the judges could use. Each judge would then place each statement into one pile or another reflecting his judgment of the relative favorableness of a given statement. Not all of the judges would assign the same statements to the same piles, however. This variability of the judges allowed Thurstone to make a selection of statements that, by and large, or "on the average" belonged at a given scale position, but which were not always and uniformly judged as having a particular value. In other words, because the judges disagreed so some extent, the possibility arises of defining a just noticeable difference among the judges. If a given statement is placed in category or pile 6, for example, by 50 per cent of the judges and in pile 7 by the remaining 50 per cent, and no judge places it in pile 5 or pile 8, we can be certain that the statement belongs somewhere in the 6 to 7 region. If the judges had the privilege of placing the statement between the two piles, they might have done so. Because they do not have this opportunity, we can adopt the position that there is no noticeable difference among the judges for this statement. It belongs in pile 6 or 7 and no other. If we wanted to use this statement in our scale we would assign it a value of 5.5 (the midpoint on a 11-point scale). Actually such a 50–50 distribution among the judges is a most unlikely finding and we would be more likely to find some spread of pile selection among the judges for almost every statement. We would then select those statements that came closest to such a 50–50 distribution and assign them a value based on the average position assigned by all of the judges. A 51–49 distribution, for example, might justify our conclusion that a statement was just noticeably stronger or weaker than some scale value.

In effect this procedure translates just noticeable differences in the percentage of judges to values of statements. It results in a scale value for each statement, and now a series of statements can be selected with values running from low to high. If we wish to measure anyone's attitude toward capitalism we simply ask him to read the statements and check those with which he agrees. We then examine the checks and note the highest valued statement he endorses. Theoretically he should endorse only favorable statements if he is genuinely procapitalism. His score is then described as that of the highest valued statement he endorsed. With such a scale at hand we are in position to suggest numerical equivalents for attitude strength, with the understanding that any point along the scale is equivalent to any other point in value, i.e., the distance between a score of 2 and a score of 3 is the same as the distance between a score of 9 and a score of 10. Whether this is actually so may be debatable. At the present time, however, it represents a notable advance in the measurement of attitudes, an attempt at turning subjective values into numbers. The student is cautioned to note that there are many other techniques for the measurement of attitudes. Thurstone is not the only one to attempt this difficult task. We have used his work only as an illustration of the application of mid-nineteenth-century psychophysics to modern problems.

RELATIVE ASPECTS OF STIMULATION: THE GENERAL PROBLEM

The above account of relationship of stimuli to standards of comparison described merely one feature of a more general concept of relativity in the behavior of the organism in connection with the physical world. By and large it is impossible to provide single or isolated stimuli and detect their effects, at least not with the intact organism and without special contrivances. Suppose we wish to show someone a red object. The object must appear somewhere in space where there is an absence of the same degree of redness or the subject will not be able to report the presence of the stimulus. Similarly a tone must be heard against a background of silence, noise, or other tones. The classical illustration is to place one hand in cold water, one in hot, and then plunge both into tepid water where the hands now feel the opposite temperature from that just previously experienced. Such an effect is called a contrast effect and we can illustrate it in any sense sphere. Red looks redder against a green background and vice versa; watermelon tastes sweeter if just the right amount of salt has been added; the banquet coffee tastes bitter after the ice cream dessert; and so on. But these illustrations only highlight the characteristic nature of sensory activity. It is always occurring within a background of simultaneous or just prior additional or different stimulation. The Gestalt psychologists have taken such observations to represent a basic principle of behavioral analysis and insist on attention to the background in which a given stimulus is presented. A dramatic story told by Koffka [5] might illustrate their point of view: a horseman rode over the frozen Lake Constance during a snow storm, presuming it to be an open field. When he discovered what he had done, he fell dead. A lake is a field if it appears so to us. The Gestalt psychologists have taken great pains to demonstrate that appearances are deceiving and indeed they are. If we are not to be misled in our appreciation of sensory activity we must take the background into account, not only the physical and immediate background, but also the prior experience of the individual involved.

The investigations of psychologists interested in such relative factors have given rise to a slogan which might well be remembered: "We see the world not as it is but as we are." Like all slogans this one must be taken with the usual salt dose, but it keeps us from forgetting to take the organism's nature and structure into account and not rely exclusively on a physical description of the outstanding (to us) features of a stimulus. Taking the slogan at face value, however, we can consider in the next few pages, how the organism brings its own nature to bear on the energy exchanges that go on in its environment. There is some need for worrying about the life stage of the organism being considered. An adult reacting to a given situation is obviously not the same sort of observer or reactor as is a child or an infant. In much of what follows we will be

[5] Kurt Koffka was a leader of the Gestalt School. His major work is *Principles of Gestalt Psychology*, 1935.

unable to pinpoint the contributions of experience or learning and the contribution of the biological organism as a hereditary given. To err in one direction is as bad as to err in the other. Neither error can be condoned.

Gestalt principles of perception

The figure-ground proposition

As already indicated earlier, no stimulus exists in a vacuum. It occurs as a change within a field of already ongoing energy changes and the nature of this background may facilitate, inhibit, or alter the reactions to the particular stimulus object considered as a unique or novel

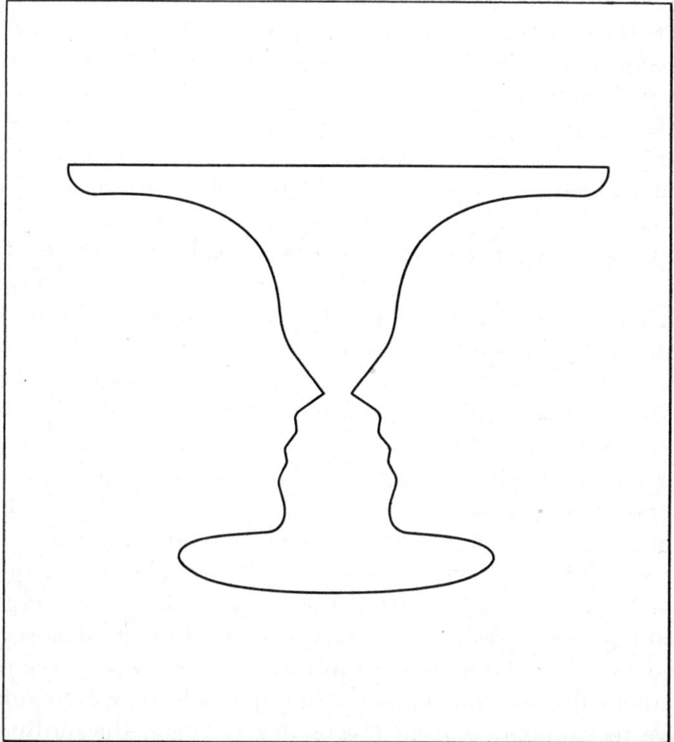

Figure 2 Figure and ground. This familiar illustration (after Rubin) demonstrates what appears to be a fundamental perceptual tendency: to see a figure against a background. In this particular illustration we have a choice of figures (facing profiles or a vase) and a related choice of backgrounds. Both figures cannot be seen at the same time; as soon as one is viewed or perceived, the other automatically becomes "ground."

item. A single note on the piano might be a modestly complex array of energy patterns with its overtones, but it does not, by itself, without special training, arouse much of a response. The same note occurring as the fourth major item in the opening bars of Beethoven's *Fifth Symphony* is something else again. It is not heard or listened to because of its own special identification but because of its location, because of the background into which it fits or against which it is presented. Similarly with all other sensory experiences. The proverbial black cat in the coal bin of the celler at midnight amounts to a visual nothing. Crossing the sidewalk in front of you at midday it may be a very obvious and, if you are superstitious, important stimulus. The significance of background as a basic determiner of the stimuli which will be reacted to cannot be overemphasized. The background can be made to hide objects as is well appreciated by magicians and camoufleurs or enhance their appeal as advertisers have learned; but the basic psychological importance lies not in tricks and puzzles (find the faces in this picture), but in what appears a basic aspect of our sensitivity to the environment. Out of what William James referred to as a "big, buzzing, booming confusion," the infant must learn to react to items of consequence to its survival. To some extent, the confusion will always be there, but there appears to be an elementary capacity or sensitivity to differences within the patterns of stimulation that effect us on which we build our discriminations of objects. Perhaps it is no more than some very simple native or inherent capacity of sense organs to differentiate out some gross characteristics of stimulus objects such as their outlines against another type of stimulation upon which we build through experience. The baby reaches for the moon; he has not developed any sense of distance, but he reaches for the moon and not the sky. The moon is a figure against a ground. Wherever we look, we automatically perceive objects, things, or outlines against a background. The speaker picks out a face in the sea of faces before him, the rest melt into a background, a framework. Books, pencils, other objects are seen lying on a table, the table being taken more or less for granted as a ground. Hebb (1949) suggests that the human organism is ready and equipped by nature to react to such stimulation as is provided by contours or lines. We may have to learn to perceive objects, that is to identify them in some manner, but it is possible that even infants are responsive to stimulation from the boundary edges, the outlines of objects, which set them apart from other objects or broader (background) areas like walls, floors, tables, the sky, and so on.

GOOD FIGURES

Besides emphasizing an innate figure-ground perception, Gestalt psychologists have argued forcefully that not only do we see figures, but we somehow strive to see as "good" a figure as possible. We tend to ignore details that do not contribute to a well-organized perception and supply missing details when these will help out. In a sense, we see what we want to see or what we are led to see, perhaps by some dominant aspects of a stimulus pattern. When a given pattern is poorly "structured," we will make the best possible figure out of what is offered. Not only do we perceive the best structure possible but, claim the proponents of this principle, we also remember in terms of a good figure. Over a period of time, the previously perceived pattern becomes organized for us. Much of the

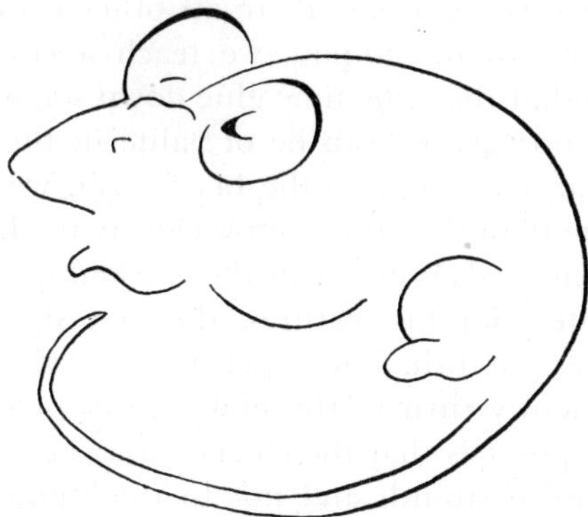

Figure 3 The rat-psychologist, an ambiguous figure. Here the viewer supplies his own background in terms of a "frame of reference." If he sees a rat, it is because he has adopted a "point of view" or attitude toward the stimulus object. If he sees a man, he must have a different "set" or orientation. Again, as with the Rubin illustration (Fig. 2), the two figures cannot be observed at the same time. Some individuals have difficulty seeing one or the other of the two figures. Past experience can determine what will be seen first or more frequently. (See Leeper, 1935.)

work done in this area has made use of ambiguous figures, patterns which result in different perceptions depending upon various conditions of previous experience, instruction, mood, and attitude. (See Fig. 3.)

Relativity in stimulation

As a necessary and obvious next step from the above we are forced again to note that a particular, specific, fixed kind of stimulation is not required to produce essentially the same reaction on successive occasions. This is so obvious in every sense field that it is hardly necessary to illustrate it, but the underlying problem is so crucial in psychological theorizing as to require making the point as fully as possible. We can start simply. A child is small at home, but large among his playmates.

Is he large or small? There are no absolutes to such terms as hot, cold, mean, cruel, light or dark, heavy or light, loud or soft, etc. But this is only part of the obvious.

We do not respond to absolutes either, but rather to relative features of the stimuli that impinge upon us. We can and do respond to such features of stimuli as better than, louder than, prettier than, etc., even though none of the stimuli can be absolutely described as loud, pretty, or good. When we choose the lesser of two evils, we are responding to a relationship and it is the capacity for responding to such relationships that now concern us. The best and simplest illustrations can be drawn from experimental investigations where all other confusing factors have been deliberately removed. Suppose we teach a chicken to peck corn from a gray dish and at the same time glue down some pieces of corn in a black dish so that no pecking can be of value in the black dish. When the chicken has learned to ignore the black dish, we introduce another dish, lighter in tone than the gray one previously used, but not yet white. The black one is removed. Where will the chicken peck? If it has learned to react to absolute stimulus features, the hen should march over to the formerly rewarding dish, but experimental evidence indicates that chickens will frequently turn to the now lighter of the two and ignore the gray dish. Our point is that the chicken appears to be responding to a relationship between stimuli and not to the stimuli themselves.

Similarly, children can be taught that candy is always to be found under the larger of two boxes (Alberts and Ehrenfreund, 1951). If training is done with one pair of boxes and tests carried out later, we might find the children selecting a larger box than the one previously rewarded. Here they are reacting to a relationship of "larger than." There is no question that similar demonstrations could be arranged in taste, smell, audition, and all of the other senses if anyone wanted to bother. The point is that here we have a problem. How can a creature respond to a relationship? A relationship is not an absolute stimulus feature, by definition. In the early behaviorist days, such findings were very distressing because psychologists were trying to explain behavior in terms of stimuli and responses and concentrated on describable, measureable features of a stimulus. The physical energy in the stimulus was supposed to lead to the behavior, not to some hypothetical or mathematical relationship. A relationship appeared to be somewhat mystical, mentalistic, subjective, unscientific, but unfortunately significant even though not palatable. Various attempts were made to fit the response to relationships into a stimulus-response framework and these attempts have become more sophisticated as psychology has grown up, but the exact and universally acceptable answers have not been developed. Some psychologists still like to talk about a response to relationships as some sort of given or native talent of organism or of the brain, something like an instinct. Other psychologists while learning to live with responses to relationships have speculated about possible ways in which such reactions are developed. We can consider two such attempts.

In the case of adults and older children who are capable of verbalizing while solving problems, the subject may say to himself: "It's under the larger, or darker," etc. Faced with a new but similar situation (some stimulus elements in the pattern the same), the subject again repeats to himself: "It's under the larger"—and thus solves the problem. The word "larger" might be thought of as the important clue, the identical element, in the two situations and a stimulus response theory would be saved. When the same findings occur in investigations with animals and small children incapable of the verbalization, some other absolute element would have to be found. Here we can imagine or hypothesize any kind of process we like but would be wise to keep it in the realm of the presumably possible. Hebb (1949), for example, suggested that perhaps the nervous system is so structured as to provide an absolute process which is generated whenever an organism responds to two separate but closely related stimuli. Thus, when the chicken, for example, looks at a dark dish and then at a lighter one, the resultant neural activity must be of some regular and specific kind; similarly when it glances from the light to the dark, another specific, but different neural after effect can be imagined as occurring. To simplify our discussion we could label a neural trace or process as reflecting a change from a higher level of stimulation to a lower level—we could even give this a name and thus help to give it specific identify—let us term it, that is, the neural process involved in going from dark to light as "upgrading" and the neural adjustment that follows changing from light to dark as "de-grading." Now we have two theoretical or imaginary neural processes. When one occurs the chicken pecks; when the other occurs the chicken turns away. When we test the chicken with any other pair of stimuli, a similar process of de-grading or upgrading will occur if the chicken looks from one to the other. If the chicken has learned earlier to peck after an upgrading process occurs, it will now again peck when a similar, perhaps identical upgrading process occurs. Again the day might be saved for a basically stimulus-response psychology without involving the chicken's mind in the act. To make such a theory hold, it would be necessary to be able to identify and perhaps record such differential neural processes and perhaps, have chickens peck or not peck as we initiated them. This has not been done.

Another explanation has been offered which will be understood better after some principles of learning have been examined. We can give a rough outline of the hypothesis here, however, and it may be enough. The view consists of the notion that such responses to relative features are only apparent and not real. The organism is still responding to absolute aspects of the stimulation but is at the mercy of forces generated by the two stimuli which work to a resultant positive value for the stimulus object that suggests response to relationships. If the problem is one of a small child picking up little boxes, for example, we might find the child picking up the larger of two boxes in a test, but if we try the child out with rather unusual boxes, much larger or smaller than the ones used in the preliminary training, we might find that there is no evidence of a response to a relationship. The explanation for this is based on the assumption that there is some spread of rewarding and punishing effects from the original items in the pair and that the spreading effect gradually diminishes as we go out to extreme values. At some middle value the negative spread to the next larger stimulus might not be as large as the positive spread to that stimulus and the consequent resultant would dictate the choice of the larger box. Out at an extreme point the spread of the negative effect would have died out and the positive effect might be so tiny that a smaller box (with more positive spread effect) would be chosen.

Constancy

Another aspect of the problem of relativity in stimulation is the rather perverse way in which the organism tends to ignore the physics of a situation and reacts to stimuli in ways that are difficult for the stimulus-response psychologist to handle effectively. Here we could again raise the question as to whether this is an innate peculiarity of human nature and its equipment or a matter of experience. The question is probably to be answered in favor of experience since it is possible in most instances to force the organism to respond in physical terms, that is, in terms of the actual stimulus situation. Let us quickly get to the point in terms of illustrations.

When a person crosses the street to meet us and we follow his progress he does not appear to grow in size as he approaches. It is a physical fact that the image formed on the retina does increase as the distance is lessened and we are all familiar with the fact that an airplane in the air is a tiny object compared to the same plane on the ground. But within ordinary conversational distances, objects do not grow as we approach them. Similarly if we know something to be round or circular it does not change in appearances and become ovoid or ellipsoid as our viewing angle changes. It remains a ball or dish or whatever it was. In the realm of color, similarly, a red dress might continue appearing red to us if we know the actual color even though the color disappears as the light diminishes and the day at the picnic comes to a close. The illustrations could be multiplied in all sense fields and we are faced with explaining a general and genuine enough sensory phenomenon—the constancy of the reaction in the face of changing stimulation (Wallach, 1948).

Now it can be shown easily that the red will be seen as black or gray by a stranger, or that the approaching person looms even larger on the eye if we look at him through a mailing tube, but those are the physical facts. What about the psychological facts? Here again we run into the problem of relativity and background. The background is changing at the same rate as is the stimulus object in terms of our focus, and the relationship between the figure and ground may remain some type of absolute as far as the nervous system is concerned. We could postulate a neural process that would accommodate itself to the behavioral facts and still represent an absolute or specific type of stimulation, but doing so would not necessarily eliminate the problem for us. Constancy is such a pervasive aspect of our reactions to stimuli that we might well accept it as one of the principles to be taken into account in our explanations of behavior. Some psychologists speak of a law of constancy. This is putting it rather strongly as most laws are stated in terms of potential measurement or at least as formulas. Here we have no formula, but rather a principle which states that, by and large, organisms will respond to stimuli in terms of other features or relationships than their own physical characteristics per se. The principle may not have much predictive value without mathematical statement; it might account for various illusory and even hallucinatory reactions which make us see things we know to be there in some given form or fashion without their actually corresponding in fact with our biases. We might extend the principle in a general way to help account for the perceptions we have of our friends, our parents, our country, and various foreign groups, modern art, anything new, etc. Mama is always a sweet, dear old lady, even as she wipes her fingerprints from the bank vault. The juvenile will still be the juvenile after he is married and has little juveniles of his own.

Closure

Another general principle, again without a formula, calls our attention to the fact that there is a characteristic tendency, presumably acquired through learning and experience, although this might be argued by some staunch nativists, to see or otherwise sense things in their entirety even though, in fact, some elements may not be present or are otherwise altered. In the typical experimental example, if a person is given only a glance at some stimulus made up of three lines which appear to join at angles a strong impression of having seen a triangle might be reported. The actual triangle need not be complete. Grammar-school children like to play at writing their names in block print with some of the lines omitted. The resulting lettering may be easily read even though the letters are incomplete. What we are saying, of course, is that we don't

Figure 4 An illustration of closure. Can you fill in the missing details? (After Street, 1931.)

pay attention to details or that not all the details in every situation are scrutinized before we are ready to react. We must be careful not to over-emphasize this proposition. It may amount to no more than saying that we rarely stop to examine carefully or insist upon a full measure of stimulation. A part, a vague hint, a suggestion may be enough. Many hunters lose their lives annually because of the tendency to respond to only a fragment of a stimulus on the part of other hunters. Actually, to require a full measure of stimulation would leave us quite helpless as it is unlikely that we would ever see the same stimulus twice in the same way. Situations are constantly changing and we put as much order into the world as we witness therein.

The fact that we react to parts of a situation is not a novel or revolutionary proposition. It has been observed from ages past and gone under various names. In the early behaviorist days it was described by a rather formidable term: "redintegration." This term was meant to indicate how part of a situation could serve to re-establish or institute the whole or large part of a reaction previously given to a larger or more complete stimulation than is now present. All learning seems to partake of this behavioral feature. We are given a cue and come through with the answer. Earlier we had to have the answer given to us. A disturbed war veteran dives under the bed at the sound of an airplane. The sound is enough to reinstitute the original terrifying situation. Closure might be a little difficult to illustrate in other senses except perhaps negatively. When Mark Twain sat on his bed waiting for the other shoe to drop in the room above, he was having a no-closure experience of an auditory variety. When someone starts to sing or play a song we find ourselves waiting for the next note, the high C, or whatever, and failure to produce it leaves us distressed. Perhaps more weight could be given the principle by saying that we behave as if we demand closure. This does appear to be the case in many broader aspects of behavior quite removed from the sensory realms—we may wait for the call that tells of the safe arrival, we may keep returning to the unsolved problem, we can't wait till we get there and so on.

Grouping and patterning

Still another tendency almost universally exhibited in connection with sensory stimulation is that of organizing elements or units into groups or different arrangements. The tiles on a bathroom floor may be only a collection of hexagonal little blocks, but simply gazing at them will result in an automatic flow of patterns, lines, rows, columns, small squares, large squares, and so on and on. We rarely see or react to any single elements—they come in more or less organized patterns; we do not see rows of clapboards or bricks—there stands a wall. We don't see the trees for the wood, nor the leaves for the tree. A miscellaneous assortment of isolated detail is somehow unpalatable or unacceptable; we make sense out of our world, even though we are frequently wrong. While nature does not really abhor vacuums, man apparently abhors unorganized punctiform stimulation and automatically groups, arranges, or organizes his world. The patterning effect is so automatic and unconsciously arranged that we commonly accept various combinations of stimulation as single or unitary events. We might congratulate the host on the result of his bar-tending activities with a "That's a mighty nice drink" without recognizing the individual sensory components of temperature, sweetness, bitterness, and various odors as well as the visual appeal and the auditory clink of the ice. The taste of celery might be more suitable as an example for teetotalers and vegetarians. The texture, temperature, the auditory crunchiness and snap, as well as the salt or cheese or other stuffing, make up a unitary effect of a rather involved combination of stimulation elements. The tendency to organize or pattern is obvious in familiar melodies which are readily recognized when whistled, hummed, or played on any instrument in any key. Sometimes

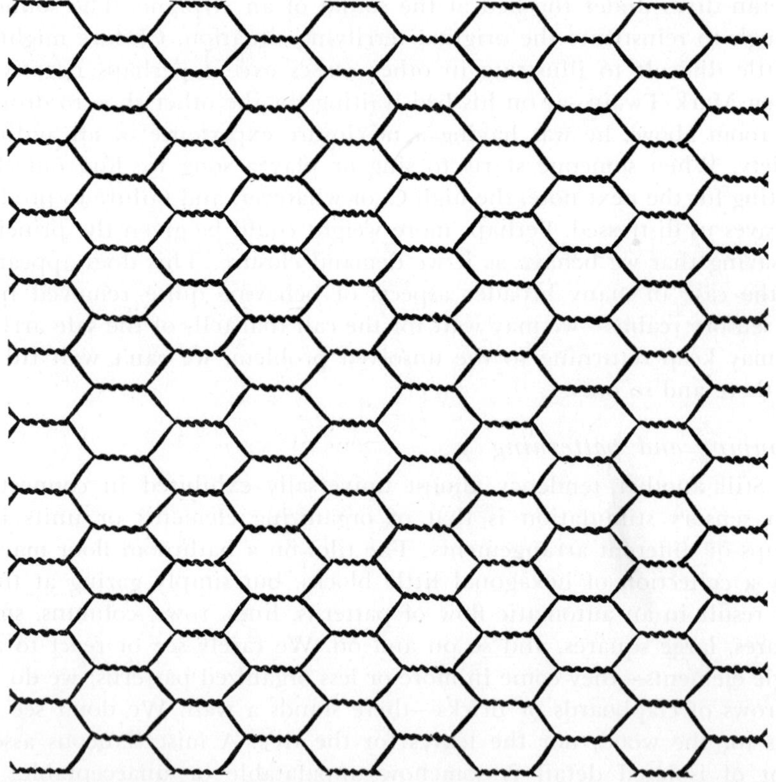

Figure 5 The dominance of patterning in perception. Try to look at just one segment of the wire-fence pattern. You will find it quite impossible to do so. Almost immediately you will find yourself seeing one pattern of segments after another—rows, columns, diagonals, pairs, and a variety of groupings. Gestalt psychologists consider this a fundamental principle of perception, a basic, innate tendency to group and organize the world of stimuli.

even the rhythm can be recognized without benefit of melody as children play in tapping, with sticks or blocks. No element by itself has any virtues, but as part of a pattern, the totality of elements makes an effective stimulus (Köhler, 1930).

It is essential that we recognize the role of patterning before we launch into a consideration of the nervous system. Failure to attend to the complex nature of the stimulation entering the nervous system may mislead us into picturing the system incorrectly as a simple assemblage of connecting circuits functioning as single units unrelated to the rest of the brain. The principles briefly reviewed above—constancy, patterning, and general relativity—must be taken into account in our appreciation of the next stages of the behavioral process. Before we get to the nervous system itself, however, it is important to lay one ghost that inevitably pops up in discussions involving patterning and organization of stimulation effects. It is sometimes proclaimed with authoritative profundity that "the whole is greater than the sum of its parts." This ringing slogan has an appeal for those who like to think in slogans or play around with paradoxes. It is obvious from any logical considerations that the expression is fraudulent. The term "sum" is being misused. If the intent is to indicate that when a number of units are added together in some particular fashion they will create an effect that is different from some other organization or from the effect of merely throwing the parts about, then there is no question about the difference. But it is a difference we are talking about and not a sum. Two single sticks separated in space are two single sticks; placed in various juxtapositions they can make a T or L or X or a cross, to be sure. But the point to observe is that nothing greater has emerged from the placement of one stick next to another. A rim, hub, and spokes scattered about do not make a wheel unless the spokes are inserted into both the hub and the rim. If the spokes are inserted into the outside of the rim and the hub hung on one of these, we will also have an organized, patterned, and somewhat unique object. It is not greater than its parts, but neither is it lesser. It is merely different. No stimulus acts in a vacuum or in isolation; we have already made this point. It is now important to mention that the nature of the background or the arrangement of elements in the background must also be taken into account when we consider stimulus energies, whether these are relatively isolated, more or less single elements, or whether we have a complex assortment to deal with.

We have reviewed now the general nature of external stimulus energies, their sources, the related sensory structures, the concepts of thresholds of various kinds and how they are measured, some of the associated effects such as contrast and adaptation, and the more general principles of constancy, closure, patterning, and the basic figure-ground proposition. As soon as we cross the sensory threshold, we have entered the realm of neural action and control over behavior. It is time now that we talk about that very incompletely understood machinery.

CHAPTER 5

The Basic Equipment 2— The Nervous System

Neurons · Neural function · The specific energies of nerves · The nervous impulse · Refractory phase and the "all-or-none law" · Frequency and intensity · The volley theory · Intensity of stimulation · Gross anatomy of the nervous system · The reticular formation · Brain waves · The autonomic nervous system · The conceptual nervous system · Reflex action and the synapse · Cell assemblies · The phase sequence · Conditioning in terms of assemblies and phase sequences · The motor aspects of behavior · Muscles · Glands

In our consideration of the nervous system we shall deal with the physical structures only superficially. It is presumed that the student has already learned something about the nervous system in a proper biology course or that he will proceed to do so before long. To attempt an adequate description of the nervous system would take us too far afield in this introductory excursion into psychology. For all that is necessary for psychologists, it will suffice if we do not make too many erroneous statements of what the nervous system must be like in the following hasty sketch. What it is actually like does not make too much difference to psychologists as long as it behaves itself the way they would like it to. Sometimes these likes must be tempered by fact, but it is unlikely that many facts that will definitely support or refute these likes will be available for a long time to come. Hebb (1958) provides a description of the nervous system that suits the needs of psychology students most effectively.

NEURONS

The nervous system is incredibly complex. It consists of nerve cells or neurons, billions of them, perhaps as many as twelve billion, with the disturbing feature of being somewhat different in various areas of the brain. Each neuron or nerve cell contains its nucleus and other cell structures and may have branching extensions emerging from it of varying

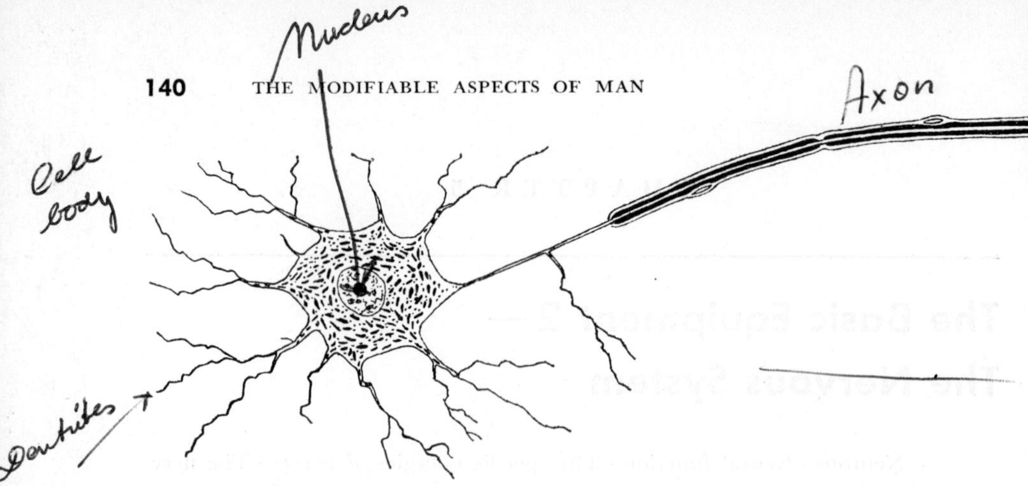

Figure 6 A motor nerve cell. The neuron consists of a cell body, shown on the left, out of which extend many short processes, the dendrites. The long process extending to the right is the axon, which terminates in fine nerve endings. In this schematic drawing the axon is shown medullated, i.e., covered with a segmented sheath. (Courtesy of Bernard Katz and *Scientific American,* November, 1952.)

numbers and lengths. At one end the extensions may be profusely ramified or branched with tiny end-bulbs or boutons which serve to pick up stimulation or activity which is then transmitted to the cell; these branches are called "dendrites." Some cells have only a few or no dendrites. At the other end the extension may be quite long, from the spine to the toe, for example, and serve to conduct neural energy to the dendrites or cell body of another neuron or to a muscle or other structure. These longer extensions are called "axons." Fibers carrying impulses to the central nervous system (the brain and spinal cord are called "the central nervous system") are called "sensory" or "afferent" fibers. The fibers carrying impulses from the central nervous system to muscles or glands are called "motor" or "efferent." While the neural energy can travel along in any direction in a neuron, the characteristic action is to have the energy or "impulse" flow from dendrite to axon and across a gap to another neuron's dendrites, and never the other way. This is referred to as one-way transmission of neural energy. The gap between axons and dendrites may be real or may represent a point of contact which may be physical or chemical in nature. We have in the nervous system only neurons and gaps. There is, of course, a constant blood supply providing nutriment and removing wastes, and in the brain and spinal cord there is watery cerebro-spinal fluid circulating through ventricles and the spinal canal. The neural cells themselves appear to be gray in color—thus, the "little gray cells" of Agatha Christie's Hercule Poirot—and the axons, when they are of substantial size, are covered with a sheathing or membrane, the myelin sheath, which gives them a whitish appearance—the "white matter." The axons are generally referred to as nerve "fibers" and many fibers join up to form cable-like structures, the nerves.

We can pause now and note a few negatives. There is nothing else in the skull beyond the brain with its protective layers of membranes and supporting cells, the circulatory mechanisms and their products, and the "nerves" which join up at the base of the brain and form the spinal cord. There is nothing inside the skull that corresponds to a movie screen or radio—we see no pictures in the brain and develop none; we find no sounds in the brain, no hammers and anvils, nor little men directing things and sending out orders as television teachers and advertisers seem intent on convincing the public. The only activity that can be discovered, or at least that has been found, is electrical and chemical in nature—oxygen is consumed and CO_2 given off. There is some heat generated but of a low order. So far, we know of little else that is pertinent to psychology as we think of it today. The nerves themselves seem to be rather stable structures although we presume they are modifiable in some way or we would have no learning; they will carry impulses along at fairly rapid rates of stimulation. Impulses will travel along some of the larger nerves as fast as 150 yards per second but that is a slow speed in the modern world. Impulses do not travel with the speed of light, nor can we respond with "lightning flash" rates. A nerve fiber will continue to respond to separate stimulations for hours on end and require only a tiny fraction of a second to recover fully (for a brief instant, it will be in a "refractory phase"), but by and large, the nerves will not "break down." There is no such thing as a nervous breakdown, nor do nerves tingle, jangle, get frayed, tense, or stand on edge. When someone complains of being "nervous," of his nerves being ragged, or shattered, he is talking, but not about the nervous system.

Neural function

How do nerves function in the translation of external energy changes (stimuli) into the vastly complex and varied activities (responses) that we call behavior? The primary function of nerves is to conduct; to conduct what we call for lack of a better term, "nervous impulses." What these nervous impulses are, how they vary and in what dimensions, we can consider shortly; the more immediate question is a geographical or anatomical one. If nerves conduct, they must conduct to some place; they must make connections. These connections will be all-important in our consideration of psychological problems and we must examine them first.

The specific energies of nerves

By patient toil anatomists have traced various nerve pathways through the nervous system and have a good but limited knowledge of where various nerves begin and end. The optic nerve system, for example, can be traced from its beginnings at the front of the retina down to a location near the bottom of the cerebral hemispheres where the optic nerves from the two eyes partially cross each other (the "optic chiasm") to the thalamus, and after other connections in various nuclear bodies, to the rear of the brain, the occipital lobe. From the occipital lobe the fibers that carry impulses originating in the eyes appear to start spreading out again in a forward direction and then atomical tracing becomes so involved that the task has not been carried much further. While the information is limited, then, we do know that impulses originating at the retina are carried to various specific places in the brain with one area, in the occipital lobe, where they appear to be patterned in relation to the kind of patterns of stimulation that are imposed upon the eyes. Thus objects in the visual field that are seen as on the left, will generate neural impulses on the right side of the occipital lobe. Actually the representation is quite refined and a neurologist might be able to locate some tumor or injury in a quite specific occipital region by knowing what parts of a visual field were not being seen by a subject.

The fact that each nerve fiber has a specific origin and a specific terminus and carries impulses originating in a specific sense organ has come to be known as the doctrine of the "specific energies of nerves." This description, first advanced by Johannes Müller in 1838, is part of the tradition of neurology. While any nerve can be stimulated by contact or by electrical currents, it will conduct the impulses to its normal outlets. No matter how the optic nerve is stimulated, for example, the result will be one involving some sort of visual reaction. A knock on the rear of the head may result in the recipient reporting "I saw stars." The cartoonists who indicate such results are correct if their characters are struck on the back of the head. Should they be hit on the ear, they might hear something. The reaction to stimulation then depends, in the first place, on where the impulse is carried and this is a function of the specific fibers that have been stimulated. The pathways of fibers are presumably fixed by nature; that is, we are born that way, with a complex highway system available for the passage of nervous impulses. Such impulses themselves are, in themselves, pretty much alike. Optic nerves carry impulses, not light. Auditory nerves carry the same kinds of impulses, not sound. The fact that in the one case we see and in the other we hear is the result of where the nerve fibers end, or rather, what other fibers they become associated with, and what motor activity results.

The nervous impulse

What the nervous impulse itself is we still do not know. It is accompanied by electrical and chemical changes and these can be measured, but if anything else goes on no one knows about it yet. Because the impulse does not travel with the speed of electricity, it cannot be only an electrical event. Most discussions of how a nervous impulse originates and travels along a nerve fiber are purely hypothetical; the common, but perhaps inaccurate, description goes like this: a nerve fiber is supposed to be surrounded or encased in a membrane that is somewhat "porous," or "semipermeable." This means that ions (electrical charges) can pass back and forth through this membrane. When the fiber is at rest, the outside is supposed to be "positively charged," that is, with a large number of positive ions on the surface of the membrane, and the inside is negatively charged, with a corresponding number of electrons or negative ions on the inside of the membrane. When a fiber is stimulated, it is "disturbed," for some reason, and the positive ions at the point of disturbance pass through the membrane while the negative ions come from the inside in exchange. The negative ions, on the outside, upset electrical balance and drive adjacent positive ions inside and more negative ions emerge on to the outside systematically repeating the process. Such a succession of electrical exchanges is called "depolarization." The nervous impulse is then a series of depolarizations progressing along a nerve fiber.

Refractory phase and the "all-or-none law"

No sooner has an electron emerged to the surface of the membrane than it starts to return to its normal habitat. When it is again on the inside with the positive ions back on the outside, that part of the nerve fiber is again polarized, and ready to be depolarized. During the time the fiber is depolarized it cannot conduct another impulse. This time is called the refractory phase. As time passes the "recovery" of the nerve becomes more and more complete passing from a stage of "absolute refractory phase" through a "relative refractory phase" back to normalcy. The whole episode usually is over with in about 0.001 of a second, or at most, 0.002 of a second. One might think of this brief period as one of neural "fatigue" or a period when new energy supplies are produced. However it is interpreted, the nerve fiber is not in condition to "fire" until it is in at least a relative refractory stage. At that time a strong stimulus might fire it where a weak one might not. When a fiber fires at all, all of it fires. This is referred to as the "all-or-none law."

Different fibers have different periods of recovery: the larger the fiber, the faster the recovery and the faster it can respond to a succession of stimulations. This difference in firing frequency permits us to speculate about how the same fibers, carrying the same kinds of impulses (as far as the neural impulse itself is concerned), can handle different patterns of stimulation of the same sense organ and produce different results or end-actions in the behavior of the organism. If one stimulus source sets off one kind of frequency of stimulation and another sets off another frequency, then the possibility for two different kinds of responses emerges.

Frequency and intensity

We noted, above, the all-or-none law. A fiber either will carry the impulse or it will not. Assuming the stimulus energy is superthreshold in strength, the fiber will discharge. Impulses from several simultaneously active fibers can "summate" and jointly develop sufficient energy to initiate activity in another neuron where one fiber alone might not do so. If the stimulation continues, impulses will be carried at some rate corresponding to the recovery period of the nerve fiber involved. Because the recovery period thus sets a time limit on the number of impulses that can be carried, no more than 1,000 impulses per second could be conducted along some particular fiber that has a refractory period of 0.001 second. Suppose that the stimulus involved were supplying energy changes faster than this rate. If only one fiber were available, the organism could not respond differently to stimuli that involved energy changes of 8,000 per second from the way it responded to 2,000 or 4,000 per second stimuli. Yet organisms do respond to such higher frequencies of stimulation as in audition, for example, most people can hear tones of 10,000 cycles per second and young healthy people with good ears can hear tones of 18,000 and perhaps 20,000 cycles per second. How can this be done?

THE VOLLEY THEORY [1]

When one fiber cannot handle the frequency of stimulation in direct proportion to the input, it is argued that other fibers can be enlisted in the task so that a number of fibers working together can handle any frequency within some limits imposed by the sense organ or the response mechanism. A human being, for example, responds only to a limited range of light energy because the sense organ may not be able to respond to radiations outside the normal frequencies. Or, on the response side, it is impossible to tap with the fingers above a certain limiting speed regardless of the stimulation frequency. When different fibers are responding in sequence, each fiber taking every tenth stimulus change, for example, then the stimulation frequency can run as high as 10,000 per second and be readily handled. Such an arrangement would mean that a different pattern of impulses would arrive at the brain centers normally served by each fiber from a pattern that involved only eight or two or one fiber. The different patterns of stimulation, considering the millions of fibers available, enable the brain to take account of the great variety and complexity of environmental stimuli.

INTENSITY OF STIMULATION

The fact that stimuli differ in intensity does not mean, considering again the all-or-none law, that any nerve fiber reacts with more energy to one stimulus than another. All that can happen, as implied above, is that a fiber might fire at some earlier stage in the relative refractory phase. It will not fire more intensely, however. Intense stimuli may also excite or disturb more fibers, again providing a different distribution or pattern of impulses arriving in certain parts of the brain. The total amount of activity may vary, but each individual fiber will continue doing its one job of conducting impulses that are strong enough to initiate the depolarization presumably involved.

The patterns of stimulation that arrive in the brain then depend upon the number of fibers that have been disturbed and on which fibers they happen to be. Besides the identity or location of the fibers and the number involved, there appears to be nothing else which can do the brain's work of responding to the myriad stimulations of the environment. Because of the enormous number of such fibers, however, and the multiplicity of combinations that are available, there seems to be enough equipment to do the job with only the number and type of fibers involved.

[1] The term "volley theory" is also used to describe a special theory of hearing (Wever, 1949).

Before leaving this discussion, it should be pointed out that many parts of the nervous system will be simultaneously active, aiding (facilitating) the passage of impulses from one fiber to another or inhibiting such passages. Such facilitatory and inhibitory actions at various stages of the passage of an impulse will increase the number of patterns that can be made available to respond to external world energies. For practical purposes, there seems to be no danger of running out of neural possibilities.

GROSS ANATOMY OF THE NERVOUS SYSTEM

In gross anatomical terms, the central nervous system consists of the brain and spinal cord with the pairs of spinal nerves. The brain itself is an enlarged development of the upper end of the spinal cord and consists of numerous collections of cells gathered into "nuclei." Anatomists have described many such cell clusters as representing different structures or "parts" of the brain. Certain areas of the brain, indeed, can be talked about as geographically located in front of or above others but there is some danger in trying to be too rigid about dividing the brain into parts and implying independence of function to such parts. Some anatomists think of the brain as "the great raveled knot" and this expression might be, at present, more accurate than dividing the brain into clearly separated parts (Gray, 1948).

As the brain developed in evolution, more and more complex combinations of cells were formed. In the higher mammalian species the proliferation of cells became so great that the latest cells to develop, the cortex ("bark"), had to fold in on itself for sheer lack of space. This cortex is about all that we can see of a brain when the skull is opened. Beneath the cortex, however, are the "subcortical" structures which appeared earlier in evolution and which are sometimes called "the old brain." For purposes of talking about different parts of the brain, anatomists have labeled various sections which are marked off by more or less conspicuous grooves which result from the fact that the cortex of the brain is really a broad blanket of material which is folded over onto itself as we just mentioned. The more prominent grooves help to mark off areas called "lobes" and it has been shown that some of the lobes have separate functions, or, at least, are involved in certain activities and not in others. Thus, the back and lower parts of the brain (with no definite limiting grooves) are called the "occipital lobe," the sides are the "parietal" and "temporal lobes," the front is called the "frontal lobes." The brain is deeply grooved along the top from end to end and in effect it appears divided into two "hemispheres" which are, however, joined together by a band of nerve fibers called the corpus callosum and by other fibers. The brain appears to carry out some of its functions in terms of a reversed specialization of the two hemispheres so that the left hemisphere largely "controls" the right side of the body in motor activity and the right hemisphere controls the left. Along the lobes, various areas have been marked off geographically as the "motor" area, the "somasthetic" area, etc. Some anatomists have attempted to assign numbers to various areas for identification purposes.

Some broad, general functions have been localized in the brain but we must be extremely careful in considering such localization. For example, the occipital region is associated with vision. Injury to this area may result in blindness. This does not mean that we see with the backs of our brains, however. It means only that neural impulses initiated in the eyes do arrive at the back of the brain. From there they go on into other areas and eventually may go out into motor outlets or other channels. They need not do so, however, and the energy may dissipate with no specific effect. All parts of the optic machinery are important for vision. Each part of the eye, the optic nerve, the occipital lobe, and much of the rest of the brain are required for seeing. The best we can say is that some parts of the brain can suffer damage or removal without affecting vision. This does not mean, however, that vision is localized in any part that cannot be removed without damaging vision. On such an argument we might argue that a light is localized in a switch, a wire, or a light bulb—none of these by itself provides light. Together, with a source of power, they might, if properly hooked up. There are some areas that are more or less finely related to specific functions, but again we must be cautious about localizing. Thus a small area in the lower left hemisphere, called Broca's area, is related to the speech process but there are other areas related to speech and language functions. Tumors or other damage here might result in a variety of aphasias (disorders related to the use of language). Dr. Penfield, of the Montreal Neurological Institute, has been able to get some epileptic subjects undergoing operations, to initiate rather long sequences of "imagery" by applying a small voltage to points in the temporal lobe (Penfield and Rasmussen, 1950). His results are limited to a few epileptic patients, to be sure, but they are provocative. By touching a tiny area with an electrical needle the surgeon is able to get the subject to remember and hear songs, concerts, rather complicated sequences of events, etc. This does not mean that the events are "stored" there, but it does indicate that such sequences can be initiated by rather precise stimulation. Not all points are equally effective but the same point sometimes seems to generate the same "memories." We can look forward with much interest to more such studies.

Thus far we have been discussing the brain as if it consisted only of what can be seen by opening the skull from the top or side. Actually, as mentioned earlier, the exterior of the brain can be conceived of as a thin blanket which has spread over and around other central nervous system structures. Because the cortex came last in evolutionary development and because we are fond of viewing man as the culmination of nature's efforts, we tend to view the cortex as the highest stage of development and commit the corresponding linguistic error of associating it with the "highest functions." The cortex, by itself, however, is of no use at all, and can only function with the aid and co-operation of the subcortical structures. The cortex and subcortical areas interact, affect each other and, in a sense, control each other. All parts of the brain must be thought of as working together. We cannot single out special areas as independent operators.

The old brain which also has a "paleocortex" consists of a great many subcortical structures, centers, or nuclei, where connections are made between nerves bringing in and carrying out impulses. The old brain structures of most concern to us are the thalamus, basal ganglia, the hypothalamus, and the reticular formation, the latter only recently recognized as an important determiner of neural function. The thalamus may be thought of as a little brain in its own right or as a giant relay station which is serviced by all of the incoming sensory impulses and which shunts these around to other parts of the nervous system, including the cortex in those organisms that possess one. Although reasoning by analogy is distressingly dangerous in connection with the nervous system, we might consider the thalamus and its parts, including the hypothalamus, as maintaining the normal vegetative functions of the organism, smoothly routing routine inputs from the various sense organs (except the olfactory sense) as they come in by their millions. On occasions when the stimulation is too intense or unusual and the hypothalamus cannot handle the storm, there may be some degree of disorganization or some other type of organization established. It might be thought and has been so declared by Cannon (1929) and others that the hypothalamus is the center of emotional control. For the moment we might accept this notion with various reservations which we will come to later. It is only important to note that much of our daily autonomic activity (the functioning of visceral organs) is under hypothalamic control and many activities such as eating, drinking, perhaps sexual behavior, and a host of

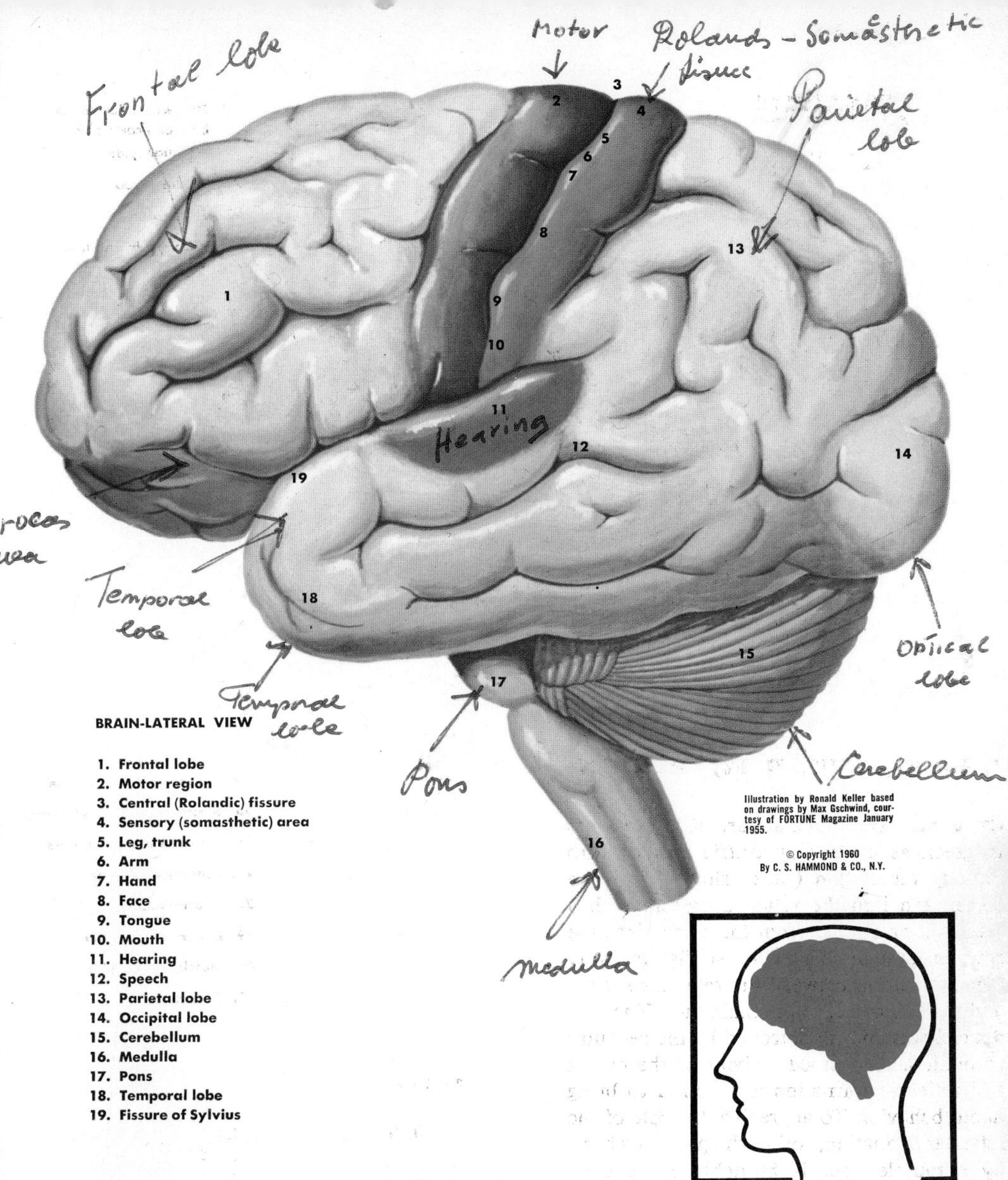

THE APPEARANCE OF THE HUMAN BRAIN

Figure 7 In this lateral view of the left hemisphere, the primary functional areas are colored to set them off from the rest of the brain. Stimulation in the motor area results in bodily movements; stimulation originating in bodily movements, in turn, is "projected" onto the sensory-motor area. The Fissure of Sylvius separates the temporal and parietal lobes. The Fissure of Rolando separates the frontal and parietal lobes. No distinct fissure separates the occipital lobe at the rear of the brain from the rest. The indicated functions are those suggested by Penfield and Rasmussen (1950).

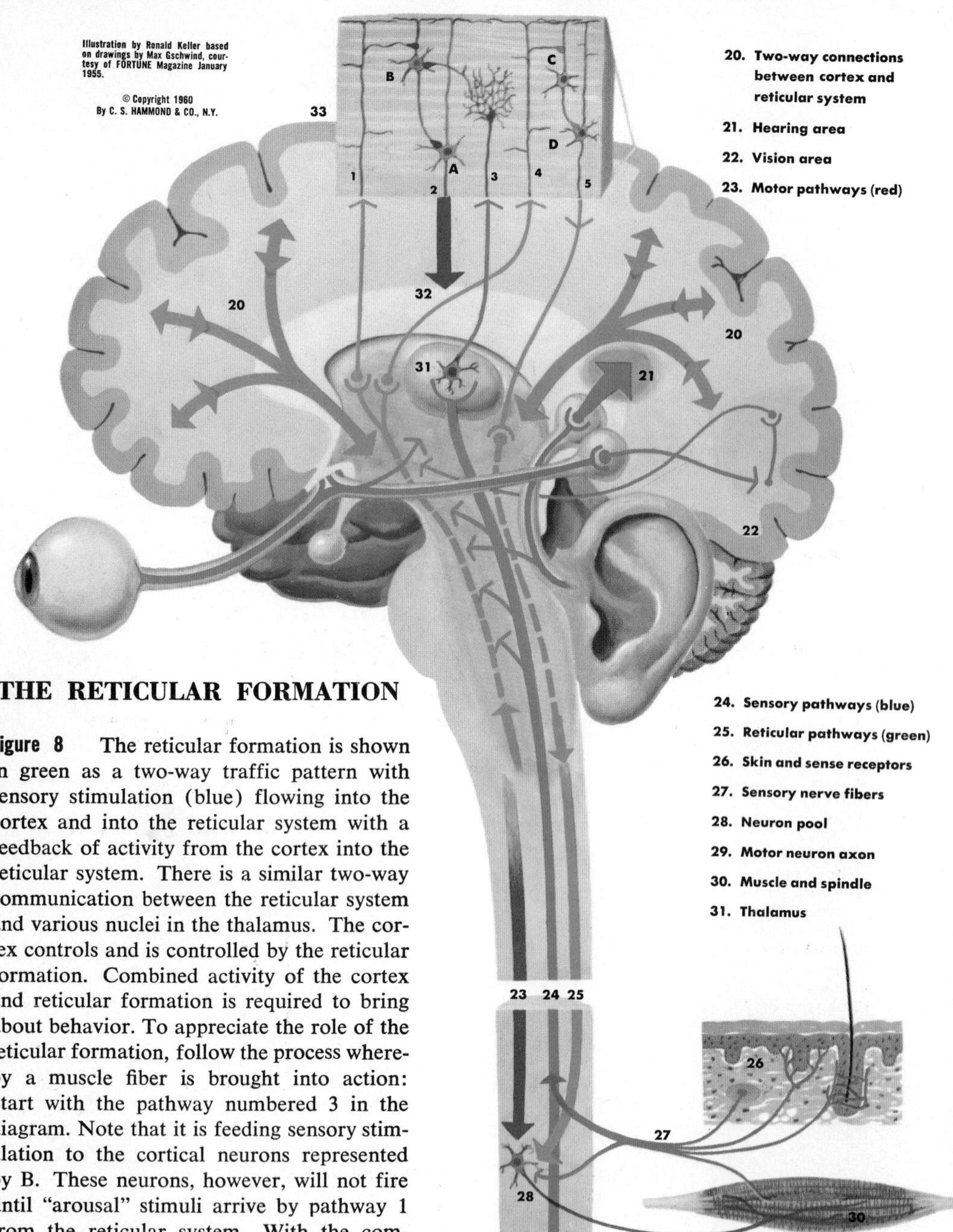

THE RETICULAR FORMATION

Figure 8 The reticular formation is shown in green as a two-way traffic pattern with sensory stimulation (blue) flowing into the cortex and into the reticular system with a feedback of activity from the cortex into the reticular system. There is a similar two-way communication between the reticular system and various nuclei in the thalamus. The cortex controls and is controlled by the reticular formation. Combined activity of the cortex and reticular formation is required to bring about behavior. To appreciate the role of the reticular formation, follow the process whereby a muscle fiber is brought into action: Start with the pathway numbered 3 in the diagram. Note that it is feeding sensory stimulation to the cortical neurons represented by B. These neurons, however, will not fire until "arousal" stimuli arrive by pathway 1 from the reticular system. With the combined stimulation, B fires and sets off A (motor neurons), and impulses then travel down motor pathways (red) in the spinal cord to an appropriate level where a motor axon connects with a muscle fiber. In this diagram the brain is shown divided down the middle. The light-colored area in the middle of the brain is the corpus callosum, a broad band of fibers that joins the two hemispheres of the brain. The pituitary gland is shown as a small bulbous structure attached to a stalk. Just above the pituitary gland we would find the hypothalamus.

glandular reactions are related to conditions that prevail in the hypothalamus and associated subcortical structures. Again caution must be urged against overspecifying the localization of functions.

The reticular formation

Just above the medulla (a bulbous development of the spinal cord near the base of the brain, an area containing many reflex centers which control such activities as breathing and temperature regulation) is a complex arrangement of neural structures consisting of neurons with connections in all directions with the midbrain, the cortex, and the sensory structures—the "reticular formation" (French, 1957). From the reticular formation pathways lead back and forth to the cortex and subcortical centers so that complex interactions can occur. The reticular formation can activate the cortex and the cortex can activate the reticular formation which can then modify the activity of the cortex and so on and on. Because the anatomical detail of the reticular formation is so complex its limits are difficult to establish. Because it is not obvious as a solid lump or well-defined body, nothing much was known about its function until only recently when we have come to regard it as a sort of "activation" center. If the reticular formation is not receiving impulses and is relatively quiescent, the rest of the brain is quiet, too, and the owner of the brain is asleep. With activity in the reticular formation or "arousal" center, the brain can be wakened and set into action. The reticular formation is apparently activated by receptor activity. Our diurnal patterns of waking and sleeping, of eating at more or less regular periods and consequently developing other conditions also may have much to do with the amount of activity in the reticular system. If there is any self-controlling mechanism in the brain at all, the closest approximation to one may be the reticular formation. We can think of it as a governor of the level of activation in the brain as a whole. The reticular formation may very well determine what sensory inputs are processed to the thalamus and get to the occipital lobe or temporal lobe or other way station. It can determine to some degree whether motor activity will be initiated and how energetically. Whether we think of something, and whether one action will lead to another, may be functions of this area of the brain. Enough has been established, however, to make us look to the reticular system, a lower brain level "structure," as a regulator of the activity that goes on in the cortex to make us question whether the cortex is necessarily related to higher mental activity or whether, in fact, it merely facilitates such activity going on at lower levels, with perhaps greater elaboration and integration with past experience.

Brain waves

We can now make some general observations about the brain's activity and then proceed to our speculative interpretations of what the brain is doing in the head. About 1929 it was discovered that if electrodes were attached to the scalp of an animal or human, minute changing electrical potentials could be detected. When such potentials are amplified, oscilloscopes or other recording devices show them in the form of waves, the so-called "brain waves"—the next time you have an idea, don't say you "had a brain wave"—you nearly always have brain waves unless you are in a coma or dead. The waves can be described in terms of frequency and amplitude. Different kinds of frequencies may be picked up under different conditions, for example, when you are asleep, the waves are slow (up to 4 per second and rather large); as you waken to the day's activities, the brain waves become faster and smaller and a typical waking wave (resting with eyes closed) will run off at about 8 to 12 cycles per second—this is the alpha wave—the slow wave mentioned earlier is called the delta wave. Between the alpha and delta waves we have other names (none of these names mean much, the frequencies are continuous)—beta and gamma—to describe decreasing frequencies. When an alpha wave is being recorded and the subject opens his eyes, the alpha wave usually disappears and is replaced by waves of high frequency and low amplitude. What the meaning of this disappearance ("desynchrony") is cannot be stated with certainty. When the waves disappear, it is assumed that there is a loss of synchronization of neural firing and that whatever potentials are present are organized in some different fashion. The point is that the disappearance of the waves does not reflect lack of activity in the brain, but does on the contrary, indicate a more specific kind of activity than that involved in resting with "the mind a blank." Any kind of stimulation is likely to disturb the pattern of brain waves and special kinds of stimulation, for example, a light flickering at about 12 times per second, can initiate and to some extent control the brain wave pattern—photic driving (Walter, 1953). Our concern here is not so much with the nature of brain waves as with the fact that they are, that they exist. They indicate as clearly as any evidence might that the brain is alive, that it is active, that it is using energy, and that any additional neural activity initiated through sensory stimulation must take its chances on getting past the reticular system and finding its place or function in an already active brain. If the brain is not ready for such stimulation it either will become disorganized in its operations or it will not accept the new entry. In short, we are insisting that the brain determines whether external energy changes are entitled to the term "stimulus," or merely external energy change.

The autonomic nervous system

There is another anatomical division of neural operation that we can now look at briefly. The various organs in the visceral cavity as well as some in the head are of a vital nature. An automatic system has developed for taking care of such things as the regulation of temperature, circulation, and digestion and various glandular secretions both of the endocrine (ductless) variety, e.g., the adrenal glands, as well as the other secretion-producing organs, e.g., the liver. Much of the functioning of the visceral organs and glands is mediated through the so-called "autonomic nervous system." This is essentially a "motor" system. This system consists of efferent fibers starting out from a number of ganglia (large clusters of nerve cells) attached to the spinal cord. From the spinal ganglia the nerve fibers go out to the heart, lungs, kidney, liver, spleen, pancreas, intestines, stomach, and all of the glandular and other visceral organs. The function of the nerves is to stimulate or to inhibit (regulate) the action of these organs and the nerves are distributed nicely according to these functions into three more or less distinct groups, the cranial, sympathetic, and sacral divisions. The middle group, the sympathetic division of the autonomic nervous system, tends to control the inhibitory aspects of those structures which are stimulated by the upper (cranial) and lower (sacral) sections (together these make up the parasympathetic system) and vice versa. Thus, normally, the heart beats away at about 72 times per minute—this must be thought of as a somewhat inhibited rate because if the sympathetic division fibers supplying the heart get control they eliminate the inhibition and the heart speeds up. Normally, again, the sacral division of the parasympathetic stimulates the intestines in their digestive and eliminative functions, whereas the sympathetic fibers inhibit both digestion and elimination under some conditions or disturb the entire system of control as sometimes happens in extreme "fear" conditions. The sympathetic fibers can excite greater adrenal gland secretion and indirectly force the liver to release more sugar into the speeded-up circulation than might be good for us, but which might be helpful if a bear is chasing us down a mountain road.

The autonomic system normally controls our vegetative existence with reasonable efficiency and for the most part can be thought of as automatic. It is, however, very much under the control of the central nervous system via the cord and the hypothalamus and is subject to hormonal effects. The organs of the viscera are subject to central control and learning operations just as are other organs although the difficulty or awkwardness of their use in ordinary experiments tends to keep them out of the psychological laboratory. We need only to observe the fact that everyone establishes reasonable control of the bowel and bladder sphincters early in life, that we can, to some extent, regulate our internal functions if we go in for Yoga exercises. Some individuals can slow down their heart beat to an abnormal degree, others can blush or blanch and otherwise control autonomic functions. In American laboratories one of the standard measurements in a variety of experimental procedures is to record the galvanic skin response or "psychogalvanic reflex" (GSR or PGR). This response is usually held to be associated with an increase in activity of the sweat glands which makes the skin less resistant to the passage of an electric current. A drop in skin resistance is then interpreted as a sign of emotion for fear, embarrassment, etc. Unfortunately, skin resistance will drop with pleasant reactions as well as with such ordinary activities as coughing or laughing or any movement. Almost any kind of stimulation can bring out a PGR and its interpretation is consequently difficult. It is sometimes used as part of a lie-detection set-up, either by itself or in conjunction with breathing, heart rate, and other measures. Needless to say, lie detectors do not detect lies. They measure autonomic activity and nothing more. Any interpretations based on more or less autonomic activity at different stages of an interrogation of a prisoner become only interpretations. We must be careful not to associate autonomic activity with "emotion." All behavior includes autonomic components and as we will find later, all behavior is emotional.

In Russian laboratories there is more interest in autonomic activity as a research tool; measures are taken of bladder and intestinal activity quite commonly. Another autonomic response, the secretion of saliva is a standard tool in Russian conditioning laboratories. It has not found much favor in the United States although some research is done here with it by measuring salivary absorption by cotton pellets placed in the mouths of subjects. The cotton is weighed before and after stimulation (Razran, 1936).

In our considerations of neural action in the future we will include autonomic activity along with the rest of the nervous system without considering it a special little activity area of its own, functioning by itself without regard to the rest of the system. It should also be noted that there is a feedback from autonomic action into the rest of the nervous system although this is frequently slow and sluggish. Visceral organs are notoriously insensitive, as far as the subject is concerned, to any but neural stimulation. Cutting intestines or burning them, for example, can be quite painless. The visceral feedback is not easily interpreted or localized by the subject. Patients are frequently unable to help their physicians about what hurts or how.

THE CONCEPTUAL NERVOUS SYSTEM

We are now finished with the real nervous system. The general description of the actual neural structures has not provided answers to any psychological problems. To do that we must now impose a more hypothetical physiology upon the structures that have been described. It has to be hypothetical because we do not actually have the physiological evidence about the role of the nervous system in behavior, at least not to the degree of nicety and elaboration that we require. What we shall proceed to do now is to set certain demands upon the nervous system. We shall require that it behave in certain ways which we hope will someday be demonstrated to be correct. In other words, we are now going to *create* a nervous system that suits our fancy. We shall call this the "conceptual nervous system" (Hebb, 1949), because it is a "conceived" or imagined one. The only restraints we shall impose upon ourselves are that we be guided by whatever facts seem important and reliable, and that we not include propositions which have no conceivable way of being tested or demonstrated in the even remote future. This kind of exercise might be considered foolhardy by some, tommyrot by others, and most undesirable and unnecessary by still others who believe they can develop a psychology without references to the nervous system at all. We have already indicated our disagreement with the latter position and regard it as limited, at best, in that it takes a dim view of the interrelatedness of science. Ignoring the nervous system cannot lead to a conviction of having laid bare the whole truth, even if some of the truth can be described. To start with the world of external stimuli and end with the world of externally observed responses with no reference to the nervous system leads one into a series of contortions and indirect, backdoor usages of internal mechanisms that makes the psychologist appear just a little awkward, at best. It does not prevent the psychologist from unwittingly theorizing in terms of his own appreciation of the nervous system's role, and if he does not make this clear to his audience, there is no way of checking on the reasonableness of his views. To ignore the active, dynamic, and controlling nature of neural actions on behavior is to exclude from psychology most of its important traditional problems and to adopt a position which tends to preclude prediction of new behavior. If we depend on observations of behavior alone, no predictions can be made until the behavior has been observed in the past often enough to provide a statistical or actuarial basis, even when the observations are postulated to be adequate because of careful experimental controls.

So long as we label our assumptions clearly and continually remind ourselves about the speculative nature of our enterprise, there can be little harm and perhaps great advantage. With these considerations before us, we can proceed to speculate. In what follows we are adopting the proposition that the nervous system is a mysterious "black box" such as was mentioned earlier (p. 52). Wires come into and out of the black box and things happen at the output end when switches are closed at the input end. The engineer's job is to deduce what the inside of the box must contain. From now on our job will be to fill the black box of the skull with the mechanisms that are required to account for behavior. To some degree we have cheated a little because we have looked into the skull and learned a little about what is and is not there.

We can start traditionally and assert that the whole function of the black box is to connect the input with the output. We can regard the nervous system as a great connecting system. The traditional analogy has been with a telephone exchange. You dial a number in your house and a phone rings in another house because of a "connection" made in the exchange or "central." We used to have operators at the central exchange but now with dial systems and other kinds of automation, the role of the operator has been greatly modified. Even long distance calls are automatized to a considerable degree and we can anticipate the day when there are no operators at all, at least in so far as connections are involved. In the great tradition an operator was also postulated to reside in the head. He was called "the mind," but nowadays we are automatizing the mind out of business too, and in our conceptual nervous system there are no operators. All connections are made automatically.

The telephone analogy is a rather weak one and has many faults which we shall try to consider, but for the moment we can play around with it. To do any good at all the analogy must include the notion that all potential users in a given community have phones already in the homes and that all the necessary wiring has been done in advance. All that is required for a conversation is to make the central connection. Here we find the first weakness in our analogy. In the nervous system, some connections are already made when we are born, or develop shortly after through the process of growth (maturation). In some organisms these connections are quite perfect and complete and we have patterns of behavior emerging with the first input of a given kind (instinctive or tropistic behavior). In humans such connections are rather limited and restricted to segmental systems that we have already identified as reflexes. Thus a tap on the knee (even in an unborn infant, or the six-month fetus) will result in a knee jerk. Food in the mouth will be followed by automatic salivation and swallowing. A cinder in the eye will initiate tearing, a gun shot will develop a rather complex but still co-ordinated "startle reaction." Thus we start out with some connections already there and ready for use whenever a specific input is provided.

Reflex action and the synapse

We might pause and examine the nature of these reflexes for a bit. The usual description involves a number of distinct steps: first an energy source impinges on a receptor. Then a nervous impulse is initiated which travels up an afferent or sensory nerve to the central nervous system. In the case of a knee jerk, the impulse would arrive at the spinal cord, coming in at the back. Here it would make connections with intermediate (internuncial) neurons which would transfer the impulse to cells at the front of the cord and from there the impulse would travel along the efferent (motor) nerve to the quadriceps muscle in the thigh. Contraction of this muscle would pull the patellar tendon and extend the leg. The knee, itself, does not jerk, of course; the leg is extended. This simple picture leaves much out of the story which we shall try to fit in, but our immediate interest is in the connections in the cord. Such connections, between two neurons, are called "synapses." In the case of the knee jerk, the synapses have already been organized, and need only to be used. The impulse arriving from the patella or knee cap goes across the necessary synapses to initiate impulses in the appropriate motor cells. Similar appropriate outlets are available for all other innate patterns that can merit the label "reflex." For most inputs some kind of outlet will be made available although it need not make any sense from an observer's point of view. Thus touching an infant's leg might lead to an eyeblink and shining a light into its eyes might be followed by a leg or arm movement although there might very well be some eye activity in the case of the light and some leg activity in the case of the touch. In some instances a given input might result in quite a general activity throughout the body. In infants the motor activity is likely to be gross and general, and, with growth and learning, more and more individuation or specialization of movements will occur to specific stimulations (Pratt, Nelson, and Sun, 1930). If the stimulation is excessive, the behavior involved is likely to be un-co-ordinated and excessive too. We are not yet ready to discuss behavior, as such, but we can anticipate a bit and suggest that the behavior, in general, appears to follow a pattern which might be described as "trying to get rid of excessive stimulation."

If we let reflex behavior more or less take care of itself, what about the stimulation that does not have handy little reflex outlets? Here we have inputs but no outputs. If we take the point of view suggested above, that the reflex gets rid of the stimulation, then we can assume that stimulation that is not gotten rid of will continue to circulate about in the nervous system until it does find an outlet, that is, until it arrives at a synapse which leads to an outlet, however farfetched. This will occur only if the stimulation is continued for some period, and, if it is strong enough not to die off (we have no good ways of describing this "dying off" process other than refractory phase or some inhibitory conditions that might tend to reduce the stimulation). As a general working proposition, however, we can assume that any stimulation that enters the nervous system will eventually be dissipated and this may take place through some outlet into the muscular equipment. A synapse or several synapses might be involved before such outlets are reached.

When a synapse is traversed it is now generally believed that either it has some natural, inherent capacity for enabling an impulse to cross from one neuron to another, or that, if it is crossed, such a capacity tends to be established. Most speculators about synapses conceive of them as becoming more amenable to being traversed with continued stimulation at the input side. To alter the readiness of a synapse might require thousands of such traversals. Thus we read about nervous pathways as if these were paths through jungle thicknesses beaten-down through the simple process of being used. Perhaps some chemical secretion occurs when a synapse is crossed, or perhaps some neural tissue (the "boutons") swells or even moves and by establishing physical contact with the intertwining dendrites of the next neuron facilitates the passage of the impulse or energy. We must accept as a working notion that repeated crossings of a synapse make it easier to cross on succeeding occasions and that this facility increases to some optimum level of automatic, uninhibited traffic.

We must not make the simple and simple-minded assumption that such activity is a limited and local one, with one impulse across one synapse from one neuron to another. It is far more likely that stimulation as it enters the nervous system spreads widely and that hundreds if not thousands or even millions of impulses are crossing synapses at widely scattered points in the central nervous system, making for a rather general activity and one that might be extremely difficult to localize. When we have arrived at the behavioral stage where a given stimulus elicits a given response, we might very well be dealing with a neural state of a most complicated combination of neurons simultaneously and successively discharging sometimes all over the brain (Sherrington, 1950). With continued practice of the particular sequence, with perhaps thousands of impulses having been involved, it might be possible for a given sequence to occur, behaviorally speaking, and have a great many of the potential contributors to the sequence unnecessary for the completion of the behavior.

The above considerations are made necessary by the facts of neurophysiology. It has been demonstrated by Lashley (1929), and others that it is quite possible to slice into any section of the cortex of a rat and still have the rat perform adequately in some trained, "intelligent" response. This forces us to the observation that while various parts of or even the whole brain, or what you have of it at any given time, may be employed in any given behavioral sequence, it might be possible to get along without any particular connections between cortical segments because enough of them are left to provide for the learned behavior. In this connection it might be mentioned that humans, too, can get along quite well without some of their brain matter. The frontal lobes particularly are referred to as "silent" areas because no one seems able to find a use for them. They can be removed or separated from the rest of the brain without necessarily interfering with intelligent or learned behavior. (See Hebb, 1945.) It is possible that they participate as much as any other part in the initial learning of some sequences but that they can be dispensed with later on. Some sections of the brain are particularly involved with some sensory function and damage or removal of such sections may interfere with some behavioral sequences or eliminate them altogether. Damage to the occipital area may interfere with visual reactions; the blind cannot perform in response to visual cues.

Thus far we have our picture of the central nervous system as operating to some degree as a whole, or at least with many parts of the brain involved in almost any kind of input-output sequence. This might be called something like a "field theory" interpretation although it involves specific neurons or fibers participating with varying degrees of importance in specific sequences of behavior. In terms of our telephone analogy, the above view would have phones ringing all over the community if we dialed any number at all. This would obviously put the phone company out of business, but the brain is not a phone company and it takes better care of the subscribers.

Cell assemblies

An additional physiological fact, and this one is of major importance to psychology, must now be noted: once the neural energy is initiated, it does not immediately cease but continues to excite neurons for some time after. There is, in short, a neural afterdischarge which amounts to continued firing of some neurons. Now, we make another assumption: for any given stimulus, suppose that a large number of neurons in the brain are fired, perhaps in the millions, and at widely different loci; suppose further that these neurons fire other neurons which in turn refire the original ones and thereby set up what might be called a recurring neural firing circuit. In other words, for many kinds of stimuli,[2] a circular chain reaction is set off which may maintain itself for some little time (Eccles, 1953). Such a repetitive chain reaction might be called, after the manner of Hebb (1949), a "cell assembly." Other psychologists might prefer to talk about such circuits in traditional S ⟶ R terms and might call them S ⟶ R "bonds" or "associations." Because the "cell assembly" is just as hypothetical as an association or S ⟶ R bond, it might be a matter of opinion as to what term is suitable. We should note, however, that S ⟶ R bonds include a *response* feature which may be somewhat restrictive and force us to think about externally observable behavior. "Associations," on the other hand, are traditionally bound up with "ideas" and may, again, divert or prejudice our thinking. Cell assembles specifically refer to neural behavior or internal neural events and the use of this expression has the virtue of specifying the nature and locus of the behavior under consideration. The student should be warned that the use of Hebb's terminology does not necessarily correspond with his current usage or commit us to adopt the changes that Professor Hebb may choose to incorporate in his concept of the cell assembly. Its use in this text is to suggest only a neural mechanism which will carry the heavy burden of learning and mediation. We can picture this assembly as consisting of a core of neurons which fire every time the particular stimulus is effective with many other neurons that participate once in a while, or which participate at first and not later, or with various additions from time to time, depending upon varying conditions of the organism. Our assumption is still not complete; it needs two more steps. The first is that because stimulation never occurs in isolation, there will be other stimulation arriving in the nervous system at the same time and shortly before and shortly afterward. It is consequently assumed that each of these stimulations will develop its own cell assemblies and that cell assemblies that are occurring more or less together will become interconnected with each other and that one assembly can fire off another assembly that normally follows it, even if the stimulation which might originally set off the second does not occur. In this way we picture one stimulus setting off not only its own assembly, but a se-

[2] Some reflex and autonomic activity may not involve recurring neural circuits or at least not for extensive periods. The concept of recurring circuits is important in connection with learned behavior. If learning is to involve a modification of the nervous system, there must be some period of activity in the parts of the nervous system involved where the modification can take place. This must take time; recurring neural circuits might be the means by which such growth or change can take place.

quence of assemblies within which its own assembly will fire every so often. The second step is to include motor neurons. Because motor activity will normally follow the introduction of energy into the nervous system, we must assume that the firing of motor neurons will also occur at the time the initial postsensory effects are still active and that the cell assembly may include a number of motor components so that the initiation of assembly action will ordinarily, but not necessarily, lead to motor action. If motor action does take place, a motor component *must* have been fired. There is no reason, however, why the motor component cannot be sidetracked or short-circuited out of the assembly action on one occasion or another.

The phase sequence

Following Hebb, again, we will call a chain of assemblies which fire each other in some order, not necessarily a fixed one, a "phase sequence." For the present, then, we have a picture of the nervous system such that whenever an external world stimulus breaks into the neural equipment via some sense organ and when an afferent nerve carries the neural impulse to the central system, a chain of neural events is initiated which may or may not, but usually does, initiate some motor activity. The sequence of events which is established depends upon the sequence of stimulation to a considerable degree, and if the external arousal is always in sequence, then we might expect the neural activity to parallel this sequence, with one thing leading to the other in the neural world just as it does in the external world. We are still not through with our picture. The stimulation that initiates the assembly need not occur outside the skin. Visceral conditions such as a dry mouth, empty stomach, distension of intestines or bladder, etc., might also initiate assemblies and phase sequences. And, perhaps, most important of all, we must recognize that neurons are living things that fire off by themselves when not otherwise invited to do so because of nutritional or other conditions, so that it is conceivable, and it will be insisted upon here, that cell assemblies can be initiated by environmental conditions within the brain itself, its circulation or lack of it, oxygen levels, blood pressure or temperature changes, various chemical constituents of the blood that may alter from time to time because of hormonal deposits, different components in the diet of the individual, and so on. We postulate then, a principle that permits us to attribute some behavior to the function of the nervous system itself based on physiological changes. Such changes might be traced to external stimulation if one follows a painstaking and indirect route (one could argue that a bladder becomes filled because we take in liquids from the outside) but such attempts are hardly worthwhile and may involve extremely devious speculations.

We have just given the nervous system a license to act by itself. Since it does so anyhow, giving the license may be a purely gratuitous act, but for many years psychologists have refused to grant this license and have restricted the operations of the nervous system to the function of connecting the outside world with the muscles. This limitation can no longer be tolerated. If a human has pellagra or too much alcohol, we can expect him to hallucinate. The pink elephants are not in the outside world and no amount of argument or postulation by the psychologist will put them there. They are the results of a physiological condition involving the brain. While the dietary deficiency can be blamed on the outside world, to be sure, and the alcohol came from a bottle, the pink elephants came from the brain. Because it might escape the notice of the student, we should point out that the license we have just given includes the privilege of having rather clever and ingenious behavior occur by virtue of the brain's action just as freely as bizarre activities have been licensed. Such action is presumably related to changes in the "internal environment" (oxygen, nutrition, etc.); it is not *uncaused,* but we are unable to identify the specific factors involved.

The above discussion of cell assemblies and phase sequences may have proven a bit confusing and the student should be worrying about the reasons for all these assumptions. We can drop a broad hint or two now. The cell assemblies and phase sequences are going to carry a heavy load. They are going to be used to account for what in ordinary parlance pass for "ideas," thinking, anticipations, attention, expectancy, and purpose. The explanation of how they can do all of these things will take up the rest of the text. For the moment, and as a sample, we can tease the student with the suggestion that what he calls an "idea" is nothing but a "phase sequence." While the phase sequences initiated by this remark are running off (while you are mulling this idea around in your mind), we can embark on our journey with the first and most serious step. We shall attempt a preliminary account of some simple learning, usually termed "conditioning," not because we are ready to talk about learning, but because the operation of cell assemblies and the development of phase sequences need to be illustrated in a context that we will be forced to call upon very frequently in the rest of our considerations.

Conditioning in terms of assemblies and phase sequences

By now most people who attend college have heard of Pavlov (see Konorski, 1949), the great Russian physiologist and his dogs that salivated when a bell rang. We will have many occasions to refer to these dogs and the student must know a great deal more about them than that they would salivate when bells rang. We will defer discussion of the many facts and principles which developed out of Pavlov's laboratory until the proper time. For the moment we are interested in a very oversimplified theoretical appreciation of Pavlov's work. To meet this need we must look briefly at the bare facts involved and try to determine what they must mean conceptually.

First, the facts. In the typical "conditioned-reflex" experiment, some response is selected which can be readily *elicited* by some stimulus. We might select some simple reflex like a knee jerk or an eyelid blink. The response at this stage would be a simple, direct, natural, or "unconditioned" response. The stimulus would be, correspondingly, an "unconditioned" stimulus. Thus, a puff of air directed at the eye (unconditioned stimulus, or UncS) would be followed in "reaction time" speed by a closure of the lid, or unconditioned response (UncR). With a suitable unconditioned response available, the experimenter now selects (and proves by preliminary tests) a stimulus that does not elicit the same response, for example, a brief tone or buzzer. If it is clear that the new stimulus does not result in the appearance of the unconditioned response, it can be used now as a conditioning stimulus or CS.

In the Pavlovian laboratories, probably for historical reasons (Pavlov was originally interested in the physiology of digestion), the favored unconditioned response was the salivary discharge to the natural, unconditioned, stimulus of dry food powder blown into a dog's mouth by means of a bellows. The saliva was collected in a graduated tube and the amount could be measured. To gather the saliva directly, the dog was first surgically prepared with a fistula through the cheek through which the saliva was brought outside the mouth. Conditioned stimuli in Pavlov's work ranged through a great variety of lights, sounds, touches or shocks to the skin, odors, and temperature changes. Pavlov used almost anything you might think of. We need to note only two more facts of immediate concern and one which will interest us later. The first two are that the conditioned stimulus normally brings out its own "unconditioned response" (and this is usually ignored as of no special interest); the second fact is that the conditioned stimulus is normally presented first in a time sequence. It has been reasonably well established that best results will be obtained if the CS precedes the UncS by about a half-second. The third fact, which we will not worry about at present, is that the dog is normally hungry when a session begins.

When an experimenter is ready to "condition" an organism he tries to eliminate any disturbing circumstances. He isolates the subject as nearly as possible so that only the CS and the UncS will be effective. He then begins to present the stimuli, the CS first, followed by the UncS, and awaits developments. As the trials follow (the time between trials can be of crucial importance) the response to be conditioned begins to come forward in time. After about seven to ten trials (in Pavlov's arrangements) the formerly "unconditioned response" would occur *before* the unconditioned stimulus was presented. When this happens, the response is considered to have been conditioned, i.e., it has been brought under the control of conditions arranged by the experimenter. For this reason Pavlov (1927) called such responses "conditional." The term "conditioned" is an American usage. For our immediate purposes we should note the fact that the conditioned response, CR, has *antedated,* that is, preceded the UncS. Later we will emphasize this antedating as the basic feature of learning.

What we have described above is what you can see. If we now ask what really happened or how this novel event came about we are forced to speculate. The nature of these speculations has formed a large part of the psychology of learning. At the moment we will look at three different kinds of speculation or attempts at explaining what must have happened. None of these is necessarily correct; on the other hand, all of them may be partially correct. We can consider them possibilities.

In Figure 9 we have diagramed three different accounts of what goes on during conditioning. In each case we show the situation during and after conditioning. In I, during conditioning, we show the CS preceding the UncS, each being followed by its own response. After conditioning, it is suggested that a "connection," a "bond," or an "association" has been developed so that the CS is followed directly by the formerly unconditioned response. It should be appreciated that in this diagram, the CS is thought of as some finite set of neural events initiated by the actual external world stimulus, bell, buzzer, or whatnot. Similarly the US represents the finite neural aftermath of the unconditioned stimulus, food, air puff, or whatever was used. R_{cs} and R_{us} similarly are neural events involving motor neurons which when activated are followed by the externally observable response. According to this account then, the neural events initiated by CS have, through the process of being active at the same time as the motoneurons for the UncR, have acquired the capacity for activating these motoneurons in their own right. They have, in effect, come to substitute for the UncS. Such a view was supported by Guthrie (1952). He argued that any stimulus that was actively present at the time a response of any kind was occurring would come to elicit that response by itself. We should note that a chain of

DURING CONDITIONING

AFTER CONDITIONING

I

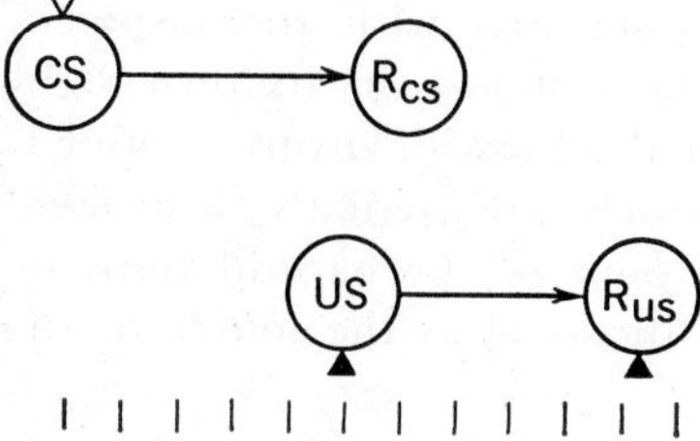

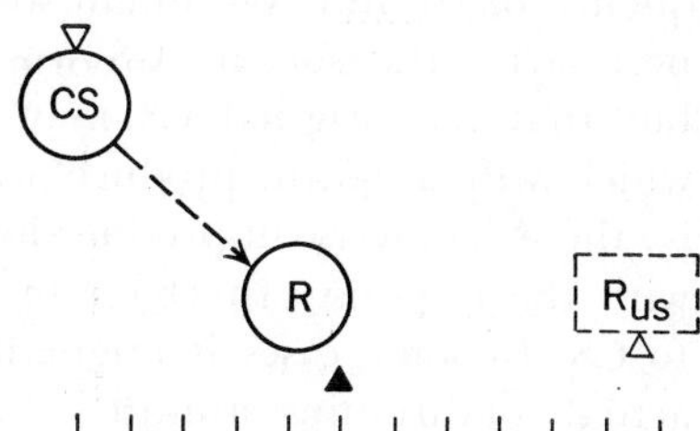

II

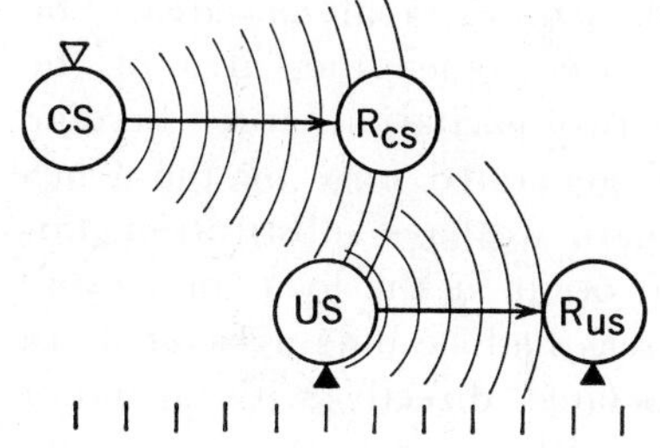

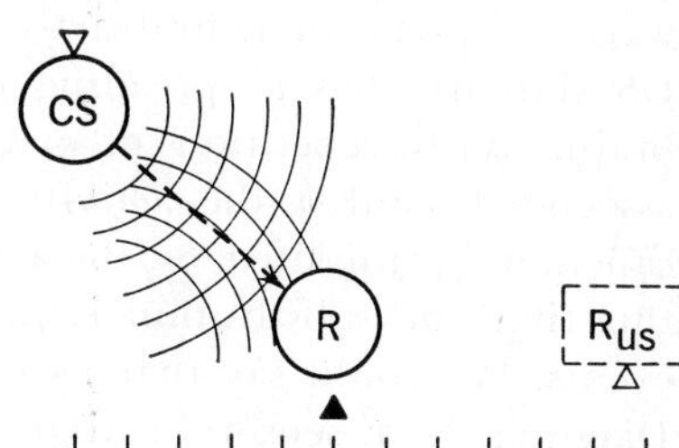

III

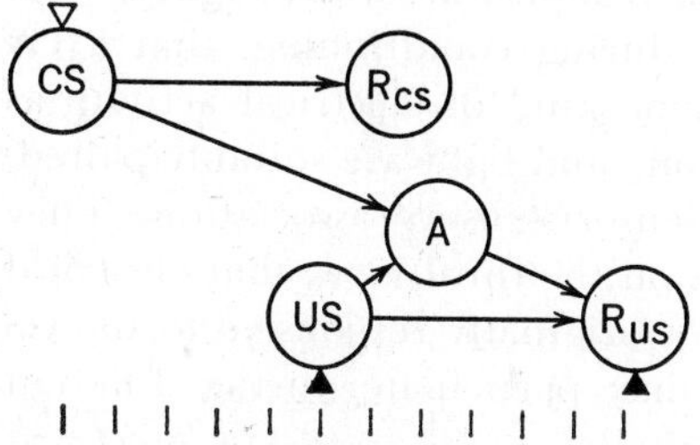

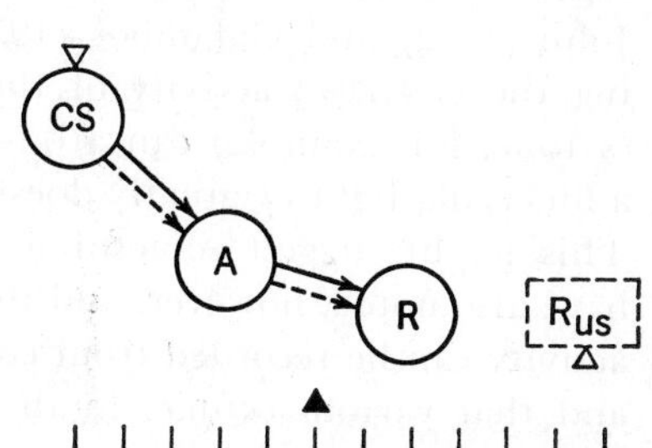

Figure 9 Conditioned reflex models. In all cases CS refers to the conditioning stimulus, US to the unconditioned stimulus; R_{cs} and R_{us} refer to the original responses to these stimuli. Time is represented in the base line in 0.1 second intervals. Open triangles indicate time at which CS is presented. Filled triangles show when the UncS is or would be presented. After conditioning, there is no need for the UncS. Note that the response moves forward in time. R_{us} in the boxes at the right indicates when the response would normally have occurred if there had been no conditioning. In Diagram III, A is a pool of association neurons. Collaterals from CS and US are shown connecting with this association pool. In Diagram II, the response has not moved forward quite as much as in I since it is still necessary to arouse the neurons involved in normal US activity before R can occur. In Diagram III, the association neurons begin to fire earlier. In all instances, the dashed line indicates a learned connection; solid lines indicate original connections. For further explanation, see text.

neural events can persist in time as a "neural trace" so that there will be temporal overlap of all of the neural activity initiated by the sequence of stimuli. We might also note, as Guthrie claims, that it is not necessarily the specific CS used that is associated with the response, but that the original CS may arouse some response in its own right which will, in turn, produce stimuli from the muscles involved, and it is these "movement-produced-stimuli" which are actually associated with the response. In Diagram I we have omitted the natural response to CS. In some cases it might have to be included as the source of the actual conditioning stimuli.

In Diagram II we show a view that, in general, reflects Pavlov's own thinking on the problem. Here the CS must be thought of as a wave or spread of neural activity in some sensory (analyzer) area. The US similarly has a spreading excitation over some other area of the brain. With repetition of pairing, the two excitation areas become associated so that the activity originally generated only by the UncS can now be initiated by the CS. Here again we have substitution, but this time the substitution is presumed to occur at the locus of sensory events. We could say that two sensory areas had become associated. In Diagram I, a sensory activity was associated directly with a motor outlet. Pavlov also suggested that the CS might operate through arousing cells in motor areas that formerly were aroused only by the UncS. John (1959) and Galambos (1959) have demonstrated, through recording the electrical activity of the brain during conditioning, that a CS (a tone, for example) can arouse the same kind of electrical activity as a flickering light originally does if the tone and light are suitably paired. This might suggest something like a sensory-sensory association. They have also noted, however, and this bears on the third view, that electrical activity can be recorded from centers not originally responsive to the CS and that various centers in the brain may participate during different stages of a learning series.

The third view, shown in Diagram III, is that favored by Hebb (1949) and Eccles (1953). It is based on an assumption that conditioning occurs through the medium of some pool of "association" neurons. These neurons are of such a nature that they can be "fired" by either the UncS or the CS, but normally such an effect cannot be produced by the action of only one of the stimuli. There is neurological evidence to indicate that it takes the simultaneous activity of two or more neurons to cross a synapse, that is, to initiate activity in a third neuron, at least at first. If such an association pool of neurons is regularly activated it can eventually be set into action by the CS activity alone. The association neurons are presumed to have connections with a variety of potential responses, including the one about to be conditioned. Through the regular and repeated activity of the association neurons, the response eventually can be initiated by their firing alone.

In the case of all three views, it should be noted that the response that is observed may not be *exactly* like the original response to the UncS. We could hardly expect such a duplication inasmuch as the stimulation is not identical and some components of the original response may be intimately dependent upon the original stimulation.

As indicated above, we do not know which of these hypothetical pictures bears the closest resemblance to the neural facts. They are simply conceptualizations, attempts to account for the behavioral observations. They are steps on intellectual ladders or scaffolds that have been erected in the process of building a theory of behavior. We can let these views rest a while and return to Pavlov's dogs to get another start on seeing how our conceptualized nervous system might work. We will try to restate the general nature of conditioning in terms of cell assemblies. But, first, another look at Pavlov.

Although a great deal of psychological literature has developed around Pavlov's dogs, much of it is very misleading, if not actually wrong. The great difficulty with Pavlov's work, and this with all due respect to this great scientist, was that he started with mature dogs and stopped with a salivary reaction instead of investigating the complete sequence of eating as it develops in a puppy. Suppose that we start by taking a new born puppy from a litter and plan on feeding it by bottle, to see what we can learn by observation. Inserting a nipple into the puppy's mouth is followed by a reflex sucking response, fortunately for the puppy. This results in a flow of warm milk which results in another fortunate reflex for the puppy, swallowing. The swallowing is preceded by, and accompanied by, salivation from the salivary glands, also reflexly excited. To some primitive degree the puppy also engages in what will come to be chewing movements when it gets to be a little older. It is still blind, the eyes have not yet opened and it cannot see the nipple, and wouldn't know what it was if it could "see" it. (We have already noted that organisms with eyes have to learn to see.) So far we have the puppy stimulated by warm milk, a cutaneous and temperature combination which initiates corresponding cell assemblies some place in the brain. The location does not matter to us or to the puppy. At the same time that the milk is brought near the puppy, various olfactory cues from the human, from the nipple, and from the milk itself will also be present and initiate cell assemblies of their own. There may be some auditory assemblies activated by the sounds of sucking or noises made by the feeder. All of these assemblies will gradually develop as the feeding routine is repeated and external events that go together will result in the formation of assemblies that go together—in short, phase sequences will develop. The neural motor components involved in the sucking and swallowing or chewing activity will become "associated" with the several cell assemblies so that whenever the puppy is stimulated with the odor of milk, it may start sucking, salivating, and swallowing even though the milk is not present. If this happens too often, we will have an unhappy puppy on our hands. For the early days of its life, however, we could insure that the odor of milk will be followed by the presence of milk in the mouth. The puppy has started its education. It has learned to suck, salivate, and swallow to an external world stimulus—the volatile action of milk molecules in the atmosphere. Pavlov recognized the fact that dogs have learned to salivate to odors and appearance of food, but he more or less ignored this fact as somewhat irrelevant to his work. He described salivating to food in the mouth as a natural or "unconditioned reflex" which it is, true enough; but this unconditioned reflex was already being accompanied by an earlier "conditioned reflex"—salivating to an odor. Since this latter conditioned reflex is so naturally formed and such a constant companion of food in the mouth we might forgive Pavlov. Such prior "conditioning" is not unimportant, however. In a few days, the puppy's eyes open. Now when food is presented a complex visual stimulation is introduced and begins to form its cell assemblies. After a number of repetitions, the visual stimulus can initiate the salivation in the absence of milk, i.e., the puppy will salivate to an empty bottle, free of odors. Here we have a true novelty in the natural world. An irrelevant, an inadequate, an unnecessary, but not immaterial stimulus has acquired control over behavior. As with the visual stimulation of the bottle, so any other visual stimulation that consistently accompanies milk in the mouth, can acquire control over the sucking, salivating, swallowing activity. Not only other visual stimulation but any stimulation of any kind, sounds, touches, even electric shocks can acquire the same control. And again, we must not forget internal stimulation. The puppy can be considered hungry at eating times. Hunger, for us, and for the moment, consists of phase sequences initiated from contractions of the stomach walls and from chemical conditions in the blood and in the brain, and these phase sequences are no different qualitatively from any other kind. The puppy can and does learn to swallow, to salivate, and lick its lips when it is hungry, in the same way it learns to swallow to visual, auditory, olfactory and cutaneous stimulation. It is no surprise for us, especially after Pavlov's demonstrations, that dogs can learn to salivate to bells, buzzers, or the sound of bubbling water or electric fans.

But we said that Pavlov stopped too soon. He should have noted that much surrounding activity develops around the eating. As the puppy matures, many additional stages of stimulation precede the entry of food into the mouth. The feeder may bring the milk from the refrigerator, opening and closing same, he pours the milk into a sauce pan, turns on the heat, stands around a bit, pours the milk into a bottle or, now a pan which itself must be produced from some hiding place; slowly, as the puppy grows, each step in the process becomes incorporated into a routine, a phase sequence of almost unendurable length for a puppy, each step being learned in a "backward" fashion, i.e., the pouring of the milk into the bottle may be one of the early features of the sequence that is learned, the opening of the refrigerator may be the last. At the other end of the eating pattern, new sequences develop as the milk slowly fills the stomach, the animal picks up various additional responses of relaxing, of toying with the food, of licking its chops, of stretching, of taking a final survey of the situation and wandering off to bed or high adventure. The pattern slowly fills in until it becomes an involved and complicated bit of business, and through it all cell assemblies are being activated and reactivated, following in various degrees of orderliness. We assume that the picture drawn above represents the basic pattern that is followed in the early learning of organisms. It is by no means a complete picture and many details must be added in our future study, but our concern was not with the learning problem per se but with the operations of our conceptualized nervous system. The basic assumptions involved in this system have now been laid bare and arrayed in various garments which while somewhat *avant garde* in fashion are as serviceable as we need them to be. From now on we will proceed as if the assumptions represent genuine processes and make cheerful explanatory uses of them as they appear to be applicable.

THE MOTOR ASPECTS OF BEHAVIOR

It has been impossible in the above discussion to avoid use of the terms "motor" and "response" and "reaction." These terms we have not explained beyond some modest distinctions drawn between movements and acts. We must now get down to more detail and complete our picture of the basic behavioral equipment.

We have already admitted that psychologists have never defined behavior adequately. They speak vaguely of a response, a reaction, or activity but just what is meant by any particular term is rarely specified except as some specific experiment calls for some detailed description of what was being measured. Frequently such events as a person vocalizing a word or a pigeon "pecking" or a rat "pressing a bar" are referred to as responses. In practice, the psychologist might not concern himself greatly with how the vocalization is produced, or how the bar is pressed but merely takes note of the fact that a subject makes an appropriate noise, or in the case of the bar-pressing rat, that a mark was made on a recording chart. This may prove to be adequate for most psychological purposes. The actual muscles involved in pressing the bar may not be too important and it may not make much difference how the vocal chords vibrated just so long as "Good morning" or "Good afternoon" emerged at the appropriate times of the day. The same muscles may be used in reaching for a pencil as for a cigarette or revolver and the importance might lie in the object and not in the muscles. It is still important, however, to emphasize that it is muscles that move, that behavior is mediated via muscles and bones, tendons, and glands and we might miss a great deal of psychologically important matter if we devote ourselves to the outcomes of such movements and secretions and ignore the movements and secretions themselves. Some areas of behavior, such as the acquisition of motor skills may be impossible to appreciate without due regard to muscle action. The situation calls for some closer scrutiny.

Muscles

Muscle matter is usually classified as smooth muscle or striate from its microscopic appearance. Striate muscles are the working muscles of the body and the appendages, the muscles that move our bones about. Smooth muscle is found in the visceral cavity and makes up the bulk of the internal organs like the stomach and intestines. The iris of the eye is also smooth muscle and reacts directly to light. In general, we tend to ignore the visceral organs in our considerations of behavior, but they are most obviously there and active, and their action will be found to be of extreme importance in many phases of psychological problems. The general characteristic that distinguishes the two kinds of muscles, behaviorally speaking, is that smooth muscle reacts more slowly, i.e., has a longer reaction time than skeletal muscle. Further, the smooth muscles do not ordinarily do anything with respect to externally observable behavior in any direct fashion (the pupillary contraction mentioned above is an exception). Their operations have to be indirect. They can slow down in their activity or speed up, e.g., a pounding heart, but the effects of these activities must be indirectly processed through the nervous system before they emerge as behavior. The heart, by the way, is a special kind of tissue called "cardiac" muscle, but this does not alter its indirect function in behavior.

The "antagonistic" action of the visceral organs has already been described in connection with the autonomic nervous system divisions. Skeletal muscles, too, work in opposition to each other. Muscles are arranged in pairs which oppose each other. When one contracts, the antagonist relaxes, and vice versa. It is possible to tense or relax both members of a pair, but the characteristic action is a co-operative one where one muscle bunches up and its opponent stretches out. The important fact to observe about muscle action is that the body works pretty much as a co-ordinated whole, except in some kinds of "conflict" situations. We sometimes overlook this basic fact when we talk about a finger flexing as if nothing else were happening, but it should be immediately obvious that at any moment other muscles are busy supporting the head and the body and that a tremendous amount of co-ordination must be arranged for by the nervous system if we are to do anything even as simple as sitting down. The co-ordination of the body is learned slowly through the infant years as the child slowly matures (and learns, in part) to keep its head up, then sit, then stand, and finally walk and run. Many parts of the nervous system are active and much sensory stimulation is present at any moment. One of the parts of the central nervous system we have ignored up to now, the cerebellum (a large division below the hemispheres of the brain and in back of the medulla), is alleged to be largely concerned with balance and co-ordination of bodily movement.

The muscle fibers are supplied with sensory receptors, as we already have learned, and these play an extremely important part in co-ordinated movements as well as in behavior generally. If the sensory cells in the spinal cord leading from the leg muscles are destroyed as by the spirochete of syphilis, the individual cannot walk without watching his legs, and in effect, guiding them visually. So long as these receptors are performing their function we can walk along, swinging our arms, as a matter of course. Each muscle, when it contracts, initiates such self-generated stimulation, the movement-produced stimulation which Guthrie emphasizes. These stimuli, of course, initiate their own reflex reactions and fit into phase sequences which make serial behavior possible. The important feature of muscular action is its totality, its co-ordination. We should think of the muscles as forming a system, and not be misled into fragmentizing this system into individual units. We might miss what is going on, just as we do when we follow the right hand of the stage magician while his left hand is putting the rabbit into the hat.

Glands

The muscles, taken all together, are described as "effectors." They produce the effects in which we are interested. They operate on the environment and modify it. The glands are another important group of effectors. These, as already mentioned, are two types, duct and ductless (endocrine). We will not attempt to enumerate all of the body's glands but can point out that they too form a system. We are concerned primarily, in this connection, with the endocrine glands which secrete their products into the blood stream and thereby affect each other as well as the nervous system as a whole and at the same time differentially affect various internal organs. The various glands have their individual roles to play in the process of growth, reproduction, nutrition, and general activity. An underfunctioning (hypo) thyroid gland will result in a slowing down of bodily metabolism with many subsequent degenerative effects. The overactive (hyper) thyroid will speed up the body's metabolism and have its own side effects in terms of "nervousness," excitability, and so on. The adrenal glands we have already mentioned as the releasers of energy via the sugar in the liver. Each gland has its job to do and cannot do its own work without the others being affected. So long as everything proceeds normally, the glands are of little interest to the psychologist. Malfunctioning of any kind immediately alters various body balances and changes the action of the brain with resultant influences on behavior. Such changes in behavior are frequently attributed to nastiness, just plain orneriness, or to learning experiences which may have nothing to do with the case. We cannot be excused from taking the glands into account as important determiners of neural activity and consequently behavior. At the same time, not much is known about the behavioral effects of glandular secretions and we can, for the moment, hope for their normal functioning while we try to discuss normal behavior. Later on we will have to take some special gland functions into additional consideration. The endocrine glands must then be viewed as a system with each gland interacting with the others. The responses of the duct glands, like crying and salivating, must also be reckoned with as effectors. The power of tears in our culture is of the highest order of behavioral controls. The tear glands are really effective effectors. The secretions of the duct glands also have their stimulus functions. These are sometimes ignored unfortunately when their importance should never be overlooked. The presence of saliva in the mouth of our puppy or our grandmother is an effective stimulus for a number of possible response patterns. (See Williams, 1958.)

With this brief discussion of glands and muscles we can bring to a close our consideration of man's basic equipment for behavior. We find him possessed of a number of systems neatly organized for what might be called "behavior as a whole." We find the muscles dependent upon sensory stimulation and sensory stimulation dependent upon the muscles. Similarly, the nervous system is dependent upon both and supervisory of both. Integration appears to be the keyword in our appreciation of this basic equipment. If we can maintain this appreciation we can now embark on the study of behavior expecting to find it also integrated and not readily subject to segmentation.

CHAPTER 6

Psychometrics—The Problem of Measurement

Intelligence as an intervening variable · The problem of measurement · Trans-situational traits · The nature of tests · The construction of tests · How good are intelligence tests? · The reliability of tests · Coefficients of correlation · Procedures for determining the reliability of tests · Validity of tests · Standardization of tests · The nature of intelligence · The constancy of the IQ · Intelligence—general or specific? · Human engineering

In our review of the basic equipment of organisms we touched on sensory equipment, neural mechanisms, and effectors. Earlier we considered the role of heredity, and in the next chapter we will consider how the basic equipment is modified and used in the process of interacting with the environment. Before we get involved with the complex problems of learning, however, we must pause once more to view the organism again as a whole, as a member of a species, but a unique, individual member, one that changes in the process of growth and development, one that differs from every other member of the species in manifold ways. We are facing the question of, given the basic equipment what can be expected of a given individual? What can the organism do?

In our study of sensory structures and motor equipment we thought of the nervous system as a mediator between the inputs and outputs. It is now necessary to examine this mediator in more psychological and behavioral terms. In Chapter 2 we discussed the nature of hypothetical constructs and intervening variables. These, too, we described as mediators. We can now begin to make a rapprochement between the neural mediating mechanisms and mechanisms that have usually been treated from more mentalistic or behavioral viewpoints.

Given standard equipment, for example, eyes and ears, nervous connections, and fingers, do we need to postulate any other mechanisms, entities, or processes to account for performance or behavior? Does the mathematician possess, in addition to his physical equipment, anything else? Does he have a gift for handling numbers, for logical reasoning?

Does the novelist have some special capacity for using language, a "gift of gab"? Are some people just naturally smarter than others? Do some people have more intelligence than others? Finer memories? In short, are there special capacities or abilities that must be postulated as somehow possessed by, or characterizing, individuals in different amounts if we are to understand behavior more effectively than can be done by strict preoccupation with physical structures?

In addition to the abilities, capacities, or skills that might be thought of as important, are there other characteristics, features, or mechanisms that must also be taken into account in order to explain otherwise mysterious behavior? Are some people just naturally lazy, energetic, stupid, excitable, timid, aggressive, and so on, and do these "personality traits" somehow determine performance? Or, does performance determine the use of such trait names? The brightest college students do not always earn high grades. Inventors commonly assert that their success is due to "one-tenth inspiration, nine-tenths perspiration." If aptitudes and attitudes determine performance they must be taken into consideration. But how do we proceed to take them into account? How do we evaluate the role of intelligence, for example, in any behavioral sequence?

In this chapter we will consider the general problem of aptitude or "intelligence" and leave the question of other characteristics or traits for later (Chapter 14). The same general theoretical considerations apply to any attempts to measure characteristics of organisms, but the problem of measurement of aptitude involves the nature of tests, i.e., instruments which can be thought of as having definite right or wrong answers. Other traits are measured with instruments that do not necessarily have correct answers. Such devices (questionnaires, inventories, rating scales, "projective" tests) can be appreciated better in their own context. Any attempt to measure aspects of behavior or personality can be thought of as "psychometrics." While this is a general term for any psychological measurement operation it is normally restricted to more or less formal attempts to measure capacities or aptitudes.

Intelligence as an intervening variable

Unfortunately intelligence cannot be observed directly. It may be what we earlier called an "intervening variable." If aptitudes and/or attitudes are to be considered as intervening variables, we must talk about such constructs only in terms of inferences we make from observations of responses made to stimuli. If our inferences are to have any merit, the observations we make must be reasonably clear-cut, objective, repeatable, and communicable, in short, operational. Our first inferences will more or less inevitably be based on hunches, casual or inadequate observation, or at least limited observation. As we become more and more concerned with any particular intervening variable, we must refine our observations and probably, inevitably, circumscribe our inferences. Thus, when we see two children perform differently in some situation, as in school, we look for some difference in the children. Generally, and again perhaps unwisely, we try to explain the difference in the behavior by an assumed difference in the nature or equipment of the children. Because of a long history of animistic thinking, we easily attribute to the children some characteristic or feature such as intelligence or stupidity or laziness and are satisfied as now having explained the difference. When one child remembers something another has forgotten, we readily explain the difference by assuming that one has a better memory than the other. It is, of course, clear to the critical observer that we have explained no more than the physician in Molière's *Le Malade Imaginaire* who explained the effectiveness of a sleeping potion by pointing out that it contained a soporific substance.

THE PROBLEM OF MEASUREMENT

In attacking the nature of such intervening variables, psychologists have turned their attention to the possibilities of measurement as a first step in the scientific analysis of these assumed mechanisms or relationships. As psychological and statistical sophistication developed, the kinds of measurements became more and more complex without the riddle of the reality of the mechanisms themselves having been solved. But the activities of psychologists in the development of the measurements have led to the accumulation of many facts, much practical information, and a great deal of theoretical speculation which will eventually find its place in the psychology of the future.

Trans-situational traits

The basic difficulty in attacking an intervening variable arises from the presumption of its relative generality and independence of time and circumstances. Thus an assumption of intelligence involves some notions or concepts about its playing a role in more than one situation and existing over a period of time, perhaps from birth to death. It is "trans-situational" (see Spiker and McCandless, 1954). Proud parents look for signs of intelligence in their newborn offspring and as the child grows they expect to observe intelligence working in this situation and that as a general supervisory mechanism that somehow controls behavior. Similarly with any personality trait: "He was born with the gift of laughter" and he is expected to be cheerful throughout his life history in all sorts of circumstances. If an aptitude, indeed, possesses such generality, then it appears logical to observe the individual in some sample of his behavior where the variable is presumed to operate and generalize from this sample to the variable as a whole. Thus, to determine something about the nature of intelligence, we would examine a sample of "intelligent" behavior and try to derive some logical conclusions about the nature of intelligence from our observation. Placing an individual in a situation that calls for intelligent behavior would then amount to putting the person to a test. A test is a sample of something more general, larger, or broader. It is, of course, obvious that if the chosen sample is inadequate or deficient in some regard, then the conclusions drawn from the observation are going to be limited or incomplete or inadequate. Because one sample might be unique or unrepresentative it is clear that somewhat more than one sample might lead to more substantial conclusions.

THE NATURE OF TESTS

Anyone who can read is already familiar with tests. Our newspapers and popular magazines are cluttered with so-called tests. Are you a good husband? Are you a proper wife? Do you have a good personality? Answer the questions supplied by the imaginative author and earn a score. School children's lives are one test after another. We are all familiar with tests for cancer or tuberculosis, "physical examinations," driver's tests, occupational tests, and blindfold cigarette tests. Whatever else the test might be it is an occasion when the tester looks over the subject, or asks him questions to answer, or assigns tasks to be done. Each answer or task is then evaluated by the tester, frequently the items are totaled, and a score is assigned. Commonly, some standard or criterion is adopted, as, for example, 75 per cent, and the subject is told that he has passed or failed. As suggested earlier, the term "test" is often misused. It should apply to situations where there is an established "correct" answer or response which no one can give without having some required skill or knowledge. One should not be able to lie himself into a good score, nor should a rater's judgment be accepted as necessarily correct.

Considering any kind of test at all, a number of questions might occur to the curious student. On what basis were the questions or tasks chosen? In some cases the answer might seem obvious. If you want to know if a person can multiply, you ask him to multiply some numbers. In this case all that is being done is to sample the actual behavior in question. In other cases a person might be asked to sit in some "simulator," for example, a device that more or less resembles the front seat of an automobile or airplane and be asked to respond to various lights and sounds. He might then be told that he will make a good operator or a poor one. Here the resemblance between the task and the ability presumably under test is not quite so apparent. The physician might ask for a urine sample in order to diagnose a possible case of diabetes. The patient willingly complies, assuming that something that is somehow done to the urine will have some bearing on whether he has diabetes. In the case of the diabetes test, the patient is quite sure that "the doctor knows what he is doing." Does the psychologist who administers a personality test or a test of musical talent, or an intelligence test know what he is doing? How do you determine whether a test, even a multiplication test, has anything to do with some assumed ability?

To determine whether a test is any good we have to examine the nature of tests more closely. We also have to examine what we mean by the expression "any good or not" more closely. We can start by learning how tests are made, the assumptions that are involved, and what the limitations of tests are. As a general sample of test construction techniques let us consider how the most famous intelligence test was created.

The construction of tests

In 1904 Alfred Binet (see Garrett, 1930) was asked by the French government to see what could be done about separating lazy children from retarded or backward children in the schools. When Binet took on the task of measuring the intelligence of French children he began by recognizing, as many observers before him had, that children differ in their performances in many different kinds of tasks that by tradition might be considered "intellectual." In schoolwork children earn different grades; some children are very slow in getting their lessons, others are able to advance rapidly and give teachers no trouble. Some children are completely unsuited for schoolwork and must remain at home or be kept in institutions where they might live for a long time without ever learning to dress or feed themselves, without ever learning to read, or do as much for themselves as an animal might. Still other children surprise adults by their unusual and adult-like performances. Binet also recognized that one could not depend upon the opinions of parents or teachers about the performance level that a given child might achieve. A child might do effective work for one teacher or under some conditions and not under others. To account for the differences in performance Binet assumed that underlying such differences there must be some basic, possibly innate, structure or "equipment" of some kind which might be called "intelligence" or intellectual ability. The intimate nature of this ability was never described but the concept was an old one in the history of man, corresponding to the anciently assumed faculty of "intellect."

To get at or measure this intellect directly seemed impossible, but indirect methods might succeed. Binet embarked upon such indirect methods.

It should be noted at this time that Binet was working in terms of what we called earlier a "hypothetical construct," that is some real mechanism or process. He was not obliged to do so, however, and could have worked in terms of a mathematical relationship type of intervening variable; that is, he might have thought about expressing the relationship between problem situations and the relative efficiency of solutions in terms of some mathematical function, a function that was itself related to some other kinds of measure, e.g., age, efficiency, or school grades. Binet stuck with the tradition, however, and most of us today still think in terms of people having some amount of some *thing* called "intelligence."

We come now to another assumption. Because most or "average" children progress at about the same rate through the school system, one might judge that the majority of children have about the same amount of intelligence; some more, some less, some a great deal more, some a great deal less. Therefore, it might be possible to construct more or less standard tests by observing what the average child can do and accepting this as a standard performance. Another consideration must now be taken. We have been talking as if all children are of the same age, an obvious absurdity. We recognize that older children can handle situations that are apparently more difficult than younger children can cope with. Our tests, therefore, must take age into account. From these considerations it follows that tests must be designed so that the average child of each age will be able to handle the situation. Here we have another assumption: intelligence grows with age, and apparently, on the average, a constant amount is added with each passing year. Each child gets brighter every year, but every other child gains in proportion, and the net effect is an average gain for the population as a whole.

Children above average should be able to do better and children below average should do less well. This would be indicated by some children being able to handle problems above their age-grade, while below-average children could function only at some point below their age level. The only remaining problem then, is to define the average child. Here Binet resorted to psychophysical practices in defining thresholds. It will be recalled that a threshold can be determined in various ways, that it could be defined as a point (or range) at which an observer might report some phenomenon as often as he failed to report it. This would be a 50–50 point. The choice of such a point is purely arbitrary; in the 50–50 case it would represent the point at which chance is operating. Any stimulation intensity below this point should be reported less often than chance; any above would be reported more often than chance. It appeared to some psychophysicists that a meaningful value might be defined as some half-way point between chance and certainty. A 75 per cent point, for example, would represent such a value. The subject's threshold would then be stated to be the value at which he could judge something accurately, or report the presence of something, 75 per cent of the time. Such a point has no absolute meaning, but is an arbitrary convenience.

Binet and his collaborator, Simon, adopted the 75 per cent value as a suitable average for the selection of his test items. If 60 to 90 per cent of the children of a given age could correctly respond to an item, that item was considered suitable for that age level. Most children of a given age would pass all of the questions asked of that age group. They would then be considered normal, or in other words, they might be thought of as living up to the expected level of their age. Such a procedure almost automatically invited the development of a concept of "mental age." A child of five who was normal for his age in terms of passing all of the questions suitable for his age was considered to have grown or matured intellectually to the five-year level, or have a mental age of five. The description of intellectual strength in terms of mental age led to the practice of scoring answers in terms of mental-age units. If a test had six items, each item might be worth two months. Passing all the six items would result in earning a year's mental age.

Because some children would attain mental-age scores below their chronological age while others would pass items on scales designed for older children, it was always necessary to mention both chronological age and mental age in considering a test score. Thus an eight-year-old child who scored at the twelve-year level would be superior while a fourteen-year-old who scored at the twelve-year level would be subnormal, even though both had the same mental age. It was not until about 1914 that Stern (see Freeman, 1934) hit upon the convenient device of dividing the mental age by the chronological age and multiplying by 100 to develop an Intelligence Quotient or IQ. The term "Intelligence Quotient" was invented by Terman who revised the original Binet tests and standardized the revisions for use with American children.

The student is cautioned to appreciate that an IQ is not anything but the result of the division of one number by another. It expresses a relationship between these two numbers, each of which in turn derives from a measurement operation. There is no excess meaning here. Only a mathematical relationship is involved. The IQ is a good example of an intervening variable. For a given child it expresses a relationship between two measures. Each of these measures, of course, must be accurate if the relationship is to be meaningful. Any error in the original measures will be reflected in the IQ.

It has already been indicated that the Binet test was so constructed that about 10 to 40 per cent of the children of a given age group would fail one or more items. It is possible, of course, to fail more than one and we can expect that smaller and smaller percentages of children would fail more and more items until we find some children who cannot pass any items for their particular age level. Such children would then be tested for the age items just below their chronological age. If they failed these also, one could go down as low as necessary and establish the mental age, if any, of even the poorest possible performers. Because of the nature of the items, children below the age of three could not be tested. (While there have been many attempts to develop tests for infants, these have not met with notable success if we judge them as predictors of later intelligence test scores.) A child that failed to pass items well below his age would then be considered subnormal; if he did very poorly one might label him retarded, backward, feeble-minded, or with some more technical label such as moron (IQ between 50 and 70), imbecile (25 to 50), or idiot (IQ below 25).

Similarly if children could pass items above their age level they would gain mental months and their IQ's would rise above 100 as far as their mental age gains would take them. Unfortunately Binet was unable to invent suitable items for children above the age of fifteen. A top limit, then, was set as far as IQ is concerned. A seven-year-old child who passed all the fourteen-year items would have an IQ of 200, but with each succeeding year his IQ would drop as an arbitrary function of dividing a fixed amount by increasing age. In the Terman revisions (known as the Stanford Revisions of the Binet-Simon test) new scales were added for the Average Adult and the Superior Adult (three scales). These scales use a basic age of fifteen for IQ calculations. Most testers are very cautious about interpreting scores earned by older children (above twelve) and adults. It should be apparent from this practical decision to use age fifteen as a terminal age that there is an assumption involved underlying such a decision, namely, that intelligence stops growing at this age. There have been many attempts to test this assumption or to determine whether there is a true stopping point to mental growth with no final answer. Most measurements of skill, strength, endurance, and efficiency appear to reach a peak sometime about the age of twenty-five after which they show declines (Wechsler, 1942).

While there are many kinds of intelligence tests for adults (the military services, for example, use a "General Classification Test" and high schools and colleges use a variety of "aptitude tests") these are not scored in terms of IQ, although sometimes such test scores are "converted" into IQ equivalents. Because the IQ is directly measured only with certain tests, like the Binet-Simon, it is improper to refer to intelligence tests in general as IQ tests.

The number of children who exceed 100 in IQ becomes progressively smaller just as is true of the number of children who earn lower and lower scores so that if a graph is made of a large population of children, we will find a bell-shaped curve of distribution of IQ scores with very few children who might be described as retarded (below 70 we would have about 2 to 3 per cent) and very few who might be called very superior (above 130 we again find about 2 to 3 per cent) (Jordan, 1933). (See Fig. 10.) Such a distribution is commonly found whenever any natural or chance phenomena are measured, for example, height and weight, number of tomatoes per acre, number of heads in 1,000 tosses of 100 coins, and all kinds of psychological and physiological measurements. The bell-shaped curve is called a "curve of normal probability." Because

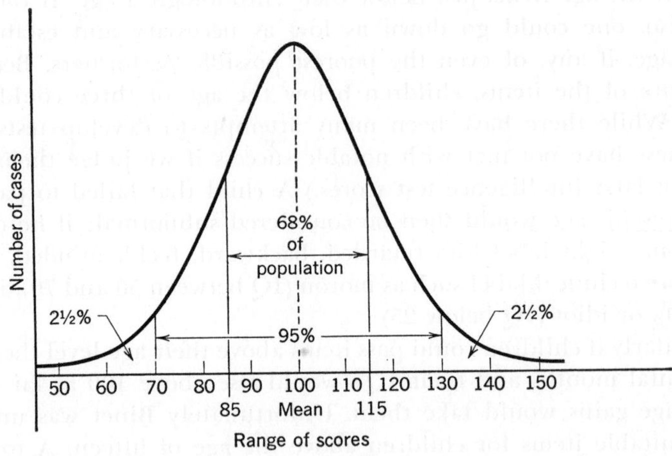

Figure 10 A normal distribution. The mean or average is shown in the middle of the distribution. Half of the cases are at or above the mean and half at or below the mean. In such a distribution the probable percentage of cases at any point can be readily determined by consulting probability tables in statistics texts. Scores on intelligence tests might follow such a distribution with a mean IQ of 100. About 2/3 of the population (the middle 68% of the cases) would be found between IQ's of 85 and 115. IQ's of 90 to 110 would be considered "normal." About 2 1/2% of the population would score below 70 and the same per cent above 130.

IQ's follow this distribution pattern it might appear that intelligence is randomly distributed in the population as a consequence of a large number of unknown (chance) factors. With the average IQ measured at 100, the student might wonder about the absolute amount of intelligence the nation enjoys. Just how smart is the average man? We frequently read that Hollywood producers and television moguls create their offerings for a mental age of twelve. How much ability does this represent? Probably not enough to complete a legitimate high-school program, and certainly not enough to complete college. The student should recognize, however, that an average twelve-year-old can learn a great deal and that experience can substitute for ability in many situations. He should also recognize that IQ's are relative measures, not absolute ones and that tests are so constructed that the average IQ will remain 100 no matter how "intelligent" the population might be or become. Even a nation of geniuses would earn an average IQ of 100 if testers had their way. It is an arbitrary figure determined by convenience.

How good are intelligence tests?

In developing the intelligence test did Binet stumble upon a magical technique for measuring something that has always appeared to be a mysterious faculty? When a psychologist administers a test with what confidence can he then advise the parents about a child? One thing he should not do is tell the parents the IQ. Most parents are not prepared to appreciate the tenuous nature of such numbers and more harm than good is accomplished. On the positive side, his advice is only as good as his test and the value of this remains to be discovered. When we begin to question the value of tests what kinds of questions would be most pertinent? We would certainly want to know if the test really measures "intelligence." Or, we might ask the question in another way, "How do you know the test really measures intelligence?" The moment we ask this question we should recognize that it carries the assumption that there really is such a thing as intelligence, or that we ourselves know what it means, or that there is some difference of opinion on the subject.

But even before we try to answer this question of truth or "validity," we should ask a prior question. Regardless of what the tester might say he is measuring, we should be interested in his measuring device itself. Does it really test anything? Does it measure accurately, does it measure dependably, or is it like a rubber ruler? When we measure a room or table for length we commonly measure it twice or even more often to make sure. What would happen if we gave the intelligence test again? Would we get the same score? If we do not get the same score, we might begin to question the value of the test on that ground alone. A test must be dependable, whatever else it might be claimed to be. Such dependability is called, in statistical language, reliability.

The reliability of tests

What does happen if we give a test over again? Commonly enough the scores improve. There is some "practice effect." People remember the answers they gave the first time and this perhaps saves time for other items previously missed, or permits them to try out some other answer if for some reason they now think of alternatives. But if we wait a month or so most of these immediate effects may vanish. What can we expect to happen if we do wait for some period and then repeat a test? Should we expect to get exactly the same measure as before? Perhaps we should allow for some possible errors of measurement; most testers are willing to consider plus or minus five points in an IQ measurement as normal variability to begin with. On a repetition of the test it is possible that a previous plus five is replaced by a minus five and the subject now earns an IQ of ten points less, all due to normal variability from unknown causes.

Allowing for normal variability from errors of measurement, do tests "stand up," that is, do you get about the same score as before? The question is still too rigorous for the field of intelligence testing. For individual cases almost anything might happen, but taking whole groups of subjects, what would we find? Being reasonably loose or generous in our views we should not expect to find identical scores but we might have a right to expect that those who were bright on the first occasion not become dull on the second, and vice versa. We would or might expect the people tested to maintain their relative standings. If A is brighter than B, then all things considered, he should remain brighter the second time around. In effect, this is how reliability is measured. But, note that our expectancies involve an assumption about the nature of "intelligence," an assumption that it is a relatively permanent thing, quantity, or relationship, that it is, in short, constant, at least within limits. We do not assume intelligence to vary at random. It is not "here today and gone tomorrow." We shall examine this constancy of the IQ a little later.

When the reliability of a test is measured, individuals are ranked on the first performance from low to high and their ranks on the first performance are compared with the ranks earned on the second. If the ranks are maintained without any change, it is concluded that the test is a reliable one. If the ranks vary a great deal, the test is considered unreliable. These rather general remarks can be given a more mathematical expression by calculating the actual rank differences and evaluating them by various statistical operations which result in numbers indicating the degree of relationships of such rank positions. Such members are called "coefficients of correlation."

COEFFICIENTS OF CORRELATION

To appreciate the nature of coefficients of correlation we can consider the examples in Table 1. Here we have worked out four sample correlations with only five subjects involved to simplify the presentation. Actually such calculations are quite meaningless and would not be performed with so few cases (for this particular technique statisticians would advise at least twelve cases). It should also be noted that this is a very simple technique, known as the Rank Difference method, and other techniques used with much larger numbers of cases are generally preferred. In all of the examples in the table, the scores are converted into two sets of ranks (I and II) representing the order, from high to low of the original raw scores. Once the scores are converted into rank positions, we ignore the actual scores and work only with the ranks. Rank I represents the scores earned by the subjects on the first test, ranked from high to low, and Rank II represents the scores earned on the second test when these are arranged according to the appropriate ranks they represent. Once the scores are ranked the ranks are examined for any Difference (D). Such differences (RI—RII) are squared (to get rid of the minus signs that might be found if a subject ranks higher on the second test than on the first). The squared differences (D^2) are then added together and substituted in the formula

$$R = 1 - \frac{6 \text{ (Sum of } D^2)}{N\,(N^2 - 1)}$$

The sum of the squared differences is then multiplied by a constant of 6 and the total is divided by a factor which takes into account the number of cases. Note that if the number of cases is large, the quotient resulting from the division will be relatively small and vice versa. The quotient is then subtracted from 1. The highest possible value a coefficient of correlation can attain is 1.0. Observe that in order for this to happen it is necessary that the total value to be subtracted must equal zero and this can happen only if there are no differences in the ranks. If the total to be subtracted is greater than zero then the correlation coefficient must automatically be less than 1.0. It is impossible for this total to be greater than 2. Should the total actually amount to 2, the subtraction would result in − 1.0, a perfect negative correlation. A negative correlation coefficient indicates a reversal of ranks. Those who were high on one test are low on the other and vice versa.

Table 1 Sample Rank Difference correlations

Perfect Positive				*High Positive*				*Perfect Negative*				*Zero Level*			
Rank I	Rank II	D	D^2	Rank I	Rank II	D	D^2	Rank I	Rank II	D	D^2	Rank I	Rank II	D	D^2
1	1	0	0	1	2	−1	1	1	5	−4	16	1	4	−3	9
2	2	0	0	2	1	1	1	2	4	−2	4	2	1	1	1
3	3	0	0	3	4	−1	1	3	3	0	0	3	3	0	0
4	4	0	0	4	5	−1	1	4	2	2	4	4	5	−1	1
5	5	0	0	5	3	2	4	5	1	4	16	5	2	3	9
Sum of D^2			0				8				40				20

$$R = 1 - \frac{6\,\Sigma D^2}{N\,(N^2 - 1)}$$

Perfect Positive	High Positive	Perfect Negative	Zero Level
$R = 1 - \frac{6\,(0)}{5\,(25 - 1)}$	$R = 1 - \frac{6\,(8)}{5\,(25 - 1)}$	$R = 1 - \frac{6\,(40)}{5\,(25 - 1)}$	$R = 1 - \frac{6\,(20)}{5\,(25 - 1)}$
$R = 1 - \frac{0}{120}$	$R = 1 - \frac{48}{120}$	$R = 1 - \frac{240}{120}$	$R = 1 - \frac{120}{120}$
$R = 1 - 0$	$R = 1 - 0.4$	$R = 1 - 2$	$R = 1 - 1$
$R = 1.0$	$R = 0.6$	$R = -1.0$	$R = 0$

How can we interpret the coefficients appearing in Table 1? The perfect positive and perfect negative correlations are easy to understand. They mean simply that if we know a person's rank on one test we can predict perfectly his rank on the next text. In practice, such coefficients are never found. In the case of the negative correlation we have to reverse our thinking 180 degrees but we are still able to predict perfectly. In physics the pressure-volume relationship for gases would show a perfect negative correlation if all other sources of error were eliminated. In the case of zero correlation we are still able to say something, namely, that there is no possibility of predicting anything better than chance. Some people who were high become low and some stay high with no way of discovering who will do what. The troublesome case is the high positive correlation, or indeed any correlation between zero and 1. What does such a correlation coefficient mean? Students commonly jump to some percentage implication of correlations, that 0.6, for example, means that you can predict 60 per cent of the cases or that 60 per cent of Rank II is somehow related to Rank I with the rest scattered or some other interpretation. Actually the value of correlations for prediction purposes has been calculated by Hull in terms of an efficiency score (E) where E is defined as the extent to which a test reduces the error of prediction made in terms of a correlation (see Shlien, 1959). Hull's efficiency formula runs as follows: $E = 1 - \sqrt{1 - r^2}$.

It can be appreciated (and see Table 2) that if the correlation is perfect, then prediction of any individual's position will be perfect, but if the correlation is less than that, and it always is in human measurements, then prediction will suffer and it will suffer as a function of the square of the correlation coefficient, not simply of its size. This means, in effect, that prediction is radically and drastically impaired if the correlation drops at all from 1.00. A correlation of 0.4 or 0.5, which is not infrequent, in correlating psychological measures means that there is only an 8 per cent and 13 per cent improvement over chance guessing in the prediction of positions. With such a correlation, say of 0.5, we would be able to guess the rank of about 13 people out of a 100 (in addition to any guessed by chance) with complete accuracy if we predicted the same rank as they held before; the other 87 individuals we might expect to be normally distributed about the guessed rank with any particular individual being found any place along the line of ranks. Table 2 shows the *E* values of a range of correlation coefficients and points to the relatively low usefulness of the correlations below 0.98, which includes the vast majority of correlations reported in psychological literature. In his highly critical article, Shlien cautions against too ready acceptance of tests which show correlations around 0.5 against other criteria.

Table 2 Relation of correlation coefficient (r) to per cent of forecasting efficiency (E) from Hull's formula

$$E = 1 - \sqrt{1 - r^2}$$

r	E
.10	1/2%
.20	2%
.30	5%
.40	8%
.50	13%
.60	20%
.70	29%
.80	40%
.90	56%
.95	69%
.98	80%
1.00	100%

The meaning of a correlation coefficient can be made somewhat clearer if we recognize that so long as there is any correlation at all between two tests or other measures, our chances of guessing the probable rank an individual would earn on one test is improved over what we might guess by chance. If the individual actually scored at an average value on one test, we would do best, if sheerly guessing, to estimate that he would score an average mark on the second. If he scored high on one test, we would expect him to score high on the second and, similarly, if he scored low on the first test we would expect a low score on the second. All these expectancies are based on the assumption that there is some correlation between the two measures. The higher the correlation the more likely we are to be right. However, the statement that we expect the person to score high on the second test because of a high score on the first must be carefully modified. He could (unless the correlation is perfect) actually earn any grade at all. We are talking about probabilities. By taking advantage of normal probability tables, it is possible to calculate the probabilities that any particular score will be earned on the second test if we know the score on the first. To do this we must first transcribe the scores into some kind of comparative or relative ranks. In Table 3 we have translated two tests (*x* and *y*) into decile scores (10 per cent divisions) and have tabulated the probabilities that we would obtain if there were a correlation coefficient of 0.6 between the two tests. To read the table pick some decile rank for the *y* test, say that of 8. A person earning such a score on Test *y* equals or surpasses 70 per cent of the population taking the test. What will he be likely to score on Test *x*? Reading across the table we see that he could score at any decile from the first to the tenth. But his chances of scoring at higher deciles are much stronger than of scoring at low deciles. He has only two chances in 100 of scoring in the first decile and 15 out of 100 of scoring in the top 10 per cent. He has 72 chances out of 100 of scoring in the upper half of the population on Test *x*. If we consider a person in the lowest decile on Test *y* we can be certain that he will not score in the top of the population on Test *x* and that there are 87 chances out of 100 that he will score in the bottom half.

We should be careful to note that the table shows the probabilities that would obtain for cases in which the correlation was 0.6. With a higher correlation the probabilities would conform more and more to fitting the rule that a high score on one test would be matched with a high score on the other. We should recall the values of Table 2, however, and not expect too much in the way of prediction precision unless the correlation is close to 0.9. With correlations lower than 0.6 there would be more uniformity to the numbers in each cell in the table so that as one approaches a zero correlation, all the numbers in all the cells would be the same, namely 10.

There is still another way of looking at the correlation coefficient. Suppose that we found that with some special test of intelligence, we had a correlation of 0.6 with success in a course in mathematics or some other subject. In accepting students for such a course we would want to select only those who had some likelihood of success. If we measured success by scores on the *x* test at the 65 per cent level, we can see that only 6 students out of 100 scoring at the lowest decile on test *y* could succeed and 94 would fail. It would appear unwise to sacrifice 94 for the 6 that might succeed. If we excluded all those at the second decile as well, we would be excluding 13 more who might pass out of an additional 100. If the class population were limited and we wanted to take only those who had some 50–50 chance of passing, we would have to exclude everyone scoring below the seventh decile on test *y*. Even at this level, taking only those who score in the top 30 per cent, we will still have a 50 per cent failure record. If we selected only the top 10 per cent there would be about a 30 per cent failure. Of course, if we set the passing score lower, we could have a greater measure of success. The student is cautioned to remember that our selection has been based on a correlation of 0.6. There are a few correlations that run that high between tests and other measures of success.

Table 3 * Percentage of distribution in deciles on measure *y* for various deciles of measures of *x*

y	*x*-Decile rank represented by midpoints									
Decile	.05	.15	.25	.35	.45	.55	.65	.75	.85	.95
10	0	1	2	3	4	7	10	14	20	36
9	1	2	4	6	9	10	12	15	19	21
8	2	5	6	8	10	12	14	15	16	15
7	3	6	9	10	11	12	13	14	13	10
6	5	8	10	12	12	13	12	11	10	7
5	7	10	11	12	13	12	12	10	8	5
4	10	13	14	13	12	11	10	9	6	3
3	15	16	15	14	12	10	8	6	5	2
2	21	19	15	12	10	9	6	4	2	1
1	36	20	14	10	7	4	3	2	1	0

* The author is indebted to Dr. Kenneth H. Kurtz for computing the values in the table. Similar values for different levels of correlation can be computed from tables published by Peters and Van Voorhis (1940).

If the student has scrutinized Table 3 carefully and has made the proper allowances for higher and lower correlations, we can assume that he now knows how to interpret a correlation coefficient when he sees one.

PROCEDURES FOR DETERMINING THE RELIABILITY OF TESTS

With the concept of correlation now available, we can return to the question of reliability. If repeated measures correlate below 0.9 most test users will regard a test as unreliable. While this may seem a rugged criterion to achieve, it actually is not too difficult to attain if the test-maker is willing to keep changing his test, eliminating items and replacing them with more suitable ones. It is largely a matter of labor. A reliable test can be developed by persistent replacement of items that make for unreliability, items that are too easy or too difficult or too ambiguous or where the scoring is difficult. Sometimes it is inconvenient to repeat a test and reliability can be measured by comparing one half of a test with the other half (the so-called "split-half" method). This procedure is based on the assumption that a test should be reliable all the way through, not only as a whole, i.e., it should be "internally consistent," and if the test is a long one, say 200 true-or-false items, partial scores can be obtained by scoring odd-numbered items and comparing this total with the score obtained on even-items. If a test is too short to split up in this fashion or if other considerations make it unsuitable to split into two parts, it is possible to make a "duplicate form" of a test, asking very similar questions or calling for the same kinds of operations on both forms. The two different tests can then be compared for reliability as if the same test were taken twice.

We have treated reliability as if it were specifically of interest only to testmakers and users. Actually any measurement that is used in any aspect of science must be proved reliable as the first step in any investigation. If the measuring tool is unreliable, there is no point in going on. We might as well measure by guessing or sampling opinion as to use an unreliable test. We will have occasion later to question the reliability of various kinds of tests or tools designed to measure some other aspects of behavior or of individuals. Such things as inventories, questionnaires, rating scales, and a variety of diagnostic devices that are frequently called tests must also be shown to have a respectable reliability or the student has the right to refuse to consider the alleged findings. It should be of some concern to the student that the average teacher blithely proceeds to make out tests for various subjects without ever calculating the reliability of the tests. In fact, it is possible that a student has never taken a test of known reliability in any course from kindergarten through graduate school. (Standardized tests of intelligence or achievement are not subject to this criticism.)

Validity of tests

We return now to the question of validity. Do the tests measure what they are supposed to measure? Does the state examiner for driving licenses actually evaluate driving skill or aptitude? Does an intelligence test measure intelligence? Does a musical-talent test measure musical talent? The only way to answer such questions is to compare the test results with some other indicant or measure or information about the relative worth of the individual in driving skill, intelligence or musical talent, and so on. If such measures are available, there is no problem. One simply correlates test scores against the criterion, and if the correlation is high (above 0.9 would appear suitable), the test is measuring what it is supposed to measure. But such independent criteria are difficult to discover. We have already hinted at this in connection with intelligence. How do we know how intelligent a person is without giving him a test? Yet this is what we must know if we are to find out if the test is any good at all. What other signs of intelligence can we use? Bank account? School grades? Height of forehead? Ability to succeed? In what, when, where? Nothing has yet been suggested as a suitable independent measure of intelligence with the paradoxical situation arising that new tests are correlated with old ones, and if the correlation is high, some modest claim is made for validity. No matter what intelligence test scores are correlated with, the coefficients fall short of a desirable strength. If you consider that learning ability should be correlated with intelligence you might be somewhat dismayed to find that the correlations reported for college students learning nonsense material are in the region of 0 to 0.02. Correlations with school grades run about 0.3 or 0.4. The student should not jump to the opposite conclusion, of course, that "intelligence" has nothing to do with learning ability. It may be that other factors are also important, e.g., motivation, study habits, and previous history. Furthermore, college students are a highly selected group compared to a general population. Perhaps they do not differ much in learning ability or in intelligence. To get a high correlation coefficient, there must be a broad spread of scores. When the scores on two tests are bunched together, the correlation will automatically be reduced. When a broader range of subjects is tested, correlation coefficients between tests and rote learning or memory span are somewhat higher, about 0.4. There are, however, few strong (0.7 to 0.9) correlates of intelligence test scores. Very little if anything positive can be said about their direct relationship to anything. There are "reasonable" coefficients found between IQ and parents' scores, socioeconomic status, and a variety of other tests, but other factors must always be taken into account. Lest the student now judge that test scores are worthless, he should be cautioned to recognize that it might be very important, in individual cases, to discover that a given student has a high IQ even though his grades are poor. This may lead to a search for other factors in low grade-attainment. He might have poor vision, for example, or little interest; perhaps he needs different kinds of activities to bring out his "potential." If a student has, in fact, a low IQ, then one might not expect the kind of attainment from him that is expected of others and special methods might be introduced for the lower-level students. For some occupations a high IQ is not necessary and perhaps undesirable for reasonable adjustment to the job. A person working below his level might well benefit from suitable counseling.

Standardization of tests

After the reliability of a test is established and some indication of validity developed, it is customary to give the test to representative population samples to determine its general limits and usefulness. Average performances are determined for different age, sex, educational, or economic groups. The range or "spread" of the scores is discovered and percentages of a given population that score at different points are determined. Such data are then described as "norms" or normal expectancies. Once a test is standardized, an individual's score can be interpreted. If the score is higher than that of say, 85 per cent of a given population, the person can be said to be at the eighty-sixth "percentile" or in the ninth "decile." A score exceeding 93 per cent of a comparison group would be in the ninety-fourth percentile or tenth decile. Standardization of tests also involves careful descriptions of who is qualified to administer the tests, specific instructions, time limits, permissible answers, conditions under which the test may be taken, and all precautions to be observed.

THE NATURE OF INTELLIGENCE

By now the student should recognize that he is not going to find out what intelligence is if he persists in viewing it as a something he possesses. If he regards it, instead, as some hypothetical construct which is presumably measured by tests, he will be somewhat better off. He can now begin to examine the nature of the tests and begin to understand some of the findings of testgivers when tests are given to different racial groups, economic groups, girls and boys, parents and children, siblings, twins, etc. Examining such tests and scores should reveal that whatever the attempt to measure innate capacities or potential, the test itself consists of exposing people to a broad assortment of items, with vocabulary items and familiarity with language and with numbers heavily emphasized. Testers rely heavily on vocabulary items, and, in fact, in some tests a vocabulary subtest correlates highly with the rest of the test and might be given alone for all the difference the rest makes. A good vocabulary, then, is a sign of a good intelligence test score. The tester reasons that the intelligent person will learn the meanings of more and more words as he grows and develops, as a matter of course. Those who learn more words must have some advantage in aptitude over those that do not learn as many. Some tests call for simple items of information, like, who is the President of the United States, or what are the colors of the flag? Other items involve repeating numbers in sequence or backwards, interpreting pictures or proverbs and so on. It is easy enough to make out a case for the claim that the kind of training (environment) a person enjoys can have a great deal to do with a test score. The argument is not readily resolved, of course. In the same environment, whatever that might mean, individuals can differ widely in their scores; not all poor, uneducated persons score low on tests, nor do all rich children "with all the advantages" score high. There are enough confusing and contradictory data to permit almost any conclusion from prejudiced interpreters, and, often enough, unprejudiced interpreters can accept facts as facts without necessarily concluding anything that is permanently or necessarily true. Thus, it is common enough to find girls earning higher scores than boys on vocabulary tests at certain ages. What does this prove? Or it can probably be established that one part of a country's population will score less well than another. Such findings are grist for propagandists' mills but cast little light on the nature of intelligence.

The constancy of the IQ

If intelligence were some kind of unitary and hereditary affair, one would expect it to remain more or less stable throughout life. If it is shown that the IQ does not change much as one grows up, this might support a nativistic theory of intelligence. The actual facts appear to support the generalization that when fairly large groups are tested, the average IQ will remain the same. This is true for average populations as well as for gifted and retarded populations (Terman, 1954). It should be recalled, however, that tests are so constructed that the average IQ for any age will be 100, regardless of age group involved. An average child of seven passes items designed for seven-year-olds; when he becomes eight, he is asked eight-year items and his IQ remains the same. Thus a mechanically necessary and arbitrary operation is imposed on the testing situation which more or less guarantees that average IQ's will not change. Again, it should be noted that tests are standardized on a broad population which more or less generally remains in the same environment from year to year and is exposed to the same influences (going through the public schools, for example) so that little change would be expected. If an individual moves out of his usual surroundings into an environment that differs markedly from his original background, for better or worse, there is no necessity for expecting his IQ to remain the same and, in fact, remarkable changes have been reported on many occasions with radical environmental changes. In any event, as we have tried to emphasize, intelligence is an abstraction which most of us have come to think of in terms of something real, a possession of individuals. When we reflect on the procedure involved in trying to measure this abstraction, we recognize that it cannot be a single, unitary thing or object. At best we must consider that intelligence is only a convenient expression for describing some relative or comparative aspects of behavior. Some psychologists advocate only the adjectival use of the word—they would approve of the term "intelligent" but not "intelligence." What the individual possesses, of course, is a body, sense organs, a nervous system. If these are all healthy, well-nourished, and suitably trained, a person might be intelligent in some situations. The jungle savage is far more "intelligent" in the jungle than he is on Times Square. Some people are, to our observations, more intelligent than others. This might mean, as Hebb (1949) suggests, a generally healthier brain, one free from a great variety of possible kinds of defects or deficiency of supplies. It might be that inheritance of structures sets some kinds of limits on the intellectual heights that individuals might reach. A damaged, abnormal, unhealthy brain might be expected to achieve but little distinction for its owner. With a properly developed and healthy brain, environmental experiences might determine other kinds of limits.

Intelligence—general or specific?

In the great tradition of philosophical and theological inquiry it has been customary to think of various assumed components of man's nature as more or less unitary matters or "faculties" (see p. 46). Thus, it is convenient and customary for us to think of "the will," the "mind," or the "intellect" as units or, at least, as separate and integrated entities. We like to think of someone as being either intelligent in general or stupid in general. It is awkward to think of a person as being very smart about this, rather mediocre at that, and somewhat average about something else. The notion that intelligence is a general, all-around ability or capacity has been broadly accepted, historically speaking. The facts of life, however, are sometimes difficult to force into our prejudice patterns and psychologists began to question the effort or attempt exemplified by Binet's approach as a measure of "general intelligence." Some held that, at best, it was a measure of scholastic aptitude to some limited degree, that it did not measure other kinds of skills and capacities that have some right to be thought of as pertaining to intellectual activity. It was held by some, Spearman (1904), for example, that intelligence must be thought of as consisting of what might be called a general component (G) and some unknown number of specific aptitudes (s). Various combinations of G and s's would account more suitably for the successes or failures of individuals in the great variety of the world's occupations and problem situations. As statistical sophistication developed and was applied to testing situations, it was possible to calculate the relationship between all kinds of tests. If two tests correlated strongly, they might be thought of as measuring the same thing. If many tests correlated strongly they might be considered to be measuring something that deserved to be called general intelligence or G. Then any tests which did not correlate with this group of tests would, if reliable, be thought of as measuring something else, an s, some specific aptitude.

The correlational technique was applied to all sorts of tests for which various claims had been made by Thurstone (1938). He discovered that the correlation coefficients between a large number of tests could be most appropriately thought of as representing different groupings or factors. Some tests would correlate with each other but not with other tests. Tests that did correlate together could be thought of as measuring some kind of relatively specific aptitude. Because the groups of tests did not correlate highly with each other, no general or G aspect to intelligence could be supported, but the groups themselves were more general than the specific or separate aptitudes they were originally designed to measure. By analyzing results of over sixty tests taken by the same children, Thurstone arrived at some seven clusters or groups of highly intercorrelated tests which he felt meant that there are at least seven *primary abilities*. Those listed by Thurstone are shown in Table 4.

Table 4 Thurstone's seven primary abilities

Ability	*Symbol*	*Measured by*
1. Verbal comprehension	V	vocabulary tests
2. Verbal fluency	W	rhymes, anagrams
3. Number	N	arithmetic tests
4. Space	S	drawing designs
5. Memory	M	recalling paired items
6. Perceptual	P	seeing similarities and differences in pictures
7. Reasoning	R	drawing inferences from facts

When subjects are tested with a battery or group of such tests it is possible to determine the correlation of each subtest with various criteria. It can and does turn out, for example, that one subtest will correlate with one activity and not with others. Chemistry grades, for example, were found to correlate with N while English composition grades correlated better with V, as might be expected. It is, of course, difficult to establish appropriate criteria against which to match any kind of test and much more research will have to be done before we are able to determine if the factor approach is more efficient as a predictor than a general-test approach. Many general tests are, of course, loaded with some of the factor items and these may contribute to correlations with criteria to the extent that the factor is important. Without suitable analysis we can easily be misled. The combination of factors that Thurstone employed reads like a list of the kinds of items one finds in so-called general intelligence tests. While this might make us properly suspicious of the value of a general intelligence test score, in that such a general or total score might obscure some special abilities, it is now quite generally appreciated that different people demonstrate different degrees or levels of proficiency in various fields, and efforts are normally made by professional testers to establish such individual differences. Children can earn the same IQ by passing and failing different items. Most college counselors, for example, stress the commonly found difference between quantitative (numerical) and verbal abilities that entering freshmen bring with them and attempt to counsel students along appropriate lines.

HUMAN ENGINEERING

The intelligence test movement received considerable impetus in the United States during the past two World Wars. Military examiners expanded the area of testing in many directions hoping to "fit the man to the job." Such practices have also been widely applied in business and industry where it is felt that a suitable selection of men will result in greater efficiency. During a war, however, and in times of maximal employment, it is not always possible to find enough suitable or qualified people for all the jobs that have to be done and lesser levels of talent must be employed. In the face of pressing need, another approach has been tried. If a man cannot be fitted to a job, perhaps the job can be fitted to the man. This latter procedure of trying to arrange the best possible combination of man and machine has come to be known as "applied experimental psychology" or "engineering psychology" and perhaps unwisely, but more commonly, as "human engineering."

In its main outlines the human engineering approach follows most directly from the early beginnings of experimental psychology in psychophysics and the later applications of such psychometrics in the measurement of intelligence. It involves an expansion of the testing program beyond the scope of intellectual aptitudes into sensory and motor acuities and skills. The general approach can be described somewhat as follows: there is a job to be done (e.g., tracking a submarine and arranging for its destruction by suitable action which might consist of pressing a particular button at a crucial moment). There is available a certain amount and kind of equipment for doing the job. Men who can do the job, however, are not available in suitable numbers, or even if numbers are plentiful, the job is not being done well enough. Too many submarines are undetected or inadequately tracked and lost, or they are not destroyed. The psychologist in such a situation, working in conjunction with equipment designers and engineers, attempts to analyze the job in terms of what the job calls for in all human respects, that is, he observes, records, or otherwise determines what the man must do. The operator must, in the illustration chosen, be able to see with some determinable degree of accuracy; he must be able to hear, perhaps while he is watching; he may have to work for long, tiring periods; he may have to select knobs, switches, levers, and buttons in rapid succession out of an assortment of such and should do so within specified time periods and without error, and so on. The psychologist must know about the visual capacities, auditory capacities, fatigue resistance, muscular control, finger discrimination capacities, the relative usefulness of switches, buttons, and knobs and their proper arrangements. In a complex operation there may be hundreds of "human factors" that have to be taken into account, factors that have to be measured and compared against abilities or limitations. It is sometimes possible to change parts, dispositions, or the very nature of the machines and instruments employed if this is necessary for the job to be done. If the machine cannot be changed, the man might be trained to work effectively if one discovers what he is to be trained for and how he should be trained (what mistakes to avoid, the most effective pattern or combination of movements, and so on). It might be discovered, for example, that it is very important to determine how long one can stay below the surface in a submarine or in the air in an airplane and the only information provided is how much fuel is available and its consumption rate. The time can be calculated, but if a decision must be made before the calculation can be performed, it would be necessary to provide an instrument reading in time-available rather than two instruments reading in terms of consumption and amount.

The employment of psychologists in military and industrial operations is expanding rapidly as the devices for modern living or survival become more and more complicated. Handbooks of data are now available telling about how well a man can see, what he can discriminate, what he can hear, smell, or sense in other ways, how tall he is while standing or sitting, how far he can reach, etc. [See the Tufts *Handbook of Human Engineering Data* (1952) and texts by Chapanis, Garner, and Morgan (1949) and McCormick (1957).] More and more such information is accumulating and jobs are constantly becoming more simplified even while they grow more complex. As one aspect of a job becomes simplified or eliminated, another is added in the constant effort to increase the output or efficiency of a man-machine combination.

As man begins to operate in formerly unsuitable or impossible areas (the arctic regions, outer space) more and more scientific effort is expanded and wider areas of talent are tapped. Anthropologists, physiologists, clinical psychologists are all called upon to test and measure, to fit the job to the man by taking into account his nature, his propensities, his talents, and his limitations. How much heat can he stand? How much cold? How much radiation? How many dials can he monitor? How much can be remember? How much information can he process in a given time? Such questions and measures are a distant cry from Binet's pioneer efforts but they are directly related to the attempt to measure man.

CHAPTER 7

The Modified Organism. The Nature of Learning

The social determination of learning · A definition of learning · The necessity of extinction · The habit-family-hierarchy · Extinction and learning · The principle of reinforcement · Learning in the laboratory · Instrumental and operant learning · Classical or Pavlovian learning · Drive and motivation in learning · Derived drives · Rewards and punishments in learning · Secondary rewards · Are rewards necessary for learning? · A hypothetical neural account of learning · Punishment · Punishment as a deterrent · Generalization · Discrimination · Subsidiary principles · Spaced as opposed to massed learning · Reactive inhibition · Whole as opposed to part learning · Active as opposed to passive learning · Meaningful as opposed to rote learning · The nature of understanding · Early and late learning

Psychologists know the importance of learning. At least they spend enough time considering the matter. No text of any importance ignores the subject or tries to suggest that the topic is not of greatest consequence. Some responsible texts devote as much as a third of their space to learning problems. The interest of psychologists in learning is a twentieth-century affair. Before that only a little had been done in terms of trying to observe the nature of learning or get at the fundamental principles. Perhaps it takes more than half a century to solve some kinds of problems. Certainly the principles of learning have not yet been found. For all the talk about changing human nature or improving adjustment, we do not yet know how to manipulate principles of learning to achieve such ends. We might manipulate something and have some modest successes but only the rash claim that they are manipulating learning processes.

THE SOCIAL DETERMINATION OF LEARNING

In order to change human nature we should know what human nature is. That we still do not know. Studies of primitive tribes in isolated areas of the world and comparisons with the most advanced civilizations do not lead to a catalogue of universal human traits. Almost any kind of behavior can be found and considered natural by the people of whom it is characteristic. Anthropologists who have been brought up in other cultures like to think of themselves as representing real humanity and attribute barbaric practices or novel customs to "cultural" differences of unknown origins. It is difficult if not impossible to determine what humans do naturally because of the long period of helpless infancy which characterizes human development. During this period of helplessness, the family and general culture begin their work and by the time the child is ready to behave and be observed we find that we cannot decide that anything he does is natural any more. We might argue on logical grounds, since men survive and multiply, that it is natural to eat and to reproduce, but even the behavior in eating and sexual relations varies so much, individually and culturally, that we would not recognize natural eating if we saw it. Similarly with other behavior patterns that we observe. How much is natural, inherited, dependent upon maturation and structure, and how much has been altered by learning? We are hard put to it to decide. Children in France learn to speak French. Italian babies learn Italian. But we know that these same babies (or their little brothers) would have learned Japanese if brought up in Tokyo by Japanese-speaking foster parents. We also assume that if someone can spell a word such as "syzygy" he was not born with this response pattern. He has to learn it as he learns multiplication tables, the words to "The Star Spangled Banner," and a list of Presidents or state capitals. But even here we run into difficulties. Some people learn better than others, or at least faster than others; some remember better than others. Do they differ from each other in some natural respects that make for this difference or did they acquire or learn the ways in which they are different? Do scores on intelligence tests result from different learning experiences? Can we make all children equally intelligent, or will some always be a little "more equal than others"?

What kinds of things are learned and what kinds come naturally? In order to find out what learning is, we have to know where to look for it. Do we have to learn to talk, ride a bicycle, fly an airplane, do algebra, play a piano, read? Are you sure about any of these things? Some children seem to be able to ride bicycles with little or no instruction. They get on one, in one way or another, and while there may be a little trouble, in a little while they are off riding with passable grace. Did they learn quickly? Or did they "get the idea"? Is "getting the idea" learning or is it the natural use of a native intelligence or other equipment? But algebra, that's different, that you have to learn. Do you? Somebody had to invent the stuff—he did not learn it, it was not there to learn. Does the student in an algebra course repeat this process of invention for himself, to some extent at least, or does he learn algebra? Some students never learn to handle algebra in any reasonable fashion even if they manage to attain a passing mark. Others continually find fault with what has been "taught" and find new ways of handling the assigned problems. Are they learning? We would be a lot better off if we could describe the characteristics of learned behavior and discriminate it from other, nonlearned behavior. Our trouble is that we do not know the characteristics of either in any unequivocal fashion. Our best attempts betray us because learning, whatever it may be in a physical, neural sense, is a hypothetical process, an inference, as far as the psychologist is able to talk about it, and his hypothetical speculations result in a condition that is best described by the poet: "He is hoist with his own petard."

A DEFINITION OF LEARNING

Before we explain this difficulty we might essay a description of a learned pattern of behavior. Assume you are at a party where some of the guests are strangers. You are conducted to a man in a gray flannel suit and he is presented to you as Mr. Quicksell. You say, "How do you do Mr. Quicksell," and are taken off to meet someone else. Before the presentation you could not say the stranger's name upon seeing him. He did not look like anything you would normally call "Mr. Quicksell." You had to wait for your host to make the necessary noises, and having in the past learned to produce noises other people direct at you, you repeated the noises. Sometime later you bump into Mr. Quicksell again and spill his cocktail out of his hand. You smile with your best charm and say: "So sorry, Mr. Quicksell." Now, the sight of Mr. Quicksell, his visual stimulus value was sufficient for you to call him by name, something you could not do before, when you needed the help of the noises of your host. When you are able to perform some response in the absence of the stimuli that were necessary before you would perform this response, we usually say you have learned.

We can try another example. Assume you have never baked a cake, but now have some need to do so. You ask someone to show you how. Mama obliges and directs each step. You follow "instructions" and the cake eventually results. Without mama or a cookbook, you might be relatively helpless. Of course you could have created something without mama or the cookbook. You know that flour, eggs, sugar, milk and butter are required, and you might even have heard about baking powder, the odd notion that a little salt might prove useful, something about mixing batters, and numbers referring to temperatures of baking ovens. It might even be edible in a rough sort of way; ducks might eat it. But the cake baked with mama's help is a good one. Next week you decide to bake a cake by yourself and, if you are lucky, it turns out fairly well. You have learned to bake a cake according to our definition of learning; you are able to do something in the absence of a stimulus that was formerly necessary.

This definition is not free from objections. We will examine the objections shortly, but it does cover most of the situations that you are likely to equate with learning. You recite a poem "by heart" *after* first having it said to you or after reading it in printed form over and over. You recite your multiplication tables, your Latin vocabulary, you drive a car by yourself, you teach someone else, all of these things are now being done in the absence of a teacher or notes or other stimuli that were formerly necessary.

We can remind ourselves now of Pavlov's dog who "learned" to drool saliva when a bell rang. Dogs do not drool to bells naturally. Something else, food in the mouth, is the natural stimulus. When the natural stimulus is accompanied by some other, nonnatural stimulus, and the individual then makes the response to the nonnatural stimulus which was formerly made only to the natural stimulus, we say that learning took place. For the moment we will not concern ourselves with how the learning took place. We do not care if the dog learned or if it "got the idea." The point is that the dog now did something to a stimulus which formerly was not done to this stimulus. You can look at Mr. Quicksell all day long and never say his name until after you have been told what it is. Even in the fairy tale, the miller's daughter could not tell Rumpelstiltskin his name until someone told her first.

Now we come to some difficulties. In the above examples we had you saying a person's name, and making a cake, and we had a dog drooling. In case you had not noticed it, the illustrations required that you already have the capacity for saying names or putting ingredients into bowls and ovens, and we did expect the dog to be able to drool, or at least to drool when food was put in its mouth. What this amounts to is that you already can do anything you are going to learn whether it is flying a kite or an airplane, the multiplication table or calculus. You must have the capacity for making the required responses before you go about the business of learning any particular behavior pattern. You observe that we do not say that you already know how to bake the cake or whatever, but you are able to make the proper noises or move things about in the necessary manner before the learning starts. A child that has never been on a bicycle knows how to make all of the movements involved in riding said vehicle before he ever gets on. His trouble is that he does not know when and in what sequence to make these movements, or what movements go with each other and which ones do not. In other words, he has natural responses aplenty, that is, responses to "natural" stimuli, but the stimuli to which these movements must now be made are unnatural or nonnatural, certainly different from the ones to which he normally makes the movements. The child knows how to ride the bicycle and he does not at the same time. But riding the bicycle involves making responses to cues or stimuli which do not naturally call out these responses, which, in fact, might call out responses that lead to falls or other disasters. The point, however, is important nevertheless. It tells us that we cannot teach anyone to do anything of which he is incapable, or more practically, we cannot teach anyone any new sequence of movements if we cannot elicit the movements themselves. Putting it in even more practical terms, it is useless to teach the child to run before it can walk.

The necessity of extinction

Even more important is the fact that any stimulus will tend to evoke a natural response (or a response strongly learned earlier in its history) and if we are trying to teach someone to do something new to this stimulus, we are in that much trouble at least. The child, if it is a child we are considering, will do what comes naturally. Consider what this means in terms of our normal concepts of education. Much of what we do naturally (spit, grunt, hiccup, snore, run around dirty and naked, wipe greasy hands on hips) is frowned upon in civilized life. Children are supposed to be seen and not heard, especially after certain hours of the day; they are to wear clean collars and keep their little necks and noses clean, and above all they are supposed to visit the bathroom on proper, and not improper, occasions. They are to say "yes, mam," and "no, mam," and "please" and "thank you" and a whole host of other unnatural, revolting, unreasonable, and civilized things. These "unnatural" responses must be transformed into normal, routine behavior and associated with "unnatural" stimuli, making the problem doubly difficult. The natural thing to do when someone gives you something is to grab it and absorb it, engulf it, consume it or smash it (see any child's behavior at Christmas). Instead of this we want our children to accept a package gracefully, bow, and say "Thank you" even before the child knows what is in it. How do we manage to accomplish such a miracle? The answer to this question is the story of learning.

We have made the point that a stimulus, any stimulus, is more or less readily or rapidly followed by a natural response to that stimulus. If the response is adequate, i.e., *gets rid of the stimulus,* the organism is ready to react to the next invasion of its nervous system from the outside world. If the response is not adequate, if the stimulus remains, if the social world is frowning, some other response must be made or the stimulus will remain. What other response? We have argued, in discussing the nervous system, that any input will normally find an output, and this output will either be along previously prepared or inherited pathways or through other available channels. We can expect that if a stimulus continues to initiate neural activity, then the organism will respond in a succession of ways until the stimulus does cease to exist. Suppose that we illustrate this by a rather strong example. Let us place a rat in a box with a grid floor through which we can shock its feet. Let us further decide to educate this rat to make an unnatural, but civilized response. We will turn on a light and after a few seconds we will turn on a shock and we will leave them both on until the rat pulls a chain in the middle of the box. The chain is hooked to a switch which turns off the light and the shock. Our rat is ready. The light goes on, the rat does whatever rats do when lights come on, perhaps it turns away or ducks its head. The shock comes on, the rat pulls up its paws briskly, it hops, it bounces, it whimpers, it squeals, it starts to bite the bars and jumps back more briskly, it runs about, it climbs the walls but finds no footholds, it goes through this repertoire over and over again, varying the sequence from time to time, but certainly not repeating any particular response to the exclusion of other behavior. We might somewhat cavalierly say that "the rat varied its behavior pattern," but we must note that there are many things the rat does not do: it does not kneel; it does not stand on its head or invoke the Fourteenth Amendment. The behavior, though variable, is limited in its variability. If we wait long enough and if the rat is lucky it will sooner or later (and we always hope it will not be too soon) bump into the chain and start to climb it. Its weight will pull the switch, the light goes out, the shock too, not that the rat "knows" this, and the rat hangs on. After a while it drops off the chain and there being no more stimulation to the feet for agitated behavior, it goes about its ratlike life again. If we now turn on the light again, and the shock, we will have, usually, a repetition, although probably a briefer one, of the above pattern of limited variability. The pattern will be repeated time and again, but each time more briefly with more and more elements of the repertoire dropping out, until finally, the light comes on and before the shock arrives the rat is up the chain. If the time between trials is fairly long, the rat will not stay on the chain for long either, but will drop off and resume its affairs. We have seen a picture of learning taking place. Now what have we seen? Let us abstract the elements.

In the first place, the rat gave a natural response to a natural stimulus. This, society decreed, did not work. The rat made a succession of other natural responses to the continuing stimulus. These were different, one from another; some of these occurred only rarely in the total number of trials, some frequently, some came sooner in the sequence, some came late, some very late. Climbing the chain was the latest, though not necessarily the most frequent up to the time it began to occur regularly.

The habit-family-hierarchy

If we wanted to, we might plot the frequency and reaction time of each response to a given persistent stimulus and arrange the various responses in some order of probability of occurrence. We would then have a "hierarchy" of responses to the same persistent stimulus. One of the members of this hierarchy we can roughly describe as climbing the chain. This is the one we selected for the animal to learn. We note that the animal already could do this, and, all that we accomplished in our educational program was to change the time at which this would happen. We wanted it to happen first, not later in a sequence. We wanted it to happen, furthermore, when a light came on and without a shock being applied. This we managed, as educators, to accomplish. But note, we merely managed the affair, we did not teach. No educator teaches. He manages. What does the management consist of? Only this: Arranging for the systematic appearance of unnatural and natural stimuli which bring out the desired response, and arranging for the stimuli to be eliminated by virtue of this response. If any learning was done, it was done by the rat. Nobody taught the rat anything, just as no one has ever taught anyone anything. Words referring to teaching or training, or education, are just convenient and conventional noises which actually refer to the management process and have no other actual or real denotation. This is quite clear in the case of the rat. No one showed it how to do it or told it what to do. In the case of a child it might appear somewhat different, but basically the same story will unfold. The teacher may have to make noises in order that the learner is managed into making certain noises too, but making the noises is not teaching, it is still making noises and if the learner does not make them, no learning will take place.

Now, we go back to the rat. We saw that the rat learned to pull the chain when the light itself came on and before the shock. But before that, the rat learned to pull the chain when the shock was present. And it did learn. We know this because the time that elapsed between onset of shock and chain-pull gradually got shorter and shorter. But chain pulling was very low in the hierarchy of the rat's responses to shock. We deliberately chose it because it is so low. Had we chosen to terminate light and shock when the rat jumped in the air, for example, the learning would take place so fast that we couldn't follow it and we might even say that no learning took place, that the rat had done what rats naturally do to shocks and lights. But jumping up is a *natural* response. Can you learn to do the natural thing? You can certainly improve in time or efficiency. This is the difficulty we referred to earlier. You can learn to do the natural thing as well as or better than the unnatural thing. And to talk about learning to do what-comes-naturally seems paradoxical. Yet consider such things as thumb sucking. It appears to be natural enough and yet there also appear to be learning features to it. Within limits, the longer a child sucks its thumb, the better it gets at it, the stronger the "habit" becomes. We can even learn to sleep more effectively, and to eat better (more efficiently and, perhaps, greater amounts), but all of these natural "habits" get so thoroughly involved with unnatural stimuli that it is difficult to conceive of improvement in the basic activity itself. In an interesting experiment Sheffield (1948) watched the time it took rats to get started running (a natural response) to a shock. As soon as they had started to run, the shock stopped. The rats learned to run almost at once; they learned so rapidly that Sheffield argued, as does Guthrie, that learning can and does take place in one trial. We are normally so inefficient about arranging and managing conditions that the proper stimuli are not presented at the proper time and consequently learning is delayed, or the wrong things are learned, or we try to "teach" one thing and test in some other fashion which we mistakenly assume is appropriate. We find that we do not get the "correct" answers, and so we call the learner stupid. Only teachers can be stupid, it might be assumed from the remarks of Guthrie or the conclusions of Skinner.

Extinction and learning

If we stop and analyze a bit more closely we will find that we have learned a great deal more about learning from our rat. Perhaps the most important thing, however, is that in the usual educational situation we are not content with what comes naturally—that is not considered education. What we want or hope to get is some response which is lower down in the hierarchy. Now, in order to do this, the responses higher up in the hierarchy must be eliminated. Eliminating a response is sometimes a ticklish business when the response is high in the hierarchy and persists in recurring. We can introduce a technical term to facilitate discussion. The process of eliminating a response is called *extinction*. Sometimes the term is restricted to the dropping out or elimination of a learned response but the process by which the elimination of "natural" responses occurs is possibly the same and the distinction need not be observed if the term actually covers both instances. We start out a learning process, then, by extinguishing superior members in a hierarchy. If there are no superior members in a hierarchy, then we simply strengthen the most natural response. This might be illustrated in situations where one organism does something that *looks like* learning quite readily, almost instinctively, while another organism, perhaps of a different species, takes a long time getting around to making that response. Pigeons will learn to peck at unnatural objects much more effectively than will elephants even though elephants have longer noses. Dogs will learn to come to their trainers on signal more rapidly than will rats. Certain breeds of dogs will learn to point or retrieve; others can hardly be trained into such activity without the most exhausting efforts on the part of all concerned.

Within the same species one organism may have no response tendencies which interfere with a given performance while another may have many; these may be "natural" or learned; in any event, they must be eliminated. The child that is afraid of the water cannot learn to swim. The fear must be eliminated first. Adults learn fixed patterns of speech and sound sequences so thoroughly that they have difficulty with foreign languages. They might eventually learn to speak a passable French with a Boston or Brooklyn accent. Rarely can an adult master a foreign language to the native level except by years of life in the foreign land with little or no contact with his former speech. An untutored "natural-born" athlete may give endless trouble to professional coaches who try to make a reasonable professional out of the diamond in the rough. Before they can make much progress all the wrong, natural, things he does have to be eliminated; sometimes the former ability disappears in the process, but the new learning can not go on until the old habits are gone. The wise teacher first finds out what the "natural" responses are and proceeds to eliminate them. This is clearly evident in the work of the golf "pro" who may not even supply a ball for the student until he is satisfied that all the natural interferences are out of the system.

THE PRINCIPLE OF REINFORCEMENT

Our rat has taught us to view the learning process as a two-faced operation: we eliminate the negative and accentuate the positive. Both steps are ordinarily required because we ordinarily do not look for learning when natural responses are socially permitted. Any primitive tribe will provide evidence of differences in cultures where one tribe approves of belching after a meal as a complimentary expression to the cook or host and another regards it as extreme crudity. We have already called the process of eliminating one response as extinction. We have not tried to explain it, however, and will not until later. The corresponding process of strengthening the desired response also has a technical name provided by Pavlov: it is called "reinforcement." The term "reinforcement" refers to the process whereby a given response is made more likely to occur. This is imagined to result from some sort of strengthening action, which presumably must occur in the nervous system. Two kinds of confusion have come into psychology in connection with this term: in the first place, the term is used sometimes by the experimenter to describe what the teacher is doing, on the grounds that what the teacher does is somehow related to the learning. Suppose that the teacher decides, for whatever reason, that by being nice to a child, the child will learn faster or even that the child will not learn at all unless the teacher is nice. The teacher then starts being nice when the child performs the right response, and the teacher then can say: "I reinforced him." In connection with animal experiments a common way of being nice to a hungry animal is to give it some food. If you drop a pellet of food to a hungry rat, you might say that you reinforced it. In the second place, if you get sloppy and careless, you might say that you gave it *a* reinforcement, and the term has now slipped over into a description of some physical object, like food or money or other frequently desired things. The term has been used in both of these ways but we might be a bit more careful and refer to reinforcement as the hypothetical neural process which underlies the development of a new response to some stimulus which does not ordinarily produce it. If we could find evidence that when learning takes place some change occurs in the nervous system such as the growing closer together of some units of the neurons involved, a swelling of terminal boutons, or some permanent chemical change in the synapses, then we could point to the process and name it reinforcement just as the building contractor does when he braces a wall with angle irons or buttresses. He can show us his reinforcement in position or being put into position and we know what he is talking about, because we believe that we understand how the operation is a strengthening one. To call a piece of food a reinforcement is simply making us accept an arbitrary verbal ruling in a game that we have agreed to play. The game becomes confusing if other players want to change the rules.

Learning in the laboratory

With the terms extinction and reinforcement now available for use we can be a bit more formal about discussing the learning process. Research psychologists over the years have devised many ways of studying the acquisition of new responses. One of these you are already familiar with to some degree if you remember Pavlov's dogs. Other techniques have been developed which, to some researchers appear more natural or more clearly analogous to some hypothetically conceived learning process. Thus the average man thinks of psychologists as people who run rats through mazes; actually mazes as commonly conceived are rarely used in psychology laboratories. A much more common tool is the T-maze which is a maze only by courtesy as it consists of a simple runway (a piece of 2 × 4 lumber will do) with a crosspiece attached to one end to form a T. The animal is placed on the starting leg and watched as it comes up to the "choice point." From here, if it is to go at all it must turn either left or right. Psychologists are by no means agreed on what happens in the rat or what the external variables are that must be controlled in order to predict which way the rat will turn. But we notice, with the T-maze that the animal is given a limited sort of freedom. It, hypothetically, does not have to walk down the starting leg, and it is free to sit at the choice point until it starves to death. It is free to turn one way or another or so it might appear, except that no psychologist believes that the rat is free to do anything at all, but responds in ways which conditions prescribe, and when we know what the conditions are and how they prescribe we shall be able to tell which way the rat will turn, and it had better not turn the other way (or we will start to look for new conditions!).

Another very popular device that has helped sweep mazes out of the laboratory is the so-called "Skinner Box." [1] Skinner devised a technique whereby a rat in a small box or cage could press a bar or any gadget which operated a device outside the box which, in turn, released tiny pellets of food to the rat. Pigeons work in similar boxes by pecking at little disks which are wired to grain dispensers. The animals, thus, in a sense, feed themselves or earn their keep, but only in a sense. We must not forget that they merely press or peck. What happens after that is Skinner's doing, and not that of the rats. Other boxes have been arranged in which the animal escapes by pulling a chain or pressing a lever. This kind of box has dropped out of the picture perhaps because psychologists are too lazy to chase after the dogs, cats, rats, and chickens

[1] Skinner (1956) describes the development of his widely used "box" in an engaging autobiographical article in which he also includes some interesting advice to researchers.

or pigeons, and the Skinner type of arrangement has been adapted to the study of a great many problems. (See p. 217.)

Instrumental and operant learning

In the kinds of devices described, it will be noticed that the animal or learner does something and this is followed by some resulting action in its environment. Food or drink appear, or a door opens. With human behavior we have many analogous situations. We ask the child who received the gift "What do you say?" and wait for him to say "Thank you." He might take all day about it, but usually we run out of patience and try to force him to hurry the process, but there is no way that we know of that will make the child actually say the desired words. *He* has to say them. We can assist the process by saying them ourselves; this still does not necessarily initiate the desired action. We do not know what buttons to press or where to squeeze the child or what neurons to stimulate electrically to initiate the "thank you" response. We must wait. So with our rats and dogs. We wait for them to do something; when they do it something happens. The something may be considered good or bad (reward or punishment) or nothing much at all, but if something is to be learned, something had better happen.

The kinds of situations we have just been describing have been classified as "instrumental" behavior because the response is instrumental in having something happen. There need not be any logical connection between what the learner does and the subsequent event, but there must be a temporal relation and there must be an event which follows the response. The psychologically important point about the kind of learning involved here is the one we made above: the organism is not literally or obviously forced to perform the response. It is said to "emit" it; that is, sooner or later, the response emerges from the potential repertoire of the learner.

Classical or Pavlovian learning

Instrumental learning is alleged to be different from the kind of training Pavlov (see pp. 161–167) initiated where he more obviously forced the animal to respond by using a natural stimulus which could be counted on to be followed by the response. The unnatural or artificial stimulus was then said to be associated with or substituted for the natural one. This kind of learning was dubbed by psychologists "Pavlovian" or "classical" learning; the other kind was called various terms, such as "operant" because the organism was "operating" upon the environment or "instrumental" as mentioned above. It might appear a little gratuitous to say that the organism was operating on anything or being especially instrumental. The organism is, after all, doing what it does naturally with the kinds of stimulus objects that are provided. It walks, it pulls, it pushes, it presses, or in the case of the child and "thank you," we can be pretty sure that a child of four or five is quite likely to co-operate and say "thank you" if we demand it strongly enough on the simple language pattern learning that it has acquired through its earlier years as more or less automatic operations. The child need have no more conception of what "thank you" means than the rat does of the electronics involved in controlling his food dispenser, and we might very well be forcing the responses out of every learner who ever learned. The amount of obvious or apparent forcing may be varied. If we use a large Skinner Box, the bar pressing will take longer than if we use a small one. If we want our rat to pull a chain in the shock box sooner rather than later, we use a big chain and a long one, one that it can scarcely avoid bumping into in its gyrations. By carefully restricting the environment and other sources of conflicting stimulation we can reduce the waiting time to seconds. That is what Pavlov did. He did not care to wait. Had he cared to, he might have observed how the animal, after having eaten and smelled food, now began to salivate to the sight of food and the sounds of food preparation. No one "forced" the dog to salivate in the first place. It is a natural reaction to food in the mouth. Can we say that the pigeon pecking at a target is not performing a natural reaction or that the rat leaning on a bar (pressing is a term that might more correctly be employed to describe what goes on rather late in the game) is not doing something that is forced upon it by its nature?

We can accept the distinction between instrumental and Pavlovian learning as a laboratory convenience, but we may be misled if we assume that some different kinds of events occur in the nervous system when a dog learns to salivate, compared with learning to push a lever which allows it access to food or brings it food. The distinction between instrumental and Pavlovian learning has been popularly accepted by psychologists in the past but it has proved more than troublesome because of attempts made to suggest that different events do occur in the nervous system. For example, it was argued for a long time that Pavlovian learning took place quite automatically as a sheer matter of *substitution* (Guthrie, 1952), whereas instrumental learning depended primarily upon the nature of the outcome of the behavior. This outcome was usually thought of in terms of rewards and punishments. If the outcome was favorable, i.e., rewarded, or reinforced, an instrumental response was somehow strengthened. The nature of the outcome in Pavlovian learning was supposed to be irrelevant. Recently one of the most prominent learning theorists, Spence (1956), proposed that the picture of learning previously advanced had been hung upside down and that it was really Pavlovian learning that depended upon the outcome and that instrumental learning did not. In the face of such a complete reversal, one might very well wonder whether either view has much to offer and if both of the views might not be incorrect. At the present time it would be folly for a student to believe very much at all of what is said about the significance of a reward for learning. Yet rewards play such a role in training practices and, hypothetically, at least, in education, that we must pay some attention to them as well as to punishment. We are almost ready to do this now, but must first prepare the ground a little more by bringing up the currently popular concepts of "drive" and "motivation."

DRIVE AND MOTIVATION IN LEARNING

At this time we shall treat the subject of drive and motivation only lightly, reserving a fuller discussion for later on. For present purposes it is enough to note that American learning-psychology developed in terms of an emphasis on reward. Now a reward is an abstract, conceptual term, and not an object or event. Objects or events can be rewarding to organisms only under specified conditions. A dime or a dollar or a hundred-dollar bill will be accepted or rejected under various conditions. A dime tip for a waiter at a banquet will be accepted with sneers and scorn; a newsboy might smile gratefully. A high-level operator in some racket might sneer at a "C note" with a snarling "Why the punk tried to cool me off with a bill." The conditions that make an object or event rewarding have usually been interpreted in terms of wants or needs or desires. Now wants, needs, and desires, are not easy concepts to handle by an objective psychology and a search was instituted for some biological foundations upon which such concepts could be based. Common experience suggested that bodily conditions can be powerful determiners of behavior and some bodily conditions were singled out as possible foundations of needs. Thus, we have always known that people eat when they are hungry, drink when thirsty, sleep when tired, and go to the toilet when bowel or bladder pressures are above some suitable level. It was but a step of logic to draw a causal inference and to argue that hunger *leads* to eating, and so on through the list. When activities of interest are somewhat more complex, as in sex behavior, it was easy enough to add a prior condition which generated sex behavior. These prior conditions of a physiological nature, tissue conditions of depletion or oversupply, were labeled "drives." Now that a term was available, it was simplicity itself to explain why an organism behaved in a particular way: it had a drive to do so and the drive somehow led to an appropriate activity which "reduced" it, or eliminated it completely. The sequence would be something like this: sometime after the last meal, the stomach becomes empty and the digestive system stops supplying nutrients to the blood stream, the blood-sugar level decreases. This changes the environment about the body cells; some cells, particularly in the brain are especially sensitive to this change and become disturbed in some manner which results in restless, and more and more agitated behavior on the part of the organism; some of this activity brings the organism in contact with food. It eats, the digestive system begins to supply nutrients again, the sensitive brain cells quiet down and the sequence shortly begins all over again. A similar set of events could be imagined for a variety of body conditions. A number of particulars should now be spelled out.

It should be noted that the drive, in this case hunger, develops periodically and automatically. Thirst, elimination, sleepiness, and perhaps some other conditions might also develop in this periodic, cyclical way.

At first the activity generated in the organism is unsystematic, disorganized, undirected. Gradually organisms become more oriented with respect to drive conditions and do the appropriate thing sooner and sooner. They look for food instead of a bed when hungry. This, in turn, indicates that drives get involved in some fashion with learning and the logic of the argument requires that the drive state, whatever else it may be, produces specific stimuli which can become associated with more or less specific behavior. Stimuli arising from drives might be labeled S_d to distinguish them from external energy changes. What the nature of these stimuli is can only be guessed at—perhaps our best approximation is to identify drive stimuli with the activity of specific neural structures which react in specialized manners to changes in the constituents of the blood stream. This leaves drive stimuli in a rather hazy conceptual state. How the drive stimuli come to initiate specific behavior we will postpone to a later page.

It is sometimes claimed that drives "energize" behavior. We must be extremely careful in the use of this term. The drive cannot create energy out of nothing. The organism already possesses whatever energy is potentially available. The drive does not produce any new energy; it can only be the basis on which energy is redirected or converted. If the adrenal glands secrete adrenalin and initiate more sugar release by the liver, no energy has been created, but more is now available for direct use by the muscles. Drives might be responsible for a general condition of restlessness or irritability, but not for more energy. To talk about drives as "the main springs of men" is just a figure of speech.

Body conditions like hunger, thirst, or pain, appear to be at least potentially describable in physiological terms. When we recognize that organisms that are not hungry, thirsty, or hurt also engage in activities we are faced with a problem. Either there are other drives which we have not considered, or else the basic drives have become expanded in some fashion, presumably by learning, to cover a lot more varieties of behavior. Consider the first alternative first.

A refreshed, well-fed, and otherwise apparently happy monkey is given a mechanical puzzle to play with. He does so. Does he have a drive for play? Or if we wish to sound a bit more sophisticated, does he have a manipulation drive? Or, if the monkey examines the inside of a box or pipe or wanders about some area of his enclosure, is he exploring? And if he is exploring, is it because of an exploratory drive? If he engages in courting behavior with another monkey is it because he is now under the influence of a sex drive? If he picks away at his skin is he under a masochistic, self-destructive drive, a skin-picking drive? How many drives are there? Can any limit be placed upon the number? The student will recall the similar problem in the discussion of instinct. A drive can be invented for each and every situation that might appear to qualify. Drives have indeed been postulated for all the situations mentioned as well as many other such as gregariousness, a drive for using the sense organs (Nissen, 1954), and a drive for using the muscles out of sheer good feeling (euphoria)—this has been called a drive for exercise. There may indeed be physiological conditions that could be spelled out as underlying the several kinds of behavior listed, but the current stage of our knowledge does not permit such descriptions. In any event, we would soon run into greater problems. These are purportedly handled by the second alternative, learned drives.

Derived drives

Unwilling to speculate ad infinitum about specific innate drives for the multivaried aspects of behavior, some psychologists have postulated that drives can be learned, that is, the organism learns to respond in certain ways which provide stimuli, functioning like those arising from basic tissue conditions, and which play the same role in behavior. Suppose that, for the time being, we assume that what we commonly call fear at least involves some activity of the visceral organs; we all more or less accept the notion that when we are afraid things happen to our hearts, lungs, intestines, adrenal glands, and so on. We feel "stirred up" inside. Assume further that this stirred-up-ness is a tissue condition that initiates stimuli that alter the conditions in the brain, especially the hypothalamus and its various centers, and, consequently, some kind of action results. In a young infant, this action is likely to be a sort of generalized withdrawal with various amounts of crying and "cowering." Assume further that this is a more or less natural reaction and one that is comparable to the restlessness previously mentioned in connection with hunger, a restlessness which sooner or later leads the organism out of the danger situation, just as in the case of hunger, the organism stumbles onto food or food is brought to it. The food reduces the hunger; in some similar way, the passage of time or the removal of the threatening stimulus situation might be thought of as reducing the fear. Again as with hunger, we found the organism showing more and more orientation with respect to food-type stimuli, so we might postulate that with experience, the fearful organism becomes more systematic about getting out of troublesome situations—it learns to run or dash about, to strike out wildly, in short, to "escape." We have now built up a picture of a potentially useful drive. Suppose that some organism, a rat, say, is shocked in a rather small box; the sudden painful stimulation initiates a "natural" fear reaction, and the animal begins to move about somewhat briskly. If one asks: "Why does the rat run?" we can answer: "It has a pain drive, accompanied by 'fear.'" The combination is making it run. Now suppose that every time we shock the rat, we also turn on a light just before the shock. In due time, with experience, we find the rat beginning to run, or shrink and huddle as soon as the light comes on. Because there is no shock, and therefore, no pain, and yet the rat reacts in some specific, yet unnatural way to the light, we are ready to make our next assumption: the rat has learned to fear the light; it has acquired a fear response to a previously innocuous stimulus, and, because the rat becomes active (we assume this is because of the fear), we might describe the rat's situation as one of being driven by fear. Such a fear, based on learning, can now be thought of as a "learned" drive (Miller, 1948; Mowrer, 1940).

A great deal of psychological experimentation and speculation has been based on acquired drives of fear. At the moment these do not concern us. The basic point is that if a drive can be learned, that is, attached to or associated with external stimuli, then it is not necessary to wait for natural periodic tissue changes; these can be evoked directly by other, external stimuli, and thereby provoke behavior that is related to the specific drive involved. On the other extreme, new responses might be learned which might appear quite afield from the original drive, but which, because of the environmental conditions under which the drives are acquired, still serve the original function of reducing the drive. Just such a suggestion was proposed by J. S. Brown (1953), for example, when he described the possible development of behavior related to acquiring money. Suppose that some child learns to be afraid in connection with words related to poverty, "We have no money," "I told you we can't afford that," "We're poor," etc. These and similar words are heard in circumstances which may be distressing or threatening; if the child is frightened when such allusions to poverty are heard and heartened by the appearance of money on the scene, we might imagine that in the future, signs or words relating to poverty might inspire some sort of uneasiness, if not quite fear, and that this uneasiness (previously dispelled only by symbols of wealth) will lead to activity related to the acquisition of money. The example may be far-fetched, but the line of reasoning is in accordance with the hypothesis of acquired drives. It has been argued that if one drive could be so acquired, then, presumably so could any other. There is no actual experimental evidence that this is actually so. It is common experience to "suddenly become hungry" when seeing others eating. Children are notorious in this respect and begin to starve at the sight of someone else eating ice cream or candy. We are all familiar with the salted nut problem. So long as we leave them alone, they are rather unimportant decorations at the party. Start munching a few and there appears to be no end to the "need" for this type of refreshment. Such observations, however, do not constitute support for a learned hunger drive, nor for any other. Fear has been the only acquired drive to receive some experimental support.

So long as we stay at the level of biological drives, the term "drive" seems to be of some value when restricted to descriptions of tissue conditions that produce some sort of stimulation or disturbance leading to irritability and restless activity. When we leave the immediate area where we can convince ourselves (perhaps "delude" would be the more appropriate term) that we are dealing with physiology that could be quite readily demonstrated if the physiologists would just get busy and find what we want, we get involved in more complex speculations. Why do men go to war? Is there a drive to fight, to aggress? Why do women like to have "exclusive" hats and dresses, or the latest from Paris? Surely there is no drive for the latest from Paris? Why do men continue working after they have achieved security for themselves and the following three generations? Why do some men paint and others write books that no one reads? Or poetry? Are there drives to create? To be famous? Are all of these activities based on acquired fear? Here we enter the difficult area of what most psychologists describe as motivation. The answer to *why* is what intrigues most of us. Why did she shoot him? Why did he jump off the bridge? Instincts? Drives? Motives? The term motive is usually reserved for more complex, primarily learned, often culturally determined behavior. We shall examine it more closely in a later chapter. For the present we can accept it as a generic expression which includes the notion of drives which may be only a class of motives. The basic proposition, however, is that some sort of motive is presumed to underly any but the most reflex behavior and the motive or motives involved are supposed to account for the reason for the behavior; they might answer questions beginning with "why," and the answer starts with the term "because." We have already learned earlier that scientists do not generally think in such "cause and effect" terms and the whole question may prove to be unworthy of our attention from a scientific viewpoint. We will return to it, however, because so much of modern psychology appeals to one form of motivational concept or another. For the present we have served our purpose, which, if you recall was to introduce an account of the function of rewards and punishments in learning.

Rewards and punishments in learning

We have made the point that whether something is a reward depends upon circumstances. These circumstances amount to wanting the item or event. Wanting something, in turn, in our present frame of reference depends upon having a drive (the tissue condition). This is not intended as a full explanation of wants or desires (see p. 341) but for the moment we recognize that rewards and drives (or motives) are fundamentally related. A reward eliminates, gets rid of, reduces or diminishes a drive. We are now ready to see how this combination of drive and reward might operate in a learning situation.

Early in this century, Edward Lee Thorndike,[2] a great authority in American education, announced that on the basis of his experiments with various kinds of animals, he had discovered a general law of learning. He called this the Law of Effect. This law stated, in general, that organisms tend to repeat those responses which are followed by satisfying states of affairs (rewards) and tend not to repeat those responses followed by annoying states of affairs (punishments). Thorndike attained great prestige in educational circles and his law was widely accepted. Actually the Law of Effect was stated in terms of the strengthening of bonds or connections between stimuli and responses, so that we can think of it in the terms we have previously used. In this framework, we can see that in a learning situation, an organism cannot learn unless

[2] Edward Lee Thorndike is one of the great historical figures in psychology. His *Animal Intelligence* (1898) is a classic in psychological literature.

it has a drive; otherwise there can be no rewarding consequence. Assuming that a drive is present, the organism then will engage in various activities some of which will reduce or eliminate the drive; these activities will then be strengthened and rise in the hierarchy of probability so that on future occasions, they will occur more readily until, finally, having been strengthened sufficiently by repeated rewards, the response will be the first to occur. Drives, then, have a dual function in the Thorndikian or instrumental learning type of situation (Thorndike himself did not talk about drives): they get the organism into action, and, by being reduced, they strengthen learning.

In the above paragraph we have been restating Thorndike's views in words he never used. The language we have been using is that of Hull (1943). Hull thought that Thorndike's "satisfyers," although defined objectively by Thorndike, were still too subjective and divorced from a natural science view. Hull restated the Law of Effect in a Law of Primary Reinforcement. According to this law, a "bond" between the neural consequence of a stimulus and the neural initiator of a response is strengthened whenever stimulation from a drive is reduced or diminished. By restating the Law of Effect in quasiphysiological language, Hull hoped to bring the psychology of learning closer to physiology and to require psychologists to initiate more molecular types of observations. The observations would have to be reduced to measurements of latencies, amplitudes, and directions instead of simple labeling such as "the cat pulled a string."

It is appropriate at this time, too, to indicate another variation on the Thorndikian theme. Skinner (1938) also found fault with the definition of satisfiers. Unlike Hull, however, Skinner felt that a definition of reinforcement in terms of drive reduction merely substituted one mystery for another. Skinner chose a more empirical approach. He presumed that, in a sense, reinforcement can define itself in terms of the behavior involved. If some behavior sample is selected for observation it can be watched for any changes that become manifest. If the behavior appears "stronger" because of something that happens after a response, it is proper to define whatever happened as a reinforcer. Thus, a rat, if given an opportunity to press a lever in the Skinner Box, will do so only occasionally and sporadically if nothing happens after a lever press. A count of such presses over a period of time is known as the "operant rate." If we now arrange for each bar press to be followed by a bit of food, the rate of pressing will change. The rat will begin to press faster and faster until it is pressing about as fast as it can eat the pellets of food. If the "operant rate" increases because of some consequence of pressing, this consequence can be termed a "reinforcer." It should be noted that, for Skinner, the strengthening of a response consists of a change in rate. A reinforcer, then, is anything that changes the operant rate. If the rate rises, the reinforcer is positive; if the rate drops, the reinforcer is negative.

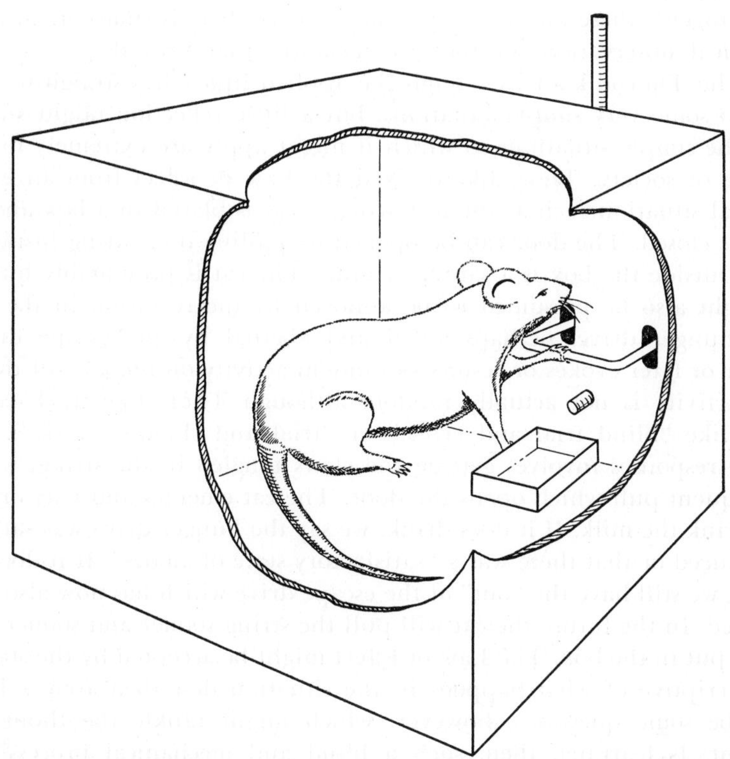

Figure 11 A Skinner Box. When the rat depresses the bar a small pellet of food drops into the tray below the bar. The food dispenser can be set to deliver food after each press or after any predetermined number of presses (a Fixed Ratio schedule), or it can be set to deliver after a Fixed Interval of time since the last press. The food tray can be located at any position in the box; locating it on an opposite wall delays the acquisition of the bar-pressing response.

While Hull and Skinner were in profound disagreement in terms of approach, they were both in the Thorndikian tradition that the consequences of behavior had an effect on the behavior itself. One additional point should be mentioned before we return to our general discussion of rewards. For Hull, a reward worked because it reduced a drive. For Skinner such an interpretation, based as it was on a theoretical inference, was unnecessary. He preferred to rely again on observation.

Instead of a drive, Skinner substituted the concept of "deprivation period," because, again, of an empirical observation that a reinforcer, e.g., food, would not alter an operant rate if the animal had just finished eating, but it would alter the rate if a period of time elapsed since a feeding period. For Skinner, then, it is not necessary to talk about drives or "hunger"; these are not empirically observed. It is sufficient to make empirical observations of the circumstances that prevail.

The Thorndikian view might be applied in a fairly straightforward way to some very simple situations, but a little reflection might suggest that the simple situations to which it might apply are extremely rare in nature or society. Thorndike derived the Law of Effect from an experimental situation such as the following: a cat is placed in a box and the door is closed. The door can be opened by pulling on a string inside the box. Outside the box is a saucer of milk. The cat is presumably hungry. It might also be presumed to be annoyed by incarceration in the box. The hunger drive, perhaps aided and abetted by an "escape drive," sooner or later evokes or results in random activity on the part of the cat (the activity is not actually random although Thorndike used expressions like "blind trial and error," or "trial and chance success"). One of the responses involves getting the claws tangled in the string, with a consequent pull which opens the door. The cat emerges and may or may not drink the milk. If it does drink, we say the hunger drive was satisfied or reduced or that there was a "satisfactory state of affairs." If it does not drink, we still have the "out" of the escape drive which has now also been reduced. In the future the cat will pull the string sooner and sooner after being put in the box. The Law of Effect might be accepted by the student as descriptive of what happens in the situation described above. There may be some questions, however, which might rankle the thoughtful student. Is learning, then, such a blind and mechanical process? Are some cats smarter than others? Thorndike would say "yes" to both these questions. All learning is blind, stupid, if you like, mechanical, certainly. Whether you are smart depends upon the number and kind of habits you have acquired, the responses that have been strengthened for you by the mechanical operation of rewards. If you have had rewarding experiences in a wide number of situations you will be smarter than someone who has not. If you happen to know the answer to some question, it is because it was strengthened for you in the past; you deserve and get no credit. If you do not know the answer, it is because you did not have the happy fortune of having such a response strengthened in your past. Forget about your heroes and do not condemn your villains; they are equally innocent victims of their behaviorial histories. Anyone can be taught anything by suitable application of rewards. As Skinner (1955) remarks: all students should get A grades; if not, the teacher is poorly prepared or has not been given the authority and the means by which to teach correctly. (In fairness to Skinner we should note that this authority and means include such difficult-to-attain conditions as having one student at a time, control over the student's "deprivation schedule" and control over the rewards to be administered.)

The serious student will ask: does the Law of Effect kind of principle apply to all kinds of learning by all kinds of subjects or only hungry cats and chickens? The Thorndikian answer is again: yes. It applies to college students and kindergarten pupils. But, as soon as we go beyond the hungry cat we run into problems of specifying the drives and the rewards, because most college students and kindergarten pupils are reasonably well fed and will not study when hungry! It becomes necessary to devise "corollaries" or additional principles which can be invoked to save the Law of Effect. One such corollary we have already examined; it is the principle of derived drives, especially the derived drive of fear, or, as it is more generally called in connection with human learning, "anxiety." Without much difficulty, it is possible to convert the concept of "anxiety" into "curiosity" as Dollard and Miller (1950) have done. With a derived curiosity drive we can handle the learning of anyone at the highest levels.

Secondary rewards

Another corollary, analogous to derived drives, is the concept of derived or "secondary" rewards, or secondary reinforcement (Hull, 1943). In its most general sense, a secondary reinforcer can be anything at all that frequently accompanies a primary reinforcer and takes on its capacity to reduce or diminish a drive or, if it does not actually affect a drive, it might strengthen some kinds of S ——→R bonds, that is, it might reinforce some behavior. Consider a feeding situation where a mother fondles the baby, while holding the bottle, and croons away to the child, frequently saying, "that's a nice baby," "what a good, good, baby," "wonderful baby," etc. How many thousands of times does a baby hear the words "good," "nice," "fine," "wonderful," before it gives up the bottle? Assuming that the milk is a drive reducer in its own right, we might and do find that the bottle (and the mother) also becomes a treasured item. We can presume that the terminology of endearment might also become associated with responses involved in drive reduction, such as relaxing. The bottle and the words have become secondary reinforcers which can then operate outside the original learning situation and strengthen responses made to other drives. Thorndike used such reinforcers as saying "right" to college students when they chose the correct response out of a number available. For Thorndike, "right" was a reward. It might have been one for some of the students as well. The educational system makes use of a variety of "secondary" reinforcers—gold stars, honor rolls, medals, prizes; the world of business uses money, checks, bonds, and Christmas turkeys as secondary reinforcers for performance.

Do gold stars and dollar bills actually reinforce learning? Do secondary reinforcers of any kind really work to reinforce learning? Perhaps their role has been misinterpreted (Bugelski, 1956). Certainly they have powerful influences over behavior. The child that does not get the gold star may throw a fit, and an empty pay envelope may result in no end of trouble. There is no question about the basic desirability of such features of our culture. But how does the gold star at the end of the month or the paycheck on Friday affect the behavior of the child at the beginning of the month or the worker on Monday? Must we start assuming that with each new item of learning, each new word to be spelled correctly, the gold star is always symbolically present in the child's imagination? Or that the child says to himself, "Ah, k-n-i-f-e, knife, another step toward the gold star." This might conceivably happen, but that it is general seems absurd. Yet just such a proposal has been advanced by reputable theorists who picture a succession of secondary reinforcers working backwards in time toward the early stages of an achievement history. It may be that so-called secondary reinforcers are more likely operating as stimuli for other kinds of responses that normally follow them, and might better be conceived as motivators than reinforcers. This is a difficult problem which psychologists have yet to resolve. The concept is extremely powerful in that it purports to explain how the great majority of human learning occurs. It is obvious that we do not reinforce human learners with food. As a matter of fact, humans do not learn well when hungry, cold, or tired, all situations that require primary reinforcers.

The concept of secondary reinforcement arose from observations that animals might continue working at some task which formerly brought about a primary reinforcer if some feature or aspect of the original reinforcement situation was retained. Thus, if a rat pressed a lever which operated a food dispenser, and this food dispenser made a noise when the food was delivered, the rat would continue to press the lever if the noise made by the dispenser continued to occur, even if the food no longer was delivered. The noise of the dispenser could be interpreted as maintaining the activity. Because a noise is of no primary value to a rat, it might be called a secondary reinforcer. Skinner (1938) showed that not only would such a noise maintain activity but a rat might *initiate* lever pressing and continue it for some time with only a noise for a "reward" if it had previously been fed by the experimenter manipulating the dispenser from the outside—no bar being present for the rat to press. Other experimenters (Saltzman, 1949) have shown that rats might learn to run to a white box (with no food in it) in preference to a black box if they had previously been allowed to enter and eat in a white box. Such experiments have suggested that almost any kind of stimulus or condition (colors, sounds, food trays, surroundings in general) can all come to work like primary reinforcers in that learning can occur in their presence, and in the absence of a primary or drive-reducing object or condition.

It is commonly accepted that before a stimulus of any kind can serve as a secondary reinforcer it must first accompany a primary reinforcer on a number of occasions (perhaps often enough for some original learning). It has been argued by some of Skinner's supporters (Schoenfeld, Antonitis, and Bersh, 1950) that another condition must be specified: the secondary reinforcer must *precede* the primary reinforcer if it is to work as a reinforcer in its own right. Thus, if a light comes on *after* a bar press, but before the food appears, the light can later serve as a secondary reinforcer. On the other hand, if the light *follows* the food, even by as little as a second, it will not acquire reinforcing properties. By spelling out this condition Schoenfeld, Antonitis, and Bersh have, in effect, identified a secondary reinforcer with what Skinner (1938) called a discriminated stimulus (S^D). A discriminated stimulus is one which precedes a response. In the absence of this stimulus, the response will not normally occur. In the Skinner Box situation, for example, it can be arranged so that no food will drop from the dispenser unless a light has come on. Any presses of the lever in the dark will not be reinforced. Any presses in the presence of the light will be reinforced. After a time, the rat will stop pressing when the light goes off and return to the lever and start pressing when the light goes on. The light has become a discriminated stimulus.

In most situations in which the concept of secondary reinforcers has been applied, it can be argued that the stimulus involved is operating only as a discriminated stimulus and is not reinforcing anything. It merely leads to the next stage in a sequence of activities. In the bar-pressing situation, for example, the noise of the dispenser becomes conditioned to moving to the food tray. If there is no food the animal returns to the bar because it has been conditioned to press *after* leaving the food tray. If the noise does not occur, the animal may not get to the tray and consequently the stimuli for returning to the bar will not occur. We must await the verdict of more research. For the present we can keep our reservations active and regard secondary reinforcers as stimuli that occur at certain phases in a sequence, terminating one and initiating another. In a spelling bee, for example, the tester may say "right" after a correct spelling of one word. This is a signal for the contestant to relax, for the next in line to get tense and so on. The presence or absence of satisfactions may be rather incidental to any learning that goes on even if some of the stimuli like "right" come to acquire other kinds of values.

It should also be noted that there is a strong correspondence between what Hull might call a secondary reinforcer and what Pavlov (1927) called higher order conditioning. If a dog, for example, were conditioned to give a salivary response to the sound of a bell, a new conditioned response could be developed to some other stimulus, a light, for example, by turning on a light and following this shortly with the bell. If the bell were occasionally reinforced by food, it could serve as a reinforcer in its own right for conditioned responses made to the light. We now must face the question of whether the bell is a secondary reinforcer, a higher order conditioner, or a discriminated stimulus. We appear to have an embarrassment of riches in terminology and a comparable degree of poverty in our appreciation. If we recognize that behavior might well be described in the expression: "one thing leads to another," it might not be too difficult to fit secondary reinforcers into our picture of behavior. Secondary reinforcers, whatever else they may be, terminate one phase in a sequence of activities. Perhaps if we examine such sequences from our conceptual neural view we may make some small gain. We shall do this in a moment, but first we might note that some theorists take a dim view of rewards and reinforcers having anything to do with learning.

Are rewards necessary for learning?

Some authorities in the learning area take a rather negative view of rewards. Guthrie (1952), for example, argues that subsequent events cannot influence prior events and claims that rewards or "satisfiers" have no function other than to eliminate the stimuli which resulted in the behavior. The pleasantness or unpleasantness of rewards or punishments would be irrelevant for Guthrie. Any new stimulus or means by which the stimulation that led to the behavior could be eliminated would serve the purpose. It just happens that if a rewarding object or event is present, the learner becomes distracted and engages in consummatory or other behavior, thereby preserving the relationship which was automatically established between the original stimulus and response. Because rewards are peculiarly suited to distract, they serve this function of preserving the learning very effectively, not because they are rewards, however, but, because they are distractors. Because some of the stimuli involved may be of the nature of drive stimuli, the reward removes these too. This last point makes Guthrie's criticism an academic or semantic quibble if it can be shown that a drive is always involved in learning.

Tolman (1949) has an interesting view of rewards which may be pertinent here. He claims that rewards have nothing to do with learning either, just as Guthrie maintains. For Tolman, rewards confirm "expectancies." What an expectancy is has never been made quite clear, except that behaviorally, it is possible to argue that when certain events (stimuli) follow each other regularly, the organism seems to behave as if it were ready to react to the succeeding one of a series after the initial one appeared. In terms of Pavlov's dog, the bell rings and the dog salivates before the food arrives. Tolman argues that it is theoretically fruitful to describe this sequence of events as an "expectancy." This does not mean that we are attributing some sort of mentalistic powers to the dog, but rather that we should view the entire sequence as a unit, the sequence itself meriting the descriptive term "expectancy." When the food arrives, the sequence is fulfilled, or "confirmed."

Perhaps all of these different views of the nature of the effect of consequences that follow responses are helpful to an appreciation of the role of rewards. Some students are content to accept an *"empirical law of effect"* (McGeoch and Irion, 1952), arguing that it does not make much or any difference how rewards work, so long as they do. This seems an inadequate position for theoretical psychology and we do not expect that such a position will be acceptable to many.

A hypothetical neural account of learning

In considering the functions of the conceptual nervous system we described the general operations of this system in a way that more or less readily incorporates the concepts of drive stimuli and the operations of rewards without doing violence to any of the views described above. It will be recalled that we postulated a fundamental reaction of persistent neural firing whenever stimulation entered the nervous system. We also postulated a fundamental process of association such that two circuits in more or less simultaneous function would tend to develop connections in common so that one circuit would set off the other. Such activity could be presumed to continue for some little time, at least a few seconds after stimulation ceased outside the organism. So long as the stimulation persisted without being eliminated via an appropriate motor outlet, the organism would find itself being stimulated into a variety of activities. Should one such activity get rid of the external stimulation (environmentally speaking, lead to a reward), the circuits firing at this time would tend to become integrated with each other. This hypothetical neural scheme might be an approach to the handling of the reward problem. We can turn now to some other facts and speculations about learning which are of significance.

It has been stated above that the important behavioral fact about learning is to get the organism to do something, something that it already can do but does not ordinarily do in the situation. Any child can spell k-n-i-f-e, if it can mouth the letters of the alphabet. The problem is to mouth them in the correct order. To get the child to do the mouthing is part of the problem of education. Here we found it helpful to introduce the concept of drive. But we also noted, in connection with human learning, that ordinarily, biological drives have little or nothing to do with human learning problems. To get a drive into the act, we considered derived or learned drives, and found that learned fears or anxieties could be suggested as stimulating agencies. To make the anxiety palatable socially, we dress it up as "curiosity." We can argue now, that a child will not learn to spell unless it has some curiosity about the problem of spelling, some anxiety. Under the stimulation arising from the anxiety condition (which includes its own neural counterparts), and additional stimulation from book or teacher, the child now responds; if the response is correct, the anxiety dwindles, the teacher may or may not say "correct." It is probably irrelevant; there are other ways in which the stimulation from the cue word are eliminated. If the teacher does keep saying nice things, a child might learn that the teacher says nice things, but that may be about the extent of the function of being nice on the part of the teacher. It might be just as effective for the teacher to introduce the next word or problem; that would eliminate the influence of the earlier one. We should note here with Guthrie that if the child gives the wrong answer and the teacher says something nice, the wrong answer will be learned. If the teacher goes on to the next problem without saying "good," the wrong answer will also be learned. We might draw from this argument one practical application about learning: never let the learner do the wrong thing last. The last performance should be a correct one.

The practical application just mentioned might suggest that any system where a teacher calls on children in succession until a correct answer is offered is a violation of learning theory. This may be the case if the children lose interest in the problem under study as soon as they are passed over. If they continue to observe the rest, they can benefit as much as the last one from a correct response made by someone else because they too are making it subvocally. The teacher's problem is to keep the whole class trying. Since this is so difficult, it might really be a waste of time and a poor procedure.

We have indulged ourselves with the concepts of drive and reward or reinforcement long enough. There is, as should be quite clear, no direct factual evidence about the nature of drive and its relation to learning. We have been very speculative in all of our treatment of learning thus far. We might point out that drives, if they function at all, function in terms of the stimuli that are generated from the various bodily conditions that might be labeled "drive." This means, in effect, that any stimuli which might impinge on the organism also function as "drive" stimuli (Miller and Dollard, 1941). In short, the distinction is quite unnecessary, and all that we need to postulate for a learning situation is that some kind of stimulation gets the organism going through a repertoire of behavior. This repertoire must contain the response to be learned, either to the stimulus that, in effect, generates it or to accompanying stimuli. Rewards, as such, mean no more than the cessation or elimination of the stimulation that originated the activity. They have little or nothing to do with the learning itself except, perhaps, to allow it to go on in terms of some sort of neural consolidation which cannot take place if the original stimulation is still disturbing the brain in its action at various, potential synapses. Note that we do not say that the stimulation is "seeking an outlet." Such talk is magical. But if no synaptic outlet leading to a response which removes the stimulus is crossed, the neural activity will persist if the stimulation persists. As soon as this neural activity ceases, some progress has been made toward strengthening the connection between the stimuli involved and the final behavior. In some cases the synapses that are available are readily crossed and only one or a few trials are necessary for learning. Other kinds of responses, being low in hierarchy may take a long time or require a great many trials to strengthen.

Punishment

It will be recalled that Thorndike included a negative aspect to his Law of Effect. Annoying states of affairs following a response were supposed to weaken the bonds involved. This agreed with popular prejudice but over the years did not seem to square with experimental fact. Punishment, insofar as it was feasible to use it in the laboratory, did not appear to weaken undesirable responses or their assumed connections. Later on Thorndike (1932) had had enough of punishment and dropped it as a principle or determinant of learning. This new view was quickly adopted by teachers' colleges and an era of permissiveness in training followed the announcement that punishment had no effect in learning. Newspapers and popular magazines took up the idea and parents learned that they were not supposed to punish children for misbehavior as it just did not do any good.

To claim that punishment, loosely defined as some sort of painful or disagreeable treatment suffered by someone, had no effects, seems unreasonable, and it is. Certainly punishment has effects. The question is what kind and on whom. The problem must be analyzed much more carefully than it has been. On what basis did Thorndike reach his conclusions? He conducted numerous experiments with college students wherein he asked the subjects to pick out one out of five Spanish words which might mean the same as an English word appearing next to the Spanish ones. Two hundred such choices might be exacted. If the wrong choice were made, Thorndike punished, i.e., he said "wrong." Examination of the data showed that saying "right" improved performance, saying "wrong" or nothing at all had no effect on performance. In fact, to the extent that saying "wrong" had any effect, it tended to be followed by repetition of the incorrect choice. Conclusion: punishment is ineffective in learning.

Is saying "wrong" to a college student in such a situation punishment? It appears that some students might not be at all alarmed at being informed that they had missed in a 5 to 1 choice situation. They might feel quite indifferent, or even informed at hearing "wrong." Certainly the punishment, if it is that, was very mild. What about stronger punishment? We are already familiar with the practice of some psychologists who shock rats. In some of the situations we described, the shock is a painful stimulus, well enough, but is it a punishment? The rat has been quietly minding his own business and all of a sudden it is shocked. We can conceive of the shock not as a punishment, but rather as a strong stimulus, a drive stimulus to get the organism to do something other than sit there. If it is punishing, it is not qualitatively different from any other strong drive like hunger which might be thought of as stressful, unpleasant, disagreeable, painful, etc. Pain, when introduced as a drive, is not punishment in the sense of some sort of retribution for incorrect behavior, yet it does have some retribution characteristics if we choose to call sitting around minding our own business the undesirable thing to do. If we do so choose, then what does the punishment do? It provides the stimulation for a variety of responses which differ drastically from sitting around, and one of these new responses has been decreed by society to be right or desirable. The response that is approved, e.g., pulling a chain, is now learned, and punishment was certainly involved.

We can probably assert with confidence that punishment will, if appropriately controlled, facilitate the learning of responses which terminate the punishment. Children learn to cry in a reasonable time after a strap has been applied. They learn to time the crying quite nicely. Crying too soon is not appropriate and taking more than a nominal amount of strapping would be undesirable. With the parent to be appeased it is necessary to delay the howling for a number of whacks. Children also learn to cry at potential threats because the crying brings the parents on the scene. Such crying is presumably learned as a response to previously experienced punishment. But much of this kind of learning is frowned upon by parents. They do not want the children to run when punished. They want them to learn to be nice, to obey, to hang their clothes in the closet, to speak politely, and thousands of other silly, unnatural things. Does punishment work here? We take a sample problem: the child rushes into the house, throws clothes and books on the floor, knocks over a vase, opens and slams the refrigerator, spills some milk and crumbs over the floor and finally, mama takes a whack at him, meanwhile unleashing a torrent of "don'ts." "Don't do this," "do it right," "can't you ever learn?" "where were you brought up?" (as if she did not know), "just like your father," "you're just no good," and so on. What does the child learn? Not to slam doors, throw books and clothes, spill milk, etc.? By no means. The routine is repeated at the next occasion, with an "I forgot" in case the lecture is repeated, or even a promise to try to be better. Punishment in such cases does not appear to have much effect, if any. It will still have the effect described above; the child will learn to say, "I forgot," "I promise," "I'll try," and many other formulas. If the punishment is especially severe, the child will learn to avoid mama, to run when she turns or raises her arm or voice, to escape, in short. But our interest is in other kinds of changes. How do we go about getting a child to hang his clothes? By punishment for not hanging them? If this behavior is consistently followed by punishment frequently enough, it might even work, but the learning would be rather insecurely restricted to very narrow circumstances involving the specific situation and call for a great deal of policemanship. The child would have to learn to pick clothes off the floor and hang them. Unless the clothes were on the floor in the first place, he would not hang them. The important clues are involved with coming into the house and responding to the hallway or the clothes closet, with a clothes-hanging response. This is what is desired. The way to bring it about is to meet the child at the door and get him to hang his clothes as the first response to the business of coming into the house. This may or need not be followed by cookies or candy. The clothes in the closet are enough to establish the learning. The cookies merely strengthen positive behavior toward the cookie giver. Since meeting the child at the door may be inconvenient or annoying, the average child does not learn the appropriate responses and the battle between the natural enemies (parents vs. children) flourishes.

The above illustration can be altered to suit the behavior involved but we might do better with a description of an experimental example. Estes (1944) tried to test the effect of punishment on the behavior of rats. He chose to train rats first to press a bar, a response that was followed by food. When the response was strongly established, he decided to punish the rat for pressing the bar. (The assumption here is that such responses as tossing jackets on the floor or the nearest chair are strongly established, i.e., they may have been reinforced frequently in the past. Using profane language, e.g., may also be strongly established in the juvenile delinquent who gets reinforced by his little juvenile delinquent friends.) When the rat was an accomplished performer in pressing the bar, Estes arranged for the response to be followed by a shock. The response was now altered to withdrawal or escape, as we might expect. With a few more shocks, the rat stays away from the bar. But note, again, as with the clothes on the floor, the shock does not come until after the bar is pressed. The stimuli for pressing come *before* the pressing. The stimuli for pressing may be very varied; they include the general appearance and feel of the box, the hunger drive stimuli, the possible odor of food, the sight of the bar. The last item is possibly of not much importance, as the rat's pattern vision is not especially acute and rats will press bars in the dark just as well as in the light. The only stimuli associated with escape from the bar are the kinesthetic ones from pressing and the rather weak visual stimuli. The rat is put into some degree of conflict. The conflict is resolved for some time by staying away from the bar end of the box, but all of the stimuli in the box and in the rat are forcing an approach to the bar. The rat can be made to stay away for weeks at a time, but stronger hunger stimuli and a rest from the punishment eventually bring the rat over to the bar and it begins to press again. Now reinforcement by food will quickly re-establish the pressing habit. What was the effect of the punishment? Suppression of the behavior, and only suppression. It is quite probably true that severe and frequent punishment might suppress the behavior for so long that the organism dies without repeating the punished response, but this might very well work out because escape behavior is sufficiently reinforced to the cues involved in bar pressing so that the animal has learned something new on the basis of reinforcement of the pain or fear drives.

In most situations involving humans, we are not punished for responding to the same stimuli which normally lead to reinforcement as was the case in Estes' experiment. The behavior is not of the repetitive type to a single set of cues. The child might be punished for using foul language in the street, but the punishment is not given in the street. It is given in the home where the language involved is never uttered anyway. Stealing goes on in stores or dark streets; the punishment occurs in courts or jails. The two situations have nothing in common. We can expect no effect from such punishment. The only way we can even get a suppressive effect from some punishment is to catch someone red-handed and punish him on the spot in the presence of the stimuli that normally lead to the undesirable (to authority) behavior. This can rarely happen—the milk is spilled, the deed has been done, the stimuli for it are usually gone and cannot be effectively reinstated. The punishment of such behavior has no value unless we consider the possible therapeutic effect on the punisher who might feel better after getting rid of his own frustrations via the exercise involved in shouting, screaming, or beating the miserable culprit.

We might end this discussion of punishment by suggesting a technique for preventing undesirable behavior. In the case of the clothes-on-the-floor routine or banging doors behavior, it might be desirable to send the child outside, fully dressed, and have him come back and dispose of the garments in the appropriate fashion. One such exercise might do more good than a life-time of screaming. Two or three such exercises might even teach the child. The door banger might be asked to open and close his door a number of times in the desired fashion. This might not work unless the complex of stimuli is about the same as when the door banging occurred originally, that is, when the child was in a temper. If he closes the door often enough he might also get into the temper which might help. Because it is easier for a parent to shout at a child than to stand over him as an educator, we can expect the shouting to continue for the next few generations of parents.

Punishment as a deterrent

A word might be ventured regarding possible deterrent effects of punishment. The punishment of criminals by hanging or imprisonment may keep them out of the crime market, but the punishment of others rarely seems to work in deterring unpunished criminals or the heretofore innocent. It may be that no genuine escape or avoidance tendencies can be developed in the absence of the necessary stimulation, and if one has not yet been punished in connection with some kinds of stimulation, there can be no deterrent effect from the punishment of others. To the extent that a potential wrongdoer has the capacity to "imagine" or otherwise verbalize the punishing situation for himself, and this would have been based on prior punishment of some sort, there may be some possibility of deterrent function from seeing or reading about others being punished. If the prior history does not make for effective self-stimulation prior to some possibly criminal action, then we can hardly expect deterrent action. If a child has been consistently protected by parents or "big brothers" when it did get into trouble, then we might find that talk about what happens to others in such situations might be rather empty of effect. The roles of reward and punishment are not without their controversial aspects. The same is true of other features or characteristics of the learning picture. At this time we would like to consider some other aspects or alleged principles of learning, noting that we can expect difficulty about interpretation of what is actually going on even if we can agree about the basic facts. There is really only one additional principle of any magnitude but an appreciation of it is rather important and so we will spend more time on it than on some other hypotheses. It is the principle of generalization.

GENERALIZATION

The child's identification of the milkman as "daddy" is a standard American joke. The underlying principle, however, is a very serious problem in learning. The child may be mistaken, but the joke illustrates how readily we respond in a specific way to nonspecific stimuli. In the laboratory we find that Pavlov's dog will salivate to any bell that more or less approximates the tone of the bell used in the original condition. And, we can say with some confidence that, by and large, we are usually responding to approximations of the original stimuli to which we learned to respond in some specific fashion. It is a common observation in philosophical discussions that things are always changing. We never step into the same river twice says the philosopher Heraclitus. Similarly, we rarely see or hear the same stimuli in the same settings from exactly the same position. A dish looked down upon may be circular; from any other angle it is an ellipse. We have already considered this in connection with the principle of constancy. Yet, we have no trouble identifying objects, whether they be dishes or lions. The tendency to respond to some stimulus value which is not exactly the same as the original training stimulus is of extreme value for organisms. If this "generalizing" effect did not occur, we would have to learn millions of additional responses to those we are already forced to learn. We would have to learn to identify every spoken word individually as each new speaker uttered it because of the voice peculiarities that distinguish each speaker. Each new example of an apple, or a cake, or a female, would become a new learning problem even of identification. Man could not possibly survive if he had to learn to behave so precisely and specifically that he would not know his mother in a new dress, or in the kitchen, or in profile.

Of course, the fact that we respond to different values of the original training stimulus has its disadvantages, too, to the extent that society insists on some degree of specification. Calling a cow a horse, for example, will not do, and in some circles, confusing a composition by Bartok with one of Hindemith's will result in raised eyebrows. When the teacher asks: "What is 8 × 7," the child that gayly sings out "54" earns a frown. In the social realm, troubles can arise from reacting to a member of some race or creed as one might have learned to react to some other member of that group. When a crooked politician is sent to jail, all politicians may shoulder some of the public's censure for a while. Similarly, attitudes established in connection with social classes, institutions, professions, and all aspects of social life may be erroneously based on specific learning to one misrepresentative of the whole.

Generalization is so pervasive in all our life adjustments that it requires close scrutiny. What actually happens when we "generalize"? Two interpretations have been advanced by theorists in this area: the first, by Thorndike [3] and his successors, was based on the principle of identical elements. We have already encountered this proposal in connection with the concept of closure or redintegration. According to this view, we are seriously misled when we talk about any given feature of a stimulus situation as *the* stimulus. In Pavlov's laboratory, Pavlov might regard a bell or a light as the stimulus. Certainly it was the stimulus that concerned Pavlov. But was it the stimulus that concerned the dog? The dog, was after all, strapped in a special harness in a special position, he was hungry to a more or less fixed degree, there were various temporal factors involved in the picture and what the dog was responding to might not actually be the bell, per se, but bell plus a lot of other things, or a lot of other things with or without the bell. In conditioning situations, organisms often respond with the so-called conditioned reflex without being stimulated specifically with the conditioned stimulus. Guthrie (1952), for example, argued that the bell might set off some reaction of the head, neck and shoulders which leads to a postural shift which in turn might produce some kinesthetic stimulation which would be the major element in the conditioned response. The dog, i.e., might have learned to salivate to the kinesthetic stimulation produced by a movement of his right hind leg. Henceforth, any pattern of stimulation that led to this movement and its consequent stimulus would generate the salivary response, with Pavlov none the wiser. If a rat is trained to jump when a light goes on, and if turning on the light is accomplished by

[3] The concept of "transfer of training" is introduced here because of the necessity for discussing "identical elements." The next chapter will continue the appreciation of the "transfer" concept.

a clicking switch, the rat may jump when the switch is turned even if the light does not go on.

Similarly, when the child calls the horse a big doggie, the child may be responding to the furry appearance of the hide or the quadrupedal structure of the equine. Again, identical elements to a degree. The milkman is called "daddy" because both wear pants or glasses or bow ties or tower over the child. The determination of what is and what is not an identical element can lead to a lot of controversy. Thorndike, for example, was concerned at one time with the question of "transfer of training" in educational circles. The question in crude form was: does taking "hard" courses like Latin and mathematics train the mind? The answer Thorndike and Woodworth found was that, to the extent that training in hard courses teaches a person to use certain procedures, develop specific study habits, attitudes toward problem situations, etc., then, transfer would take place to other tasks calling for identical procedures, study habits, and the rest. If the new situation did not contain the identical elements, there would be no transfer.

Because it is possible to argue, as above, that identical elements can be of a very general nature and include emotional, attitudinal, procedural, and situational factors, it is very difficult to prove or disprove the argument. If transfer takes place, it was because of identical elements. If it does not then the identical elements which matter were not present even though numerous other physically identical elements are present.

The other interpretation of generalization is a more physiological (Wolpe, 1952) approach, at least hypothetically. It is argued that a given stimulus energy will excite certain specific fibers in the nervous system over a relatively broad range. Other physical energies which are close to the original in some dimension, will excite some of these same fibers or neurons and bring about the same or a similar reaction. Thus, a given tone serving as an original stimulus will have a certain intensity and frequency and other physical characteristics. Suppose that the conditioned response is one of salivation. Another tone, close to the original in any one of these physical dimensions, will presumably excite some of the original neurons and bring about salivation, perhaps of a lesser amount. Touching the dog on the flank as a conditioned stimulus might serve to illustrate the point more clearly. Any touch in the neighborhood of the flank might excite some of the neurons involved in the original touch and bring about the response. To some degree this view also involves identical elements, but now we are dealing with identical elements in the nervous system and providing for lesser amounts of the reaction, if that should prove to be the case. The Thorndike view is an all-or-none type of argument—the element is there or it is not.

There has been a prolonged debate about the course of generalization in this respect. Does the response diminish in quantity with "distance" from the original stimulation, and if it does, does this follow any particular kind of pattern, such as dropping off more rapidly at first and more slowly later (negative acceleration) or does it follow some other course. Those who hold to some variation of the Thorndike view claim that there is no real drop-off at all so long as there are identical elements. Evidence supporting each view has been accumulated but there is not enough to support a final answer. (See the evaluation by Osgood, 1953.)

Whatever the course of generalization and whatever the basic physiology, the facts are clear that we do not expect to ever reproduce the same stimulus in all detail (including the condition of the organisms) in any test of the hypothesis, yet we can be reasonably sure that we can predict (or at least account for) numerous, if not the majority of, reactions upon the basis of generalization. Sometimes the enthusiastic application of the concept will lead us into difficult situations where nothing can really be proved but where argument can flourish in a lively fashion. Suppose we take the popular illustration stemming from psychoanalytic views that young men, in search of a wife, will find themselves attracted to women who are "like" their mothers. The view is supposed to be based on some development of the Oedipus complex and to hold more or less universally. Thus, your wife will resemble your mother, like it or not. How can this hypothesis be tested? Certainly your wife will be like your mother in some respects—they are both females. If their eyes differ in color, their hair or size might not; if they are very unlike physically, they may be "identical" in attitude, mannerisms, or smile in the same way. It would be very difficult to prove that any two people are completely unlike in any respect. To find some respect in which they are similar is no trick at all, but very possibly of no consequence whatsoever.

DISCRIMINATION

Because generalization is limited in its usefulness in adjustment to situations condoned by society, and because it regularly can lead us into error as well as salvation, it is necessary to combat generalization effects with specific training procedures to develop "discriminated" reactions. Generalization will take us only so far, and we can easily wind up in trouble in a highly complex civilization. "Don't spit on the floor" posted in a hall might not transfer to the subway, the street, or your living room. "Daddy" might work all right for a while when applied to anyone in pants but sooner or later daddy himself wants to be the sole nominee for the position. The process by which we learn to make more specific responses to stimuli that invite a response based on generalization is called "discrimination." How do we learn to discriminate?

Earlier we described the principle of extinction. If the stimulus is retained or persists in spite of a reaction (or if the unconditioned stimulus, or perhaps the reinforcer is not present) the organism is forced into some new reaction to the stimulus in question. We can not afford to rush to the door every time the phone rings. The phone keeps ringing and there is no one at the door. Gradually the new value of the stimulus acquires its own response. The process is not a simple one because the new learning will also generalize to the old stimulus which must retain its own value or there will have been no gain in learning. If the child is learning to call a cat, a cat, instead of a doggy, it might now start calling the doggie a cat. In the laboratory, if the dog is being trained to respond to a dim light and not a bright one behavior with respect to the dim light might suffer when the bright light is not "reinforced." A rat might be trained to jump toward a black card and not toward a white one; this is relatively easy to do. Now if we change the black card to a gray one, the behavior might get a little disturbed. If we start out with two grays, not radically different from each other, training will be long drawn out, because of generalization from one to the other in both positive and negative directions. Pavlov (1927) trained a dog to react to a metronome beating 100 times a minute. By generalization the dog would respond to a metronome beating at 60 or at slower rates. Gradually the negative metronome beat was stepped up forcing a finer and finer discrimination upon the dog. When the metronome beat at 96 times a minute the dog was no longer able to maintain the discrimination. The dog would salivate to either or to neither, and, in addition, appeared extremely disturbed, fighting the situation. Pavlov termed the condition "experimental neurosis." Many enthusiasts immediately jumped to the conclusion that other instances of disturbance, among humans, were similarly created by difficult discriminations. There is little if any evidence that such is the case and we should be careful to emphasize the "experimental" term in the process of developing "experimental neuroses."

It should be clear now that the processes of reinforcement and of extinction are the presumed major factors in the development of learned behavior. It should also be clear that both processes are working together, almost from the very first, if indeed not from the first, in the acquisition of any learned pattern. If the response called for by society is a highly specific one, we can expect trouble from generalization; if no great specificity is required by society, then we can expect that there will be little discrimination developed. If the organism can survive peacefully in such conditions, no great harm has been done. In a complex environment where verbal responses are the primary basis for interaction, we can expect that only those who develop rather fine discriminations of a verbal nature will be effective contributors to the society. Most of what passes for education is the acquisition of a more and more refined vocabulary. Students sometimes complain that some subject, e.g., psychology, is nothing but a lot of definitions. This is certainly true. But it is equally true of physics, chemistry, mathematics, or any other phase of education. The engineer requires a finer vocabulary than the mechanic. The mechanic needs a better working vobaculary of mechanical terms than the music teacher who has his own troubles with musical terminology. Instead of complaining about the definitions to be learned, it would be far wiser to start learning them. Only then can the necessary discriminations be labeled and communicated to others, problems identified, and work pushed forward.

With the principles of reinforcement, extinction, generalization and discrimination behind us we can now attend to some subsidiary principles. None of these have been sufficiently well spelled out in terms of the various dimensions and factors that might have to be taken into account but they may be of some help in comprehending some of the many complications of learning experiences. We can deal with them somewhat more summarily than the important principles already discussed.

SUBSIDIARY PRINCIPLES

Spaced as opposed to massed learning

Most of our learning experiences are sporadic. The stimuli to which we learn to respond in specific ways come upon us at unpredictable or at least irregular intervals. How often do you see a dog and try to get a child to learn its appropriate label? On the other hand, some activities are practiced more or less regularly and systematically. The piano lesson is practiced daily at 4:00 P.M. for one hour, or whatever schedule has been established. The poem to be learned for class is rehearsed a number of times in succession. The school play is rehearsed daily for a month, and so on. How often, how regularly, for how long should any such activities be practiced? Actually no one knows the answers to these questions. But from laboratory studies with rats and humans, some general information has been accumulated, much of it contradictory and specific to the dimensions of a given task.

It is generally agreed that spacing trials over a period is a more efficient way of studying than devoting the same amount of time to a single, massed session. In a massed session, the learner gets tired, loses motivation, gets confused about what he knows and doesn't know, and may develop various kinds of "inhibitions." In spacing his trials, the learner recovers from fatigue, finds out what he knows and does not need to practice any more, and may find additional motivation from progress as well as from the relatively brief study session. This may all be true, but there is no way to determine how much time to skip between trials, or how long a given trial should be. Certainly it takes time to warm up and one warm up is less expensive in time than a whole series of warm ups. The lesson should be at least longer than the warm up period; beyond that it is difficult to decide. No lesson should include so much material that by the time the end is reached the beginning is forgotten. Times between learning sessions cannot be spread out indefinitely; a month between rehearsals of a poem might result in its never being mastered. Practical affairs will probably interfere with any well-laid plans, but in general, it might be wise to plan on spreading out any learning task into several sessions rather than to leave study for a long "cram" session. The chief difficulty with the cram session is that the student cannot trust himself to retain what he might very well know and wastes time going over it. Having had the benefit of a series of self-tests he can afford to skip known material and concentrate on the remainder.

Reactive inhibition

When study or learning is not proceeding well, in fact, when something like extinction might be occurring because of failure of reinforcement, the learner may begin to undergo some "fatigue" or what Professor Hull (1943) called "reactive inhibition." The fatigue condition or reactive inhibition may function as a drive and will tend to initiate resting responses or avoidance of the situation; the books, papers, and other impediments and circumstances of study may be conditioned to withdrawal. On the next occasion, the withdrawal stage may be reached sooner, and eventually the student may learn to avoid books completely. This situation might be labeled "conditioned inhibition." It might be sound advice, possibly impractical, that one should never study when he does not feel like it. The more positive approach would be to develop study habits such that one does feel like studying sufficiently often to do as well as might be expected.

Whole as opposed to part learning

In earlier days of learning psychology it was argued that learning by the "whole" method was better than the "part" method or the "part-progressive" method. Such a principle might apply most usefully to the memorization of poetry and very little else, if it applied there. It can be shown with materials of certain length that going over the entire material as a unit can be more effective than breaking it up into sections, verses, or what not. Because rote memory drills are not very fashionable in schools nowadays, the method is not frequently tested and most grammar school children rely on learning a bit at a time, adding more as they learn until they can manage to stumble through the whole thing. Such adding of sections (the part-progressive method) obviously involves a considerable overlearning of the first part with progressively less mastery of the end. If sections are learned separately, the end of one section becomes associated with the beginning of that section instead of with the beginning of the next and may result in the common situation of getting "stuck." Many children are able to romp through any section if they can get a start on it. If the starts are learned as thoroughly as the intervening material, there should be no trouble in using a part method. With a long assignment, like memorizing the Bible, one could hardly go through it as a whole; by the time the final verses were reached, Genesis would be forgotten. Using the whole method is not very productive at first, the student is not confident that he is learning. In general, we might say that a student with practice in the method, a lot of "intelligence," and with reasonably short materials to master, can do better using the whole method. If the combination fits, it might well be used. Actually, there is little we can say without more analysis of the dimensions involved—difficulty, length, practice with the method, and probably many other factors the very nature of which is yet unknown.

Active as opposed to passive learning

The learner who sits up and takes notice, who knows he has something to learn, who wants to learn it, and who actively works at the task learns much more rapidly than the student who does not know that he is to learn something, who does not care to learn, who has no intention of remembering or passing a test on the subject, and who sits or lies in a relaxed fashion. This much we should know from common experience. This common sense appreciation is compatible with experimental findings and the theoretical speculation which has developed from the laboratory work. A number of kinds of laboratory study support the active as against the passive attitude for learning. In recent years there has been some newspaper discussion along typical science fiction lines of possible use of sleep time for study purposes. Popular novelists describe the horrors of population control via pillow speakers which fill the naive ears of innocent sleeping babes with great lies which the wakened children find themselves believing. Children believe enough lies told them while fully awake and the prospect of endowing them with more when they are asleep is rather horrifying. Fortunately for mankind, at least this particular kind of abuse of psychology does not appear to be possible. Of course, one could teach the truth, too, if he knew it and had the freedom to do so, but today's students, in whatever country, had best forget any notion that their chemistry or French lessons can be learned while enjoying a good eight hours in the Land of Nod. There is no evidence of any merit that would justify the conclusion that anything can be learned while asleep. The reliably controlled experiments (Simon and Emmons, 1956) that have been done in this area indicate that unless the subject is awake, he learns nothing. Proper control involves an adequate check on whether the subjects are in fact asleep. In some early experiments this control (electroencephalograms) was lacking and enthusiastic claims were made on the basis of subjects who, for reasons best known to themselves, were faking the sleep condition, or were not really asleep when the experimenters thought they were.

Other kinds of laboratory experiments involve asking the subject to exert some pressure, or tension, on hand dynamometers (strength of grip testing devices). If the subject exerts some tension against such resistances, he tends to learn better than while sitting in an ordinary way without any exertion. Too much tension, of course, calls for attention to the tension task and interferes with learning. How much is too much may be impossible to prescribe for any individual, but if the activation stimulation source calls for some degree of attention in its own right, then it is too much (Courts, 1939).

We have already mentioned that some degree of intersensory facilitation is possible and we can expect a more rewarding learning period to result if the learner receives additional stimulation from any source so long as he does not have to deal with it separately. Thus the student who studies while the radio is playing may be assisting the learning process with the additional energy input. Should the radio blare or emit verbal materials that might interfere, there might be a loss of efficiency. A foreign language broadcast in an unknown tongue, on the other hand might not prove harmful. Most people are overly concerned about the possible distracting value of extra stimulation. Numerous experiments have indicated that even rather severe attempts at distracting people taking intelligence tests and solving problems are not especially harmful. The subjects may work harder, but not necessarily less effectively in taking IQ tests in a boiler factory. Susceptibility to such distractions may be an individual problem with some more "sensitive" than others, and no hard rules can be proscribed. Some people even learn to study in bed although this would hardly be recommended if the bed is also to be a place for sleeping. In any event, asking other people to creep about the house because Johnny is studying receives no support from the experimental laboratory.

In considering the active attitude, we recognize again the role of the reticular system, the arousal or activating system. Without this system functioning in an optimal fashion, we cannot make use of the rest of the brain. Overloading this system, on the other hand, will lead to a disorderly operation of the brain and result in inefficiency. Because we are unable, at present, to tune in the proper degree of co-operation from the recticular system, we have to leave it at the level of practical individual experience with the general suggestion that a casual, relaxed attitude, overstuffed furniture, complete silence, and no distractions should quite generally lead to a soporific condition, and one highly unconducive to study.

The active method, like the spacing method, provides ample testing opportunities so that the learner can check his progress instead of waiting for it to "soak in." Nothing "soaks in," as many experiments on "incidental learning" demonstrate (Jenkins, 1933). In the typical such experiment, the real subject serves as manipulator of materials for someone else to learn; thus he might keep a record of how well someone else is doing in reciting poetry or a list of words. When the "regular" subject has learned, the "incidental learning" subject is tested and usually found to have learned little or nothing even though he saw or heard the materials as frequently as the presumed official learner. Most of us have had experiences of a related nature. If we take a long city bus ride to school everyday we may hear the driver call out the streets in sequence every day for months and have little or no knowledge of the sequence, or, indeed, of the existence of some of the streets. Grammar school children who answer to a roll call everyday learn a few names just before theirs is reached and can give only a poor performance when asked to recite the names in order, especially the ones that follow their own. All in all, the intention to learn seems a positive requirement. Reading a chapter in perfunctory acquiescence with an assignment is an unproductive process and must be supplemented with a search for answers to prepared questions.

Meaningful as opposed to rote learning

We will not stop at this point to worry over the nature of meaning. That will occupy us in Chapter 9. At the moment, however, we can point out that trying to memorize an unrelated set or series of responses which had no previous connections is a relatively difficult task. Ordinary verbal materials arranged in sentence form are much more readily acquired. To the latter type of task we bring to bear a great many verbal habits. For example, if a sentence should start "There is . . ." we know without learning that the next unit is likely to be "a" or "an"; if it's an "an" we know the next word most likely will start with a vowel; many other such tricks of sentence structure are acquired which set restrictions on the possible errors one might commit if the material were unrelated. When subjects learn such connected materials better than unorganized lists of nonsense syllables or words, it is argued that meaningful material is better learned than nonmeaningful. This is probably not well advised and quite inexact. It is possible to learn a sentence like: "The table laughed uproariously at the zephyr in the tweed suit," with perhaps one repetition. There appears to be very little meaning in the sentence, however, and until we consider meaning, itself, we can say little about the value of meaning in learning. In the kinds of experiments which compare connected discourse with unconnected discourse, we might observe that the connected discourse (meaningful or not) is better learned than unconnected discourse.

In some experiments the concept of meaning is restricted to the use of principles or general formulas as opposed to "blind trial and error" and again, it is argued that knowing the general principle facilitates performance. The usual kind of evidence is drawn from the principles of physics, like the principle of refraction. In one old experiment, boys were allowed to practice shooting at an underwater target at one depth. Then some were told about refraction and others were not. When the target was changed to a new depth, those who were told about refraction scored better than the rest. This kind of experiment is used to support the practice of teaching principles rather than rote memory or drill, on the grounds that "understanding" aids learning.

In a famous series of experiments Katona (1940) tried to demonstrate the superiority of meaningful learning or understanding over rote learning or trial and error problem solving. In one of the experiments, for example, the learning task consisted of reproducing a series of numbers. The series ran: 581215192226293336404347. At first glance the task appears formidable. Katona, however, divided his subjects into two groups. The first group was told that there was a principle involved and that they were to study the series until they discovered it. The principle is simple enough: add 3 to the first number; to the result add 4, then 3 again, 4 again, and so on. Three weeks afterward 23 per cent of the subjects were able to reproduce the list correctly. The other group of subjects was instructed to break the list up into groups of three numbers, thus, 581, 215, and so on, as the experimenter read the numbers to the group. The numbers were repeated five times. Three weeks later, none of these subjects were able to reproduce the list correctly. Katona concluded from this study that learning by understanding was more effective than rote memorization. The critical student might find much to question in such an experiment. It is obvious that the first group had to remember only that the series starts with five and that the rest is formed by alternately adding 3 and 4. This is far less than the second group was asked to remember. The only justifiable conclusion to be drawn is that it is easier to remember a little than a lot. Whether there is any essential difference between memorizing a verbal rule and memorizing a series of numbers has not been demonstrated. Many people can solve fairly difficult problems in algebra and geometry by following memorized verbal rules and be unable to give a coherent or logical reason for the steps that are followed. Memorizing rules is not necessarily different in nature from memorizing lists of Presidents or state capitals.

The nature of understanding

The concept of "understanding" has never been accounted for or explained. If we ask someone if he "understands" and he says "yes" we do not know any more about him than if he had said "no." If he replies, "I get the idea" we might be encouraged, but we still know nothing about his understanding. The final proof will lie in his performance. If he now misperforms, we or he can say that he "misunderstood" and start all over again. Those educators who deprecate drill may produce students who understand everything but can do nothing. If we examine the concept of understanding a bit more closely, we may discover that it amounts to verbalizing a sequence of responses and that such sequences have to be learned like any other sequences. One can understand something to be true which is not at all true and be far worse off than never having understood at all. When one understands the Pythagorean theorem or the principle that it is perfectly proper to add the same things to both sides of an equation, has something different happened to the person than when he learns that Mary had a little lamb? Certainly where verbal rules cover a variety of instances, one should learn the verbal rules and also, learn the cues that evoke the subvocal recitation of such rules. Trying to teach a child to understand that one and one make two is an absurd venture and leaving such things as 9×8 to understanding rather than to rote drill is folly. Knowing the rules is not a guarantee of successful performance. Many a student fails to solve a problem because he did not know which rule to apply, although he "understood" the rules well enough. The problem is too complex to be handled yet and we will delay consideration until later (see p. 311).

EARLY AND LATE LEARNING

A great deal of confusion has developed in the psychology of learning because until relatively recently the nature of the learning assignments submitted to animal or human learners was not carefully analyzed. It was recognized in a general way that past experience would seriously affect the performance under observation, and attempts were made to keep the material strange and novel. Humans would be asked to memorize poems they had never seen before or words from some foreign language or even manufactured words (nonsense syllables). Similarly, animals would be put into wooden or metal contraptions completely foreign to their natural modes of life. By placing a cat in a wooden box, Thorndike felt more or less confident that he had set a new problem for the animal, as indeed he had to some extent. Of late, we have become somewhat more sophisticated about this factor of past experience and strive to control it more effectively. It is quite obvious in the case of the human learner, for example, that if he is to learn a list of words, he must first know a word when he sees one, that he must be able to read, and that a great deal of past experience with letters and words must have been accumulated by any human reader. It is quite impossible to stamp any verbal material as completely new for any subject. Even when children are beginning to read in the first grade they have had various degrees of experience with letters and words. Many children learn to read some of the advertising materials on television programs before they ever go to school.

It appears that a logical inference can be strongly made to the effect that one is bound to misinterpret the learning process if materials are used which have had unknown degrees of previous experience associated with them. Yet the search for pure, unadulterated novel material has not been fruitful and we might be forced into heroic measures of rearing organisms in various kinds of deprived environments in order to be able to "start from scratch." When this is done, as we have seen with dogs, rats, and chimpanzees, as well as cats and pigeons, we find that even simple responses to sensory stimulation must be learned. The chimpanzee raised in the dark and brought out into the lighted world after eighteen months has to learn to see. Similar deficiencies in other senses have been observed if organisms are deprived of their use from birth and tested at a later age. Thus, while it might be argued that one must be able to see to learn reactions to visual stimuli, and therefore, learning depends upon a prior condition or capacity to sense or perceive, when we discussed perception it was argued that the organism must learn to sense or perceive. It might look like the hen and the egg problem, and the solution as to which came first may prove equally difficult. Our best guess, at the present, might be that both, or many kinds of processes develop simultaneously as the organism grows and develops, and indeed, the processes might not be as separate as we have presumed them to be. Thus, the child in its crib is learning to see, and hear, and smell, and feel, and taste at the same time that its behavior is changing toward such things as the odor of milk and mother, the light rays reflected from the furniture, structure, and people in the room, the pressure of the mattress and clothing, etc.

When we say that a child knows its mother we must mean that the infant has developed discriminated responses to a particular complex of stimuli, and we recognize that this took place over a period of time. It is doubtful if anyone would argue that learning had not taken place, that children intuitively or innately know their mothers—the imprinting experiments cited earlier indicate that goslings, at least, do not know their mothers from golf balls. But the average student believes that knowing involves something more than overt behavior, that something takes place "inside his head" which is the real knowledge. This too is true. The real question, however, should deal with what does take place inside the head. Our present best guess is that a specific number of particular neurons discharge over a period of time. These neural discharges do not secrete any knowledge or mental, non-material "ideas" but lead ultimately to some kind of effector response, perhaps of a very cursory and modest nature. Prior to the acquisition of speech habits, these responses are likely to be, in infants, approach or avoidance, clinging or rejecting operations. With speech, the overt behavior can be short-circuited and drastically reduced. The child may merely utter a noise "no" as the discriminated response in a given situation. From this noise, we make *inferences* as to the child's knowledge. Our inferences, however, are not equal to the child's knowledge. That consists of the responses he has learned to make.

In the present chapter we have used illustrations from both early or novel kinds of learning and from learning situations where past experience obviously played a role, mostly of an undefined and unknown nature. While experimental techniques have been developed to control past experience, to a considerable degree the control frequently consists of measures to equalize past experience effects. Equalizing such effects does not eliminate their influence. They might be presumed to work uniformly upon the learners. The point, however, is that if past experience is playing a role, it should be taken into account and not ignored, just because it was balanced out of the picture. We do not have a clear or clean appreciation of basic learning principles at work when we use subjects who have had any relevant past experience. It may prove that the learning of novel kinds of responses, new learning, primitive, or early learning operates in a manner quite different from that operating in the mature organism. Certainly college students do not learn like the small fry in the kindergarten. The background of the student is of the highest importance. As has been stressed throughout this chapter, learning is a two sided affair: we must unlearn or extinguish our natural responses, or previously learned but now interfering responses, before we can make progress with the new material. How well the new material will be assimilated depends upon the background the learner brings. The professor of psychology should be able to master the contents of a psychology text in a fraction of the time the beginning student needs. Some teachers practice as if they had never considered this principle and make assignments that would have been impossible for them to complete in the allotted time when they were students, but which now look like child's play to them. In the next chapter we will consider the effects of past experience on new learning as well as the effect of current learning on future performance. For the present purposes we will conclude that such operations as association or conditioning, reinforcement and generalization, extinction and discrimination, as they have been studied in the laboratory, apply primarily to early, primitive, first learnings. Once the learner has acquired a background, these same principles might be operating in new learning situations but they will be heavily obscured by the background and new considerations might have to be added to account for the behavior.

CHAPTER 8

The Influence of Past Experience— The Transfer of Training

The principle of mediation · The goal gradient · The shaping of behavior · Fractional antedating responses · Mediated behavior · The role of practice · Memory and transfer · Factors in forgetting · Recall, recognition, and relearning · Warm-up · Reproductive Interference · Forgetting and disuse · Interference and transfer · Positive transfer · Learning how to learn · Mediation and transfer · The function of prior experience · Remembering, forgetting, and emotional factors · Persistence of uncompleted response sequences

In this chapter we will consider the effects of past experience or previous learning on present performance, and, indeed, on future performance. While it might not be evident from the preceding sentence, we are going to deal with the problem of memory or, in its negative aspect, forgetting. We shall try to find out why the professor seems to know more than you do about some things, why some kinds of subjects seem easy, others difficult, and what the point of going to school might be inasmuch as you seem to forget everything you learn almost as fast as you learn it. Before we can hope to offer intelligent comments on these important problems, we need more help than the last chapter supplied. Some rather useful observations have been made about what might appear at first glance to be side effects or incidental events in the course of learning. We will examine these in some detail because without them we shall be rather hopelessly lost in trying to account for your ignorance and the brilliance of that other fellow.

THE PRINCIPLE OF MEDIATION

The goal gradient

The late Professor Clark L. Hull, in some of his first observations on learning behavior, was struck by what he came to regard as a most vital and essential feature of learning. He watched and timed the speed of running in rats when they were placed in a long alley (twenty feet long) with food at the "goal" end, and noticed that they ran faster and faster as they approached the food. He interpreted this as indicating that the running behavior was more strongly conditioned or reinforced at the food end, and that the strength of conditioning fell off with distance from the food. Such observations were described as illustrating a "goal gradient." But, the important point was that if the rat ran at all from the starting end it could only be because it was conditioned to run at that point too, even though it ran slowly because of the low conditioning strength. Now, here we have a problem of the greatest importance: how can we account for the rat's starting to run from a point in space to another point in space, twenty feet away, where food is hidden, and cannot be thought of as a stimulus for the rat? If we ask the mythical man in the street for an explanation, the answer comes easily: The rat knows that there is food at the other end, it's hungry, and it decides to go running down the alley. If you agree with the man in the street you have not yet learned to think as psychologists think (not that the man in the street is necessarily wrong—psychologists like to believe that the man in the street doesn't know very much, but the opinion may be mutual). In any event, the learning psychologist is much more cautious about outfitting the rat with knowledge and decision-making capacities. If we do not want to admit that a rat knows the score and makes up its mind in an intelligent, rational, fashion, what alternative can we suggest? It should be observed, that much of the behavior of any organism, including man might be described in similar terms: the organism at one time and place begins a train of activity which eventuates in its later appearance at another place where it does something that appears to be related to the origin of the activity. A man, for example, puts on his hat and coat, gets into his car, drives eighty miles, stops at a particular place, rings the bell at a door, and announces to the person who answers the door: "Here I am." The man in the street, showing no more hesitation than before, will say that the man wanted to go to the distant residence, decided to do so, and went. That's all there is to it. He made up his mind and acted upon his decision. As far as any ordinary communication purposes are involved for men in the street, such a description or explanation of the behavior is perfectly adequate. Communication is established, no further inquiry is indicated.

For the psychologist, however, the problem has just been stated. What do we mean by "wanted to go," by "he decided," by "acting upon a decision," or "making up one's mind"? We go back to our rat in the alley. Not for answers, but for hints, suggestions, clues, or cues. With hardly any reflection, we can recognize that we have little or no right to conclude that the rat "wanted food," that it "knew" where the food was, or that it "decided" anything at all. It is or should be plain that we don't know what these terms mean for humans and to attribute such functions to rats is beyond our license. The rat cannot tell us these things and this is an advantage because when a human does tell us, we, having learned the communication system, may arrive at some response of agreement and misconstrue this response as amounting to an understanding. With the rat, all that we know is that we did not feed it for some time, that it runs when placed at the start of the runway, and that it moves faster and faster as it approaches the end, at least in the early stages of training. From here on we start hypothesizing, conjecturing, inferring, deducing, occasionally finding something which encourages the speculations.

When we see the rat running rapidly at the end of the alley and slowly at the start we might make an assumption, as Hull (1932) did, that the behavior of running is more strongly associated with the food end of the alley. If we keep reminding ourselves that this is an assumption, we can proceed. As training continues, we see the rat moving more and more rapidly at earlier stages of the run, until finally the rat takes off rather rapidly and maintains the pace throughout. What can this mean? Hull took it to mean that learning proceeds backwards, from the end of the response series toward the beginning. We tend to learn the last step in any sequence first. You might recall Guthrie's emphasis on the fact that rewards merely preserve learning that has already occurred. Guthrie's argument depends on the notion that the last thing done is what is retained. If there is a sequence of events, then the learning, if it is to take place at all, must occur in reversed order, last things will always be learned first. This is a basic principle in learning, if we really have such principles, and we can illustrate it in a typical learning situation that anyone with rights to a dog or cat in his home might try. We can use an illustration of Skinner's (1951) that makes the point as neatly as any.

The shaping of behavior

Suppose you decide to train a dog to go to a particular dresser, to reach up and touch the left knob on the third drawer with his nose and come back to you. You will demonstrate this brilliant dog to your friends by saying to your dog, "go kiss the left knob on the third drawer of that dresser," and the dog will comply, after training, presumably to the astonishment of your friends. We might note, incidentally, that your instructions to the dog might be "go fly a kite" or "ticketty boo" and the same behavior can be extracted or exacted from the dog; in short, the words used are completely irrelevant and none need be used; the dog could be trained to do the same thing when you scratch your ear or his. Words mean only what the behavior associated with them amounts to. Now how do you train a dog to be so bright? You start by throwing small bits of meat on the floor at whatever point you want the sequence to end; the dog eats the meat if you have starved him for a day or so (and a hungry dog will learn faster than a just-fed one). While you occasionally throw the meat to the dog, you snap your fingers everytime he reaches down to snap the meat. After a few trials the dog will look down when you snap your fingers. We have established a "conditioned reinforcer" or secondary reward or "discriminated stimulus" as the first stage in learning. Note that the bureau need not even be in the room yet. The next thing we want the dog to learn is to come to the feeding station; this we accomplish by waiting for the dog to turn away from the feeding station, at first, a little bit, then, later, more and more until we have the dog turning completely about face. With each improvement in the turning away (in the direction of the dresser) we snap our fingers and throw the dog some meat. Sometimes the dog does not find the meat soon enough, that is why we snap our fingers, the reinforcement in that form, at least, is immediate and follows directly on any response we want the dog to make. When we have the dog turning away efficiently, we extend the waiting period till the dog gets up and moves away—immediately we snap our fingers, the dog reports to the station and we have achieved the next stage of the program. Now we wait until the dog moves farther and farther away, until he is close to the bureau, before we snap our fingers. This takes several stages which we carefully build up by reinforcement. Skinner calls this "shaping," and it is a good expression; we are shaping or carving out the behavior we want, slowly but steadily. When the dog consumes a piece of meat, it will now run over to the dresser. We wait until in its meanderings, the head touches the dresser; snap! Food. Another wait. Slowly we shape the dog's behavior until it is touching a more and more restricted area of the dresser. No snap follows poking around the "wrong" place. In time, if we have patience, the dog will reach more and more definitely toward the specific position we have decided is "right." Finally it is kissing the knob, or at least putting its nose to it. Your friends won't mind if we call this kissing; but if they are purists, all that is needed is more patience; sooner or later the dog will lick the knob and we will snap our fingers. All this time, with each of the later trials we have been muttering "Kiss the left knob of the third drawer." When we are ready to invite our audience, the dog is ready to behave as if it were familiar with at least one sentence in the English language. It "knows" what you want it to do, and does it. Or does it? The dog is just as stupid as it was before the training began. The only difference is that it responds in a specific way to a specific cue. Society or someone has decreed that this response of all possible responses is correct. When that happens, we praise the intelligence of the performer. If we had said "Go fly a kite" all during the training, and the dog kissed the left knob of the third drawer, we would clearly have an example of a rather idiotic dog, certainly one that did not understand English. Or would we?

Whatever the brilliance of the beast, we recognize that the training took place in exact reverse order to the actual performance on demonstration day. This was the point we started out to verify. It appears to be a dominant principle in learning. You might check it over for yourself in terms of anything you might have learned. The last event in the sequence, which is learned first, also appears to be learned most strongly; this feature can be observed if any steps in the sequence can be slighted or skipped. Frequently circumstances force an orderly progression of events; the rat, for example, cannot skip the middle of the alley, it must move through every foot of the distance, but the dog can skip the kissing routine or at least shorten it. The kiss will soon turn into a mere pass and often enough, if it is not checked, the animal will barely wave its nose in the direction of the knob in its hurry to get to the food station. Similarly, the dog can hardly wait to eat and starts to seize and swallow the food even before he gets to it. The familiar "many a slip twixt cup and lip" has a firm psychological foundation—we begin to enact the final steps in a sequence before we are actually in position to do so; in short, the presumably universal tendency in learning any sequence is to anticipate the final, mostly strongly learned stages.

We have already referred to one such anticipatory response quite frequently in previous chapters—the salivation of Pavlov's dog, or indeed the salivation of anyone is an anticipatory response. In this case the anticipatory response, coming at the time it does, has a biological value in its own right as it prepares the mouth for accepting the food and making it suitable for swallowing. This biological value, however, does not gainsay the psychological fact of the anticipatory nature of the event. The dog comes to salivate sooner and sooner to a conditioning stimulus and when it finally does so *before* the food itself is in evidence, we say the dog has learned. The point, however, is that the dog has learned an entire sequence of events even though Pavlov may have curtailed the total possible performance to a brief scene in the laboratory harness. The far more interesting thing about the whole conditioning affair is that the response is anticipatory in nature, just as are all learned responses.

Fractional antedating responses

Some responses, like salivation, swallowing, or making a "pass" at some object with actually touching it in some specific manner can be thought of as parts of a sequence, or fractions of the whole. If we find some such fractions appearing in anticipation of their normal or original point in a time sequence, we can call them "fractional anticipatory responses" (Hull, 1930). They are fractions of some more complete affair that we might label "goal behavior" or a "goal response" (if we followed Hull's terminology). Such an expression—fractional anticipatory goal response—is rather awkward to repeat frequently and Hull invented a symbol to represent it—r_g (pronounced "little argie"). We might now make one additional point about such r_g's—we have been using the word "anticipatory" to describe them. Such a word might have some undesirable connotations and we can save ourselves a lot of trouble by changing this term to "antedating" which is an objective description of the tendency for the fractional response to come forward in time. With such an antedating, fractional response we are almost in business.

We are ready to ask some questions about the behavior of our dog and the drawer knob. We can dismiss out of hand any notion that the drawer knob means anything to the dog. It is, if anything, a nuisance, something that must be taken care of before the food is available. Yet the dog does make a pass at the knob, or even licks it. What good is it to the dog? Such an activity sets the stage for the next activity which is to drop to all fours and run to the food. The run to the food is not authorized or permissible until the knob has been touched. Touching the knob or at least straining in its direction, like any response, initiates proprioceptive stimulation in the dog's muscles and joints. Such stimulation, preceding as it does, the next response in the sequence, becomes associated with the next response and cues it off. The value of the behavior can now be appreciated. It has no other value than to provide stimuli for the next step in the sequence. Hull called such responses which serve primarily to generate stimuli which call out the next step in a sequence "pure stimulus acts." They are pure because they have no other function. They are stimulus acts because they produce stimuli. Some r_g's, as already brought out, may have additional value in their own rights as in the case of salivation and swallowing, but even these responses are unnecessary as we could feed the dog directly by placing food in its stomach through some tube or other device. We need not concern ourselves too greatly over the purity of the behavior; the really important feature is that of stimulus production. Even in the alley, the middle sections must be traversed, to be sure, but the rat gets little value out of running the middle eighteen feet of the alley. They only serve to bridge the gap to the food. Each step taken provides the stimuli for the next step and is otherwise of no value. This stimulus function of fractional portions of a behavior sequence is the basic value.

Mediated behavior

Whenever we have some operation occurring which, in and of itself, is of no consequence but merely serves to bring two sides or items together, serving as a bridge or thread, we might speak of a *mediating function*. In psychological settings such mediation will be achieved or accomplished by some activity, and such an activity can be called a "mediator," if we wish to attach a name to an event. In Chapter 2 we talked about mediation in general, theoretical terms. Now we have just described mediating operations in terms of r_g's which we were careful to picture as responses. The response may be of muscles or of glands as in the case of salivation. Some of these responses such as running, or licking knobs, or salivating, we can see without difficulty. When we have reason to suspect that a sequence of behavior has taken place, but where we have been unable to observe the operation of muscles or glands, we take the license and freely assume that some kinds of intervening mediation reactions took place inside the organism, even if we were quite unable to see them or even to speculate about what they might have been with any conviction. Suppose that we ask someone to tell us what 42×87 amounts to. He may just sit there blankly and stare at us. It is quite possible that he will start moving his lips unless he has learned not to do so. He is more than likely to start wiggling his tongue about; he might even reach for a pencil and paper and start scribbling. Some time later, depending upon a lot of things, he might announce "3,654." From the point of view of the questioner, that "3,654" is the only important response, but it is apparent that many other responses were made between question and answer. All the intervening responses were mediators, each providing cues to the next step in the sequence until the final cue released the final response. We note, among other notes, that the outside world provided only one stimulus pattern, the question; everything else was provided by the succession of responses. We might note also and incidentally that "4,654" or "3,745" or even "How do you expect me to know that?" would also be final, terminal responses which could occur; these might not be correct or satisfactory answers, but they would be arrived at on the same basis, mediated responses providing cues. Thinking correctly is not different from thinking incorrectly in terms of the machinery involved.

We can now take an additional argumentative step. This one will not be too difficult if we recall our discussion of nervous action. While we have been talking about responses of muscles and glands we did not forget, of course, that muscles do not initiate activity by themselves but must be stimulated into doing so. In other words for every mediational step there is a corresponding neural action, presumably in a circuit of the kind we described as cell assemblies. These cell assemblies are set in action by stimulation and initiate action in turn as motor components become active. Should the assemblies be organized into sequences, as we would expect to be the case in any continuing action of a sequential sort, then each assembly could set off the next assembly in the sequence. In some kinds of sequential activity where strict environmental control does not direct the precise order of events, assemblies can get out of order, or out of sequence; some that should not occur till later might occur earlier, and there might be considerable repetition. It is also conceivable that when the cell assemblies are well organized and integrated some of the motor components may be bypassed so that no overt behavior or any muscular or glandular action takes place and consequently various stages of a sequence might not be observable in any way unless we sometime arrive at the happy stage where the physiological events in the brain can be pinpointed. Such a chain of assemblies running off with little or no overt action would be a train of thought. We shall return to this notion when we consider thinking processes. For the present our concern is with recognizing a more or less purely neural event as a mediating mechanism, one that can function to bridge gaps between overt actions without the benefit or necessity of r_g's. Again, we take pains to point out that such neural events are strictly hypothetical and we have no evidence that any such processes occur in the manner described; they are to be considered as the product of working assumptions. In some support of the assumption is the apparent necessity for making it. There is a need for some such mechanism if we are to account for all that psychologists hope to explain.

It is not out of order, in any case, to posit some underlying neural mechanism for the r_g's and some form of implicit action or movement which generates stimuli is a common assumption of learning psychologists. Guthrie could not get along without what we have described earlier in his terms as "movement produced stimuli" or MPS. Hull's r_g is an attempt to specify one class of such movements with more detailed consideration of their origin and function, and the cell assembly notion merely adds the possibility that the movements or r_g's themselves might be short circuited out of action in some instances. Such short circuiting, as we pointed out, will lead to difficulties in situations where the environment requires a strict adherence to a sequence and probably many of our errors in ordinary behavior are traceable to such skips. When a sequence requires a "feedback" from a response, that response itself must run off at least to the point of supplying the required amount of feedback. This may, of course, be something less than a full-fledged movement and a rat in a Skinner Box may frequently make a "pass" at the lever without actually depressing it at all or enough to let the environment work; the rat, heedless of the experimenter's devices, goes on to the food tray and is ready to eat. It is a form of slip twixt cup and lip.

With r_g's, MPS's, and cell assemblies we have modified the traditional $S \longrightarrow R$ approach to the analysis of behavior by inserting some intervening processes. By inserting these unobservable, assumed operations we have greatly extended the range of problems with which we can now deal; at the same time we have greatly increased the risk of being wrong. Finding out that we are wrong, however, can lead, hopefully, to correcting errors and arriving more closely at some approximation of what we fondly think of as the "truth." The limitations of a strictly environmental analysis of stimuli and observed responses involves such circumlocutions and difficulties that the risk seems worthwhile. We can only take it and see where it leads us. To anticipate our future discussions we can suggest that the mediation concept will be of importance to us in connection with thinking and problem solving, especially with the interesting concepts of insight and meaning. Our present interest is with the problems of memory and transfer of training. With the mediation construct as a working tool to be used when we need it, we can return to the present concern.

THE ROLE OF PRACTICE

Up to this time we have not raised the issue of the effect of repetition or practice on habit formation or learning. It is commonly assumed that "practice makes perfect" and just as commonly that learning is a slow, cumulative process. Most textbooks illustrate the course of learning by showing graphs indicating the progress of learners at such tasks as memorizing nonsense syllables, poetry, mazes, typewriting, etc. Most such curves show an initial period of fairly rapid learning, then a slower rate of progress as the criterion level is attained. There are no such illustrations in this text as recent studies and criticisms (Hayes,

1953; Spence, 1956; Rock, 1957) suggest that these curves are misleading. They commonly are based on *group* results of a number of subjects, or, if they are based on one subject, they may show how much of a total amount has been learned per trial. In either case, the curves may obscure the facts of learning. In a group, for example, one subject may have learned everything on the first trial while others learn varying amounts. Averaging out the gain for the group will show some change from a starting point, but in no way will it reflect individual performance. Yet, it is individuals who learn, not groups. If a single subject has to learn ten things, he may learn two or three of them perfectly on the first trial and add more items with succeeding trials. On each trial he may learn whatever he does learn *in one trial,* yet a graph of his acquisition of the material *as a whole* may show a slow, gradual acquisition. It behooves us to be careful in assessing the role of repetition on learning.

We have chosen to discuss the role of practice at this time because of the intimate relationship between practice and retention, or remembering. While it is possible to measure various aspects of performance while observing a learner (e.g., reaction time or amplitude of response) what we are basically interested in is whether the learner will make the response at all, regardless of speed or magnitude. Will the dog salivate if we ring the bell now? Will the child recite his poem correctly this time? Such questions are raised only if we have, in the past, reinforced the dog or observed the child in an incorrect performance. In short, every time we watch a learning trial we are also raising the question of memory or retention. In a sense, the only test we have of learning is one of retention, however this manifests itself.

It will not surprise the student to learn that psychologists are divided in their opinions on the role of practice. Some, like Hull (1943), support the popular opinion and argue that learning is a slow, cumulative process. A response gradually acquires strength from a below-threshold level until it advances in the hierarchy to the point where it can overcome the natural response to a particular stimulus. Others, like Guthrie (1952), claim that learning will occur in one trial, as an all-or-none operation. Guthrie is famous for his conclusion that you will always do what you did the last time in any given situation. This principle, called "postremity" by one of Guthrie's students (Voeks, 1948), is held to be more potent than mere repetition or "frequency." Guthrie explains away the practical need for practice in many kinds of situations by arguing that he is talking about the association between one stimulus and one response whereas most people are prone to think in general terms about "acts" which are properly conceived, says Guthrie, to consist of many responses to many different stimuli.

For an "act" to be learned, the individual learner must practice, that is, he must appear to be repeating something, but he is actually making slightly different movements to slight changes in the stimulus pattern. When he has learned some simple act such as opening a door, he has actually learned hundreds, if not thousands, of individual stimulus-response patterns, all of them related to door opening.

How are we to resolve this dilemma? Do we learn all at once or gradually? The answer, like all psychological answers, is not easy. We can begin by reassuring the student that if he practices he will remember better. There appears to be no controversy on this question (Rock, 1957). Whether he learns all at once, quickly, or slowly, depends on many variables. We have already hinted at the fact that our data are misleading because experimenters have confused the issue by grouping either the subjects, or the materials, or both. When a college sophomore is asked to learn pairs of nonsense syllables, for example, the experimenter will not ask him to learn only one pair. The student can learn one pair immediately, so fast that the learning process can not be observed. Here we have a hint as to a possible approach to our problem. It may be that the controversy exists only because of the way in which learning is measured. If the experimenter adopts an all-or-none criterion, then it is obvious that the results will show that learning took place all at once. Any efforts not reaching the criterion will be dismissed with a zero score. A child learning to spell, for example, will get no credit for an almost-correct attempt. Sooner or later, however, if he ever does spell the word correctly, it will be done on some one particular trial. If he *retains* the word, the experimenter will then support the one-trial conclusion. On the other hand, if the experimenter is measuring something that is not so discrete as a right-or-wrong verdict, i.e., if he is measuring something like time that can be broken down into finer and finer units, he might find a gradual speeding up in the response with practice and he will favor the cumulative conclusion.

Two other factors must be considered. Usually the base line for graphs of learning rates consists of some time measure, frequently, the number of trials. A trial, however, can consist of one exposure of some stimulus or a whole series of exposures. The time of each exposure can vary extensively. In learning pairs of words, for example, the "trial" or exposure of materials might last for three or four seconds; there may be an equal interval before the next pair is exposed. In some experiments, a total of eight or ten seconds might pass during one trial. In such a period the learner could repeat the material many times. Did he then have only one trial? The other, and perhaps more important, factor involves the nature of the material. It may be very novel (as almost anything might be for a baby) or quite familiar, often encountered in the past, and readily learnable, in the sense of being associated with some other event or stimulus. Thus, one needs no practice to remember a pair like *hot* and *dog*. These words have been frequently associated in the past. A little later on we shall attempt to show how more novel-appearing combinations can also be quickly put together on the basis of mediation. In general, we might suggest a resolution of the one-trial versus frequency controversy on the basis of the distinction we have already drawn in the last chapter, the distinction between early and late learning. Early learning may require many repetitions. Late learning may occur in one trial. With this preliminary orientation about the role of practice we are ready to talk about memory.

MEMORY AND TRANSFER

We usually think of memory in a negative way, that is, we are concerned with our failure to remember something we have some reason for believing we should not have forgotten; our concept of the influence of past experience appears to have been split off into what might be called "logic-tight compartments" so that we view the past as something that fades out and dims with the passing years. At the same time we are constantly invoking past experience to explain current behavior. This man, we say, behaves in this fashion because of something that happened long ago, perhaps when he was three years old. We constantly run into contradictions when we try to segregate the influence of past experience according to our interest of the moment; yet there are two sides to the story of past experience, and each must be taken into account. Because we can not discuss each aspect at the same time, we will treat them separately at first and then try to develop an integrated picture. We can start with memory first.

Students are among those most strongly concerned with practical problems of remembering; the educational system with its periodic examination exercises forces the student to consider whether he is prepared to undergo the test he faces. Until the test is over, the student is plagued with the question: Do I know my stuff? And his usual confessive answer is: not well enough. He finds characteristically that much of the material of a given course seems not to be available—it has been forgotten. With no particular feeling of guilt, many students recognizing a weakness in performance attribute it to a "poor memory." Others sympathetically agree and lay claim to an equally poor or poorer memory. It has become an acceptable excuse in our culture to admit to or claim a poor memory. Somehow it places the blame on our ancestors instead of upon us. According to students, people come equipped with good memories or bad ones; some exceptional people are unusually blessed, they have "photographic memories" or "photographic minds"—one glance, and poof! They have it. When asked for proof of photographic minds they talk about having read about it somewhere, in a magazine or Sunday supplement. Psychologists do not appear to have unearthed such gifted individuals. There are differences among people, of course, in the ability to remember what has been heard and seen. Children sometimes are quite astonishing in their ability to recall details of some experience such as the items in a picture briefly seen. When the talent is of a high order, the term "eidetic" imagery is used to describe the presumed exceptional capacity. Not much work has been done in this area, however, and we know little about the basic retentive capacities of individuals and still less about the functions or operations involved. Children might well best adults in the card game *Concentration* when all the cards are laid out face down and the players take turns in exposing briefly two cards to find "matches." Unmatched cards are replaced. Children can astonish adults by their "memory" of the location of cards under such circumstances, but, again, we have little useful data. It cannot be said that we are all equally endowed in this respect but the problems of remembering are not solely related to basic capacity. It might be assumed with reasonable safety that college students do not differ radically in their retention capacities. They are a selected group of those who managed to remember enough to get into college. Any differences in retentiveness among them are quite probably due to other factors.

Factors in forgetting

Assuming a reasonably healthy brain, how does it happen that we forget some things and remember others? We might note that some of the items we remember are from an earlier period in time than some of the items we forget, so that a simple answer in terms of fading with time is not very useful or precise. Before we accept the confession: "I forgot," however, we must ask a very pointed and pertinent question: "Did you ever know the material in the first place?" The common remark: "I can remember faces but I can't remember names" illustrates our point. When we meet someone for the first time we are stimulated by his visual appearance for thousands or millions of times, neurally speaking. If his name is mentioned once, and we do not even bother to repeat it, there should be no wonder at a future lapse of recall for the name. The name was never learned! Certainly if a name were repeated with each glance or visual fixation we would do much better. The same argument applies to course content and other events which are more or less promptly forgotten—we have not learned them in the first place. If the student insists that he has gone over the material, say a chapter in a text, three times, and still forgot, all we can hope to judge from this is that three times is not enough. Now, the student has the right to inquire: "How often do I have to go over something in order to remember it?" And here the psychologist has no answer other than to be smug and say: "Often enough so that you'll remember it or until further practice does not result in any improvement." Concert pianists frequently work on a concerto for a full year or longer—some have worked decades on a single composition—and still feel insecure about various features such as interpretation, timing, and touch. Of course, they are striving for perfection. The student may be satisfied with remembering a passing percentage and can adjust his study level to the aspiration he has. No one can predict with utter certainty that some failure or error will not occur at the time of a test performance, but it is reasonably certain that the average college student will be able to mumble through the words of "America" in chorus with others and probably by himself. He has learned this well enough never to forget it for practical purposes. Even though we cannot prescribe how well something must be learned in order not to be quickly or ever forgotten, we can recognize that if it has been learned only to a degree, it will be remembered only to a degree at best, and in any case, if it has not been learned at all, it will not be remembered at all. The reverse of this statement has sometimes been claimed to be true, that is, if something has been learned to any degree, it will be remembered to some degree, or, in other words, that we never forget entirely something that we have experienced or learned. (See Penfield and Rasmussen, 1950.)

Recall, recognition, and relearning

The above statement hardly makes any immediate sense in the light of our normal experiences of forgetting past events, but that is because we tend to identify remembering something with the ability to describe or recite, what is technically called "recall," "reproduction," or "reinstatement." Frequently we are unable to recall with any effectiveness, yet it can be shown that the material involved is not completely erased or "gone." Suppose that you are offered "reminders" or allowed to "refresh your memory" by hints, notes, or other devices. With suitable stimulation you might be able to "recognize" certain facts or events or descriptions thereof. The typical "objective" test is a test of recognition. The student has merely to check in some manner one of several items with which he has presumably had prior experience. True, the process by which he decides may require some attempt at recall, but as in a "line-up" he has merely to identify one out of several items. While a person might not be able to recall many items that might be scattered on a table and briefly exposed to view, he might well be able to state which items had been there previously and which had not when given an opportunity to study the table again with some old and some new items now arranged for inspection. The ability to recognize items that cannot be recalled argues for some form of existence of the former experience.

Sometimes when we can neither recall nor recognize material that was learned earlier, we may have the opportunity to *relearn* the material anew. It is commonly observed in laboratory experimentation that such relearning occurs with a considerable savings in learning trials or time to learn. Assuming that interest and attention (motivation) have been controlled and that no other aids to learning have been allowed to operate, the fact that it is easier to relearn than to learn originally again argues for some residual effect of the earlier experience.

The facts of recognition and relearning experiments have been interpreted sometimes to mean that you never forget, at least not completely, anything that has been learned. This is not actually the case as circumstances and conditions can be arranged to make recognition and relearning more difficult than they might otherwise have been and we will have to take account of such factors. For the present, however, we can play with the suggestion that learning something leaves some permanent change in the nervous system which can be made use of in one way or another. McGeoch (1942), who made many studies of human verbal learning, argued that the passage of time by itself was quite irrelevant with respect to what was remembered. If some material appears to be forgotten, it might be revived or restored by proper techniques. Some of his advice may be worth examining.

In the following considerations, it must be noted that McGeoch assumed that the material had been learned to some degree in the first place; there are no psychological tricks by which you can hope to remember material that has not been learned. Even material that has been learned has to be learned in a certain way if it is to be remembered, argued McGeoch. While evidence is vague, ambiguous, and scanty to this point, McGeoch claimed that if one is to remember material about to be learned, the learner must have an *intention to remember*. How an intention to remember can influence the material to be learned is not at all clear, but we might relate such intentions to what we have already described as an active attitude toward learning in the previous chapter. It possibly involves taking notice of points that are of importance and points that need special attention in order not to be confused with other items—in other words, items must be discriminated from each other sufficiently so that generalization effects are reduced. Responses must be associated with the specific stimuli that might be presented in the future and any tendency to react with a specific response to an incorrect stimulus must be noted and extinguished. In learning a man's name, for example, we should not associate the name with a gray flannel suit as the next time we see the man, he may be in swimming trunks. Only permanent features should be marked off for attentive scrutiny. The learner must be aware of the fact that forgetting is likely to occur and actively try to isolate the significant factors in the learning situation that might introduce confusions. This will be made a little clearer in a later section. For the present we can leave the remark as it stands.

Another factor in remembering is that of *proper stimulation*. Unless the question involved is correctly stated, it may not reinstate the desired response. If a given response is to be exacted, the proper stimulus must be presented. If we have learned the name of a woman while looking at her, we might not be able to recall when someone asks "Who was that woman I saw you with last night?" The visual stimulation might be necessary for the response. One might not remember much of a place in which he passed his childhood but revisiting the neighborhood might be a great help in bringing out responses that could not otherwise be given. Students frequently write at great length answers to questions that were not asked and earn little credit. Sometimes they may know the essential information required but misinterpreted the question, or, from the student's viewpoint, the teacher asked the question in a queer, odd, or improper way. It is not possible to state what the proper form of a question should be because one rarely knows the stimuli which affected the learner. In trying to recall names, for example, it might help to run through the alphabet a few times trying various combinations of sounds; one of these might produce the rest of the desired name—without such a cue, the name might never be remembered. As a practical hint for students in examinations, it often helps to jot down any associations that occur at the time of reading over a question even if they do not directly relate to an answer. Coming back to such cues may initiate other associations which may be of pertinence.

The nature of the cues that can initiate some response cannot always be specified, as just mentioned, but it might be pointed out that a great variety of features of some stimulus pattern might serve the purpose. One frequently hears in a joke-telling group "that reminds me . . ." when there is no physical or other resemblance between the two stories. A song might remind you of another song when the similar elements might be hard to trace; something like a subtle resemblance in rhythm might be enough to initiate a whole new train of events. People frequently claim that some person reminds them of a given individual when no one else can see any basis for the alleged resemblance. If one pattern does initiate another pattern in any individual there is reason to suppose that some common reaction has been evoked by a feature of the stimulus pattern which it might be impossible to specify. The McGeoch position is unassailable in this respect. If we cannot remember, it is perhaps due to the fact that the proper stimuli are not available. If these are presented, there will be no difficulty. The question is not of a good memory or a bad one, but of stimulus identification. It should be noted here that most memory systems are based on methods for developing the appropriate stimulus. To this extent the memory system makers are on sound grounds. The systems they develop for making sure that the appropriate stimulus arises, however, are so devious and time consuming to learn and apply that they are of little real value. If one spent the same amount of time rehearsing the material as the memory system requires for producing a suitable stimulus, there would be no need for the system. For those who would rather do it the hard way, the system has some appeal. Actually, only those who are looking for quick tricks will turn to systems and they will find these too difficult for their tastes. There is no real substitute for an interest in the material and a little rehearsal if one is to remember.

WARM-UP

As part of the general business of appropriate stimulation we should include the concept of "warming-up." It is relatively difficult to switch from one problem area to another or from sleeping to waking, from one activity to another. It usually is found that whatever the activity, performance improves for a short time as we "get into" the task, whether it be football, pitching baseballs, dancing, or reciting poetry. To do an adequate job, we must expect an initial period of less than peak performance. It turns out from laboratory studies that getting busy with some type of recall task, even naming colors, helps the recall of verbal material. Getting going may prove the major difficulty and until one does begin working, there may be some felt difficulty. In examinations, a flow of associations may begin after the student has started to write even if his first writing is of little value (and is done on scrap paper). The same seems to apply to reading and other intellectual tasks and the benefit involved may result from getting rid of interfering kinds of activities and associations from the preceding tasks.

Reproductive Interference [1]

Even when the learner applies himself with the best intentions, learns reasonably well, and has the proper stimulation (within limits, to be sure), there will be difficulties in remembering some kinds of materials. Phone numbers we used daily a few years ago may no longer be remembered. The names of students in grammar school classes may no longer be available; content of courses seems to vanish with the passing semesters. Even the best students in a given course might have difficulty earning a passing grade in that course, with the same examination after ten or twenty years, or even shorter intervals. When failure to remember cannot be accounted for on the grounds described above, McGeoch argues that what has happened is that the stimuli in question have become associated with other responses which now intrude and prevent the reproduction of the original responses. In other words, we forget because we learn something new. Superficially this might strike the student as an inadequate account as most of the time he argues that "my mind was a blank." A little examination of this phrase should be sufficient to reveal that it is quite impossible to be "blank" and remain so for any length of time. Try it. What does seem to happen when we try to recall something which does not "want to come" is that a whole series of responses is made, many of which are irrelevant, vague, and incomplete; others are quite definite but recognized to be incorrect and foolish to announce. When students are learning some material which is new to them and are specifically instructed to "take a chance" they come through with any number of incorrect responses to the stimuli; they are by no means blank just because they cannot give the correct response upon demand.

It might be difficult to accept the notion that new learning is what is responsible for failure to remember but a great deal of evidence has been accumulated from laboratory studies to demonstrate that there is a strong tendency for such new learning to prevent adequate recall. We must be careful to note before we go further with this discussion that not all new learning interferes with recall of the old. That is not the point and it is certainly not to be inferred that one should immediately stop his education for fear of losing everything learned up to now. The point is that *if* forgetting occurs, it may be due to new learning, and not that new learning always interferes with retention of the old. It may, on the

[1] McGeoch's term "Reproductive Interference" is preferred to the traditional expression "Retroactive Inhibition" which refers to the same effect on retention from interpolated learning. The student is likely to encounter the traditional term in his explorations of learning literature.

contrary, improve the retention of the old or have no effect whatsoever. We shall examine such other effects of new learning in a later section. At the moment we are considering the situation where forgetting does take place.

It is unusual for the same stimulus to become associated with new responses when old responses are already well established to this stimulus. This consideration may give the student some pause. Much of our discussion of the topic will bear on this point. As should be expected, it is not necessarily the same stimulus that we have to worry about, but a *similar* one. It is actually quite impossible to describe what is meant by "similar" in any objective terms. In connection with words, for example, we might say that "mush" and "much" are similar. They differ by only one letter, but one might well question the amount of similarity actually present. We have no way of measuring this parameter (or factor), as we brought out in discussing generalization. However, it forces us to consider the possibility that many stimuli besides the specifically named one may evoke a response that has been associated originally with a particular stimulus. When a new response is learned to one of the many possible generalized stimuli, there will be a corresponding tendency for the original stimulus to now evoke these other responses instead of the one originally learned. If the new learning is stronger than the original, the subject may find himself coming through with a response which is inappropriate and conflicting or interfering with the original. Not being able to respond in an acceptable fashion because of such interference, the subject says "I forgot." To tell the truth, the subject should say "I keep thinking of this and that instead of what you want me to think of." Because "I forgot" is simpler and readily accepted, we keep using this expression and this in turn leads to an erroneous interpretation of what goes on including such statements as "I guess I've just got a poor memory." When investigators set about looking for poor and good memories instead of examining what is actually taking place, a great deal of time is wasted to no purpose.

We are now ready to consider some of the implications of an interference explanation of forgetting. Suppose that we start with a simple example or two. The student is quick to answer "Columbus discovered America" when asked what happened in 1492, and "the battle of Hastings" when the 1066 is mentioned. He has learned these responses well in connection with the questions asked. But, most students know very little else that happened in either 1492 or 1066 and consequently have no interfering responses in connection with the dates. The dates represent almost the sum total of information. When a student is asked what happened in 1957, no specific and definite answer occurs to him. He might ask, "What do you mean?" or "What kinds of events are of interest?" but he does not ask these questions when we ask what happened in 1492 or 1066. Similarly, if a person reads but one book, sees but one movie, or stops attending school in the eighth grade, he may remember the features of the book or film or the names of his classmates much better than those who continue reading, movie going, and attend high school and college. There is little or no interference. When new responses must be made to somewhat similar stimuli, the opportunity for interference arises.

From the above discussion it should be evident that interference will operate only if generalization effects are strongly present and from our earlier discussion of discrimination we might infer that if a specific stimulus has been strongly discriminated from other (generalized) values of that stimulus, less interference will be present. In other words, if you learn something very well, with specific reinforcement of a particular aspect or value of a stimulus, it will take a great deal of new learning in connection with similar stimuli to make you forget. If you learned poorly, if, in fact, you never really did "discriminate" the stimulus, then interference can occur easily. Well-learned material is not forgotten as readily as poorly learned. This might appear to be spelling out the obvious, but the basic processes involved must be appreciated. The learning might appear to be quite strong, yet if there has not been special attention to discrimination factors, it might readily suffer interference.

Experimental data appear to indicate that it does not matter when the new learning takes place. Some solidly learned material from childhood might undergo interference in middle age when new responses become associated with stimuli that in some manner can be generalized onto the original. When students learn in college that the Jews were expelled from Spain in 1492, their efficiency in connection with Columbus will be somewhat impaired. If they went on to make a specialty of the year 1492 on a worldwide scale they might come to mentioning Columbus rather late in a hierarchy of responses that might be developed. In general, no learning is ever safe from possible interference. We cannot learn something so well that it can be guaranteed to be "on tap" forever; all we can do is to learn it well enough to serve the purposes involved. The one saving grace appears to be that of the efficiency or ease of relearning. Once something has been learned we can relearn quickly. If this were not the case, the entire educational procedure would be one grand waste of time. The student who has decided that it is a waste of time to learn what he will more or less readily forget has drawn the wrong conclusion. Recognizing that we will forget, we still must go through the original learning experience in order that we can relearn when we want to or need to. Even this position is not the only virtue of education as we shall soon recognize. Some aspects of our studies are mutually supportive and cumulative, that is, they build on earlier foundations which are constantly renewed. When we learn to extract square roots we maintain all of our arithmetical skills of multiplication, division, and subtraction. Each new operation may, in fact, does, depend on prior learning which is constantly reinforced. Instead of forgetting, we get better and better at studies which involve a progression. But this is another topic and we will examine it more fully at the proper time.

Forgetting and disuse

The above analysis has ignored the factor of time as essentially irrelevant. If forgetting can be explained on the grounds of poor learning, of improper stimulation, of new and interfering learning, then we can regard time as of no consequence. Certainly there is sufficient evidence to support the observation that some events or experiences can be recalled after decades. A foreign language learned in childhood and never used in intervening years may be brought back to a fairly efficient level in a few weeks in the country where the language is the native speech. Such reports are relatively common. With sufficient work and careful probing, people do recall authentic information about their early years on psychoanalyst's couches. When some report remembering being born or conceived (as has actually been reported by some enthusiasts) we can probably ignore such reports with a sympathetic smile. Such people do need help. Some childhood "memories" can be dredged up with concentrated effort. The effort is frequently too taxing to make it worth while and consequently we give up trying when the prize is inadequate.

The principle that time, by itself, is irrelevant is challenged by some who believe that physiological changes can take place in time which are unrelated to the lack of new learning. Just as unused muscles may atrophy and lose efficiency, so it is argued, unused neural connections may show what might be called "regressive" changes. If, as we suppose, neural changes do take place when learning occurs, there is no reason to presume that such changes will remain as permanent modifications of the neural structure if they are no longer used. Since we do not know the nature of the changes involved, it is improper to take an absolute position and claim that the changes cannot be reversed or that alterations cannot take place as time passes.

The view that physiological changes can be reversed or that the original condition, that is, the prelearning condition, is restored with the passage of time has been called the hypothesis of "disuse." We cannot deny this hypothesis without being ready to demonstrate the nature of the other variables that might account for the forgetting of some given experience. There is some reason to believe that disuse of a synapse does result in some impairment of efficiency, at least on the spinal reflex level. Eccles (1953) has shown that when sensory input is eliminated by cutting afferent nerves, the reflex as tested by electrical stimulation at the stump of the severed nerve is not as adequate as previously after three weeks of disuse.

The disuse hypothesis is not the only physiological possibility, of course. There is no reason to reject the proposition that many other kinds of factors might operate to change neural structures and thereby result in inefficient recall. Disease, faulty nutrition, or trauma can also cause degenerative changes and impair efficiency. Whether disuse is an important factor in the kinds of behavior normally of concern in forgetting, or whether the interference explanation is more important, the lesson is clear in either case for those who want to retain a particular response: it must be practiced from time to time, or, in effect, relearned from time to time.

INTERFERENCE AND TRANSFER

The influence of new learning on retention of old learning has been presented thus far as a basically negative operation, that is, the old learning suffers when new learning takes place. This is only a partial view, and, while not basically erroneous, it must be carefully modified in relation to several important aspects of the learning situation.

Up to now we have discussed the matter as if all that the subject did was to learn something which we might conveniently summarize or symbolize by the expression $S \longrightarrow R$, i.e., a given stimulus has, through learning, brought about some tendency for a given response to follow. We had better identify this stimulus as the first stimulus involved if we are to talk about other stimuli and interfering connections, and we may as well label the response in question as the first response, thus

$$S_1 \longrightarrow R_1.$$

When the same stimulus is later associated with a new response, we symbolize the new learning as

$$S_1 \longrightarrow R_2.$$

We have already made the point repeatedly that S_1 is not readily describable in all possible regards and that identical elements of a stimulus pattern or generalizable aspects of a stimulus may be present in some future learning so that an R_2 might be learned to such an identical element or generalized stimulus which might then interfere with $S_1 \longrightarrow R_1$ since R_2 would now be evoked. Since S_1 is so difficult to specify, we might find that almost any kind of new learning might interfere with almost any old learning. There is some evidence to suggest this. Where the kinds of new experiences are left to chance and are quite uncontrolled, there is typically some loss of retention. In a famous experiment by Jenkins and Dallenbach (1924) students learned some material and went to sleep as soon thereafter as possible. On different nights they were awakened at various intervals after the learning and it was found that they forgot some of the learning if they were awakened after one or two hours of sleep, but that further sleeping time did not result in additional losses. If they learned the material in the early hours of the day, however, they kept losing steadily with each waking hour throughout the day. No analysis was made of the daily routine or of what was being learned, but presumably just being awake and going about the day's activities results in a systematic increase in forgetting. It is true that less and less was forgotten per hour, but the degree of forgetting did increase.[2]

We can expect to have some loss in retention from almost any activity following learning, but the amount of loss does appear to be related to the kind of activity so that a passive state like sleep keeps the loss at a minimum and the amount of loss increases as we approach the condition where exactly the same stimulus is used in association with a different response. Even this, however, is not precisely the case, although this view is commonly described in standard discussions of the subject. It is usually argued that when the new response is very different or "opposite," "opposed," or "antagonistic," that interference will be greatest. This might appear to be logical, but it is not necessarily psychologically the case. A very different kind of response might be more readily discriminated; it will be recalled that the point was made that if the discrimination were securely established there might be less interference with recall. This seems to apply in the present argument in that a subject learning to call something "black" and now having to call the same thing "white" might have an easier time of it than he might with having to call the item different shades of gray.

In order for a newly learned response to interfere with an older one, then, the new response must be somewhat related to or similar to the original response. Similarly, when the stimulus in the new learning is quite similar to the original stimulus, we can expect considerable inter-

[2] Newman (1939) found similar results for nonessential elements of stories. Essential elements, however, showed no differences in retention as a function of waking or sleeping experience.

ference. When the new learning is a combination of somewhat similar stimuli and somewhat similar responses we will have the greatest negative effect on recall or retention. As the stimuli get less and less similar and the responses, too, get less and less similar, then we will have less negative effect. Hypothetically if the new learning is composed of neutral (no connection with) stimuli and neutral responses, there should be no interference whatsoever. We can summarize our findings about forgetting now in a few rules, but our rules will have to include both stimulus and response features.

1. If the stimulus is identical and a new response must be learned, then we can expect trouble in retention of the old response, but there will be less and less trouble as the response differs from the original through some hypothetical neutral state to an opposed one. Most of the difficulty will come from learning more similar responses.

2. If the new learning involves a similar stimulus, then we can expect trouble in retaining the old unless the new combination involves an identical response. In the latter event we can expect relatively better retention.

3. If the new stimulus is only somewhat similar, that is, less similar than presumed in Rule 1, then the negative effects on retention will still prevail but in lesser degree. Again an identical response will benefit somewhat in retention.

4. If the stimuli are neutral the effects on retention will be only mildly negative if the responses vary, and slightly helpful if the response is identical.

Positive transfer

The rules listed above deal only with the problem of forgetting because of new learning. It may have been observed, however, that when the responses involved are identical, there is no difficulty about retention which is generally improved with such new learning. Here the subject is practicing the same response even though the stimuli vary. The benefit enjoyed by the learner in such cases is commonly called a "transfer of training" effect, or, more specifically, "positive transfer," just as forgetting because of new learning is called "negative transfer." To illustrate: if someone showed us a modern art painting by a chimpanzee and called it "Woman in White," and then showed us another painting and gave the same title to it, we would later on recall the name of each of the paintings better than if they had different names. In the one case, the new learning improves the retention of the old; while on the other hand, the old learning improves the learning of the new. Frequently we are interested more in the future than in the past and ask the question as to whether this or that subject will help in the learning of something still to come far in the future. Will Latin help in law school or will math help in future good citizenship or wholesome adjustment? When we raise the question of the effects of present learning on future learning we are dealing with what is traditionally called the "transfer of training" problem. We can get some leads to an appreciation of this problem by considering the same general situations we have just reflected upon in connection with forgetting. It appears justifiable to infer from the conclusions drawn above in the form of rules that we forget one thing only if we have learned something that might interfere with it either because the stimuli or the responses varied from the original. We have, however, not examined what happens to the "interpolated" learning under such conditions and this we can now proceed to do.

Learning how to learn

Again we have our $S_1 \longrightarrow R_1$, $S_2 \longrightarrow R_2$ situation except that we are now interested in how well $S_2 \longrightarrow R_2$ is learned and not in how well $S_1 \longrightarrow R_1$ is retained. Within certain limits, learners generally show improvement in the learning of new materials that are of the same general context with practice. For example, when monkeys or children are given a series of problems to work, they solve the later problems much more readily than the early ones, assuming equal difficulties. This phenomenon has been labeled "learning how to learn" (Harlow, 1949) and may have broad applications in many kinds of simple learning tasks, particularly at the early stages of practice. Once we have had some optimum level of practice at some kind of learning we do not improve noticeably with practice. William James (1890), for example, found that he was unable to improve his memorizing ability even with a great deal of practice. This might have been true for him at the mature age at which he conducted his experiment, but, it has been pointed out, he might have reached a peak level of memorizing ability before the experiment above which he could not improve.

Assuming a general "learning how to learn" effect to be present, and a consequent facilitation or improvement in new learning, what specific effects of old learning can we expect after practice effects are accounted for? If, as we found, new learning interferes with the recall of the old, should not the old learning interfere with the acquisition of the new? Is there not some likelihood of a "proactive" inhibition or interference? Can a subject learn $S_1 \longrightarrow R_2$ as easily as he might have if he had not already learned that $S_1 \longrightarrow R_1$? Here again we find that the answer depends on the nature of the S and R involved and their relative similarity to the originals. If we take the number of trials to learn the original material as a base, we will find, in general, that the new learning will be accomplished with less effort, that is, there is a general facilitation effect. This effect, however, masks the fact that interference may have been present. In other words, although there is a gain, it is not as large as it might have been without the interference. If we are to talk about positive transfer or facilitation, we must talk about it in relative terms. If the new is learned *at the expense* of the old, perhaps it, too, is not learned as cheaply as it might have been. If we find the new learning relatively easy, we can presume that the old did not interfere with it to any serious degree. We can summarize what might happen to new learning in terms of the old by again taking account of the nature of the stimuli and responses involved in both cases (see Bugelski and Cadwallader, 1956).

1. Assuming for this and the following rules that a given number of trials was taken for original learning, and using this as a base, there will be an obvious facilitation effect if the new responses are identical with the original. The facilitation will be less and less, however, as the stimuli differ in degree of similarity from the original. Neutral stimuli will have the least effect. The facilitation will be observed in terms of fewer trials to learn the new material. The decrease of facilitation can be interpreted as an increase of interference even though fewer trials are taken to learn the new material.

2. As the responses vary from identity there will be less facilitation (greater interference) at first, then greater facilitation as the responses become more and more different. The greatest interference will result from learning slightly different responses to identical stimuli. As the stimuli differ more and more from the original, the interference will be less and less as the responses also become more and more different.

3. With completely neutral material (both stimuli and responses completely unrelated to the original) we should expect neither facilitation nor interference from the material itself. Methods or attitudes might show either effect. Completely neutral material cannot be defined a priori, nor, for that matter, can degrees of similarity. In general, neutral stimuli will facilitate learning if the responses are identical, interfere somewhat with similar responses, but less than similar stimuli might.

In general, we see that the learning of a new task may be facilitated to some degree by our having learned some related material in the past, but this facilitation is confounded or reduced by interference effects. If the new material is easy to learn (large positive transfer) it will not interfere with the retention of the old. If the new material is difficult to learn, suffers a lot of interference, it will also, after it is learned, interfere more seriously with the retention of the old material.

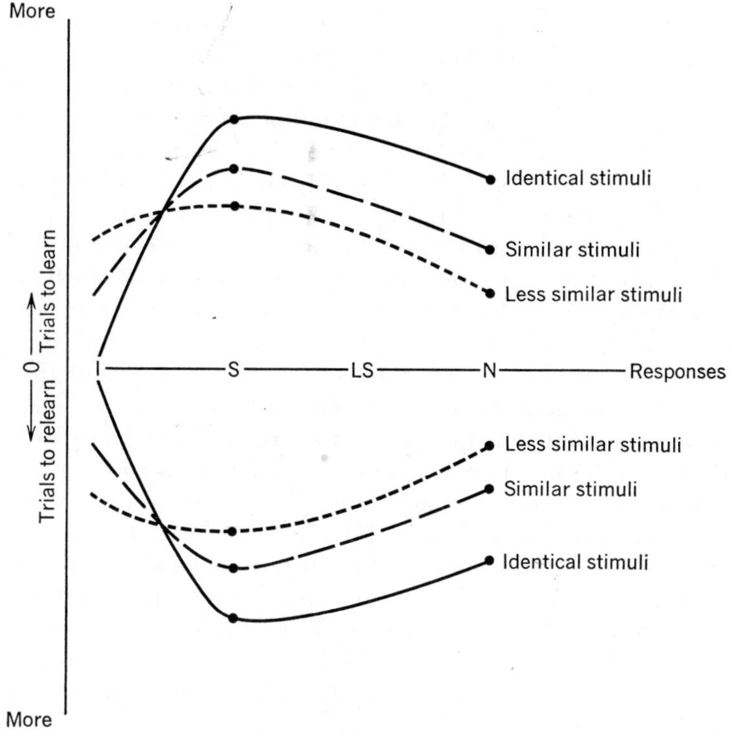

Figure 12 Hypothetical relationships between interference with new learning and forgetting. When forgetting can be attributed to new learning, the amount forgotten is proportional to the difficulty of learning the interpolated (and interfering) material. Earlier learned material will interfere with new learning, which in turn will interfere with the recall of the original. Note that when stimuli and responses are identical, there is no need to practice the new material, and no forgetting. As stimuli become less similar there will be more trials required to learn even if responses are identical. As the stimuli and responses get less similar and approach some hypothetical neutrality, there will be less trouble in learning the new and recalling the old. The greatest difficulty is found with identical stimuli and similar responses. Neutral stimuli and neutral responses would not interfere with recall but would not benefit either. They are not shown in the figure because their relative ease of learning cannot be established and would depend upon the nature of the material. Only the general or relative positions on the curves should be considered. Actual values cannot be expressed without taking into account the nature of the materials, practice effects, and, most importantly, the way the degree of similarity is to be measured. (Based on an experiment involving learning word responses of varied similarity to nonsense figures of varied similarity; Bugelski and Cadwallader, 1956.)

The rules, as stated above, have been modified from a similar set of rules proposed by Osgood (1949). They may not be of great practical help but they do tend to bring some order into the picture and may help us to appreciate the comments about forgetting and new learning. We need not fear that some learned connections will automatically be wiped out just because we learn something new. If the new learning bears no relation to the old, then we are unlikely to undergo any loss. If anything, we might benefit slightly from having gone through the new learning exercise by picking up tricks or modifications of procedure which might help in recall of the old material. We do not normally go around learning the same responses to different stimuli until we have somehow characterized the stimuli as really the same in some "abstract" sense. The child learning to say "Pardon me" or "Thank you" must learn to say these words in very different circumstances and frequently shows a failure of generalization. According to Guthrie, we must learn many different ways of being polite, that is, we must learn to make a specific polite response, to each and every situation in which we are ever going to be polite. In a famous study (Hartshorne and May, 1928) of honesty it was found that school children tended to be very specific in their honesty behavior. Some would cheat but not steal; others would do the reverse; some might copy but not ask for information; others would only cheat if they had a chance to change answers in self-correction procedure. Many otherwise honest people do not hesitate to accept an overchange at the expense of the clerk; others save felonious activities for the income tax collector. Practicing neatness at school does not appear to transfer to the home. When failure to transfer is observed, it is sometimes argued, and we now see it to be an empty argument, that nothing transfers. Broad generalizations are made about school curricula on the basis of observations of failure of transfer to take place. We can now appreciate that positive transfer does take place when the responses involved in the two situations are alike. If the responses are different, then we may have negative transfer.

Mediation and transfer

In introducing the topic of retention and forgetting we stopped by the way to discuss the mediation principle. We can now return to an examination of this principle as it might function in the transfer situation. Our general problem is to account for satisfactory adjustments or the ease of new learning in the light of past experience. It is readily recognized that when we have experience with some subject matter we are able to assimilate advanced studies in that area better than if we attack the advanced material first. This does not necessarily mean that there will be a saving in total time, but as far as the new learning is concerned, it will be more efficiently learned when there is some background. We might illustrate with the problem of learning to fly airplanes. It is customary to start with light, single-engine planes without many instruments and with relatively easy and stable handling characteristics. When such planes are mastered, the trainee proceeds to more involved aircraft with more and more instrumentation and control devices. He may end up flying transatlantic jets with such complex instrumentation and intricate controls as might well frighten a novice; yet there is no principle that dictates the order of learning and the novice might start with a transatlantic jet aircraft as his first plane. We can presume that given enough time and practice he might eventually learn to fly the machine and that in total time there might even be a saving, but there is no question that the gradual procedure will lead to more rapid mastery of the final aircraft involved. Our problem now is to account for the benefit of background (and to point out how background can sometimes prove unhelpful, that is, how background can generate wrong answers as well as correct ones).

We can start with a simple experiment which might "structure" the situation for us. Suppose that a subject is asked to learn some material presented in pairs of words such that the first word is supposed to serve as a stimulus and the second as the desired response. We might select some combinations like

stimulus	*response*
wall	mush
bale	milk

When the subject has learned these to some set criterion or standard, we might ask him on some subsequent day (week, year) to learn another set where now the former response words are used as stimuli for new words as responses, thus

stimulus	*response*
mush	tray
milk	clown

When these in turn are learned, we could ask the subject at some later time to learn still a third set where the stimulus words of the first learning experience are used as stimuli and the response words of the second set are used as the response words, thus

stimulus	*response*
wall	tray
bale	clown

If we symbolize the first stimuli as A, the first responses as B, and the second response words as C, then the subject first learned A-B, then B-C, and in the last situation, he is asked to learn A-C. In such an experiment it is likely that the third learning will occur quite rapidly when all other beneficial effects from familiarity with the words and procedure are controlled. Why should this be so? If we assume that there is some neural counterpart of A, B, and C, then we can imagine that when the learner is faced with learning A-C, something like this goes on: A sets up its neural counterpart; this is already associated with B which becomes active, but B is associated with C and sets that into activity; within a few trials, the subject is able to respond correctly because he has advantage of the neural activity that took place quite automatically and with no necessary recognition on his part that anything was going on. It would not be unreasonable to expect that in some instances the learning takes place immediately and that the subject when asked to give a C response to A might report the correct associate of B on the first trial (Russell and Storms, 1955).

In the situation described above, the neural activity involved in the hypothetical operation of the B unit can be described as a mediator. It comes between the two end-items and joins them functionally. If the experimenter requires a C response to A, we can say that learning has been facilitated by the mediator, and when such facilitation is present, we have learned to label it positive transfer.

As described above the mediation process can work quite automatically and the subject may be unable to report any of the alleged neural activity. It is also possible for the subject to verbalize such activity and to make deliberate use of it as is done in various memory improvement systems. Here is how a memory system can work (and all of them do make use of such devices): Suppose that your assignment is to learn some new association, say a name to a face or a phone number to a name or whatever; the basic principle involved is to allow the stimulus to initiate some action in the form of a free "associate," which means some normal, dependable response. If this response is now used to initiate some other association which normally arouses the desired response, the problem of remembering the desired information is solved. We can illustrate with a verbal example. The assignment is to learn to say "maypole" when the word "cat" is used as a stimulus. It would be unlikely that anyone would have a normal, free association of maypole to the word cat. Suppose, however, that the learner reacted in this fashion: to the word cat the associated common response of "nap" occurs. "Nap" now evokes the association of "sap," "sap" now in the context of "maypole" may give rise to "maple" (maple sap) and "maple" can be used with a slight pronunciation twist to evoke "maypole." Once such a routine is gone through, the subject may be able to give the "maypole" response to "cat" without any practice of any kind. We have one trial learning, and a basis for a memory system which might work quite well for this item.

It is possible to follow this kind of routine for almost anything that one wishes to remember. The difficulty lies in the fact that the normal associates that occur when one tries to pin down a particular new association may be of such a nature that they lead the learner away from the subject instead of toward it. Suppose the problem is to remember that some man's name is Jones or Brown. To try to find the chain of associations that would lead from the visual or imaginal stimulation of the face or figure of the man to the final verbalization might be awkward indeed. It might be far better to practice the name in connection with the stimuli involved directly by repeating the name several times while looking at the person, recognizing that it is more than likely that the name will be forgotten and looking for discriminated cues which would set this individual apart from others of the same name. If the name itself is a difficult or awkward one, that too must be practiced by asking for the spelling, by writing it down, by repetition of the name frequently. All of this is far too much trouble for most people who are more interested in having their own names remembered than remembering the names of others and consequently we have a culture pattern which permits us to freely confess "I can remember faces, but not names."

Let us return to the mediation hypothesis once again. We recognize that something new has been added to our S ⟶ R arrangements. The mediator is a response or a series of responses that comes between the external world stimulus and the observed response. The assumed mediator is frequently unobserved, unconscious, and need not necessarily involve any motor aspects; it is essentially what Osgood (1953) referred to as a second stage of events included within the broad stage described by S ⟶ R. A two-stage S ⟶ R theory involves a mediator and can be diagramed as:

S ⟶ r ⟶ s ⟶ R where only one mediating circuit is suggested.

If we return to our cat—maypole illustration we can symbolize the series of mediators as:

$$\begin{array}{ccccccccccccccc} S & \longrightarrow & r & \longrightarrow & s & \longrightarrow & r & \longrightarrow & s & \longrightarrow & r & \longrightarrow & s & \longrightarrow & R \\ \text{cat} & \longrightarrow & \text{nap} & \longrightarrow & \text{nap} & \longrightarrow & \text{sap} & \longrightarrow & \text{sap} & \longrightarrow & \text{maple} & \longrightarrow & \text{maple} & \longrightarrow & \text{maypole} \end{array}$$

It will be noted that the same element functions as both stimulus *s* and response *r* on the internal level. It is of most importance to emphasize this dual nature or dual role of internal events. We symbolize them by *s* and *r* but they are more properly conceived as processes which lead to other processes. Here the *s* and *r* are really ways of distinguishing events in a temporal order rather than in any other respect. The example chosen took advantage of a series of steps that can be verbalized and readily appreciated. We should now note that there is no reason to presume that mediational steps must be in verbal form, that basically they are neural processes and some of these processes may have motor outputs to various parts of the body, the external musculature as well as internal organs and glands, that one of the *r* steps may well be or be accompanied by a frown,[3] an increase in bile or adrenalin, a contraction of the stomach walls, or any other organic function. This brings us to the point that what we have previously described as r_g's are also *r*'s of the type described above, that they, too, are mediational devices or mechanisms, in a more motor form. In any sequential type of behavior, we can expect r_g's to occur if it is possible for any aspect of the sequence to become more or less "detached" from the final features of the sequence and appear earlier in the sequence. Here they can play the part of mediators by generating stimuli which can be associated with any other activity taking place, and we emphasize here the neural activity which we have suggested as carrying through the mediational process.

The function of prior experience

The student who has thought carefully about the cat and the maypole will have noticed that the capacity for remembering the response after one exposure was based on other associations. These other associations were previously learned and were being put to work in a new situation. Without such a repertoire of earlier learned associations, each new fact would have to be learned in its own right. This we do not have time to do in any ordinary lifetime. Our past experience is always

[3] The motor accompaniment to such mediation might "give away" your thoughts. Prize fighters occasionally "telegraph" their blows—i.e., some small move or gesture indicates what they intend doing next. Such motor activities can be the basis for some small success in "mind reading."

with us, available for employment in new acquisitions. To argue as some people do that there is no transfer of training, that everything has to be learned in its own right is manifestly absurd. We could never have learned all what we know. It is true that young animals and young children have less past experience to go on and consequently have to learn many things *de novo,* but once a foundation of any kind is established, it is used. Frequently the use leads to errors, as when the child calls a horse a "big doggie" or a dandelion a "pretty flower," but that is the price that is paid for the benefits that are enjoyed when the past experience is helpful. Once we have learned to use the word "polite" to describe certain operations such as kissing a lady's hand or taking off hats in elevators, or in general addressing women as "ma'am" and men as "sir," we have also established the mediators which will permit the use of such responses to new representatives of the stimulus patterns involved. This is where we must leave Guthrie's highly specific learning emphasis which may very well apply at the level of early or primitive learning and recognize what the facts of behavior dictate, that many kinds of behavior can be predicted in advance of any description of the stimulus other than that it can be classified as belonging to a group which initiates a particular kind of mediator. We have arrived in our analysis at the stage where we can now deal with classes of stimuli regardless of their specific features, at least to some degree. When we learn that the whale is a mammal, we are ready with certain expectancies which the neural correlates of the terms "mammal" dictate. While the physical resemblance between a bat and a whale to external observation is rather meager, we are equipped to handle certain kinds of problems on the basis of the mediator involved. Similarly in other areas of activity. A child can spend a lively afternoon with a soap box or a broomstick if these are not really soap boxes and broomsticks but forts and horses or rifles or airplanes. We shall return to such applications of the mediation hypothesis when we deal with thinking. For the present, the concept of mediation has served its purpose. It is the mechanism of transfer. It is the tool by which we remember. It is also the means or mechanism which, when leading us astray, makes us forget.

Remembering, forgetting, and emotional factors

It has been noted for centuries that other people have convenient memories. They forget things which are to their advantage to forget and we are irritated when they cite their poor memories. Freud (1938) extended this common observation to important proportions in founding or resting his system of psychoanalysis on the concept of "repression" (see p. 431) which, basically, is a proposition that events and experiences which disturb us and make us "anxious" are in some unspecified manner pushed back out of our conscious life. Such events would, in general, merit the description of "unpleasant" and many investigators have, without endorsing the concept of repression in its Freudian use, tried to test the hypothesis that, in general we tend to forget unpleasant events, and, in contrast, remember more pleasant experiences for longer periods or in greater number.

The general findings in such experiments are equivocal; some finding evidence for and some against the hypothesis. We might expect great difficulties in conducting a proper experiment in this area. To define an unpleasant event is not a simple task; to measure the degrees of unpleasantness even more difficult. It is probable that almost anyone can recall unpleasant experiences when asked, although he might be reluctant to describe them and sometimes, even to admit having any. This raises the difficult question as to why some unpleasant experiences are remembered when others might be forgotten. Are there peculiar features to the kinds of unpleasant experiences we forget, and if so, what are these? If one argues that the experience that is forgotten is one that makes you anxious when you think of it, then we are caught in a circular reasoning trap out of which there is no exit. Without an independent specification of the kinds of events that should be forgotten and the kinds that should not be, we are in no position to deliver a scientific judgment. The contradictory nature of the data leaves us without a safe and reliable conclusion on this subject.

Should it turn out that some kinds of unpleasant events are actually forgotten in a greater proportion, or that even one peculiarly suited unpleasant event is forgotten, the question remains as to whether there is any need to specify any special conditions beyond those already described to account for it. Do we need a concept of repression when the concept of interference is available? The concept of interference from new learning might be sufficiently broad to cover any special kinds of forgotten events or responses. If a person finds himself uneasy and anxious in the presence of certain stimuli and is responding in terms of some anxiety symptoms like perspiration, flushing, stomach upset, or general tension, and if the stimuli do not, in effect, call for any kind of specific response, the individual will inevitably find himself doing something. If he is religiously inclined, he might begin to pray; those otherwise disposed may decide to garden or work in their shops, review their stamp collections or read mystery stories. They might even count to ten. In time, if the activities hit upon do ease the situation, and get rid of the stimuli to anxiety, the new activity might well advance forward in time as any other learned response and eventually be the characteristic

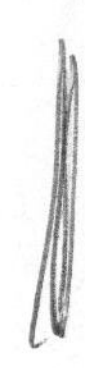

response to a former anxiety-arousing stimulus. New learning has replaced the old response, and the subject's behavior has been changed. Without special effort, relearning, prevention of the substitute activity, etc., he might not "remember" the original event or response (anxiety) that he used to make. Freud might call this repression: it appears to be only a special case of forgetting due to new learning.

At this time we might take special pains to note that what has been forgotten has not disappeared without a trace. Our consideration of relearning speed and the importance of correct stimuli suggest that much that appears unavailable to ready recall can be brought back or relearned quickly. This suggests that a neural basis for the associations involved still exists although in less accessible form than the more recently learned associations. Such associations we have described as organizations of neural cells in cell assemblies which might well have numerous associations with other assemblies and might be activated at various times whether in the interests of some current activity or quite randomly. In other words, it is not uncommon for us to have rather random thoughts (activity of cell assemblies in sequences), to be reminded of things that no one else is reminded of by some commonly shared experience, to dream about things or events long "buried" in our past. This much we can readily grant. To jump from this position into one which suggests that memories are themselves possessed of some kind of energy which demands expression, that they seek outlets, that they resist "repression," and that, perhaps, they are in some kind of conflict with other alleged agencies is something else again. We must not allow a small fund of fact to be expanded into a justification for uncontrolled speculation. To picture the organism as equipped with an "unconscious mind" which is a virtual storehouse of repressed memories, illicit urges, and conflicts with guardians at the gates to the "conscious mind" appears to be pure fabrication. What little fact we have is difficult enough to appreciate without an elaborate mythology being imposed upon it.

From the argument presented, there is no more reason for an unpleasant event (in our terms, a response) being forgotten than a pleasant one, all other conditions being equal (importance, time, opportunity for new experience, etc.). If we were to concede any hypothetical structure like an unconscious mind, it would be no where near as interesting as the Freudian picture. All kinds of "memories" would be included, none of them would be fighting or struggling to emerge, and any of equal strength would have an equal probability of becoming involved in some conscious associations without themselves evoking any motor activity that would enable us to identify them or note their existence. In this context we might even accept an ancient notion of the mind as a storehouse of ideas. If we translate this to say that the brain is made up of neurons which have become associated in complex ways as we have undergone various learning experiences and that these learning experiences are represented by altered neural structure some of which can be activated by stimuli involved in the learning, then the old expression is conversationally acceptable. If we can make a case for the notion that an idea is a phase sequence of cell assemblies, then we can hardly deny that the brain is a storehouse of such "ideas." It is a rather queer storehouse, however, as the stock will not always stay on the shelves but has a characteristic of wandering off and getting mixed up with all kinds of other goods. The direction of such wandering, however, is under the control of stimuli and physiological conditions and not a willfulness of the ideas themselves. To put the matter in the most dogmatic form, an "idea" could not care less about whether the owner of the brain "had" it or thought of it or not.

Persistence of uncompleted response sequences

When a subject is given a number of things to do and begins to go through a sequence something akin to what we have previously described as "closure" has been postulated to occur as the tasks are finished. If a task is interrupted, and left unfinished while the subject goes on to other jobs, it is argued that there is a tendency for the unfinished tasks to lack this closure or "need it." In any event when a subject is asked to name each of say twenty tasks on which he has worked (ten of which were interrupted) he might list more of the uncompleted assignments than of the completed. The tendency was first reported by Zeigarnik and is often referred to as the "Zeigarnik effect."[4] Later investigations disclosed that what is remembered depends to a great extent on the nature of the subject's personality, his goals, how much he enjoys success, the challenge of the tasks, etc., so that no definite predictions can be made about what a specific individual will do. Without some study of the individual under at least related circumstances we cannot argue that incomplete tasks will tend to be remembered or "seek expression." This does not, of course, negate the possibility that some individuals may behave as if they must complete everything they begin. Nor can we deny that some events persist (the song running through your head) despite changes of stimulation and activity. One can resume humming the same song late in the afternoon after lunch and some work if the "running through your head" routine started in the morning. Similarly, when one thinks of something to say in a meeting

[4] Osgood (1953) presents a critical analysis of the Zeigarnik type of experiment.

or conversation but gets no opportunity to say it at the time, he may find himself saying it eventually, even if at the time it is somewhat if not completely irrelevant. This is an area of behavior that has not received experimental analysis to the point where we can do much more than recognize it and allude to the probable persistence of neural circuits which are once aroused but not effectively completed.

PART II

The Integrated Aspects of Man

CHAPTER 9

An Introduction to the Traditional Problems of Psychology

The problem of classifying behavior · Faculty psychology · Other attempts at classification · The concept of integration

THE PROBLEM OF CLASSIFYING BEHAVIOR

Up to now we have been concerned with the nature of man's equipment and how it is modified through experience, or learning. We have seen that the modification of the initial hereditary contribution begins with conception and from that moment on continues through the processes of growth, maturation, and learning. At no time of life can the hereditary contributions be ignored nor can we treat lightly the structural and physiological changes that underlie any behavioral manifestations. Our problem is to discover what the modifiable organism can do and actually does with its equipment. Given a modifiable and modified nervous system, how does man behave? Man does many things, behaves in such diverse ways in so many kinds of situations, that any attempt to catalogue behavior seems doomed from the start. Until we begin to think about classifying behavior we do not appreciate the complexity that appears in following a single individual's activities over a day or even a briefer period. To say that Individual A went here and there, interacted with so and so, did this and that, would be an extremely superficial account. The report would be a bit of history, not psychology. We might watch a housewife shopping at a supermarket, picking things off shelves, pausing at some, passing others hurriedly, replacing items previously selected, and we might report that we had observed some "consumer behavior." The observations might serve some practical or general conversational purposes, but psychology has long concerned itself with a much more molecular approach. We would like to know the factors underlying or related to the selection and rejection of items and the display features that halt the shopper and those that do not. Answers to such questions would be more in the realm of traditional psychology.

It is obvious that we cannot examine in detail each individual response that any organism might make and that some sort of classification scheme must be adopted from which we might proceed to a determination of some, and perhaps the more important, principles that operate in a variety of behavioral situations. When we are finished we might still be unable to do much with a particular individual's specific behavior but might have some general appreciation of various classes of activity and some general explanatory (theoretical) principles.

Classifications of behavior have been attempted from ancient times as interested observers have attempted to penetrate the mysteries of man's behavior. The classifications have attempted to compartmentalize behavior in convenient packages of types of activities with common features or common governing agencies, and none has ever proved satisfactory so that new conceptions are advanced with each new attempt to view the behavior of man. The most ancient classificatory scheme was that of the early Greek philosophers who thought of man's functions as divisible into three broad classes of cognitive, conative, and affective operations (see Allport, 1954). The cognitive function included all intellectual activity—thinking, reasoning, and its precursors, sensing and perceiving. The conative function took care of the causes of action, wishes, urges, desires, choices, and decisions. The affective function involved the emotional aspects of behavior and included the various states of feeling and temperament. Special classifications of temperament were developed by the classical philosophers and early physicians who related various characteristic temperaments to the liquids or secretions of the body and indeed to body structure or type. Individuals were said to be sanguine, phlegmatic, choleric, or melancholy, depending upon the oversupply of, or imbalance among, the body's "humours." We still use the expression "good (or bad) humor."

Plato's three-fold ancient classification is still to be detected as the background from which modern psychologists work. They no longer talk about cognition, conation, and affection in those particular terms, but they do tend to subdivide behavior into categories which stem from the original three. Thus we have in the typical text chapters that might be classified as dealing with "cognitive" matters (sensation or sensory processes, perception, intelligence, concept formation, thinking, and reasoning); chapters dealing with conation include discussions of "motivation" and "drives," aspiration and ego involvement, conflict and defenses; affection is represented with the typical chapter on emotion, and sometimes, a chapter on feeling, anxiety, and stress.

The ancient classification did not work well because it was apparent that, however intriguing the magic number of three might be, man's behavior could not be divided into neat and separate categories. Subsequent attempts to enlarge the number of functions were not much of an improvement either because they perpetuated the notion still dominating our texts that man can be at one moment a thinker, but not a feeler or that when he wills or chooses, intellectual and emotional factors can be set aside. If any one concept that psychologists have developed has value, it is the concept of integration of behavior, in the view that the whole man behaves, that he does not function in parts; nor is he merely the tool or means by which separate functions express themselves.

Faculty psychology

The ancient view that man was controlled by or possessed separate functions or "faculties" is no longer accepted as a working assumption by psychologists. At one time such a "faculty psychology" dominated the entire approach to an understanding of man. Whatever was done, was done by the temporary operation or dominance of some special faculty. When a man loved, it was because the faculty of love was in the ascendant. When he tortured, it was because the faculty of cruelty held sway. When he worked on a problem, the faculty of intellect or reason was busy; when he selected or chose a course of action, the faculty of will did the work. We still have the remnants of such a psychology quite dominant in our ordinary vocabularies. When we talk about a "memory" or "intelligence," of a "capacity" or "talent" or "ability," we are using the vocabulary of faculty psychology. Modern texts tend to avoid such terminology and prefer to emphasize verb forms referring to processes that might conceivably be taking place, or they use adjectives to avoid the almost inevitable tendency to slip into the error of establishing an agency to govern a function. Thus we read about emotional behavior rather than about emotion or intelligent behavior, or problem-solving behavior, remembering rather than memory, and so on. These are probably wise precautions, but they do not avoid the real problem.

Other attempts at classification

Neither the three-fold classification of the ancients nor the uncontrollable ramifications of a faculty psychology proved satisfactory to critical observers of behavior; they had to give way. Always behind the attempts of classifiers we can detect the interest in simplifying, in reducing behavior to some workable number of principles, in easy solutions to a complex problem. Over the years the efforts at simplification took various turns ranging from bold efforts to reduce behavior to the operations of some single universal principle to more pragmatic efforts in which principles would be added *ad hoc* as they proved to be necessary. We can profit by examining or at least mentioning some of the more energetically advanced proposals. A simple enumeration should reveal that where so many different kinds of principles are alleged to be all-important (or at least of prime significance) that quite possibly, none of them is actually so. We have had a parallel situation in the history of medicine where at one time bleeding a patient was the cure-all technique, giving way in due time to other panaceas. Even today we find some specialists arguing in effect, although no one is quite so naive as to say so directly, that all illnesses are psychosomatic or due to allergies (or that none are); that we need more fat in our diets or less; that we should exercise more (or less) and so on.

We have already mentioned the attempts of early psychologists to reduce behavior to instincts. William McDougall (1915) found that seven instincts and their accompanying natural emotions would neatly handle most behavior. What could not be taken care of with the basic instincts was referred to other additional instincts of a lesser generality or significance. Following McDougall we have Freud (1938) basing his psychology on life and death instincts and emphasizing the role of sex and repression as the foundations or keys to psychological problems. Among Freud's original supporters we encounter such analysts as Adler, Jung, and Rank who began to question the master and developed their own views of what was truly fundamental. Thus Adler argued that sex was overemphasized at the expense of the truly significant "will to power" or a need to dominate, to be superior. Jung became interested in folklore and mythology and began to emphasize a "racial unconscious" or a universal nature that must be appreciated if behavior is to be understood. Rank became interested in the hypothetical importance of a "birth trauma." Other analysts began to emphasize as universal or basic other kinds of events or forces. The search for a universal principle is still going on in analytic circles with some emphasizing infantile or childhood experiences, others looking at more current situational factors.[1]

In the more direct historical development of psychology other kinds of first principles were advocated. Walter B. Cannon (1939), for example, argued that psychology should be built around a principle of "homeostasis," that is, the proposition that organisms seek to maintain some kind of status quo or physiological balance, that all behavior is

[1] The student interested in various schools of psychoanalysis might begin with Hall (1954), proceed to the biography of Freud by E. Jones (1953), and continue with Horney (1939).

an attempt to maintain or repair the body. Under such a principle, an organism might be expected to sit or lie quietly until some injury, danger, or need stirred it into activity. Such activity would be calculated to restore the original condition. The homeostatic principle is in the line of theoretical development stemming from Darwin's evolutionary theory of adaptation and survival of the fittest. Many psychologists adopted the homeostatic view and textbooks have been written with this principle as the underlying foundation. It is the view from which modern drive and motivation theories have sprung. Unfortunately, like any single principle it runs into difficulties when the complexities of behavior are considered and it is difficult to stretch the principle without obvious forcing. It begins to explain too much without explaining enough.

From our concern with the problems of learning we have already found out how some learning psychologists hope to stretch a single proposition into a blanket explanation. Pavlov's conditioning and Skinner's reinforcement have been applied to the most complex abnormal and social behavior. How successfully this has been done cannot be appraised by asking the supporters of such views, nor yet the critics who have their own pet postulates.

From the welter of prime principles (and we have listed only a few) can we begin to describe the problems of psychology, to say nothing of the principles? Is it instinct, or sex, or repression, or organ inferiority and compensation, a racial unconscious, or a birth trauma that accounts for behavior and misbehavior? Is it homeostasis or adaptation, conditioning, or reinforcement, or is it still some yet-to-be-discovered principle that will provide the answers?

Another problem that plagues us in attempting to get at the general principle or principles on which a scientific psychology might proceed in an orderly fashion is the fact that many psychologists have only cursory interests in theoretical problems. They become concerned over specific practical issues and applications of psychology to special fields. Thus we have school psychologists and legal psychologists, psychologists in industry, advertising, vocational guidance, military work, marriage counseling, clinical activities, child, and social welfare, and other more theoretical but still specialized psychologists who are called social psychologists, or physiological, comparative, or abnormal psychologists.

Is it true that each of these fields represents some unique kind of psychology? Are the principles of child psychology different from those of industrial psychology or social psychology? It is obvious that data gathered by workers in each of these fields will differ in terms of the kinds of activities and stimulus situations each studies. But, are the underlying principles different? Cannot the general theoretical psychologist step into a military situation and work effectively without having studied "military psychology"? It has been done. In fact, before World War II, there was no military psychology to speak of. Now there is, but it is staffed by psychologists who received ordinary psychological training and who happen to be working in a military situation. Do military problems involve some special kind of psychological principles or is it more a matter of recognizing the special features of stimuli in a military situation and working with the same principles one would follow in a nursery school or advertising office?

The fact of special interests both in the field of principles and in the field of practical affairs has led to a more or less chaotic state. On the one hand, psychology is beset by proponents of one universal principle after another; on the other, every area of practical work from setting off guided missiles to fish breeding and prevention of forest fires is asking for some kind of specialized psychological lore. One group or another is interested in winning friends and influencing people, selling tomatoes or phonograph records. We have the psychology of the laborer, the farmer, the college student, the housewife, the consumer, the audience, or whatever group happens to concern anyone.

In the face of the situation we have just considered, it is not surprising that not much success has been achieved in a classification of psychological problems and principles. There are too many cooks all cooking different dishes in the same kitchen and in many cases in the same pots, quarreling over the ownership of the pots. The result has been that we have divided and subdivided the human race and the rest of the animal kingdom into smaller groups looking about for either the same principle to apply to all or for special principles to apply to each segmental group. We have even broken up the unit organism into smaller and smaller functions and postulated one entity or principle after another to handle each function, getting, inevitably, a distorted and one-sided view of whatever function has been so isolated out of context.

Throughout the range of attempts at classification of functions, principles, or problems, a persistent tradition has prevailed throughout history with respect to what is really interesting about man's behavior. However practical interests or special prejudices sway us, we cannot escape the fact that what we are really concerned about is what goes on under the skins of other people or organisms. We want to know what the other fellow is thinking about, how he feels, and what he plans to do. In some measure we apply the same questions to our dogs and cats, and quite commonly to ourselves. The ancient Greek philosophers were not so different in their interests from modern psychologists. We are still trying to explain the same kinds of events. But when we do approach these phenomena we are handicapped in our approach by the failure to recognize a major problem.

The problem referred to above is that behavior is a function of the whole individual and that any attempt to break it up into segmental processes as if they occurred in isolation is likely to distort the analysis and lead to the wrong interpretation. We might picture two men playing chess, for example, and infer that they were engaged in a "reasoning" or "thinking" process. But even a moment's consideration reveals that the men are not *just* "reasoning." There is first of all some reason for their playing, a "motivation" factor. Each man wants to win. Such a want is not an abstract intellectual thing. It is an emotional affair; and in some games it dominates the reasoning, if any, that goes on. As the players engage in their game they sense, they perceive, they imagine, they choose, they fret, they decide. They work quite intensively though the outside observer might regard them as lost to the world. A one-hour chess match can be a grueling, exhausting affair, leaving the combatants, and the word is deliberately chosen, limp. The whole body plays chess, it is not a game for the "intellect" or the "intelligence," nor the "thought processes" or any other imagined agency. We tend to identify the game with "reasoning" or "thinking" because of certain characteristics involved in the situation, but we are unlikely to arrive at any analysis of thinking if we study chess players. What we will get is something that involves "thinking" plus a great many interacting functions and activities. Similarly with any other behavior pattern, there will be complicated, simultaneous, interacting processes that prevent our observation of an isolated or separate function.

The concept of integration

Whenever we try to study a given behavior pattern, say anger, panic, a decision, or bliss, we must recognize that there are numerous interactions present involving the entire history of the organism, its perception of the present situation, its thinking activities, and its needs or motivations. If we try to study the perceptions of the organism, emotional, motivational, and thought factors will be present. This situation is not peculiar to psychology. It prevails in any complex operation in the physical world when many parts of an apparatus must function at the same time in some co-ordinated fashion. It does make the study of psychology and other sciences difficult. It is quite impossible to talk about everything at once and as soon as you begin to concentrate on one aspect you may lose sight of another. This is the price we must be prepared to pay. In the following chapters we will frequently, if not constantly, lapse from a thoroughly integrated analysis of what is going on, but if we keep reminding ourselves to synthesize at the same time that we analyze, we may make some progress. With this warning before us, we can begin to break up the behavior of organisms into categories that might help illuminate some of the processes that underlie the molar or externally observable operations. Because each kind of process will be found to be related to all of the other kinds, it hardly makes any difference where we start.

In the remainder of this text we shall restrict ourselves to what might be called the traditional areas of psychology: cognition, conation, and affection. As indicated earlier, each of these terms covers a multitude of problems and we shall have to be content with what appear to be basic and fundamental issues. To get too deeply involved with some special facet of one of these major problem areas will inevitably force us to lose sight of the role of other processes. When we have finished our examination of the general principles that appear to be of interest in thinking, motivation, and the complicated area of emotion, we shall attempt a more molar approach and consider the problems involved in trying to appreciate the whole man, the "personality." Finally, an even more molar problem, that of the social man, will require some attention. If the student will now consider himself properly warned, we can begin to examine psychology in its traditional framework. Because the previous chapters have dealt with learning and mediational processes, and since these are basically related to the analysis of thinking, we can start with an examination of what goes on when we think.

CHAPTER 10

Cognitive Functions—Symbolic Processes and Meanings

Thinking · The characteristics of thinking · The delayed response experiment · Symbolic behavior · Double alternation · Novel combinations in thinking · Insight · The tools of thinking · Ideo-motor action · Thinking and meaning · Discriminated responses · Language and meaning · An association theory of meaning · The semantic differential · Thinking and concepts · Concept formation in animals · Thinking and consciousness

THINKING

We have no doubts about the fact that we think. Indeed, as we have seen, Descartes convinced himself of his very existence by recognizing that he was able to think. Most of us have learned to regard man as a thinking creature and we have various reservations about the capacities of "lower animals" to think. Thinking is generally regarded as one of the "higher processes." What this "higherness" consists of we are not too sure except that it somehow distinguishes us from lower forms which, presumably, do not think or, at least, not as well. Thinking is somehow identified with something above lowly material things, something essentially unanalyzable, a nonsubstantial activity going on in a nonsubstantial mind. Physical activity is presumably absent or minimal. Rodin's "The Thinker" is a monument of impassivity and immobility. The figure in the sculpture has settled down for a good, long, hard, thinking session. He is not to be disturbed. Whatever is going on cannot be observed. When the thinking is finished, perhaps we will be told about its outcome.

If psychologists were to accept such an interpretation they would close the discussion at this point and leave the subject to philosophers, logicians, and sculptors. Logicians, particularly, concern themselves with one aspect of thinking, that of reasoning, but while they appear to be concerned with the processes of thought, they are actually concerned with the products of thought, and not with the nature of the activity itself. Two thousand years of preoccupation with the logical or nonlogical aspects of syllogisms has not thrown any light on the nature of the thinking process itself. In the last fifty years we have acquired a little information about it. What information we have is not very complete or even competent, but perhaps a start has been made. We can now examine what we have.

The characteristics of thinking

How do we know when thinking occurs? If we could answer this question, we might have what would approach an operational definition of thinking and would help inform us about our subject. We might put the question in another way: under what conditions do we think, and contrastedly, under what conditions do we not think? Here again, satisfactory answers would help to restrict the subject. The answers to those questions that might be supplied by a layman are not very helpful. He might tell us that we think when we have or generate "ideas." Unless he tells us what an idea is we are not much better off and most attempts at defining an idea will leave us with more questions than answers. If we persist in our questions the layman or anyone else is likely to come up with something that might be a little more helpful. "You think when you don't know what to do." This might suggest that when you do know what to do you do not think, but that is something that may merely be a minor obstacle to our analysis and we might start with the notion that we think when we do not know what to do.

John Dewey (1910) expressed the same proposition by saying that if we had enough habits we would not need to think. If we interpret this correctly, then much of our behavior which is of a routine nature and runs off more or less automatically, like typing or repeating some factory operation time after time, does not involve thinking. We can skip for the moment the fact that the factory operator may be thinking about how he will meet the monthly payments on his home and car or about more pleasant affairs; at least he is not thinking about what his hands are doing. But when does he think about what his hands are doing? When he first started the job the hands did not know what to do and some period of learning and practice had to be gone through before the habitual responses were acquired. At first, then, the worker had to think, but now he does not have to, and presumably does not think about the work unless something goes wrong for which he has no automatic adjustment in his habit repertoire.

This may be something to go on. We have a start. Thinking occurs when a situation arises for which we have no automatic and immediate response. Such a situation might be called a problem and we might be justified in presuming that thinking does go on in the problem situations, although it might also go on in other situations which we have not yet considered.

But there is more to a problem situation than might appear at first inspection. We note that the habitual course of action has been stopped, that now there will be a delay before the course is resumed, and that what goes on in the delay period may include some thinking. The delay is a purely objective affair, a temporal period to be measured by a clock and has nothing to do with the thinking, to be sure, but if we look at the behavior during the delay period we may make some useful observations. One way to do this might be to artificially create delay periods in the normal courses of action and see what goes on.

The delayed response experiment

It is common knowledge that some animals bury bones or secrete food and later return to regain the treasure. Psychologists have applied this information to a form of investigation that has been called the "delayed response" experiment. In such an experiment an animal is first trained to go to one of two sides of a divided area for food. This area is identified by a light and the animal learns to go to the lighted side. When the habit is strongly established, the light is turned on briefly while the animal is restrained. The light goes out and after some desired interval the animal is released. It now has no present cue to serve as a guide. If it selects the correct compartment, it has demonstrated a capacity to delay action and to solve a problem. If it cannot delay this action, if the performance becomes a matter of chance then the animal is considered to be incapable of handling the delay situation. Comparative studies have revealed that animals like the rat have practically no capacity to delay. When released moments after the light goes out they chose the wrong compartment as commonly as the correct one. Raccoons and dogs do better. It is noted however that dogs will orient themselves toward the light and "point" toward the correct compartment all through the delay period. If they are released while pointing they will perform well. If their orientation is disturbed by turning them about during the delay period, they will be as helpless as the rats. Raccoons seem to be fairly successful even though they are not characteristically pointers and even if they are turned about. None of these animals can delay the response for any length of time, however, and a minute is more than enough to wipe out any benefits from the signal. Monkeys, chimpanzees, and children can delay for very long times and generally speaking, indefinitely. The adult human would have no problem in such a task.

When a delayed response is successfully achieved, it raises the question of how the performance was guided to its successful conclusion. With the man we learn very little when we ask how it was done. He simply tells us: "I knew it was on the right." We are no wiser than before because we are concerned with what he means by knowing and his remarks do not help. If we press for details, he might say something like, "Well, I remembered that the light was on the right" or "I told myself that it was on the right." Perhaps we are getting closer to something here. If we go back to our dog we noted that the dog could not solve the problem without pointing. By pointing the dog is, in effect, telling itself that the food is on the right. The rat apparently does not tell itself anything since it is an incompetent in this task. Does the rat know nothing, remember nothing? In this kind of task, the rat is no thinker. But the raccoon is at least a little better. How does the raccoon tell itself?

SYMBOLIC BEHAVIOR

We recognize, at least with the man, that the behavior is completed successfully because of something that takes place during the delay interval or just before the test performance. We have already learned to call such intervening or interpolated behavior "mediation" and we can assume for the present purposes that the problem is solved by some kind of mediational device. Because such mediated behavior is not commonly observable (except in the dog) we have to describe it as "internal" and since it substitutes for such things as pointing, we can add that it is "internal substitution." When one kind of event or item substitutes for another, we frequently use the term "symbol" and it might be legitimate to refer to the mediation activity as "symbolic" behavior. We have to be extremely careful here to emphasize that the symbolic aspect derives only from the fact of substitution and that we are not introducing some new and indeterminable structure to get out of a tight spot. The nature of symbols must be carefully appreciated or we will get into more trouble than we had without them. If we count library cards instead of counting books directly, we are still counting things. We can say that the cards symbolize the books, but all that we mean is that the cards are serving as substitutes for the books. The use of such symbols does not at all permit the addition of any surplus adornments to the events. When we described Pavlov's dog responding to a bell by salivating, we did not imply in any way that the bell made the animal "think" of food or that the bell "stood for food," or symbolized a banquet, or had any other excess reference. All that was implied was that the bell now served the same function as the appearance of food, that, in effect, it was a substitute for the appearance of food as far as salivation was concerned. Similarly here and in all our future discussions, the term symbol or symbolic will be restricted to the function of a substitute process. When we speak of thinking as symbolic behavior, we will still mean that it is behavior, that some kinds of processes are going on which substitute for other kinds of processes. We will not mean the thinker is "manipulating symbols" or doing anything else with the kinds of things we identify as symbols in the external world. In the brain we have only processes occurring and no one is doing any manipulating. The processes either occur or do not occur because of the conditions that have been established.

In man, the use of language apparently serves the symbolic function required in the delay situation. The man tells himself at the time the light is on, that "it's on the right." Later, in the test, he is in the same situation as before, and again he tells himself, "It's on the right" and proceeds to go there. This is not the complete story, of course, and we shall have to return to it later, but for now it might be enough. A deaf mute has a sign-language to employ. What can a speechless animal like the dog or raccoon do? When the animal points and maintains the point, there is no problem; we recognize the pointing behavior as symbolic for running in a given direction. When the animal does not point and still solves the problem, then we must look for other kinds of symbolic behavior.

Suppose we make the situation quite easy for the dog but do not permit him to maintain a point. If it solves the problem at all, it might conceivably do it by something akin to what man does for himself. Let us assume that the dog, seeing the light, is ready to eat (the previous training has been such that the appearance of the light has been conditioned to moving forward and seizing food). We can assume that in such circumstances, fractional parts of the behavior would move forward (r_g's) and that on the appearance of the light the dog would begin to salivate, chew, and swallow in an anticipatory manner. All of these responses would produce stimuli which would be present at the time the animal was orienting itself toward the right in straining to get to the food. Sometime later, in the test interval, the animal is again exposed to the separated chambers, and some of the situational stimuli will initiate the r_g's previously set into action. The stimuli from the r_g's have been conditioned to straining to the right and the animal might well turn in that direction. We cannot expect to get much accuracy out of the animal because we are depending upon one trial learning to stimuli that are not likely to be especially potent and which will, when the animal is next tested on the left light, have to serve to direct the animal in an opposite direction. When there is no such confusion, the animal might be quite effective in delay behavior. The dog might easily find old buried bones because there might be only one or a few places where such behavior has occurred; a particular spot may have been dictated by conditions of the environment to begin with, and if the appropriate r_g's should occur, the animal might proceed directly to the spot. If we saw the animal getting up, stretching, and setting off in a fixed direction to the bone pit, we might say that it "thought of its old bones and went to dig them up." What we should say, perhaps, is that r_g's associated with chewing and crunching old bones occurred; they produced stimuli which were associated with moving in a particular direction and the dog moved.

Another form of delayed response experiment (Tinklepaugh, 1928) might make the above analysis more or less credible. A monkey is shown a piece of banana and this piece is hidden under some cover while the monkey is held under restraint. Behind a curtain the experimenter exchanges the piece of banana for a grape or some lettuce or other fruit. Now the curtain is raised and the animal is permitted to pick up the cover. Under such circumstances, the animal often gets quite furious and refuses to eat the otherwise acceptable food. How are we to analyze the behavior? It is obvious to us that the animal "thought" it was going to find banana. It expected banana. During the delay period, the animal must have been thinking of banana and not something else. This may well be; our problem is to account for the thinking.

Again we resort to symbolic, substitutive, mediational behavior. While the animal is watching the experimenter hide the banana, the responses associated with eating bananas are initiated but, of course, cannot be completed. This does not prevent the occurrence of r_g's associated with eating bananas from taking place. These r_g's consist of salivating to a certain degree, of preparing lips and teeth in appropriate positions for bananas and no other food. These r_g's become associated with the cover and with the situation generally so that when the animal is later released, the r_g's again occur. When the cover is snatched off and the food reached for, the animal is disturbed because it is not ready for grapes or lettuce. It is ready for bananas. The student might question such readiness for specific foods but a little reflection ought to convince him that different foods do require special approaches. One does not chew steak the same way that he chews potatoes; drinking soup requires a different approach from drinking whiskey. To find whiskey in a teacup leaves most tea drinkers quite unprepared and even the accomplished alcoholic is not quite happy with a teacup as the medium. The true gourmet could not bring himself to drink brandy out of a bottle or use anything but the proper utensil for caviar or oysters. As soon as any habitual mode of response becomes integrated into a pattern, the pattern elements must occur at the right points in the sequences or else we are at least momentarily upset. We are quite willing to eat chicken held in our fingers but probably most of us are not so ready to eat spaghetti or gelatin without the proper tools. Who has not been disturbed at finding on the dinner table something that he would normally be quite pleased to eat but which is different from what he had been told earlier was to be the *pièce de resistance?*

Double alternation

We can look at still another form of the delayed response experiment. This one is known as the double alternation experiment and involves forcing a subject to repeat some pattern of responses where two or three steps must be repeated in sequence if the experimenter is to be satisfied. In the form used with animals, an animal might be required to traverse an alley to a choice point where a right or left turn is permitted. Taking the turn only brings the subject back to the original starting point where again the alley must be traversed to the same choice point. This could be repeated ad infinitum but suppose that the experimenter decides to reinforce the pattern: right, right, left, left. That is, the animal must turn right on the first two runs up the alley and left on the subsequent two. Now, the point is, of course, that there is no change in the appearance of the end of the alley at any stage of the exercises and the animal must, if it is to follow the correct sequence, respond to a cue by one movement on one occasion and by a contradictory movement on the next occasion. It is easy enough for a rat or dog to learn to keep making right turns at the choice point, but animals like cats, dogs, and rats cannot master the double alternation problem. It is claimed that raccoons are somewhat more successful but require a great many trials before they begin to show any reliable scores. If the problem is mastered at all, how is it done? For humans there is not much of a problem. They tell themselves, twice to the right, twice to the left. Again, language is being used as substitute behavior. Humans can count, rats cannot. The counting process generates the necessary cues for the correct behavior in the human. He could learn to go seventeen times to the right and twenty-one times to the left if that is what the experimenter required and the effort would not be different in nature from the two and two problem although it would take much longer.

Lacking the capacity to count, the animal must use other cues if the problem is to be solved. One such cue might come from the kinesthetic feedback from action. It might be possible to base new responses on such muscular inputs from previous action. In many kinds of repetitive tasks, we get to recognize about how much work was done without measuring the work simply by what we refer to as the degree of fatigue. Rats have been trained to turn at a predetermined point by training them to run down an alley and turn at some cut-off point. Later on they are forced to carry little weighted saddlebags and it is found that the animals turn off sooner. Presumably they have run far enough to build up a given state of fatigue. This has provided the cue for turning behavior and the animals turn even though the turn has now become premature (Solomon, 1947).

Where cues from fatigue serve to cue off a response, they are, again, substitute or symbolic cues. They play a part in the solution of a problem, even though the solution may not be a correct one. It should be pointed out here and will be repeated frequently that solutions are solutions even though not correct. Perhaps a better way of stating the case is that there is no essential difference in the nature of correct or incorrect behavior. The same kinds of processes lead to both. Thinking is the same whether the thinking is good, bad, or mediocre. Solutions depend upon society or nature and have nothing to do with the nature of the thinking that goes on. If a solution is reached through cues of a fatigue origin, then these are the symbolic mediators that brought about the behavior.

In the above illustrations we have tried to describe some of the kinds of events that mediate between the situation and the final solution of a problem, that is, a situation involving a delay. The delay period is taken up by action. Our problem has been to describe this action which is by and large unseen, symbolic, substitutive, and either of a minimal nature as far as external observation is concerned, or wholly internal. We do not see the salivation, the chewing movements, the set of the teeth, the cues from fatigue, all of which have been posited as playing some role in thinking. No more do we see the man talking to himself, although most men will admit that that is how the time is spent in a delayed response situation. Sometimes we can see people mumbling to themselves with their lips moving just as we can see a dog pointing, but much of the behavior is of a restricted, internal nature, so that we are forced to infer the occurrence of events which may be difficult to establish as facts.

Our discussion of mediators in the previous chapters included the neural processes themselves which are set into action as phase sequences. These we certainly are in no position to see, yet they may be the basic tools of thinking. After all, the observable or potentially observable reactions we describe have to have a neural base. Without the neural activity they cannot occur. The question is, can the neural activity that normally precedes or accompanies such responses go on by itself quite indifferent to whether motor expression occurs? It is held by Hebb (1949), for one, that neural activity of a problem solving nature can occur without any overt activity. This is not too likely to occur with a beginner at any problem. There will be much overt searching and trial and error activity in the presence of unusual stimuli. Later on, however, the thinker may skip many stages in a sequence while the sequence runs off as a neural series of events. In mathematical exercises, for example, we might at first insist on paper and pencil and go through a very physical sequence of overt activities even in simple addition. Later on we might be able to add up a column of figures by grouping numbers into 10's or larger units. Instead of 7 and 8 are 15, and 2 are 17, and 3 are 20, we might quickly add the 7 and 8 as one unit of 15, and the 2 and 3 as a 5, and the total as 20 in a series of two overt or observable steps. There is no need to make the additional steps listed earlier. Similarly, there is no necessity for the neural action to proceed step by step; it might be quite cursory and still serve the net purpose of bridging the gap between situation and response.

Novel combinations in thinking

Insight

Even though there is some delay between stimulus and response and even though mediation might be presumed to have occurred, there may be reluctance to identify such activity as thinking. We have tended to reserve the expression for something more commendable than routine action—it is "higher" activity, as we have mentioned earlier. The highness seems to reside in doing something new, solving a problem where previous specific experience is lacking, "putting two and two together," or, in general, coming through with a new combination of responses never previously employed in the specific situation. The solution to a problem may not be novel to anyone but the thinker, but if it is novel for him, such novelty is taken as a sign of thinking having gone on. Thus, when someone has a toothpaste tube cap drop into a sink drain and cannot get it out easily, he might note that his trouble comes from the fact that the cap was small enough to drop into the drain. "Why don't they make them larger (or sink drains smaller)?" might occur to the victim, and a new invention has been effected. Large caps are familiar enough objects from jars and wide-mouth bottles, toothpaste tubes are also familiar. The combination is the novel factor and we freely assert that a "thought" was born. How do such novel combinations come about? It should be recognized at once that if we stipulate that a combination of elements must enter the definition, then the elements themselves must be available, presumably from past experience, and no one is going to have an original thought without the prerequisite experience. We might presume with confidence that no one is going to invent a system of algebra who is unfamiliar with arithmetic, and, hypothetically, we might entertain the hypothesis that anyone who is familiar with arithmetic might invent algebra either in its present form or in some other. As a matter of fact, students learning algebra go through a good deal of inventive activity and some of them arrive at ways of solving problems long before they hear about such techniques from the teacher. They independently arrive at procedures that have been taught for generations because the procedures are, in effect, inherent in the elements to which they have been exposed. There is no guarantee that such invention will occur in any particular case, but there should be no special surprise involved when it does.

How do we account for such more or less spontaneous solutions of problems? How are elements of past experience put together in a novel manner? In the long history of psychology this has been a serious stumbling block because "thought" has always been identified as some sort of mental activity not readily translatable into physical terms which the psychologist might like to employ. Traditional answers came from resorting to references to an intellectual faculty, the use of intelligence, "using your head" as we still instruct our friends and children, or to some reliance on some vaguely appreciated "creative faculty" or creativeness. We might at this time examine a famous instance of such creative thinking and see what can be said about it.

During World War I, the German psychologist Köhler (1925) was experimenting with chimpanzees on the island of Tenerif. He was concerned about the apes' ability to work with problem situations, and, in general, arranged problems which involved the use of tools to secure food. For example, a banana might be hung out of reach of the animal and a box might be left lying around in the vicinity. Placing the box under the fruit would permit reaching the bait. Some problems involved stacking several boxes on top of each other to build higher platforms. In an alternate form of the general experiment, a banana would be placed on the ground outside a chimpanzee's cage, again out of normal reach, and a stick left lying about. The stick could be used as a rake to drag in the fruit. Köhler found that the chimpanzees were quite capable of using sticks and boxes as tools in their tasks. In one particular instance, Köhler thought of an ingenious test (he does not explain how he thought of it) for his chimpanzees. He placed the banana beyond the reach of the ordinary stick but now placed two sticks in the cage. One of the sticks was hollowed out so that the other could be inserted like an extension rod to make a longer stick out of the two. In the experiment involved, the chimpanzee at first struggled with one stick at a time, finally giving up and facing away from the fruit. It then picked up both sticks and played with them. In the playful manipulation of the sticks, one was inserted into the other, presumably by chance. Immediately, says Köhler, the animal turned around, extended the now longer stick through the cage, and raked in the banana.

How did the chimpanzee manage to arrive at such an intelligent solution to the problem? It will do no good to say that he thought of the problem, recognized the need for a longer stick, recognized the longer stick when he had one, and "saw" the solution. It is just these events that we are trying to explain, namely thinking, recognizing, and seeing solutions when they occur. Köhler's statement of the case created a virtual revolution in psychology and in education. According to Köhler, the solution to a problem comes from a reorganization of perceptions; a "dynamic reorganization of the brain" occurs in which a new orientation emerges which is recognized as a solution. Köhler called this dynamic reorganization "insight." Insight, it soon proved, came to be used as a principle of explanation. Whenever a solution to a problem occurred, it came because an organism had had an insight. Until insight did occur, the problem could not be solved. The characteristics attributed to insight in an attempt to make it look like some sort of process were that it comes about suddenly, after a period of attempted solution, and it is relatively perfect in use thereafter; that is, there is no gradual improvement in the application of the insight. There would be little or no forgetting once the dynamic reorganization of the brain had taken place.

Traditionally trained psychologists did not look with favor upon the new principle. American education had been strongly influenced by the trial-and-error and chance success-plus-reward approach advocated by Thorndike. From that point of view, solutions to problems come about slowly as the correct S ——→R bonds are strengthened. A variety of negative views developed. It was argued that no such thing as insight occurred, that insight was no more than the last (and successful trial in a series of trials) and therefore no more meritorious or worthy of special consideration than any other response in a series. It was also argued, as we have noted with Guthrie, that there was no reason why learning should not occur in one trial. In fact, said Guthrie, it always does, and if the situation is repeated there should be no mystery about the retention of the so-called insightful solution. Others argued that even if something novel and unique did take place, calling it "insight" was only supplying a label and not an explanation of anything. Still others chose to deny that insightful solutions ever occurred in the absence of specific experiences that might have escaped the notice of the observers and that nothing was occurring other than a simple application of some earlier learned behavior (see Birch, 1945).

Over the years the traditional attacks have waned somewhat in their fervor and insight is no longer a forbidden word to American psychologists. There still is the tendency to regard it as a label and of no explanatory value, but the phenomenon is not denied, i.e., it is not denied that two (or more) separate and specific experiences can be brought to bear on one situation where the two experiences were never combined before in an orthodox learning situation. Instead, propositions are advanced which purport to explain how it is possible. We have already laid the groundwork for such an explanation and now can attempt to apply it.

In our discussion of mediation it was pointed out how one association (represented by a cell assembly set into action by some stimulus) can initiate another association, and this in turn another and so on so that a train of associations (assemblies) or "thoughts" can originate and continue. There is no preconceived or predetermined end to such a chain of associations and if one is asked to start associating to some stimulus, there is no predicting where the subject will end when he is finally interrupted. Suppose the chain is initiated by a word like "water." This can lead to almost any other kind of assembly since water will have many associates. Each associate in turn can lead to a great variety, and, if we catalogue them all we will have quite an assemblage. One subject gave these associations in the space of one minute: waterfall, Niagara Falls, honeymoon, hotel, expensive, go south, Texas, cowboys, hot, dry, Canada Dry, ginger ale, Scotch, cheap. (It is interesting to note that if one is allowed to continue, a great variety of categories of words can emerge, and if one has some preconceived notions about the process of association as did Freud, for example, it can readily be proved that you can find sex associations to almost any cue word.) If we had stopped the subject at "honeymoon" and required more associations in that area, we would soon have the subject responding with more sexual allusions or references than of some other variety, especially if we "reinforced" such references by murmuring, or saying "yes," or otherwise demonstrating an interest in that class of response. Similarly if we wanted our subject to respond with financial terms we could change the course of his associations by showing a reinforcing sympathy for terms like "expensive," "cheap," etc. In simple experiments in this area, subjects have been led to respond with adjectives, plural nouns, personal pronouns, and other parts of speech when the experimenter did no more than mutter "mm mm" at such responses (Greenspoon, 1955).

The point we are making is that a chain of associations once started, can be slanted or controlled to some extent by circumstances quite outside the subject's ability to identify. Normally we do not associate at random, we are constantly being held in check as by a rein, by the circumstances which started the train of associations. This is what we mean by "keeping our mind on the problem"; the associations that do occur tend to remain within a given frame of reference and others are quickly checked. If the solution to a problem is within a readily tapped reservoir of associations, the answer will come quickly and we will say that the subject happened to "know the answer." If it comes slowly, we will say that he had to think of it. Frequently enough, if our repertoire for a particular stimulus pattern is limited we will come back to the original association. In every student's experience we can find instances where in attempting to solve a problem, say a mathematical exercise, he kept coming up with the same wrong answer. This is also the factor behind the pun, the practical joke, the O. Henry ending for a story. A train of associations is set up which normally can be expected to lead to a given conclusion; when this conclusion is not presented, we have the "sock finish" or the "punch" line which makes the story or joke unique. It might be funnier to see somebody step on a banana peel and not slip than the reverse. It is the new twist, the odd association, that is required under some circumstances to solve a problem, and if the odd association is not in the repertoire, the problem will not ever be solved. If it is in the repertoire but not readily available, the problem may be solved, but it might take a long time.

Coming back to our problem of accounting for insight, the point seems already to have been made and needs only spelling out. Insight occurs when some association that has merit in the situation occurs to the puzzled or struggling thinker. When this association does occur, it must lead to action or it will be lost in turn as it leads to a new association which may be inappropriate. There is no way for an individual to guide his own train of thought in such contexts, because, if he knew what associations were required, he would have no problem. The efforts of others, however, can be guided as we do when we give hints in guessing games. In one laboratory study (Maier, 1933), the experimenter hung two pieces of string from the ceiling at some distance apart and asked subjects to tie the ends together. When the subject picked up one string and started walking toward the other he found that he could not quite reach the other. Here was a problem. Many of the college students serving as subjects could not solve this problem. Lying about in the room were various objects like a pair of pliers and other tools, but so long as the student concentrated on his string problem as a matter of the strings being too short, he could not solve the problem. Of those who did solve the problem, the solution came about through giving up trying to tie the ends and searching about the room, possibly for more string. Some of the students, seeing the pliers might think of tying the pliers to the end of a string, thereby making it longer. This might lead to the association of a weight on the string, and the almost inevitable association of a pendulum. This, in turn, solves the problem because it permits you to hold one string, walk with it, toward one that will be brought to you by pendulum action. Without the pliers, the subject might in his search for more string think of other sources of string, his shoes for example, these then might be used in various ways, including a pendulum to bring about a solution. Many students did not think of the pendulum solution until the experimenter brushed against a string and set it in motion. This was a sufficient hint to initiate the necessary association.

In mathematics, and in the string problem as solved by humans, we presume that the associations involved are largely of a verbal or language nature. The chimpanzee has no language to speak of and cannot employ such associations. There is nothing in the explanation suggested, however, which precludes the use of cell assemblies involved in experiencing events in other ways. Language associations are so facile and numerous that they lend themselves to a great variety of problems; chimpanzees and other animals without language are restricted in the kinds of problems they can solve; the same kinds of neural processes, however, are presumed to operate at all levels. What kinds of activities they "symbolize" depend upon the sensory and motor equipment of the animal involved and its previous experiences in situations that may, through generalization, through r_g's, or through other mediational media, be brought to the fore.

THE TOOLS OF THINKING

As just noted above, there has been a great deal of emphasis on language in the analysis of thinking. The use of language by humans in problem situations was recognized in ancient times, and indeed, will occur to anyone who stops to ask himself what he is doing when he is thinking. He will inevitably find himself talking to himself. We do not wish to overemphasize the function of language in thinking but it is so obviously a factor that its role must be appreciated. We will shortly examine other modes of action that might serve thinking purposes, and indeed we have already hinted at some of these above, in the suggestions about chimpanzee problem solving. But language, for humans, is par excellence the mechanism of thought. The initiator of Behaviorism, Watson, was so convinced of this that he described thinking as nothing but implicit speech, or subvocal speech. Much of the research stimulated by Watson's views was designed to demonstrate that thinking involved actual movements of the tongue and the vocal structures. It did turn out, as might be expected, that such movements could indeed be observed and recorded but the pattern of movements made no particular sense and did not by any means correspond to the phonemic structure of words. While a subject might find great difficulty in thinking about one thing while saying another, thereby pre-empting the vocal equipment and, according to Watson, being unable to think, it could be done. It is difficult even to write one thing while saying another, yet professors frequently do this while working at the board. Are they thinking about what they are saying, what they are writing, or what they are about to say? In some early experiments, subjects were instructed to solve problems like multiplying two-place numbers by two-place numbers while saying over and over "banana, banana, banana, banana," etc. This kind of preoccupation of the tongue did interfere devastatingly with the capacity for such problem work, but it did not prove the essential point. Many years before, in Germany at Wurzburg, early experimental psychologists (see Boring, 1950) had introspectively analyzed what went on during brief intervals in experiments involving reaction time to different kinds of stimuli. They came to the conclusion that some kind of control over the behavior, which they equated with thinking, could go on in an apparent absence of any kind of internal activity. At that time they were investigating the role of imagery in thinking and came to the conclusion that images were not necessary for thinking. Their findings have been summarized by the slogan "imageless thought." Similarly, it has been argued that speech need not occur in the thinking process but that it may and commonly does.

Observations of young children indicate that they frequently carry on rather detailed verbal accounts of their behavior while at play. The child, quite alone, may, while going through the motions, say, "now I put you down on the bed," or "now I pour you some tea," etc. This activity is of the utmost importance in human development even though parents and teachers attempt to discourage it almost as soon as it appears. Parents may not care for the continual assault on their ears from the rambling utterances of their children, and teachers regard the use of lip movements, both in reading and thinking, as characteristic of some lower form of life. Despite the discouragement, many adults still move their lips, although silently, while presumably thinking. Observations of bus passengers may be very illuminating in this connection, and practically everyone on occasion gives vent to an audible, "now where did I put that" and similar expressions. Some of us talk extensively in our sleep, presumably when we dream. Even briefly "thinking" over the material just read will involve considerable subvocal speech. Think it over.

Ideo-motor action

The significance of speech, whether vocal in the child or subvocal in the adult, is that the stimuli leading to the speech activity occur at the same time that the subject is performing some actions. As the speech is emitted and heard as a feedback, the stimuli from this combination involved in talking to yourself become conditioned to the other performances involved. The child who says, "now I take off my sock" learns, then, to take off its sock when those words are spoken either by itself or another or when some symbolic (neural) substitute or surrogate for this remark occurs. When the poet says, "the thought is father to the act" he is giving us a bit of psychological lore, as the thought, now identified as the verbal expression or its neural substitute, does initiate the response. This kind of activity used to be identified by the expression "ideo-motor action." Perhaps we now have a basis for using such an expression.

Not all words, of course, are "action" words and the language might have to have frequent assists from other neural activity associated with sensory experiences either from the external world or from internal responses. In playing chess, a player might have difficulty in preventing himself from moving a piece to some square; he hesitates because danger may come from many quarters and he has difficulty "visualizing" how the piece would look if placed in the square involved. The rules of chess demand "hands off" until you are ready to move. If the player has the assistance of seeing the piece in position before he definitely places it on the square, he may profit. Such sensory or imaginal processes aid the language operation in which the chess player like any problem solver is continuously engaged.

Many kinds of responses are involved in thinking besides those of language. These may include such response patterns as movements of the eyes from side to side or up and down when we "think" of positions of objects. If you watch someone's eyes closely and ask him to think of some geographical location which the person has never visited and only knows through a map, he is likely to show an eye-movement corresponding to a search of a map; e.g., children in the eastern part of the United

States will move their eyes leftward when asked to think of California. Thinking of an airplane may be accompanied by actual eye-movements or tendencies to move the eyes up. Thinking about ice-cold water may be accompanied by a tightening of the skin, hair-raising, and "goose-flesh" if the thinking is rather seriously done. On the other hand, a person who has no familiarity with ice-cold water or ice of any kind, cannot think about it except of a verbal level. In laboratory experiments psychologists have been able to condition the constriction of blood vessels (a characteristic reaction to plunging the arm into cold water) to various external cues and to the self-stimulation produced by thinking of a particular nonsense syllable (Roessler and Brogden, 1943). In such experiments the subject is instructed to say a particular syllable out loud and some means of constricting the blood vessels is applied—it could be electric shock or cold water. After pairing of these events, the spoken sound is enough to elicit the vasoconstruction. Later on, the subject is told merely to say the syllable to himself, to "think" it, and the vasoconstriction occurs just as before.

Deaf mutes have been observed while asleep. When their fingers begin to move about, the subjects are awakened and admit to dreaming. When awakened at other times when the fingers are "silent," they deny having been dreaming. To some extent, then, mutes dream and/or think with their fingers (Max, 1935). In some now famous experiments, Jacobson (1932) attached recording electrodes to muscles of subjects and recorded muscular action currents which could be detected even though the muscles themselves were not observed to move. A subject might be asked to think of hitting a nail with a hammer three times—the record would show three sharp bursts of activity coming from the muscles of the right arm, but not the left. When asked to throw a ball when given a signal, the right arm would show a burst of activity while the left arm was "silent." There appears to be no question about the fact that subjects think with their muscles, glands, skin, blood vessels, both separately and probably in some kinds of patterns, or, putting it more properly, the brain is assisted in its thinking activity by various parts of the body at one time or another. An even more correct position might be the statement that the whole body is involved in thinking.

An interesting question arises in this connection. What happens to the thinking capacity of people who lose the use of various organs or muscles? If an arm is amputated can you no longer think of pitching a baseball? If your leg is paralyzed can you no longer think of kicking a cat or a football? Would the deaf mute be unable to dream if his fingers were locked in a plaster cast? If someone were paralyzed from the neck down would he be unable to think, particularly if his tongue and vocal cords were immobile? The famous philosopher-psychologist William James was inclined to believe that the mental life of such a person would certainly be seriously impaired. If such a person received no stimulation from his internal organs, James argued, he would be unable to have any emotional experience. Until recently we were unable to say much about such incapacitated individuals. There was information from amputees who would complain about pains from missing toes ("phantom limb" reactions) and who could report dreams about walking as they used to before legs were lost but such information has not been systematically collected and organized under controlled conditions. A more careful approach was employed by S. M. Smith, *et al.* (1947), who made use of the South American Indian arrow poison, curare, which paralyzes muscles very quickly and leaves a victim helpless as far as movement is concerned. A volunteer subject was carefully dosed with curare while resting in an "iron-lung" respirator which would permit him to breathe when his chest became paralyzed. The subject was instructed to listen to questions which could be answered by "yes" or "no" and signal his answers by speech, finger movements and eye movements until these were blocked off by the drug. When the subject was completely paralyzed, as far as any voluntary movements were concerned, the questions continued even though the subject was unable to answer them. Later on as the drug wore off, the subject was able to report on the questions that had been asked and indicated that he could think of the answers while drugged even though unable to communicate with the questioners. Such an experiment indicates that the role of the muscles and other organs may be only facilitatory and not essential for thinking. There may still be need for some sensory input, i.e., there may be some basic requirement that the activation or arousal system be functioning at some minimal level and this may depend upon some visual or auditory or other stimulation source, but as far as motor activity is concerned, it apparently is not necessary for the processes involved in thinking about verbal and mathematical problems at least. It is still likely that a paralyzed person cannot get a very effective thinking process operating about such events as diving into an ice-cold tank or pitching a baseball. What thinking he might do about such subjects might be of a rather different kind; he might, for example, "visualize" the ball in flight or see somebody else throw one. We are quite unable to arrive at rigid conclusions on this point. On the other hand, we can hardly accept the science fiction writer's description of a criminal brain in a chemical bath plotting and scheming to take over the world. Without some sensory inputs and feedback from the body, such a brain, even if it could be kept alive would have nothing to think about and what thinking it could do would be random and chaotic as neurons fired in disorderly sequences without the control of external stimulation or response feedback.

THINKING AND MEANING

The nature of "meaning" has been a continuing puzzle for philosophers and psychologists ever since speculation about man's nature began. We are all preoccupied with the meaning of things or events, and meanings are identified in common parlance with the operations of the mind. Meaning, for most people, represents some sort of psychic manifestation, an illumination (the cartoonist illustrates the drawing of an idea with a light bulb), some kind of "understanding." None of these terms or approaches makes any sense to the scientific psychologist and he attacks the "meaning of meaning" in other ways. We have already examined the concept of "insight" which to most people who use the term carries some connotation of "understanding" or penetration into a mystery or puzzle. When an organism has achieved insight, the problem is solved or, at least, great progress has been made. Those who deal with disturbed people commonly strive to get the patient to achieve insight, referring here to some alleged appreciation of his own true nature or difficulties that must be attained before therapy can be successful. An insightful person grasps meanings. This beautiful phrase does not communicate much to the scientist who would like to arrange conditions under which he could observe both the grasping and the meaning. Frequently it amounts to a patient saying things which meet the therapist's approval.

Much of our time is spent in talking about the meaning of some event, someone's behavior, a symptom, symbol, or facial expression. Frequently all that is involved is a question of prediction as to what the next step in a sequence might be. A runny nose, high temperature, and spots on the inside of the cheeks may "mean" measles. Obviously the signs or symptoms here are being used to predict the future course of events. "Where there's smoke there's fire" again indicates a predictive relationship. Also when people get involved in arguments about words, someone is sure to suggest a dictionary to get the real "meaning" of a word. None of these illustrations bears on the problem of meaning but rather each deals with a predictive relationship to be established by further investigation of events. But the use of the term "meaning" in such situations as smoke meaning fire, or a rash meaning measles, or a dictionary containing meanings, does help us in examining the problem. Meanings are put into the outside world and to that extent taken out of the brain or mind. This may be a very valuable step. If the meaning of a word is in the dictionary, it is not then in someone's mind. But, when some people look up a word in the dictionary they may report "I still don't know what it means" and we have not made much progress.

Discriminated responses

We resort to our dogs and rats again. They at least will not confuse us by telling us they do not know what something means. Yet when Pavlov's dog salivates to the bell, the naive observer may say, the bell means food to the dog. If we look into this matter more closely now, we may be able to make progress. All we have to go on is that the dog salivates to a stimulus that formerly was ineffective, i.e., a specific stimulus evokes a specific response. When the bell rings in this situation the dog salivates. It does not struggle to get away, it does not sit up and beg or do any of thousands of things it might do to other stimuli. Similarly, if a rat goes to a lighted compartment where it has been fed before and ignores a dark compartment where it has not been fed, the naive observer may report that the lighted compartment *means* "food" to the rat, but again all that we have is a specific, perhaps discriminated response. When a child misuses a word we say it does not know the correct meaning. When it later uses the same word "correctly" we now say or assume that the child knows what the word means. But, again, all we have is a specific response in a specific situation.

Language and meaning

It may be that the only "meaning" of "meaning" resides in such discriminated response activity. The person who uses words correctly (i.e., in correspondence with usage as defined by society's authorities) is using them meaningfully. The person who uses words incorrectly, like Mrs. Malaprop, is not using them meaningfully. The meaning resides in social approval and not in the uses or responder. If Pavlov did not supply food after ringing the bell, then the bell did not "mean" food. But, says our student, the dog thought the bell meant food, regardless of what Pavlov did. To this we can only say that the dog responded to the bell as it does to food and whatever meaning there might be in the situation resides in the relationship between the stimulus and the response. When the food no longer follows the bell, the dog stops salivating. Now the bell no longer means food to the dog, not because the bell has lost a meaning, but because the bell no longer leads to salivation but to some other kind of behavior. The bell now "means" something else, and what that something else is depends upon the behavior of the dog.

In recent years psychologists have paid little attention to the nature of meaning with one or two notable exceptions and have left the subject of meaning to language specialists, linguists, anthropologists, and communications experts. In all of these special studies there is considerable preoccupation with the nature of meaning but this work has yet to show promise for theoretical psychology. The current psychological approach has concentrated primarily on the analysis of reactions to words. We can examine two such approaches and see how much they might help.

AN ASSOCIATION THEORY OF MEANING

In a new approach to the subject of meaning, Noble (1952) decided to ignore all prior mentalistic approaches and tried to get at some way of measuring meaning. He assumed that meaning is primarily a matter of verbal habits, and, to this extent, whatever might be said about the meaning of events or nonverbal stimuli may have to be omitted from the present consideration. If meaning is a matter of verbal habits, then association techniques and procedures might be successfully applied in the measurement of meaning. Noble accordingly asked subjects to respond to each of 100 words with the first word that occurred to the subject, then with the next word that occurred to the same stimulus word, and so on for 60 seconds. The total number of responses generated by a single word in one minute was defined as the *meaningfulness* of that word. Some of Noble's words were "paralogs," i.e., manufactured words of two syllables which do not appear in any dictionaries, like, zimlac or tormil. Such words would elicit very few responses from any subjects and would have a low meaning score. Other words like "master" might elicit a great many words and consequently have a high score, or high meaningfulness. According to this view, then, the meaning of a word resides in the sheer number of associations which it can arouse. What is the meaning of the word "spring" for example? If you start associating responses to this word as a stimulus you might come up with "season, bed, jump, coil, scale, pool of water, surprise, tide, onions," and perhaps a great many more. The 60-second limitation need not be disturbing as it would merely be an arbitrary limit to standardize the measuring situation. Noble was able to show that lists of words that were high in meaningfulness were learned more easily than lists of low meaningfulness words. He interpreted this as supporting this interpretation of meaning.

Osgood, Souci, and Tannenbaum (1958) criticized Noble severely for the use of this association technique. According to Osgood, it measures nothing but associations and throws no light on the nature of meaning. For example, Osgood argues, a common association to Mary as a stimulus might be Sally, or to white might be black. Does Sally *mean* Mary or does white *mean* black? This is obviously nonsense to Osgood, who goes on to point out that associations are so controlled by context and by the nature of the stimuli presented that any association technique can be only partially helpful. For example, the word "red" might elicit a number of associations when spoken to a subject, and these associations might differ quite dramatically from those elicited by a strip of red paper, red cloth, a red box, red liquid, etc. Different subjects would give different associations to the same stimulus and Osgood argues that this would imply that there were different meanings for the subjects whereas Noble might count the number of associations, find them to be the same in number and, therefore, in meaning. In Noble's system the stimulus words that have the same number of associations are interpreted as having the same degree of meaning. Such arguments present serious if not insuperable obstacles to an association theory of meaning. It still may be that by carefully structuring the situation and limiting the kinds of responses (as we did with the illustration of "spring" above) the association theory may prove valuable. In a given situation, for a given subject, with a given stimulus form, and with restrictions governing the range of responses, the associations that are elicited might represent the "meaning" of a given stimulus. For the dogs in Pavlov's laboratory, a given bell might "mean" food in the sense described earlier where meaning was described as reflecting a relationship, approved by society, or through reinforced personal experience, between a stimulus and a response. The bell could have no other meanings in that precise context. There need be no objection, however, to the bell having other meanings in other contexts or for other dogs who might have been shocked shortly after hearing the same bell.

There is nothing especially damaging about the argument that Sally cannot *mean* Mary. If Mary is what occurs to you when Sally is presented as a stimulus in verbal form, then Sally may be an occasional "meaning" of Mary at least on a verbal level. It is one of the potential discriminated responses one might make in a given context. To deny that Sally means Mary implies that one has a different appreciation of what "meaning" means. We can turn to Osgood's view of meaning and learn what he thinks meaning is.

The semantic differential

Osgood's contribution to an analysis of meaning has to be treated in two parts because he first presents a theory of meaning and then a method of measurement which may or may not be appropriate to his purposes. Each contribution must be examined separately. Fortunately we are already prepared to appreciate the theoretical contribution. For Osgood, meaning is essentially a representational process. This is the same kind of process we have been describing in various ways in our earlier discussion of mediation and substitute activity. The responses made by the organism, whether these be neural cell assemblies running off in sequences or fractional antedating responses, have been called upon to serve as substitutes or symbols of other activity which itself may or may not occur. We can examine the example used by Osgood to illustrate his theory of meaning.

Suppose that a buzzer is sounded and shortly thereafter a shock is administered to a dog's footpad. The dog is strapped down and unable to escape. After a number of trials the dog raises its paw when the buzzer sounds even though no shock is given. To the lay observer, the buzzer has come to "mean" shock and the instrumental behavior of the dog in raising its paw is a natural, intelligent thing to do under the circumstances, although, since no shock is experienced, some other observer might regard the dog as just a bit stupid.

How does Osgood analyze this event? He argues that a reaction to shock, although it involves raising the leg, includes many other responses. For one thing, the dog begins to breathe a little more rapidly, or at least, there is a change in breathing rate and probably in breathing depth. We need not worry about the nature of the breathing changes so long as we recognize that a change takes place. There will also be other responses such as a change in heart rate, a possible change in digestive processes, and perhaps some canine vocalization will also be noted. Now all of these things can occur without the leg being raised at all, that is, these responses of the visceral organs, vocalizations, and perhaps many other activities can be thought of quite separately from leg movement. We can, in Osgood's language, think of these separate or *separable* responses as "detachable" responses. In earlier discussions we have labeled such responses as r_g's. These "detachable" r_g's have the characteristic of antedating, that is, they move forward in time and will precede the final response of leg raising which might normally control our interest and attention. It is these detachable responses, however, when they are detached, that are the important items of interest if we are concerned with meaning. Again we should be careful to point out that the actual physiological process involved in glandular or muscular action need not take place; it can be short circuited out of the activity pattern by its neural antecedents which initiate other neural activity without the actual motor processes taking place. Osgood does not commit himself on this point and is willing to accept the neural mediational processes as sufficient for the purpose. Now, as we have already learned, the mediating processes or reaction will generate its own stimuli either for succeeding neural responses or for some motor outlet. We can symbolize the process thus far as

First training S_u (shock) $\longrightarrow R_u$ (leg withdrawal)
S_c (buzzer) $\longrightarrow R_c$ (listening reaction)

Later training $S_u \longrightarrow R_u$
$S_c \longrightarrow r_g \longrightarrow s_{rg} \longrightarrow R_{u2}$

It will be noticed that this diagram is somewhat different from the typical diagram of conditioning in which S_c is pictured as leading directly to the original unconditioned response R_u. Here we have indicated that the antedating, detachable features of R_u have come forward in time, that they generate stimuli, and that these stimuli in turn lead to a response that is not exactly the same as the original response to shock. Since there is no shock present, we could hardly expect the dog to act as if it received a shock. It *must* act differently because there was no shock stimulation to force a particular kind of response. We label this new response R_{u2} to indicate that it is a different response. It will be recalled that some theorists might call this an instrumental response (although if there is no shock to be given, it can hardly be instrumental in accomplishing anything) but there is no need to use this terminology here. Because we do not wish to insist on an actual effector response in the concept of mediation, we can change the labeling of the mediating response from r_g to r_m and its generated stimuli to s_m so that we can now have a new diagram, as below, to indicate the operations involved. When the dog is raising its leg to the sound of the buzzer, the sequence can be diagramed as follows:

$$S_c \longrightarrow r_m \longrightarrow s_m \longrightarrow R_{u2}$$

We are now in position to talk about the meaning of the buzzer. The buzzer S_c now elicits a mediating or "representational" process ($r_m \longrightarrow s_m$) which can be said to be the meaning of the buzzer to this dog in this situation.

According to this view, the first part of the pattern ($S \longrightarrow r_m \longrightarrow s_m$) is a "decoding" process or "interpretation" aspect of meaning. The second part of the pattern ($s_m \longrightarrow R_{u2}$) is an "encoding" process or "expression of ideas" aspect of meaning. Both aspects are necessary to meet the ordinary conception of meanings. It might also be remarked in passing that this conception rests on a foundation of learning. Meanings are learned. There can be no innate meanings. Any innate reflex or instinctive response patterns must be regarded as meaningless.

One additional feature of this theory must be included to complete the picture. It is obvious that much of our behavior is involved with words in spoken or printed form and that many synonyms or verbal substitutes come to have about the same meaning. Thus a small child learning to cross streets is first physically restrained from racing across a street; later on he is held back only gently (symbolically) without sufficient restraint to hold him if he should really break away, still later a verbal caution will suffice, and finally the visual patterns involved or signs like "Don't Walk" on red lights will stop the walker. Here we see a piling up of stimuli or "signs," each of which leads to the same behavior of stopping. According to the view described, these second-, third-, and higher-order learnings or conditionings amount to the association of these signs with the same mediational process and thereby the meaning of the signs is shared to the extent that the same mediational process is reproduced. Nuances, "shades of meaning," represent deviations from the original mediational process involved in some primary learning situation.

We can now turn to the measurement procedure developed by Osgood for the analysis of meaning just presented. It will be recalled that Noble simply asked his subjects to give verbal associates to key words and then counted the number of these responses in a minute as his measure of meaning. Osgood reasoned that a closer approach to meaning would be obtained by getting a sample of all kinds of possible reactions to a stimulus. Again we are dealing with meaning in a verbal form although Osgood's system permits the use of pictures or objects. We might wish to determine the meaning of some object, event, person, or "abstract" term for any individual. One way of doing this might be to ask the subject to tell us all that he thinks of when this item is present or mentioned. We might ask: "What does Franklin Delano Roosevelt mean to you?" In reply we might get a wide variety of reactions from different individuals as well as a conglomeration of responses from any one individual. We might find him using a variety of adjectives to describe his presumed internal reactions or "meanings." Thus he might say: great, sly, clever, ambitious, noble, humanitarian, strong, active, etc. Hitler and Stalin might earn such adjectives as: clever, crafty, strong, cruel, nasty, evil, hard, cold-blooded, ambitious, dictatorial, etc. From this assortment of adjectives we might begin to recognize that Hitler and Stalin mean pretty much the same thing but that they differ in meaning from Roosevelt, although there may be points at which the same adjective could be applied to all three, for example, clever, ambitious, strong.

Most people are not very articulate when it comes to emitting adjectives and Osgood believed there was no danger in supplying a representative list of adjectives covering a wide variety of characteristics that might be applied to common objects or people and concepts. He arranged such lists and asked subjects to check off the adjectives that applied to a given stimulus item. Because an adjective might apply, more or less, an opportunity was given to the subject to indicate the degree to which a given adjective did apply, on a seven-point rating scale. When a subject had finished checking off his reactions he would have also indicated what the concept or stimulus item meant to him. This technique, which amounts to taking advantage of the "encoding" feature of mediational processes (that is, discovering what s_m leads to in terms of some R_{u2}) has been called by Osgood the "semantic differential." The semantic differential refers to the differential in linguistic associations (including the intensity dimension) that exists among stimuli. Osgood refers to a "semantic space" in which the meaning of a given stimulus could be located if we knew exactly what adjectives to employ in testing the subject and if the subject could indicate with reasonable precision just how much or in what degree each adjective applied.

As soon as subjects are tested with any great number of adjectives, and with any extensive range of stimuli, it becomes apparent that there are many adjectives that are in effect synonyms for each other. These, of course, can be dropped out to simplify the picture. But even after these are eliminated, it is observed that a great many terms still tend to go with each other. (In statistical terms, they are highly "correlated.") So that if a subject uses a word like "good," he is also likely to use words like "up," and "light"; bad things are "down" and "dark." The use of words like "good" would also tend to elicit words like, "harmonious," "beautiful," "successful," "true," "positive," "reputable," and "wise." If a subject called something bad, it would be likely to be accompanied by the opposites of the words listed for good. Osgood recognized this tendency to group words of this type into a single class as an "evaluative" factor, or prehaps, in our terms, an evaluative reaction. In general, we might say that one class of reactions to almost any stimulus would include an acceptance or rejection tendancy, an approval or disapproval or an approach or avoidance kind of reaction.

Another class of words that tend to go together includes words like: hard, masculine, severe, strong, tenacious, heavy, and mature. If an item is classified as meriting one of these terms it is also likely to merit the rest. If an opposite of one of these is used, then the rest of the words used would include the opposites of those listed. If the stimulus item were a popular motion-picture actress of a blonde, blue-eyed, curvaceous nature, subjects would tend to check off: soft, feminine, lenient, weak, yielding, etc. Osgood described this class of terms as making up another strong cluster or "factor" and named it a "potency" factor. Words like fast, active, excitable, rash, and heretical and their opposites make up another extensive cluster or factor which Osgood labeled the "activity" factor.

If enough words are used and sufficiently analyzed by statistical techniques many other factors can be derived in varying degrees of interrelatedness. In much of Osgood's work, however, the three factors described, the evaluative, the potency, and the activity factors were most prominent. If we ignore the possibility that other powerful factors may be present but unknown, we might then define the meaning of any given stimulus as the degree to which the S in the mediational formula elicits evaluative, potency, and activity mediational processes which, in turn, as ($r_m \longrightarrow s_m$) mechanisms elicit R_{u2}'s of varying kinds. In other words, when a subject tells us what something means to him we are getting at the mediational processes that presumably are occurring within him. We do not expect him to be able to describe these well since he can hardly observe neural activity or even internal organic activity or incipient but inhibited muscular reactions. But, if when asked to talk about his father, he uses words like strong, kind, large, heavy, hard, etc., we presume that sometime in his history these words occurred as reactions to s_m's that were aroused by r_m's, which in turn had been associated with the father as an S. It might be noted also that many of the words that the subject uses have no present accuracy as descriptive of his father who may now be old, decrepit, merely fat, not heavy, and soft in many ways. Yet the subject uses these terms because many of his r_m's were conditioned in early life when the father was hard, strong, large, etc. This observation may help clear up the eternal mystery of "what does she see in him?" and vice versa, and may also clarify why people using the same words may be talking about entirely different things with the usual difficulties which we find among our friends at all levels of human intercourse. Consider the political terms "radical" and "liberal" for a moment. The party label of "radical" refers to extremely reactionary and conservative groups in some other countries. The term "liberal" is no longer of any value for communication purposes. Its only function in the language is to serve as an example of how one word can mean many things, depending upon time, place, occasion, and speaker. It is awkward, of course, to have to depend upon words for ascertaining meanings. Perhaps we might sometime be able to measure ($r_m \longrightarrow s_m$) more directly.

THINKING AND CONCEPTS

When Hull developed his propositions about r_g's they were designed to fill the role of "pure stimulus acts," it will be recalled. As such, r_g's were surrogates or substitutes for the mentalistic "ideas" of an earlier psychology. We now have expanded the r_g notion to include hypothetical neural processes, the cell assemblies of Hebb, or the still more general hypothetical mediational processes of Osgood. These hypothesized activities represent our best approach toward accounting for the tradition-honored "idea." Ideas, because of their mentalistic flavor were never popular with American psychologists and much of the earlier work in attempting to cope with thinking was done in terms of what appeared, apparently, somewhat less mentalistic, namely "concepts." Over the years occasional studies would appear in which the formation of concepts was studied in the laboratory and some general behavioral principles were developed which were of some interest even though they never seemed to come to grips with the subject matter as the mediational view does. No one ever defined a concept in any acceptable terms, any more than an idea could be defined, but it did appear to be possible to work as if everyone knew what a concept was to begin with, and start from there.

It was possible on a superficial level to talk, as lexicographers or grammarians might, in terms of "concrete" and "abstract" concepts, although, in the light of the analysis presented above, the terms concrete and abstract do not appear to differentiate any kinds of events that might occur in thinking. The same kinds of mediational activity go on whether the subject thinks of physical objects, social movements, "peace," "freedom," or "justice." The degree to which evaluative, potency, or activity factors (as well as a hypothetical host of others) enter into any specific "concept" cannot be specified without special attacks on each such term or concept, but we can assume that, in principle, visceral and muscular responses participated in the original learning experiences and are still involved either directly or by neural substitution when we speak of "love," "honesty," or "automobiles."

In the early experiments on concepts, the interest lay in the process by which concepts were formed, that is, in a learning approach. It was recognized that the function of concepts was to ease communication by developing class names for individual instances. A child has to learn that the great variety of objects to which it is exposed can be be labeled by a finite and limited number of terms. Any object which when shaken results in a cascade of salt is a "salt shaker" even though it may look like an elephant, a tower, or a vase. Similarly, the word "red" or "blue" may be applied to thousands of instances of occurrence of a particular range of light rays reflected from objects differing in shape, or use. On the other hand, the child must learn not to call every man "daddy," every flower a "rose," or every toy "mine." The twofold function of concepts or, rather, labels, is to permit grouping of many instances of some events or items on the basis of some common but specific features, and, on the other hand, to isolate or segregate specific items from a mass with some other features. The twofold function was described as the process of abstracting (discriminating) and generalizing and the classical question about the hen and the egg occurred in this problem area. Do we first generalize and then abstract or vice versa?

It is difficult to set up experiments to follow the process of concept formation with adults because they already have so many concepts about anything that can be presented to them as experimental learning material that the development of a concept from some zero stage is practically impossible to achieve. In a famous attempt at an analysis of concept formation Hull (1920) used Chinese picture language as his learning materials. Subjects were asked to learn the names of separate ideographs printed on individual cards. There were 72 such cards and 12 names. The subjects were not informed that a common element was present on each of 12 cards which had the same name. Hull observed that the subjects learned the names of the cards in a rather slow but regular manner in what appeared to be an orthodox trial and error learning situation. The subjects, college students, seemed to use both abstraction and generalization techniques more or less from the beginning, apparently recognizing the situation as a problem situation instead of merely a routine memory experiment. In effect, the subject would respond to some element of a card, and if this response proved to be correct, he would use the same name for another card with the same element. Thus, he was in the first instance, abstracting, and in the second, generalizing. If the generalization test proved successful, the element itself would then be more specifically isolated from future test cards. Eventually most of the subjects were able to report on the elements themselves after a series of successes and failures. Hull said the element had been "dissociated" from the context, that is abstracted or discriminated through this history of success and failure. It was of interest to Hull that some subjects were able to name the cards correctly without being able to specify the element, and could even name new examples of the element without being able to point it out. Some elements were somewhat complex and involved a number of components in themselves and some subjects were never able to detect or point out the complete element. In other words, their concepts were only fragmentary. This latter observation appears to be a common failing among people who are quick to identify items or events as instances of classes to which they do not really belong because they possess some fragment or single common feature where a number of features might be required. While it is unlikely that a rose will be confused with a lily, it is not unlikely that daffodils might be confused with jonquils by the uninitiated.

In other experiments the interest lay in how quickly various kinds of concepts might be learned, for example, concepts of number, color, shape, etc. Children apparently handle color concepts fairly readily, with form or shape next, and number more difficult (Heidbreder, 1946). It is impossible to state a principle with any conviction in this connection because the arrangement of the experiment, the types of materials, the "set" of the subjects and their backgrounds would have to be taken into account, and this has rarely, if ever, been done with adequacy. We still know very little about how children form concepts of number, shape, or color. There seems to be a strong maturational factor involved as well as a powerful influence of specific training. Children of seven, for example, when taking an intelligence test might be asked to copy a diamond. Some of them draw squares standing on end and fail the item because the distinction involves one long and one short diameter. Before the age of seven, apparently, children do not react to such niceties. Perhaps they verbalize the figure as a square and proceed to draw one. Reacting to or perceiving a diamond comes a little later in childhood, perhaps not until someone calls attention to the proportions of the figure. Children's drawing of human figures show similar difficulties with bodily proportions. Parents and teachers continually correct such "errors," not always successfully, if we judge by adult drawings. Many adults, for example, do not locate an ear in proper relation to eyes in their drawings of human profiles.

Concept formation in animals

Many discriminations studies have been done with rats, monkeys, dogs, and other animals to evaluate their capacities for dealing with abstractions like triangles, elipses, horizontal versus vertical lines, etc. Usually the experiment has a specific purpose in which the symbolic cues play a role. We have noted Pavlov's findings about experimental neuroses developing in dogs severely tested with ellipses and circles. The general results seem to follow an evolutionary pattern of higher and higher ability with the development of species. Monkeys are able to discriminate readily between various visual forms including colors. Rats are restricted to blacks and whites but can respond to triangles, squares, and circles as such, and to vertical and horizontal arrangements of lines or other visual patterns. Presumably such abilities are heavily dependent upon learning and involve the processes of generalization and discrimination which we have already considered.

THINKING AND CONSCIOUSNESS

The concept of consciousness is not a popular one in psychology. Most psychologists prefer to get along without talking about it and more or less push it into the family skeleton closet. It is not the kind of concept, however, which can be easily locked up or hidden away and our ability to deal with it is not of a very high or satisfactory level, especially when scientists in other disciplines accept the concept without any qualms, perhaps assuming that psychologists either regard it in the same way as they do or have some satisfactory account to give.

To most American psychologists "consciousness" has always been a stumbling block to a scientific appreciation of behavior. It was inherited along with much of the introspective technique and findings of the German structural psychology and when psychology was the study of the mind, it was a concept in good standing. With Watson's behavioristic approach, consciousness became anathema. Watson dismissed it as an archaic notion of little merit and relegated it to the status of an "epiphenomenon" of no interest to a scientist analyzing behavior.

To the average person, consciousness is the most immediate fact of life. His awareness of his inner feelings, his private reactions, his perception of the physical world of sounds, lights, odors, pains, etc., makes consciousness a near and dear possession. Yet no satisfactory way of dealing with this private world has ever been developed. When visual or other sensory activities are studied a variety of subterfuges may be employed to avoid contact with (or because contact cannot be made with) the conscious experience. Thus, when a subject shown a blue light says "I see blue," the psychologist puts this down as a bit of behavior, a "verbal report" which is recordable or observable by objective methods. Those psychologists who are willing to talk about consciousness as such, at all, deal with it on an "as if" level. That is, they take the report of a subject or, indeed, of their own experience, and admit that something is going on that might be described *as if* some kind of unique, nonphysical operation, located basically in the head, but also involving the rest of the body is occurring. If one is touched on the back of the hand, the subject reports that he has a "feeling" which "appears" *as if* it were located on the back of the hand. But, says the scientific psychologist, this is only an "as if" operation and it is subject to eventual explanation in purely physical terms. In what follows, we will not presume to have accounted for consciousness in any final and universally accepted form, but we can state the physical monist position and see how well it accounts for the facts and how well it meets individual tastes and expectations.

The attack on consciousness must begin with an account of the earliest squirmings of a fetus. If we attempt to analyze the experiences of an adult we are lost in a hopeless maze. Starting with a fetus, however, in a dark environment, we can select the problem of dealing with visual aspects of consciousness as a sample, with the assumption that any other sensory activities would follow the same principles of development and the same kinds of learning effects. If the newborn organism is transferred to a lightproof environment at birth and reared there until some degree of maturity, we might have some basis for evaluating the contribution of the sense of sight to consciousness. As we have seen (p. 55), this has been done with a variety of organisms like cats, pigeons, and chimpanzees. We can now re-examine the study by Riesen (1950) involving chimpanzees who were so treated. Riesen feared that the visual structures themselves might fail to develop in the absence of light and so he fabricated translucent plastic helmets which fitted over the chimpanzee's head so that light could enter the eyes but no *patterns* of visual stimulation would be transmitted through the domes. It is still possible that there may have been some organic damage or failure of development. When the chimpanzees were mature, the helmets were removed and the animals exposed to the visual world. How did they behave? According to the observations reported they behaved as if there were no visual world. They stumbled into obstructions and by every practical test were "stone blind." Various kinds of tests were employed to discover the extent to which the chimpanzee could react to any visual stimuli such as approaching objects, threatening gestures, etc., but to no avail. Milk bottles which were recognized by touch remained untouched though close at hand and eagerly grasped when the nipple was inserted in the mouth. Now a program of training was introduced. A large yellow disk with an electric shock device was brought toward the face until contact and shock were experienced. The chimpanzee made no movement to avoid the large disk until some eighteen or more trials had been made. Normal chimpanzees would avoid the disk after the first trial, and, in fact, would try to draw back from the approaching object even before any shock had been given. On the basis of this and similar observations, Riesen concluded that the chimpanzees had to *learn* to see. We might extend this conclusion logically to read that if they had to learn to see large yellow disks, they might also have to learn to see every other kind of object that ever comes into experience.

If we accept the proposition for the sake of argument that we learn to see (and by extension, learn to hear, smell, feel, and every other sensory reaction) where does it leave us? We note that learning to see means learning to do something with respect to some stimulus. In the case of the yellow disk, it involves an avoidance response. In the case of milk bottles it involves an approach response. If no response is made, we assume that nothing was seen. With the eyes open for a large part of the day and with millions of light pattern stimulations rapidly following each other, the organism has the opportunity of reacting repeatedly to some patterns in one way, to other patterns in another. Presumably, it spends much of its early life in learning to react with eye movements and incipient approach or avoidance movements to various patterns. How much a baby sees is difficult to establish. The time when a baby recognizes various objects or reacts to visual cues has to be established by objective procedures because babies do not talk. Even when quite mature, the young child continues to learn to see and it is some time before it is able to make use of little black marks on paper in reading. Discriminating word shapes, one from another, does not occur till around four years of age and many letters are not clearly discriminated from each other until five and six years. F and E, K and X may represent the same thing to a child for some time and specific practice is involved in learning each of the letters. The practice opportunities are countable in thousands, if not millions, of instances and by the time we are adults we have learned to see so well that it seems like we always had the capacity and we look upon results like those of Riesen with some alarm.

Let us back up a bit in the discussion. When the light rays from some object enter the eye, processes that eventually result in seeing begin. Light on the retina, however, is not enough; this light must effect photochemical reactions which in turn must effect electrochemical actions in fibers of the optic nerve. These reactions or impulses are not *sight* either; the impulses arrive eventually at the occipital lobe and from there initiate further neural activity in more forward sections of the brain, but we do not see there either. All of this will happen in the chimpanzee's brain, even though it was reared in darkness. Eventually the impulses will initiate some activity which may or may not eliminate the visual stimulation. If it does, there will be that much more of a tendency for that activity to recur on the next occasion and the process of learning to see will have begun.

As each new type of stimulation (in terms of intensity, wave length, pattern, extent) enters the nervous system, new reactions are associated with the different kinds of stimulation. We say that the organism now sees or is a "seeing creature." With animals we have no other way of testing. On the human level we presume the same kind of process takes place with an added feature that slowly enters the picture with the acquisition of language. In addition to the eye-movement and approach or avoidance behavior patterns we begin to indulge in verbal behavior associated with certain objects or events. We begin to name the stimulus situation or some of its features and seeing has taken on a new dimension —that of verbal discriminations. When the process of abstraction and generalization begins, we begin to discriminate more and more finely among the various visual patterns. We begin to name colors, for example, in terms of the neural mediational activity that develops along with our customary reactions to the stimuli. Eventually we are able to say "red" when a given kind of light wave enters the eye, not because we "see" red in terms of some kind of psychic phenomenon, but because we have learned to make that noise when similar stimulation initiated the mediational pattern before and we were led by one means or another to say "red" on the previous occasion. There is presumably nothing particularly "reddish" about "red." We could just as well learn to make any other noise as users of other languages do when such a mediational process occurs. It might be interesting to consider how the generalized concept of redness occurs as it is obvious that in nature many objects will emit the same wave lengths. Osgood (1953) suggests that primitive man, developing his language, probably reacted to red objects in about the way he would to more important red items like blood. His word for red might then be close to his word for blood. As a matter of fact, in the Polish language, one kind of red is described by the equivalent of "bloody" and in that same language, the "sky" and "blue" are equated verbally. With changes in the languages the original words become modified out of all recognition and we lose this clue to the original behavior. In the area of olfactory experience, however, science has progressed but little and we still talk about odors as flowery, fruity, spicy, resinous, burnt, hircine, rubbery, etc. This indicates that the mediational activity has not yet been "abstracted" sufficiently for us to have developed abstract terms for specific elements.

The experiments with animals reared in the dark receive some support from observations of people born with cataracts which are removed in later life. Where such cataracts are complete and truly prevent any vision, the human reacts in a manner comparable to the chimpanzee when he is given "the precious gift of sight." In some cases the patients do not want the gift and continue on in their blind habits, refusing to *learn to see* because the process, for an ambulating adult is extremely frustrating and unrewarding. It takes months to learn to recognize people seen every day and it is extremely unrewarding to be faced with repeated exposures to the same stimuli and be unable to do anything about them as far as naming them correctly is concerned. There are few such cases nowadays, as cataracts are treated early in life, when recognized, and we are dependent upon some cases histories collected by Von Senden (see Hebb, 1949) who collected about 100 such cases. Unfortunately in most cases little or nothing was available in terms of psychological information and many of the cases were not especially intelligent and reports of their incapacity might be misleading. The gist of the information collected, however, indicates that when first exposed to visual stimulation such cases are unable to perceive objects as such, have no sense of visual distance, and do not react in any manner other than to indicate that something is happening, that is, a new form of stimulation which they cannot describe is occurring. When facing an object with an examiner who traces the object they are able to report differences in stimulation when a change in direction is occurring, but very little else. In other words, something akin to a figure-ground relationship is available, but without any real definition. After some practice in looking at things, the subject might be able to see a square or a triangle but would not be able to say what he was looking at. If allowed time to count the corners, that is the number of times a line changed direction, he might be able to say the figure was a triangle, but shown the same figure a moment later, he would have to start counting all over again. Eventually the learning process is so complete that the individual does not even have to have a triangle present in order to react as if there was one before him; he can imagine it. We have previously described the image as a conditioned sensation. We can now include it as a representational process in our mediational formula. With such mediational processes occurring more or less constantly, many simultaneously, as we are bombarded by stimulation, we begin to have difficulties in responding effectively to everything going on about us. At times we stop, in a sense, to name some of the mediational processes, and in fact, make use of the naming function itself, speech, to carry out rather extensive adjustments. Much of what we refer to as consciousness is the activity of talking to ourselves.

It would be improper to restrict the concept of consciousness to some sort of inner or subvocal speech as many of our mediational responses are not yet suitably named. Yet, they occur, and lead to additional sequences of mediational processes or motor responses. To restrict consciousness to speech factors, would make speechless children and animals nonconscious, yet we have no reason to suspect that their behavior is carried out by any qualitatively different processes. It might be wiser to be more chary in the use of the term if not to dispense with it altogether. A vague term is likely to be employed in so many devious ways as to mean many things in general and none in particular. Consciousness is frequently used, for example, as a synonym for "awareness." It might be possible to reach agreement on the use of the term "awareness" if we set up some standards or criteria for when it should be employed. If by "awareness" we chose to describe a state which permitted a verbal description of some aspects of behavior, then awareness might be equated with the use of language. If someone gives an account of his behavior saying: "I thought of this and that and then did this because . . . ," we might be free to say that the speaker was aware of at least some features of his behavior. No one can give a complete account of any moment's activities of the various parts of the body and the mediational processes taking place; consequently, we would be forced to treat awareness as a concept of limited applicability.

There are other synonymic usages where the word "consciousness" is sometimes employed. J. Miller (1942) listed some sixteen different usages of the term "unconscious" and we may assume that consciousness has at least that many references. If a person is awake he is deemed conscious; if asleep, he might be called unconscious. It might be more useful to develop a scale involving sleep and the wakened state (and this is already available in the form of brain wave patterns that parallel different degrees of receptivity to stimuli). No purpose is served in referring to the sleeper as unconscious since no one can know precisely what you mean until you go through a more specific description. Similarly if a person is knocked out by a blow on the head or by an anaesthetic, he may be unconscious enough, if we define the term somehow, but he is not in a state of normal sleep, however much the two conditions might resemble each other, and again a separate term might be more useful.

In psychoanalytic practice, the term "unconscious" is used to describe alleged activities of a motivational nature which the individual cannot describe, which he might well deny, or, at least, oppose when they are suggested to him. Thus, the person might be accused of harboring ill wishes toward his father, sexual desires toward his mother, and a variety of emotional states toward himself and society. The delinquent is accused of having an unconscious hate of society which reflects his unconscious hate of his parents, which in turn represents an inner hatred of himself, this latter also being unconscious. The delinquent might argue himself blue in the face, saying, "Naw, I don't hate nobody, we was just havin' fun," but this denial would only confirm the intensity of the various hates to the orthodox practitioner and psychoanalytically oriented social worker. We shall deal more directly with such claims in a later discussion but for the present we are concerned with the matter of definition. It is apparent that in psychoanalysis the term is used as an equivalent of "awareness" as discussed above. Perhaps the expression "the unaware" is not as flavorful as "the unconscious." In any event, the psychoanalysts must equate consciousness with some state that permits accurate verbalization of motivational states. Because motivational states are notoriously complex and irrational as well as involving many considerations we might not like to verbalize publicly, the analysts have given themselves plenty of working territory.

From the discussion above it might be clear why Watson was anxious to get rid of the term "consciousness." The term has acquired considerable status through synonymic usage in describing a wide variety of conditions. It will probably remain in the vocabulary for a long time and no point is served by trying to discard it. We can probably learn to live with it by reserving it to cover such representational processes as we are able to communicate to others with some degree of satisfaction and we need not restrict it by fiat to only so-called higher forms of life since mediational processes presumably can occur in the nervous system of any organism that has something corresponding to a ganglionic system and which shows evidence of learning. Consciousness might be equated with mediational processes which take up some time between observable stimuli and responses. Reflex responses like eyelid blinks would then represent some low degree of consciousness while more involved responses occurring after a time lapse would be at the other extreme of a consciousness range. On the human level we might take note of the fact that thinking behavior, especially such thinking as involves words and thereby permits of some intercommunication with others, might be regarded as "highly conscious." Eventually we might develop suitable scales to describe various levels of activity, starting, perhaps, with some factors of sensitivity of receptivity and ending with precise communication. That day is still far off.

CHAPTER 11

Conative Functions—
The Determiners of Behavior

The causes of behavior · Determinism and causation · Drives and motives · Social motives · Attitudes · Attitudes as preparatory responses or "set" · Wants and desires · Characteristics of motivated behavior · Social motives in our culture · The desire for prestige · Other social motives · Emotions as motives · Motivation and frustration · Reactions to frustration · Frustration and aggression · Displaced aggression · Self-aggression · Motivation and attention · Interest · Concentration · A review · Unconscious motivation · Techniques of controlling motivation · Brain washing · Hypnosis · Advertising and propaganda

It will be recalled that the ancient Greeks divided behavior into cognitive, conative, and affective functions. We have explored to some degree the cognitive aspects of behavior, noting that these could not be separated from motivational and emotional activities. As we turn now to a consideration of conative matters we will find again that they do not occur in a vacuum, divorced from cognitive and affective processes. And again, as with our observations about thinking, we will find the operations of learning and transfer of overriding significance. It is important to keep warning ourselves that behavior is not made up of isolated operations, that we cannot give a satisfactory account of any kind of behavior pattern by looking only at isolated fragments when other functions are not kept "constant." Nor can we expect to hit upon some master principle or universal key which will account for all or much of behavior. In the present context we will be dealing with some concepts advanced by some searchers for such keys and will have to remember that it is most unlikely that any all-powerful single factor will be found. Not all behavior problems are to be explained by sex or the "will to power" or the "achievement motive." The student is warned that there is no easy, effortless road to the comprehension of behavior.

THE CAUSES OF BEHAVIOR

We are going to concern ourselves with what our culture has led us to talk about as the "causes" of behavior. This is perhaps the most fascinating area of psychology for the layman. All his life he has heard about and given reasons for his activities. And all his life he has been exposed to arguments about the causes of crime, delinquency, alcoholism, maladjustment, divorce, even economic ups and downs. People have always been interested in "why" someone does something and our courts have been built on a foundation of psychology which pictures man as sometimes being responsible for his acts, sometimes not, as having good, bad, or accidental reasons for his behavior. While it is not, in fact, necessary to "establish the motive" for a crime in order to secure a conviction in court, much of the interest of the public and courts lies in "the motive." Motives are the keys to behavior as far as our culture is concerned. It is this area of behavior we can now try to explore.

Determinism and causation

Modern science has come to be less and less interested in "causes." There is no generally accepted philosophical or logical analysis of what a "cause" is. We must be careful not to fall into a linguistic trap and identify a cause as some independent, real entity. Without getting ourselves involved in a philosophical discussion of the nature of causation we can recognize that the term is employed to describe a relationship in a sequence of events, and that we are usually selecting some one or several *antecedent* events or conditions for special emphasis when we say that something was the cause of something else. In John Dewey's (1938) illustration of the conditions that lead to malaria, he pointed out that natives had attributed the disease to the night air because people who slept with their windows opened at night might get the disease because the night air came into the room. This much is obviously true, but, of course, only part of the truth. Along with the night air come the mosquitos. Are the mosquitos the cause of malaria? They are necessary, to be sure, but only those who are bitten by females of the species might get malaria, but again, the bite of the female is not always followed by malaria. Certain other conditions must also be present in order for malaria to develop. When all the conditions that must prevail have been described for some given event to occur, we find that we usually have a complex situation involving a series of events where no particular event can be labeled as "the cause." In another of Dewey's illustrations, the question is raised as to the cause of death when someone shoots someone else with a revolver. What is the cause of death? The penetration of the heart by a bullet? This does not always lead to death. The fact of the pistol having been fired? Of the trigger having been pulled? Or the fact that someone sold the murderer a gun? Or the fact that the murderer hated the murderee? Or the fact that the murderer had not been brought up right? That he had not joined the Boy Scouts at age twelve?

Because one question usually leads to another, most scientists are wary of talking about causes at all and prefer to analyze the circumstances that must be present or the sequence of events that has taken place in order to make their predictions about future events. They ask th question "what" rather than "why" because the latter question is fruitless and unrewarding. In our inquiries we will concentrate on antecedent conditions, on current interactions, on sequences of activities, rather than on causes (see Pratt, 1937).

In a scientific orientation it is necessary to assume that events in nature follow an orderly course and that this course can be described and detailed if sufficient and careful inquiry is made into the event under consideration. The first part of this statement is usually known as the principle of *determinism* and it is taken as a working assumption by every scientist, at least while he is working as a scientist. The orderliness of nature is assumed to follow the pattern expressed, for psychological purposes, in the S ——→R formula, which we can spell out to read: given a certain set of conditions or events, S, a certain other event or set of events, R, will follow, regularly and repeatedly. It is further implied, and this negative emphasis is important, that nothing can happen to disturb the S ——→R sequence which is not also explicable in scientific terms. In effect this means that we expect the same rules to apply from day to day, that no unobservable kinds of operators or energies of an unknowable nature are expected to intervene in the regular course of nature's ways.

The second assumption indicated above as applying to a scientific orientation is that all factors relevant to the observation of S ——→R sequences are potentially, or in principle, knowable, and measurable. The amount of measurement that can be applied may be limited to simple statements of yes or no, but the whole object of science is to describe (in terms of some kind of measurement) the relationships between antecedent and consequent events, with the implication that once such relationships are known, prediction is possible. Given the S, the R can be stated. Sometimes attempts are made to state the S, given the R; this process is one of "postdiction" in contrast to prediction and it should also hold, in theory. In practice it becomes difficult to establish as correct because we cannot hold historical events under control. After they have happened, they are beyond our grasp. If we were to try to describe the "causes" of the Civil War, we would have to operate postdictively and we cannot go back and test the alleged "causes" by holding everything else constant. Historians are forced to operate on a postdictive basis. Clinical psychologists too, when delving into someone's background and seeking factors that presumably were involved in someone's current difficulties, also work postdictively. By and large, postdictive types of statements are of little scientific value because proof is virtually impossible. Some sort of "evidence" for almost any interpretation can be mustered. One theory can be made to appear as plausible as another by "selecting" pieces out of the past (London, 1946). Postdictive speculations might serve as sources for experimental research involving variables that can now be controlled.

It is important for the student to examine the full implications of the determinist assumption. If behavior is a function of antecedent conditions that have operated on the organism, the organism inevitably and necessarily must behave in the manner that it does. Hydrogen and oxygen suitably combined become water. There is nothing the hydrogen or oxygen can do about it. Analogously, if someone's knee jerks when suitably stimulated, that is the necessary and inevitable consequence of the conditions that have been established by the nature of the organism and the stimulation or conditions involved. Presumably no one will strain at swallowing this gnat. But the determinist position holds equally strongly that George Washington crossed the Delaware because he had to, literally could do nothing else; that Lincoln wrote the Gettysburg Address in just those wonderful words because he had to and could not have written anything else; that the rapist who assaults your sister was helpless to do anything else; that juvenile delinquents who murder cripples by kicking their heads in are completely bound by their past histories and present conditions and can do nothing else; that the lad who sits on the fifteenth-story ledge and, after hours of pleading from mother and police, jumps, was a helpless victim of his past and the stimulus situation as it operated on him. No one is to merit blame or praise for his behavior as his behavior is a natural consequence of the conditions. You do not blame hydrogen and oxygen for changing into water. Similarly you cannot, as a scientist, praise Shakespeare, Shelley, or Beethoven.

If the student now feels he is being asked to swallow a camel, it should be noted that the position described has been rather generally spreading throughout the culture, particularly in the areas of health, mental adjustment, criminal behavior, and economic adjustments. When there is a large amount of unemployment throughout the land, it is no longer customary to blame the unemployed as shiftless or lazy; it is quite generally accepted that they are helpless victims of a situation and merit no personal censure. Similarly, judges and juries are quite ready to accept pleas of insanity as a defense in murder cases. The accused is sent to a hospital instead of a prison if the psychiatrists involved in the trial are willing to classify the defendant as "insane." Even when the criminals are sent to prison, the culture would like to "reform" the really blameless victims of slums, broken homes, faulty rearing and frustrated childhood. One judge in New York City, in his enthusiasm for the new look in criminology, sentenced the mother of a juvenile delinquent to a prison term on the grounds that the youngster was not guilty; his mother was. With a little more enthusiasm the judge might have sentenced the grandmother because she brought up the mother of the child. We need not belabor the point, but merely note that judges, psychiatrists, social workers, and other professional groups act as if they firmly supported the deterministic view. Parents, too, are generous in forgiving their own children's misbehavior on the grounds of youth—"they don't know any better." Here, there is an implication that someday the child will know better and somehow a change in behavior will take place; but the age is never specified, and when the child of twenty-five or thirty is arrested for murder, treason, or some other heinous crime, the parent bewails the situation saying, "Where have I failed?" Parents characteristically accept the responsibility for their children's faults. Everybody seems to be guilty of something except the criminal. He is the innocent victim of circumstances, inadequate training at home, in the school, "bad companions," and in general, a poor environment.

When someone does attain some distinction in a more positive manner as in some spectacular achievement in sports, science, or the arts, those less favored by nature (and circumstance) are quick to account for how he had the "breaks," good training, fine home, or a "pushing" parent. In general, it appears safe to say that society as a whole, in modern American culture, subscribes rather fully to a deterministic view about other people. Individuals themselves, on the other hand, in their private human relations, do not behave as if their wives or children or friends are blameless or unworthy of praise. A husband and wife may find fault with each other for many years never once raising the question of whether the other person is responsible for his behavior. Frequently enough some irate father beats an infant to death (presumably he did not "want" to kill it) because the "damned little brat wouldn't stop crying" and many of us extend to inanimate objects some perverse intentions to annoy us when we kick at machines that won't run or throw away tools that "refuse to work."

The perversity of frustrated individuals notwithstanding, the deterministic viewpoint prevails as the scientific working orientation of psychologists. If the psychologist could not depend upon a given R to follow a specific S because some unknowable force interfered on any occasion, there could be no hope of prediction, and therefore no science. Those who cannot accept this position will presumably indulge themselves in a variety of other views, which, according to a deterministic view, they cannot help doing. It should be appreciated that the deterministic view does not exclude the possibility of changes in S ⟶ R relationships, but such changes when they occur will be determined, necessary changes such as occur in the course of learning. An important corollary to the deterministic assumption is that unless special learning experiences occur, we cannot expect an individual to change his behavior patterns by appeals to his better nature, threats or promises, or by some act of "choice" or "will." When people appear to have changed, the determined deterministic psychologist will be prone to search for new circumstances and, perhaps, previously undetected learning experiences, that have effected the change. If new learning cannot be legitimately shown to have occurred, then a new, or more powerful *motive* has entered the picture. We had better turn to an examination of the nature of motives.

DRIVES AND MOTIVES

In our discussion of learning we found that the concept of drive was a helpful explanatory device in accounting for the initiation of activity in a learning situation. At that time we identified drives with bodily changes which resulted in stimulation (S_d) which led either to random or reflex activity, and which could be associated with specific responses that developed out of the habit-family-hierarchy or through arrangements forced upon the organism by the experimenter. We also observed that it might be possible for some drives (that is the responses, muscular or neural, that are involved in bodily states) to be learned, that is, associated with previously irrelevant stimuli. One such "derived" or learned drive, that of anxiety, was suggested as the basis for a variety of behavior patterns including "curiosity" and many operations involving some kind of "insecurity."

In discussing the relationship between drives and learning we noted some complexities such as the tendency among psychologists to add drives ad libitum to some basic list that might include commonly recognized physiological states such as hunger, thirst, pain, fatigue. Thus we mentioned manipulative drives, exploratory drives, and drives to exercise the sense organs, the brain, and the whole body. We might have included specific hungers, as for starches or proteins, salts, vitamins, etc., which have apparently been demonstrated in self-selected diet studies on rats and children. We noted that drives tend to be periodic in nature, with cyclical rises and declines, but this applies only to drives that are also periodically "satisfied." There is nothing cyclical about pain, for example. In describing the acquired drives we noted that drives were apparently able to function as innate responses and learned responses. We saw that drives might have no particular directional orientation, i.e., they might lead only to random activity. On the other hand, the stimuli arising from drives could be channeled into specific outlets. Whatever else a drive might be, we emphasized its stimulus-producing function. A drive, then, is a bodily state or a response pattern that produces stimuli; these stimuli can be conditioned or associated, hypothetically, with any kind of subsequent response. In terms of our present concern in tracing the antecedent-subsequent relationships subsumed under the S ⟶ R formula, we must include drive stimuli (S_d) in the stimulus portion of the formula.

Social motives

Our problem, however, is not to explain why people eat or drink, or sleep. It is to explain why they eat or aspire toward eating in fancy restaurants with flowers on the table, damask tablecloths, sterling silver, and filet mignon. Again, not to explain why they drink, but why they drink Scotch or imported sherry; to explain why they sleep or might like to sleep between silk sheets on king-size circular beds and with assorted companions. In other words, the problem for psychology is to account for the wide deviations that occur in the nature of the drive satisfiers, in the indirect satisfactions, in the effort that goes into the acquisition of satisfactions, and in the unusual deviations that are observed in some individuals who develop forms of satisfaction from activities that have no direct biological survival significance. Why do people strive against great obstacles for an education? Why do they sacrifice their lives for their children, their friends, or their country? Why do they adorn themselves with diamonds or rare metals? Why do they give up all sorts of material goods for posthumous fame? Obviously to answer these questions is quite an order and we should not expect to be able to come up with much more than tentative and suggestive answers. Moreover, we cannot consider each and every line of activity which men might follow but must look for general principles which might account for at least grosser groupings of data or observations.

As soon as we leave the area of basic, physiological tissue conditions and start talking about why people seek company (and certain kinds of company), how they vote, how they interact with their fellows and their culture, we enter an area that has been described by most writers as that of *social motivation* or socialized motives. The fact that we are dealing with the impact of cultural forces on the organism does not make such impacts any less physiological in nature, but the description of the stimulus conditions will have to be couched in other terms than the physical characteristics of the objects in terms of wave-length, decibels, pounds, etc. When we have contact with a man of another race, whose skin color may be different from ours, the problems that arise are not functions that can be plotted against the wave-length of light reflected by the skin. Several novelists have described the involved consequences that follow the revelation of the fact that a person who has lived all of his life as a white man is actually one-sixteenth Negro.

Attitudes

Our problem will be to discover new techniques for describing stimuli and to extend our appreciation of the mediational processes that intervene between stimulus patterns and behavior. The kinds of mediational processes that will concern us are commonly called *"attitudes."* We have already considered the question of how attitudes are measured (p. 123). The concept of attitude has for a long time been the mainstay or working tool of the social psychologist. Much of what we know about social factors in behavior comes from attitude studies. The general psychologist has not paid much attention to this concept, at least not under this name, and the social psychologists have come to regard attitude studies as primarily social problems. While it is certainly appropriate to study attitudes of members of various kinds of groups, there is nothing especially or exclusively social about attitudes—they are normally defined rather vaguely as "everything that a person thinks and feels" about any object, person, institution, or doctrine. Frequently enough, social psychologists are not too concerned about the *nature* or characteristics of an attitude so much as they are in measuring the differences that prevail among groups; they are content to define the attitude in terms of some measuring scale—thus, your attitude toward the church or capital punishment would be represented by your score on an attitude scale that was labeled "attitude toward the church" or "attitude toward capital punishment." Our concern is not with these scales, however, but with the nature of attitudes. We have already indicated that they must be individual affairs, something characteristic of a person, whether a group is involved or not. A child may have an attitude about taking medicine or a bath. While cultural factors are commonly involved, we want to know what having an attitude means and how it functions in motivation.

The social psychologist measuring attitudes toward politicians believes that the attitudes he measures will be reflected in the voter's behavior on election day. The attitudes are presumed to "predispose" a person to certain lines of activity. It is reasoned that if you know the attitudes of a group you can predict what the group will do. Studying the attitudes of a group will then, presumably, reveal something about the motives of the group. While it is not commonly asserted as such, it appears that in their predictive analyses, social psychologists are identifying attitudes with motives. This might be an interesting lead for us to develop in connection with individual motivation.

What do we mean by attitude? Ordinarily psychologists speak of a "relatively permanent predisposition to respond" in certain ways to certain situations or stimuli. The "relative permanence" need not concern us unless we are involved with long term propositions covering substantial periods. We must be careful, however, to avoid any trap that would equip an individual with a collection or assortment of attitudes that function independently or "dynamically" in the absence of stimuli. A predisposition to respond in a certain way simply refers to the probability that a certain response will be made to a given stimulus pattern. In other words, the attitude bears a relationship to the stimulus, a relationship, that in effect, sets limits on the possible varieties of response. We can presume at once, that attitudes are learned affairs, that as such, they have response characteristics themselves. Attitudes are actually forms of response which, while not normally observable, restrict or otherwise control the actually observable response. Stated in another way, attitudes are mediating responses which intervene between a stimulus and a response and which account for the differences in response patterns to the same stimulus pattern which we find among different individuals. The translation of attitudes into intervening, mediating responses, however, does not distinguish them from other kinds of mediators such as we described in connection with the problems of transfer and thinking. We will have to look at attitudes more closely.

Attitudes as preparatory responses or "set"

In many behavioral situations "attitudes" are aroused when no direct action of an overt nature is called for. In terms of political attitudes, nothing much can be done until Election Day. Sometimes an argument might develop as the consequences of some stimulation which has political aspects or overtones, but frequently enough, a person might encounter political stimulation from newspapers, radios, billboards, etc., when quite alone and no suitable mode of expression is available, permissable, or expected. Here an attitude has been aroused and no suitable outlet has been provided. In such cases the attitude may prevail for some time and interfere with other activity or simply be sidetracked by the next form of stimulation.

As an obvious kind of illustration of attitudes at work we might select the sprinter about to engage in a footrace. The starter calls out "On your marks," and the sprinter responds by dropping himself to finger and toe tips in a tentative fashion. The starter then signals "Get set" and we see the runner tense himself, lean forward, *ready* to spring into action at the sound of the starting gun. In this leaning-forward position, the runner has responded to a specific stimulus ("get set") within a more general stimulus situation of a racing meet (people do not get down on all fours if someone shouts "get set" in their living rooms). But being set is of only indirect consequence. The runner is prepared now, or "predisposed" to react in a given way to a particular stimulus. If the shot is not fired, the runner will remain tensely poised for a time, but if much more than the customary interval elapses, he will begin to fidget and lose the nicely co-ordinated launching position. A gun shot at that point will result in a poor start. If the shot comes at the appropriate moment when the runner is most finely set, the start will be an efficient one. Should a fly land on the runner's nose when he is "set," he cannot react to it in his customary manner and is very inefficient in his fly-chasing behavior while being efficient in race-starting behavior.

We have now pointed out two aspects of a "set" response. It makes you efficient for one kind of behavior, while at the same time, it makes you inefficient for a vast array of other kinds of behavior. We had occasion to illustrate such muscular sets before when speaking of kinesthesis (p. 117) where the work of watch repairmen was described. It will be recalled that repairmen do not like to switch from wrist-watch work to alarm clocks because they waste so much time getting "set" for heavy or light work. Another aspect of set behavior that emerges from our illustration of the sprinter is that the set, by itself, does not normally lead to any specific pattern or behavior—another stimulus is necessary in order for the action to develop.

Watching our sprinter on the track reveals that the task of "getting set" is a rather complex one. Track coaches have worked for years on the problem of developing starting techniques that would enable their best runners to reduce the total time of the run. A slight improvement in the set might result in a broken record. The same considerations apply to all the effort expended in the development of "form." "Form" is a matter of properly "predisposing" the body to respond in some specific way to a given stimulus situation whether it is with a vaulting pole or a basketball. In basketball we even speak of the "set-shot" which the player is able to make if he once gets into a certain position. In pole vaulting the athlete carefully measures and counts each step in his approach; if there has been the slightest deviation from some hypothetical optimum, the jump will not be a satisfactory one. The fact that improvement can occur in the development of preparatory sets is again an indication of the role of learning. What we are dealing with in terms of set we could just as readily talk about in terms of habits, or we might define sets as habitual modes of response to particular stimuli. These habits, however, are of value only in terms of controlling the next stage of behavior, the next response to follow upon the occurrence of another stimulus.

The behavior of an athlete may illustrate the nature of preparatory sets well enough but the student might well wonder what this had to do with motivation. We can come a little closer to this question now that we have brought out the physical features of set in at least one area. To make the position quite clear it will be argued in the future that the term "motivation" actually amounts to the process of initiating preparatory sets—predispositions to respond—which then facilitate the behavior engaged in when appropriate stimuli are present. To make it doubly clear, it will be argued that motives themselves are *responses* (preparatory) made by the individual organism to specific stimulating circumstances, that without such circumstances present they do not exist; that, like habits, they represent or are represented by neural patterns that are not normally active until specific stimulation occurs of components of such patterns. One comment that seems to be a weasel-like attempt at dodging issues or seeking loopholes must also be made at this time to avoid misunderstanding in the future: it is possible for a "motive" or preparatory set to be aroused by generalized forms of the originally appropriate stimulation, by second-order or higher-order conditioning stimuli and by still unknown physiological conditions, presumably of a chemical nature which might initiate activity in the neural processes involved, giving an air of "spontaneity" to the motive under consideration. There is no reason why any particular motive could not be aroused by a great variety of what for us, at the present time, must amount to "random neural activity." The "spontaneity" however, is only a reflection of our ignorance, and just as we considered in connection with the phenomenon of "insight," we have no reason to doubt that a proper sequence of antecedents and consequences was followed.

One more complication must be added before we can proceed. If motives are in fact responses, then like other responses they will inevitably generate stimuli from the response activity involved. Such stimuli might be rather vague and undirected as we suggested for the runner on the track who is waiting for a long-delayed gun shot, or, if the pattern is repeated sufficiently often for learning to take place, the response generated stimuli may become associated with some specific behavior which is normally evoked by adequate stimuli that normally follow the initiation of a set. In other words, the motive-produced stimuli can also lead to highly specific responses after learning has taken place. In order for some kinds of behavior to occur, then, all that is necessary is that the set (motive) be aroused; the rest will follow automatically. We have already encountered this principle in connection with drive activity; we can now transfer it to the motive area.

It might be most helpful to start our analysis with a popular form of romantic activity, that of kissing. This kind of activity has the virtue of being readily observed by most students. It has the additional virtue of playing a role in a rather prominent motivational area in western culture. We kiss, get kissed, or watch someone else get kissed in movies or television shows. What motivational factors underlie this behavior? If we ask the participants why they indulge themselves in this manner, they might say "Because we want to." This, of course, is no answer if our real question is "What does it mean to want to kiss?" or to want anything, for that matter.

Wants and desires

In examining this example of social-sexual practice we are beginning our analysis of "wants." We start by asking how we identify wants. If the young lady does not want to be kissed it is quite apparent to anyone but the extreme neophyte. She stands aloof, arms outstretched defensively, face averted, *set* to defend virtue and honor. If she wants to be kissed it should be equally easy to observe. She makes no defensive gestures, she is *set* to relax in many bodily areas, her face is uplifted, her lips puckered, *set* to press and be pressed against. Anyone who has kissed anyone who did not care to be kissed can readily appreciate the role of a kissing set versus a nonkissing set. Considering the time, place, and general situational factors, we are ready to draw some generalizations about this kind of activity:

In the first place we do not find people going around with urges to kiss in the absence of appropriate stimulus objects. When there is no one around to kiss, there is no kissing motive in any real sense (we shall treat of variations of wants and what shall be termed pseudo-wants later). No amount of observation would reveal that some isolated individual had a kissing want. When a suitable partner appears on the scene and other situational features are equally suitable, e.g., social isolation, the stimulus situation begins to approximate the necessary conditions. It is of greatest importance that no interfering sets be established as by the appearance of pain, tears, terror, great excitement, etc., in the partner. If now, for any reason, a suitable proximity having been established, and other things being equal, some stimulus is introduced that bears on the behavior of kissing, either or both of the partners will begin to develop responses that are the precursors of making contact with the lips. When such responses are observed we can infer that a want exists. Without such responses there is no want. As the preparatory activity continues, the stimuli generated by such responses may lead to the consummation of the overt response. With inexperienced partners nothing may happen because the stimuli generated by the preparatory responses have not been associated with the consummatory response. If novices do manage to make contact, their result may prove strange and perhaps disappointing, abortive, and even disturbing.

CHARACTERISTICS OF MOTIVATED BEHAVIOR

The illustration developed from the factors involved in kissing is intended to suggest a paradigm of motivated behavior. Many other illustrations could be presented all incorporating the same general features which we can now itemize as generally applicable to motivated behavior:

1. There is no behavior which does not display some motivational features as we are always under the influence of some kind of stimulation.

2. If we attempt to abstract from the general ongoing pattern of behavior some specific motivational sequence we observe that:

a. there is a time dimension involved such that organism is not at the moment indulging in a particular consummatory pattern.

b. a specific stimulus related to the consummatory pattern impinges upon the organism.

c. the immediate response to this stimulus is not consummatory behavior but an attitudinal or set response which restricts or limits the possibilities of other stimuli becoming effective and facilitates the response to stimuli bearing on steps in the sequence leading to the consummatory pattern.

d. the attitude or set may generate response-produced stimuli which directly or because of learning lead to subsequent steps; in other words, the motivational pattern may be self-sustaining once it is initiated.

3. Motives are themselves responses to stimuli; they do not arise spontaneously or independently in the absence of stimuli; they are like habits in this respect, and like habits, must be thought of as organized patterns laid down in the nervous system through a process of training. They can, like the habits they are, be made functional when the appropriate stimulation is present.

4. The kinds of stimulation that can become appropriate depend upon the individual's life history. Like any other kind of association, motives can be aroused by generalized stimuli and by any degree of remote association that can be brought to bear upon the neural structures involved through a mediational process.

5. While many kinds of motivational responses are important to individual or species survival, and, hence, involve or originate in physiological tissue conditions (drives), the construct of "motive" is the more general case and we need not try to derive motivation from drives; quite the contrary, we find drives only one example of how behavior sequences that originate in some kind of stimulus situation develop through mediational processes to terminate in some form of consummary behavior. We note that the concept of consummatory behavior is not restricted to such activities as eating or drinking, but covers the more general activity of eliminating a source of stimulation through one of many possible forms of behavior such as retiring, attacking, or merely waiting for time to pass and for the stimulation to be removed by other means.

6. It is obvious from the above description that motives are conceived of as temporary response patterns that are set into function through immediate stimulation. Motives are frequently thought of as long-range operations extending over years, as the motivation for becoming a psychiatrist which involves years of study, or the setting aside of savings against the damp and rainy days of retirement, or the motivation for an extensive journey. In this connection it is necessary to argue that the long-term motivation does not actually exist as a functional affair throughout the many and long sequences that may intervene between initial stimulation and final consummation. What does happen is that the immediately important motivational pattern is eliminated by some response which commits the organism to a given future pattern of sequential stimuli. Boarding a plane or ship com-

mits you to staying aboard for the duration of the trip and upon arrival at a destination, the new stimuli will further commit you to some course of action. The student who *signs* up for a program leading eventually to psychiatry puts himself in a position where stimuli relating to other kinds of programs or activities are ruled out or otherwise become ineffective (if the program is to be completed). Every morning he may be roused from his bed, go through his ablutions and dressing routines, breakfast, and head for the institution involved at the particular stage of his program, not because he has any motivation for psychiatry at any given moment of the day, but because he once *had* the motivation and it led to this routine. If we now ask him why he goes to school, he can give us an answer of the "I want to be a psychiatrist" type. This may or may not have any bearing on his actual day-to-day behavior and his current motivations may be as distantly removed from psychiatry as possible—he may be concerned with a TV program or about a new car, a new girl friend, etc. His motive for psychiatry is only one of his habits. He has, of course, many others, and only one is likely to be functioning efficiently at any one time.

SOCIAL MOTIVES IN OUR CULTURE

In western civilization many cultural patterns have developed which make the business of social living function as well as it does, or, at least, in the way that it does. One generation prepares the next for the practical business of living in the culture as it is known to the parents. Ways of earning a living, permissible pleasures, appropriate patterns of social intercourse, and knowledge about personal privileges are gradually acquired by the growing child. In the course of this education, both in and out of school, the child acquires a code of ethics (suitable for his use) and a familiarity with objects and situations which permit a degree of adjustment to his environment. In our culture such situations and objects tend to be heavily loaded with *status* features because of the heavy emphasis in our society on individual dignity and worth which is expressed in adulation of historical heroes, the pioneer, the adventurer, the self-made man. The heros of politics, industry, science, or finance (or the motion pictures) have status. With status come many of the material comforts and security which the child has learned to value. By acquiring material comforts and security, it is possible in such a culture to attain the status that itself might have brought about or insured the values involved; and, in our culture, the motivational patterns that are of most significance have to do with the acquisition of status. Since status can be developed in a wide assortment of fields (athletics, science, business, politics, entertainment, etc.) the manifold ways in which motivational patterns are developed present a bewildering complexity. We can attempt to show how a prestige motive might be the normal consequence of routine educational practice in our culture and consider other motivational patterns to follow essentially the same lines.

The desire for prestige

Perhaps the dominant motive in western culture is that of individual prestige (see Packard, 1959). The constant battle for keeping up with or slightly ahead of the Joneses is probably familiar to anyone old enough to be reading this. Much of our economic life is tied to the concept of staying ahead of our neighbors through the acquisition of the latest model of automobile, vacuum cleaner or vacuum bottle. To a considerable extent the directions of action involved depend upon the nature of the "Joneses" close at hand so that some individuals aspire to prestige with the local neighborhood gang or bowling alley circle; others, already in or close to the country club set, have their own prestige targets. Probably no one, or only deluded people, aspires to a general prestige; certainly there are groups in any society which are not courted for favor by members of other groups.

The practical development of the prestige motive presumably starts in the home as soon as any differential treatment is encountered by the growing child where his own immediate and current motives are thwarted. The child that has to go to bed, while grown-ups can stay and watch the late show on television, learns about one kind of power and authority and the privileges it confers. The child that wears hand-me-downs from an older sibling begins to learn about the power of money. Comparison of one's own toys with those of neighbor children again point up the value of money as parents explain why Johnny cannot have a pony or a sports car, when Jimmy can. Along with the negative and punitive aspects, Johnny witnesses the varying patterns of rewards that accompany certain kinds of individual achievement in school sports, spelling bees, and classroom performance on tests, and in general. The medals, the gold stars, the praise, and the financial compensation that occasionally get into the pattern become stimuli that arouse attitudes or sets, sets that at first are rather vague and disorganized as well as disorganizing—emotional reactions that we come to know as rage, fear, envy, jealousy, etc. These sets are uncomfortable and stimuli generated from them lead to random activity unless someone older and wiser steps in and presents other stimuli leading to a more specific and socially acceptable reaction, such as the thoroughly unnatural response of congratulating the winner or the "it's not whether you won or lost, but how you played the game" routines. Because competition is rampant in many cultures from the cradle to the grave (even the tomb must be carefully considered), the occurrence of prestige symbols is virtually a constant feature of the environment, and the sets that develop in connection with such symbols are constantly exercised and eventually find regular outlets. The typical outlet is some state of distress with an accompaniment of verbalisms such as "I'd like to have that" or "I'd like to be like that." The torrent of advertising that pours forth from the inexhaustible dams constantly exercises the prestige set or attitude and patterns the behavior of multitudes of citizens. The pattern of stimulation becomes increasingly complex as the child grows older. The basic discomfort reaction is associated with almost every aspect of life through combinations of stimulus patterns that have no intrinsic connections, such as the advertising of automobiles in terms of attractive women models, cigarettes with baseball stars, etc.

In a competitive culture the citizens are constantly bombarded by prestige symbols which create dissatisfactions and lead to actions designed toward the acquisition of such symbols which become important reinforcers of behavior. Once such reinforcers have played their role, they become potent reinforcers for many kinds of attempts at excelling the members of immediate community in various competitions. An occasional victory, like a periodic reinforcer, will keep the individual at the game for a long time. The culture itself manages to provide some modicum of victory for many individuals—there are second and third prizes and there are always condolences from friends, alibis, and rationalizations to keep the door open for the next attempt.

In our culture the competitive motive pervades most aspects of life. The wife we choose cannot be just anybody—she must be more than passing fair; our children have to be the brightest, our homes the most expensive on the block, our clothes and food from the better stores. The range of the competitive area is so great as to permit everyone to get a prize. If a child is not very bright, he might be a "regular little devil" or a "normal" boy. Even being "normal" is twisted into a prize-winning status. "Who wants a nasty little egg-head around the house?" asks the parent without egg-head children.

If we stop to analyze the operations of the prestige or status motive, we see it functioning in the same manner as the sets we described in such grosser physical operations as sprinting and kissing. We recognize the role of learning, the functions of reinforcing situations, the role of status stimuli in arousing the sets, the function of set-produced stimuli in associations developed with responses that eliminate the stimulus pattern that aroused the set in the first place. The point to be underscored is that a status motive is a learned response, like any other learned pattern of behavior. It is not based on any particular physiological need like hunger but on a more general stress situation which involves thwarting of any kind of behavior by authority figures, who, in the first instance, will be parents, then teachers, and our peers. The role of status symbols or stimuli is such that the acquisition of such symbols eliminates the thwarting for the time being. At the same time these symbols become associated with and in time lead to the stress reaction so that an organism is uncomfortable in the presence of such stimuli and learns to strive or respond in such fashions as are calculated to eliminate the stress through the acquisition of the stimuli.

What we have been referring to as stress in the preceding paragraphs has also been described as anxiety. The reader will recall from our discussion of drives, that the anxiety state has been postulated by some psychologists as the basic condition out of which much of the social motivation develops. The desire for money was cited as an illustration. We hesitate to adopt the term anxiety because of its clinical connotations, but the present analysis is not essentially different from that previously described. By referring to thwarting of some ongoing behavior we have a more general principle which may or may not involve some aspects of "anxiety" and frees us from the burden of handling such excess meaning as might be involved. We proceed directly from a thwarting situation (whether or not anxiety is involved) to the development of some mediating condition we have described as a set on the basis of which competitive behavior can develop.

In spite of the pervasiveness of the competitive motives in our culture, we still insist on the description of sets or motives of this nature as habits, as responses that are aroused by stimuli. The motives have no independent dynamism. One does not go around struggling for prestige unless he is stimulated into doing so. Because much of our time is spent in this general orientation, we must conclude that the culture provides many occasions (profuse stimulation) for such reponses to come out of the habit systems of its citizens. We are not competitive by nature, but rather by culture.

Other social motives

Many attempts have been made in the past to develop the concept of social motives and various lists of such motives have been produced. Such lists include references to such behavior patterns as gregariousness, play, co-operation, achievement, dominance, pugnacity (motives for war), and many others. In some cases attempts have been made to trace such motives to some basic biological or instinctive need. The social behavior of insects, for example, is examined to suggest parallels to human gregariousness. Some theorists try to develop systems whereby much if not all behavior is tied to some singled-out biological need, e.g., sex. Others try to postulate a biological foundation for achievement or "power."

One of the most recent such attempts is that by Schutz (1958) who argues strongly that in our culture, and perhaps all over the world, man is dominated by three fundamental needs: the need to love and be loved, the need to be interested in others and have others interested in him, and the need to be respected by or control (and to respect or be controlled by) others. In describing these three needs Schutz has incorporated much of what other students have emphasized singly. How effectively this new attempt to categorize human motivation will succeed remains to be seen. It is possible to set up all kinds of broad categories of traits or needs of such generality that they are made to appear as plausible frameworks for "explaining" behavior. The fewer the categories the more general they must be, and the more they pretend to explain, the less they fit the individual case. On the other hand, if a list or catalogue becomes too specific and extensive it loses any generality and flexibility.

The history of attempts to catalogue human motivation constantly reminds us of Procrustes and his attempts to fit sleepers to his bed. No such attempts in the past have won any general favor, nor do they appear likely to do so because of the many contradictions involved in our social activities. Rather than to try to trace a given social pattern back to some assumed biological or social needs, it seems the better part of wisdom to take the behavior itself under scrutiny and examine its historical development in the individual concerned. When this is done, it appears that we do not need any kind of "prime mover" to help us appreciate the factors and functions involved. There does not appear to be any class of energizers of action functioning as independent agencies which we must call on to account for our observations. The concept of habit and the inclusion within this concept of the mediational response (itself a habit) appears to be adequate to the occasion. There is, in fact, considerable doubt as to whether there is any need for introducing a concept of "motivation" as a special feature of behavior, if the use of this concept is to include a listing of individual "motives" as independent agencies. Such a practice involves us in a confused philosophy of causation wherein we lose sight of the conditions that must be present for certain behavior patterns to emerge because we are looking for an agency that does not necessarily exist. To say that reference to some alleged motive like "sex" is only a short and convenient way of referring to important and limiting conditions may appear reasonable and acceptable, but since we do not always remember that we are using a term as a convenience, there is some danger of reification which can be avoided by not resorting to such practices. If we are to retain the term "motive" at all, it should be used only as a general expression dealing with arousal or activation of the organism; in this sense it does no particular damage to our thinking even though it may not help. The danger lies in singling out some alleged agency like sex or achievement, and presuming that it represents some common set of operations for every individual. We then run into a situation where we begin to measure behavior and deduce that someone has a high or low or no such motive. While such action cannot be denounced as unscientific, because we are all free to postulate anything we like, we get into great difficulties if we first postulate a universal motive and then find no evidence of its operations in any direct observations. If we are sufficiently convinced of having arrived at an eternal truth we then say the motive is there all right, but it has gone underground, or into the "unconscious," or it is obscured or otherwise denied a role by other motives. When we have reached this stage of argument we are on a merry-go-round from which it is difficult to get back onto a straight course. Instead of trying to present the world with a neat package of motives, it might be better to forego the entire concept and see if an adequate account of behavior can be developed without the help of motives.

EMOTIONS AS MOTIVES

The nature of emotion will occupy us in the next chapter. For the present it is of some interest to relate the two concepts even before we attempt to describe emotional phenomena and behavior in any formal fashion. It is common (layman) practice to account for behavior by reference to various alleged emotional states. People are said to kill other people because they *hate* them, or *fear* them, or *love* them (as in euthanasia cases). In almost any behavioral pattern some emotional features can be cited, and, in some instances, magnified into a causative role. One person fights for his life because of fear; another cheerfully gives his life because of patriotism. Mob behavior is accounted for by a "frenzy that seized the crowd." Jealousy, love, fear, hate and various stages of these "primitive" emotions have been used by novelists and poets to account for the majority of human behavior. So powerful has this approach been that we are all ready to account for our behavior in these terms. While it is unquestionably true that emotional factors play a role in behavior, the nature of that role must be assessed and not misinterpreted. As we shall see later, emotional patterns of behavior are subject to maturational and learning factors and their primitive, innate, aspects are considerably modified before they begin to function in any systematic way in behavior.

There have been various approaches to describing the role of emotion in human affairs which range from a denial of any significant causative importance to emotion to acceptance of innate drives and accompanying emotional patterns as of primary significance. The latter point of view announced by William McDougall (1915) is no longer widely considered and we will ignore it here. The other approaches have adherents of varying degrees of loyalty and require our notice.

The view of William James (1890) was that emotions are aftereffects of behavior and of no causative importance. In his classical illustration, James discussed what happens when we encounter a bear in the woods. The usual explanation would be: we see a bear, we become frightened, we run (because we are frightened). James reversed the argument and said: we see a bear, we run, we become afraid (because we run). While this view may appear paradoxical, there is much to be said for it and we will examine it more closely later. For the moment we are considering motivational properties of emotion and need go no further with the James view.

In the opinion of John B. Watson (1930), man is born with three basic innate emotional patterns which he labeled "fear," "anger," and "love." These patterns are evoked by specific stimuli and later can be conditioned to other stimuli, but the reactions involved are responses in their own right and no causative agencies were incorporated into Watson's views. Fear, for example, was a reaction to sudden stimulation like that of a loud noise and consisted of a withdrawal kind of activity; anger was the result of thwarting of bodily movement and consisted of thrashing about; love involved relaxation as a response pattern. Whatever happened as a result of withdrawal, thrashing about or relaxing would be in the nature of physical aftereffects and not the result of emotion as motivating anything in particular.

Walter B. Cannon (1929) proposed the view that is most closely akin to that described earlier where motivation was treated as set. Cannon regarded emotions as primitive reactions of visceral organs to simulation in the hypothalamus and operating through the autonomic nervous system to activate some visceral organs and to inhibit others. The body was prepared, according to Cannon, for reactions to emergencies. What behavior did develop would depend upon additional stimulation of an external nature. The organism was prepared to fight or flee on the basis of visceral activity but this visceral activity did not dictate the course of events; it did not cause anything in particular to happen. In one famous experiment, Cannon injected adrenalin into a number of athletes, thus artificially creating a visceral pattern that might normally result from hypothalamic origins. The athletes did not become active or do anything but sat around and reported that they felt like they "ought to be afraid" or that they felt "tense." They were ready to respond to additional stimulation in a way they might normally react when excited because of the now "emotional" visceral condition, but they did not actually do anything. From our point of view, they were "set" to respond, but there was nothing to respond to. Presumably the responses they would make to additional stimuli would be related to the nature of the stimuli and their historical associations for the individuals involved. The responses might very well be more extreme, more active, or energetic, because of the emotion, but not, because of the visceral condition, any more specific.

In recent years, Leeper (1948) has advocated the view that emotions energize any ongoing activity, in fact, give it some direction in the sense of restricting the field of action, thereby providing some degree of organization to the behavior. A professional boxer in the ring might lend more authority to his blows if he were somewhat more emotional than if he were calm and bored. Leeper argues that emotions are organizing in the Cannon sense of aiding and abetting the activity involved. In this sense, emotions play a role in motivation by adding energy which might not otherwise be called upon. There appears to be general approval of this view, but we notice, again, that no directive feature of any independent nature is conferred upon emotional activity.

In his argument Leeper attempted to reconcile the more classical (and common sense) view with the simple energizing theory. He sees no essential difference between appreciating how hunger (as a drive) might lead to food-seeking behavior, and how fear (also as a drive) might lead to behavior that we might describe as "taking precautions." Two campers in the woods, for example, might illustrate the similarity in motivational processes. One, "driven by hunger," looks about for food or makes preparations for such action; the other, "driven by fear," looks for a safe spot, builds a shelter, and starts a fire to keep animals at a safe distance. In these examples, however, we are dealing with older organisms; we are dealing with situations that involve learning.

It is only when we come to deal with learned emotional reactions in the derived drive sense that emotions come into the picture as motivational agencies. Here, it will be remembered, the argument runs that an emotion like fear can be conditioned to some stimulus. The fear (or anxiety) at first generates stimulation of an undirected nature, that is, a variety of random responses may emerge. If one of these responses eliminates the fear-producing situation, the organism learns to repeat this response on future occasions. We note here that a highly specific response pattern is singled out by the experimenter, and it is this response pattern that is displayed in subsequent tests. It could be argued now that anxiety or fear does, as a result of learning, call out a specific response, and therefore functions as a motive. The specificity of the response, however, restricts the role of emotion in motivation to those kinds of responses that the organism learns to make to emotion-produced stimulation. In the absence of learning experiences, we would be restricted to using emotional patterns as motivators of rather random activities. To use emotions as motivators, then, we must be prepared to limit them to either specific responses learned in connection with a specific emotional pattern or to a wide variety of random activity of a rather un-co-ordinated, undirected variety. The French "crime of passion" might fit our case. In an agitated condition a person might *accidentally,* that is, as a basically *random* response, do something which resulted in death or damage to someone or something and the behavior might legitimately be ascribed to the agitation.

The role of emotions in motivating behavior, then, is a complex one, involving, paradoxically, the two extremes of highly specific responses and random, disorganized reactions. While there is no evidence on hand about any other kinds of derived drives of an emotional nature (we know nothing about love as a derived drive, for example), we might tentatively propose that other emotional patterns might function in similar ways. We should also note that generalized stimuli might evoke the common emotional reaction learned to some specific stimulus and thus lead to some behavior that might otherwise be quite inexplicable. There is also the whole problem of possible additional mediating functions from the labeling of responses so that what is learned as a specific response to a given stimulus might later show a great variety of possible behavior patterns learned to the mediating response. Thus, a frightened person might learn to label his response to the fear situation as one of "got to get out of this jam." If he learns a variety of ways of getting out of jams, he may behave in some novel fashion in the given situation because he is responding to the label and not to the situation per se.

MOTIVATION AND FRUSTRATION

The picture of motivation as we have drawn it thus far includes, to some extent, the notion of thwarting, interference with an ongoing activity, leading to what we have called discomfort or stress, and which we have described as a set. This set, in turn, may produce stimuli which at first lead to random activity and through learning to more specialized response patterns.

The thwarting or interference with ongoing activity is commonly labeled *frustration*. Sometimes the term is used as if it referred to some internal state ("I feel frustrated"), and sometimes only to the facts of interference, the existence of some obstacle to progress. Presumably both factors are involved. The presence of an obstacle to progress will inevitably arouse response patterns (sets) of a general disorganized nature (if the apparent obstacle is not really such, the subject will handle it in automatic fashion—the traveler in the jungle hacks away at the obstacles in his path in routine fashion, regarding them not so much as obstacles as "jungle"). We can picture the general pattern into which an obstacle intrudes as an interruption of a normal $S \longrightarrow R$ function by some kind of barrier, of whatever form, in this way: if the original stimulus to some sequence of behavior is labeled S_o and the final, consummatory response in the sequence is labeled R_{fc}, then typically $S_o \longrightarrow R_{fc}$, but when a frustrating event or obstacle (S_F) appears any place in the sequence, we have this pattern:

$$S_o \longrightarrow S_F \text{ rather than } S_o \longrightarrow R_{fc}$$

When the frustrating stimulus appears we have to presume that it will lead to responses in its own right, and that these responses will, in the absence of habits which would eliminate S_F readily, be dependent upon the great variety of variables, particularly the history of the organism, but also on the strength of the original $S \longrightarrow R$ association. Thus, if the frustrating stimulus is a familiar one, i.e., it has been encountered frequently and methods of dealing with it have been developed, then the stimulus is dealt with in the habitual manner and the course resumed. Here we have the response to the frustrating stimulus functioning as an ordinary mediating mechanism with merely a delay in the R_{fc}. If the original association is very strong the organism may persist in direct progress as if nothing were present in the form of an obstacle as a child might struggle forward toward some tempting bait even though held back by an adult so that no progress was taking place. We can presume that if the original association is strong enough and supporting conditions (deprivation) powerful, the organism will continue for some time to, in effect, crash through the obstacle, and only after some loss in the strength of the forward tendencies, will the obstacle even be percieved (reacted to) as such. We might state this as a principle to the effect that other things being equal, an obstacle or frustrating event will not begin to initiate reactions to itself until a change in strength of the original association toward completing the sequence has occurred.

Reactions to frustration

When the obstacle does begin to affect the organism we can expect a variety of possible reactions, one of which we have already mentioned (ignoring the obstacle, taking it in stride on the basis of previously learned maneuvers). If no routine responses are available in the repertoire of the organism, we can expect random behavior such as might be characteristic of the set or mediational reaction initiated by the obstacle. If the obstacle represents a threat, such as the sudden appearance of a huge dog when a boy is reaching for apples in some farmer's orchard, we might expect flight. If the obstacle is a physical barrier such as the apples being out of reach, we can expect mediational behavior resulting in the labeling responses which would generate such solutions as throwing stones, climbing trees, jumping, etc. On the other hand, if the obstacle represents some more restrictive stimulus, such as being held back physically, we might expect some thrashing about and struggle or "aggressive" behavior, designed more or less to demolish and destroy the thwarting stimulus. In the remarks just made we notice that the nature of the reaction to frustration depends on the nature of the frustrating stimulus. We cannot then conclude that frustration will necessarily lead to any particular class of behavior, such as aggression, that, in fact, each class of responses if we can so characterize responses, depends on the class of stimulation. Further, we must recognize the role of the individual life history in the various kinds of frustrating situations that might arise. If the individual has had a series of failures in dealing with some class of frustrating stimuli, we might expect an apathetic, perhaps disgruntled surrender to circumstance, with a possible sour-grapes dismissal of the virtues of the final consummatory response. To other individuals, the frustration situation might represent a challenge such that the original $S \longrightarrow R_{fc}$ situation itself is of no further interest while eliminating the frustration might become a goal in itself. We see this frequently when children (and adults) get involved in fights or arguments where the final outcome of the battle becomes the end in itself and the original problem is forgotten. "I don't remember what we were fighting about, but it was a great fight, mother." In general, the nature of the response to a frustrating stimulus cannot be predicted from the simple fact of the occurrence of the frustration. On the other hand, given additional information of the kinds to be detailed below, we might be able to appreciate rather unusual forms of behavior which are commonly witnessed.

Taking the case where no routines are available, and where no direct fear responses are generated by the frustrating stimulus we are left with the situation where the frustration amounts to thwarting of progress with resultant struggle responses. When there is evidence of struggle, we can infer frustration, or putting it in terms of a formula: frustration may lead to aggression; aggression, when present, presupposes frustration. We should be careful to note that it is not being asserted that frustration always leads to aggression, but rather, that aggression, when seen, was preceded by frustration (see Dollard, Doob, Miller, Mowrer, and Sears, 1939).

Frustration and aggression

We can symbolize the situation where aggressive behavior is observed as:

$$S_o \longrightarrow S_F \longrightarrow R_m \longrightarrow s_a \longrightarrow R_a$$

where the frustrating stimulus leads to an emotional mediating state or set from which stimuli (s_a) are generated leading to responses (R_a) of an aggressive (destructive, attacking) nature. In some situations the aggressive behavior is immediate and successful in terminating the frustrating stimulus; this would be the case when the S_F was not especially powerful and could not stand up to the aggressive activity. A frustrated parent spanks a child and resumes his interrupted pattern of reading the newspaper or whatever. This of course does not help the child who was frustrated by the parent and we can presume that now the child will engage in aggressive behavior such as howling, banging doors, kicking the cat, or whatever happens to be available and receptive. Similarly if an adult is frustrated in getting into his automobile because someone else parked too close for him to open the door of his own car, we can expect to observe, in some individuals, some verbal aggression of a name-calling nature, and perhaps some moderate attack on the neighboring car in the form of a kick or some bumper activity in the course of withdrawing from the parking space.

DISPLACED AGGRESSION

In many instances, perhaps the majority, the frustrating stimulus is protected by size or authority from any aggression directed toward it. When the policeman stops the speeder, there is little to be done by way of aggression that will help the situation. The policeman eventually removes himself but the emotional set that was aroused may not disappear rapidly or completely for some time. During this interval the frustrated individual is still under the influence of stimuli from this set and may engage in aggressive behavior which is not directed at the frustrating stimulus but may be directed at anything handy, just as the spanked child slams doors. When aggression is directed at some object or person not directly responsible, we speak of *displaced* aggression. There is apparently a great deal of such displaced aggressive activity in our culture; so much so, that it is commonplace to assume a bad day at the office when the husband growls at his wife as soon as he arrives at his home. It is important to note that there is nothing inevitable about such displaced aggression. Some writers make it appear that aggression will inevitably come out if there has been a frustrating incident; this is not necessarily the case. We cannot presume that the mediational response will last, forever generating aggressive stimuli. It will eventually cease as new stimulation comes into the picture calling for new responses. We can only agree that so long as such mediational stimulation is present, the possibility of aggressive behavior also exists. It is most unlikely that without additional frustrating stimulation the husband who might have growled at his wife and children will do so the next day if for any reason he was unable to do so the night before—if the family had been called away, for example. Had he been under the influence of mediating stimuli for aggressive behavior he would have expended it in the process of getting his own supper or tearing open his newspaper. When it is argued that various gross social phenomena such as wars, race prejudice, industrial strikes, etc., are forms of aggression resulting from frustration we had best be extremely careful in appraising such conclusions. Frustration is, of necessity, an individual affair, and while a great many people might be frustrated at the same general time, it is unlikely that the frustrating stimuli are the same or that there is any great similarity in the patterns of response to the stimuli from mediating sets that are aroused. It is possible, of course, to frustrate a group of individuals in about the same way and to the same general level and to supply the same general scapegoat and thereby observe a mass displaced aggression. This does not mean that the same behavior would have ensued if it had not been engineered to follow those lines. In one study (Miller and Bugelski, 1948) some young men were frustrated and it was arranged for them to indicate their attitudes toward Japanese and Mexicans immediately after the frustration. Their responses indicated that some aggression had been displaced on these innocent victims. We must be careful in generalizing from such experiments not to conclude that race prejudice is due to frustration. At the time of measurement, the frustration might have just as readily been displayed toward George Washington or the Constitution. The young men in a prefrustration test had already demonstrated a low opinion of "foreigners." We cannot be sure such low opinions reflected previous frustration experiences.

Self-aggression. It is common enough to observe instances where people deliberately injure themselves or their possessions when frustrated. This, too, is a form of aggression stemming from the frustration but the special factor here is the recognition of the frustration as due to one's own behavior which in such circumstances is frequently called stupidity. When the housewife is faced with late-afternoon callers when she is busy preparing dinner, she might reluctantly make the gesture of inviting the callers to stay and eat. When the callers take up the invitation with only modest demurrers, the housewife may be ready to scream, but makes the best of it for social purposes. The parting of the guests releases the aggressive behavior that has been nursed throughout the evening. But the frustrating agent was, unfortunately, herself, and the aggression is turned inward with such comments as "How stupid can I be?" or "How did I ever let myself in for that?" In the process of preparing the dinner, the housewife could very readily manage to cut herself, burn herself, place hot plates on her unprotected table, etc. We have chosen only a mild illustration. There is a wide range of self-punitive behavior from such mild demonstrations to the extreme of suicide, which is presumed to be the ultimate form of self-aggression and to be due to personal failures of one kind or another, which are perceived as self-frustration.

MOTIVATION AND ATTENTION

In some of the earlier presentations we were obliged to bring up such considerations as expectancy, curiosity, and, without going into the matter in any detail, the concept of attention. Such terms have a mentalistic flavor about them which has led many psychologists to avoid their use or at least to apologize for such use. We are now in position to welcome them back into the realm of respectable language for these terms are only other labels for what we have been describing as mediational responses or sets. Let us start with the concept of attention. We cannot define attention independently in subjective terms that would communicate effectively; yet we all use the term in a rather specific way—especially in a negative sense. We recognize occasions when someone is *not* attending to us (even though he claims to be and is actually doing so). When we see a person to whom we are talking sitting with his eyes closed, there may be some question of his attentiveness. If he is snoring, there is no question. If he is closely examining some object or scene while we are talking about something else, we are hardly pleased with the amount of attention we are receiving. In general, if someone is following *our* movements with his eyes, is oriented toward us, cups his hand to his ear and strains forward when we speak, we are inclined to think that he is attending, even if he is not, and is actually putting on a show for some peculiar reason of his own. The schoolchild quickly learns to put on such a show for his teachers even while he is imaginatively centuries and leagues away. Granting that some deception is possible, the behavior of the attentive person is something that can be roughly described as above. Such a description, however, omits the essence of the situation, namely, that the attentive person is *prepared* to respond to a succession of particular stimuli and not to others. We cannot attend to two sources of stimulation at one time with any great degree of success. We cannot attend to two conversations at once at a cocktail party, even though we can hear quite well any particular conversation in the midst of the hubbub. To do so we watch the speaker, his lips, his gestures, and, in effect, "tune him in." Other conversations then form a background which we can note but not detail.

Our picture of the sprinter "on his marks" showed us a real "attention" in action; the sprinter could just as well be called to this position by the shout "Attention" as is done in the military services with well-known results. From the position of military attention, the soldier is ready to engage in certain maneuvers or drill responses which would be awkward from some other position. In other words, the disposition of the bodily parts prepares the soldier for a certain course of action, and, like the sprinter, he is poorly disposed for other lines of action. Again we note that the attentive posture is primarily preparatory in nature, the soldier is in the most efficient "attitude" to respond to certain signals about to come. This is what the teachers have been calling upon students to do for centuries. We note that the attentive response is just that, a response, that it has no consummatory function of its own, that its sole purpose is that of facilitating other responses about to be made to other signals. It is therefore, a mediational response. Such mediational responses have to be learned in connection with specific commands and stimuli (as to sergeant's commands or teacher's entreaties) but they are also learned automatically by every individual in his growing-up period.

Through the process of repeated exposure to any sequence of events, we can expect the neural mechanisms involved to become closely integrated so that the externally observed sequence will be preceded and accompanied by a neural sequence. In the process of learning we can expect the neural sequence to become somewhat antedating in nature so that the neural events will be occurring slightly before the external events in the sequence. When the proper event occurs in the external world, the neural processes involved will be nicely timed to receive the new stimuli as they arrive. If we are picking up one object at a time out of a series and are counting, with the foreknowledge of the total number, then as we reach for each object in turn all the necessary finger and arm adjustments are ready to operate when the hand reaches the object. If you are picking doughnuts out of a bag which you were told contains a dozen, you can dip into the bag without looking and extract the doughnuts without difficulty; the slight cues from a fingertip contact are enough to institute the entire grasping pattern. As the number of doughnuts in the bag decreases, new anticipatory movements are instituted involving some small degree of search; the fingers are ready to encircle the object no matter what its disposition. Such antedating preparatory reactions reflect "attention" or "expectancy."

It should be appreciated that the attention or expectancy can be on a purely neural level and no motor phenomena need be involved although in most cases of attentive behavior we will be concerned with a succession of external events and will be making some kinds of motor responses if only on a low level of activation. When listening to a familiar piece of music, for example, we may not be too active in terms of muscles, yet the attention or expectancy is there. If the musicians play a wrong note, our nervous system is not ready for it and an "expectancy" is violated, leading to some modest degree of neural disorganization.

It is possible to anticipate or expect disaster, too, if disaster has been previously experienced in a given situation. If the small child always gets stuck at a certain point in his recitation, we can come to expect his getting stuck and our nervous systems will be prepared or set for the faulty performance; should the child be successful on this occasion, the nervous system will be "disappointed" even though the proud father is not.

Being set, or attentive, for a given stimulus prevents normal ongoing behavior to other stimuli, frequently bringing everything else to a halt.

We have already described the failure of cats to respond neurally to auditory stimuli when mice were being observed (p. 116). Prolonged anticipation or frequently reinitiated attention can be very exhausting. Listening to a halting speaker who just does not say the next and obvious word on time can be a distressing experience. When the stimuli do arrive on schedule, our efficiency is markedly increased. In simple reaction time experiments, the subject is told to get set and to respond as rapidly as possible to the onset of a light. His reaction time can be seriously modified by radical alterations in the time between the "ready" signal and the light. Too short a time catches him "off base" as does too long a "foreperiod."

Interest

Being interested in something basically amounts to having an attitude (a habit) with respect to the matter involved of such a nature that attentive sets can be readily aroused. Interest is essentially a long-term proposition and involves some probability of repeated experience with the particular stimuli. Thus, a philatelist has an interest in stamps. To say this does not imply, any more than having any other motive, that the philatelist is always and eternally interested in stamps. When sleeping, eating, camping, or working in his garden, the philatelist is displaying other interests; the arrival of a letter may immediately initiate a set (attention) to the stamp involved, but once this is taken care of the interest may also disappear until the next philatelic stimulation. If Susie is "only interested in boys," then Susie has a low threshold for attentive responses to stimuli associated with young males. Again we point out that such interests are learned as are all sets and interest patterns to appropriate stimuli. To say that someone is not interested in algebra or Spain or swimming, means that the person has not learned to be interested in such matters. He has no way of making preparatory responses if he has never made the consummatory responses involved. The obvious practical implication is, of course, that a person can become interested in anything if he can be brought to make such consummatory reponses to the stimuli involved. This is the basis for the slogan: "Interest comes from doing." This slogan has much merit as an explanation for lack of interest—you can hardly be interested in anything you have never done. How to bring a particular person to do something may be a problem especially where lack of skill or capacity prevents any highly attractive level of consummatory behavior.

Concentration

Students frequently complain about a "low power of concentration." What they usually fail to point out is that this low power is highly specialized with respect to some course or courses. They can concentrate with high power on athletic events, the opposite sex, automobiles, etc. What appears to be the explanation of "low power" of concentration is a lack of interest, that is, the lack of attentive sets to the "uninteresting" stimuli. Rather than concern ourselves with improving concentration capacity, we might better investigate the deterrents to participation in the activity and the resultant failure to develop appropriate sets.

A review

In the above discussion of interest and attention we find enough parallels with our earlier discussion of motivation to include the mediational activity involved in interest or attention within the general framework of motivation. A motivated person is interested, an interested person is motivated. With both words or labels we define a situation where an organism is ready to react to some special stimulus in a more or less special way (depending upon what responses have been associated with stimuli from mediational reactions). When the laboratory psychologist starves a rat, he is motivating the rat through the process of making the rat interested in food and nothing else. A rat that has not eaten for twenty-four hours has little interest in social life or sport. Depletion of nutrients in the blood stream has affected neural mechanisms that control eating behavior. The rat is set to eat. Since there is no food in the place where the rat is, the rat moves, because of stimulation from the neural feeding center and associated neural assemblies that have been active in prior feeding periods. Where it moves, and how, is largely up to the experimenter's devices. The point is that hunger drives or hunger motivation amount to a set, an interest, or an attitude relating to food taking behavior. Other chemical conditions such as occur with glandular secretions of sex hormones may make the animal interested in sex activity. Watching sex behavior alter as a function of such hormonic secretions reveals to some extent the degree to which behavior (and interests or motivation) depends upon physiological controllers of neural mechanisms. Some sets or motives depend to a considerable extent upon such physiological preparation. Others are strongly related to external stimulation. In the area of sex, particularly, we run into a paradoxical situation. The human male is much more subject to the development of sex interests or motivation from external stimulation (e.g., sight of nudes, photographs, sex stories) than is the female (Kinsey, *et al.,* 1948). Advertisers of body-building courses sometimes show photographs of well-muscled males attracting admiring glances on the beach from women bathers. There is apparently considerable question about the sex-stimulus-value of muscles. Female sex interests are a complicated pattern of physiological and cultural influences and not as readily subject to arousal as are those of the male. In some animals, the sexual motivation of both males and females is strictly regulated by physiological changes, and neither sex has any use for the other except at certain seasons of the year.

Because some interests, sets, attitudes, expectancies, or "motives" have some degree of dependence upon glandular and other physiological operations, we cannot fully equate any particular motive with any other. In some cases external stimulation alone is enough; in others physiological change alone is enough. In other cases there must be a period of learning where physiological factors play a role in the early stages and then are no longer necessary. In still others, some kind of physiological state must be also present if external stimulation is to have any functional significance. We see that motivation is a complex subject matter and not one that is readily reducible to formula. The best we can do is to emphasize the central importance of set or preparatory responses as an apparently common factor in all forms of motivation that have been considered.

UNCONSCIOUS MOTIVATION

In the previous chapter we identified consciousness with the presence of mediational processes which we could communicate to others with some degree of satisfaction. Such communication would normally take place via words or gestures but could include other responses of a discriminative sort. We were careful to indicate also that not all mediational processes of the vast number that can be presumed to occur are thus singled out for communication, and consequently might be legitimately called "unconscious." There is probably no question about the proposition that much if not a major part of our behavior is "unconscious" in a variety of senses, including the sense of our not being able to describe it or not remembering much of what occurred in our presence (such as how often we brushed away at a fly or even that we brushed at all).

We now come to the question of whether motivational activities (defined now as sets of a preparatory nature) and, perhaps, some of the consummatory behavior that such sets might lead to, can be unconscious. It is widely believed by many practicing psychologists (and by all psychoanalysts) as well as by many educated laymen that much of the most important aspects of our lives is dominated by unconscious motivation; that we often behave as we do because of unconscious wishes, desires, urges, or whatever, and that we do not recognize these motives or remember having had them later. Before we try to answer the question as to whether such motives can exist, we might consider the nature of the evidence for the belief. The evidence is basically of a clinical nature in that a patient fails to or is unable to account for some of his behavior but after a process of therapy, which might be quite extensive, the patient finally admits or reveals, or the therapist states, that the motivation for some behavior must have been unconscious. Frequently patients deny interpretations made by their therapists that they have harbored some socially unacceptable motive. This is put down to a defensive attempt on the part of the patient. Some alleged evidence is claimed to result from the analysis of dreams (see Hall, 1953) which are regarded as a demonstration, in Freudian psychoanalysis, of unconscious wishes masquerading in disguised (manifest) form while their true (latent) meaning reveals the actual unconscious wish. Since such evidence is the result of interpretation alone, it is far from acceptable in a scientific sense. It is admittedly difficult to experiment with people on matters of personal motivation especially in the realm of personal troubles, and interpretative evidence may be the only kind we can get. If this proves to be the case, the argument for unconscious motivation will remain unproved.

There are other forms of attack on the problem of unconscious influences on behavior which demonstrate with some degree of satisfaction that subjects would react in specific and predictable fashion even if they were unable to describe the nature of the influence. It is significant to note that such studies (Rees and Israel, 1935; Siipola, 1935) are based on the formation of sets to respond in a given way without instructing the subjects specifically about the way in which the response is to be generated. Thus subjects might be instructed to solve a series of anagrams. The anagrams might all be arranged in a specific fashion as "first letter in the middle, last letter in the fourth position," etc. Later on, subjects would be asked to solve more anagrams where other solutions would be possible. Some subjects would proceed to solve the new anagrams in the way in which they had become accustomed and never notice what they were doing and be quite unable to state that they had noticed any special arrangement. Similarly subjects can be misled about the factors to be employed in a problem (Luchins, 1946) and fail to notice what would have been obvious without the misleading instructions or exercises. There is no reason to doubt that subjects can act under the influence of a set they are unable to identify or even recognize as having existed. It should be noted, however, that the subjects were engaged in a task to which the set was related and that they were not being led into other kinds of activities by a simultaneously functioning but different set. You can easily demonstrate the influence of a set on behavior. Write an I and X on a piece of paper and show it to someone, asking what it is. The ordinary answer will be a 9 or a Roman 9 (IX). Now ask the person to *add* one symbol and "change it to six." Many educated and intelligent people cannot solve this simple little problem. They are caught in the grip of a Roman "set" and cannot free themselves. While trying to solve the problem they are *unconscious* of why they cannot solve it. Later on, of course, they will tell you "I kept thinking of. . . ."

We can agree that unconscious sets or motives can operate to determine behavior. There is probably an endless series of such sets going on in daily life. The question that has not been answered, however, is whether two different sets, one conscious and one unconscious, involving the same general stimulus situation can operate at the same time. Thus, when a person is being friendly and polite and saying sweet things to someone can he at the same time be under the influence of a set which involves hating the person, wishing him ill, and intruding itself into the conversation as slips of tongue, etc.? We must be careful to note that the polite and friendly remarks are supposed to represent a conscious liking or friendliness for the person. It is certainly possible to be reasonably polite to someone you do not like and know you do not like. How well your efforts succeed may be related to your skill at dissembling, but if you know you do not like the person, then we are not dealing with unconscious motives in the usual "clinical" sense.

It is difficult but not impossible to carry on two kinds of motor activity if one of these is habitual or can be made automatic such as patting your head while rubbing the belly. It is less easy, in fact, quite impossible, to listen to two conversations at one time or handle two kinds of verbal material like reading one thing and listening to another. Despite our best efforts we find ourselves alternating in "attention." To the extent that unconscious motives involve verbalisms of any kind, it is unlikely that they could flourish along with any conscious verbal activity. The problem to be answered really is: can two sets for mutually opposite types of reactions function at the same time? The answer on a conscious level seems to be quite definitely not. There is no reason to assume that an unconscious motive could function any better than a conscious one in such a case. We cannot presume that unconscious motives would have any degree of independence from stimulation or that they could function in the absence of stimulation so that both conscious and unconscious motives would always have to be aroused at the same time.

As far as unconscious motivation is concerned then, we can readily agree that much of our motivated activity is "unconscious." Unconscious motives, however, are not qualitatively different from conscious ones. There is no reason to suspect them of being nefarious in nature, primitive, ugly, evil, unethical, and so on. Most of us have plenty of conscious motives that could easily earn these epithets. To say that we do something and cannot give a clear rational account of why we did it is not the same as saying there was an ulterior motive. Ignorance is an adequate excuse in such cases. When someone informs us that we chose a certain woman for a wife because she unconsciously reminds us of our mothers or maiden aunts or kindergarten teachers he may be close to some mark. We cannot always clearly explain why we like some people and not others. The expression "She's not my type" may have some sound psychological basis even though the speaker cannot define his type. Yet if we find him frequently associating the females of a particular variety, e.g., short and fat, we might suspect some common determinant or set is aroused by such individuals. If the person does not recognize this to be a fact, assuming it is one, then he has been motivated unconsciously. Love at first sight presumably rests on some such foundation.

We can conclude our account of unconscious motivation by noting our emphasis on the fact that there is nothing qualitatively different between such sets and the more conscious ones. We are never completely conscious of any sets, for that matter, and would be hard put to describe even the simplest motor sets in anything like adequate terms. To make anything more out of unconscious sets than we do out of "conscious" ones, however, we find no justification. It is questionable that any "evil" urges we might have had in childhood reside in "the unconscious." Again we have to be careful not to exclude the possibilities that some attitudes formed when we were very young may have shaped the course of our development or that they can become active at later stages under suitable stimulation without at the same time becoming conscious. We should be particularly careful to note that our relations with people, especially families and loved ones, can become extremely complex and involve us in situations in which both positive and negative attitudes can be developed about the same persons. Analysts speak of this as "ambivalence." Few people grow up without some kinds of difficulties with their parents which might occasion some fear, distrust, even hate, of people who otherwise merit, earn, or demand our love or affection. It is unwise in our culture to announce that you hate your mother or father (yet what child has not said this to the parent at least once?). Such experiences may have important repercussions in later life and cause some discomfort, especially when one tries to avoid discussing such events or attitudes, because of cultural restrictions. Such ambivalence, however, may be all too conscious, and there is no point to assigning all negative "memories" and impulses to some "unconscious mind." The conscious mind can give us trouble enough. In considering the nature of unconscious motivation we must be careful about avoiding dynamisms of any sort other than that provided by stimulation from sets or motor outlets of neural mechanisms involved in the mediating responses involved. Certainly there is no license for cloaking the discussion of unconscious motivation in mythological language, in making entities of processes or developing *ad hoc* explanations to account for weaknesses in the original description.

TECHNIQUES OF CONTROLLING MOTIVATION

In every culture techniques are developed by which behavior is controlled to various degrees of success. Parents attempt to control children and children try to control parents. In some cultures groups develop which try to control other groups either in terms of political or economic life. No purely anarchical society has ever flourished or lasted long. Whether we, as individuals, approve or disapprove, techniques are developed, laws, rules, regulations, moral principles, and customs and mores come into being which regulate to some extent the behavior of the members of a group. The individual is "socialized" by being forced to conform to an acceptable degree, at least superficially. In a general sense, we might refer to the net efforts of the society in controlling its members as an "educational" process. Within the general social framework the activities of any one individual or group may interfere with the activities of other individuals or groups. This clash or conflict of interests or motives underlying the activities results in varying patterns being developed to eliminate the conflict either by physical annihilation of the opposition, or some forms of compromise. In some cases a form of action is developed which is designed to get some people to comply, "co-operate" with, or surrender their own interests to those of others. Such attempts to manipulate motives of others occupy a great deal of the time of large segments of the population (both of the manipulator and of the manipulatee). Much of our social life consists of "brain washing" or being "brain washed," or resisting such efforts.

Brain washing

The term "brain washing" has only recently come into common usage as a result of the practices of Chinese Communists who tried to "convert" American prisoners of war to their own points of view about politics, economics, and society. The practice of brain washing itself, however, is as old as history. Only the techniques differ. The ends have always been the same. The brain washer tries to influence those whose motives and interests do not correspond with his, to make them conform, give up their own views, and subscribe to those of the washer for the benefit of the washer. It should be recognized that the brain washer may be fully convinced of the virtues of his own views and that he might regard the process of brain washing as for the washee's own good and for the ultimate good of society. It is, of course, pointless to condemn brain washers for their activity even if we happen to disapprove of their particular type of goals—the washer's own brains have been washed and he is in no position to do otherwise. Some methods of brain washing are more gentle than others and if the goals involved correspond to our own social practices and beliefs, we are likely to call the process education, or "missionary" work. Communists too send "missionaries" into the field and non-Communists or anti-Communists might be revolted by their use of the word because of its religious connotations. But missionaries are only emissaries. If they represent our own point of view, they are "patriots." If they are the enemy, they are "spies," "fifth columnists," etc.

How do we get others to change their attitudes or motives to conform with our own or lend themselves to our goals? There is a general air of mystery about this problem that has been fostered by newspapers and other writers of fiction as well as by people directly concerned in large-scale efforts to manipulate the public—advertisers, publicity or press agents, and by the gullible public itself, which, apparently, likes to think of magical operations by which the mind can be controlled. Our slow historical development has been beset by lies, superstition, hasty generalizations, and general misinformation for so long that we have grown accustomed to accepting and enjoying authoritative pronunciamentos which simplify complex problems. While most of us no longer believe in witches and ghosts and goblins, many of us are still willing to accept equally magical or mystical explanations for much that we do not understand. We anxiously await the new miracle drug in just about that sense and fail to recognize the amount of painstaking research that must precede the miracle if it is to come about. The discoverer of the drug becomes the idol of the masses even if he honestly disclaims most of the credit and tries to emphasize the many efforts of his predecessors who made his particular contribution possible. Because there is so much to be learned, so much to know that no one is able to independently investigate, we learn to believe what we are told. Much of what we are told is believable and correct enough. The rest we believe because we are told.

What factors underlie the acceptability of statements we hear or read? How are people manipulated into believing what they are told? We have already laid the groundwork for an answer to this question in our discussions of learning. People learn to accept and repeat statements in the same way that they learn to make other responses, through what we have described as a process of association and reinforcement (in terms of elimination of the stimulus and the cessation of the neural patterns aroused by stimuli). Our present interest, however, is not with the fundamental learning process itself but with more or less deliberate attempts to circumvent the learning process or to increase the efficiency of learning by the use of special techniques. Perhaps the use of the term "learning" in this connection is not fully legitimate as the new behavior involved, although representing or due to a changed attitude or set, may not follow the typical course of learning and may lack some of the features of a normally learned activity. It may, for example, be only a temporary modification of behavior that is likely to extinguish quickly;

discriminative features might be lacking so that erroneous responses are made (erroneous from the viewpoint of the manipulator) or they may be heavily dependent upon a pattern of stimulation that cannot always be presented when the manipulator wishes to evoke the response. To the extent that sound learning practices and principles are violated, to that extent we can expect failure of retention, improper kinds of transfer, confusion, and failure when previously learned responses are elicited in a situation where the manipulator hopes to see the newly learned behavior functioning.

In contrast with what we might legitimately call learning or education, the manipulators of public attitudes or motives try what amounts to a crash technique consisting of the use of what might be called psychological tricks. Their efforts can be described, as above, in terms of "brain washing," or more gently as "advertising," or somewhat less gently as "propaganda" or "hypnosis." The modern student of psychology must be able to appreciate these terms and evaluate the techniques involved for their relative efficacy. Because of their prominent role in any culture they must be understood if the culture itself is to be understood.

Hypnosis

We can start with what appears to be the most bizarre technique for controlling motivation and behavior and perhaps the most extreme form of "brain washing" that has been developed by man. The very subject of hypnosis has a fascination for students because of their own growth and development in a culture that fosters mystical and romantic attitudes. Much of what the average student believes about hypnosis is arrant nonsense because most of our information comes from Sunday supplements and popular magazines and movies. The stage hypnotist is basically an entertainer who puts on a good show and very little will be learned from observing such performances. A good deal of nonsensical talk about hypnotic eyes, control of the will, and "now you are in my power" is a feature of such entertainments. The subjects "go under" and make love to brooms and engage in other farcical activities for the delight of the customers but how much hypnosis was present, if any, will not be determined in theaters.

Hypnosis is a genuine enough phenomenon with many interesting accompanying effects, some of which are quite startling in terms of our ordinary expectancies. It is quite possible, and has been done many times, for mothers to give birth under hypnosis without the aid of any drugs and with no great amount of pain. It is also possible to have dental work done on patients under hypnosis, work that would ordinarily require some kind of anesthetic drugs. Surgical work too, such as amputations and abdominal operations, has been performed under hypnosis with some success. We should immediately note that all of these kinds of activities have also been done without hypnosis (and without the benefit of drugs) with varying degrees of success. Women had been giving birth to infants for centuries before drugs to ease pain were discovered. Many of these births were relatively quiet and "bearable" events, with no outcries, and possibly not too much pain. There have been instances where surgeons removed their own appendix commenting all the time about their progress. Even amputations have been done without drugs when the situation was crucial and in some instances the event occurred without screams or other manifestations of pain. Farmers who get their hands or arms tangled up in machinery have been known to cut themselves loose and animals caught in traps have been known to bite off their own legs in the struggle for freedom.

We should also note that some subjects who plan to undergo childbirth or dental surgery under hypnosis fail to behave properly and require drugs, perhaps in smaller dosages; the practical obstetrician may be willing to have his patients hypnotized but he does not rely on a smooth performance and keeps his drugs at hand. Since he knows that childbirth is a normal enough process and that neither drugs nor hypnosis is necessary for a successful delivery, he can afford to let patients indulge themselves to some extent if he happens to be interested in hypnotic effects. Similarly, the dentist is familiar with how much the fears of his patients interfere with his work and any measure which reduced the degree of terror is highly appreciated. If time factors are not of great importance, and if the nature of the problem is not going to be interfered with by the patient's not being drugged, hypnosis can be quite useful.

Before we describe in more positive terms what hypnosis is, we need to point out some things which it is not. It is not a form of sleep, for instance, even though a person can readily pass into a sleep state while hypnotized. Brain-wave patterns of hypnotized subjects are not similar to those of sleep. The subject may or may not be relaxed—that depends on what you ask the subject to do. The subject cannot do under hypnosis anything that he cannot do otherwise unless his normal ability is obscured or limited by doubts, uncertainties, or other forms of inhibition. The subject cannot, for example, perform miraculous athletic feats like high-jumping nine feet (the world record is a little over seven). It is generally argued, although almost impossible to prove, that a subject will not commit crimes or engage in other kinds of immoral or unethical behavior under hypnosis. The usual weasel argument applied here is that you will not do under hypnosis what you would not do otherwise.

Only a fool would hand a hypnotized subject a loaded pistol and ask him to fire it at someone; in such demonstrations the pistol is not loaded and the subject does fire, but it can always be argued that if it were loaded, the subject would not have fired. If a girl under hypnosis discards some of her clothing, she is a hussy anyway, runs the argument, and nothing serious is proved. Weitzenhoffer (1953) argues that hypnotized subjects might be induced to perform antisocial acts, but only if the subject's perceptions are first changed. He suggests, for example, that a hypnotized soldier might attack an officer if he were first convinced that the officer was an enemy. A "perceptual alteration" is the first requirement; the subject must see the act as not really antisocial. It should also be pointed out along these negative lines that there is no evidence that anyone can raise a blister on his body under hypnosis. Stage demonstrators sometimes make use of a "pencil" which they take from their pockets and touch the subject telling him it is hot; a red spot or blister then forms. The point is that the pencil is hot. It is heated by a battery in the performer's pocket and the blister is a very proper resultant of the application of heat.

We can now consider the phenomenon more positively. It is generally agreed that hypnosis is a heightened state of suggestibility brought about by a temporary suspension of critical judgment. We can all readily adopt some degree of such a state as we do when we accept someone's proposition that "for the sake of argument, let us assume." If we do assume, then we have removed an obstacle, we have eliminated an area of criticism, and we are bound to accept certain conclusions. Commonly enough we then say, "Yes, but I don't agree with your original assumption" which only goes to indicate that a lot of time has been wasted. If we do not hark back to the original assumption, however, we are now committed to accept certain propositions.

Normally we are all susceptible to suggestions if the suggestions do not immediately indicate future discomfort or difficulties and if the suggestions do not embarrass us by revealing our ignorance (assuming we do not wish to be exposed). Suggestions are accepted more readily when we are ourselves in doubt as to a course of action and someone who is giving the suggestions is presumed to be in a position to know. Even a geographer will take suggestions from a local farmer about how to get to the next town if the roads are unmarked, though he might resent suggestions about how to draw a map. The acceptance or rejection of suggestions depends then, on doubt, uncertainty, and a reasonable degree of confidence in the suggestor. This is the condition that the hypnotist uses to develop a state of trance or hypnosis. His first requirement is to command confidence or respect (prestige). This he can easily do in our culture by calling himself "Doctor" and announcing his long history of successes; or, if he is a college sophomore, by indicating that he has had a successful history, with an appeal to good sportsmanship. The subject on his part must be ready to accept suggestions or at least not fight them actively. To facilitate such a condition, the hypnotist advises relaxation, looseness of limbs, sleepiness (not that sleepiness has anything to do with the matter—it is only one of the conditions under which people are used to thinking about relaxation—a lot of sleep behavior is far from relaxed). The hypnotist now introduces a series of suggestions related to motor behavior which he can watch and thereby test progress. He suggests that the eyes are closing—if the subject hearing these words thinks about closing eyes there is a strong likelihood that some tentative closure will begin and if he co-operates fully he may begin to close his eyes more or less tightly. Similarly, if it is remarked that the arms are limp and relaxed, the subject who has ever gone through response patterns that result in limp and relaxed arms may follow through in the sense we described in talking about ideo-motor action in an earlier chapter. Having complied with a number of such suggestions, the subject is inclined to comply with or at least not resist actively other suggestions until he has complied so frequently that he would be embarrassed not to comply further. In this state of co-operative compliance, the subject is willing to entertain suggestions of a nonmotor sort as well as suggestions about direct muscular actions. He will accept with varying degrees of conviction the suggestions that people who are obviously present are not there, or that he cannot see, hear, feel, etc. To a large extent the hypnotized subject is portraying a role, he is acting—not necessarily in a "phony" sense—he is playing his part as described to the best of his ability. With some people this ability is rather well developed in the sense that when they are sufficiently imbued with some set, other stimuli get in with difficulty, if at all.

Demonstrations of hypnosis have pointed up very strikingly how many of our reactions to painful stimuli are due to "imagination" or expectancy, or set. Presumably much of what we describe as painful is heavily dosed with what we have described as "anxiety" or learned fear. The coward dies his thousand deaths and the dental patient cringes with every movement of the dentist, tensing himself in dreadful anticipation. When these tensions are removed through suggestions about relaxation, perhaps much of the pain involved also disappears or is otherwise reacted to. Instead of crying out, the subject may become interested in the pain. We have all had the experience of teasing slivers out of our fingers. It is much less painful when we do it ourselves than when someone else does it. We can relax to our own ministrations but not to the unexpected movements of others. Being absorbed with something permits us to suffer pain without even noticing the damage done as football players find when they start counting bruises while showering after the game. William James (1890) long ago pointed out, in discussing emotion, how bodily attitudes predispose us to react emotionally to stimuli. When we sit slumped, chin on breast, hangdog expression on our faces, arms limp, we invite sympathy for our despair. Try to feel despair if you puff out your chest, jut out your chin, flex your biceps in a strong-man pose. It is quite impossible argued James. Similarly in hypnosis, a bodily set can be established which facilitates one kind of reaction and inhibits another. Hypnosis is an extreme form of motivation or set. The hypnotized subject will do whatever he is prepared to do by the suggestions that are provided before the directions for any specific response are introduced.

When we recognize the importance and reality of hypnosis as a state of extreme suggestibility (fixedness of set), we do not at the same time have to take for the truth whatever it occurs to someone to say about hypnosis. When for various reasons (presumably commercial) hypnotists announce that they have observed reincarnations of long dead personalities or communication with the dear departed, we should recognize them as frauds and treat them as such. Legitimately employed, hypnosis can be a help in some professional areas; illegitimately employed, it can become a viciously harmful affair, preying upon gullible innocence that still exists far too widely in our culture. It should hardly be necessary to warn students that practicing hypnosis is a serious affair and should be left to professionals who are thoroughly trained. It is definitely not a party-stunt matter and anyone who treats it as such has not yet become quite adult.

We have not covered many of the phenomena associated with hypnosis and interested students can pursue the subject further in appropriate texts. We have spent as much time as we have because the basic procedures of hypnosis are involved in the other kinds of attempts at manipulating populations to which we can now turn.

Advertising and propaganda

The term propaganda has acquired unsavory connotations in our culture although in some countries it means only what its literal origins imply, something like "spreading the word." In some cultures it is synonymous with education and quite innocent of nefarious implications. However it is viewed, propaganda is an attempt to influence one line of action or belief in an area where competitive beliefs or lines of action are possible (Doob, 1935). In general, the propagandist strives to develop favorable attitudes for one doctrine, agent, or product, and at the same time, though not necessarily, prevent other viewpoints from getting a hearing. On a more or less innocent level we can illustrate the general orientation by the observation that broadcasting networks, by rule or otherwise, try to bring their own networks to public attention while preventing any mention of other networks. They do not go so far as pretending other networks do not exist—they do say "on another network," but never mention the name. Similarly politicians never mention the name of an opposing candidate—to whom they sneeringly refer as "my worthy opponent" as if mentioning the name were a major crime. Advertisers characteristically avoid any mention of their "inferior competitors" while they "plug" their own wares. Advertising and propaganda amount to the same thing: a one-sided effort at establishing attitudes suited to the advertiser's or propagandist's purposes.

The techniques of advertisers have changed from a rather innocent practice of announcing their wares and listing their virtues as was the practice in pre-World War I days to the much more calculated and sophisticated attempts to manipulate the public that we witness currently. Great numbers of people have been drawn into the "advertising game" and great fortunes are spent in the effort to capture the public's fancy. Experts and consultants are hired from psychological and psychoanalytical fields to prepare campaigns and programs designed to make the public favor this whiskey, that soap, that automobile, or that cigarette. Not only do advertisers try to sell products like meat and cheese, but also politicians, other "personalities" as well as ideologies or doctrines.

Just before World War II, advertisers began to develop principles and practices that appeared to work in controlling "consumer" behavior. They made use of devices calculated to appeal to presumed traditional attitudes. One such attitude alleged to be characteristic of our culture is that of being suspicious of high-brows, intellectuals, "long-hairs," "egg-heads." "Just plain folks" is supposed to be the national ideal and advertisers would slant their copy, their pictures and propaganda generally to give the impression that their product was truly American—it was just plain folks. The famous photograph of Adlai Stevenson showing his shoe to be in need of repair is a classic illustration of this approach, not that this particular incident was deliberately planned. Mr. Stevenson's campaign managers were in despair because he was unable to create the impression that he was just one of the boys or "plain folks."

Another typical device is to announce confidently that everybody is doing it. This is the so-called band-wagon approach. Give the impression that anyone who is not with you is an outsider, a member of a lunatic fringe, or miserable minority. "Puffos" are the leading cigarettes. Everybody smokes Puffos. The band-wagon approach is fostered by bringing together large crowds, even if they have to be imported from great distances to fill halls, by announcing the results of polls favoring a particular product or personality, and by lavish displays of the product, numerous personal appearances of candidates and successions of supporters. If rival candidates or products are also being given the band-wagon treatment, there may be no net gain, but the general principle is presumed to work on the assumption that in our culture, everyone wants to be on the winning side even if he has no use for it in other respects.

A third device is the use of the endorsement—the appeal to authority—or the use of prestige figures who might be presumed to serve as models for the members of the culture. In our culture movie stars and athletes appear to be the idols of the public and such personalities are employed to endorse politicians, soap, and gasoline. The fact that a particular motion picture beauty may know nothing about the subject is quite irrelevant. If she can be gotten to sing a popular song at a political convention it is assumed that some votes will be attained that way which would otherwise be lost. When a ballplayer shaves with a particular razor, it is the hope of the advertiser that young lads who are just beginning to worry about the fuzz on their faces may be inclined to ask for that razor in a year or two because of the presumed tendency in our culture to "identify" ourselves fancifully with athletic "greats."

There are other common devices which are frequently employed—the use of "glittering generalities" where high-sounding principles are announced in sonorous tones but which like a lot of other sound and fury signify nothing—commit no one to anything. President Roosevelt, for example, promised "the mothers of America" that he would "not send your boys into foreign wars"—"unless we are attacked." He could not, of course, say anything more or less, yet in making this promise, he promised nothing that the opposition did not promise. The opposition at that time was also for not sending our boys into foreign wars but obviously could not say that they would not do so if we were attacked.

It should have been observed from the above that none of the advertisers' techniques have anything to do with the subject or product. They are all side-approaches and quite irrelevant to the issues or qualities of the objects. Advertisers continue to use these techniques, but since

World War II, new procedures have been incorporated into advertising based on what has come to be known as "motivation research" or MR. Psychoanalysts are consulted to discover the motives that guide our behavior—the really and truly motives—motives that only analysts know about through their researches in "depth psychology." From such "research" it is revealed that when men are buying cars they are not really buying cars, they are buying prestige, or fancifully satisfying repressed sex urges. In *The Hidden Persuaders,* Vance Packard (1957) has described some of the alleged hidden motives that are being exploited by advertisers. To get at the hidden motives various indirect techniques must be used. To sell a cigarette that has acquired some feminine associations, the advertiser recommends that only roughly dressed, athletic men, hunting boars with bow and arrow, be shown smoking the cigarette. The man must have a tattoo on his hand, clearly evident to establish still further his masculinity. Then the purchase of the cigarette will really represent a purchase of a modicum of masculinity. Much of what advertisers are alleged to believe in this respect is arrant nonsense and should lead, not as Packard believes, to some abuse of the public, but to the downfall of the advertisers if they continue to use the indirect approach. Since there are no easy ways to verify the value of any given campaign especially when everybody else is in the act using the same techniques, there is little likelihood that the techniques will be given up until someone comes along with a new "gimmick."

Such a new "gimmick" is already being promoted in connection with what is known as the "hidden sell" or subceptive advertising. It is alleged that messages can be flashed on movie or television screens that will not be consciously seen but will be received unconsciously. The subjects watching the screen for their favorite cowboy will be bombarded with a series of unseen flashes saying "drink Wino Beer" or some such message. This is presumed then to affect some kind of unconscious motivation to respond to the advertised product, presumably later, since not even the advertiser believes that the customer will give up watching his cowboy. It will be appreciated that the "hidden sell" technique assumes that something that cannot be perceived consciously will be perceived unconsciously. This appears to be quite unjustified as countless experiments have been done with such flash techniques where it is quite clear that no intelligible message can be picked up at exposure speeds of less than 0.02 seconds, even though something is seen. If nothing at all is seen, it is dubious that any effect of any kind could be produced. Even if the message got through, there is still the assumption that an appeal to an unconscious reaction was more potent than the appeal to the conscious reaction.

For this there is no rational ground. The experimental evidence in favor of "the hidden sell" is just not available for public inspection (on the dubious grounds that "patent rights" are involved). While Congress and some public spirited magazine editors have been horrified by the possibilities of the "hidden sell," there appear to be no genuine grounds for alarm. The only people who will be "sold" by the hidden sell are the purchasers of the technique, unless more substantial proof is offered than is now available, that this procedure does in fact have an effect on behavior.

The advertising techniques we have mentioned have much in common with hypnosis. In both instances there is a strong dependence upon repetition of a message in tones of strong conviction, no reservations. The hypnotist announces repeatedly and confidently "you are falling fast asleep." The advertiser announces: "Greaso is the best." They do this repeatedly hoping that the suggestion will be acted upon. In both advertising and hypnosis there is the same determined effort to eliminate critical judgment—no counterarguments are permitted. The advertiser does not even talk about his product nowadays so that there cannot be any argument. The existence of other products or other concepts is not recognized. From the advertiser's point of view there *is* only one cigarette or washing machine. For the hypnotist there is no possibility of any counternotion to his suggestion. Only one side is presented, and that endlessly. The other side does not exist, unless it is evil or un-American.

When the techniques described above are applied in extreme form, we have the basic operations for "brain washing." Communist brain washers have the advantage of a captive audience—something advertisers can only hope for. In a literal sense they have complete physical control over a prisoner and can restrict his contact with the outside world to a zero quantity. Thus no possible opposing view can be presented unless the prisoner's own is strongly enough developed to be present. The brain washer starts out by isolating his prisoner for some time and then gradually begins to present his own point of view. The isolation process has been shown to result in many disturbing changes in an individual —he begins to hallucinate, he becomes uncritical, his intellectual capacity deteriorates, he is unable to think effectively (Heron, Doane, and Scott, 1954)—the brain washer takes advantage of these changes and presents arguments that are carefully prepared to be more or less innocuous, even reasonable. The subject is reinforced for co-operating with, for not resisting, the brain washer who as the bearer of reinforcements (candy, cigarettes, better food) becomes himself a secondary reinforcer, as the source of whatever good does arrive. The subject, like the subject of the hypnotist, becomes a victim of his training.

The remarks above apply just as pointedly to any educational system that uses the techniques of advertising and propaganda. If the educational system presents only one point of view, repeats this endlessly, never countenances critical reactions, in fact, reinforces students for mouthing what is presented rather than for asking searching or critical questions, then the system is only a form of brain washing. To some degree all societies engage in such practices. They are concerned with their own survival and with loyalties of their citizens whether such loyalties are logical or not. Every culture tries to present a one-sided picture in which it is pictured as great and good, and all other cultures are inferior or evil. American students would be surprised at some English history books, or even Canadian history books, in their treatment of American problems, the American Revolution, for instance. A German history of the World Wars would certainly be quite a contrast in the presentation of the "historical facts" and a Russian treatment of American history would be a real hair-raiser. One of the great difficulties in achieving anything that might correspond to an objective education is that the educators themselves have been thoroughly brain washed and can only give one point of view with any conviction. Even when they try to present "both sides" they are unable to do so adequately, and if there are more than "two sides," the educational process becomes a very weak effort at objectivity. While the picture drawn above may appear somewhat chastening if not distressing, the best we can do is carry on the effort at understanding how we have been brain washed so that we can make a little progress some day "toward an objective ethics."

CHAPTER 12

Affective Processes—Emotional Aspects of Behavior

Emotion · Classification of emotions · Emotion and meaning · The genetic-learning analysis of emotion · Conditioning and emotion · Indirect effects of learning on emotion · Functional theories of emotion · The James-Lange theory · The emergency theory · Functional significance of emotion · Psychosomatic disorders · The behavioral approach to the study of emotion · Directional and intensity factors in emotion · Emotional control · The control of fear · The control of anger · Frustration tolerance · Emotional aspects of cognitive behavior · Prejudice · Stereotypes

EMOTION

So far we have examined, at least in a cursory fashion, the cognitive and conative aspects of behavior. We found that the separation of these aspects was completely artificial and that neither could occur without the other. We have a third aspect left to worry over, the field of affective behavior—emotion, feelings, and sentiment. In our ordinary practices we tend to isolate such affective processes as independent operations. We name or label certain states and reify them into agencies which are endowed with motivational properties; thus we speak of hate or love or anger or jealousy as if these were agencies that existed within us and occasionally took over the business of determining our behavior or at least directing it for a time, while other behavioral processes are temporarily forgotten or somehow divorced from the activities at hand.

It should by now have become clear to the student that behavior cannot be explained quite so simply. We cannot dichotomize behavior into emotional and nonemotional. There is no time in our lives when we are free of emotional influences. There is no real zero point on a continuum from some sort of emotional vacuum to some high point, nor is there any neutral point at which various kinds of "emotions" cancel out each other. There are, of course, periods of *relative* quiet, and periods of relative excitement, but they are relative and not absolute. Even in sleep we can experience great excitement, terror dreams, sex dreams, and various bizarre conditions. We are probably misled by incidents of high levels of activity such as terror states, temper tantrums, or dramatic alterations in behavior such as crying, fainting, or screaming. One of our great difficulties in the assessment of emotional factors is that we have never learned to measure such factors with any degree of reliability or validity and we have become so confused in this area by language operations that quite commonly we use expressions that in no way correspond to any reality. In no other area of psychology do we have such an excessive vocabulary of undefined words which are frequently used in such a variety of circumstances as to make the problem almost impossible to attack.

Consider, for example, the following expressions: I love apple pie. I just *love* Christmas. I love you, I really do. I love to dance. I love the mountains. I love America. I love peanuts. Is it conceivable that the word "love" refers to the same affair in these usages? Suppose now that we introduce some modifications: I'm fond of you but I don't love you. I like Beethoven more than Berlioz. I respect you. I cherish these old things of mother's, and so on and on. With any other emotional terms we find similar proliferations of synonyms, nuances, "shades of meaning," etc. We are in no position to measure such shades of meaning; in fact, we are unable to measure the alleged entities which are supposed to have the shades.

No one has yet catalogued all the terms in the English language which have emotional connotations; yet there must be thousands of them. The mere cataloguing would be a task in itself, and by some artificial criteria some classification system might reduce the mass to a workable number. Some psychologists have attacked the problem from the other end and have assumed a classification to begin with, assuming that the shades of meaning might eventually be resolved into measurable terms. Since much of the little we know about emotional behavior has come from such attempts at classification we had best start with these.

Classifications of emotions

In the early days of experimental psychology, Wundt proposed his tripartite structure of the mind which we mentioned briefly in an early chapter. It will be recalled that besides sensations and images, the mind was supposed to include an additional kind of process—feelings. In his introspective analysis Wundt decided that feelings had properties or characteristics that could be analyzed along three continua: feelings could range from unpleasant to pleasant (with a presumed neutral), from excitement to calm, and from tension to relaxation. Presumably, again, extreme positions on these scales would represent something akin to emotions and some states like fear or anger might be unpleasant, excited, and tense in varying degrees. Love might be pleasant and relaxed, and perhaps somewhat excited, and so on. It was Wundt's hope that some scales might be developed by which such feeling states could be

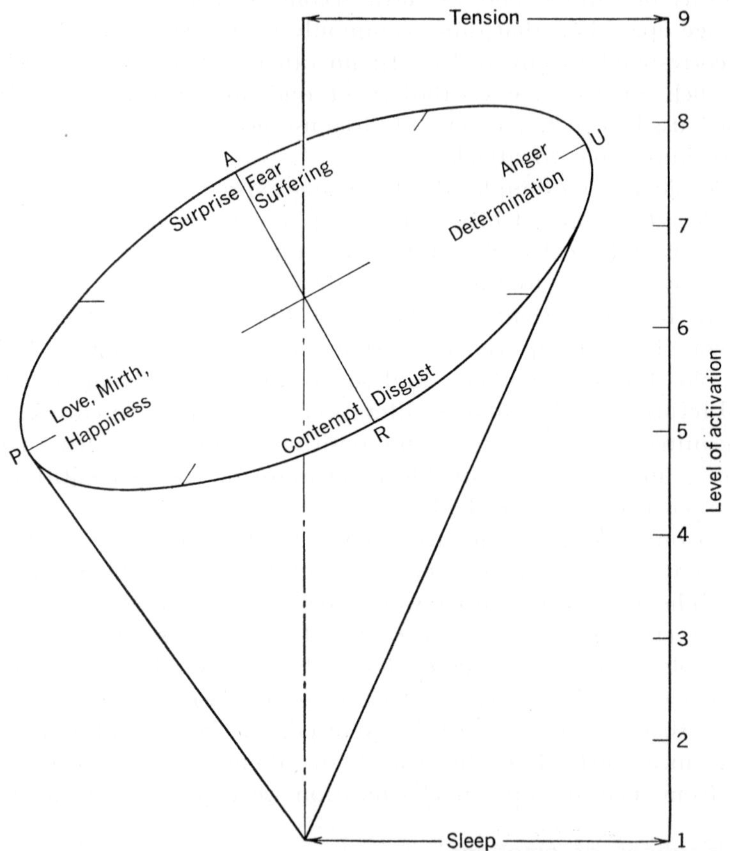

Figure 13 The three-dimensional theory of emotion suggested by Schlosberg. He found that a 6-point scale developed by Woodworth for judging facial expressions would result in a continuous circle when applied to a series of posed photographs. He then found that two axes, a pleasant-unpleasant axis and an attention-rejection axis, could be used in judging the pictures. With this two-dimensional surface, pictures could be located more reliably. A third dimension, level of activation, with a 9-point scale was then added. (After Schlosberg, 1955.)

distinguished one from another, but this hope never materialized and in the general disfavor which terminated interest in introspection, the Wundtian feeling-scales were forgotten.

Following the Wundtian decline, other approaches developed in the study of emotion and we will come to these shortly. Before we do, however, it is necessary to consider a recent approach that harks back to the Wundtian attempt. Schlosberg (1955) has presented another tripartite schema for the analysis and potential measurement of emotional states. He did this on the basis of the judgments of facial expressions, using photographs where the models tried to depict various alleged emotional experiences. After trying various schemes, Schlosberg hit upon the notion that facial expressions (and presumably the underlying emotional states) could be sorted out on a pleasant-unpleasant continuum just as Wundt had suggested. When he had subjects sort out photographs on this basis, he found that there was a tendency for one emotional pattern to shade into another and to come about full circle if enough photographs of varied emotional poses were used. Thus a subject who was portraying fear would have this picture judged as different from anger, very different from contempt, different from love, but close to surprise. Emotions could be arranged around a pleasant-unpleasant circle. Love and anger would appear as polar opposites while fear and disgust would again be polar opposites between love and anger. Schlosberg found it convenient to describe a new dimension or axis running half-way between love and anger in terms of a scale of attention-rejection. How happy a choice of terms this might become remains to be seen in future research. In any event we now have two scales for describing emotion, unpleasant-pleasant, and attention-rejection. Schlosberg found that these were not enough, and added a third dimension which he thought of as intensity. He thought of this scale as running from some quiescent state like sleep to "tension" as an opposite extreme. This recalls the Wundtian scale of tension-relaxation. Thus, Schlosberg has revived two of the Wundtian scales and substituted his new dimension of attention-rejection for the Wundtian excitement-calm.

There is a lot of vagueness about the terms employed by both Wundt and Schlosberg, yet certain consistent judgments can be made by subjects when they rate photographs which are by no means the best materials. In fact, considering the nature of photographs and the artificiality of the poses it is surprising that any agreement can be attained.

It is interesting to note that both Wundt and Schlosberg made use of an "activation" scale involving "tension" and "relaxation" (sleep in

Schlosberg's case). Schlosberg relates the function of "activation" to the operations of the arousal system (the reticular system, see p. 148) and to this degree gets away from the Wundtian psychic dimensions. The other two scales, of attention-rejection and unpleasant-pleasant, are still far from objective although the attention-rejection scale suggests some behavioral possibilities. In our later considerations we will be much concerned with the concepts of avoidance and approach. It is possible that such terms (or perhaps some more appropriate synonyms) might be at least partially useful to account for what Schlosberg calls attention and rejection. Perhaps Schlosberg's terms are not the best for what he thought he saw in his data, or perhaps his data could provide only what amounts to an attention position of an approach-avoidance scale.

Similarly, the terms unpleasant-pleasant leave a lot to be desired as far as objectivity and measurement are concerned. Inherent in such terms is the notion of approach and avoidance (just as there is with attention and rejection). If we took the unpleasant-pleasant axis to represent some general approach or avoidance tendencies and the attention-rejection to represent differences in the type of approach and avoidance perhaps we would be closer to an objective position. There are numerous ways to approach and avoid. For example we can approach tentatively, passively—let the object come to us, with gusto and enthusiasm, or only reluctantly, without at the same time having negative aspects present; we can avoid by retreating (fear), by standing still and refusing to go forward, by attacking and destroying, by merely turning away, by doing something else, and so on. In the future we can anticipate a gradually developing independence in connection with such subjective terminology as Schlosberg has been constrained to employ. Perhaps with pictures to be judged, there is no convenient language to use in instructing the subjects about their duties. In a "real life" situation, perhaps more objective terminology might prove useful and at least as reliable as Schlosberg found to be the case with his pictures.

Emotion and meaning

Before we leave the subject of such attempts at developing dimensions for scaling emotional activity we should recall the scales developed by Osgood (1957) for his analysis of meaning. It will be recalled that Osgood also used polar scales or co-ordinates and that he too found three sets of such co-ordinates of the most importance. These were: the evaluative scale—is something good or bad, pleasant or unpleasant?; the activity scale—is something fast or slow, active-inactive?; and the potency scale—is something strong, masculine, hard or weak, feminine and soft? If we examine the adjectives used by Osgood to characterize his three scales (evaluative, potency, activity) there appears to be a strong resemblance to Schlosberg's and Wundt's scales of feeling. Osgood was measuring meaning, Schlosberg and Wundt feeling, yet the two concepts appear to invite language that is pretty much of a piece. Was Osgood measuring feeling instead of meaning as he thought? Or was Schlosberg really measuring the "meaning" of his pictures? Was he really getting at what Osgood calls "connotation" as opposed to "denotation"? Judges cannot *identify* emotions from photographs. If they do succeed in making some kinds of consistent judgments, these may be "meanings." Or, is meaning so much interrelated with feeling that the two terms are not really distinguishable as having separate referents? Perhaps the point is, as we have tried to stress throughout, that we cannot separate out functions of the organism for separate analysis by some simple verbal sleight of tongue. If we deprive thinking behavior of its emotional aspects we do not have the same pattern we started out to study. Similarly if we deprive emotional behavior of its cognitive aspects, we have eliminated some, perhaps the most important aspects of emotional activity. Man's body at all times functions as a whole and behavior is a result of integrated action of the nervous system; there are no separate little black boxes that work by themselves in the absence of activity in the other boxes. While there may be a more-or-less condition, there does not appear to be an all-or-none condition. If we lose sight of this integrative character of behavior we may lose contact with the problem for good. In what we turn to now, we will have frequent occasions to be reminded of the various aspects that must be considered together if we are to offer a reasonable account of an approach to the study of emotional activity.

The genetic-learning analysis of emotion

The contributions to our understanding of emotion have not followed a smooth logical pattern of systematically building up on crude foundations. Theories pronounced in the last century are still in some good standing. Various aspects of the subject have been studied or speculated about by a great many individuals without any systematic development. We shall try to organize some of the contributions in some orderly manner but cannot follow a chronological pattern.

In picking out approaches to the study of emotion we can begin with a study which pictures all emotion as developing out of a single original state of excitement. A baby is born with the capacity for this excited form of behavior but has no other emotional capacities or categories. No love or hate or fear. For two months or so, according to Bridges (1932), no other emotional condition can be observed reliably. At about three months of age, the infant is still excitable (now called "distress") but can also demonstrate something that merits the label "delight." Distress continues to be displayed but by about the fifth month seems to break up into separate patterns that might be called "anger" and possibly "disgust." From these patterns, at about the seventh month the infant develops something like fear. Delight continues all this time and about at a year or so, seems to differentiate into what Bridges calls "elation" and "affection." Other observations on children born blind seem to suggest that such patterns as crying and laughing also follow a more or less innate pattern and come into being as the results of growth and maturation.

From Bridges' observations we might assume that emotional patterns of quite some complexity are inherited characteristics of the human species, and there is no reason to doubt that the physiological mechanisms underlying the states we label emotional should show such maturational characteristics. From the knowledge that emotional patterns are more or less innate and natural, however, we do not profit much except to recognize that we are equipped for such activities and that we are very likely to use this equipment in our ordinary daily lives. Occasionally some one comes out with suggestions for emotional control which appear to be based on the assumption that emotions are undesirable or abnormal or in some fashion reflect maladjustment. It is far better to recognize how much more primitive man really is and deal with realities than to try to pretend that emotions are something we can or should do without. We commonly hear about "the thin veneer of civilization" without fully appreciating the thinness of the veneer. Man is extremely susceptible to rather strong emotional reactions. It does not take much to scratch through the veneer. A scratch on the fender of your new car by some other motorist is likely to result in a rather frenzied situation regardless of all the poise, gentility, and culture that has been imposed on you in the process of growing up. Human beings in automobiles are not far removed from savages. In handling their own children, the thin veneer may grow thinner with the passing years.

Conditioning and emotion

Bridges' observations are generally accepted although they do not conform with earlier observations of Watson (1920), the behaviorist. Watson, on the basis of his observations of infants, decided that three emotional patterns, or, at least different kinds of reactions are inherited —he labeled these fear, anger, and love. We need not concern ourselves with the fact that his observations could not be supported by other investigators—Watson's purpose was merely to provide some basis for further elaboration of emotional life from whatever was inherited. According to Watson, stimulating the infant by holding his limbs tightly together provoked a struggle pattern that could be called rage or anger; dropping the infant or making a loud noise resulted in whimpering and crying or "fear," and caressing the infant, particularly in erogenous zones, resulted in smiling, cooing, general relaxation or "love." With these three basic reactions as a foundation, Watson argued that all our future emotional life develops on the basis of conditioning. Thus, if we are shown an animal, such as a rat, and a loud noise is sounded behind us at the same time, we shall become conditioned to fear rats, and by generalization, all small, white, furry (perhaps) active objects, or, perhaps, even all animals. If our limbs are pressed together by some fat, redheaded, mustached man, such men and some generalized range of variation will come to be hated, and so on. Watson's views are quite unassailable when the generalization principle is accepted, and, indeed, the vast amount of experimentation on anxiety is based on just such an argument as Watson advanced. In many experiments with animals, a shock is given (innate, unconditioned stimulus for pain and fear) just after a buzzer or light is turned on. After a few trials the animal behaves as if it feared the buzzer or light and indulges in agitated behavior when these are presented in the absence of shock. Presumably, if the fearful subject can be forced into some other kind of response by some new unconditioned stimulus presented at the time it is afraid, the fear reaction can be made to disappear. Such was shown to happen by Jones (1924) who presented candy to a child that was afraid of rabbits when the rabbit was brought into distant view. The rabbit eventually became a conditioned stimulus for responses associated with eating candy and the fear was eliminated. (See, also, Wolpe, 1954.)

INDIRECT EFFECTS OF LEARNING ON EMOTION

While Watson may be correct to some degree—we may fear lightning because it is normally followed by the crash of thunder—his views are probably too simple to account for all our fears and other emotional patterns. Hebb (1946) argues, for example, that it is quite normal for most of us to fear things we never had a chance to be conditioned to fear, as for example, dead bodies, parts of bodies (imagine someone handing you an arm), various insects, snakes, the dark. Very few, if any, infants are afraid of the dark, yet most of them become so about the age of four or five. It is not likely that they have all been exposed to loud noises when the lights are turned off, yet they generally develop the fear. Hebb's position is that it is not only loud noises or loss of support that initiates fear, and indeed, it has frequently been argued that the stimulus for fear need only be a sudden, unexpected, stimulus of any variety. What is interesting about Hebb's hypothesis is that it requires that a certain amount of learning has to take place before we are able to react to unexpected stimuli in the fearful fashion. A stimulus is novel only if it is not usual and expected. For something to be usual *and* expected a certain amount of learning must go on. We learn how to respond to stimuli in ordinary daylight, for example. Stimuli emanating from chairs, tables, the walls, etc., become part of the environment to which we have suitable adjustments. When we are four or five years old, however, and are in some semidark situation, the stimuli from tables, chairs, and walls are not the same as they were in the daytime. We have no adjustive responses to such stimuli and the lack of proper, habitual response leaves us in a somewhat disorganized state which we label fear or apprehension. Similarly we become accustomed to living people with the customary allotment of heads, arms, legs, etc. Living people move about; even when sleeping they toss around, snore, breathe, and so on. When we see people without arms or legs or without life, we are again uncomfortable; there are no familiar responses to make. The undertaker eventually gets to the point where he welcomes corpses as part of the day's routine; the rest of us remain uneasy in the presence of death. It is not unlikely that our reactions to strangers generally and to members of other races or nationalities (if they are sufficiently distinctive in some feature) are also determined in part by learning which has been restricted to one type of race or nationality. We learn to accept the people with whom we are reared. Later on, "the stranger" is received gingerly, hesitantly, or fearfully, depending upon whether we have adequate reactions in our repertoires for dealing with him. Children are quite obviously unafraid of members of other races, or, for that matter, of most of the things which they will come to fear later on with no specific negative conditioning. Babies will play with snakes or glass eyes which will disturb an older child. It becomes a question of suitable habits.

According to John Dewey (1910) if we had enough habits, we would never become emotional (nor would we ever have to make up our minds, nor—as we saw earlier, p. 299—even think). This opinion of Dewey's seems to be related to Hebb's analysis. It does help us appreciate how the medical student gets over his first aversions to working with his anatomical specimens, how firemen and other professional people get to be able to handle situations that strike fear in the layman. When college students liven up a dormitory bull session by dining on fried grasshoppers they create an emotional carnival by requiring someone to react to an unfamiliar stimulus. Even when the challenged subjects do eat the delicacy, they find it difficult to chew and swallow what in effect should be no more of a problem than a small piece of bacon or peanut. The native populations in areas where fried grasshoppers are considered desirable items of consumption surely eat with more efficiency.

Failure to become familiar with a variety of stimuli or situations results in an inadequate background for dealing with such stimuli when they occur at some later stage in life. When dogs are confined from birth to very limited quarters and have no opportunity to become adjusted to the great welter of stimulation that does exist in a normal dog's world, they also show bizarre patterns of behavior when released in such a world (Melzack and Scott, 1957). They do not know enough to be bored, for example; they explore and investigate more or less continually; they have not learned to fight and do not do so when a bone is thrown between them and a normally reared dog. They have not even learned to suffer pain and appear insensitive to pain stimuli that send normal dogs yelping away. To put the matter briefly, we do not acquire all our fears through direct learning; rather, we learn to live in a regular, conventional, or routine world. When the regularity, conventionality, or routines are violated, we are left incapable of reacting appropriately and the resulting uneasiness or even panic is the consequence of an inadequate preparation.

We should note, before leaving the subject, that many of our fears can be readily eliminated by the presence of adults whom we have learned to trust; they can even turn the situation to appear amusing and associate other values with the stimuli involved such as ("you are a big boy, now"; "you're not afraid"). Such positive but extraneous values can lead to behavior which involves putting one's self into situations that elicit some mild (and quite safe) disturbing situation such as embarking on roller coasters and other "rides" at amusement parks. The confidence that nothing will happen and the extraneous rewards involved invite youngsters to these "adventures." Older youngsters engage in other risky activities such as mountain climbing, presumably for the same kinds of extraneous rewards. We can be pretty sure that people do not climb mountains for the view, especially mountains whose peaks are above the clouds where the view is of dubious value. When the conquerors of such mountains say they climbed the mountain "because it was there," we have to interpret this in terms of extraneous rewards that come to such conquerors. There will be many volunteers for the first trip to the moon and it is doubtful that "scientific curiosity" will be the motivation. Thrill seekers have learned to enjoy situations that panic others and the knowledge that others are panicked is probably an important source of support for such activities. It provides the basis for the extraneous reinforcement that follows the "adventure."

Functional theories of emotion

Attempts at measuring and classifying emotional dimensions are only incidentally, if at all, concerned with the role of emotions in behavior. The Wundtian structural approach leaves emotions as a unit of mental life but without any role. The primarily practical approach of American psychologists has been to appreciate what emotions do to one or for one, to analyze their functions. William James (1890), the pragmatic philosopher, was the first to attempt such an analysis as the forerunner of the "functional school" of American psychology, later to be developed by Dewey and his students.

The James-Lange theory

It will be recalled that James raised the question of the motivational role of emotion and found a negative answer. The typical analysis of the average man—see bear—become afraid—run—was partially reversed to read: see bear—run—have fear. James (and at the same time, but quite independently, Lange, a Danish psychologist) arrived at the theoretical view that emotional experiences are the aftermath of bodily activity. James recognized the important role of visceral activity in emotion—activities related to the operation of the autonomic nervous system. For James, such activities as well as movements of skeletal muscles, postural adjustments, and the stimulation that arose from these activities constituted the very basis for emotion. James was primarily interested in explaining the nature of emotion and put it in this way: *the awareness of bodily change, as it occurs, is the emotion.* In order to have an emotion, then, bodily changes would have to occur first, and these would occur only if some external stimulation was present. When the subsequent stimulation from the bodily responses reached the brain, the individual would properly be said to be emotional because then he would be aware of reactions of his body. Such awareness would not necessarily be very specific, but it would include appreciation of a pounding heart, sweating palms, internal queeziness, etc.

According to James, if such behavioral changes could be induced artificially, an emotional experience would develop. Actors on the stage, for example, who "put on" a pattern of clenched fists, loud voice, aggressive posture, etc., would necessarily begin to feel "outraged" or angry. Similarly if they slumped in their seats, dropped their chins on their chests, etc., they would begin to experience some degree of depression. Because the actors would also have some responsibility to their fellow-players as well as the audience, they could not be concerned solely with the stimulation from their own reactions. Similarly, if a person is already experiencing some emotion, it should be possible to eliminate it by changing the pattern of reactions. A crying child, for example, might be turned into a laughing one by being tickled or forced into some other activity. Candy dries more tears than sympathy.

James can be credited with calling attention to the role of response-produced stimuli ("feedback") on behavior and with recognizing the role of visceral or autonomic activity. Subsequent theoretical approaches to emotion have relied heavily on the latter, and today, most psychologists view emotion as a primarily physiological affair. While James was concerned with the psychological "experience" of emotion, that is, with the characteristics of emotional processes as part of mental life, modern psychologists are no longer keenly concerned about the psychic aspects and dwell more on the role of neural structures and functions.

The emergency theory

We have already mentioned the work of Walter B. Cannon (1929) in connection with his "emergency" view of emotions in the discussion of motivation. Cannon too relied heavily on visceral activity, particularly on secretions of glands, such as the adrenal gland in emotional behavior. But Cannon believed James mistaken in restricting emotions to the feedback from bodily activity. Such feedback would occur, to be sure, but Cannon was concerned more with the original source of stimulation for such visceral activity. In his analysis of emotion, Cannon looked for neural centers of emotion and came to believe that the hypothalamus was the important locus for emotional activity. The hypothalamus, it will be recalled, is a part of the midbrain, the old brain, and a primary relay center for all incoming stimulation before it is routed around to other brain areas and to motor outlets. All visual stimulation, for example, passes through the thalamus on its way to eventual connections in the occipital lobe. Similarly, auditory and other stimulation is channeled through the hypothalamus. According to Cannon's views, the hypothalamus serves as a rather busy exchange center which normally handles considerable traffic without difficulty. When strong or novel stimulation or excessive inputs arrive and the hypothalamus cannot handle the load, changes are initiated in the autonomic nervous system either directly or via glandular secretions from the pituitary gland. The body functions that are concerned with mere routine operations such as normal heart beat, normal blood pressure, digestion, etc., are then altered to cope with the "emergency," and the pattern of excitement that emerges is a result of the sympathetic division of the nervous system taking over while the parasympathetic functions are halted. Thus, the adrenal glands discharge their hormones which affect the liver to discharge more sugar into the blood. Coagulants are also discharged through adrenal secretions; blood pressure rises, the heart beats faster, the breathing becomes more rapid and shallow, digestion stops, and so on. The organism is ready for "fight or flight"; it is on an emergency footing. Cannon's theory has been labeled "the emergency theory" of emotion.

Cannon and his successors (Bard, 1934; and Lindsley, 1951) have engaged in much supportive research in order to develop the original thalamic theory. Much of the early work was related to demonstrating that James' view was incorrect. It was demonstrated for example that animals would display emotional patterns of behavior (sham rage) when the cortex had been removed (decortication) and, presumably, no stimulation from the viscera could then be appreciated by "higher centers." It could be argued by supporters of James that just because a cat looked afraid or angry was no proof of its actually *feeling* that way and the decortication argument can be considered at best, indirect, negative evidence. Cannon's own theory involved an awareness of the turmoil in the thalamus and the sham rage experiments are equally pointed at that view. The important distinction between the two views was that for Cannon the visceral stimulation did not have to return before the subject would become emotional; it was enough for the thalamic disturbance to initiate such changes as well as the disruption of the systematic routing of stimulation to higher centers from the hypothalamus itself.

Cannon's views did not include any specification of the physiological patterns underlying different emotions. It was a general theory that dealt with emotional behavior but not with separate kinds of emotions such as rage and fear. Subsequent physiological attacks have been concerned with determining the factors which might account for such specificity. The attacks have been by direct investigation of neural structures that might be involved in such states as "fear" as well as indirect approaches through the measurement of bodily changes under presumably different emotions. In the latter case, subjects in laboratories have their blood pressure, breathing, and galvanic skin responses, as well as various chemical reactions (blood, urine) tested while undergoing stimulation calculated to arouse fear or anger. It is obviously difficult to establish reliable states of fear or anger in a laboratory; the subjects are normally quite confident that there is no genuine danger and that no matter how they are treated, it is part of an "experiment." Consequently the results obtained are likely to be of questionable value. The actual results obtained have usually failed to result in any clear-cut patterns of visceral activity underlying separate emotional states such as fear and anger. We are faced with assuming that there is no internal difference, viscerally speaking, between these two states or that current measurement techniques are not equal to the refinements involved. In one study by Ax (1953) a large number of different measures were recorded from subjects who were made angry and fearful. Many of the measures showed no differences but some seemed to be reliable differentiators although these are not clearly understandable. For example, in anger, there were more galvanic skin responses recorded, but in fear, the galvanic responses were greater in magnitude. Why such a relationship should appear is not evident. Similarly, in anger, more heart rate decreases were noticed, while in fear, respiration rate increased. These changes were statistically reliable but in view of the number of measures that involved breathing, circulation, and skin conductance that showed no differences, they may turn out to be artifacts of some kind. Chemical analyses have not been too helpful.

It appears that there might be some differentiation in physiological function in emotion from two separate secretions of the adrenal glands—adrenalin and noradrenalin; the first kind seems to be related to a fearful pattern; the second to an anger or aggression pattern. How glandular secretions could pattern the rather rapid behavioral changes that occur to external stimuli is still a big question. The general argument that parasympathetic functions are related to normal, quiescent activity is also doubtful. In times of rather strong tension, it is common to experience a need to urinate frequently. This has been reported by pilots when on military missions as well as in more humdrum activities like those involved in making speeches or taking examinations. In fact, defecation and urination are used as tests of emotionality in rats and dogs and these are parasympathetic functions. The indirect approach through laboratory measures of visceral function may not prove definitive although it does testify to the importance of visceral action and points up the chemical influences on behavior.

The approach through evaluation of neural centers may prove more fruitful eventually. It is already known that electrical stimulation of certain midbrain centers can result in patterns of behavior normally controlled by hunger, thirst, "fear," or "anxiety," and even something that has been called, perhaps unfortunately, a "pleasure" center (Olds, 1956). By implanting electrodes in the brains of rats, cats, dogs, and monkeys, it is possible to control some emotional patterns. Much of the evidence is of very recent origin and it will be some time before enough reliable data have been developed or accumulated for us to speak with confidence on just what is being observed. But there appears to be no question that such electrical stimulation of limited areas of the brain can, in effect, force an animal to approach some mechanism which will provide such stimulation (reward? pleasure?) even in competition with food when the animal is hungry, or to approach a device and manipulate it in order to turn off or avoid such stimulation in another part of the brain.

Operations involving the destruction of some parts of the brain or of cutting pathways from one part to another also seem to be related to emotional behavior. Patients with intractable pain, for example, have benefited from the cutting of pathways between the frontal lobes and the thalamus; destruction of other areas can make animals ravenous, agitated and aggressive, or docile and sleepy. Such experiments do not directly indicate the nature of emotional function but they help to limit the problems to be explained and with the development of microrecording techniques we may be in position to note what is going on in various parts of the brain when animals are under different kinds of stimulation from the external world.

Functional significance of emotion

What is the role of emotional reactions (and here we emphasize the physiological changes which we have been considering) in daily life? We have already noted the motivational aspects of emotional behavior where we found that it was quite impossible to separate out such factors. We have also noted the function of emotion in providing the enthusiasm for risky undertakings, the search for adventure, the "zest for living." At the same time, most of the discussion has been heavily weighted in the direction of a negative evaluation of emotional factors —psychologists do not know much about what most people would regard as desirable states—their efforts have been largely restricted to laboratory studies involving fear and anger.

Charles Darwin (1855) at one time raised the question of the survival value of emotion and argued that emotional expression—the baring of teeth, for example, was of some value in scaring off enemies (assuming they were not baring their own teeth) and that such emotional expressions as humans indulge in may also have "survival" value. The curling lip, the sneer, may fend off undesirable consequences. On the other hand, it may also invite such consequences. In raising the question of survival, Darwin, of course, anticipated the emergency theory of Cannon and should be credited with this proposition. It appears, in spite of some maturational evidence, that much of our emotional expression is a learned business and differs widely from culture to culture (see Klineberg, 1938). Its value may lie more in the field of economical communication than in the area of survival, but there is doubt even here. It is common enough to misunderstand the emotional attitude, mood, or condition of others even though stereotyped patterns have developed which are commonly used in the theater. Actors in the "silent" movies had to communicate an emotional response to the audience in the most economical way and managed to do so quite successfully by exaggerated rolling of the eyes, chest-heaving, leering, etc. In most daily-life situations we get our cues to how people are responding from an appreciation of the situation or stimulus conditions. When we hear of the death of a member of someone's family, we are ready with condolences and may be quite astonished to hear something like: "It was about time—good riddance." Gross responses are fairly well discriminated, some even from photographs, although detection of more subtle reactions usually calls for a report from the emoter.

Psychosomatic disorders

The negative aspects of emotional reactions are frequently related to various kinds of illnesses, sometimes as causative factors. It is commonly believed for example, that ulcers of the digestive apparatus can result from frequent and chronic emotional reactions. It will be recalled that in strong fear, anger, etc., the sympathetic nervous system takes over the dominant role and normal digestive functions are upset. The details of what goes on are not quite clear but it is argued that digestive secretions which are normally under parasympathetic control become excessive under sympathetic dominance—this appears to be a contradiction of the roles of the systems, but there is some evidence from observing the tissues of stomachs that they become inflamed and engorged under strong emotion and they may also become excessively acid. If this is the case, a chronic hyperacidity could result in something akin to the stomach digesting itself—i.e., a lesion might result as a consequence of frequent or chronic emotional stimulation. When such a physiological disorder does occur and can be attributed to emotional "tension," it is called "psychosomatic" (mind-body) and presumably calls for a different kind of treatment from that which would be given a person with a simple infection or disorder resulting from some external agent.

The psychosomaticists have not limited themselves to ulcers but the more enthusiastic (see Alexander, 1950; Dunbar, 1943; Weiss, 1950) among them have traced all sorts of ills to "mental" factors. It is commonly argued for example that asthma is of "psychogenic" origin and that high blood pressure and various internal aches and pains are due to excessive worry or conflict. Whether a person heals quickly or slowly is related to his basic emotional organization by some psychosomatic speculators and even such factors as susceptibility to diseases of legitimate virus origin is sometimes attributed to "psychological factors." Many physicians claim that a majority of their patients are neurotics and that their symptoms—skin rashes, backaches, headaches, etc.—are of mental origin.

How various illnesses or symptoms can develop from emotional disturbance (so-called "psychogenic" disorders) is not clear. Psychosomaticists have not provided a detailed, step-by-step description of how anxiety or chronic worry is translated into physical symptoms. It is easy enough to gather empirical data—many people who consult physicians for treatment of physical ills can be shown to have troubles, problems, various difficulties. There is certainly plenty of latitude in the domain of troubles. If the patient does not appear to have "trouble-enough" at present, it can always be shown that sometime in the past he did have a difficult time, a period of unhappiness, a failure or a series of failures, etc. Who can report a completely happy and successful past? On the theoretical side an account can be given which is plausible enough for many adherents of the psychosomatic school of thinking. The psychoanalyst Weiss (1950), for example, argues that symptoms might develop as symbols—a paralyzed leg prevents you from taking a *step* in the wrong direction; a patient may *identify* in his symptoms with those of a friend or relative or he might build up on a previous history of some physical ailment—a bronchitis in the past may turn up as asthma in the future under some emotional stress. A patient might be conditioned to respond with symptoms to stimuli that originally accompanied some physical distress. These are possible avenues by which psychological stress may end up in physical malfunction, but, until we have more detailed experimental observations they cannot be accepted as anything but possibilities.

There appears to be no reason to doubt that emotional factors, conceived as changes in the operation of autonomic functions, can have some effects that amount to or correspond to illness. What illnesses, or to what degree some illnesses, are related to emotional functions is still debatable and it could be a very serious error to presume that any illness was purely psychological, psychological in origin, or even related to psychological factors. A mistake in diagnosis could lead to serious consequences; some cancer patients have died while being treated psychologically. Many so-called psychosomatic disorders have been traced to allergy and it might be just as arguable that "it's not all in your mind" (Berglund and Nichols, 1953) as it is to argue the other way. It is perfectly true that emotional stimuli (a telegram announcing the death of a son) can result in faints and other, perhaps, violent reactions. People under prolonged emotional stress can have serious alterations of their sleep and dietary habits and various eliminative functions may be disturbed. How common prolonged periods of significant stress are is a statistical question for which we have no answer. It is common, however, in battle conditions for men in action. While some of these do develop symptoms of a physical nature, there does not appear to be any particular kind of symptom that does emerge, nor is there any excessive proportion of such reactions as ulceration. Certainly not all of the people undergoing the same external stress conditions come down with symptoms. Why some people should develop psychosomatic difficulties and others do not then raises another question: are some people constitutionally predisposed to illness that might arise from autonomic hyperfunction and others not? Or are the individual histories of people such that some are able to withstand the ravages on their digestive apparatus by learned techniques of adjustment while others have not learned appropriate techniques?

Experimental evidence is difficult to obtain in this area. One experiment (Brady, 1958) that may lead to fruitful attacks on this subject has been reported in which four monkeys were put into a situation in which they had to make an avoidance response every twenty seconds for six hours at a time (followed by six hours of rest, then another six-hour session of avoidance, etc.) for six or seven weeks in succession. Each of the monkeys developed gastric ulcers. Four control monkeys who did not make the avoidance response and only got shocked when the experimental monkeys failed to make the avoidance response did not develop ulcers or any other apparent ailment. It should be noted here that such a prolonged period of presumed tension—six hours at a stretch—may not be comparable with any other situation of which we have heard. To be provoked into some degree of fear every twenty seconds regularly and systematically does not begin to compare with any troubles known to man. The fact that the control monkeys did not develop ulcers may be due to the fact that they could get more rest and enjoy uninterrupted sleep for almost as much time as they felt drowsy. The experimental monkeys had to stay awake; or, putting it the other way, the experimental monkeys never got more than six hours of successive rest. This may itself be a factor in ulcer production. Other experiments of this type are in progress and we may get more precise information about the relations between anxiety and physical symptoms before too long.

In the examination of people who have one kind of ailment or another it should also be noted that the ailment itself can lead to considerable anxiety and it might be difficult to establish in some cases which came first. In no case do we have the kind of clean-cut evidence that would make everyone happy. It is known, or alleged to be known, for example, that such a physiological function as menstruation can be affected by emotional factors so that the cycle may be interrupted if a woman is unduly worried or anxious. Since it may also be interrupted for a variety of other reasons, there is no proof in any individual instance. If a girl is worried about pregnancy and does not menstruate, an obvious, but not necessarily correct, conclusion can be drawn.

On the somatopsychic side, it is again alleged although systematic, well-documented proof is lacking, that the menstrual cycle in women results in various alternations of mood and levels of agitation. One physician described women as reacting to certain phases of the cycle (just before menstruation) in terms of three grades of witches. The most disturbed would be one that was just about impossible to live with, with lesser degrees of uncontrolled irrationality in the other two witch grades. On the other hand, many women appear not to be especially affected by the menstrual cycle and show no excessive agitation at any phase.

There is little point to taking sides on the psychosomatic or somatopsychic interpretation of behavior. It is obvious that any claims have to be spelled out clearly and reasonable evidence has to be advanced in any case. Until such evidence is presented there is no point to wasting time in treating an infant with asthma like a psychological problem. It is doubtful that infants have psychological problems. On the other hand, it is unwise to argue that no physical changes can result from prolonged or frequent bodily disturbance such as is associated with strong emotion. It should, of course, first be established that such emotional disturbances were in fact occurring in frequency and severity sufficient to create the damage involved. Most emotional experiences tend to be shortlived in nature, and highly dramatic descriptions of daily strife between husband and wife, for example, have to be examined carefully. There is not only the question of whether there is strife and how much, but why the wife does not get the ulcers. The romantic description of the "executive" ulcer seems to be more romance than fact. Executives usually can afford to have ulcers and medical help, and thus may represent an abnormal selection in the statistics. It must also be established sooner or later why some people who undergo abnormal experiences and great degrees of stress do not develop symptoms. It may be, of course, that some people learn to adjust to various kinds of frustrating circumstances (they may have greater frustration "tolerance") or they adopt defense mechanisms (see p. 428) that do not involve debilitating physical symptoms and they never come under medical or psychological scrutiny; they may live out their lives as worried, unhappy, or "nervous" people who just won't have anything to do with doctors.

In fairness to those who emphasize a psychosomatic approach we should point out that they do not suggest that illnesses that appear to involve psychological factors should be treated by only psychological methods. Psychological therapy might be only incidental or additional. In some cases the psychological treatment might be designed to prevent recurrences of the difficulty. The combined term "psycho-somatic" dictates attention to both bodily and environmental or behavioral factors.

Until we have answers to all these issues, it is best that we proceed carefully before diagnosing our friend's ailments as due to worry, anxiety, or impossible living conditions. Too many people live under impossible conditions without getting ulcers to make the psychosomatic theory especially attractive. We should also be careful to ask for a more precise statement of the theory than one that involves "psychic" factors. We cannot separate the human organism into mental and physical divisions. There is nothing mental about the body and the psychosomatic theory must be stated in terms of physiology, or if that is not quite possible, in terms of behavioral principles that reflect observations of some substance. It is not "worry" for example that we should worry about, but the functions of the autonomic nervous system and the factors that control its activity. If some of these are environmental, then we can trace the influence of such environmental (psychological) factors in the development of disorders of the body if such can be found. The hypothetical possibility is quite logical. All we need is the evidence.

The psychosomatic theory has recently been restated by Hans Selye (1950) in terms of what he calls "the general adaptation syndrome." Selye pictures the reaction of the organism to stress (any trauma, infectionary invasion, etc.) as following a regular pattern which consists of three stages. The first stage is an initial defense response (a homeostatic reaction—i.e., an automatic, more-or-less reflex reaction of an adjustment nature, e.g., shivering to cold or perspiring to heat). The initial defense reaction he labels the "alarm-stage" where the organism's adjustment forces are mobilized following an initial period of underactivity. A second stage—that of "resistance"—then follows, and finally a stage of *exhaustion* in which the defenses fall apart if the defenses have been inadequate. While the picture drawn by Selye may be appropriate for many ailments which beset us, it is generally accepted as a description of how psychosomatic disorders develop and mature.

Some evidence for this view has been accumulated in observations on rats put into chronic stress conditions and the Selye view is presumed to apply to all stress situations if these continue long enough for the several stages to develop. We shall have additional occasions to concern ourselves with the problems of stress later in the text (see p. 425).

The behavioral approach to the study of emotion

The psychologist who is not inclined to investigate emotional phenomena by physiological techniques (or concern himself about introspective reports) is forced to rely on observations of behavior. When such behavior appears to have emotional overtones (as the psychologist infers on the basis of his own introspections and biases) he tries to relate the behavior to the stimuli involved and determine to what degree manipulation of stimuli can result in controlling the response patterns of the organism. Because he has only behavior to observe, he has to employ some dimensions of measurement that are adaptable to observable responses. If he is preoccupied with *rate* as a measure (as is Skinner, 1938) he will tend to consider emotional factors as those which change the rate of some selected pattern of behavior either in the direction of more or less of the response in question. Such factors will have to be related to controllable stimulus situations so that the analysis of emotional behavior will amount to recognizing and evaluating the role of special kinds of reinforcers. If the reinforcers increase the activity in question, they will be positive (approach) reinforcers; if they decrease the activity, they will be aversive reinforcers. If the reinforcers are themselves learned in connection with more direct kinds of reinforcing action, they will be labeled "secondary." Thus, if a dog is shocked after a buzzer sounds and raises a leg to the shock, the withdrawal movement is considered an aversive or avoidance response. The presence of the shock certainly changes the rate of leg withdrawal from a relatively low operant rate to a dependable one. When the dog begins to raise the leg when the buzzer sounds, the buzzer has become a secondary aversive reinforcer. Its presence or absence also changes the rate of withdrawal of the leg. From this point of view, then, the study of emotion is really the study of secondary aversive or nonaversive reinforcers and their role in changing the rates or responses. This system has the obvious merit of being strictly objective but it appears awkward to employ or to apply to specific cases where the rate of the original behavior involved is not easily measurable.

Other psychologists, too, make use of the notion of aversion or avoidance and approach, but they are also willing to attribute to the animal the existence of some internal condition which they want to label as the emotion involved and which is presumed to have energizing and directing properties (in the sense of drive). Thus, in the case of the illustration just employed above, the buzzer is thought of not as a secondary aversive reinforcer but as a conditioned stimulus which evokes an emotion (presumed to be fear or anxiety). The fear or anxiety, as a "hypothetical construct," is then endowed with stimulus-producing characteristics which generate activity as we have described earlier (see p. 224). Such a view has some possibilities of accounting for behavior of an avoidance or escape type but has been severely limited in the area of more positive emotions. We shall have to delay examination of this approach till the next chapter. We cite it now merely to fill in the pattern of attacks on the subject of emotion that psychologists have employed in the past. At this time we can content ourselves with examining the logical nature of this approach.

To reduce the rich patterns of emotional life to tendencies to approach or avoid stimuli appears superficially to be extremely modest and unlikely of success. On the other hand it may prove the "breakthrough" in the analysis of emotion that will lead eventually to a greater success than will other attacks on the problem. Its very simplicity offers the possibility of some kinds of testing, a feature not readily discernable in some of the other views we have examined. If we are careful not to fall into the difficulties involved in the Watsonian approach to which this one is obviously closely related, we have here a view which traces the specific emotional patterns in which we indulge to a history of learning and reinforcement. It will be remembered from our discussion of drive and learning that when anxiety is treated as a drive and by that means related to a number of different initiating stimuli and different consummatory responses, a great many daily life situations seem to be handled with some satisfaction. The theory leans heavily on anxiety and kindred negative states as a basis for much of our behavior, but, perhaps, we all are as anxiety-ridden as the theory seems to require. The whole culture can be described as anxiety-ridden. This would not be a new appellation, either. Henry Thoreau (1854) described the average citizen of his day as leading a life of "quiet desperation." If his description was apt in his time it is probably more so today. Perhaps much of our behavior consists of reducing rather frequently initiated states of anxiety.

Directional and intensity factors in emotion

In most considerations of emotion it is held that emotion is largely a disorganized response. The organism is taken by surprise and unable to react effectively. We have noticed this interpretation with Dewey and Cannon. Darwin, too, probably had some influence in this connection because, besides the survival principle, he saw some emotional behavior as basically disorganized, diffuse nervous *discharge.* In laboratory experiments where a pistol shot is fired behind a subject who is quietly sitting amidst the recording equipment hooked to him we can observe what has been labeled a "startle pattern" (Landis, 1924). The subject reacts as he might and does when a chair in which he is sitting suddenly gives way. His entire body reacts in a typical, but ineffective way. We are all familiar with some approximation of this "startle pattern" which is commonly experienced when we think we are alone in a room and on turning around find someone near us regardless of how friendly he might be. It is possible that a startle pattern plays some role in any novel situation and may be a basic kind of fear response to sudden, unusual stimuli. But pistol shots are momentary and once the chair has collapsed and we are on the floor the situation is altered—we are no longer frightened; in fact, we may be amused, if not angry. And most novel stimuli do not disappear: they remain and may require some action. The startle pattern does not get rid of them nor do they disappear when the startle pattern has faded out. The rat that is shocked may be startled too, with the first tingle of the shock, but only rarely is the tingle all that happens. The shock continues and something has to be done about it. Later on, the rat learns to avoid the shock entirely but it may still be emotional. If a light comes on signaling the shock, the shock will not be surprising or novel; the light itself is not eliciting startle patterns either; on the contrary, in the well trained rat, the light elicits a nicely organized response involving varying degrees of complexity depending upon what the experimenter has introduced as the necessary instrumental response. The rat may jump over a hurdle, turn a wheel, pull a chain, press a bar, or do a number of things, and do them in an organized fashion, or at least an efficient and systematic one.

The fact that responses can be quite efficient under emotional stress has led some psychologists to argue that emotions, far from being states of disorganization, actually (within limits) represent organized, integrated, co-ordinated behavior and, in effect, amount to the same operations as do motives. Emotions would then be the same as sets, or attitudes, controlling the responses to other stimuli. We have already encountered this notion in the previous chapter where we saw Leeper arguing for the inclusion of emotion as "organized response" of a motivational nature. Duffy (1951) has been arguing for a long time that our entire approach to emotion has been misdirected by the concept of emotion as disorganized behavior. She insists that a more appropriate course would be to ignore the usual process of classifying emotional states and making entities out of them, and recognize that a more objective study of behavior would result from finding appropriate parameters actually descriptive of behavior. She suggests, for example, that any behavioral sample can be described along at least two parameters, those of direction and intensity. There may be other parameters, of course, but in the present context we might restrict ourselves to these two. In any situation, then, an organism is seen as moving toward or away from some stimulus or situation or can be so conceived even if there is no actual movement at the immediate time of some observation. There will be a directionality about the behavior, something like approach or avoidance as we described above. Many psychologists, particularly those who follow Kurt Lewin (1935), are attracted to the idea that organisms can be best understood as being in a "field" of forces with various influences on the organisms, such as attracting and repelling forces or "valances." Other psychologists like to emphasize "goals" which can be negative or positive. Whatever the orientation of a psychologist, the concept of directionality of behavior is a common one and Duffy does not lack for support in this emphasis.

The other parameter Duffy advocates is intensity. Here again there is no lack of support. We have seen how Schlosberg found an intensity or activation dimension necessary for his tripartite analysis of emotional expression. And, we have also observed the current physiological emphasis on the functioning of the reticular or arousal or activation system. Activation or intensity can be measured in various ways depending upon a given situation; in one case it might be measured in terms of energy expenditure [J. S. Brown (1942), for example, harnessed rats to a spring and measured the force with which the rats strained against the spring when a rat was in an avoidance situation and when it was in an approach situation]. Another popular measure of activation level is that of speed or reaction time (latency) and we have noted above how Skinner would measure the influence of emotion in terms of the changes in the *rate* at which some response was performed.

By combining the measure of intensity with the measure of directionality, Duffy would hope to eliminate any need for the very concept of emotion and would simultaneously incorporate much of what we have discussed in connection with motivation in this objective analysis of behavior. There would be no need to debate whether a particular sample of behavior was organized or disorganized, rather vague terms, at best. It would only be necessary to relate the intensity and directionality of the responses to the stimuli involved. This may be the eventual line of development, which may be followed in the study of behavior. For the present we are hampered by our historical development, by the difficulties of language and communication which have created emotional entities such as jealousy, sympathy, and the whole gamut of expressions we have learned to use. Most of these words apply to situations and not to persons behaving in a particular fashion. Psychology has to take account of situations, to be sure, but it is concerned with studying behavior. By observing a person while ignorant of the situation, we would be most unlikely to discover what "emotion," if any, he was undergoing. This was demonstrated many years ago by Sherman (1927) who would stimulate an infant behind a screen (by pinching it, dropping it, "thwarting" it, etc.) and then expose the child to groups of nurses, physicians, and psychologists. The judges were uniformly poor in their judgments of the "emotions" on display. No one has done this with adults, but the expected results are not much in doubt. We would not be able to state that a given subject was being shy, timid, fearful, frightened, terrified, frantic, or horrified (is this an intensity scale of some sort?). In our ordinary, daily-life interpretations, we take the situation into account and *assume* the existence of an emotion on the interpretation of what the situation calls for, regardless of what we actually see or what the subject is doing. If someone has just been "insulted" we presume he is annoyed or "peeved"; if he has received "bad news," he must be "worried," and so on. This kind of interpretative psychology has not been very fruitful and today most psychologists are quite close to giving up the concept of separate emotions as entities or patterns of some specific and universal kind in favor of some variation of the intensity-directionality analysis of behavior. The position that is coming into favor might be summarized as: there are no separate emotions; all behavior is emotional to some extent; behavior can be represented along a variety of continua, such as intensity, direction, and perhaps a continuum of organization with a disorganized extreme at one end of an efficiency continuum.

Emotional control

In our culture, for better or worse, emotional control (usually interpreted as "self-control") has a high value. Somewhere along the educational line we learn to admire the steady, solid citizen and we mumble in unison with the class: "If you can keep your head when all about you are losing theirs——." Only righteous wrath is approved by the culture; other kinds are infantile or signs of immaturity. Similarly, fear of any kind is poorly regarded. It might be all right for women to demonstrate a modest fear of mice, but men are supposed to be brave and it is a law that Boy Scouts be courageous. Yet, as we mentioned earlier, the veneer of civilization is very thin and our daily language is full of emotional terminology in the discussion of our neighbors, colleagues, national policies, world affairs and women drivers. Our own position is usually noble, rational, virtuous, eminently justified, and correct. It is the behavior of others that is out of line and which should be controlled. Our devotion to self-control usually amounts to a concern with how to control others. In our remarks on the subject we will concentrate on the control of others, as self-control is an unlikely outcome of any individual's private efforts. Someone else might be able to improve your behavior (and thereby your self-control). You are not going to be able to do much about yourself.

Presumably all of us have faults in the eyes of others. Marriage counselors wisely advise that young people about to get married give up any notions of anyone changing his personality or his ways after marriage. People living together as married partners will encounter hundreds if not thousands of situations that will result in some disagreements and counselors have discovered that in spite of threats, abuse, pleading, and entreating, nothing seems to work in bringing about perfect harmony where there is any fault-finding on one side or the other. Nor will any easy path be found to elimination of the fault-finding to begin with.

Why is emotional control so difficult? The answer should be obvious from our previous discussion. All behavior is emotional and to eliminate emotional aspects we would pretty much have to eliminate the behavior! It should be clear that we cannot eliminate emotional aspects of behavior; all we can hope to do is to change the direction, and perhaps the intensity of behavior in some situations where we have some control over the situations or the responses involved, i.e., where we control the reinforcement features in the behavior patterns in question.

Since we cannot hope to discuss all possible directions and intensities of behavior in this context of "control," let us examine two kinds of situations that are presumably commonly considered undesirable and which we might want to control, the patterns of fear and anger. Experimental studies involving fear have been generally restricted to animals where some strong stimulation like shock can be employed without social difficulties. When rats or dogs learn to perform an avoidance response in an "anxiety" situation, it is normally observed that the animals are extremely persistent in the behavior patterns involved. If dogs are shocked in the presence of some signal like a buzzer until they jump a hurdle, they will continue jumping the hurdle after only a few trials until the experimenter gets tired of sounding the buzzer. In one well-known study (Solomon, Kamin, and Wynne, 1953), the experimenters deliberately set out to eliminate the hurdle jumping behavior and watched dogs jump and jump until they had cleared the hurdle 800 times in succession with no sign that they were ever going to give up. Some experimenters (N. Miller, 1948) report similar persistence with rats in avoidance learning, the rats repeating some pattern for hundreds of trials even though they have not been shocked since trial ten or trial four. Even when the animals are prevented from jumping by additional barriers or by being punished for jumping, there is difficulty in eliminating the behavior, and, in the case of punishment for jumping, the animal has not lost any fears, it has acquired new ones. It appears that avoidance behavior is extremely resistant to extinction. This observation has led to the conclusion that in avoidance behavior there is a source of reinforcement which is strengthening or maintaining the behavior, and, if this is the case, the behavior will get more solidly established with each presentation of the stimulus than it was before. Actually there are many studies in which avoidance behavior has been successfully extinguished and we should be careful in evaluating studies where extinction fails to take place. There may be conditions present whose influence has not been taken into account. It may also be that only the observable behavior extinguishes, while the conditioned fear remains in some degree.

Taking the observation of persistence of avoidance behavior at face value, however, we might examine the problem from the point of view that assumes a reinforcing operation. If the organism is actually being reinforced for having been frightened into doing something, then we can expect the behavior to persist. The reinforcement involved in avoidance learning is based on the following theoretical explanation: the signal initiates the fear pattern via ordinary Pavlovian conditioning. The fear response that ensues serves as a drive and the stimuli from the fear response lead to some kind of behavior, at first somewhat random, then more directly, as determined by the experimenter, to some response which terminates the signal while the fear dissipates. The dissipation or reduction of fear amounts to a reinforcing state of affairs, strengthening the behavior that took place while it was being reduced.

In the case of a child who is frightened and runs to mama, the pattern would presumably be the same. Some stimulus arouses the fear, the fear leads to a response, the comforting arms of mama eliminate the signal, and the fear is reduced, leading to a strengthening of the "run-to-mama" reaction. Nothing has been done about the efficacy of the signal to initiate the fear and so in the future the child will continue to be frightened by the signal and will continue to run to mama. From this point of view nothing much can be done about the elimination of fears. If mama does not provide the comfort, something else will have to, and usually something else will be found that will eliminate the fear signal sooner or later.

The control of fear

From the theoretical sketch presented above, the only way to get rid of a fear response is to work on the fear response itself, and not on what the fear leads to as a consequence. The organism must be gotten to make a different response, something other than fear, to the signal. We have already considered Watson's original hint, and Jones' demonstration of how a fear might be deconditioned by arousing another, contradictory response in the presence of the fear signal. Jones was able to bring the child around to liking rabbits instead of fearing them by associating chocolate with the rabbit. A child can be gotten to enjoy thunder by having a parent who takes advantage of the period between the lightening and the thunder and cajoles or otherwise gets the child to treat the thunder as a big drum beat or other pleasant noise. If the parent shows disappointment at the weakness of some thunder claps and joy at the louder ones, the child may be propagandized into mimicking the parent in some fashion and also learn to show disapproval of quiet thunder and approval of the house-shaking variety. In general, the prescription for elimination of fears is to countercondition the fearful organism by forcing it to deal with the signal itself rather than by permitting it to avoid the signal or terminate it in some fashion. The medical student who has to dissect his "subject" eventually gets over his qualms and squeamishness. A professional ballplayer who feared airplanes maintained his fear as long as he could avoid air travel. With the help of hypnosis he was cajoled into riding in airplanes and found them less distressing. A few flying lessons would probably have helped even more. The big problem, as should be evident, is to be able to engineer the appropriate counterreaction when the basic tendency is to flee. This calls for a degree of control over the behavior as well as skill in selecting countermeasures that is not commonly available. Presumably the above analysis applies to any situation involving fear. We cannot spell out the procedures for every possible instance such as stage fright, fears of high places, sharp objects, dark cellars, etc., but the formula is simple enough; it requires only that the organism be forced to deal with the signaling stimulus in a manner that does not eliminate it or permit the avoidance of the unconditioned stimulus. That this is difficult to apply is obvious. It calls, for instance, in the case of fear of the dark, to send someone into a cellar and keep him there doing *something* instead of or besides being afraid *in the dark.* If what he does turns out to be to have a heart attack, the cure might be worse than the problem.

There are other suggestions that might be of some modest merit in the control of fear. Many fears that are enjoyed by some people are of no real significance as they manage to avoid the situations in which these fears might be aroused. If such control can be developed or arranged, a fear that never is aroused can be dismissed. Even when the fears involve relatively common kinds of signals like dogs and cats they need not be magnified into significance as it is generally possible to avoid these animals. A fear of tigers is of no real consequence to a resident in a civilized community. For that matter, it is probably a healthy kind of fear to have in case of any possible encounter. It is unlikely, however, that anyone who fears tigers is going to lose much sleep about it unless he lives in an Indian village in "tiger country."

The only kinds of fears of any real consequence are those which interfere with everyday activities and result in inefficient adjustments to one's environment. These fears sometimes develop to the point where major changes are affected in one's style of life, such as never leaving the house, for example. Here again, the situation must be evaluated carefully to determine whether any great service will be done to the person or the community if such a fear is removed considering the effort and probable additional anxiety that will be involved. We will concern ourselves with such neurotic fears later in more detail.

It is important to note that various kinds of maturational effects will occur in the process of development and aging. Children will pass from a more or less fearless state into a fearful one and eventually emerge from that with some reasonable success. Most adults are still somewhat afraid of the dark (sometimes with good reason) and do not particularly enjoy groping around in dark cellars or strange places. Because such experiences are not frequent they never learn not to be afraid, nor does it matter too much that they are. Due to the influence of Freud, many people become alarmed at the possibility that some "traumatic" experience in infancy or childhood will manifest itself in neurotic anxiety in later years and such people worry about the fears displayed by their children only to find that many such fears disappear in the general process of growing up. Since no one is in position to say in any individual case what the future effects of a given experience may be, it is impossible to offer any panaceas or even recommend any specific action. On a probability basis alone, one could presume that most children will grow up with some assortment of relatively unimportant fears and that any reasonable amount of protective arrangements should prove adequate. When the fears get to the point of interfering with normal adjustments it is time to take action, presumably along counterconditioning lines.

It is interesting to consider that some cultures promote a general fearful orientation among the citizenry with respect to foreign enemies, the threats of war, air raids, Communist or capitalist infiltration, etc.

How much harm is done to a child that is forced to crawl under his school desk for an air raid drill cannot be estimated. Yet a government may feel forced to institute such practices lest it be accused of a lack of interest in "civil defense." To see enemies behind every bush and to keep a constant aura of suspicion hovering about the activities of scientists, teachers, labor leaders, and any sponsors of international amity may also be an unhealthy approach to group living. Yet a government that does not take such action may find itself accused if difficulties arise. The great danger lies in allowing such "scare" activities to come into the hands of a small group of professionals who might then find it necessary to exaggerate danger or manufacture suspicion in order to stay in power. On the other hand, placing the responsibility with unprofessional people might lead to general havoc. This is the kind of problem for which no easy and ready solution is at hand and for which solutions will probably never be satisfactory.

The control of anger

It would be very convenient if no one ever got angry, especially with us, and our own lives would presumably be more peaceful if we did not lose our tempers. In our considerations of frustration we learned that anger, when it is evidenced, is a consequence of frustration. The obvious solution, then, to the control of anger is to eliminate the possibilities of frustration. This simple solution calls for a rather major reorganization of the world's ways and is not likely to be adopted by any sizable proportion of the population of the world. It is clear that the way to eliminate frustration is to remove obstacles to consummatory behavior that has been initiated by stimulation. This suggests in turn that stimuli to consummatory behavior be restricted to those categories that can be successfully pursued. To the extent that stimuli for consummatory behavior are present when consummatory behavior cannot be practiced, there will be frustration and possibly, anger and aggression.

Any attempt to eliminate obstacles to consummatory responses calls for rather major modifications of social practices as they have developed in our culture. Even such simple activities as footraces involve competition for first place, a position that is normally attained by only one person, barring dead heats. In effect, anger develops where there is any likelihood that the consummatory behavior that has been initiated cannot be completed and this situation prevails in any competitive setting. A competitive setting need not involve the same consummatory behavior. It can also be established in any situation where one person's consummatory behavior interferes with another's consummatory behavior although the behaviors in question may be quite different. When a parent wants to sleep while a child wants to stay up or vice versa there is a competitive situation where each person is frustrating the other. Since it is unlikely that our culture will ever arrive at a philosophy and educational program entailing the submerging of individual interests, we can expect to have competitive behavior continue to flourish and along with it, frustration, anger, and aggression.

What measures can be taken to eliminate or reduce the amount of frustration that we experience? There are techniques for reducing aggression through more or less innocent forms of displacement of aggression such as chopping wood or smashing objects specifically designed to be smashed—one enterprising manufacturer did place on the market a glasslike bauble to be thrown against the wall when the mood took you. But the problem is only indirectly solved by working on the reduction of aggression. The real attack should be directed at the factors involved in frustration. A hermit who renounces civilized activities at the same time eliminates many sources of frustration (while developing, perhaps, one big bargain package). Any procedure which results in the renunciation of some kinds of consummatory behavior will reduce frustration to a degree. People who have no interest in classical music are not frustrated when every radio station provides the latest popular form of music. If we do not train people to want what they cannot get, they will not be frustrated. If they already want what they cannot get, they might be trained not to want it so often or at all. This is, however, a re-educating process and extremely difficult to effect. The direct education is more potent. One mother trained her children to dislike her, to have no use for her, and to favor other relatives so that they would not miss her when she died. The training seemed to be quite effective, but not likely to prove popular with mothers generally.

The problem of changing consummatory interests or "goals" is not insoluble. Children, in the process of growing up, are continually changing their interests. The doll the little girl could not live without is thrown into the garbage can when the little girl grows up. The difficulty is that with growth and development many more and more difficult goals are introduced into the life history, and to settle for lesser goals is the mark of the inferior person in our culture. What must be effectively established in the growing youngster is a respectful attitude toward the probability of success. If half the college population wants to acquire medical degrees there is going to be a tremendous amount of frustration generated in the academic environment for the simple reason that medical schools do not accept all of the applicants. The immediate suggestion is to have an assortment of "goals" which can function as acceptable alternatives. Learning how to bow gracefully to the inevitable should be assiduously practiced and parents should foster such learning by introducing verbal formuli which can be tapped in future instances. When the child wants to see two different television programs at the same time, it must inevitably bow to the facts and such an occasion can be used by the watchful parent to spell out the advantages of broad interests and suitable substitutes in adjusting to the limitations of the real world.

FRUSTRATION TOLERANCE

The above remarks are sometimes incorporated in discussions of frustration tolerance. This expression refers to an acquired capacity for accepting disappointments, delays, and the more or less inevitable obstacles that intrude into our lives. Some psychologists advocate a deliberate program of training for frustration tolerance (see Skinner, 1948) by introducing delays and obstacles into such behavioral arenas as dining-rooms. There may be some merit to such a suggestion but there seem to be enough obstacles to go around without creating additional ones in most cases. What a program of frustration-tolerance education amounts to is educating the growing child to accept reality and to live with it. This might include some attempt to keep children from accepting mythical and magical views along with Santa Claus and good fairies. How much would be gained from such an effort is debatable. Most children manage to get along without Santa Claus after seven or eight years with no serious aftereffects. Perhaps other fantasies that do not correspond with reality also are eliminated for the same reason. Those fantasies that are retained are probably of the nature that they cannot be tested by matching them with reality and there might be some question of their frustration capacities. They might, in fact, make some kinds of frustrations tolerable. To develop an adequate appreciation of reality is a difficult task. The parents of a retarded child find it extremely difficult to accept suggestions that the child might never go to college. Blind individuals and those with other handicaps show more tendencies toward magical thinking, miraculous cures, and in some cases resist making any effort at coping with their present situations in a realistic fashion.

It has been emphasized that frustration tolerance is something that has to be learned and presumably such learning would follow the principles that apply to other kinds of learning. The learner must be reinforced for coping with situations in realistic ways. If the learner is also taught to set realistic goals with suitable alternates as well as to perceive the situations in which he operates realistically, his frustration frequency and intensity might be reduced. There are no simple rules that apply to any particular kind of obstacle or situation and general advice would be of little value. By anticipating obstacles it is occasionally possible to reduce or eliminate certain sources of frustration. If one is frequently waiting for someone else who "is always late" a ready remedy may be available in employing the waiting time in reading. The habit of carrying a pocket-sized book as part of basic equipment might well save a lot of waiting-induced frustration. Much frustration is generated in circumstances that make it difficult if not impossible to keep appointments. It might be possible to reduce the number of appointments that are made and to make those that must be made on a looser basis than pinpointing a time. Outside of business responsibilities, there seems to be no reason why a young man should promise to be at some young lady's house at 8:15 P.M. on Thursday. To keep such an appointment might involve considerable difficulty and much would be saved (and possibly lost) by some more flexible agreement for merely social arrangements that do not involve many people or upset other preparations. A variety of interests is the best antidote for frustration; rigid habits are most likely to lead to frustration.

Emotional aspects of cognitive behavior

Prejudice

In considering learning, thinking, and motivation we had frequent occasions for bringing up affective or emotional considerations. We have repeatedly made the point that no behavior is free from affective features. Our viscera are always with us and their activities "color" our thinking and everything else we do. In some instances an emotional tone or coloration is the major feature of whatever might be passing for thinking with us. Much of our daily life reflects an emotional packing whether we are choosing a necktie, applying for a loan, or simply picking out the items on the menu that we will have for dinner. Our likes and dislikes are continuously being stimulated into existence and determine our reactions.

The American culture officially fosters the development of tolerance and mutual respect for all individuals regardless of creed, race, color, age, sex, economic status, etc. Yet each of us has his private reactions to all other individuals, of whatever variety, colored by extraneous influences which may have nothing to do with the worth of the individual involved, but depend, rather, upon emotional conditionings which have been imposed upon us. The vast amount of prejudice that prevails in our culture reflects the degree to which emotional loading has been incorporated in the rearing of our citizenry.

A prejudice, as the term implies, is a prejudgment, a decision for or against something or someone. By its very nature of for-or-against-ness, a prejudice involves an emotional aspect when the decision is made in advance of an evaluation of a case on its merits. Prejudices are no different in nature from any attitude or set except for the possible intensity-dimension involved, and even here we have to consider relatively mild prejudices like "preferences" or relatively low levels of approval or disapproval. In ordinary discourse we reserve the word prejudice for marking out more important kinds of prejudgments that are shared by many members of one group, usually against another, as in the case of racial prejudices where we can assume both groups to be negatively oriented when any problem of interaction develops. We sometimes lose sight of the fact that very often the prejudice is equally strong on both sides, and that solutions to social problems cannot be attained by working only in one group. Prejudices, while commonly shared by many members of a group, are necessarily reactions or attitudes and are presumably learned by the individual in the ordinary routine of growing up. There may be some special predisposing factors to the development of some kinds of prejudice especially if members of some group are seen as sources of frustrations or obstacles to individual consummatory responses, but, frequently enough, such prejudices are generated without any individual experience of frustration. Parents can easily innoculate a child with the parental attitudes toward religion, economic status, racial origins, even fruits and vegetables. The devices of propaganda are commonly used in the home and the parents' commitment to some opinion which is not a universal one but which is opposed by some other opinion is enough to initiate the process of propagandizing the child. Thus parents who subscribe to one religious affiliation may find that affiliation threatened by members of some other faith. The challenge to their own religion is a frustrating circumstance and can invite aggressive behavior. Such behavior is normally restricted by police and social conventions and is then displaced in talk at home. The child who has frequently been reinforced for mouthing the opinions expressed by the parents will now acquire new opinions on subjects he knows nothing about.

Stereotypes

If the members of some group are distinctive in some respect such as skin color, uniform, or other identifying characteristics they come to be identified abstractly in terms of the distinguishing feature instead of being taken for individuals in their own right. The attitudes developed toward one individual can be transferred intact to another with the same characteristics. Such *stereotypes* are convenient techniques for dealing with many individual cases as one although the process of thinking in terms of stereotypes is, of course, a gross perversion of realistic thinking. Sometimes a well-developed stereotype is of service to a group as when a policeman carries the weight of authority of all police officers even though he himself might be quite an inferior person and far from the dominating figure his role places him in. On the other hand, the police in our society carry the burden of being identified as frustrators or obstacles to personal pleasure regardless of the kindly intent of any individual officer. In a similar vein, the most rascally judge is treated with dignity because all judges are revered figures who uphold the law regardless of the possible conniving which resulted in their march to the bench, and bankers are solid conservative people even though we occasionally read of one who got tired of looking at all that money and ran off to Miami with his secretary.

Perceiving all members of some group in terms of a stereotype enables a frustrated individual to displace his aggressions over a wide population area in an indirect fashion without risking encounters with individuals of the group. He can blame politicians, foreigners, "capital," or "labor" for his troubles without facing individuals or individual issues directly. Such displaced aggression is usually called "scapegoating" (G. Allport, 1944) after the Biblical practice of putting all your sins on the back of a goat and driving it out into the desert.[1] Occasionally the displaced aggression is not enough to fully discharge the frustration or it gets out of hand and leads to more direct aggression against some group. But even when the aggression is directed against individual members of a group, it is done in an abstract way—it is not the individual who is being aggressed, even though he is left cold and dead, it is the stereotype that has been attacked.

The stereotypes in our thinking are usually developed as convenient devices, mediators for a habitual action which is more readily functional than having to develop separate responses to all individual representatives of a group. As such they result in endless confusion when they prove to be inadequate to the actual individual stimulus. When the anti-Semitic person becomes friendly with someone he has no reason for believing to be Jewish and later discovers this fact, he may become uncomfortable with his new knowledge. His attitudes toward the stereotype conflict with his attitude toward his friend. In some areas in our culture it is not considered polite to have prejudices and we sometimes hear someone say "some of my best friends are. . . ." This can be readily interpreted as the mark of prejudice because of the use of the label which identifies the person as having a well-developed stereotype as his usual method for dealing with members of the group in question who are not his friends.

[1] Lev. 16:10.

While prejudice of any kind is undesirable in social interactions, it is extremely difficult to erradicate. We are all prejudiced in some areas, if not in all, to the extent that we engage in stereotyping and classifying ideas or people under convenient labels instead of handling each case on its merits. To do the latter is virtually impossible in view of the convenience we earn by use of the label and the common set. It is probably easier to change one prejudice into another than to get someone to think without prejudging items that can be placed in classes. It is far easier to be for or against than to be neutral. Not all politicians are crooks but the average citizen will have his suspicions. Not all Latin lovers are romantic, and not all Italians sing "all over Italy," but it is easier to think so than to constantly be considering the boring and realistic facts. Even scientists, for whom the stereotype consists of a devotion to objectivity and to research, are prejudiced, not only about members of other groups, but even within their own areas. One group or school of scientists may combat another school for years and years with the rather fixed view that whatever the opposition proposes is *ipso facto* wrong. The facts of one school are termed prejudices by the other and much of the effort of the devoted and objective scientist is devoted to building fires under the opposition. On the creative level such prejudices may be of value—they are called "heuristic" that is, stimulating and provocative of new ideas and more research. To dream of a world without prejudice may be a noble aspiration but it appears an unrealistic goal. To break down prejudice involves working on an individual basis with individuals and eliminating stereotyped behavior. To the extent that this is done without creating basic frustrations, the dream can be approximated.

CHAPTER 13

Conflict and Adjustment

The nature of conflict · Experimental neuroses · Experimentally produced neuroses without discrimination · The Miller analysis of conflict · Approach-approach conflicts · Approach-avoidance conflicts · Avoidance-avoidance conflicts · Double approach-avoidance conflicts · A classification of conflicts · Defense mechanisms · Personality disorders and psychotherapy · Structural and functional disorders · Normal and abnormal · Neuroses and psychoses · Psychotherapy · Psychotherapeutic strategies · Interpretative therapy · Nondirective therapy · Evaluation of psychotherapy · The need for counseling

In our culture people have troubles. Possibly this is true in any culture and possibly the amount of trouble is exaggerated but the media of mass communication, the pronouncements of national leaders, the advertisements in our magazines, and the conversations of our friends all point to a great preoccupation with problems of an emotional nature. On the one hand we are told that our chances are excellent of entering a mental institution (one out of five in New York State, according to some prognosticators) and on the other hand we are informed that we will probably die of cancer of the lung if we do not give up smoking, if we have not been killed in an automobile accident. Add to these threats the fears of atomic attacks and the national disturbance over our "inferior" educational system, the growing delinquency rates, the growing divorce rates, the fluctuations in economic life, and the picture is indeed a gloomy one. The front page of your morning newspaper is no invitation to gracious living.

Even when the news is good it is accompanied by a threat. When medical scientists report a cure for a disease they raise the question as to whether new forms of cure-resisting viruses will not now develop. Elimination of one form of threat exposes us to others which formerly had no chance to flourish. The general level of dissatisfaction is maintained at a high point. Even in such simple matters as transportation an effort is made to keep the purchaser dissatisfied with last year's car in favor of the current model which is promoted as being longer (or shorter), with more chrome (or less unnecessary ornamentation). The practices of women's clothing designers have become part of the culture pattern and the seasonal changes are something we look forward to, but the constant pressure to change our ways and standards in the milk we drink, the bread we eat, the wives we marry, and the schools our children attend is symptomatic of a general theme of unhappiness and preoccupation with adjustment which pervades the culture.

It is logical for psychologists to interest themselves in this trouble-beset culture and its victims, and many attempts have been made to understand the nature of the culture and the factors that underlie human misery. Out of these attempts has grown the concept of conflict. Around this concept have developed various theories of how conflicts develop, the roles they play, and the nature of the defenses that are attempted to cope with conflicts. These interesting questions will occupy us now.

THE NATURE OF CONFLICT

What is a conflict? Under what conditions can we be said to have one? The term has been rather uncritically adopted into technical usage from general popular usage and we have no "official" definition. We can appreciate, however, even in the absence of a formal definition that a conflict calls for an opposition of two (if not more) factors, a struggle between contestants. It is the nature of the factors or contestants that concerns us here. For psychologists, the components of a conflict might be ideas, wishes, impulses, tendencies to respond in opposing directions, instincts, emotions, even percepts. In one way or another all of these have been proposed for combatant roles. The original emphasis on conflict was developed by Freud (1938), and for him, the conflicting agencies were urges, wishes, and instincts; in the case of instincts, for example, Freud conceived of a major battle of a more or less continuous nature between a Life instinct and a Death instinct. In his more specific preoccupations, Freud was concerned with conflicts between desires, wishes, or urges.

In our own everyday experiences we are familiar with the *kind* of affair which concerned Freud. We can illustrate with innocent examples (Freud was occupied with less innocent types) of more or less casual conflicts: should we study or go to the movies, should we have a Manhattan or a Martini, a blue necktie or a maroon, read the paper or a magazine, beef or pork, and so on and on through the day. These conflicts are normally short-lived, the decision is quickly made, sometimes forced upon us, but, the momentary hesitancy involved in the choice indicated the conflict was present. Perhaps a little later the choice is regretted, again indicating that a conflict had been present. Such conflicts as just listed are quite conscious affairs as might be more serious problems like should we buy a house or rent, this school or that one for the kids, this job or that one, this wife or that one? Not all aspects of such conflicts would necessarily be conscious matters but the fact of the conflict itself would be quite conscious. The subject involved could easily report if we asked him while he hesitated, "I have a conflict" or "I can't make up my mind between. . . ." The subject involved might not be able to tell us *why* he was having a conflict and a fuller examination of the life history might provide some basis for an explanation, but superficially, at least, such conflicts might be classified as conscious ones.

In his own views, Freud was concerned primarily with unconscious factors in conflict. He arrived at the conclusion that in the human organism many forces were at work which did not operate at a conscious level but which nevertheless affected behavior. He postulated such forces as unconscious wishes which could compete or interfere with decisions or behavior presumably related to conscious wishes. Thus, in one of his famous cases, a young lady sought treatment for a paralyzed arm. Such paralyses, if it can be shown that there is no "physical" cause, are referred to as "functional," "hysterical," or "conversion" symptoms. Presumably, physical cures are of no value and the problem must be attacked "psychologically." She reported a desire to marry a young man but found this inconvenient because she was responsible for the care of her aging father. After working with the girl, Freud decided that she wanted to get rid of the burden her father represented. This wholly natural "unnatural" wish functioned only on an unconscious level where it was held under restraint by culturally acquired inhibitory forces (Freud thought of such forces as "conscience" or "Superego") which also operated for the most part unconsciously. Here we have a young lady with a conflict on a conscious level which she could discuss with anyone "I'd like to marry but I can't" (Should I marry or not? Can I leave my father?) and an unconscious conflict (the wish to get rid of the burden opposed by a daughter's sense of duty).

We will not concern ourselves further with the Freudian approach. We mention it only to point out that conflicts have been conceived of as taking place between conscious components, between conscious and unconscious components, and between unconscious components. The kinds of approaches or attacks on these conflicts that have been developed in clinical practice have not resulted in scientifically satisfactory evidence relating to the nature of conflict and the factors involved. The case studies are interesting and we need not deny out of hand that something in the nature of what has been described might occur, but laboratory studies which are admittedly difficult to carry on have failed to confirm Freudian postulations with anything like acceptable precision (Sears, 1943). While most psychologists are friendly to Freud, they have not accepted Freudian theory as anything but suggestive in nature and have turned to other methods for more objective data about the nature of conflict which might eventually result in a scientific analysis.

The basic objective type of approach to conflict stems from a stimulus-response orientation toward behavior analysis. From an S ⟶ R view, a conflict will result when an organism is simultaneously stimulated to make two different responses. To study conflict, then, all that is required is to present two different stimuli and observe the results. A number of interesting developments have originated from this basic procedure and we shall look at these. The first contribution in this area was made by Pavlov, and we can start with him.

Experimental neuroses

It will be recalled that in ordinary conditioning experiments involving such stimuli as lights and tones, it is commonly observed that the subject responds not only to the specific stimulus used as a conditioning signal but also to variations of that stimulus. This process is called "generalization" (see p. 230). If the experimenter uses a metronome as a conditioned stimulus and has it set at 60 beats per minute, the animal will respond to this rate but also to a wide range of other rates. If it is desired for some reason to restrict the range of stimulation to which the organism should respond, a systematic program of reinforcement of the standard and extinction of any other stimulus value must be initiated. The animal receives no food when the metronome beats at 70 or 50, but does when it beats at 60. Over a period of time, the "discrimination" involved can be narrowed down to the limits of the animal's capacity to discriminate. When these limits are reached, let us say that the animal now behaves appropriately to 60 and 57 beats per minute, any further discrimination is too difficult and if the animal is "forced" to respond in the 58, 59, range, it may begin to show signs of disturbance. In some cases the disturbance may be very severe so that the animal "breaks down," refuses to enter the laboratory, gets nasty and un-co-operative, and shows signs of great agitation. The disturbances in some cases were sufficiently distressing for Pavlov (1927) to have considered them genuine neurotic states. With the publication of such findings, psychologists began to see the possibility of an experimental approach to abnormal behavior. The dog was considered to have been put into a state of conflict and the conflict in turn was presumed to have resulted in the neurosis.

If this could be taken as a suitable paradigm for human behavior, the human neuroses could be interpreted also as due to conflicts. To be properly strict about it, human neuroses should be interpreted as resulting from systematic stimulation from two highly similar sources calling for a response to one and not to the other. It is difficult to conceive of any situation like this in human affairs and even more difficult to relate it to the behavioral situations that precede human breakdowns of a neurotic nature. There is no known case study which would exactly parallel Pavlov's routine on a human level with a neurotic outcome. To fit the vast variety of human neurotic situatons to the paradigm proposed by Pavlov would indeed be an achievement. But Pavlov's work was of value in encouraging additional research in the area of conflict and we can turn to some American work that has for some unknown reason not received the attention it merits.

Experimentally produced neuroses without discrimination

The American psychologist Liddell (1944) adapted Pavlov's techniques to the study of farm animals (pigs, goats, sheep) and made use of avoidance responses instead of salivation as his experimental routine. He too observed the development of experimental neuroses in his animals but found that such disorderly behavior as Pavlov described could be developed without putting the animal into a discrimination situation. All that was required was to carry on a systematic program of securely fastening the animal to a frame, as Pavlov did, and proceed to administer the unconditioned stimulus itself in a regular, periodic fashion. If the animal were shocked every seven seconds, for example, for an hour at a time, and nothing else was done to it, the animal after some extensive period of such daily practice might develop the symptoms Pavlov described. Liddell proposed, on the basis of his observations, that the ingredients for a neurotic condition consisted of a prolonged, persistent, regular course of stimulation (presumably of an unpleasant nature) where the subject could do nothing about the "inevitable reinforcement." An additional factor was the restriction of the animal's movement by the harness and the narrow stall. Liddell referred to the restriction of freedom as "encapsulation" and the combination of the encapsulation and inevitable reinforcement was sufficient for the development of the neuroses. The parallel to Liddell's animals that is suggested by the role of the educated housewife is striking. A housewife with small children might very well feel encapsulated under certain restrictive conditions, and if her lot consists of an inevitable succession of unpleasant duties over a long period of time we might expect rather disturbing results. It is presumed that the housewife that shows neurotic symptoms must dislike making beds, cooking, and washing dishes, and that her encapsulation is rather complete in isolating her from time-consuming cultural activities she might have been brought up to enjoy. If a housewife has never learned to enjoy freedom before marriage the encapsulation might actually be a positive reinforcer with no occasions for maladjustment.

It should be noted that Liddell was careful to establish the fact that if his sheep or goats had company while in the Pavlov frame, or if they were free to move about, the systematic "inevitable reinforcement" was not sufficient to produce neurotic behavior. The important point to notice in Liddell's work is that no conditioned stimuli (barring a temporal interval) and certainly no combinations of positive and negative stimuli were employed. There was no choice of reaction. There would always be a shock to the foot. Yet under these circumstances, maladjustments of a serious magnitude developed. Such findings force us to be extremely cautious about the nature and role of conflict as the sole instigator of neurotic behavior.

THE MILLER ANALYSIS OF CONFLICT

Perhaps the most influential studies of conflict behavior in the United States have been done by Neal Miller (1944) of Yale University. Miller combined the principles and observations of Hull and Lewin and applied them to an analysis of conflict behavior from which testable hypotheses could be derived. Miller began his analysis with a consideration of approach and avoidance tendencies such as we have already discussed in the previous chapter. Such tendencies had already been studied to some extent and an important feature of approach and avoidance behavior had been isolated in the recognition of *gradients* of approach and avoidance, that is, it had been observed that organisms approaching a positive stimulus location move faster and faster (the positive goal gradient) while organisms retreating from a negative stimulus location move slower and slower as the distance from the negative goal increases. Miller raised the question of what would happen if two such gradients were elicited at the same time in what could be conceived as a conflict situation. It is unfortunate that the interest in gradients was so dominant a factor in Miller's analysis because it forces a more or less "geographical" orientation onto the problem. "Goals" are considered to be located in space and the organism is presumed to be motivated to move toward or away from these spatial goals. Miller, of course, was concerned with possible experimental attacks and behavior could most easily be observed in terms of locomotion toward or away from fixed positions. The concept of "goals" may prove to be awkward and to speak of negative goals appears somewhat contradictory. Observations of behavior in terms of locomotion in space may also prove to be of limited value. With these precautions before us we can consider Miller's analysis. By pairing various combinations of approach and avoidance gradients, Miller arrived at the following classification of conflicts:

1. Approach-approach. Here the organism is thought of as being between two positive goals with a tendency to approach each.
2. Approach-avoidance. Here the organism has a tendency to approach a positive goal, but there is also a tendency to avoid the same locus.
3. Avoidance-avoidance. Here the organism is caught between two negative goals, with a tendency to avoid each.
4. Double approach-avoidance. Here the two goals are positive, but attaining one will result in the loss of the other. In the simple approach-approach conflict, one goal can be approached at a time; the other simply remains there.

We can now explain each type of conflict in terms of experimental observations and notice the kinds of solutions that appear to function.

Approach-approach conflicts

This is the kind of situation that we face daily in the selection of some item from a number of alternatives. Shall it be orange juice or tomato juice for breakfast. We can have either, perhaps both, and if one is adequate, we can have the other later, perhaps tomorrow. Experimentally, Miller could place a rat in the middle of a long alley where food was available at each end and observe what the rat would do; or, alternatively, a child might be presented with a pointer and asked to point to whichever of two items it might like to get, the choices being between such things as candy or a toy, or the choice might be between orange juice and grape juice. The movements of the pointer could be observed, and were, in fact, recorded in such experiments. In general the findings were that there was but little hesitation; the rat would run toward whatever end it happened to look at or start toward first; the child might hesitate a bit and move first one way, then the other, but more or less quickly indicate a definite choice. Miller concluded that such conflicts are not especially serious; they are quickly attended to by a definitive commitment. It is difficult to establish genuine equality between alternatives and a slight preference decides the outcome. The movement of the rat's head in one direction is enough to commit the animal to a course of action. It is unlikely that any serious personal disturbances arise from approach-approach conflicts.

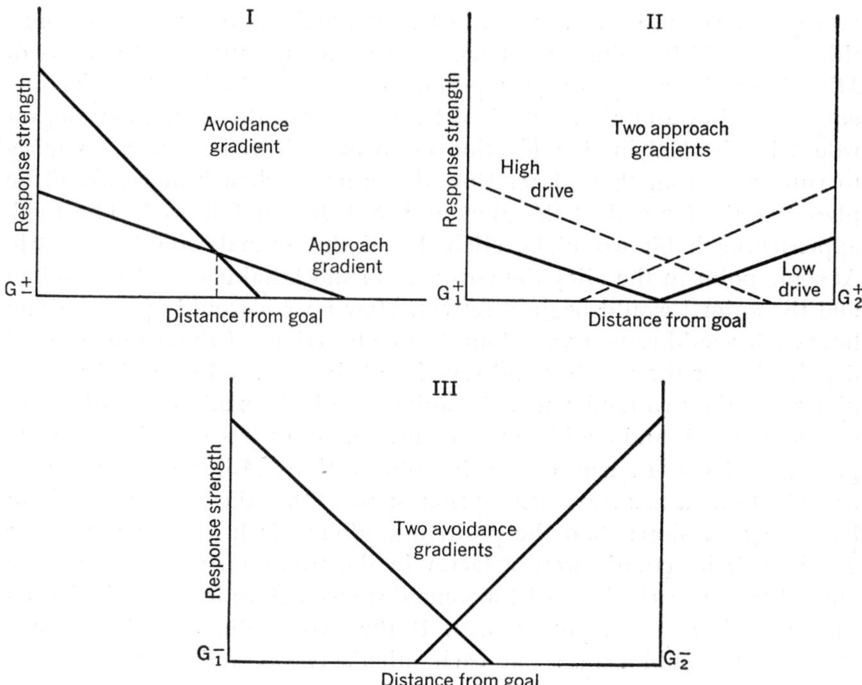

Figure 14 The Miller analysis of conflict. In I, the subject has a tendency to approach the locus of the goal, but he has a stronger (steeper) tendency to avoid it. The avoidance tendency, however, does not begin to be effective until some progress toward the goal has been made. Other things being equal, the subject will stop, in conflict, where the gradients intersect. Here he will vacillate indecisively. In II, the subject is attracted toward separate positive goals. He can be in only momentary conflict, because the moment he moves in the direction of one, he lessens the tendency to approach the other. If the subject is under a higher drive, he will merely move faster. There will be no more, nor less conflict. In III, the subject is caught in the "sphere of influence" of two negative goals. He cannot leave either without getting nearer the other. He will vacillate uncomfortably in the limited area shown as the intersection of the gradients. Note the relatively steeper gradients Miller assumes for the avoidance tendency. According to Miller, the slope of the gradients will not be altered by changes in drive or goal attractiveness; only their height can be changed. (See N. Miller, 1944.)

Approach-avoidance conflicts

Here we have some language or semantic difficulties. This kind of conflict is sometimes loosely described as wanting something and not wanting it at the same time. It is unlikely that such a state of affairs ever exists. We want something, to be sure, and we may not want something else which trying to get what we want may involve. In terms of Miller's spatial analysis and experiment, food would be placed at one end of an alley and after a rat had learned to run there for food, the rat would be shocked in that location often enough to initiate a tendency to run away from that place. Now the animal, when hungry, could be placed at the far end of the alley and its behavior followed. The food-approaching habit would be elicited and the animal would approach. At some point in the alley the escape-from shock habit would be elicited and the animal would begin a retreat. How near it would approach and how far it would retreat were found to be functions of the degree of food deprivation or the number and severity of the shocks. By careful manipulation of the two tendencies, the animal could be made to vacillate between approach and avoidance, stay away more or less completely or approach and eat. In considering his observations Miller made what he thought to be a necessary assumption, namely that the negative gradient had a steeper slope than the positive gradient. Such a steeper negative gradient, if it actually were a factor in the situation, would permit an animal to approach the goal for some distance before it would find itself in a negatively more potent area. If the two gradients had the same slope, they would cancel out each other's effects and nothing would happen (see Fig. 14).

Miller considered the approach-avoidance conflict the prototype or paradigm of human neurotic conflicts. The person with a conflict is considered to be stimulated along some course of action (toward a positive goal) but the closer he gets to achieving this goal, the greater the threat to him of failure, rejection, or disaster of one kind or another. As a consequence of the interplay of such positive and negative factors the person finds himself unable to attain his ends although always striving toward them; he becomes inefficient, vacillates, and gets nothing done. Because the goal is not attained and the negative factors may be difficult to face or talk about and some kind of adjustment must be made to the situation, the organism is likely to develop one kind or another of such adjustments, none of them really adequate and necessarily indicative of the conflict that must be present. Such inadequate adjustments are called "defense mechanisms" and will be discussed later. We might illustrate some possible human conflicts that appear to reflect the approach-avoidance paradigm: a young man may wish to propose to a young lady but fears being turned down on the basis of, to him, satisfactory evidence. He may hem and haw and just about "pop the question" but never does get around to it. Or, the loyal employee would like to ask for a raise, but for reasons good enough for him, is afraid that raising the issue is likely to result in being rebuffed, perhaps even fired. He makes up his mind daily that today is the day, but somehow, he never gets to the point. A student would like to be a star on the football field or in other sports but does not go out for any team because he fears he will be dismissed as incompetent. A young lady knows she could be a star in New York but her family will be hurt or outraged. Sexual intercourse is attractive but consequences might be dangerous. Such examples can be made up ad infinitum and we can all find illustrations in our own histories.

Avoidance-avoidance conflicts

Here we have the classical "between the devil and the deep blue sea" situation. When the command "Follow that sergeant" is given, the unenthusiastic soldier may have his troubles. The bigamist whose wives find out is caught in the middle. If you marry the girl your family will disown you; if you don't, her father will "fix you good." The laboratory rat is placed in the middle of the alley at each end of which it has been shocked. There is no place to go but up and that is prevented by the apparatus. The only solution that appears to do any good is to "leave the field." Such a solution has its own disadvantages and possible dire consequences and is in effect, no solution. Somebody is likely to come after you. Doing nothing is frequently out of the question if events themselves determine the issue. Miller uses the example of the boy caught in the pasture between two charging bulls. You just can't stand there; if possible, you leave the field. The avoidance-avoidance situation is an intolerable one; to the extent that time is available, nothing will be done because any move in one direction brings you closer to another danger. The laboratory example is not especially appropriate to use as an analogy for human situations. The confined animal is unable to leave the field or develop any other defenses. On the human level we can imagine avoidance-avoidance conflicts generating considerable anxiety from double sources of fear stimuli. The relation of anxiety to such double-avoidance has not yet been adequately traced.

Double approach-avoidance conflicts

In this situation some kind of appreciation of potential loss must be present and a laboratory demonstration with infra human organisms is probably impossible to establish. In this type of conflict, the subject is attracted to two different goals but can have only one of them. If you marry Mary you can't have Susie. The familiar "you can't have your cake and eat it" seems to cover the situation. While some frustration from the inevitable loss may be anticipated, the compensations resulting from attaining one goal may make up for the sacrificed pleasures. Because it is impossible to evaluate realistically "what might have been," a double approach-avoidance conflict may have repercussions at some later period when dissatisfactions and recriminations may develop. "I gave you the best years of my life" is a common refrain in soap operas and perhaps in "real life." The double approach-avoidance conflict may generate hesitation of a much more profound degree than a simple approach-approach conflict. When an individual gives signs of hesitation in approaching an obviously attractive goal we can suspect another attraction somewhere in the background, just as we might suspect a negative factor which might not be obvious to us in other cases of vacillation and hesitation or other evidence of some "defense mechanism."

Miller's analysis of conflict behavior is the most thorough one available. We have already discussed the limitation involved in the geographical orientation which the emphasis on gradients forces onto the interpretation. The gradients may not actually exist in the manner and form that Miller assumes. There is some evidence (Rigby, 1954) that the negative and positive gradients do not have different slopes, a vital necessity in Miller's view. The laboratory restriction to spatial studies is again a weakness. An individual can enjoy a fully developed conflict in the quiet of his own home in the absence of any but symbolic, self-generated stimuli. He might at one time consider certain consequences and later consider others from separate courses of action. To have to think in terms of gradients may be very restrictive. Such gradients may indeed operate in the confines of an alley but need not play any significant role in an ordinary environment. There is no problem in approaching a boss and offering him a cigar. His geographical proximity is not frightening. It is the proximity of the raise-asking response that generates the trouble. It might be possible to restate the findings of spatial experiments in temporal terms and to examine the approach-avoidance tendencies in other experimental settings. In one such attempt, for example, rats were trained to make two separate kinds of avoidance responses to separate stimuli (light and tone). When both stimuli were presented at once (the double-avoidance situation), the rats did not vacillate or hesitate or leave the field—they performed one response or both in succession. The principles which apply to the approach and avoidance situations are still to be discovered. At present we have only suggestions from which to proceed.

A CLASSIFICATION OF CONFLICTS

In considering the several types of conflict described by Miller we indicated some of the "normal" solutions of some of these. The approach-approach situation is usually quickly and definitely solved by acting on one or another of the alternatives. The avoidance-avoidance situation is solved by "leaving the field" if this is possible. The other two kinds of conflict have no real solutions and even accepting one of the positive alternates in the double approach-avoidance situation leaves room for recriminations and regrets which might involve the individual in further difficulties. In the approach-avoidance situation no easy solution is readily available. Before we raise the question of what the individual does in such cases, let us restate the general nature of conflict. A conflict exists when the individual is being stimulated into two courses of action at the same time and where these actions are incompatible with each other. Actually, on a human level, the routine circumstances of daily life, the normal requirements imposed by social or economic obligations and a host of other factors act to delay any immediate action in many kinds of conflicts and it is hardly correct to define conflicts in terms of simultaneous stimulations. Such conditions might be arranged in a laboratory. In ordinary life situations it is more likely that the individual's conflict behavior takes place in more symbolic terms; he thinks about one course of action for a while, then about its consequences. It is difficult if not impossible to think of two things at the same time. Thinking about consequences of one action might lead him to think of other courses and their consequences. At times he might concentrate for hours on one course only, and even reach decisions, before something comes up to restrain him and force attention to another alternative. If "deadlines" can be delayed, a conflict can be entertained for years; on the other hand, if events are forcing an issue, the individual in conflict may panic and be unable to indulge in anything like thinking behavior, giving way to a "Oh, what shall I do, what shall I do?" routine.

The possibility of delay, in fact, is what makes a conflict possible. The kinds of behavior studied by Pavlov and by Miller are more typical of panic states generated by the forcing of events by a deadline. A human conflict is much more of an "instrumental" situation in that the stimuli involved are not nearly so clearly evident. Even in the "shotgun" wedding situation, the young man can be riding out the storm in his own home with no shotguns in evidence other than those which he conjures up for himself. And again, in such a situation, he can delay the wedding march for at least a short period. During this delay he is going to be preoccupied with what he wants to do (and this may be very negative) and what he does not want to do. To state these alternatives as approach and avoidance may not be quite close enough. It is possible that he does not want to approach anything, the status quo might be quite satisfactory; his only problem may be in devising techniques which keep him from doing something or which keep something from happening. Even the schoolchild with the bad report card may not care about receiving praise—he may be quite content if papa never finds out. In other kinds of conflict, the subject may definitely want something, as for example, a raise in pay, and he may fear discharge for asking; but again, to express this as an approach-avoidance situation may be somewhat incomplete or misleading. The person is not approaching anything—he wants something and this is a specific kind of response of a mediational sort as we described in connection with motives. To say that he fears discharge is to spell out another specific mediational response, a fear or anxiety reaction. This is not necessarily adequately defined as "avoidance" or even as another want. A person who is afraid, is afraid, and to say that he wants not to be afraid, or that he wants peace and serenity to prevail, is gratuitous and unnecessary.

In view of these considerations then, we must try to redefine the concept of conflict to indicate what it includes or may consist of; this turns out to be a rather broad assortment of possibilities which we can now state as follows:

1. There can be a conflict between one want and another want if two separate stimuli are present to initiate such wants (approach-approach). On the human level such stimuli can be self-generated through verbal mediators. A person might want to buy one brand of car or toothpaste and think of other brands that might be equally acceptable. This kind of conflict will not trouble him for long. Such conflicts are probably rare as the stimuli are presumed to be equal in strength and such equality is difficult to arrange. Most people have fairly strong preferences and equally strong stimuli acting at the same time would be unusual. The individual in conflict will flip a coin or consult some acceptable authority and take action. If the action proves satisfactory his conflict is over. If unsatisfactory results develop he may have occasion to regret his choice, call himself a fool, and perhaps seek ways

out of his choice if that is feasible and if the problem is a serious one. This may lead to other kinds of conflicts.

2. There can be a conflict between a positive want initiated by some stimulus and a negative state like fear in varying degrees of potency. The fear may be intermittent or persistent and prevent any action that the want might generate or it might be of a low degree of activation when the situation is merely thought about and grow more serious when action leads the individual closer to the source of want satisfaction. The little boy on the diving board may want the plaudits of his friends for his courage, but his actual state is likely to be one that generates avoidance behavior. In his own bedroom the plaudits can sound more sweetly in his imaginary dreams; the fears do not arise, or if they do, they are only of modest intensity. He may wander over to the swimming area, examine the board, estimate its height and otherwise appraise the situation. The closer he comes to getting into a situation which calls for diving, the stronger the fear becomes. Here the conflict is between a wanting response and a fear response. Approach-avoidance may not be quite suitable a description. The boy is not approaching anything in having a want. It may be incorrect to say he wants to dive. What he wants is praise or glory. Diving is only incidental, though material to the want. We may never know he had such a want, to be sure, if he never does approach the board, but that is only a limitation on our ability to detect conflict where it may exist. The nature of the conflict can change markedly if he ever does get on the board. He may then have two fears, one of diving and one of not diving. He may no longer want anything.

3. There may be a conflict between a negative state (fear or other undesirable state) and a simple status quo want; that is, the individual may be quite content with his current prospects but circumstances are forcing him toward some undesired action. He expresses this as "Why can't they just leave me alone?" This condition cannot be described as approach-avoidance as the person is not interested in attaining any goal. He prefers things to remain as they are, unchanged. The conflict, however, is genuine enough because there is some felt obligation to comply with the negative forces involved. The negative state does not have to be fear; it may involve no more than an irritation and the "avoidance" involved is not the kind that might be associated with fear so much as "annoyance." In some instances the prospective annoyance might be lifelong in duration and of strong potency in generating avoidance. The conflict can exist only because the avoidance is not easily achieved; it may involve other kinds of irritations, or as below, there may be some obligation felt to comply. To argue that complying

with an obligation is based in turn on fear of not complying seems a semantic quibble.

4. There may be a conflict between two fear reactions. Actually this is a complex state of fear where alternatives appear to be limited and where there is some felt necessity for doing something; there are undesired obligations to behave in somewhat contradictory manners. The little boy who broke his father's pipe may be afraid to go home and also be afraid to stay away from the house. He may be punished for either. The soldier who is afraid of the enemy and of the charge of cowardice faces danger from front or rear. In such situations it is awkward to speak of a conflict between fears. It is a conflict between two courses of action each of which is based on fear. There may be only one general fear involved. This fear may be maintained as the tendencies to react in one way or another fluctuate. The fear itself may wax and wane as the behavior vacillates and other emotional reactions may intrude. The person may become angry at being caught in such a mess or may begin to want a more desirable state of affairs, escaping for a while into some fanciful Nirvana. Again we cannot afford to restrict ourselves to an avoidance-avoidance analysis as the individual can enjoy such conflict without apparently avoiding anything. He may eat, sleep, and carry on some routine (doing none of these very well, perhaps) and still be in a more or less chronic state of panic because of two or more sources of impending doom.

There may be other kinds of conflict than these listed here, but these are enough to account for most people's ordinary troubles. It will be appreciated that unless someone chooses to tell us about his troubles we may not be able to discover that he has any. Some reasonable inferences can be drawn from behavior but these will remain inferences until otherwise confirmed. The kinds of behavior that suggest the inferences can now be considered (we can more or less ignore overt approach and avoidance activities as these are not the most likely operations to be witnessed).

Defense mechanisms

What do people with conflicts do about them? If no solution of a direct nature is available and time permits, the individual must make some sort of adjustment to the stimuli that normally initiate the conflict if he is to do anything at all besides sit and worry. Must something be done about a conflict? Do they cry for solution? Perhaps most conflicts are not ever really solved. People do sit around and worry and sometimes, if they sit around long enough, conditions change and the conflict disappears along with the stimuli. When indirect attempts at adjustment are tried they may not be satisfactory but may be the best that the individual involved can achieve for himself in terms of his own skills, previous background, and the prevailing conditions. Indirect adjustments to conflict have been labeled "defense mechanisms" on the assumption that they serve to reduce the anxiety or fear or protect the person against a greater anxiety that a more direct attempt to cope with the situation might develop.

The term defense mechanism is usually associated with Freudian psychoanalysis (A. Freud, 1937) and over the years a number of such "mechanisms" have been described. Some of these are no more than popular folklore has long cherished in homespun psychology and these may have as much or as little merit as folklore normally has. Because these alleged mechanisms are so popular in literature and even in ordinary conversational psychology as practiced by housewives over the back fence, we must review them or attempt at least a cursory appraisal. Among the more popular defenses, the Freudians list:

1. *Rationalization.* This is an attempt to make one's own behavior (which might be subject to criticism) appear reasonable. Usually such attempts at explanation are manufactured *after* a decision or some event. It may or may not be a truthful statement. Freudians sometimes describe rationalization as an unconscious kind of lying. We all do enough rationalizing to be familiar with the process on the conscious level of lying. Why we should also be motivated to lie unconsciously is a pretty question. To prove that a lie is unconsciously motivated one would have to rely on some interpretative procedure incorporated in psychoanalytic therapy. Folklore knows rationalization by the expression "sour grapes." The person beset by conflict might find many occasions for "sour grapes" types of thinking although he is usually concerned about demonstrating his own sweetness and nobility. Rationalizing does not solve any conflicts. It may help make the period of difficulty more endurable.

2. *Projection.* Another bit of folklore that has been dignified into the status of a defense mechanism is that of projection. This is the same as scapegoating which we examined earlier. When we project, in the defense connotation, we place our faults (guilt, sin, weaknesses, undesirable traits) onto others. It is possible that we do indulge ourselves in this way without necessarily reflecting a conflict within ourselves. To blame others for our faults or mistakes is such a convenient explanation for our current status that it is a quickly learned operation, familiar to every school child. It may serve as a defense if we are under

attack or scrutiny without in any necessary sense indicating that we have any conflict in the area involved. If the teacher "is a big dope" and grades us poorly we may still be quite unconcerned about the grade. If we are very concerned and want the better grade, then we might begin to suspect some dissatisfaction. To speak of dissatisfaction as a conflict, however, may again be twisting a term out of shape. Besides, the teacher may be a "big dope." All too frequently a justifiable accusation or assertion is put off by the hearer as "he's only projecting." Projection is known to us from the old saw "It takes a thief to catch a thief" or "only a woman can understand another woman." While there may be some obscure merit to these bits of folk wisdom, specific scientific support is not available to back them up. To suspect all our criminal investigators of a felonious history when they catch thieves is obviously out of order and women's observations about other women are not necessarily of the highest validity.

There is some evidence (Sears, 1936) that when people are asked to rate themselves on undesirable traits some will assign themselves much more favorable ratings than they will earn from other raters. Yet these same people, who might be unaware of their own social image, tend to assign more derogatory ratings to others. Such studies, usually carried on with fraternity members, are not too convincing. The trends, although in the direction indicated, are not especially strong. It is obviously difficult to obtain true judgments from fraternity brothers even when anonymity is guaranteed. Even with highly objective ratings, we would not expect extreme degrees of undesirable traits in the membership. The additional requirement that the subject be unaware of his own faults and have a distorted self-perception makes difficulties for researchers in this area.

We should be careful in assuming that a person is projecting and should securely assess the behavior and statements involved. Only if we can establish the facts in a given instance can we be justified in assuming that the fault or weakness is within the projector and even then the question of conflict remains to be demonstrated. Sometimes "projection" takes the form of displaced aggression and can be expressed as "kicking the cat" (Preston, 1940). If this is expressed in an extreme form with a nicely developed logical argument we might suspect the individual of a serious personality disorder, a psychosis called paranoia. In paranoia the victim accuses others of "trying to get him" or "stabbing him in the back." While many of us use such expressions, we do not normally accuse George Washington or Winston Churchill or men from other planets of nefarious designs on us. Such accusations more or less obviously establish a person as having delusions (organized systems of false beliefs). Should the person restrict his range of accusers to more likely candidates and list a series of apparent facts, then, again, we have to establish the facts, before diagnosing a paranoid psychosis. We will return to a consideration of such more serious states a little later.

3. *Repression.* A person in conflict may sometimes show evidence of having forgotten something we might presume he should have remembered. We have discussed such "convenient memories" before and will not repeat here the earlier comments (see p. 277). Here again we must be careful not to refer to every case of forgetting as a repression. Nor should the fact that something unpleasant has been forgotten lead to any interpretation that the forgotten material is still actively seeking expression. If it is genuinely forgotten it might be just as innocent in its forgotten status as what we had for dinner on the third day after our fourth birthday or the name of the fourteenth President of the United States. Nor should we necessarily assume that repression is "bad." One psychologist (Klein, 1956) has argued that it is a very healthy kind of reaction to learn how to think about something else when thinking about the affair in question is likely to lead to trouble. When playing bridge one should play bridge and not "footsie." Neither will be very effective if both are practiced at the same time. One should be repressed.

The above comments are not to be interpreted as indicating that repression has had no effect on the personality. In order to forget an unpleasant or traumatic experience, the person may have had to develop new reactions to the stimuli involved; these new responses may not have been most suitable and may lead to awkward behavior patterns suitable to cause an observer to wonder. If a bitter experience with females has lead a person to associate strictly with males, his entire life pattern may have been altered. The fact that he no longer remembers the instance is inconsequential. His behavior is abnormal. If through some process he can be led to recall the original experience it might be possible to re-educate him. It might be possible even without such recall, or alternatively, even with recall, that no changes might be effected by attempts at re-education. Whatever the outcome, if he has forgotten the incident we presume it has the same characteristics as other forgotten experiences and is not fighting to get out of the unconscious any more than is Franklin Pierce. Freudian psychoanalysts make repression the keystone or foundation of their systematic thinking. Many attempts have been made to demonstrate Freudian repression in the laboratory. So far none have succeeded.

4. *Regression.* Some people when seriously disturbed fall back on earlier forms of meeting frustration. Again we have to be careful not

to assume that a conflict is involved when people act in what we classify as an immature fashion. There has presumably been a serious frustration involved but the frustration might be on a rather simple level and no particular conflict might have been in operation prior to some calamitous event. To find the tires on one's new car slashed by vandals might result in a primitive reaction on the part of the owner of the car. He might even sit down on the curb and weep. Since in our culture weeping by adult men is considered unmanly, the behavior might be called regressive. For women to weep is considered a reasonable use of basic equipment. A clever man might also resort to tears on occasion if he is concerned about reflecting a truly grievous injury. If the behavior is put on it can hardly be categorized as regressive. Actually any kind of aggressive behavior by civilized people is presumed to be not quite adult in our culture. If the provocation is clearly great we condone it. If the provocation is not clearly great we tend to look beyond the immediate incident and attribute the behavior to some unrecognized conflict that the less adult activity apparently makes more tolerable. Freud expressed the concept of regression as the pattern of going back to previously prepared defenses as is done by an army in retreat. When we cannot solve our problems in an adult fashion we may be forced to resort to techniques that solved problems for us in our past. The last resort in such a campaign or retreat might be a complete reversion to childish behavior. Here again we have to evaluate the individual history. If a person never became an adult, he can hardly have regressed. Only when we see a drop in the qualitative level of characteristic adjustments can we label behavior as regressive and begin to suspect conflicts. The conflicts might well be at some "deadline" point if genuine regression has occurred. A retreat is not the first course of action in most cases.

5. *Reaction formation.* One of the more extreme devices for defense that have been described by Freudian psychoanalysts is the suggestion that sometimes a conflict is so powerful within us that mere rationalization or projection will not do. In order to keep from giving in to some urge or strong wish we attempt to devise a world, at least in the miniature (or for ourselves), which would automatically prevent us from falling victims to sin. If we should have strong urges to consume alcohol or drugs or engage in illicit sexual activities, we might become very active in efforts at establishing "prohibition," closing up saloons, wiping out the "dope traffic," driving the prostitutes out of town, etc. By removing the possible means to the satisfaction of temptations, we might be able to control the impulse to sin. Somerset Maugham described the operation of reaction formation in his short story "Rain."

Here a missionary is pictured as condemning Sadie Thompson, who is entertaining military personnel, for her lewd and sinful life. He "protests too much" and finally reveals his own "repressed" urges. By "protesting too much" we are alleged to reveal our own "unconscious" interests. If we should accept this postulate of "reaction formation" seriously, we find ourselves in the difficult situation of never being able to evaluate the motives of any campaigner for presumably good and morally approved causes. Perhaps the saloon smasher is only a repressed, potential, lush. The man who proclaims his love and brings his wife flowers is really disgusted with her and wants someone else. The parents who shower their children with toys really hate them, and so on and on. Since there is no scientific evidence for such a mechanism and we have only literary and interpretative evidence from clinical cases, we cannot accept the proposition with any confidence. To deny that some cases may have merited the description of "reaction formation" would be improper also. No one has been able to or bothered to produce evidence against it. When tin pan alley song writers tell us "you always hurt the one you love" we can only shudder and suggest that it might not be "always" and perhaps you do not really love her anyhow. When the principle of reaction formation percolates down into an ordinary citizen's actions and wives suspect husbands who bring home flowers, things have come to a pretty pass. It should be noted that theoretically the reaction formation concept works both sides of the street. If you hate somebody fiercely, it suggests a hidden attraction. If you are always attacking religion and proclaiming yourself an atheist, it is because you have hidden religious feelings. The spinster and the bachelor, however confirmed, really want to get married, deep down inside. Such is the "stuff as dreams are made on" and novels written. Whether it is the kind of stuff a science of psychology will mature on, is debatable. With this mechanism, as with others, it will be appropriate for us to have some evidence to examine. Unfortunately, this is not available.

6. *Sublimation.* In the Freudian dogma, considerable emphasis is placed on a concept of energy which has its basis in sexual sources. There is no adequate description of this libidinal energy other than the suggestion that it is somehow rather kinetic and seeking expression. If normal sexual gratification channels are blocked, the energy will somehow be transformed into other arenas of action and be the support or source of energizing other kinds of activity. The kinds of activity apparently have no limit and can be observed by Freudians in any kind of creative activity—in science, politics, sports, art, literature, etc. Sexual energy has been transformed in terms of its outlets into a base for ac-

counting for anything from the Mona Lisa to the Golden Gate bridge. It is held by some speculators that all creative people are basically neurotic and psychoanalysts hold all neurotic potentialities to be basically disturbed in sexual adjustment. Considering the alleged amount of sexual frustration and the small amount of creativity the postulate of sublimation does not appear well supported. To suggest that all creative people are neurotic is again a proposition that cannot be proved in any scientific manner when neither term in the equation is ever adequately defined and when so many neurotics fail to be creative—in fact, one of the presumed characteristics of the neurotic is his alleged inefficiency and inability to produce up to his capacity. Here again, we have a suggestion about behavior, and one that cannot be proved or disproved. As a literary device, a conversation piece, it works well. How well it works in behavior is another question.

There are other suggested defense mechanisms. The proof for their operation is just as hazy and fuzzy as we have found with the ones described. We have taken a strongly negative attitude about such propositions because they are normally presented, even in elementary textbooks, quite uncritically as if they were well established mechanisms instead of rather loose hypotheses. While they may be great insights into human personality, they have not been put in scientific, i.e., testable terms and are quite outside the scope of a scientific psychology. If they flavor our novels for us, perhaps they serve some purpose. For the student to accept them as principles of behavior is another matter. We should be just as critical of proposals in this area as we are in any other. In no other aspect of psychology would a proposal receive so much courtesy and consideration. It is time to raise a serious question about the contribution of mythologists and *littérateurs* to a scientific psychology. The lack of evidence about such contributions suggests that they be properly ignored until someone begins to spend some time advancing proof rather than argument. It is customary that the burden of proof be on the shoulders of the advocate. It might be wondered if the time of scientifically oriented psychologists should be spent in testing assertions confidentially presented by people who claim to have "insights" into human behavior when such insights are not expressed in testable language.

Personality disorders and psychotherapy

We have suggested that many of our citizens get themselves into difficulties, some of which can be described as "conflicts." Such conflicts have been illustrated with rather mild little situations like those arising in a restaurant when we examine a menu, with more serious interpersonal clashes between parents and children, husbands and wives, obligations to behave in some undesired fashion, and even more serious and crucial situations that determine the courses of our lives for many years to come. In some instances, action is delayed or postponed while the conflict *situation* remains more or less alive throughout making life difficult and resulting in temporary adjustments, some of which might resemble what we have talked about as defense mechanisms, others unsatisfactory compromises or ill-considered, unrealistic solutions which frequently get us into even greater difficulty. When we start borrowing from Peter to pay Paul, we are hardly making progress. The horse fancier who keeps "borrowing" from company funds in order to make the "one big killing" that will enable him to recoup his losses frequently winds up as the victim of the "one big killing." Our prisons are full of people who adopted inefficient ways out of conflict situations.

Not all people in prison are there because of conflict in a personality sense—they did have a conflict with "the law" to be sure, but there may not have been any indecision about the behavior that preceded their arrival at the gates. Some people live with their troubles more or less quietly. Sometimes they divorce their troubles. (It has been reported that three out of four marriages are "unhappy" and that the current divorce rate is climbing so that we can expect about half the marriages that occur to terminate in one kind of separation or another.) But not even all divorces represent personality clashes and psychological conflicts; some of them are probably rational solutions of problems of a nonpsychological origin.

What is the eventual outcome of serious conflicts which do not get solved realistically and for which "defense mechanisms" are inadequate? The answer to this question is of vital concern to the citizenry of the entire world. It is no trivial question. Many of our tax dollars as well as private medical fees go into attempts at answering this question and mistakes in answering this question can be very costly. The question is really that of the causes of mental illness. We cannot hope to consider all aspects of the problem in this text but can only examine some of the claims and proposals that have been generated in investigations of this major social problem. Our own approach will be limited to a consideration of the role of psychology and the attempts of psychologists to solve the problems involved. It is perhaps unnecessary to point out that these attempts are honest efforts, that in many cases they are preliminary steps, that they do not bear a guarantee of correctness and that psychologists are self-critical enough to recognize some of each other's errors so that we will someday arrive at a more realistic appraisal of the contribution of psychologists to the solution of the problem of mental illness. At present, they can only be described as working at it. It is our current purpose to look at some of this work.

Psychologists did not become seriously concerned about mental illness until World War II when many of them were in service and had the opportunity to see many cases of disturbed military personnel. Prior to such intimate contact, most psychologists had a merely academic interest in the problem arising largely from familiarity with Freud's system of psychoanalysis and the controversies that originated as some of Freud's colleagues rebelled against him and started their own "schools." Psychoanalysis, although purporting to rest on a biological foundation and a biological approach to the nature of man, was the first system of therapy to hold that people's troubles originated in conflict, but, what is important for us, the conflict was between biological urges or natural instincts and social forces. It was held by Freud that people could become sick, i.e., mentally disordered, not because they were infected by some disease germ or because of a malfunction of some internal structures or processes like digestion, circulation, or even neural difficulty, but because of conflicts originating in their experiences in their environments. Without spelling it out in learning psychology terminology, Freud, *in effect,* traced the development of at least some kinds of ills to traumatic experiences and inappropriate kinds of learning and forgetting (repression). And, again, *in effect,* his system of therapy was based on the principle that a patient could *relearn,* i.e., be re-educated to lead a more appropriate kind of existence. Psychotherapy became a matter of re-learning, a replacement of the wrong kinds of reactions by learning new ones.

The Freudian principle that described some kinds of mental illness as related to personal experiences in the environment and as unrelated to brain damage or other physical or physiological agencies of disease or malfunction, was not an original insight into the nature of behavioral disorders. For centuries it was held, by one kind of authority or another, that a mentally disordered person was being punished for sin or was invaded by an evil spirit; that he was the victim of a curse, a witch's spell, or some other nonphysical agency. By the middle of the nineteenth century, medical science had made some advances and certain kinds of behavioral disorders had been identified or classified as related to "organic" or "structural" agents. Indeed medical practitioners from the days of Hippocrates had concerned themselves with physiological questions concerning the "humours" of the body and their functions. The prevailing orientation had always been to find an "elixir" or tonic, to "bleed" the victim so that the disease would be discharged along with the befouled blood, to apply poultices and proffer "medicines" derived from herbs and berries which magically or otherwise would cure or heal the victim. With the discovery of bacilli and the development of the "germ theory" of disease, medical science had arrived at a position from which it was able to diagnose or classify some diseases as to the presumed causative agents. Some diseases, however, chiefly those of a behavioral nature could not readily be classified as "organic." Nothing could be found to be wrong with the "structure" of the patient, and by default (or ignorance) such disorders were classified as "functional." A functional disorder was identified as one for which no organic cause could be discovered. This kind of identification more or less naturally led to the conclusion that there was no organic cause and many mental illnesses were then classified as functional disorders which could not be treated by surgery, by drugs, or other physical techniques. The victims were more or less abandoned to the ministrations of their families or put away in "hospitals for the insane" where they received varying degrees of custodial care.

Into this area of functional disorders Freud stepped with at least the hope of helping some of the victims, those who were within reach of the methods he had developed. At first Freud was forced to accept only those patients who could communicate, who would talk, and talk more or less freely, who would "associate" freely (i.e., report any and everything that "came into their heads") so that Freud could interpret from what they said what must have gone wrong in their early experiences which resulted in their current difficulties. In recent years, some of Freud's followers became willing to extend the theory to the treatment of patients that are not quite as easily reached through simple verbal methods.

Structural and functional disorders

We will not concern ourselves now with Freudian psychotherapy but rather, consider the larger question involved. Can we continue to assume that there are disorders of personality or behavior that are not related to some physiological, anatomical, structural change in the organism? It should be clear by now that we are not raising the question of "mental" versus physical disorders. Psychologists no longer speak of "mental" disorders. They prefer the expression "behavioral disorder." A human organism is a living structural physical affair and any disorders he has will have to be expressed by some kind of physiological function. This is not to say that the habits of this organism, how it has been changed by experience, may not be poor ones for coping with a given environment or set of problems. But the habits are presumably alterations in a physical nervous system and they are expressed through the activity of various effectors. Any disorder then will involve structure. The structure need not, however, be diseased or deficient if we are merely concerned with the reactions an organism makes to different stimuli when the reactions themselves are normal enough and only their effects or outcomes lead to difficulty. Saying "yes" or saying "no" may have violently different effects at different times. The mechanisms of the body which are employed in saying these words may not be particularly important. If a person, however, says "yes" when he should say "no" (and the *should* is a reasonable inference from other evidence) then we might conclude that anatomical factors are not of primary importance per se, at least not those in the vocal apparatus. But this might be a very dangerous and improper conclusion. Why the person happened to say "yes" might be the result of abnormal states or conditions in many other parts of the body, including the nervous system, even though the vocal cords are in good condition.

We have already touched on a number of factors involved in such matters in discussing psychosomatic disorders, the operations of the sympathetic nervous system, and the processes involved in mediation. The relative probability or likelihood of a given response may very well be a function of the nutrition supplied to the nervous system, to its relative irritability, or to factors that inhibit some activities and facilitate or permit others. The sex glands of the female rhinoceros permit a "yes" answer once every three years. The glandular secretions of the human may similarly permit or prohibit a given kind of response. There is no virtue in detailed speculation and we shall not indulge in it but the presence of some chemical or anatomical change in the structures of the brain need not be large enough to permit ready detection but more than large enough to disturb or disorganize the organism seriously enough to permit defective functioning. Before we are ready to accept a given behavioral disorder as "functional," meaning nonorganic, we must be very careful to exclude the possibility that we are dealing with a tumor, a virus, a glandular malfunction, a circulatory disturbance, a nutritive imbalance, an allergy, or some other lack. A simple lack of oxygen in the brain for only a few minutes is enough to produce a very disorderly person. Unfortunate victims of pellagra can behave like chronic alcoholics, and diabetics without their insulin have sometimes been jailed as drunks when found in a stuporous condition. The consumption of tons of aspirin and, currently, large numbers of tons of tranquilizing drugs might suggest that chemical factors may play far more vital roles in our behavior than we have been able to recognize in years past. On the other hand, we cannot conclude that chemical or physical therapy (for example by chiropractors) has been the actual responsible agent when some patients "improve" or are "cured." A strong argument can be made to the effect that psychological factors were also at work—the patient needed to have someone take an interest in him, give him reassurance, perhaps suggest that the new treatment would work, or, in some cases, give the patient an excuse for getting well. Actually the use of miracle drugs, so highly praised when they were first introduced, has not resulted in the hoped-for success they appeared to promise. They have been found most useful in bringing people into a condition where traditional psychotherapeutic techniques can be attempted. The evidence on the issue is not clear-cut enough for us to adopt a rigid position. The easy logical dichotomy of functional and structural disorders is not necessarily a correct classification.

Normal and abnormal

The failure to find a physical reason for some behavior that does not appear desirable, healthy, adjusted, or socially approved has, as we have seen, led to the assumption that some, if not all of these conditions, are functional, i.e., represent deviations that are due to personal experiences in an individual's history, and therefore, subject to analysis through a learning approach. Since all of us have experiences and learn, and since the kinds of experiences that humans undergo are (within reasonable limits) pretty much the same, it is sometimes asserted that all of us are more or less abnormal. Behavior disorders are viewed as perhaps the end of a continuum running from some hypothetical neutral or normal point through increasing degrees of disorder or maladjustment. Such a view is usually supported by reference to the distribution of other human characteristics such as height and weight, or intelligence, which, as we have seen (p. 180), is normally distributed. Actually the possibility of a continuum running from normal to abnormal does not by itself require any assumption other than that abnormality is "normally" distributed. We might note, in passing, that the same argument that is used to prove that "we are all more or less abnormal" can be used to prove that we are all more or less normal. Nothing of consequence is determined by such playing with words. Before we accept any assertions about the distribution of abnormality in behavior we should note carefully that normal probability curves are based on the operation of a great many variables coming to bear on any particular instance in such a complex fashion that no one can pinpoint the individual operation of any of them. We do not know why a coin falls heads up and so we put it down to "chance." There is, of course, no such thing as "chance." This is just the name we give to an unknown collection of factors.

In connection with illnesses like tuberculosis or syphilis, normal probability arguments do not apply. We either have the disease or we do not have it. We may or may not have a broken arm. We do not have a little syphilis, nor do women get slightly pregnant. Our question now becomes: can we be slightly maladjusted or slightly abnormal? Of course we can recognize degrees of severity in some diseases, that is, the tubercular patient may have just the beginnings of a case or a serious development. There can be, in some kinds of illness, a "normal distribution" among the sick but this distribution would be quite cut off from a normal distribution of the healthy; the latter distribution would be all of one degree and not at all spread out, at least as far as tuberculosis was concerned. If it should turn out that psychological disorders are also due to specific structural changes then we would not expect a normal distribution of maladjustment or adjustment. We would be either adjusted or not. If we were either, then we might be described as more or less *within* the group to which we belong but the two distributions would not overlap.

What are the facts of the matter? Here we run into trouble. The usual approach has been to devise sets of questions that can be asked of people listing all kinds of items like: Do you like your father more than your mother? Do you sleep well? Do you have headaches frequently? and so on. It is probably impossible to answer any of these questions fully or completely and meaningfully. How well can you sleep? How much should you like your parents? That might depend upon the parents. If you do have headaches, what is meant by frequently? Is the kind of headache of importance? Similar questions could be asked about most such "inventories." If enough questions are asked, some people will answer a few affirmatively and some will answer many affirmatively. This will usually result in a distribution that more or less approaches a "normal probability" curve and the investigator might conclude that we are all neurotic to some extent. At no point will he say, from here on all people are abnormal, because there will be no gap in his data. The fact that most people will endorse a certain number of statements is not taken as an indication of a normal population tendency but as a sign of normal amounts of neuroticism. A total score on such a test might be by far less meaningful than the endorsement of a single item. If somebody hates his father violently and loves his mother in a fashion that no mother should be loved, that person might be extremely neurotic but quite capable of honestly answering many of the items in a questionnaire in the negative. He might sleep well, have no headaches, no stomach trouble, be quite sociable, etc. If such questionnaires are to be used at all, they should be used with already diagnosed neurotic populations and already diagnosed normal populations to determine whether there are reliable differences between such groups. Unfortunately there is no way to define such a population. Frequently group differences are found on the basis of one test or another but there is also a lot of overlap among individuals so that people diagnosed normal have scores like those of the abnormal group and vice versa. This either means the test is not adequate, the diagnosis was inaccurate, or both. Commonly enough, the firm believer will defend the test and venture that the cases involved were victims of incorrect diagnoses. In other studies a "normal" distribution is found leading the investigators to support the view that adjustment is something that is normally distributed.[1]

The suggestion that we are all somewhat abnormal, only some are a little more so, may be comforting to some but it throws little light on the problem of diagnosis (selecting the people who need treatment) and less on the problem of therapy. What kind of treatment can you give someone who is only a little more so of something than someone else who does not need treatment? The whole problem becomes an extremely vague and subjective one with psychologists disagreeing among themselves, with psychiatrists testifying in court on both sides of the aisle, and with few acceptable standards for classification.

Neuroses and psychoses

When people are sufficiently miserable or irritating to their families so that either they come themselves or are sent by their families to seek "help," we have that much basis for separating normal from abnormal. This basis, of course, depends upon how tolerant a person's family might be, but those who appear for treatment willingly or not, can at least be separated from those who do not come (whether or not they "need" it). The individuals who do appear for treatment are usually classified in some fashion as to their relative ability to remain in the community or the advisability of having them sent to an institution. Ordinarily, if they are extremely troublesome or unapproachable they will be classified as psychotic and institutionalized. But if they can communicate with the therapists and can carry on some minimum of functioning, they will be

[1] The widely used Minnesota Multiphasic Personality Inventory (MMPI) has been very carefully standardized, and the criticisms given of many other tests do not apply to it. In scoring the MMPI the fact that most people will endorse a certain number of statements is taken as a *normal* population tendency. The test has been used with already diagnosed groups, hospital populations, etc.

called neurotic and treated as office patients of one kind or another.

Psychotics, then, are more seriously deviating people. They might be quite violent, aggressive toward self or others or more or less withdrawn so that they do not really make contact with their environments. Sometimes psychotics are diagnosed as people who have lost a sense of reality. They do not appreciate their own status or position in the community, in a sense they do not know who they are. They might be able to give their names but the name might not refer to a person formerly known to his friends as having certain views, skills, friends, etc. He is different from the person we knew. The psychotic might regard himself as a hero, a villain, a great sinner, a benefactor, and so on. If he is not, in fact, what he regards himself, then he is unrealistic, he lacks a sense of reality, and that makes him psychotic. We must be careful with this diagnostic sign, as some of us may not be too free of delusions. But so long as we keep our delusions within bounds and more or less private, we can enjoy them. If someone states that he is from outer space or has come from the seventeenth century, we can assume he does not know what time it is and that might be enough to warrant sending him away. The presence of delusions (whether of grandeur or persecution) is a primary sign of psychosis, if the delusions are not being shared by a substantial proportion of the population. When a small body of some sect climbs a mountain to await the end of the world, we can consider the whole troop psychotic. When a large population shares a belief which cannot be easily verified or is, in essence, untestable, we are hard put to it to decide whether a whole culture is "mad" (if *we* assume the belief to be a delusion) or whether some other grounds must be adopted for judging the sanity of the group. Even if a group does enjoy some delusion, the members might behave more or less realistically most of the time or at all times when the delusion is not involved. In such situations (if the delusion does not interfere with the ordinary routines of living) no point is gained, by classifying the group as psychotics.

Neurotics are of a lesser breed. Their delusions, if any, are under control. They know what time it is and who they are, but they are having trouble. They are more unhappy than normal standards would allow for the kinds of trouble they report having, and they are having so much difficulty handling their affairs that they become inefficient, they do not come up to the expected standards for people of their backgrounds or talents and they frequently report indecisions, an incapacity for deciding on a course of action. Whether they are torn by conflict or not, they may be presumed to be experiencing such states because they may show signs of defense operations and commonly they report excessive fears or vague anxieties of impending doom with no objective evidence being offered in support of the fears. To catalogue the possible symptoms would take a volume in itself. We have already mentioned some and can list just a few. Neurotics might whine, cry, complain, or boast (all unjustifiably), forget things that should not have been forgotten, work feverishly or not at all, have various fleeting physical symptoms, and, in some cases, spend a lot of time going from one medical man to another in search of a cure for poorly described ailments.

In the past psychologists and psychiatrists have tried to devise special classifications of psychotics and neurotics and such labeling still goes on in some institutions but the tendency now is more to the end of describing the behavior rather than trying to classify patients into types. Typical classifications can be consulted in any psychiatric text and we will avoid the issue here although there will be occasion to use some of the terminology that has developed in the area.

It is sometimes suggested that neurotics are people who are in an early state of psychosis, that unless some help is introduced, they will become psychotic. This is an extension of the "we are all a little crazy" notion. Actually there is no proof that neurotics become psychotic in any greater proportion than "normals." Neurotics can remain such for years, never losing a reality orientation, and never requiring hospitalization. On the other hand, people who have appeared reasonably normal can begin to show psychotic symptoms—experience hallucinations, hear voices, report systematized delusions, and become unmanageable. One form, and the most common, of psychosis, schizophrenia appears to be especially noticeable among young people under twenty-five without an extensive neurotic history, if any. Some schizophrenics have been "queer," perhaps all their lives before they come to the attention of professional people but the very youth of many cases indicates that there is no gradual development of psychosis through prolonged neurosis.

In connection with schizophrenia and some other kinds of psychoses, evidence has been accumulating that there are strong hereditary or constitutional factors to be taken into account. Studies of identical twins for example show that if one twin gets classified as a schizophrenic, the other twin is very likely to attain that classification as well. In a famous study, Kallmann and Roth (1956) reported that in such cases an identical twin also was typed as schizophrenic in 86 per cent of the sample. Fraternal twins showed only a 14 per cent correspondence. Slater (1953) reported 76 per cent concordance for identical twins. The figures on manic-depressive psychoses (a disturbance characterized by shifts in mood) are even more dramatic.

Other kinds of evidence are slowly accumulating that suggest more and more that schizophrenia is more likely to be an organic affair rather than the "functional" disorder it has so long been presumed. Some experiments using prisoners as volunteer subjects indicated that schizophrenic symptoms can be induced by injections of drugs derived from lysergic acid. Other drugs used in treatment seem to bring about some degree of symptom alleviation. If a chemical treatment can reverse the symptom pattern, the implication is at least suggestive that the original difficulty is also a chemical one. Kety (1959) critically evaluated the research on chemical and genetic factors in schizophrenia. He regards the problem as an extremely complex one, like looking for a needle in a haystack. He finds reason for continued enthusiasm among researchers from many varied fields. A reading of Kety's reports should be a sobering experience for the student who wants a quick answer to the difficulties involved in the analysis of abnormal behavior. There is still a long research road ahead and we must be just as careful in evaluating miracle drugs, the tranquilizers, and energizers as we are of psychological methods of treatment. It is one of the risks we take in working with some problems that the method of attack that is employed, and which at first might appear fruitful, may turn out to be completely useless and misleading. If the psychoses and perhaps even the neuroses turn out to be chemical or other kinds of organic difficulties we will have wasted a lot of time with psychological speculation and attempts at treatment and the conclusions drawn about disturbed people merely being at the extreme of a continuum may turn out to be an unfortunate analogy drawn too hastily.

Psychotherapy

"Psychotherapy" is a general term covering a wide variety of methods or techniques used in the treatment of disturbed persons or "personality disorders." The techniques range from more or less "physical" therapy—drugs, convulsive shocks, surgery, diet, and rest to more or less pure "psychological" approaches. The latter involves talking and listening to people, letting them "act out" their difficulties in "psychodramas," having patients meet in groups and discuss their difficulties (so-called "group therapy") and various methods involving suggestion and, sometimes, hypnosis. By common usage the term "psychotherapy" has been more and more restricted to what we have called psychological techniques. In the succeeding discussion we shall, unless otherwise indicated, mean by psychotherapy that the therapist has not used any of the physical techniques, or at least not deliberately.

It is sometimes argued that some disorder must have been functional because the patient failed to respond to any attempted physical therapy but was "cured" or "improved" by psychotherapy. Because some forms of psychotherapy do not involve or employ any drugs or surgery, the disorder must, it is argued, have been nonorganic. This is a most awkward kind of argument where nothing is proved without the most careful controls, and even then, questions remain. Because psychotherapy of a psychological kind is frequently extensive in time, it permits the possible recovery from a physical disorder during the psychotherapy. A person under treatment may change his way of life, his habits, his routine, get more rest, or find that the sources of his difficulty have been dissipated in the passage of time. The psychotherapist may then accept credit for having helped a patient when his actual role might have been quite incidental. Thus far the studies that have been made in this area are contradictory and confusing. Some critics of psychotherapy (Eysenck, 1952) have concluded that the same percentage of patients recover whether treated by therapists or not, quite regardless of the kind of therapy that has been given. Others find that forms of physical therapy using sedatives, diet changes, and rest are just as good as formal psychotherapy. When psychotherapists do report the results of relatively controlled studies showing improvement in treated as against nontreated controls, arguments can always be found which leave the critics dissatisfied. For example, in one study a group of potential patients was set aside as a control group, and found not to improve during the time the experimental group was undergoing therapy. The therapist concluded that his work had something to do with the results. Critics, however, can argue that had the control group also talked with *anyone* at all during the period for the same number of hours, about *anything* at all, they too might have improved. Thus, the specific kind of therapy could not be given credit for the improvement. In one study, medical students talked to a control group using no therapy techniques. The patients did not improve while a genuine therapy group was reported to improve. In other studies, control groups may show as much improvement as the treated patients, leaving the question of the value of the therapy, really untouched.

Before leaving this point the student should be cautioned to recognize that the question of evaluating psychotherapy or any other kind of therapy is an extremely complex one. It involves starting out with a well-defined population of people "needing" therapy and dividing these into equated groups. Such an equation in terms of type and intensity or complexity of disorder is itself virtually impossible. Assuming some modest success here, the question is raised of the type of therapy to be given (one might be no good and a negative conclusion might be generalized to other forms of therapy) and the kind of therapists involved. The amount of treatment must be carefully controlled and the control population must be screened from any degree of such treatment (or other potential sources). There must be some kind of relatively objective standards for deciding whether there has been a "cure" or improvement, and how much of that. No one yet has successfully defined a cure. We tend to expect something permanent from a cure, such as we associate with an appendectomy. We recognize that we frequently get colds or may get "the flu" repeatedly; pneumonia and other diseases are "allowed" to recur. If a psychotherapy patient does not stay cured, we are prone to suspect that there was no cure at all. This, of course, is not necessarily correct, as there is as yet no reason to suspect that such should prove to be the case. A person returned to the bosom of his family may find various vipers in that bosom and find that the cure cannot really "take."

It should also be noted that where physical therapy has been tried (electric and other kinds of convulsive shock treatments) permanent cures are not the rule nor are they at all expected. The patients return for more shocks. Until we find out more about the nature of cures, we are in a poor position to evaluate psychotherapy. When we hear about people who have had several psychoanalyses it is just as proper to assume that they became ill again as it is to assume that the preceding one failed.

Psychotherapeutic strategies

While the term psychotherapy may refer to any method of treatment applied to disturbed people, therapists differ in their fundamental approaches. Generally they fall into two camps, interpretative (directive) and noninterpretative (client-centered). The psychoanalytic method developed by Freud, for example relies entirely on having the patient relax and freely discourse about anything at all while the analyst listens and tries to understand and interpret what hidden meanings lie under the patient's "free associations." The procedure is analogous to dream interpretation where the dreamer reports what he remembers of a dream and someone else tries to find some significance in it. The famous dreams of Pharoah in the Bible which Joseph interpreted have set a pattern for our culture where it is frequently assumed that dreams have meanings. The usual emphasis, however, is on the predictive nature of dreams. The dreams are supposed to foretell the future. Freud's emphasis was on the present and the past. His patient's dreams told him what the patient wanted to do or what he feared. Whether the patient reports real dreams, manufactured dreams, or anything at all does not make too much difference in psychoanalysis, as anything that is said may have a "latent" meaning which the analyst might be able to decode or "interpret."

Interpretative therapy

The psychoanalytic techniques which Freud and his followers developed over the years since around 1895 set a pattern for "psychotherapy" from which other forms or emphases developed. We will not concern ourselves with the various off-shoots and separate "schools" that broke away from Freud. These modifications have developed separate interests and emphases while retaining the central emphasis on *interpretation.* The basic operation is to discover what is troubling the patient and point this out to him so that he can, with the help of the therapist, arrive at a new outlook, a new system of reactions, and thereby cope with the circumstances that brought him to the point where he needed help. The principle involved is that the roots of a patient's troubles are not known to him. They are "unconscious" and they must be made "conscious." The patient has developed defenses against their becoming conscious and these defenses must be broken down. The process of breaking down defenses will be resisted because it is painful and anxiety provoking; the patient does not want to discover what is really troubling him but until he does there is no cure possible. The patient is brought to feel dependent upon the therapist (one aspect of the process known as "transference") whereby he can feel somewhat secure and supported so that as the formerly unconscious threats begin to emerge he can face them more effectively than he could by himself. The therapist will not condemn or blame the patient no matter what comes out of his "unconscious" and in the "permissive" atmosphere the patient finally becomes able to think freely about things he could never allow himself to dwell on. At this stage he can learn to react in a different manner, presumably a more adult one, and when he has learned his new emotional repertoire he is "cured." An important aspect of psychoanalysis is that the analyst feels free to interrupt the patient if the patient seems to be avoiding issues and try to bring him back to the point. Avoiding issues means that the material is important no matter how trivial it might appear to the patient. The therapist, in other words, *controls* the therapeutic sessions. He may, if he chooses, tell the patient to talk about specific items; he may require that dreams be reported or, if the patient has none to report, the analyst may ask him to make one up. The fact that the analyst leads the way, interprets, informs the patient, and in general controls the course of therapy, has led to the process of analysis being called "directive" therapy.

Nondirective therapy

Since World War II we have seen the expansion of another kind of emphasis in psychotherapy. While this emphasis has a venerable history and has roots in various cultures, it was not till recently that a formalized program of psychotherapy has been developed which deliberately abjured interpretation and direction and left the course of treatment almost entirely to the patient. The new emphasis, under the leadership of Carl Rogers (1951, 1952), has gone by a number of names such as "client-centered" therapy, and variations of this, but the label "nondirective therapy" appears to have more discriminative value even though couched in the negative. In client-centered therapy the therapist offers his services to a patient with the understanding that the patient will come at specific times and make use of the therapy session to freely talk about himself and his problems. The therapist undertakes only to be there, to listen, but to take no active part. He will not interpret anything. His only questions will be for purposes of clarification. He will offer no advice under any circumstances, and as nearly as possible he will do nothing. The prospective patient might well wonder at the value of such sessions but he is given some modest degree of assurance that this procedure has had value for other patients and might have it in his case too. No guarantees are offered. If the patient agrees to the terms the therapy can begin. The therapist does not actually play an immaterial role. He must be there and his function is much more than that of a "sympathetic ear." As in psychoanalysis, the therapist and patient must show interest and confidence in each other and get on a footing whereby each can speak freely to the other (this is known as "rapport"). Until rapport does develop, nothing much else is going to happen. When the patient learns that the therapist is serious about merely sitting and listening, he begins to talk and is allowed to talk about anything or nothing at all. If he chooses he may merely sit for an hour. If he does talk, the therapist listens and shows an interest by occasional clarification questions. Sooner or later the patient will begin to indicate something about his attitudes or feelings toward individuals or problems. When emotional material is introduced the therapist tries to play the part of a mirror or reflector; he tries to empathize with the patient, feel something of what the patient feels and reflect this feeling. If the patient's feelings are "mixed up," the therapist tries to clarify the feelings by rephrasing the patient's statements. If the patient says "I hate my brother" the therapist has to discover what degree of feeling is involved and he might suggest "You don't like your brother very much, is that right?" The patient then can say "You're damned right I don't like him. I hate his guts." By restating the patient's outbursts, by rephrasing the statements, the therapist helps the patient to "straighten out" his feelings. By being sympathetic and noncondemning, the therapist, just as in psychoanalysis, provides the patient with an opportunity to "bring his feelings out into the open." When they are out in the open they sometimes look a little silly or exaggerated or irrelevant, immature, etc. The patient may come around to recognizing that the emotions he has been reporting are no longer significant in his current way of life and may start changing his views. It is a principle of nondirective therapy that people have inner powers of growth and maturation, that given an opportunity they will themselves come to a more adjustive orientation to their problems and that the newly acquired maturity, when come by through their own efforts will be a more lasting good. The entire emphasis in client-centered therapy is for the patient to arrive at "insight" (a recognition of his own role and an appreciation of the roles of others in the development of his problem) and to constructively develop his own solutions for the problems. Supporters of this kind of therapy are convinced that nearly everyone has the capacity to handle his own problems if they can be clarified and, that such clarification can come only through a process of self-examination in an atmosphere of permissiveness, where the patient can see at various stages that the feelings he reports are a normal or natural kind of reaction to the situation as described.

Evaluation of psychotherapy

We have previously indicated the difficulties inherent in any attempt at validating any psychotherapy. At the present time it is virtually impossible to arrive at a decision as to whether any kind of psychotherapy is of any value as far as a coldly scientific appraisal is concerned. The studies that have been reported have been both pro and con and the difficulties of evaluation are constantly being pointed out. People who are engaged in psychotherapy are interested in helping patients who are in desperate need of help. They do not have time to indulge in scientific evaluations. The people who are not active in psychotherapy do not have much more than an academic interest in the problem and can easily point to the limitations of studies that have been undertaken. When therapists are asked about the value of their work they usually report that they believe they have been helpful to many patients but they also are willing to admit that they are not sure but that someone else might have done better. A great pressure is felt by therapists to develop more effective methods and take care of more patients and new kinds of therapies are constantly evolving for use with various kinds of patients. There are systems of "group" therapy, play therapy, "psychodrama," and among psychiatrists there are complex combinations of drugs, shocks, surgery, diet, rest, talking out, and whatever else the therapist can find potentially useful. In such activities the therapist has little time for finding out what did the trick so long as the trick comes off. The situation at present appears a little more hopeful than it did just a few years ago. Many hospitals are now beginning to find room for their patients as the discharge rates increase. The use of tranquilizing drugs has had some remarkable effects. Those with a "structural" point of view maintain that eventually drugs themselves will solve the problem. The more psychologically oriented claim the drugs make the patients more amenable to talking out their problems. It is interesting to note that near the end of his life, Freud himself began to despair of psychoanalytic methods and stated that he believed the day would come when chemical methods would replace psychological methods in the treatment of behavioral disorders (Dallenbach, 1955). Should Freud's prophecy prove correct the edifice he built will become only a curiosity in the history of culture, a culture that Freud strongly influenced in many ways, in its child-rearing methods, its drama and literature, its marriage institutions, its education and even, as we have seen, its advertising.

The need for counseling

Alongside of but separated from psychotherapy, there has been a growing development of another psychological service, that of counseling. Many people have troubles of a lesser magnitude or of a different variety from those that require the services of a therapist. By this time our culture has accumulated a great deal of *information* about numerous areas of personal adjustments, information that it is too difficult and time-consuming for an individual to acquire for himself. We commonly get into difficulties which are based on sheer ignorance of the facts that should be taken into account and these difficulties might develop needless worries and minor conflicts as well as ill-considered decisions. We have learned to consult physicians and lawyers when we recognize a problem to be within their scopes but we have not yet recognized the counseling psychologists as a potential source of advice. Such counselors are in a better position to advise people on specific kinds of problems than an individual is likely to be, and various specialties have been developed in counseling areas, particularly in the areas of vocations, education, marriage and family living. When people discover that their particular problems are not especially novel and that methods of some value have been developed for handling certain kinds of problems, they can frequently be helped over a difficult period or into a wiser decision than they could reach by themselves. Some parents of feeble-minded children, for example, are tortured for years by hope that someday the child will show signs of a change, and, because of embarrassment or other reservations, they seek no help, hiding the child, risking harm to other children, and so on. This and many other kinds of problems might be more effectively handled with appropriate counseling. The counselor is slowly replacing the village wiseman, the head of the family, the older friend, and other traditional sources of advice. Where the old friend of the family had to depend upon his own experience for the advice he would offer, the professional counselor has the benefit of highly specialized experience in a relatively narrow field. Frequently a little information can prevent a large problem from developing.

CHAPTER 14

Man as an Integrated Organism—The Nature of Personality

Popular views · The self · Role playing · Stereotypes · Other type approaches · Class membership · Personality "syndromes" · The trait approach · Rating scales · Inventories and questionnaires · The rationale for trait measurement · Projective tests · Traits: general or specific? · The nature of human nature · Individual differences · The original nature of man · The Freudian man · Is a concept of personality necessary?

We have arrived at the point where we can begin to talk about "personality" with some small confidence in our treatment. The concept of personality is perhaps the haziest with which we have to deal. Like many other terms in psychological discussions this one has been taken over from general public use where it has a great variety of connotations. Psychologists have tried to give it a restricted meaning and have not been blessed with much success. At one time Allport (1937) reviewed the various definitions that had been suggested for "personality" and came up with over fifty different efforts. A term that has fifty different references or meanings is surely an awkward one. To try to get agreement among users on such a term would really be a formidable task, and one that we shall not attempt here.

POPULAR VIEWS

The strong and prevalent belief in the existence of something we call personality is continually revealed in our everyday lives. Advertisements promise us that our personalities can be improved. We get rated on our personality "traits" in kindergarten and in military service as well as on the job. We are asked to comment about the personalities of job applicants. Sometimes we draw special distinctions: "He's brilliant, but he has a terrible personality." Business leaders sometimes pontificate publicly that they are more interested in an applicant's personality than in his experience or other qualifications. Needless to say, they usually find that other qualifications are more readily appraised and probably count for more. It is not surprising that we have come to look upon "personality" as something we have or do not have, something that can stand improvement and something that is good or bad, fine or poor. We are rarely challenged on our comments about other people's personalities. Our opinions are given some weight even though they are not in agreement with the opinions of others. "That's the way he strikes you" is sometimes offered as a resolution of conflicting opinion. The ordinary use of the concept of personality seems to amount to an appraisal of an individual's social effectiveness (social stimulus value). It is a blanket reference representing our attitudes toward someone and usually is heavily loaded with our likes and dislikes.

If we push such an analysis more strongly we will find common disagreements about individuals in the attitudes of others. The young man who marries the girl obviously sees something in her that others who are asking "What does he see in her?" do not. When the sobbing mother tells the judge that her boy who is charged with rape, arson, and sundry other crimes "is really a good boy, your honor," she obviously has a different view of the lad from that shared by the police.

There are instances of honor among thieves and some gangsters love their mothers and see to it that their brothers or children go to college and become respectable. Political leaders or figures who attain some status frequently arouse rather intense attitudes among their detractors. A President of the United States can be loved by millions and hated by other millions and an inquiry about his personality can result in findings that the President is a "wonderful man," a "cheap, tinhorn politician," a "dirty, rotten crook," a "fearless leader and patriot," or a "tool of the interests." The conclusion from such findings must be that the personality of the person in question is only a product of what other people think of him and may have little to do with the person himself. If the personality of an individual, then, is thought of as his effect on other people, we would have to study these other people in order to find out something about the personality with which we were concerned. We cannot even say it is the *net* effect on other people because two violently opposed views might cancel each other out and we would be forced to conclude the individual had no personality even though he could arouse strong reactions in the population.

If it should turn out that a great majority of people tend to characterize a person in just about the same way we might be misled into believing that we have found out something about the person beyond the fact that he has a more or less uniform effect of a specific kind on large masses of people. Some female motion picture beauties have a more or less uniform effect on the male population but a somewhat different effect on the female population. The personality of the beauty is still a relative matter and not necessarily a genuine entity. "Beauty is in the eye of the beholder," the poet tells us.

It is not intended to suggest that the social effectiveness of individuals is not worthy of study or analysis, but it is suggested that asking other people about somebody's "personality" really is asking people about themselves and their reactions to an individual. This can often be important information but we must not be misled by the hidden assumption that it is the individual involved who possesses something called a "personality" and that this is what is being appraised.

THE SELF

Central to all concerns about personality is a preoccupation with some alleged inner core or unique pattern of characteristics that is sometimes called the "self," or "ego." This concept of the self is held to be a basic, integrated organization and is sometimes identified with personality. The study of personality becomes, for some theorists, the study of the self. Consideration of the problem posed by the assumption of some unitary self has led to difficulties as it quickly becomes apparent that neither we nor anyone else knows this self with any validity. The concept of a self derives from a phenomenological or introspective practice in which we all indulge, and corresponds to the description of ourselves we would give if someone asked us to describe our personality. Most of us are not very well equipped with the necessary words to give a convincing account which will correspond to the views of others. The advice of Socrates to "Know thyself" has probably never been followed successfully. We do not even know what we look like to others. Rarely do we even approve of photographs of ourselves while at the same time we say, "That's a good one of you." Our own familiarity with our physical appearance is based primarily on reversed images we view in mirrors. None of us has received the gift that concerned Robert Burns, "to see oursels as ithers see us."

We do of course have some appreciation of our physical size and general appearance. This is, to be sure, distorted by our concerns over appearing "fat," "handsome," "sophisticated," and so on. In addition to general external appearance we have, when we stop to think about it, a vague, poorly defined appreciation of personal continuity and identity that apparently persists from as far back as we can remember. While we obviously grow older, the process is a slow and imperceptible one and we rarely appreciate the change. Somehow we never feel older and we are shocked when someone tells us to "act your age." Many people fight retirement at sixty-five or seventy and argue that they are just coming into their prime. Other people change but we do not. The high-school and college freshman always looks like an infant in arms to the senior who cannot imagine himself ever having looked so immature. "What babies they let into kindergarten now," says the third-grader. We have always been the same, ever since we learned to call ourselves "me" and "I" at the age of two. That process of discriminating our bodies from the environment and from other bodies was slow, a gradual learning affair. Once such learning was complete, the personal identity was never lost. Upon wakening in the morning we do not lose contact with the past. It is the same "I" that lay down last night. This personal continuity and identity which appears changeless is what we call the self.

Because of the continuity and apparent unity we fall into the trap of believing that there is some underlying, true, inner being that makes for this continuity and individual unity. A unity implies an integration, a co-operation of parts, or a sweet reasonableness. We find it difficult to believe that the same organism can act now one way now another. We consequently think of our behavior as all of a pattern, an integrated wholeness. Our behavior is reasonable, logical, and for most of us, virtuous and proper. We then proceed to endow others with similar selves which make their behavior rational to us even though there are apparent discrepancies. The discrepancies we think are *only* apparent. If we regard someone as "basically" mean and unsympathetic and hear that he behaved generously to someone, we easily interpret this to show that it *proves* his meanness. "He's only trying to show his superiority," or "He's only establishing his power over someone."

When we examine and evaluate the views of a number of people about any particular person we find that commonly there is more disagreement than agreement. One person sees the individual in one way, another in some other way. This can only mean that there are two, three, or more selves or that our observations are unreliable, or inadequate. "After you get to know him, you'll see him differently." You probably will, but not necessarily in the same way as your advisor imagined. "One man in his time plays many parts," Shakespeare tells us, and examining the many parts we play as children, lovers, breadwinners, as fathers, as "boys of the club," has led us to the more readily approachable topic of "role playing."

Role playing

In our "dreams of glory" and in our disappointments we see ourselves as conquering heroes or misunderstood martyrs, as long-suffering and innocent victims of circumstance; sometimes we are virtuous to a fault, rarely are we appreciated. Most of us are virtuous, noble, refined, et cetera, but we have learned that others will not approve if we call attention to our virtues. In our culture you must be modest and accept awards with a humble "I don't really deserve this; it was the team that really did the job." Even with such a simple matter as looking at ourselves in a mirror we must be careful that no one is watching and some of us are embarrassed when we discover that someone has been observing us as we preened and posed or tried out an expression or a new hairstyle. We behave, superficially at least, as others expect us to. The difficulty is, however, that in the process of growing up we find out that various groups or individuals expect different kinds of behavior in more or less the same situations. In some places children are supposed to be seen and not heard. In other instances, not discriminably different to the child, he is called upon to discourse about school or even venture his opinions. Some people want your advice, others want to give it to you. The culture in which we live has over many generations developed and established certain standard practices, ways of behaving, under various circumstances. When in Rome you do as the Romans do. To learn your part and to know when to play it and not some other part takes up the greater part of an education. When we have successfully learned all the parts we have to play, we come to be so many things to so many people, that we have lost a certain amount of individuality and gained many individualities.

A father, in our culture, is supposed to play a certain role. He goes to work every day and comes home in the evening. In some subcultures he then doles out the daily accumulation of praise or punishments, or he takes the dog for a walk. He plays ball with the boys even though he never liked the game and he talks to them about camping, hunting, and heroic adventures in which he played an important part. This same person, in his employment may be "the timid soul" who is pushed around by even the office boys. In his social club, he may be the Grand Imperial Potentate who withers lesser officers with a twist of his lip. To his wife he may be a boor and a clod and behave like one. In the church choir he may be frolicky. He tries to live up to the expectations imposed upon him as a father by the cultural standards developed by the group with which he associates.

As an employee, he again has a role to play. He takes orders from one person or group and gives orders to another. He observes certain rules about when he eats or rests or with whom he associates, the kinds of clothes he wears, the neighborhood in which he lives (the address of an individual is carefully evaluated in some groups and some individuals starve in order to be able to report an appropriate address). If he is a union member, he "sticks with the boys" against the management in times of stress. If he is "with management" his loyalties are automatically presumed to be with "the company."

Whatever the situation, the group, or the circumstances, cultures decree certain codes of behavior (mores) which must be observed. The first-grader learns that you "don't snitch" on your fellows even if they beat you up. In college he will continue to protect students who have no business in college and would be much better off in some other activity. He will defend his family even when he knows them to be in the wrong and otherwise conform with what the group is presumed to expect of him.

In playing his various roles, the individual displays his various selves, or, more correctly, his various ways of behaving, his habit patterns. He will have a "social self" (and this may consist of several selves depending upon the number of different kinds of "societies" in which he moves), a family self, a professional self, a religious self, a self he displays "when he lets his hair down," in fact a self for every one of the situations in which he becomes involved. Sometimes these selves come into conflict, as when his family self calls for responses which his professional self does not sanction. A teacher with one of his own children in a class may find himself in occasional difficulties. Children often refuse to learn or accept guidance in their studies from parents. The parents simply are not "teachers." Even competent piano teachers frequently send their own children to other teachers for instruction.

There are many ways of talking about these various selves. To personify them may lead to trouble and it may be, as suggested above, that we are talking about nothing more than different habits, ways of behaving that are learned in different situations. Reifying various selves may lead to conceptions of personality that are not readily translatable into research questions. When a book is entitled *Three Faces of Eve* and the central character is pictured as being three different women at the same time (or in rapid succession), we are presented with a difficult problem of rationalizing a "multiple personality." In a sense we are all multiple personalities, but we usually do not let one get too far out of touch with the others. Those who do get into difficulty are rather rare. Case reports are not always accurate. Authors like to dramatize.

We have a right to be suspicious of such Dr. Jekyl and Mr. Hyde reports and should demand adequate evidence before accepting them as genuine. Should we be forced to accept the reality of such multiple personalities we might argue that they are only extreme examples of what all of us do, namely, behave differently at different times and places, thinking of ourselves as now one kind of person, now another. James Thurber's Walter Mitty is not far removed from the average American male. Some of us never grow up and we occasionally behave as we did years before when we *were* Snow White, or Robin Hood. When children adopt other selves, they can be deadly serious and many a mother has had to feed her child on the floor in his dog days. When we are forced to play an unwanted role by some strong pressures, we can expect some upheaval with perhaps violent and bizarre consequences. A wife who has long hated her husband but who has put up a front for the sake of the children might "reach the end of her rope" on some occasion when events seem trivial enough, and say things she might never have been predicted to say on the basis of her former role playing. She might behave "completely out of character." "I'll show you how mean I can be" might be a starting point for a series of more or less ridiculous and outlandish actions. So long as we retain a picture of the former devoted wife and mother as representing the "real" personality, we have now to view the disorderly behavior as reflecting another person. If the person is reinforced for such activities, that is, if engaging in "out of character" activities brings her some satisfaction in her original status, she might repeat the behavior on future occasions. If the act is an odd one, we may have a so-called "dual-personality" on our hands. It may be difficult for us to recognize that we are not dealing with a dual personality but with two ways of behaving demonstrated by the same individual. We keep thinking that because there is only one body and one name, there can be only one, the true personality. Perhaps such a single true self is merely a reflection of what we would like the person to be, uncluttered with cumbersome contradictions. Unfortunately people are cluttered up with different ways of behaving in what we mistakenly identify as the *same* situation. The close-fisted stingy person sometimes proffers generous gifts which his stinginess allowed him to afford. In our ignorance of the facts and with our strong convictions about the "true inner me" we are surprised at the unusual behavior we might witness. Perhaps this true inner self is no more than the habit system we are dominated by when we are alone, when certain stimuli are missing, when we feel no pressures to conform or please others. Such moments are comparatively rare, however and rapidly give way in the changing social scene. A child might be highly regarded in school as a quiet, co-operative person who always has a cheerful air. At home the child may be lazy, unruly, painfully honest, even vicious. Which is the true self? Perhaps we could argue that the true self is the habit system that is active most of the time. Because the distribution of activities in time will vary with growth and aging, occupation, marital status, and possible parenthood, we cannot expect much stability for such a "true" self. It will not usually have a long life.

Stereotypes

As we try to come to grips with the concept of personality we recognize more and more that by the use of the term, people try to convey something that is quite characteristic of the individual, something that marks him off from others, that distinguishes him from his friends and neighbors. We have already emphasized the differences of opinion among observers about the person observed. Every parent recognizes the blindness of his neighbors when it comes to seeing the positive points and values exhibited by his child. It is difficult to live with such contradictory views and we quickly settle on an attitude that suits us. Our children are geniuses regardless of what the neighbors think. Their children are stupid and nasty little brats. We have considered such easy thinking operations before when we talked about stereotypes. Much of what passes as our opinion about somebody's personality amounts to a statement of what our stereotype for this individual contains. Even when we are forced to consider contradictions to this stereotype we find it convenient to say "Yes, but . . ." and retain our stereotype. By identifying our stereotype with personality we endow individuals with an entity or identity they may not possess.

Frequently we are caught short with our stereotypes. When the gangster kisses his mother on the way to the Big House, we find ourselves uncomfortable with what to us is a contradiction. Rather than deal with the contradiction we would prefer to retain a stereotype even if we have to change it. We ask ourselves, "What is he really like?" because it is inconceivable to us that a gangster can really love his mother and still be a gangster. Either he is a mother lover or a gangster. He must *really* be one thing or another but not both. The contradictions and misunderstandings that are uncovered in the biographies of our heroes are also upsetting. We do not like to read that Lincoln stated that Negroes could never be accepted as equals with whites. It upsets our stereotypes. In our own personal histories we are frequently misunderstood because somebody does not know "the real me." The search for the real Shakespeare, the real Napoleon, the real Washington, goes on along with the search for the "real me." We find it difficult to accept that people, including ourselves, may be bundles of contradictions instead of definitive, neatly packaged units with an inherent and permanent consistency.

The tendency to type people has been practiced from the earliest times. Shakespeare has Caesar saying "Let me have men about me that are fat; . . . Yond Cassius has a lean and hungry look . . ." Hack writers in general find it convenient to describe characters in a few "well-chosen" words, words that arouse common stereotypes and save a lot of writing such as would be involved in any attempt at really describing an individual. The chap with the close-set eyes and thin lips (or sensuous lips) is obviously a villain; the receding chin marks the weak father of the girl; the tall, blonde, and tanned chap is the hero, without any question, and the fat fellow is in there for laughs because all fat men are jolly as any fool knows. Some serious attempts have been made by scientists to discover if people can be classified into any meaningful types and a number of proposals have been advanced suggesting relationships between body build and other characteristics of people. We have already mentioned the earliest such attempt made by Hippocrates who described four fluids of the body (blood, black bile, phlegm, and yellow bile) which were supposed to vary in proportions among different individuals, leading to differences in temperament. His classification of personalities as sanguine, choleric, melancholic, and phlegmatic never rose above the level of literature and today we do not use such expressions frequently even in literature.

In the nineteenth century, attempts were made to measure body build and classify people as predominantly heavy or fat, athletic, or thin and lean. These body types were called pyknic, athletic, and asthenic and were supposed to be associated with specific characteristics. The lack of any good statistical devices prevented any proper test of the theory and such attempts had to wait for the work of Sheldon (1954) who photographed thousands of college students and measured them along various axes to develop again a series of types which he called endomorphs, mesomorphs, and ectomorphs, corresponding to fat, athletic, and thin. When personality tests were given to such individuals whose body indexes were known, it was found that no reliable personality clusters or characteristics were in fact associated with body types (Tyler, 1956) and this view is now losing whatever favor it had, although we cannot expect it to die as it will receive continuing support from novelists and entertainment producers who have no time to waste developing "character" when it can be done with one picture or one sentence.

The fact that no consistent relationships between personality measures and the physical structure of the body have been found for groups of subjects should not lead to a total rejection of the hypothesis that an *individual's* bodily formation and organic functioning have nothing to do with behavior. Throughout this text we have been at great pains to point out the physiological determinants of behavior. At this time we need only mention a couple of illustrations to recall our basic orientation. If you are seven feet tall, you cannot hide from basketball scouts and your behavior will certainly be circumscribed if not determined by your height. If you are fat and find it fatiguing to move about rapidly, you might easily develop into a slow moving and deliberate sort of person. If you are a very attractive person, you will find marriage or relations with the opposite sex difficult to avoid. Sickness or health again will set the pace and frequently determine the outcome of the race.

Other type approaches

Class membership

The attempts to pigeonhole personality have been limited only by ingenuity. Various "logical" approaches have been developed along with a variety of statistical methods. We shall sample each. In the more logical vein, it has been argued that a person can be understood, in effect, from the outside, by discovering what he does with his time, the groups he belongs to and the various formal kinds of associations and environments to which he has been exposed. The concept of "class membership" (J. F. Brown, 1936) has been developed in this connection. The environment, especially the social aspects of environment, is broken down into categories and a person is classified as belonging to one or another of various divisions and subdivisions in the hope that the enumeration of groups with which he has or had contact will reveal his personality.

We shall consider the nature of the social environment more fully in the next chapter. Here we will deal only superficially with various social labels. It will be necessary to refer frequently to such terms as "society" and "culture." They will require more lengthy treatment than is necessary here and ordinary conversational meanings will be presumed for the present. Various divisions or regions of social groupings, as, for example, religious, economic, educational, professional, political, and racial or national origins can be taken into account. Suppose we know someone to be a Catholic, upper middle class, Ivy League graduate, lawyer, Republican, of Irish background, and someone else to be Jewish, lower middle class, grammar school, delicatessen employee, Democrat, of Russian background. Surely these are two different people, and just as surely, as each class membership is mentioned we respond in terms of our stereotypes for these classes and build up a picture of each person, attributing to him certain attitudes, mannerisms, habits, and sundry personal characteristics as we have picked such up from novels, movies, or family life, or other personal experience. But what do we really know about these individuals? Would we be able to pick them out of a "lineup" or even tell which was which when only the two were present? If we could do this much could we go any further? Could we make any important predictions about the behavior of either in his family or business life, in the number of friends he had, in his level of adjustment, his philosophy?

Class membership stereotypes are of questionable value. Suppose we meet someone who is introduced by name only; we react in terms of stereotypes relating to physical appearance, speech, clothing, etc. There is not much to go on. Now the introducer remarks, Mr. X is a West Pointer. Immediately our reaction pattern is altered to make room for the new stereotype. During World War II many civilians were rushed into services in commissioned ranks and on the surface it was quite impossible to tell an Annapolis or West Point man from a "reserve." As soon as the distinction was established, "appropriate" reactions were developed, regardless of any other information. You might sit next to someone in some public place and be quite indifferent to him. If someone later points out that you were sitting next to some public figure, famous athlete, actor, or other "personality," your reaction pattern alters immediately. Famous "personalities" appear glamorous, "magnetic," and somehow possessed of a "magic." When they lose their favored status the glamor, magnetism, and charm also seem to disappear. Did the fame create the magic or vice versa? Did they lose their magic with the loss in fame? Perhaps they never had it. Many movie stars starved for years before they were "discovered" and suddenly became possessed of previously hidden glamor.

Examination of individuals who are members of different groups commonly results in the conclusion that either the groups are not appropriately made up, or that membership in a group means very little. New Hampshire Republicans are not the same as California or Wisconsin Republicans. Some bankers are embezzelers. Some artists have ordinary haircuts and wear business suits. Some members of religious groups have only nominal ties with the church and the church policies or principles may have no bearing on the person's behavior. When Hollywood producers or casting directors are looking for a man to play the part of a waiter, they do not go to restaurants—the waiters there do not even look like waiters. Bankers do not look like bankers, and politicians do not look like politicians. The casting director knows his business. He knows that he is not dealing with reality but with fiction. Most stereotypes are fictional and we learn little by being told that Mr. X is a steelworker or an author or a deep-sea fisherman. There is too great a range of individual differences within any "class membership" for us to make any predictions with any reliability. Some Republicans even vote Democratic and vice versa. The current political distribution is nominally Democratic on the national level and hypothetically, a Democrat should always win the Presidency. The election and re-election of President Eisenhower should suggest that predictions based on class membership of a superficial kind are worthless. Of course, we could develop a specific class membership to include all the people who would vote for Eisenhower and a prediction might be more successful, but such a class membership would be difficult to determine and it is far easier to think in terms of already available, even though useless, stereotypes.

Personality "syndromes"

The class membership approach has given way to a more sophisticated attempt to pigeonhole personality in terms of what might be called "patterns of attitudes." It would be convenient if we could tell something more about a person if we knew one or two things more or less reliably, and if this minimal information was strongly indicative of other personality facets or characteristics. If all Southern whites were anti-Negro, for example, we would know something more about a person as soon as we found out that he was from the South. However, it is not true, in this particular instance, nor, on the other hand, is it true that all Northern whites are pro-Negro. It is argued, however, that some attitudes or behavior patterns do go together and that some kinds of "organization" or "syndrome" (a combination of symptoms or traits) can be discovered for at least some broadly conceived "personality types." It is common enough in literature to read about a "Prussian" personality or a "slave" personality. Our common language habits make it easy for us to support such views as we label others "Fascists" or "Liberals" or "Communists." When attitude tests are given to a large enough population on a sufficient range of topics, there is evidence to suggest that within limits some attitudes do cluster together so that a person might merit the label "authoritarian," "rigid," "conservative," "masculine," and so on. The "authoritarian" personality might include conservative, if not reactionary, attitudes toward racial groups, religion, economics, et cetera. We might think of such people as "rigid," power-oriented, superstitious, and prejudiced. But even here we would run into difficulties with individual differences which would prevent easy generalizations from bearing any predictive fruit. It we could collect groups of "authoritarian" and "democratic" individuals and compared their behavior in some situations we might find differences that did separate the groups on the average, but there would be other situations where no such separation would be discernible, and in all cases there would be individual variations so that some authoritarians acted like democrats in some situations and vice versa.

In the general context of type studies, some attention has been paid to the role of economic factors, or, more properly, to the economic role of a person. How an individual makes his living is presumed to affect a great many of his attitudes and behavioral characteristics. Guthrie (1944), for example, argued that because so much time is devoted to the business of earning a living, it will inevitably result in the development of habits and attitudes that cover a wide range of situations and circumstances. It will affect your mode of dress, your very manner of walking and talking, the things you talk about, the kinds of people you associate with, and so on. Going back to our West Pointer, we will find that he will have a "military carriage," he will say "sir" to some people and not to others, he will not talk about women, religion, and politics in certain places, and he will display a pattern of behavior that we will not ordinarily observe among non-West Pointers. The psychologist Strong (1943) developed what is now known as the Strong Vocational Interest Test on the basis of such considerations and was able to discover characteristic patterns of attitudes aand preferences that are shared by members of one profession but not another. There is some overlap, to be sure, but the test does tend to discriminate among the professions. People who become lawyers and find the profession a suitable one endorse a different series of preferences about hobbies, books, people, etc., than do successful physicians or authors. It is not certain whether only those who already have the appropriate patterns enter the profession or whether the business of becoming a successful member of a given profession imposes certain preferences on the members, but the pattern differences are there. There appears to be merit in discovering the pattern of interests among prospective candidates for a given profession. Those found exceptionally "unsuitable" might be advised to try something for which they appear to be more closely matched. We must repeat the general caution that despite the uniformities that do prevail, there are still individual differences that must be considered. Not all lawyers think alike, nor even psychologists.

THE TRAIT APPROACH

Rating scales

Throughout the above discussion we have been forced to talk about "characteristics," features, or aspects of personality without stopping to specify what was meant. In talking about people we commonly resort to the use of adjectives or other descriptive verbal forms. People are called kind, neat, generous or sly, mean, cruel, fat, lean, etc. There are thousands of such expressions. G. Allport (1937) counted almost 20,000 such "trait" names. The term "trait" refers to some presumed characteristic of a person which might be pointed out or alleged to exist as a feature of some descriptive value. It is sometimes presumed that if a trait does have any claim to being mentioned, one should be able to recognize it, perhaps even measure it in some way or at least to *rate* it, i.e., tell whether it is present in some small amount, average amount, or in some exceptional degree. Actually, most people tend to be rather absolutistic in their judgments and describe people as "honest," "sincere," "warm," etc., without specifying amounts. It is only when a question of comparison arises that amount or degree becomes important. Then the problem of measurement arises. For most trait-terms the measurement techniques are predominantly "subjective" and depend upon the use of *rating scales* wherein a judge is required to indicate his opinion of the amount of a trait along a continuum running from low to high. Sometimes the scales are broken up into sections labeled "very much" or "hardly ever" and so on. It is obvious that such scales are not likely to attain the degree of reliability (see p. 182) one would achieve with a ruler, but for most traits, it is the best procedure that has been developed. When judges are asked to "rate" a person, they are frequently provided with a list of traits. Quite commonly they assign about the same rating for every trait in the list. This is known as the "halo effect." It is probably due to our difficulty in separating out different traits (e.g., generous, kind) and a tendency to judge a person in more general terms, as "he's all right." If "he's all right," then he is also kind, generous, fair, responsible, friendly, etc. (and probably in the same degree).

Inventories and questionnaires

Some tests of personality are not tests in any real sense, i.e., they do not even pretend to measure what a person *can* do; rather, they are designed to discover what a person might do in various situations or how he feels about them. In such a test, more commonly called an "inventory" or "questionnaire," a person can deceive the examiner if he chooses to (there are some tests where it is possible to discover if the subject has been lying). Sometimes people try to present a picture of themselves which is more favorable than the facts warrant; occasionally people try to present themselves in an unfavorable light in order to avoid some responsibility such as military service. Usually inventories are aimed at discovering more important, "dominant" traits, or "cardinal" traits or how a person measures up in comparison with others on a selected list of traits which have been assumed to be important in our culture, such as co-operativeness or competitiveness, aggressiveness, conservatism, extroversion or introversion, sociability, emotional control, etc. Such inventories can frequently be made into reliable measuring devices but suffer in connection with validity which is sometimes impossible to discover except by comparison with ratings. In tests which are designed to determine degree of adjustment or neuroticism, comparisons can be made with hospitalized patients, diagnoses by qualified practitioners and other "judges." It is obviously difficult to determine, however, if a person is sociable or co-operative. These terms themselves are so fuzzy in meaning that nothing much (or almost anything) can be proved. A person might be sociable in one group and not in another; he might co-operate in some situations with some people or some kinds of people and not with others. It is always necessary to keep such relativistic limitations before us in considering the measurement of personality.

The difficulty of validating personality tests was tellingly exposed by Paterson (1951) when he made up a "universal" personality analysis that could be applied to anyone regardless of race, creed, color, sex, education, etc. It is quite likely that any person subjected to a barrage of personality tests and inventories would be satisfied to be told that, among other things, he "was above average in intelligence, was inclined to worry at times, liked to mix with people he knew well, disliked turning out sloppy work, was inclined toward sports but watched or read about them more than he participated, and has a good disposition although earlier in life he had to struggle with himself to control impulses and temper." Such comments along with many others Paterson included in his humorous yet serious sketch amount to trivial generalities that do not discriminate one individual from another. The weaknesses of such diagnoses have been discussed at greater length by Dunnette (1957) who warns against the "Barnum Effect" which gives a spurious sense of accuracy often resulting from this kind of "anecdotal validation" (also see Stagner, 1958).

THE RATIONALE FOR TRAIT MEASUREMENT

Underlying the whole effort at discovering what traits an individual displays and to what degree he is characterized by them is the assumption that some central core of personality can be identified by this means. The trait-centered psychologists view personality as an *organization* of traits, and by organization they intend an "integration" that *is* the personality. The emphasis is on an integrative principle, the personality is viewed as a "relatively permanent" organization of traits or reaction patterns with which a person meets his problems, and the assumption is made that this organization can be determined by finding the important or significant traits which pervade the personality or serve as a skeleton or frame around which other reaction patterns are developed. To make the task of describing personality simple enough to be practical, the hope is always to find a limited number of traits which would serve to identify the assumed basic framework or organization. No matter how diverse the behavior patterns of an individual might appear, the belief is held that there is a thread that binds, integrates, or organizes these patterns so that if one understood the pattern or organization it would make sense of the apparent discrepancies.

Projective tests

Because such basic patterns of organization are not easily demonstrated by direct observation techniques, inventories, and tests, some psychologists rely on more indirect tests which are designed to tap "unconscious" determinants of behavior. On the surface a person might appear kind, generous, and co-operative. His "true" personality, however, might be "hostile, aggressive, and anxious." By developing a picture of the "unconscious" personality it is possible to claim a fuller understanding of some apparent contradictions in behavior. To get at unconscious factors, tests have been developed whereby a person looks at inkblots, or pictures of dogs or people and indicates his likes or dislikes or what the inkblots, clouds, or other stimuli make him think of. Sometimes the subject is shown a picture and asked to tell a story about the people in the picture. The story he creates is supposed to reveal something about himself. Such tests are called *projective* tests because the subject has to give something of himself to the test in order for any meaning to emerge. An inkblot is, after all, only an inkblot. In order to see "two bears dancing," a subject has to imagine such figures and such an event. Other subjects will report "two old maids fighting" or "nothing, maybe a butterfly" and so on.

The value of such projective tests has yet to be established as far as validity is concerned. Various studies aimed at determining validity have resulted in debatable or negative conclusions. Clinical psychologists make considerable use of such tests and find them useful in some ways. It is usually possible to recognize extremely disturbed people from their reactions to such tests. Because extremely disturbed people can also be recognized in other ways much more quickly, the value of the tests might be questioned. If such tests can be established as valid devices, they may prove useful in providing more specific diagnoses than now possible. At present many psychiatrists and clinical psychologists hesitate to use precise labels for their patients. They prefer to think of them as "psychiatric" cases rather than as "schizophrenics" or "paranoids," etc. Such caution is commendable. On the other hand, "psychiatric" cases might be cases of very specific biochemical disturbances which are expressed in varying behavior patterns and which will continue to baffle those who study only behavior.

Let us examine the assumption that the use of indirect measures of personality might identify the hypothetical hidden integration or organization of the personality that accounts for the discrepancies usually observed in any person's behavior. When a person is kind to his child but kicks dogs and cats around, we cannot say that he is "plain kind" or "kind in general." When he holds doors open for old ladies, he is polite; but, if he does not give them his seat on a bus, he is not. If he is neither kind nor not kind, perhaps he is something else which would be accounted for by his "inner core" or "true personality." If he is nice to women, always bringing them gifts, but not nice to men, perhaps he has some homosexual yearnings which he fights off by being aggressive and hostile to men and generous to women, and so on. Clinical case studies are full of such interpretations but case studies are essentially postdictive affairs, not predictive ones and interpretations are not proof. In some cases a clinical patient will "admit" or endorse the interpretation of his personality given by the clinician. This, of course, is again not proof. In such interpersonal operations as are involved in diagnoses and therapy, it becomes difficult to keep a clear and direct observational path. The clinician may find himself arriving at an interpretation on the basis of other cues and believe that the test itself told the tale. Some psychologists are willing to assume almost anything rather than give up the conviction that there is an inner organization of traits that would make people understandable if only the organizational framework were laid bare. There appears to be as much reason for abandoning this assumption as there is for retaining it, at least in the light of present kinds of evidence. We can only await the results of future research.

TRAITS: GENERAL OR SPECIFIC?

Our picture of the rationale underlying the measurement of traits is not yet complete. We must include the assumption that the traits somehow exist in themselves, that when they are measured or rated, something more or less real lies behind the measurement. Why else measure intelligence, for example, if there really is no such thing? We talk about extroversion, introversion, submissiveness, hostility, aggressiveness, and anxiety, for example, as if these were realities. All we can possibly know about, however, is whether the person involved behaves in ways that might merit the *adjectives* intelligent, hostile, aggressive, etc. It is further assumed that such traits, if they exist, exist more or less absolutely. People are either generous or not generous is the argument. The fact that rating scales make provision for indicating degrees of a trait does not make traits any less absolutist. A person may be rated as only a little generous, for example. This means, presumably, that he has a small amount of generosity which he spreads thinly over all situations calling for generosity and not that he behaves generously at one time and not at another. Scale items are commonly defined or described with such terms as "always, sometimes, rarely, never." According to this reasoning a person who gives $2,000.00 to one charity and nothing to others is less generous than someone who gives $20.00 to each of 100 charities.

Even more to the point, the trait is somehow abstracted from the specific behavior of individuals and perceived as having dynamic properties, as, in effect, governing the behavior. Thus the child that says "thank you" is endowed with "politeness" and it is assumed that he says these words *because* he is polite, and not the other way around. Yet this child may kick cats and trip old ladies. We recall that Guthrie (see p. 254) argued for a very opposite kind of view. He claims that everyone learns specific responses to specific stimuli and that we do not ever learn politeness, generosity, or other general dynamisms as such. We learn only responses which are considered polite, kind, etc. The student might be inclined to shrug off the whole matter as of no consequence, but only if he has failed to recognize the serious consequences that might follow. Let us illustrate from the field of psychotherapy. If we regard someone as maladjusted or neurotic and believe that some central core or basic trait pattern (the neurotic personality) is involved, we might try to work on this central, but hidden, pattern. Thus, someone who is behaving in ways we find undesirable might be diagnosed as having a condition of "anxiety." His behavior might be thought of as reflecting hostility, rigidity, or aggressiveness or some other "symptoms" but so long as the belief in a "basic anxiety" persists, it is argued that there is no point in curing the symptoms. They will only be replaced by other symptoms if the fundamental "disease" or condition is not eliminated. This point of view might represent good standard practice in medicine which might decry reducing fevers or headaches without finding the basic cause.

Is there, however, a good analogy with medical practice to be found here? Why not treat the aggressiveness or hostility or whatever is causing trouble? Do we really have evidence that other symptoms will replace those that are eliminated? Clinical practitioners like to think so but there are no systematic studies of this presumed substitution. Guthrie 1938 (and Skinner 1948) would argue for working on the symptoms one at a time and getting rid of them; Guthrie, by new learning; Skinner, by extinction of the undesirable activity. Skinner (1953) regards a "neurosis" as a linguistic fiction. If behavior really consists of specifically learned responses then Skinner and Guthrie are correct. If we manage to remove the undesired behavior, we need not worry over the basic anxiety. The indirect attack favored by some practitioners may be very time consuming and when it works, might work for precisely the reasons Skinner and Guthrie espouse—somewhere in the process or in the course of the indirect attack, the troubled person learned new ways of behaving to previously disturbing stimuli.

In *Walden II,* Skinner (1948) suggested that if we want to discourage someone from telling "dirty" stories we need not worry over his disordered personality that somehow must tell dirty stories. All we need to do is stop laughing at his efforts and not reinforce such behavior. Presumably the dirty stories will disappear in favor of some more socially desirable behavior if we reinforce that. Similarly, any other undesirable behavior can be extinguished by nonreinforcement. This applies to simple disorderly behavior like throwing clothes on chairs and to complex patterns like "aggressiveness." In the latter case, we have to spell out just what responses we are going to include under this label and go to work on each aggressive response. The student should pause and muse over just what he means when he attaches such labels to behavior. If he derives some answers, he has arrived at the starting point for re-education.

THE NATURE OF HUMAN NATURE

The study of personality is hampered by the divergent interests of psychologists as well as by their theoretical orientations. Some are concerned with specific problems of specific people whom they would like to help in some manner; others view the problem of personality much more broadly, looking for common factors, traits, or trends in development which characterize Everyman. Some clinically oriented psychologists emphasize uniqueness and individuality, where some theoreticians emphasize basic similarities. This dichotomy of interests leads to confusion in discussions of personality when some are considering individual patterns of traits and others are thinking more broadly of human nature in the most general terms.

Individual differences

Outside of the relatively infrequent cases of multiple births, the most obvious thing about people is the wide array of differences which can be observed. How important these differences are is a separate question to which we can return, but, for the present, we can consider the breadth of differences themselves. Even without differences in training or environment, differences are provided for by nature in the simple fact that each parent contributes 24 chromosomes of his 48 to the new offspring. Which chromosomes he contributes, however, is unpredictable and uncontrollable at the present time and is described as a "chance" operation. It is highly improbable that any two children of a given pair of parents would inherit the same constitution, and while family resemblances might sometimes be quite noticeable, the differences are also assured by the hereditary contributions. Even if we all had the same parents there would be enough differences to go around; the fact that we do not have the same parents allows for more extreme variations to occur. The variations that are observable running from one extreme to another over every imaginable dimension of size, shape, and color of various parts of the body create no end of difficulty for manufacturers of clothing, furniture, and various conveyances. If we add variations in internal bodily structures, bone and tooth structure, diameters of blood vessels, capacities of stomach and bladder, glandular structures and neural equipment we have more than enough differences to conjure with. If it can be assumed that many kinds of behavior are traceable to just such aspects as size, shape, color, and other simple physical dimensions we begin to "get the feel" of the task of psychology (Williams, 1958).

One of the important considerations that hardly needs bringing out, but which sometimes intrudes itself into psychological discussions, is the fact that we tend to forget, when talking about one dimension and the range involved, that one characteristic can be at one extreme while another characteristic may be at another. The short, fat man represents two such extremes, as does the tall, thin man. We also have medium-fat, short men, and medium-fat, tall men, and tall, fat men with little feet, as well as short, thin men with large feet and long noses. In the midst of all these variations we try to deal with averages and we talk about the average man. The only difficulty is that there is no such thing as the average man in even the crudest physical sense when we take more than one dimension into account. People even differ in the lengths of their tongues, the diameter of their hair, and their body temperatures. The person who steps on a drugstore scale and finds that his height matches the suggestion of the chart of heights and "correct" weights is unique. An individual is just that, an individual. He differs in one way or another from everyone else on earth (as well as all those who preceded him and who will follow him). When we add to the structural uniqueness the characteristics he manages to develop in the course of growing up, he is entitled to resent his wife's remark that "Men are all alike." Men are alike only to the extent that a powerful culture can force some degree of similarity in some aspects of behavior. Frequently enough the areas of behavior where culture does exert a commanding influence tend to appear of little importance in human adjustments so long as we remain adjusted to the culture. We can all learn to wear clothes, visit bathrooms, wash our necks, and even obey traffic signals. These affairs become commonplace and standard. We are rarely concerned about the commonplace, however, and become interesting to others, including psychologists, when we deviate in some fashion. Even the culture would not tolerate complete uniformity and considerable effort goes into fostering and developing differences of which the culture approves. Parents try to dress their children better than those of the neighbors, urge them to win races, star at athletics or scholarship, etc. We are even horrified by pictures of "standardized" populations and if Johnny is out-of-step we are a little proud of Johnny. The fact that society may sponsor some individual deviations and that most of us tend to behave more or less uniformly, should not be interpreted to mean that societal influences are not important in *eliminating* individual differences. Through educational, governmental, and religious institutions, a great deal of uniformity is imposed on practically all individuals not only in how they behave overtly but even in how they think. Our concern here has been to point out that those features or characteristics of our behavior that are uniform, or standardized by society, set the limits for individual differences and thereby the range and nature of individual "personality."

The fact that we are all born different and that some are more different than others has been the basis for many definitions of personality. Personality is held to be that unique collection (some argue for organization) of characteristics (traits) which mark off the individual. Such a definition permits us to consider the possibility that some people have "more" personality than others, but not in any "value" sense. A two-headed, one-legged, pock-marked, half-naked individual has more personality on Madison Avenue than a chap in a gray flannel suit. In a world of two-headed, one-legged, pock-marked, half-naked people, such a person would have no personality to speak of and the gray flannel suit wearer would be the one with "personality." To the extent that we adopt common speech, common clothing, common reaction patterns we lose personality. With each item of individuality that distinguishes us from others we gain personality. In the armed services, where men are considered "units," to be *replaced* when necessary by other "units," each "unit" must be as nearly like the next as possible. For this reason military personnel wear uniforms, tuck their ties in below the second button, wear their caps at a certain angle, get their hair cut in the same style and learn to say and do the same things at certain commands. The drills that seem so tiresome to trainees are necessary to wipe out any personality that might be left after the screening and clothing process has taken its toll. The military services cannot afford to put up with idiosyncracies. They have to depend upon the "unit" to act like a cog in a machine and no effort is spared to manufacture the cogs in a uniform style. In other walks of life, like the entertainment profession, we see the practice of the opposite extreme. Actresses might have their pictures taken bathing in tiger milk, they might dye their hair green or purple, go around barefooted, with pet lions and do anything a press agent can hope will attract enough attention to get into print. Actors must have "personality," or at least this is what press agents believe.

In Western culture women try to distinguish themselves by their clothing, coiffures, and personal adornment and, in certain socioeconomic strata, insist on having "unique" dresses. In fact, the terms "unique" and "exclusive" have been adopted by the clothing trade to describe a garment which has been specially designed and which is not duplicated. When women at a social function find someone else with a copy of the same garment, it is sufficient grounds for bringing the merchants involved to court. The concerns of women over clothing and appearance in contrast to the more or less drab attire of males are presumably related to the fact that they have so few opportunities to distinguish themselves in the professions and creative areas. Women pianists, for example, even when exceptionally talented, have a more difficult time than men in obtaining engagements. Perhaps the public does not care for women musicians; at least booking agents think so. The effort to attain some distinctiveness, some individuality, is an effort designed to increase "personality" in a culture that emphasizes individualistic values. Rugged individuals are admired, envied, or respected even when their ruggedness is enjoyed at the expense of someone else. People with great talent are allowed to indulge themselves in tantrums, insolence, and other disorderly and normally unacceptable ways because they have "temperament," not just temper like the rest of us. In our culture we have a real "cult of the individual" and so important is this emphasis that many psychologists have taken individuality or uniqueness as equivalent to, if not the most important feature or dimension of "personality."

The original nature of man

In spite of the emphasis on uniqueness and individuality, some psychologists, perhaps viewing the array of individual traits with some alarm, feel that this emphasis is misplaced or exaggerated to the degree that we lose sight of fundamental and far more significant or important similarities. The dress, the adornments, the mannerisms, speech patterns, differences in size, strength, and so on are all superficial. Beneath these trimmings, they argue, there is a hard core of fundamental processes or mechanisms that define human nature, real human nature, and if these processes or mechanisms were understood in their intimate organization and interplay, we would be able to appreciate man as he really is, separating the shadow from the substance. According to this view, all men (and women) are fundamentally alike, similar, or the same or, at least, they start out the same. The differences among them are trivial and not especially worthy of attention in their own right. Of course, such psychologists are not denying differences in physical structures and whatever such differences may lead to as a matter of course or necessity. The blind cannot see and the lame do not win foot races; but such functions, in themselves, are not important for an understanding of human nature. Given certain anatomical differences, such as those distinguishing men from women and individuals from one another, there is still a basic similarity or fundamental sameness in humans which determines their behavior. Any significant deviations in behavior are to be explained as "defense mechanisms," fixations, or other adjustments which are adopted because something disturbed the normal course of development. The variations in "defenses" or other "adjustments" are, in themselves, not important and can be readily understood once the basic pattern of human personality is fully appreciated.

We cannot consider all of the many attempts that have been made in the course of civilization to understand this basic "man." Philosophers have wrestled with this kind of approach for centuries and have presented us with solutions of varying degrees of detail and sophistication. Some views are elaborations or extensions of some single basic theme such as might be held by different theologians. Thus, one will find that man is cursed with original sin and all of his life is marked with this stain which he battles to wipe out against constant temptation to behave in ways that prevent him from ever winning his battle. Another will find, as Rousseau (1762) did, that man is born basically good, a "noble savage" who is soon corrupted by society. Some will argue for one form of doctrine of predestination or another which leaves "behavior" in the clutches or toils of various forces beyond our comprehension. Some will regard man as basically an animal with a "thin veneer of civilization," while others will regard him as essentially a machine, in some instances a machine that is supplied with energy from the outside and eventually succumbs to "wear and tear," while others endow the organism with inner resources which generate energy in some undescribed fashion and permit constant growth to higher and higher aspirations.

We can perhaps appreciate such efforts better if we consider the problem of a visitor from some other planet whose assignment is to observe the creatures he finds on earth and report back his findings, limiting himself to essentials and not cluttering up his report with trivia. Assuming further that he restricts himself to humans while his colleagues might specialize in other forms, what might his report be like if he were sufficiently insightful or intelligent to penetrate the "essential nature of man"? Unfortunately, no psychologist can presume to such intellectual gifts and the best we can do is to offer tentative suggestions instead of firm conclusions. The suggestions themselves range over a wide variety of views as different psychologists cope with the problem in terms of their own biases. We will consider only one widely discussed view, that of Freud. Should our man from outer space happen to "see" in man what Sigmund Freud (1938) thought he saw, his report might include remarks like the following.

The Freudian man

Man is a warm-blooded vertebrate with a highly developed central nervous system. Like other animals he undergoes a process of development starting with conception and terminating in death. Throughout his life two basic instincts struggle for mastery within him, a Life instinct and a Death instinct. These instincts account for some contradictory manifestations in his behavior where we witness a variety of constructive and destructive efforts. Man's personality unfolds in three stages related to sexual energy or "libido." At first the infant is completely self-centered. His life is governed by a "pleasure principle" and his only interests are "narcissistic." Gradually he develops contacts and interests in other creatures of his own sex and enters a "homosexual" stage. Eventually he passes out of this stage and becomes "heterosexual," confining his libidinal interests to members of the opposite sex. Because of traumatic incidents he may become "fixated" at any of these stages and remain there throughout his life. Paralleling the three stages of sexual development will be the development of processes, still under the influence of the pleasure principle, which control or rule over the behavior; these processes are called the Id, the Ego, and the Superego. At first the Id-forces or processes are dominant. These are basic, primitive needs or urges which demand immediate satisfaction. As the individual develops, Ego-forces enter and modify the Id's urgency. The Ego represents, in effect, processes which involve compromises with an environment that will not always cater to the Id. Both Id and Ego are selfish—the Id blindly and the Ego intelligently so. The child must wait for his meals, confine his excretory activities to a bathroom, and so on. He learns to do what he must. With further development, social forces including moral and ethical principles (conscience) are acquired which further interfere with and modify the activities of the Id. The individual becomes, to a degree, civilized.

In the course of development much of the activity of the Id is forced into the Unconscious, as are many Ego and Superego processes. Ego and Superego processes, however, can exist in part on a preconscious level and can be made conscious on demand. In short, most of the forces that control behavior are unconscious and some of these forces are mutually contradictory and interfere with each other, that is, they are in conflict. The presence of this conflict is not recognized by the individual in many instances and the anxiety that is generated by such conflicts is instrumental in developing "defense mechanisms" that temporarily reduce the anxiety. Anxiety plays a dual role, sometimes generating such mechanisms as repression, sometimes operating as the result of repression.

All humans develop unconscious sexual interests in the parent of the opposite sex. They unconsciously resent the parent of the same sex who is a competitor for the pleasures that might be enjoyed. This is called the Oedipus or Electra complex. In the process of growing up the individual has to come to terms with this complex. Failure to develop adequate adjustments or defenses results in disturbances of personality in later life.

The above brief sketch of Freud's basic views would be the substance of the Freudian-type space man. Should he be wearing different spectacles, for instance those of Alfred Adler (1917), an early associate of Freud, but one who broke away from him and developed his own views, he might see all humans engaging in a struggle for power, compensating for felt inferiority. The little man with the loud mouth, the cowardly braggart are familiar to all of us from literature. Adler saw man as fundamentally driven by feelings of inferiority, derived from real or apparent weaknesses, to striving for control of his environment. Everyone, said Adler, develops a "style of life" which is his way of meeting the problem of felt inferiority (see Wolfe, 1930).

IS A CONCEPT OF PERSONALITY NECESSARY?

The nature of man our Martian would report would depend upon what he saw or thought he saw. There have been dozens of attempts to discover the fundamental formula assumed to define the nature of man. Whether such a formula can ever be found is a tantalizing question. Maybe like the search for the Fountain of Youth, it is hopeless. "Personality" has proved to be an elusive target and most psychologists have changed their orientation from a concern with the nature of man as an organized unit controlled by internal forces to an interest in "behavior."

We have already examined the nature of this concept and recognize that "behavior" is an abstraction, an inference, drawn from observation just as is "personality." We must now ask ourselves what is the value of a concept like personality as compared with a concept like behavior. Both are abstractions.

The concept of behavior appears to be somewhat closer to the observations from which it is inferred, but when psychologists speak of behavior they have difficulty in specifying precisely what they mean. Even in the most carefully worked out approaches the behavior that psychologists speak of remains an abstraction. Specific kinds of responses such as bar-pressing or maze-running are simply means to an end. The means are of little interest and no one really cares about a complete and precise description of the *movements* of a rat running in a maze. These movements are of interest only as they permit the testing of hypotheses which are related to principles or postulates which are stated generally so as to encompass *any* kinds of reactions. When the behavioristic psychologist really gets down to business he is interested in predicting (i.e., testing) the relative probability that certain events will occur. These events themselves may be rather generally described so that a prediction might read: Group A will exceed Group B in performance. The performance itself will then be measured by some "indicant" such as reaction time, or number of trials, number of errors, amount of response, and so on. A chain of inferences is then followed from actual measurements of something through several stages or steps of more and more abstract speculations to a final statement of some general principle of law. The laws themselves, however, are desired only to explain the observations of events that were made in the first place. The whole effort is thus a somewhat circular affair. This is the procedure for all science and, while not free from criticism, it is accepted as the only way to work that we know. We start with observations that interest or intrigue us. The sun rises in the east, we note. We then study this event and other events and conditions related to it and finally come up with a series of laws which explain why the sun rises in the east. The sun still rises in the east, but now our curiosity is satisfied.

To some extent the same process is followed by psychologists who are interested in personality. This concept seems to be at a "higher" level of abstraction than some others we have considered because it depends upon some presumed principles of behavior from which it is derived (these principles themselves not being firmly established, perhaps). There are probably two basic principles from which the concept of personality was derived. First is our belief or conviction that individuals are relatively consistent in the face of variations in the gross stimulus situations.

How firmly such a principle can be established is obviously questionable. What do we mean by relatively? How gross can a variation be? Is it really a variation or is there some unidentified common element? The second belief or principle is that the assumed consistency we observe is relatively durable, spanning years, perhaps a lifetime. Again we might be hard put to establish that no real changes in behavior occurred. A superficial resemblance between childhood patterns and those of an adult might be just that, superficial. A timid child might remain a timid adult but the timidity is hardly likely to be the same in degree, content, and methods of adjustment. Assuming consistency and durability, however, any such reliability and permanence must be taken into account in the explanation or prediction of behavior. Further, it must be taken into account before the prediction of a response is made in any S ——→R orientation. It belongs on the S side of the formula because it determines, to some degree, the response. This makes it awkward and difficult to define personality in terms of behavior or habit systems as we have done. Yet the concept of personality is obviously derived from behavior. We are forced to draw another inference: we assume that the behavior occurred *because* of the particular personality characteristic, trait, or feature that we constructed or hypothesized to be present. Personality, then, becomes no different from any other hypothetical construct inferred from behavior and calculated, in turn, to account for the behavior. There remains only the question of whether it is needed or superfluous. Do we have adequate constructs to carry the burden of consistency and durability in the face of alleged stimulus variation?

There might be an adequate case made out for replacing the concept of personality by the concept of "set." We have just made out a case for reducing the construct of personality to the status of a mediational mechanism. In previous chapters we have found the concept of set to be of some value in connection with motivation, problem solving, and such matters as attitudes and prejudice. Perhaps its role can be extended to cover the problem of consistency in the face of stimulus change. We have previously talked of traits and stereotypes in terms of *predispositions* to respond. Such predispositions we have earlier identified as sets. Suppose we find someone who might merit such labels as "paranoid" or "rigid," "suspicious" or, in a different vein, "generous," "kind," "warm," etc. Do we mean anything more by such labels than that the person commonly responds to a variety of situations in some specific way? If we do not mean anything other than this, it becomes necessary only to show that a common set is established by sundry stimuli. If the paranoid is convinced that "people are no damned good," then he will react to *any* representative of the human race negatively, as, in spite of the variability of people, they all have in common a single, identical feature, they are human beings. If the so-called generous person responds to any and all appeals it may be because he identifies and reacts to them with a common, identical mediator, namely, "charity." If his behavior repertoire involves "giving to charity," then he gives to any solicitor who arouses the charity set. Perhaps we need no more than a concept of set to take care of the problem of personality. How effectively this will work depends in turn on how strongly we can establish the general effectiveness of this mediating mechanism.

The concept of set was derived from behavior and has been presented as a general principle that carries a heavy burden of explanation. If such principles are not securely established, inferences from them will be even more insecure. This insecurity leads some psychological theorists to avoid or abandon observations of behavior, based on experiment, in favor of case studies, clinical observations, philosophical or theological (rational) approaches, and even "common sense." Some personality theorists are impatient with the slow progress of behavioral research; they feel they cannot wait for the halting, step-by-step accumulation of grubby results. They want answers now so that they can help people. Such intentions are commendable, of course. Which course will lead to greater success in practical application cannot be stated with certainty. It is not a matter of opinion but of demonstration. Many hard-headed laboratory psychologists disclaim any interest in helping people. Such work is beyond their personal interests, even though they have no objection if others apply their findings should they ever become useful. Some clinicians on the other hand, believe the laboratory will never provide useful facts that can be applied in real situations because these are too complex and include too many variables which have to be taken into account; that only those who are trained in clinical *arts* can be useful in such problem areas. The student may be dismayed by such conflicts of opinion but he should remember that without controversy there will be no research. While the laboratory psychologist continues his search for the principles of behavior, others will continue the search for the original (or basic) nature of man through other channels. They will continue to look for a key to the *personality,* a key that will open every door, because all doors will then really be the same.

CHAPTER 15

Man among Men—Social Interaction

The social environment · The group and the individual · The function of society · Personality and "culture" · Subcultures · The influence of groups on groups · Class, caste, and cult · The individual and the group · Crowds · Psychological groups · Face-to-face groups · The definition of a group · Dynamics of small groups · Cohesiveness · The formation of social groups · Group dynamics · The sociogram · Dominance and submission · Leadership and followership · The influence of individuals on a group · Research on group structures and leadership · Leadership and imitation · The problem of conformity · Institutional behavior · Institutional survival · Reactions to institutions · The J-curve · Experimental studies of conformity · Mass communication media · Action research—group decision processes · The psychology of social behavior

In Chapter 3 we described man's environment as a world of stimuli, a world of lights and sounds, of smells and tastes, and other sensory excitants. We neglected to emphasize then, and continued to treat lightly through subsequent chapters, the fact that many of these stimuli originate not from the sun and wind but from other men. Even when man is alone he carries the world of other men with him. When he reads, he reads what other men have written, when he eats he dines on what other men have provided, and when he listens to music, it is the music of musicians, and not of the spheres. From time to time we have been constrained to introduce this consideration into our discussions. We have talked of parents and teachers, friends and foes, husbands and wives, and even the public at large. It is time now to make amends and treat specifically of the influence of the presence of other individuals in our environments, an influence that far outdistances the importance of lights and sounds. We must talk about society and culture. Up to now we have assumed that everyone appreciated these terms and we have used them rather conversationally.

THE SOCIAL ENVIRONMENT

Man does not live alone. The occasional hermit or recluse is regarded as in some ways abnormal. The usual, the regular thing to do is to live with others, in a family grouping of some sort, to work with others, associate with them in clubs, political parties, singing societies, and participate in community efforts, in short, to live among men.

In infancy and early childhood, at least, man needs others for his own survival. No other animal has such a long period of maternal or parental care and numerous factors have led to an extension of this parental care in various human communities to the point where parents have become "legally" responsible for their children up to ages of eighteen or twenty-one. Some parents, of course, never give up their attempts at controlling their children and their children's children. With the increased educational levels that have also come into being, it sometimes occurs, and will perhaps do so with increasing frequency that parents will be responsible in some communities for housing, feeding, and clothing their children up to ages of thirty and forty, long after they have become parents themselves. While this may shock a modern teenage American it would not be unusual either historically for Americans or in other contemporaneous cultures. Our grandparents *assumed* they would live on the farm and take over when great-grandfather died. The one-family house or apartment is not the only way of life, nor is it necessarily here to stay.

In the course of childhood care, the parents and educational systems take over the task of socializing the child, making him fit to live with, preparing him for his role in the "society" of the future. By their efforts the impact of "culture" is gradually allowed to play its part in the modification of the personality through the development of attitudes, sentiments, skills and beliefs, aspirations, superstitions, and whatever passes for knowledge in the community. A "veneer of civilization" is imposed upon the developing and growing human.

We touched briefly on the role of "society" in the learning process (see Chapter 7) and now must extend that earlier discussion. Because every child has some kind of parental care for some period of time, it is impossible to discover what a human would be like if he grew up alone. From time to time we have been entertained with stories about children being brought up by wolves or, like Tarzan, by apes, but such stories lack any creditable evidence and belong in the realm of science fiction or sentimental romance. So far we have learned nothing of consequence from studies of such "wild" or "feral" children. We discussed this problem briefly in Chapter 3 and the student should reconsider it now.

The problems of group living and group influences are of the greatest importance for humans. Whether humans continue to exist as a species may well be determined by the actions and reactions of one group toward another. In modern society we have learned to think in terms of group actions. We think of France, or Russia, or the United States, in terms of people viewed rather abstractly and collectively. We ask "What will Russia do?" or "How will the South react?" when certain problems arise. We label groups of people as Democrats or Algerians, baseball fans or bus drivers, and react to these labels as if we were dealing with some reality instead of with some class-membership characteristics of individuals, all of whom have other class-membership attachments and loyalties which may also determine their behavior. The Algerian bus driver may be a democratic baseball fan, but it is unlikely that we will ever deal with him as even this much of a totality. Politicians make calculated speeches in various neighborhoods seeking the "Negro" vote, the "small farmer" vote, the "Italian" vote, the "Catholic" vote, etc. We learn, wisely or not, to deal with people as if they were labels. Frequently enough we ignore people as people. We can walk along a busy street amid hordes of Christmas shoppers, rush and fight our way through to counters and come home worn out from our struggles, not with people, but with "the crowds downtown."

The scientific effort to understand the activities and behavior of groups has been rather haphazardly divided up among anthropologists, sociologists, social psychologists, and psychologists whose primary concerns are with the individual. No clean-cut lines of separation mark off the efforts of these social scientists. They publish in each other's journals and quote each other's findings and in their courses they frequently overlap in their discussions so that a student taking sociology, anthropology, and psychology, might find himself listening to the same lecture on three different occasions as each of his professors discusses such things as postnatal care, family influences, attitudes, crowd phenomena, instinct, and a host of other topics. We cannot hope to examine all of the observations relevant to group phenomena in this chapter and must restrict ourselves to a limited sample. Because this is a general treatment of psychological principles we shall confine ourselves to problems where principles already examined appear to apply and where emphasis has always been upon the more psychological aspects of social life. We will, in short, limit the discussion to the questions of how the group influences the individual and how the individual influences the group. Questions that go beyond these broad limits will have to be examined by the student in other courses. We cannot hope to do justice to even these questions within the confines of a chapter but will rely on previous discussions to have made some contribution to an appreciation of the problems. It should be pointed out that in previous chapters we have discussed such matters as attitudes, prejudice, propaganda, the role of culture, social selves, and social motives. These topics are commonly discussed in Social Psychology courses because of the role of group interactions and pressures on the individual in connection with these problems.

THE GROUP AND THE INDIVIDUAL

In the examination of group factors in behavior, some psychologists state the problem in such a fashion that students become confused. It may be said, for example, that the problem of social psychology is that created when "protoplasm meets society." The statement is meant to endorse the notion that man is a biological organism who somehow is placed in a situation where something nonbiological or nonphysical is going to work on him. Society is contraposed to protoplasm as if it consisted of something other than more protoplasm. For us to insist that society consists merely of numerous individual globs of protoplasm might be just as absurd as to overlook the fact that society does consist of people and only people. We must recognize, however, that when we speak of people, we are no longer dealing with "original human nature" but with the activities of humans who have gone through a socializing educational process which has altered their behavior patterns to a most unbiological degree. No self-respecting animal would tolerate for one moment the latest creation from Paris or watch a quiz-show or "western" on television. But for all the modification of human beings into people, they still have to exert their effects through the ordinary physical media that separate them into the individuals. Stimuli emanate from people in the same fashion as from other objects, and we react to them in terms of visual, auditory, and other stimulus qualities and intensities. The fact that stimuli emanating from "people" have "meanings" does not differentiate people from other objects which stimulate us. They have meanings, too, and the nature of such "meanings" we have already considered.

The function of society

Human beings become people only when they live together, when, in short, they live in groups. Because, as we have emphasized above, there is no possibility of survival for human infants unless they are members of a group which supports them through infancy and childhood, group living is a necessity for humans, at least in the early years of a child. When a child is old enough to survive by himself, there is frequently another infant on hand. Commonly enough the first is enlisted in the care of the succeeding children. The biologically imposed group living involves some kind of arrangements and distribution of functions of parents and children as well as of other adults who happen to be living in, or who are likely to visit, the neighborhood. Presumably such arrangements in the early centuries of man's existence were arrived at by chance reinforcements with adequate and efficient arrangements surviving and forming a pattern for succeeding generations, while less adequate arrangements left no survivors. Depending upon climate and the nature and amount of the food supply, various arrangements of group living would prove successful or adequate so that no specific pattern of "society" deserves to be thought of as "natural" or better than another. Residents in any particular part of the earth might well regard themselves as living in the best of all possible worlds and resent the appearance of anthropologists who come to examine their "strange ways" of living. American students are sometimes taken aback when anthropologists or foreign travelers report on the American culture, thinking that only primitive tribes are appropriate objects of study, their own ways being, of course, the natural standard (Kluckhohn, 1958).

For whatever initial reasons, a variety of arrangements for living have been developed throughout the world and throughout history. It is not our intention to trace the development of "culture." That is a job for anthropologists. We wish only to suggest the apparent relationship between the biological requirements of infants and the consequent requirement upon parents to make some arrangements for their care. All such arrangements, of necessity, start with the problem of child survival. They may eventuate in simple family groupings in farm, desert, or jungle where simple manual skills are the only requirements for survival, or they may result in modern metropolitan communities where manual skills give way to automation and executive brains, with individuals depending for survival on specialized skills attained only after long educational preparation. The role of the sexes in the arrangements for living varies also with time and place. In some societies women are dominant and men are relegated to positions and duties of a "lower" level. In other societies men are dominant and women occupy an "inferior" status. In still other societies women compete with men on equal terms. (It should be appreciated by the student that beyond the obvious sex difference and function, men differ from women only in strength and height, and even here, it is only in terms of averages.)

What we have referred to above as "arrangements for living" is what amounts to what some students call "culture." [1] It should be clear that such arrangements have no independent existence of their own and no power or force in themselves. They are the rules of the game as practiced by the individuals of a group who learn these rules from infancy on through a slow and painful history, painful inasmuch as the infant, as Freud pointed out, knows no rules and respects those set up by others even less. Yet, he must learn to obey the rules. The rules are honored by individuals with varying degrees of respect, compliance, and reverence. For some, as for Inspector Javert in *Les Misérables,* the rules become the only worthwhile *realities,* for others rules are meant only to be broken, when this can be done safely. The rules become habit systems of individuals and if enough individuals live by some mutually appreciated rules, we have a "society." If only a small number of individuals can agree we have a gang, a club, perhaps a family. A "society" is a group of individuals who have a "culture."

It is important to recognize that society consists of individuals, and individuals only. If a number of individuals come together and display the same habit patterns with respect to some stimulus situation, it is convenient to talk about them in some collective terms as a group, a crowd, a tribe, a nation, even an empire, but any one of such collective terms is justified only when we have reference to a given habit system. Once we start thinking about society as a "thing" with an independent existence we lose contact with reality and become subject to speculations which, while they may appear attractive to many people (and become rules *for them*), are essentially unrealistic. Thus, someone like Karl Marx can picture some inevitable course of historical determinism leading inexorably to some foreordained end. Hitler can promise his followers 1,000 years of Nazi glory, the Stars and Stripes will wave forever, and Britons never, never shall be slaves.

Whenever any substantial numbers of individuals are thrown or come together, additional arrangements must develop or be created to handle the problems that the sheer numbers alone generate. Even when the individuals do no more than sit together, as at a theater, someone must see to it that there are enough seats, that individuals are guided to their seats, and that some general degree of order must prevail or some of the individuals will begin to create a disturbance which will interfere with the pleasures of other individuals. At the dinner table people acquire habits of sitting in certain places and resist any effort to have them change their seats when guests or other conditions involve some adjustment. Even such small matters as who is served first, where the salt

[1] Our discussion of "arrangements for living" corresponds to the definition of culture offered by Kluckhohn (1958).

is placed, and from which side one is served become a matter of habit (and if enough people learn the habit, a custom).

While the infant, in a sense, creates society, he is not alone in his influence on development of patterns of living. Other facts of life become important as the infant matures. The reproduction of the species involves the association of individuals and the competition within and among the sexes entails some new adjustments. In the ordinary course of living individuals come to acquire property of one kind or another, even if it is only a spear or sharp stone for skinning animals. Such property becomes important when the final biological fact of death is faced. Arrangements have to be made for the inheritance or disposition of the property as well as of the dead, and again there is the possibility for varying social patterns to emerge and grow into habits, to be taught to the children and to become "traditions," or, if the circumstances are too important to be left to tradition, the arrangements become "laws."

In general then, and the student will have to pursue the subject further in studying sociology and anthropology, what we call society amounts to a mutual adjustment of individuals in some more or less particular fashion for many different situations. This "collection" of patterns of adjustment, in effect, controls the ways of living and the habits that will be learned through which an individual will interact with his fellows. The collection of patterns of adjustment touches almost every aspect of life whether we are dealing with primitive savages or the most "highly" developed civilization. It will encompass rules for family structure, size, and roles to be played by fathers, mothers, and siblings. It will dictate political, economic, and religious practices. It will grade the members of the group in socioeconomic classes or castes. It will dictate the behavior patterns of various age groups from toddlers to "senior citizens." It will set limits for sexual practices. It will control the very patterns of thinking through its control of the language and educational systems. It will prescribe goals for individuals and the appropriate means for their achievement. It will prescribe the values (folkways, mores, taboos) along with "sanctions" [2] for their violation. And all of these things it will do through its "culture." If we remember that by society we mean only the habits practiced by individuals in their interactions with other individuals and that we do not intend any independent existence or thingness by this term we can turn our attention now to the business of "culture." Our interest, as psychologists, is inevitably with the impact of culture on the individual and his behavior. We have been forced to refer to it frequently in the past; it is time that we examined it more carefully.

[2] "Sanctions" are penalties for violation of social standards (or rewards for their support).

Personality and "culture"

Some psychologists attempt to understand the "fundamental nature of man" and hope that their principles will apply universally. They are concerned with a universal man, man in the abstract, man in the Australian bush and in the Paris salon, in the English counting house, and in the eighteenth-century drawing room as well as in the Viennese psychoanalyst's consulting room. The fundamental assumption that is made is that man is everywhere alike, always has been, and always will be. Individual differences are unimportant and sometimes annoying trivia. Freud (1938) was so confident of his views that with no contacts of any kind with primitive groups, he wrote a treatise on anthropology, *Totem and Taboo,* in which he described the principles of organization of tribal life of savages. With apparent serenity Freud (1947) undertook to explain the smile of Mona Lisa and to diagnose the problems of Leonardo da Vinci on the basis of the painting the master left behind and a fragmentary report of a dream. Ernest Jones (1947) similarly psychoanalyzed Hamlet, or perhaps, more correctly, Shakespeare. When a psychology undertakes to analyze both living and dead, real or imaginary people, primitive and civilized, we must perceive it as aiming at universals, as in effect, founded on a *biological* orientation and as having only cursory interest in the effects of environment or "culture."

In the twentieth century we have witnessed the growth of a sister science of anthropology which has as its domain the analysis and comparison of cultures that have existed in the past and that exist in the present all over the globe. The cultural anthropologist [3] is interested in the patterns of tribal and group living in customs, rituals, ceremonies of primitive people, how they make their livings, how they entertain themselves, their religions, language, and everything about them. But more than anything else, the anthropologist is interested in the interpersonal relations, in family organization, in child-rearing practices, in roles played by men and women, in adolescents' relationships with parents and peers, in marriage and sex practices, in conflicts, in short with all the problems that come up when we talk about psychology and, particularly, personality. While anthropology claims to be a young science and was at first strongly dominated by armchair anthropologists who wrote books on the basis of the most casual contacts with different cultures (the way travelers do today after a six-week trip to China or the Soviet Union),

[3] Cultural anthropologists are to be distinguished from "physical" anthropologists who are more concerned with physiological and physical characteristics of ancient and modern races. The student should consult the works of Margaret Mead, Ruth Benedict, and Bronislaw Malinowski to get an appreciation of cultural anthropology.

there has now been achieved a great accumulation of information about how people live all over the earth, and the outstanding single conclusion that emerges from this accumulation of data is that there are no safe generalizations that can be made about "man." What to us looks normal, ordinary, and "natural" proves abnormal, unusual, and unnatural to other peoples. The Japanese, for example, frown on kissing and consider it somewhat abnormal, if not a perversion. Some groups are dominated by males, some by females, in some groups fathers are unknown to their children while uncles are revered, in other groups fathers take to their beds while their wives are delivering children. Some groups are dominated by "acquisitive" patterns of behavior, others are communal in regards to property, some groups are hospitable to strangers, others eat them. The catalogue of differences is so exhaustive that anything we say about behavior should be preceded by the caution "In the culture of . . . ." In this text we have often felt the constraint to preface comments with "In our culture . . ." to caution the student that the remarks that followed were of less than universal import.

There is a tendency among anthropologists, in their reports, to be just as one-sided as the more biologically oriented. Almost any difference that is discovered to prevail as between groups is attributed to "culture," meaning a historical accumulation of traditions, mores, and more or less fixed patterns of human relations. In other words, the anthropologists frequently outdo the psychologists in emphasis on environmental factors, but by environment they mean pretty much what they identify as culture. The sheer physical environment is to a considerable extent, ignored by anthropologists except as the rigors of climate (or its felicity) dictate the means of earning a living, the construction of habitations, the amount of clothing, and the kind of food supply. The anthropologist's concern with primitive groups frequently takes him to relatively remote and isolated areas of the world, deep in a desert, small islands, coastal areas shielded by mountains, the frozen north, or the protected jungle. Here he finds people living in ways we might call strange, and *assuming* that man is everywhere biologically the same, he concludes that these differences are due to "culture." Biological sameness may be carried too far, however, and there are differences in characteristic size (pygmies), skin coloration (which may have biologically adaptive values and may be accompanied by other kinds of adaptive differences), and possibly in temperament. Such groups may have lived for generations in isolation from other groups and while developing their own culture they might also have inbred a great many kinds of traits which are serviceable for survival in that environment and not in others. In other words, Eskimos may be more different from non-Eskimos than in merely wearing more furs. Dwellers high in the Andes have different lung capacities than dwellers in New York City and newspapermen following political figures on tours in Bolivia and Peru must carry oxygen in order to survive, while the natives scurry about their business.

There is no a priori reason to preclude us from speculating that temperamental differences can be associated with certain body structures, and even in the absence of obviously unique internal organs, for temperamental differences to be inheritable. This appears to be true with other mammals, like dogs (Mahut, 1958) and horses, and may well be true of men. If it takes a certain kind of temperament to survive in a given part of the earth, the people with such temperament will have children better prepared to cope with the situation. Even if survival has no great current role, it may have had at one time, and isolation of a population by vast ocean stretches, deserts, or mountains will lead to inbreeding which will perpetuate traits that may no longer be adaptationally functional. The Scottish terrier no longer kills foxes even though that was its function some decades ago. The temperamental nature of the modern Scottie, however, has not been altered in all probability by generations of household pet service.

Even in modern Western civilization we find ourselves thinking in stereotypes about the Italians and French as people who "cannot talk with their hands tied behind their backs" because of the extensive use of gestures. Perhaps there is more folklore and fiction to such thinking than real observation but, should it be true, or have been true at some earlier time, it might represent a *national* kind of difference. When we speak of Russians as moody and introspective, we may be saying little more than generalizing from a few characters created by Dostoevski or Gogol. On the other hand there may be some more or less common characteristics shared by Slavic populations that vary from Mediterranean populations. The very sense of humor of the British in contrast to that of Americans is a topic frequently cited in considerations of Anglo-American relations. It may prove to be an overhasty generalization, a purely cultural product, or it may reflect something about the temperament of groups of people isolated from other groups. We must be very careful to separate fact from fiction, from popular stereotypes created by newspapers. Not all the Irish in New York are policemen, nor do all Italians drink wine and eat spaghetti. Some Italian restaurants in Italy do not serve spaghetti in any form and consider it foreign to their part of Italy. Northern Italians may differ from Southern Italians in more than geography and culture, however. It will be a long time before the twisted lines of genetics are unraveled to the point where we can say what results from culture and what is biologically true of all men or some men.

It should also be noted that in various parts of the world there are wide differences in the nature of the food that is consumed. Some live almost exclusively on grains, others on fish and seafood, others primarily off meat. Some groups also indulge almost as a matter of course in the use of drugs such as quinine, cocaine, and opium, to say nothing of alcoholic drinks, which appear to be almost universal in use. We still do not know much about the effects of diet on structure, health and resistance to disease, or temperament. Future research may result in our finding that some allegedly cultural phenomena are more chemical than cultural and will call for modifications of our views. Even within a heterogeneous culture like the United States, we find great differences in racial and national representations in different kinds of hospitals. Some groups appear to have few alcoholics, others appear to have a disproportion. The varieties of mental disease in different national and racial groups (Opler, 1957) may also prove informative about the relative roles of culture and biological equipment. It is still far too early to generalize with the freedom that some speculative theorists in both psychological and anthropological camps might like.

We should take note of the fact that anthropologists, too, disagree among themselves. Some even argue that there are no anthropological theories that have not been borrowed from psychology, sociology, or history (Morganbesser, 1958). It can be argued that when anthropologists speak of "culture" they are only referring to acquired dispositions of individuals, and, if this is so, the principles of learning (when we discover them) and the laws of physiology should be sufficient to account for the differences in the ways of life of different communities. In short, we need not expect to find our explanations for personality in "patterns of culture" but rather the reverse might be the more likely result. Lest the student at this point suspect the anthropologist of naïvete or of being blinded by his own interests, it should be pointed out that anthropologists are well aware of the fact that their "culture" is only a "convenient abstraction" like so many other concepts we have encountered heretofore. They recognize the difficulties that prevail in the analysis of a "society" and are just as cautious as any other scientists about hasty generalizations.

With this introductory preface to the problem of society and/or culture as perhaps the most significant aspects of man's environment, we can begin to look at the individual in the group.

Subcultures

THE INFLUENCE OF GROUPS ON GROUPS

Before we begin to consider the impact of groups on individuals we should take at least passing note of the fact that in many parts of the world, smaller groups take up residence (or are forced to do so) as relatively separated or segregated parts of a larger society. These groups within groups share some of the rules of the larger society but may have special arrangements of their own. Frequently they live within more or less marked-off areas or "ghettos" with symbolic if not actual walls (Hersey, 1950) separating the inhabitants from the rest of the population of the area. The basis for such segregation might be color, national origin, or religion, or simply economic status as with the residents on the "wrong side of the tracks." Within such groupings there may be further subdivisions or sub-subcultures with some groups occupying a higher social or economic status than the rest. In a mobile society, that is, one where the rules permit some freedom for everyone to become educated and obtain employment at any level at which an individual qualifies, and where membership in a subculture does not hamper an individual because of language barriers or other restrictions presented by members of a dominant group, such subcultures may gradually wither away as the members become "assimilated." When the barriers to assimilation are too restrictive and when members of the subculture cannot "pass" without recognition into the dominant culture, the ghetto life is maintained, sometimes for centuries. Frequently, members of a subculture are required to follow two sets of rules, that of the dominant culture as well as that of the more immediate subculture. When this is the case, conflicts may be generated in some individuals who cannot serve two masters or maintain two or more loyalties. Individuals with second-class citizen status find it difficult to support the arrangements of first-class citizens and where the latter prove too restrictive, intercultural conflicts break out. Such conflicts can become major upheavals and develop into wars, civil or otherwise, where the subculture includes a majority of the population as in colonial territories where the dominant culture is actually foreign to the area. In countries where democratic ideals are presumed to reign, members of subcultures might have even greater personal difficulties than do individuals living where their "rights" are clearly described by statute or custom.

CLASS, CASTE, AND CULT

Besides the minority groups described above as subcultures, people are divided or divide themselves into many other kinds of special organizations with their own rules or arrangements for living. In some "cultures," people are divided into "classes" along economic or occupational lines. The distinctions are not always clear as they become confused with other qualifications. Terms like "upper," "middle," and "lower" classes do not communicate any exact intelligence and they are frequently amended with additional modifiers like "upper-upper," "lower-middle," etc. The economic measure is not always based on income as such but upon the level of occupation; thus the "working class" might be distinguished from the "professional class." Some members of the working class wear overalls and others wear white collars. To some individuals such a distinction is more meaningful than an economic one and financial sacrifices might be made by some workers to wear white collars at lower wages. Some workers belong to unions and follow union thinking; others are "independent" and follow other rules. Class distinctions are "real" enough for many individuals who pride themselves on belonging to one group or another. Various additional values may become associated with class feelings, e.g., intermarriage might not be expected. Many people do not have very clear concepts of class structure and identify themselves as being in a middle class when economists or sociologists would classify them as lower-class members on the basis of whether they owned television sets, bathtubs, cars, and various appliances. In the United States more people have television sets than bathtubs and many lower-income individuals have expensive automobiles. Such possessions make scaling of people according to classes difficult if not impossible.

In some cultures occupational status becomes rather rigidly stratified. Sometimes religious and legal sanctions develop around such occupational differences and support the original divisions. Property rights and social privileges might also be carefully circumscribed for separate groups. In some "culture areas" the people who are "in trade" or "laborers" are expected to act like tradesmen and laborers and not like "gentry" or "their betters." When certain behavior patterns are followed rigidly and passed on from father to son, or other restrictive procedure, we have the development of a *caste system* with each caste clearly discriminated from others by one sign or another. At the simplest level, a caste system might involve a color line and people with one skin color might be prevented from voting or other kinds of practices by people of another skin color. American Indians, even if they are oil millionaires, must observe certain rules imposed upon them by a non-Indian majority. Indian Indians are the usual example of a rigid caste system with certain individuals demarked as "untouchables" while others are equally untouchable in the sense of being too lofty in the social hierarchy.

In addition to various rather broad social groupings such as class and caste, there may be such classifications as "intellectuals," the "proletariat," and dozens of other distinctions drawn for one purpose or another. We might divide people into highbrows, middlebrows, and lowbrows; upper lowbrows, and so on, on the basis of language, kinds of music enjoyed, movies attended, etc. Advertisers, merchants, and entertainers might think of their "public," the buying public, "shoppers," "browsers," and any number of other distinctions.

Religious groups often break down into smaller and smaller "sects" or "cults" with certain objections to views held by larger bodies who might be termed "orthodox," while the newer groups are "reformed" or "modern." Various kinds of associations or organizations of a religious or professional nature also set up their own rules just as do fraternities and sports clubs. An "in group" automatically involves an "out group." Outsiders are kept out while insiders follow certain codes with varying degrees of privacy, secrecy, and regularity.

The important point to keep before us is that while only individuals can belong to groups, the group rules of one organization might be in conflict with those of another and lead to difficulties for all of the individuals in one group, or for some of the individuals who find themselves trying to follow too many sets of rules, because they are trained, to some extent to function with conflicting sets of habits. Even being a "student" sometimes interferes with being a member of a family where some family "need" or ritual calls for the individual's presence in two different places at the same time.

THE INDIVIDUAL AND THE GROUP

Crowds

It is time now to turn to considering such group influences on individual behavior. We have recognized that "society" is an abstraction, a convenient shorthand to save us the trouble of describing every individual's interactions and interrelations with every other individual. Once we lose sight of the individuals involved, however, we might get caught in a trap which confused early thinkers on the subject who were fascinated by the differences in behavior observed when an individual was alone and when he was in a group. These early writers went so far as to endow a group with a mind, and we had such abstractions to deal with as the "group mind" or "the mob spirit," and so on. The obvious absurdity of such constructs did not occur to early observers of lynching mobs and street rioters who saw the group as somehow becoming more than the individuals involved because, obviously, the individuals taken alone were such "nice" people. It is still difficult for many observers to recognize that the "niceness" of people is a relatively thin veneer which is adequate for most superficial social relationships but which is easily and readily shed under frustrating circumstances. The atrocities perpetrated by the Nazis during World War II showed what a "hard working, industrial, scientific" population could do. The Nazi atrocities were perhaps unmatched for scientific refinement, but other groups and nations from the beginnings of "civilization" have matched them in fervor and cruelty. In future wars as well as in current domestic strife, we can expect more of the same. Frustration tolerance, as we pointed out in an earlier chapter, is not one of man's more highly developed attributes.

The fact that a man behaves differently as a member of a mob from his behavior as an isolated individual is no more surprising than the fact that he behaves differently with his boss, his mother, his minister, his lawyer, his employees, his poker partners, his wife, and his mistress or such females as he might wish to master. The crowd offers security and anonymity, two powerful factors that may be missing in individual relationships. The fact that crowds generate action not likely to occur when only an individual is concerned may mean only that a crowd gathers only when action is desired by a number of individuals, none of whom is capable of the effort or willing to take the responsibility alone. No one creates crowds or mobs out of nothing. The basic attitudes involved in the group activity must be available for stimulation. No "spell-binder" is able to "whip the people into a frenzy" if they are not already prepared to be whipped. A Communist can scream his head off on a street corner and attract only a handful of curious loungers when the population prospers. Under other circumstances he might be more successful.

In modern psychology we no longer are concerned with group minds; they are relics of a period when psychology was created in arm chairs. One problem that is still receiving much attention, that of morale or *esprit de corps,* is somewhat confused by out-moded, "group-mind" concepts. In investigating such problems today social psychologists try to contrive situations where group influences on individuals can be observed objectively, where interactions among individuals (so-called "group dynamics") can be recorded and analyzed, and put to further test. The emphasis in social psychology is on experiment, on prediction and evaluation of hypotheses, just as in any other branch of psychology. Admittedly the task is difficult. The variables are more numerous and frequently difficult to identify; the influences of separate cultural backgrounds create additional problems when groups are composed of a heterogeneous assortment of people with different national backgrounds, different religions, and different home influences. Part of the effort is devoted to the analysis of just such influences. In other researches, it is hoped that something akin to pure "social" factors is operating and can be observed.

Psychological groups

In all our previous discussions we have emphasized and elaborated the obvious fact that individuals do not live alone. They come together as members of families, teams, clubs, gangs, organizations, parties, classes, and all manner of groups, large and small, voluntary or involuntary. Commonly enough, the group membership is merely nominal or imposed upon the individual by the culture or economic machinery and the membership is of only casual significance or even undesirable to the individual who may regard himself as in the group but not of it. Even when the membership in a group is nominal or undesired, the fact of membership can still affect the behavior, status, and circumstances of the individual. The "status seeker" (Packard, 1959) is frequently a "joiner" and carries a wallet full of membership cards. Many individuals belong to more organizations than they could possibly visit on meeting nights. Some group life is imposed on individuals against their strongest wishes, as in a military draft. In other cases, individuals join because of more subtle social pressures. Once membership is established, group pressures can forcefully dictate how a man's time will be spent.

The organization of individuals into any pattern (society) almost inevitably (for economy and efficiency) forces individuals to spend part of their time with other people who, for the time being, will all be labeled as members of a group. Thus a child in school is a member of the fourth grade or of the senior class. Later he is a member of the Teamsters Union or the American Medical Association. As a member of such organizations, the individual normally submits to or even welcomes certain rules or practices and adjusts his behavior to that of other members even when not in their presence. Physicians or television repairmen as a group may decide what the charge should be for "house calls" and every member of the organization then charges the same fee, or at least, roughly so. For the most part, because an individual belongs to so many groups, his adjustments are rather transient and he may be many things to many people as the Sunday church-goer who embezzles on Monday, patriotically buys government bonds on Tuesday, and spends the rest of the week doing the right thing in the right place.

Face-to-face groups

So far we have been concerned with groups the individual can scarcely avoid, as a functioning member of society. His membership in many of these groups is not necessarily active, intimate, or personal, especially in relation to large organizations like the Republican Party. Large organizations, however, are normally subdivided into regional and local segments with occasionally the local group at odds with the larger or national group. It is with the local group that the individual actually functions. Even local groups tend to be too large for effective social interaction so that behavior that is subject to group influences is rather narrowly confined to smaller subdivisions or "face-to-face" groups. It is with such small groups that we look for genuine "social" or group influences.

THE DEFINITION OF A GROUP

Up to this point we have been talking about collections of people, organizations, associations, aggregates, and the like. While all of these have effects on individuals these effects can be exerted at a distance, by mail, or various media of communication (radio, television, newspapers, magazines, etc.) even when the individual is quite alone. Social influences can extend to isolated mountain cabins. A different class of influences operates when individuals are actually together, aware of one another's presence, and in position to observe and respond to others and be observed in turn. For such conditions to prevail the number of individuals involved must be relatively small, with a minimum of two, and a maximum determined by the number that can take effective cognizance of each other's presence and role. Such relatively small collections of individuals are what the social psychologist is referring to when he speaks of a group. While there are many attempts to define such groups in psychological terms, there is also much disagreement or at least difference in emphasis on various component features of a presumed group. After considering various definitions, Gibb (1954) offers his own definition which stresses the purposes of the individuals in being members. His definition is representative of social psychologists' reflections on this problem: "A group is characterized by the interaction of its members, in such a way that each unit is changed by its group membership and each would be likely to undergo a change as a result of changes in the group. In this case there is dependence of each member upon the entire group, and the relation between any two members is a function of the relation between other members." This statement serves to describe a more or less socially *structured* aggregate of people and Gibb finds it inadequate unless the motivation of the members is included. He adds such motivational features in considering the functional aspects of a group: "The term functional group refers to two or more organisms interacting, in pursuit of a common goal, in such a way that the existence of many is utilized for the satisfaction of some of the needs of each."

Dynamics of small groups

The emphasis on interactions among individuals is widespread among social psychologists, yet such interactions are among the most difficult aspects of behavior to study. Their nature depends so much on the kind of group, its reason for existence, its goals, and various formal arrangements, e.g., rules of order, customs or traditions, etc. Not all groups take too kindly to the presence of a psychological observer and when psychologists create their own experimental groups, new kinds of problems may be introduced, especially in the formative period, a time when the psychologist might be most interested in making his observations while the group is just getting over its reactions to the artificial aspects of its creation.

When a group is brought under observation, it is obvious that many kinds of interactional factors might be studied, but there is no broad agreement on what dimensions, factors, or principles are operative or important in all groups or even groups in general. So much depends upon the nature of the group, its function, history, and prospective duration. Some factors, however, appear to be important for many kinds of groups, and almost inevitable. During and after World War II, social psychologists began a serious study of the interindividual reactions of members of small groups. Among the many kinds of dimensions or functions that came under scrutiny were those of "cohesiveness," leadership, dominance and submission, and decision making, along with many other socially generated variables. We shall treat some of these briefly. For more extended consideration the student will have to consult modern texts in social psychology although a general overview of many of these subjects can be gained by consulting appropriate chapters in Lindzey's (1954) *Handbook of Social Psychology.*

Cohesiveness

The concept of cohesiveness began to concern social psychologists as a consequence of their wartime studies of morale. This is a difficult construct to work with although like many other concepts we all have a common-sense understanding of it. By cohesiveness we usually refer to the "togetherness" of a group. Do the members stick together? Do they share a loyalty toward each other and the group as a whole? Are they willing to make sacrifices for the group? Tests of cohesiveness (see Goldman, 1953) are difficult to develop because of the diversity of groups. Some groups have no occasions for sacrifice or exertion; some are only temporary and offer no real opportunity for the members to become acquainted as, for example, an appointed committee made up of representatives of other groups to whom they are responsible or which they represent. Some groups, like Great Books clubs, might consist of members who have only one special interest in common, and the cohesiveness might be strictly limited to the common interest. If a particular group of people gathers regularly for a period of years the members may develop an "in-group" attitude and regard "outsiders" as undesirables. They may try to keep the group intact, each for his private purposes, perhaps.

In general, cohesiveness is alleged to be greater when the groups are composed of people well acquainted with each other, when the group has high status, when the rewards shared by a group are earned co-operatively, and where democratic attitudes prevail (Festinger, *et al.,* 1950). Where opposite relationships are noted, cohesiveness decreases. Social psychologists are as much interested in factors or forces that tend to disrupt groups as those which keep the members together. Both kinds of factors must be assessed in evaluating the cohesiveness of a group.

THE FORMATION OF SOCIAL GROUPS

Group dynamics

The problem of how groups are formed and organized has received much attention but little experimental study. It is difficult to control a situation where strangers are brought together and observed while interactions among individuals develop to the point where a group is organized and functions as such. Unless the experimenter is a member of the group he cannot observe effectively without being hidden, perhaps behind a one-way screen (such screens obviously limit the size of the population to the number that can be observed in a relatively small room). Taking notes while observing the group is awkward at best and sets up an artificial atmosphere. Recording conversations introduces other artificialities like microphones, tape recorders, etc. Still such attempts have been made in pioneering attempts at watching group formation and interactions among individuals. A count can be taken of the number of "contacts" (how often one individual addresses another or reacts to someone), the number of remarks made per individual, the relative order of speaking, who makes suggestions and how many of them, who assumes leadership or has leadership thrust upon him, and why. Thus far, the studies that have been performed have been primarily exploratory with no strong basic principles emerging. Much of the data requires some evaluative treatment and this is difficult to objectify. One important difficulty is starting with complete strangers in a group. This is not the way in which most groups are formed. Another difficulty is created by the knowledge on the part of the subjects that they will be together only briefly if they do not care to continue the relationship beyond the experimental period. For the short time involved there may be factors operating that will not operate in prospective long-term associations.

One elementary principle seems to emerge from studies where groups of individuals are given problems to solve. So long as the problems are easy, members adopt a competitive attitude and stick to their own work. When the problems are impossible or difficult to solve individuals leave their own efforts and seek help; the harder the problem, the more help is sought from others. In this fashion interactions commence and it could be argued that groups arise when problems are met that individuals cannot solve by themselves. In passing we might note that many groups did start in this fashion, when a number of individuals had a common problem, and developed such an involved machinery for their purposes that the groups exist long after their problems have been solved or have disappeared. The group continues to operate without a cause, perhaps simply from inertia, and from a dread of giving up the elaborate apparatus that has been accumulated, perhaps through years of effort. People find themselves meeting week after week with nothing to do and in desperation initiate new projects far removed from their original causes. College fraternities, for example, may have originated for some specific mutual needs of individual students, such as eating inexpensively. The fraternity, as a group, finds it can do more as a group than simply eat together. The members get involved with buying a "house" on a long-term contract and then find that the house dictates the necessity for a fraternity. When the student population changes (as it has) in terms of age and the increasing number of married students, the fraternity finds itself struggling to survive, burdened by debt, and the members eating expensively.

The sociogram

In any group individuals are unable to react equally and in the same manner with all the members of the group. Even where the members all like each other, some individuals will be more attractive to some than to others and invite more attention, respect, approval, etc. Hierarchies of power, importance, or popularity develop because of individual characteristics of the membership and this could not be prevented even with a concerted effort if it were deemed desirable. Various attempts have been made to study the internal organization of groups and one promising technique, the sociogram method, has been quite popular (Moreno, 1934). It is easy to use with groups where the membership is small enough so that everyone knows everyone else as in a Boy Scout Patrol, for example. The technique has been used with large populations, too, but as the group grows larger the limitations become more severe. In essence the procedure involves a secret vote. Each member of the group is asked to list in order of preference two, three, or more members of the group whom he likes most, or whom he would support in an election, or with whom he would like to serve on committees, etc. He is also asked to list those he would not like to work with, or whom he would like to see leave the group, etc. When the voters are assured of complete secrecy and report honestly, the structure of group preferences and antagonisms is revealed by plotting the likes and dislikes of each individual (identified as a number) on a master chart. Arrows can be drawn from one person to another showing a "like," a different colored arrow can show a "dislike," double-headed arrows show mutual likes or dislikes, and so on. If a group is new and loosely organized, the chart will show very little concentration. One person may like another, who likes still another, and so on. After a group has existed long enough for mutual admiration and antagonism to develop, a plot may show heavy concentrations of arrows pointing to one or two popular or dynamic individuals. "Sore spots" can be identified by a barrage of arrows of the negative type and individual difficulties can be discovered when it turns out that some person likes someone who dislikes him. It may be discovered from the diagram, for example, that one person, a leader, say, dislikes some individual who is also rather popular in his own right (a competitor?). This second individual may dislike someone else who dislikes a fourth person, and so on down a long line of dislikes, winding up with some person who is liked by no one and disliked perhaps by only one other.

During World War II, some psychologists (Jenkins, 1948) studied the interpersonal relations prevailing among Naval Air Force squadrons and were able to discover situations that were responsible for some inefficiency and low morale. By reorganizing air combat teams so that they consisted of mutually agreeable pilots, they were able to restore morale in a situation where it was not considered "cricket" to complain about one's fellows. Whole communities have been planned by sociometric techniques in areas where government projects involved moving the residents of villages that stood in the way of dam projects. It should be expected that the sociometric plot that is revealed by the like-dislike procedure will change from time to time and cannot be considered final, but the procedure does appear to have some practical applicability, although it lacks theoretical development. More intensive study of interrelationships as functions of time, interest areas, age, and other factors may eventually lead to some reliable information about how groups are formed.

Dominance and submission

Social psychologists have long been interested in dominance-submission relationships expressed in the behavior of individuals. If we think of dominance or submission as personality traits, we recognize that they are socially conditioned traits, that is, they have no meaning except in terms of social interactions. Some one must be around to be dominated by somebody else. A dominance-submission relationship is commonly observed with pairs (husband and wife, boy and girl, "my best friend") but such a relationship can extend within a group in varying patterns. One person can dominate one or many others or he may dominate some but be submissive to others within the group. Various degrees and kinds of relationship can exist among members of a group. An interesting dominance-submission relationship has been reported by observers of farm animals who describe "pecking orders" among fowl and a similar pattern of aggressiveness among cattle, and monkeys (Maslow, 1936). The dominance relationship in groups is investigated by observing who speaks first, or last, who takes orders from whom, whose suggestions are put into action, who associates with whom, even the positions at a table or on a reviewing stand.

Some observers (Krech and Crutchfield, 1948) argue that there may be some primitive or insistent needs for dominance and that we all attempt to attain some degree of such status. It is commonly argued that those individuals who become leaders or who strive for leadership have a strong dominance need but there is at present no clear evidence that this is so (Gibb, 1954). We have already considered the assumptions that have to be examined in connection with the nature of traits and might safely leave the discussion of dominance and submission at this time, taking pains to point out that it might be a potential dimension for the analysis of group structure.

Leadership and followership

The influence of individuals on a group

When groups are formed, by whatever means, even when individuals are arbitrarily assigned to group formations for someone's convenience as in a prisoner of war camp, it is inevitable that some individual will come to represent the group as spokesman or leader. Sometimes leaders are simply appointed by higher authority without regard to qualifications, e.g., the first name on a list, or the first one through a gate, or when left to the group, a leader may be chosen by drawing straws, simply because a group must have a leader for efficient functioning. For some functions it is desirable that the leader be an effective one and the characteristics of leadership have often been of concern to administrators in business, military organizations, educational and recreational units, political groups, in fact, in all walks of life. Historians have spent considerable time debating the question of what makes for great leadership. Some, like Winston Churchill, endorse the "great man" theory which assumes that in the course of time some men, endowed by nature with superior characteristics, will inevitably rise to leadership no matter what their origins and by their personal actions direct the path of history. Napoleon and Lincoln, for example, both rose from obscure beginnings to historical prominence. From the great-man point of view, this was inevitable: nothing could have stopped them although events could have forced them into making their contributions to history in other ways. Other historians argue that "times make the man," that some have "greatness thrust upon them" because they happen to be in the right place at the right time. Since history does not pretend to be an exact science, we can expect no solution to this age-old question from historians. Psychologists, however, have not been especially helpful in analyzing the problem of leadership either. There is no precise answer to the question of what makes a good leader. Among the stumbling blocks are the differing needs of different groups, the previous kinds of leadership to which they have been exposed, and which they now expect. A person who might be a suitable leader in one situation might prove hopelessly incompetent in another. When groups are in conflict, whether these be political parties or national armies, the success of one group involves a failure on the part of the other. A failure inevitably reacts on the prestige of a leader. If the failures are important or frequent he soon becomes a follower, or at least an ex-leader, now, apparently without leadership qualities. One can readily question whether he ever had them.

Research on group structures and leadership

A series of studies (Lippit and White, 1943) has been performed in observing leader-group relationships in situations that have been experimentally "rigged" to create different "atmospheres." Using children as subjects, psychologists have observed the behavior of ten-year olds when a leader follows an "autocratic," a "democratic," or a laissez faire pattern of leadership. The autocratic leader, without being ruthless or harsh, maintains strict discipline and serves as the sole authority. He provides the instructions, assigns jobs (working with toys, models, etc.), permits no discussion, and, in general, keeps the boys "in line." The democratic leader (in the experiment he may be the same person with a different group) allows the boys to vote and decide for themselves what the project will be on which they will work (but they must vote for something), he permits talking and some joking around but co-operates with the boys to see that liberty does not become license and that fooling around does not replace work. The laissez faire leader does no leading and permits the subjects to do whatever they please, within limits, so long as they remain within the area; he does not talk to the boys unless spoken to and then only in a perfunctory manner.

What happens when boys are treated in these different manners? Objective appraisal of the work done shows the authoritarian leader to get more work done than any other group; the laissez faire group gets little or nothing accomplished. Interrogation and observation of the members indicates that there is dissatisfaction in both of these groups; the morale is low compared with that of the democratic group. When children under authoritarian rule are now placed under democratic leadership they do not know how to handle themselves with their new found liberties and get out of hand. In educational systems where children go from one classroom to another, there might be difficulties for a democratic teacher who follows an authoritarian, difficulties that have nothing to do with the leadership qualities of the democratic teacher. The suggestion seems warranted that whenever youngsters and adults, too, are released from strict discipline to a democratic atmosphere, they may induge in excesses which violate the limits that a democratic structure requires to survive. It takes time to learn to adjust to democratic living.

It is claimed that the authoritarian-leader situation generates either submissiveness or repressed hostility and when the leader is not present, work stops, aggressive behavior and scapegoating are likely to develop. The laissez faire situation appears a hopelessly inadequate way to conduct human affairs from the production and morale standpoint. Groups cannot function without some kind of structuring and given time, a laissez faire group would probably become organized into some other form. The experiments did not last long enough to determine if this is so. What the experiments did suggest, however, is that a leader cannot be defined without reference to the group and its background, historical factors, needs, and internal organization. As these factors change, so do the qualifications of a leader. A peacetime leader may be of no value during a war and vice versa. Someone who functions well at the beginning of a task, getting it going, putting it on its feet, and so on may be inadequate to lead a going enterprise. In the absence of strong, objective data, it is easy to be misled by popular writings, by romantic biographical sketches, as well as by oversimplifications advanced by those who would manipulate public opinion. Our traditions have been built around great men and it is much easier to view complex social conflicts in terms of heroes and villains instead of trying to assess the contribution of many factors in any difficult situation. A leader cannot exist without followers and people will only follow those who lead them where they want to go (they may be mistaken about the correctness of the path, but the goal is presumably clear enough). To place the blame for World War II on the shoulders of Hitler and Tojo is an oversimplification; on the other hand it is equally an oversimplification to presume that leaders are helpless and but tools of the masses they lead because once they are in power, they are in position to issue orders which may alter the course of history. It is alleged for example, that Hitler lost the war because he had become incensed when the British bombed Berlin. Because of a personal desire for vengeance against Britain for this insult, he decided to bomb London instead of continuing the almost successful campaign to destroy the British air arm. By this strategic error the war was lost, an error that can be attributable to one or a few men. On the other hand, if he had not chosen to retaliate against London, the German people might have started looking for another leader.

Leadership and imitation

Much if not most of our behavior is patterned on the behavior of those about us, our parents, siblings, teachers, and friends. This patterning on a model, or imitation, has not received its due share of attention from psychologists, perhaps due to the confusion inherent in the term. It is sometimes held, for example, that we learn by imitation, but the nature of such learning by imitation is not at all understood. There is no question that our behavior is modified by imitation, and that, in general, does constitute learning, but in order to imitate we must already have done some learning, acquired some basic skills, and now we proceed to apply such prior learning to a new situation. We do not learn any basic response by imitation. Such basic or "early" learning proceeds along the principles we described earlier in the general treatment of learning. Once we have a basic repertoire of skills and habits, these can now be transferred to new situations if we also *learn to imitate* (Miller and Dollard, 1941). To take an obvious sort of example, we can consider the behavior of a novice at an elaborate banquet where the array of spoons is somewhat bewildering. Unless he has arrived equipped with some formula such as "start at the extreme" he may not feel secure about which spoon to use when. He looks about him and if favorably situated, watches his hostess. As she reaches for a specific implement, he mimics her response and carries the day. He has learned to do what the Romans do. The process of learning to imitate begins in infancy as parents, in misguided attempts to teach skills, keep showing a child how to perform some response. They try to teach children to catch balls by imitation only to find that it is a waste of time; the best the child can do is stand with his hands together. That much he has previously learned. Learning to catch a ball depends on developing anticipatory clutching movements of the fingers as the ball approaches. This can be done only by making contacts with balls and not by watching someone else. The child is continually instructed to watch others and do likewise, sometimes with the modification to "Do as I say, not as I do" to be sure, but by and large, he is urged to do what some model has just done. When he does so, he is generally reinforced for such behavior and the *process of imitation* is learned like any other response to cues that can be identified or labeled as models. Unless the model is first responded to as a model, there will be no call for imitation.

The procedure of imitating others is strongly reinforced by the behavior of children who, in attempts at aggrandizing themselves, show off their new clothes, hairdos, toys, and other reinforcing stimuli to the despair of their parents. The important point to note is that in imitating, we follow models. This can be demonstrated quite literally in experiments with rats that can be trained to follow a leader along a runway, turning left when the leader turns left, stopping when the leader stops, and so on. Imitation in reverse can also be learned in that a rat can be trained to do the opposite of the leader or model rat's behavior. When the leader turns right, the follower can be trained to turn left, et cetera. Children have similarly been observed to learn to follow leaders in handling devices that dispense candy. They can be trained to do the same thing that a tall person does, the opposite of what a short person does, and, presumably, could be trained to behave in one fashion or another depending upon the behavior of some model. If it is reinforcing to follow, the subject follows; if it is reinforcing to do the opposite of what a model does, then the subject does the opposite.

Cats have been observed to benefit from imitation, just as we all do, if we are already basically equipped (Herbert and Harsh, 1944). When cats are blocked from access to food which another cat can obtain by manipulating some device, the watching cat takes less time to learn than the original animal because it goes to the right place when it has an opportunity to do so. That much it has already learned in its earlier history.

In the process of growing up, the child, then, learns to practice the behavior patterns he sees being reinforced about him. So long as he chooses models that are acceptable to his parents, he is reinforced. When the parents are not about, he may be reinforced for following other models where the reinforcements come from the teachers, the playmates, or vicariously, from fantasied reinforcements shared by a television or movie hero. When little girls play "grown-up" and don adult clothing, the indulgent parent reinforces the children by permitting liberties normally not permissible when the children are children. In numberless ways, the children mimic the parents and come to be like them in attitudes, prejudices, mannerisms, and in some cases even in such things as posture, speech, and food preferences and numerous household habits. When the father says "You're just like your mother" and the mother says "You're just like your father," they may be referring to assumed hereditary factors, but the proper reference might very well be the model the child has learned to follow.

The process of imitation is the foundation for conformity, for following the leader, for following fads and fashions, for keeping up with the Joneses, and it is a basic operation in the influence of the group upon the individual. No other operation has equivalent significance for accounting for socialized behavior. In the process of imitation we see the role of the leader to be that of providing the means to the acquisition of reinforcements. If the group already is enjoying reinforcement, the leader is that much more potent than the one who merely promises. In the absence of any reinforcers, however, even promises are better than nothing, and some followers can be stimulated into action. If the situation is desperate, a leader can even say he can promise "only blood, sweat, and tears" and still maintain a following when the alternative is death and slavery. In situations where discipline is a primary function, following the leader is the preferred operation to disobedience which will be followed by negative reinforcers.

The nature of a leader then, is seen to depend upon the characteristics of the group, its needs, its attitudes, the kinds of reinforcers that might be significant in their situations. Because all of these are subject to change with changing events, the leader of one day is the despised villain of tomorrow. In business circles some individuals are regarded as leaders until they go bankrupt. When this happens, the followers wonder how they could ever have been taken in by such a hopeless incompetent. When the pillar of the community turns out to be head of a dope ring or an embezzler, when the president of the Stock Exchange goes to jail, all of his leadership characteristics appear to evaporate and he is now someone to kick around or abuse. It is commonly alleged by historians that military leaders do not make good Presidents, for example, and presidential popularity measures vacillate with various circumstances like the threats of war, economic fluctuations, changing social problems, and even the weather. It is sometimes suggested that a wise leader knows where his followers want to go and takes them there. The nature of the leader cannot be assessed without reference to his followers.

THE PROBLEM OF CONFORMITY

When individuals live, work, and play together, they must accept (that is, learn the rules, acquire the habits) certain limitations on their "natural" reactions to the complex stimuli involved in such interactions. In effect, this is the problem of civilizing the human animal, and as we stressed in the discussion of learning, the problem of civilizing human beings is the essence of education. Through the process of learning, the behavior of the individual is brought into conformity with the rules, laws, traditions, and mores of the other individuals who make up the group. At this time we shall not re-examine the principles of learning but, instead, note how conformity itself affects the behavior of individuals. Sometimes the problem is stated in terms of such labels as competition and co-operation with varying emphasis upon innate and learned influences. Competition and co-operation are sometimes thought of as dynamic traits which cause certain kinds of behavior. We should by now be able to recognize that they are merely descriptions of responses, like other trait names and we need not worry over their possible "dynamic" properties. Sometimes the question is raised as to whether people are competitive or co-operative "by nature." They are neither. People behave competitively or co-operatively depending upon what they have learned to do in given situations. Even dogs do not compete for a bone if they have not learned to do so; this, of course, does not mean that they co-operate with respect to bones, either. Chimpanzees can learn to "co-operate" when appropriately reinforced (see May and Doob, 1937). Some critics object to the experimental demonstrations as not representing *real* co-operation. Such criticism is based on some unrealistic assumption that there is such a *thing* as "co-operation." We will examine such thinking shortly (see below: Institutional thinking).

The problem of conformity amounts to evaluating the role of habit in social, that is interindividual behavior. William James (1890) stated the case in a dramatic expression: "Habit is the great flywheel of society." He was referring, of course, to the stabilizing and regulating function of habit in maintaining a status quo, in providing a basis for the prediction of the behavior of others to which our own behavior could be adjusted. James went so far as to attribute the economic occupations of individuals to habit. Habit keeps the miners in the mines and the sailors at sea, and presumably every other profession or occupation is heavily influenced by habit. It may be, of course, that other factors are also at work. Many miners somehow do not get the habit and leave at the first opportunity. There are, of course, others who spend their lives in the mines and would not leave in exchange for many other kinds of employment. Whether this reflects the influence of habit still remains a question. There are many other variables to be taken into account. Seniority in a union often restricts whatever freedom of choice a worker might enjoy.

Whatever the influence of daily habits as far as regulating the eating, sleeping, and economic activities, there are other kinds of habits, habits of thinking, that must be added to the social flywheel. These habits of social thinking come into function in connection with the very arrangements that men make to make social life possible. These arrangements involve the creation of machinery (the buildings, the jobs, the "table of organization") which creates, in turn, its own problems. Such machinery for handling any given problem is called an "institution." We turn now to an examination of behavior revolving about such machinery.

Institutional behavior

Because of the complexities of social or group living, people become specialized in their activities. They employ or elect some individuals to look after certain of their affairs and organize their activities around such specialists who look after their educational problems, religious life, financial and business affairs, and property relationships. In due course the individuals who serve these functions pass on while the functions remain and are filled by new representatives. Because the functions are permanent while the incumbents are transient, we come to divorce the office from the individual and think of the function as the essential reality. Thus, we think of a jury as "twelve good men and true" and take no notice of the fact they may not really be so good and true as we might imagine. Similarly, a judge is the embodiment of impartial justice even if he is a wife-beating drunk who knows a lot of politicians but very little law. The policeman is the embodiment of the "law"; in fact, some groups even refer to a policeman as "the law." We think of a "university" as something that is more than the administration, faculties, buildings, and campus—it is a permanent, live, growing *thing*. When we do something we do it for the good of the University, or we are afraid that something might harm the University. The law with its courts, the church, the school, the Congress, are "institutions." They are like corporations or committees which get things done but which somehow cannot be touched. Individuals speak for or in the name of the church, the law, the university, the committee, the "company" and so on, not for themselves, they say, but we are asked to believe that it is the institution itself that is doing the talking. The committee is perhaps the most intimate illustration of the point. When something unpleasant has to be done, a committee can do it with no individual taking any personal responsibility. A person can be fired from a job, blackballed from membership in an organization, labeled a "red," or otherwise destroyed and nobody can be found who did the destroying. The committee did it.

The institutional device is a powerful tool for imposing the wishes of groups of individuals upon the growing generations (F. Allport, 1947). A father punishes his children remarking that "this hurts me more than it hurts you" because it is the institutional function of fathers to punish children. As individual personalities, they try to absolve themselves from personal responsibility by donning the institutional cloak. A person is fired *for the good of the company;* similarly, individuals are promoted for the good of the company or they are given bonuses for the good of the company. Commonly enough the "company" is not consulted. It cannot be consulted, of course. Only individuals can be consulted. It is not the intent here to suggest that institutions engage in only shady practices. They operate just as effectively for what some people will regard as social progress or the good of the community. The point is, rather, that things are done in the name of a nonexistent entity, by individuals. Sometimes the unrealistic practice does cover up unpleasant realities; at other times, it may be generally approved. It becomes dangerous only when "institutional thinking" replaces a more realistic approach to problems facing a group of people.

One of the most cherished American institutions is the United States Supreme Court. Franklin D. Roosevelt, when President of the United States, was frequently frustrated in his attempts at social reform by having legislation declared unconstitutional by the Supreme Court. Roosevelt threatened to "pack the Court," i.e., appoint additional members with different attitudes toward social legislation from those demonstrated by "the Nine Old Men." An almost universal horror arose at the idea of packing the Court. The Supreme Court *always* had only nine judges; these judges were judges, not men with what some might consider antisocial prejudices. As an interesting historical sidelight, the judges themselves began to approve the desired legislation and the effort to pack the court was abandoned. Interestingly enough, with changes in the composition of the court, the Supreme Court again began to suffer attack for being too "liberal." Still the Court retains the somewhat awed respect of most of the citizens who find it difficult to recognize a man under the flowing black gown. The black gown is a "symbol" of something that goes far beyond the wearer. Even college professors look more "scholarly" and somehow remotely detached from the world in their academic gowns at Commencement exercises than they do in their classroom garb.

Institutional survival

The degree to which institutional thinking prevails among us is a function of many factors. Great age is, of course, a primary factor. The longer an institution has survived, the more magic it possesses. A new college, without ivy, is hardly a college at all even with the best faculty in the world. Great power is an equally important factor, but primarily, institutions and institutional thinking survive because of their utility. While some institutions fail to "keep up with the times" (this is called cultural lag) and enjoy less and less respect and support, those that do survive do so because they meet the needs of those who support them. When such needs are no longer met, the institutions wither and decay or are overthrown. The royal families of Europe are dwindling in number although they were once virtually worshipped. They are no longer useful. The British monarchy survives presumably because it still meets the needs of the present British Empire.

Reactions to institutions · The J-curve

When people are observed in an institutional setting their behavior does not follow a "normal distribution." The institution sets up a standard or absolute ruling from which individuals can deviate in only one direction. One can only obey the law—it is impossible to obey it more than is called for. It is possible, however, to disobey in various degrees. The behavior of automobile drivers at intersection Stop signs provides a readily observable illustration. If you stand at the corner and watch the drivers, you will find that most people do come to a dead stop before advancing. This is compliance with the law and you cannot do any more than that. A small number of people will slow down and *almost* come to a stop, but their wheels do not actually stop rolling. The percentage of such people will be small, actually, and a plot of the observations would show a sudden drop from absolute compliance to relative compliance. Some people do not stop at all. This group will be exceedingly small as is the criminal element in general. Our jails may be overcrowded but prisoners are only a small percentage of the population. The violators can be plotted on the curve at some extreme and the total plot will resemble a J more than any other convenient symbol. Similar curves would be obtained if we plotted parking meter behavior. Most people would either move their cars or pay for another period; some would be a little late. Very few would actually overstay their time by any long period. It is assumed, of course, that normal policing prevails for both of the examples cited. At night or in quiet neighborhoods, people take liberties with driving regulations—they conform to custom then, rather than to law. The J-curve principle applies to many kinds of social activity—keeping dental appointments, dating in general, standing in line to buy tickets, coming to classes on time, tipping waitresses, returning library books, church attendance, and many other social and semisocial patterns.

Experimental studies of conformity

A novel experimental technique for studying conformity was introduced by Asch (1957). He devised a deception technique where three subjects were employed to create a social pressure on a fourth subject. We will refer to the fourth subject as the real or true subject; the other three were "stooges" working with the experimenter. (In various experiments the number of stooges might vary from one to eight or nine. The use of three stooges has become most popular.) In a typical study, the subject would be introduced to the stooges as one of the group. The experimenter would instruct the group to look at a vertical line about ten-inches high and then show them a card with three lines on it, one exactly the same as the standard, one taller, and one shorter. The subjects would be asked to select the similar line from the group of three. Two of the stooges would then report the taller line; the subject, in third position, would now be in an awkward spot. If he announced what looked like the correct line to him, he would be disagreeing with his fellows. He might choose to do this. In any event, the next report, from the third stooge would agree with the first two choices. The experimenter would continue showing new sets of standard lines and comparison lines, and always the three stooges would agree, and twelve times out of eighteen, they would select the wrong line. When the subjects are faced with this ordeal, about a third of them generally capitulate at about the third or fourth trial and echo the choices of the first two stooges nine or more times. Some subjects are influenced only slightly, and about a third remain quite independent. Women subjects tend to conform more. At first it was argued and believed by some that the subjects who conformed actually were influenced in the perception of the lines, i.e., that they began to see the incorrect lines as more similar to the standard. A lot of empty argument was generated by such an interpretation as recent results show that the subject sees as well as ever and when given the chance to mark his choices privately, he will always select the correct line even though publicly he will report in conformity with the stooges (Deutsch and Gerard, 1955).

In variations of the experiment it is possible to increase the number of subjects who will conform. When "social pressure" is great there are fewer dissenters or rebels even though the situation is simple and harmless enough. Subjects find it easier to go along with the group rather than risk calling attention to themselves or getting into an argument even in a situation where eye witness evidence is in question. What will such subjects do when pressures are stronger and issues less clear-cut but more important? Against how many stooges will an individualist stand up? Studies using seven, eight, and nine stooges show that the more stooges, the more rapidly will conformity set in but generally, no more than the three mentioned in the description of the procedure are needed. Such experiments do not prove much other than that most people conform in such situations. Many questions can be raised about conformity that might be answered eventually by such research. What would happen if the subjects were allowed to discuss the judgments before voting? What if the subject were told that he was right and the group wrong? Would he then start to vary his judgments and choose the wrong lines if the stooges chose the correct? (See Crutchfield, 1955.)

Mass communication media

In advanced civilizations with large masses of population, various means of informing or misinforming people have developed in such a way that large proportions of the population can be more or less simultaneously affected. Newspapers, the movies, television—all reach large numbers of people making it possible for a few to influence the many or at least to stimulate them. What is the result of such concentrated power? We have already considered the nature of propaganda (pp. 372 ff.), but we are now concerned with the specific problem of mass media of communication. How effective are such media? C. I. Hovland (1954) has summarized the numerous studies in the area and finds much confusion in the data and the claims made for one medium or another. There is still much more work to be done on all aspects of mass communication before we can even reach a conclusion on the effectiveness of various kinds of comic books. Attacks on such books (Wertham, 1956) are based on case studies rather than controlled studies and the conclusion that our juvenile delinquents are created by violent comic books is far from satisfactory, scientifically speaking. Newspaper editors continue to write editorials and perhaps slant their news almost heedless of the fact that most people who purchase the papers do not read the news and certainly not the editorials. Franklin D. Roosevelt was elected by substantial majorities in the face of the efforts of a great majority of newspaper publishers Hovland finds the issues fairly complex, involving as they do such factors as the nature of the communicator (who says what?), and the audience, the nature of the communication—whether it is an appeal to reason or emotion, the sequence of arguments—that is, whether a point or climax is reached first or early and is then followed by arguments or the other way around, whether arguments are one-sided or apparently two-sided (intelligent people are more likely to be impressed if offered both sides of the story). The medium itself makes a difference. Television advertisements appealing to both eye and ear seem to be remembered longer than radio presentations. Finally, mass media must deal with personalities—such factors as age, intelligence, education, sex, and various cultural factors all are important.

ACTION RESEARCH—GROUP DECISION PROCESSES

One approach to group dynamics consists of studying groups that are engaged in some effort at changing some existing social situation, for example, a prejudice of some kind. The psychologist-observer may become a member of such a group, e.g., a labor union, and participate in the activity at the same time taking note of the action and its outcomes, observing the relative efficiency of one technique or another to accomplish some social end. If a given course of action succeeds or fails it is related to whatever variables can be effectively isolated in the situation. In one widely-quoted such study (see Lewin, 1948), the investigators observed the effort made to change housewive's buying habits during a wartime shortage of popular meat cuts. Some groups were given lectures and advice about the nutritional value of less popular cuts while other groups participated in group discussions and examined the issues by much more active participation. It was found that more effective attitude changes followed the discussion technique. Other studies involved attempts at reducing racial tensions in housing projects. In some investigations, attempts were made to compare lecture versus discussion methods of teaching psychology courses (Faw, 1949). At present the status of such research does not permit definite conclusions and it cannot be claimed that psychologists know how to affect group behavior in serious issues. It is encouraging, however, to note the expansion of efforts in such directions. Action research raises serious ethical issues for psychologists whose traditional orientation has been toward observation and study rather than action. We shall touch on such issues in the next chapter.

•

THE PSYCHOLOGY OF SOCIAL BEHAVIOR

Our account of social factors in behavior has been sketchy and general. Throughout the present chapter we have emphasized the role of culture and, implicitly, the role of learning. We have further, and perhaps unwisely, emphasized the social behavior of man, ignoring all other organisms. Man does not live alone, and certainly not by bread alone, as our emphasis on "arrangements for living" should have made clear. But, very few other organisms live alone either. In our emphasis on man with his capacity for language and thereby for handing down culture from generation to generation by folktale and saga, by song and by history book, we have perhaps overlooked other factors that control and determine behavior, factors which might be *natural* to man. Can we learn from the beehive, the school of fish, the anthill, the pride of lions, the herd of zebras or giraffes? Other organisms, too, have a social life and "arrangements for living," and these arrangements have been studied for many years, largely by naturalists, but more and more commonly by biologists and psychologists and, currently, by a new kind of scientist, the ethologist. Thus far, the results of such studies have not shaken up our thinking about social phenomena, but we would be rash to conclude that they never will. In Chapter 3 we mentioned the observation of "imprinting" and dismissed it rather casually. We can close this chapter with an invitation to the student to reread the earlier discussion of heredity and environment and begin anew to explore the strange and beautiful social life of the birds and the bees. The latter at least has been described in an exciting fashion by Von Frisch (1955). If we "go to the ant" we might learn about more than industry, and if we study the social life of monkeys and chimpanzees in their own habitat (Carpenter, 1934) more assiduously, we may have much to revise in our thoughts about man and society.

CHAPTER 16

Retrospect and Prospect

Changeable human nature · Psychology and values · Problems of controlling behavior · The role of reinforcement · Freedom of choice · Determinism again—methodology or metaphysics? · Resistance to change · Is propaganda effective? · The power of education · Learning and performance reconsidered · Individual differences · Convergence and divergence · Prediction versus explanation · Suggestions for the future study of psychology

In this final chapter we shall try to answer some of the questions that were raised at the beginning of our study. Many of the principles we have examined can now be brought to bear on the issues without pausing for explanations. The student who has perused the text with care may be able to anticipate the remarks that might be appropriate for the various section headings. In any event, it might prove profitable to appraise the results of the effort involved in the study of the text. We have been amidst the trees for so long that we may have lost sight of the forest.

It is not our intention here to summarize or review the text; rather, we shall attempt to appraise the role of psychology in contemporary life. We shall treat briefly of values. Our discussion of values, however, will be limited to problems involving the feasibility or practicality of changing human nature.

CHANGEABLE HUMAN NATURE

We started our consideration of psychology by taking note of some claims, fears, threats, and promises. Throughout the text we have been concerned with the principles that might be employed to explain behavior and, incidentally, "predict and control human behavior." Now we can re-examine the threats and promises in the light of such principles to see if they can be made good. We discounted the concerns of philosophers and novelists as not necessarily pertinent and turned to a psychologist, B. F. Skinner, who promised a happy, adjusted, constructive world. We will not worry now over whether such a world is desirable, but only over whether it is possible.

It is obvious, from the outset, that whether we are aware of it or not (however dimly or acutely), most of us act as if human nature can be changed along lines we desire. As parents or teachers, husbands or wives, therapists or religious leaders, judges, pillars of the community, social workers, YMCA counselors or Boy Scout leaders, football coaches, or members of the Junior Chamber of Commerce, boyfriends or girlfriends, we are all out to change somebody's human nature. If there is a "will to believe" we all have such a will to believe that Skinner is right. Not only is the will to believe this present in huge quantities, but there is an overabundance of evidence that human nature is changeable. All over the world we find man adopting different customs and ways of living, following different traditions and practices, adopting varied religious orientations, believing in various superstitions, speaking in different tongues, wearing different kinds of clothing, swearing allegiance to different kinds of rulers, even eating with different kinds of tools. All these things and many more we are reasonably sure are learned and modifiable.

Psychology and values

The citizens of the Soviet Union learn one way of life. The people of the United Kingdom or of the United States of America learn another. The people of the United States of Brazil still another, and so on. When the ways of life of one large group of people come into conflict with the ways of another, the usual method of settling the differences involves violence and warfare, and, nowadays, perhaps a mutually annihilating kind of warfare. Another solution, of course, would be to have the citizens of all countries learn the same way of life, a way that would not involve groups of citizens in the intergroup strife. Into this situation the psychologist might be bold enough to tread with his call to action by all men of good will. We quote one such call:

> I believe that the world will either be saved by the psychologists or it won't be saved at all. I think psychologists are the most important people living today. I think the fate of the human species and the future of the human species rests more upon their shoulders than upon any group of people now living. I believe that all the important problems of war and peace, exploitation and brotherhood, hatred and love, sickness and health, misunderstanding and understanding, the happiness and unhappiness of mankind will yield only to a better understanding of human nature.

These remarks of A. H. Maslow (1956) are certainly flattering to the psychologist. It is doubtful, however, that many psychologists are anxious to take this burden upon their shoulders. Most of them are not overly concerned with saving the world or changing it. They are more interested in trying to understand it. Maslow himself admits that psychology is an infant science. He appears to be asking a great deal of an infant. The infant is involved with hatred and love, sickness and health, and misunderstanding, to be sure. Whether he should be asked to do something about these problems, however, is another matter, especially before he really knows much, if anything, about them.

It is time to reflect upon what we have learned about human nature to see if anything can be done by psychologists to improve man's lot, that being the chief concern of so many of the world's citizens (with, unfortunately, some narrowing of the concern to rather immediate family). Before we get too wrapped up in our concern over man, we should take note of the fact that most people are more concerned over a bloody nose or a bump on the head in the family than about plagues and starvation or other catastrophes that wipe out millions across the sea. A whole town in Texas can blow up and the citizens in Alaska will not shed many tears. When a hundred miners are buried in a coal mine there is less concern manifest in other towns and states than when one little girl falls into a local well. If the little girl's dog falls in with her, a dog-loving nation will wait tensely for bulletins about the rescue efforts. In short, it is quite clear that many people do not really care much for other people, especially if their skins are of a different color or if they worship other gods. This observation, whether we like it or not, does not suggest that the job psychologists are being asked to do by Maslow, is going to be easy. There is considerable question as to whether it is even realistic to expect that much can be done about it. It is difficult to think about people one does not know in a rather intimate way as real people, individuals in their own right, human beings like ourselves. The people in a distant country are people only in the abstract for most of us; even the people on the next street are not very real to us and in large cities, neighbors, even people in the next apartment, are rather vague and amorphous. Those individuals, psychologists or otherwise, who are out to save the world, are not thinking about people. They are no more capable of appreciating the six hundred million Chinese as flesh and blood individuals than is anyone else. They are dealing with abstractions, with ideals, and any action predicated upon abstractions and ideals is fraught with the danger of running up against obstacles that are unfortunately very real.

The portrait of man we have tried to draw in this text was not especially flattering. We were not concerned with determining whether man is "good" or "evil" by nature. Many observers have tried to place such value judgments on human nature, some concluding with more pessimism than optimism. One such contemporary observer, Peter Viereck (1958), considering the problems of human reform says: "But the good builder builds with the clay at hand; never does he pile up utopias from some ideal airy clay that does not exist on his particular planet. The most bloodcurdling crimes are done not by criminals but perfectionists. Criminals normally stop killing when they attain their modest goal: loot. Perfectionists never stop killing because their goal is never attainable: the ideal society." When we examine the claims of reform-type psychologists we must determine whether they are good builders or perfectionists.

PROBLEMS OF CONTROLLING BEHAVIOR

With the above general considerations behind us, we are ready to consider what the psychologist could or might do to change (for better or worse) the current social scene, presumably through the manipulation of conditions that would affect the behavior of individuals. The sheer number of individuals involved is somewhat appalling and the number of psychologists necessary to do the job might be quite prohibitive (we would still need butchers, bakers, and television-tube makers). But brushing this modest problem aside we raise the question of how the psychologist is going to get into position to put his techniques to work. In the debate with which we opened our discussion in Chapter 1, Carl Rogers (1956) raised this question. He argued that we cannot expect the world to invite the psychologists to "take over," and in this he is certainly correct. If psychologists are to achieve a position of power, they will have to be put there by fiat, by somebody who has the power to give and who will presumably give it only to someone who serves him or his values. Fortunately, or otherwise, there is no world dictator who will do this. If there were, there is considerable question that he would hire psychologists who would work toward goals not consistent with his own.

The role of reinforcement

The other alternative, apparently, is for psychologists to function as missionaries, to debate, to exhort, to plead with people to join "the movement." Nothing in what we have examined in this text supports such a venture. We do not change people in attitude or action by pleas or entreaties. According to Skinner himself, there is only one way to change behavior and that is by reinforcement (and through a converse process of extinction). When we apply this argument to any attempt to alter behavior (whether by lecture, by argument, by propaganda, or advertising, or by psychotherapy) we run into a controversial problem in learning theory. If we follow the argument of the psychologists who support a view of learning based on the reinforcement of the instrumental response, as does Skinner, we must picture the behavior as coming *first,* and then being reinforced by the psychologist (or someone) immediately. Simply asking people to change their minds is of no possible avail. This has not worked in the thousands of years that it has been tried by one individual or group, or another. The advertiser who asks the television viewer to go down to the drugstore *now* to buy the new miracle twelve-way pain reliever is wasting his time as far as that particular message is concerned. It is doubtful if he himself has any such bizarre hopes. If the advertisement is of value at all, it is for other reasons. The only basis for any individual's responding to a suggestion or plea from another individual is the previous history of the people in question. If Individual A has followed the advice of Individual B previously, and this action has been reinforced, then it is possible that A will again follow B's advice. Thus some parents have earned the "confidence" of their children who will, in such cases, do what the parents ask.

Inevitably in the course of child-rearing and education, children encounter various threats and promises which are not fulfilled. "Everybody stays after school!" says the teacher who has reached the end of her rope. Actually nobody does, and the teacher's threat-strength has diminished. "This won't hurt," but it does and mother's promise-strength has been impaired. We can assume that most advisors have not always, or even often, had their advice followed by reinforcement. The huge throngs that gather to hear evangelists or politicians are made up of individuals who have already been reinforced in some manner for attending such meetings or listening to such speeches. Very few come to "scoff and remain to pray." The potential scoffers stay away.

Threats and promises become somewhat specifically related to situations and in each new situation, new learning occurs. The baby at the beach being encouraged to enter the water by daddy may hesitate to enter the new kind of environment. If a stranger tries to entice the baby into the water he has almost no chance of success. Later when the child is urged to try something potentially dangerous by swimming teachers or athletic instructors, the child may be reluctant. "He has no confidence," we say. We mean he has no history of reinforcement in that situation or with that instructor.

In talking about propaganda, we made the point that communists get nowhere trying to enlist support from capitalists and vice versa. There is no history of reinforcement on either side. Catholics and Protestants similarly run into stone walls if they try to convert one another. We find little agreement between Arabs and Israelis, Algerians and Frenchmen, and on a lesser level, one gang of juvenile delinquents and another. In the home, brothers and sisters, and frequently enough, husbands and wives have trouble "convincing" each other about the merits of any given action. In many kinds of interpersonal relationships the tangled history of reinforcements and extinctions makes prediction difficult for any new proposition.

When Skinner addressed the American Psychological Association he undoubtedly elicited approval from those who had previously found his proposals reinforcing. Those who had not did not rise immediately and urge him on in his program. The individual most directly concerned, Carl Rogers, far from being won over by the argument essayed an argument of his own, finding approval among his followers. Skinner, of course, did not expect to convince Rogers any more than Lincoln expected to convince Douglas. Inevitably, a history of reinforcement is necessary before we take advice or follow the leader.

Only those who have lived in Utopia can follow the leader into Utopia. Since such a state of affairs is virtually impossible, we are left with a problem where we observe followers embarking upon a new course with untried leaders. We see some of the peasants and soldiers of Czarist Russia rebelling against the government with slogans proclaiming the worker's paradise. Since they never knew such a paradise, how could they have succumbed to the preaching of Lenin and Trotsky? We know the problem was not so simple. They followed not only Lenin and Trotsky but Kerensky and other leaders of various social coloring. Most of the people in Russia did not even know what was going on, including many in the active revolutionary groups. The course of the revolution was actually negative even though it looked positive. The revolutionists were *against* what they had, which they knew well enough; they were *for* something "better," though precious few could know what this meant, and while engaged in destroying the old regime, they wondered what course the revolution would take. It is easy to be against something familiar and real. To be for something new and unexperienced is quite impossible if we are talking about anything real. The *Mayflower* Puritans were escaping oppression; it is doubtful if any of them knew what they were heading for out in the Atlantic.

Freedom of choice

Inherent in any plea or request for action from anyone is the notion that the individual is free to choose or at least to select from more than one alternative of action. The concept of freedom of choice has been proclaimed for centuries as one of the fundamental verities. Deterministic psychologists must take the "experience of personal freedom" into account, or account for it. Consider Roger's statement in commenting upon Skinner's statements: "I can understand this point of view, but I believe that it avoids looking at the great paradox of behavioral science. Behavior, when it is examined scientifically, is surely best understood as determined by prior causation. This is one great fact of science. But responsible personal choice, which is the most essential element in being a person, which is the core experience in psychotherapy, which exists prior to any scientific endeavor, is an equally prominent fact in our lives. To deny the experience of responsible choice is, to me, as restricted a view as to deny the possibility of a behavioral science." Rogers goes on to compare the paradox between determinism and the experience of responsible personal choice with the paradox in physics where the wave theory and the corpuscular theory of light seem to be contradictory but necessary. Conant (1953) has indicated that physicists must learn to live with these two views, using either as the occasion requires. Rogers similarly argues: "We cannot profitably deny our subjective life, any more than we can deny the objective description of that life."

Whatever the problems to which physicists must reconcile themselves (and that may be only a temporary state of affairs—it may turn out that light is neither corpuscular nor wavelike but something else entirely), the problems of psychologists need not be surrendered to analogy. In this text we have not attempted to *deny* our subjective life. Nor were we concerned about affirming subjective experience as such. Instead we have treated the alleged experiences in terms of internal behavior. We have tried to account for such internal behavior in objective language. It is obviously customary and convenient to refer to such internal behavior in subjective terms. Ivan London (1948) has tried to smooth over the difficulty by making use of an *"as if"* postulate. He argues that while a strictly scientific description calls for objective accounts of behavior based on a fundamental determinism, there is room for accounts of behavior which can be prefaced by the use of an *"as if"* formula (see Boring, 1957). Thus, while behavior is strictly determined, man acts "as if" he could make choices, have ideas, and so on. We have tried to account for such "as if" phenomena throughout the text and need not repeat the story at this time other than to re-emphasize that man has learned to talk, to some degree, about his internal behavior. The fact that he labels certain internal behavior as an "experience of personal responsibility" does not constitute evidence for some peculiar or different and nonobjective reality.

Determinism again—methodology or metaphysics?

The deterministic psychologist is in no position to deny the existence of phenomena he is unable to observe, measure, or manipulate. Early in this book we stated that if such affairs are of significance in the control of behavior, then it was so much the worse for psychology. It should be clear that the determinism we are talking about deals only with psychology as an "empirical" science (in contrast to a "rational" theory of man). For the psychologist, determinism is a methodological assumption and not a tenet of a metaphysical system. Paul Meehl (1958) has described the distinction between methodological and metaphysical determinism in considering the relationship between psychology and religion. To adopt a metaphysical determinism, Meehl says, would be arrogant and quite unjustifiable. In this text a methodological determinism was assumed as the only *working* position an investigator of behavior could follow if he was to be guided by common rules of evidence based on empirical (sensory observation) findings. In our examination of the various topics that concerned us throughout this text there was no basis for altering that point of view.

The working psychologist in his laboratory, when faced with the problem of accounting for an "experience of personal responsibility," can say that the enjoyer of such an experience has learned to label some of his internal behavior with words like: I prefer this to that, or I'll take that one instead of this one, or I'll do this instead of that. Such labeling behavior was described earlier in terms of mediational responses which gave rise to stimuli associated with responses. Presumably such mediational responses possess characteristics which could be described as "evaluative," "approach," or "avoidance" kinds of reactions; the stimuli generated by such responses could be conditioned to overt behavior which would be related to the "internal" or mediational response. Anyone faced with a choice situation would inevitably react in terms of such mediators as "this is good" which in terms of a lifetime of experience is associated with a succeeding response of "I'll do it." The "I'll do it" is a phrase describing the initiation of an action which normally follows in the situation involved. Should the mediational response be "That's bad," aversive or avoidance behavior is, similarly, inevitable. When both kinds of mediators are simultaneously or successively initiated, the subject, we said earlier, is in "conflict." With conflict in the picture, we can expect fluctuating, vacillating behavior; neither tendency is strong enough to win out, and commonly enough, a compromise response terminates the situation. When a child cannot "make up his mind" about which flavor of ice cream to select, vanilla or chocolate, he may finally select strawberry, which had not even been a candidate for election. This means only that the apparently strong contenders were not actually as strong as they appeared in that each cut into the strength of the other leaving the "dark horse" to gain the field. Similarly an adult might have learned, when no specific response is strong enough, to "flip a coin" and follow the toss with action dictated by the coin. Such responses presumably occur in situations of no great consequence. The behavior involved, however, can hardly be considered "free."

To return to Roger's point about denying the experience of responsible choice, we can now say that there is no point to denying certain kinds of internal behavior which some people can label as an "experience of personal responsibility." We cannot deny the existence of anything we have no way of observing within the limits of scientific procedures. Not denying it, however, does not involve endorsing it, either, and for the same reasons. In some cases we can recognize the behavior that underlies the report of the experience. If patients in psychotherapy show growth in "personal responsibility" we can recognize that they now are acting and talking differently from their previous patterns; now their descriptions of internal behavior correspond more to what the psychotherapist has been trained to approve in his social history. Whether there has been evolved *more* freedom, we may never know. From this analysis we might judge that a "sense of responsibility" consists of evaluative attitudes that correspond with the prevailing mores of a group and that developing such a sense involves training individuals to label situations as "good" or "bad." An individual so trained would also normally be trained to respond positively to situations labeled "good" and to avoid those labeled "bad." Should he find himself doing something "bad" we can expect the individual to be disturbed in varying degrees of severity. The individual might report such a disturbance as "suffering pangs of conscience," being "guilty," suffering shame or remorse, and so on. There appears to be no reason to doubt that habits, appropriate to a "sense of responsibility," "character," "morality," and so on, can be effectively taught by appropriate training.

Under ordinary circumstances a person "of good character" has no problem of "freedom" or "personal responsibility." He merely does what he has been trained to do. So does the individual of "bad character." The problem of freedom arises only when a person of "good character" finds himself about to do ("tempted") something he has learned to label "bad." (The "bad character" might have similar trouble when asked to do or about to do something "good.") The problem of "choice" or "freedom" arises in such conflict situations where we can expect the hesitation, vacillation, and compromising tendencies, we have already discussed in our treatment of conflict. While the present discussion may not prove satisfying, it is about as much as psychologists are in position to say at present. The laboratory study of freedom, conscience, guilt, and responsibility is obviously an area that so far has eluded the psychologist, and, as far as serious moral problems are concerned, may continue to elude him. One does not ask subjects to commit crimes in the laboratory and it is doubtful that anything akin to a "conscience" can be developed in lower organisms.

The roundabout argument presented above was designed to bear on the problem of how psychologists are or were to get people to improve mankind, i.e., change the behavior of men. We conclude from the argument that they are not going to do it by preaching or asking for a change. If they are going to do it at all, they will have to reinforce the behavior that corresponds to "improvement" when, as, and if it emerges or is "emitted." This means, as we pointed out earlier, that psychologists or their helpers (teachers, parents, or a corps of reinforcers) must be ready and able to apply the correct reinforcement whenever the desired behavior appears. We have referred to the scope of this enterprise (considering the number of people who need improvement) as "modest." We are ready to face less modest difficulties.

Resistance to change

We are sometimes told by historians and philosophers that the more the world changes, the more it stays the same. It is suggested, of course, in such statements that man is a relatively stable organism, evolving slowly, changing, if at all, by imperceptible stages. Wars we have always with us, along with death and taxes, illegitimate children, and juvenile delinquents. Adolescents have always irked their elders—only the specific techniques have changed. Delinquents used to steal horses and buggies; now they steal automobiles for joy rides. Someday they will steal space ships. Socrates complained about the irresponsibility of the younger generation. Two thousand years later we have made no perceptible progress in the relationships between children and parents. Young people still consider their parents stupid only to find them, as Mark Twain pointed out, becoming fairly intelligent as they become older. It is still expected that young people, around twenty should become socialistic in their views, or some kind of social rebels, and change these views before they are forty. There is always a "lost" or "beat" generation.

There may be some truth in the view that "the more things change, the more they stay the same." If there is, psychologists have not been able to do much with it by way of verification or refutation. It may be, however, that years and years, generations, perhaps centuries, would be required to make actual and significant changes in man's behavior of any serious nature. This is not meant to deny that given a certain social structure such as a totalitarian dictatorship, with a powerful and secret police force, that people cannot be *forced* into lip service and public compliance with certain beliefs, rituals, and practices. Forcing people to comply involves threats, punishment even torture (in difficult cases). Such techniques are called "aversive" by Skinner, and they do work as we saw in our discussion of punishment. But we also noted at that time that punishment does not deter others (that is, those who have not been personally assaulted) very effectively and that in many situations punishment or "aversive techniques" only *suppress* behavior (if that behavior was previously reinforced). We also noted that punishment tends to develop avoidance (hate?) of the punisher or punishing situation. Should the tyrant want his "subjects" to love him (as some dictators apparently have), he has his work cut out for him. He will not achieve his ambition with aversive techniques. When the population shouts "Heil" the tyrant cannot rest easy. He cannot count on the loyalty of masses controlled by fear. How deep-rooted the beliefs and loyalties of an aversively controlled population might be is a question that is obviously not easy to answer.

In any society, the amount of positive reinforcement and aversive control is difficult to evaluate. How loyal are the citizens of the Soviet Union to the current occupants of the Kremlin? How do you measure such loyalty? By whether they fight against Hitler? How loyal are Britons to the royal house? Do we measure this by how strongly they defend their homes against invasion and prospective slavery? Were they ever actually more loyal? We can expect a basic kind of nostalgic affection in anyone for the scenes of his protected and relatively peaceful childhood. In every country childhood is exploited by educators in the name of patriotism. We reinforce affection for Washington and Lincoln by days off from school. Even so people are and always have been leaving the homeland or home town to settle on foreign shores, or more likely locations, bringing their nostalgia with them, weeping for the "auld sod," but being careful not to return if they could help it if the present situation is an improvement over the old. Patriotism is a complex pattern of emotional conditioned reactions involving nostalgia, a certain inertia to change, fear of the new and strange and "foreign." The enemy is always "foreign" with strange ways, ways we do not care to adopt because we are more comfortable with our own. Do we fight for "King and country" or because we can hardly do anything else? Is our patriotism much more than an enlightened self-interest? Does the draftee in any country put on the uniform with enthusiasm or regret? The very need for drafting young men into military service is a partial answer. Even when we enlist do we enlist to fight for our country or *against* the enemy who may destroy us if we do not take action? The lessons of history suggest that peoples can be oppressed for generations without losing their passion, capacity, or willingness for revolt, that when conditions are appropriate they do revolt. Perhaps previous tyrants have not had the services of the modern psychologist? Would they do better with modern techniques?

IS PROPAGANDA EFFECTIVE?

In our first chapter and in Chapter 10 we mentioned the modern advertisers, the men in gray flannel suits who claim to manipulate the buying masses on the basis of their "depth psychology." These "Motivation Researchers" (MR) sell their clients programs and campaigns designed to bring the consumer to his knees, buying, buying, buying. How successful have they been? When they sell an automobile as a "sex symbol" are they doing anything other than recognizing that whatever a car is, it is more than a conveyance, or "transportation"? Thorstein Veblen, in his *Theory of the Leisure Class,* explained the role of "conspicuous consumption" in buying practices long before current Motivation Researchers were born. The average car buyer knows very well what he should do when he needs "transportation." Instead of that, he looks at his two-year old car and begins to rationalize (quite consciously) about how much new tires would cost, how soon he will be stuck with big repair bills, how the "trade-in value" is dropping. He knows he wants a new car (and that he is *not* kidding himself), and aided and abetted by his wife who sees the neighbor's new car in the driveway, he lets himself get "sold" by a salesman who talks about horse-power, torsionaire, hydromatics, and other musical-sounding but meaningless matters, knowing full well that the customer is either sold or not sold on the basis of completely extraneous matters such as the rear-window rainwiper. Who is fooling whom?

How successful are the Motivation Researchers in selling their client's wares? It is very difficult to measure the effect of advertising or to determine what is doing the selling, if anything is. If someone sponsors a television show and the sponsor's products are purchased, he is happy and the Motivation Researchers are free to attribute the success to anything they choose to consider, yet such a show (to say nothing of consumers' behavior) consists of numerous factors that are not experimentally appraised. The entire increase in sales may be due to the failure of some other sponsor to entice the viewers with his own quiz or cowboy show or to resentment of some competitive sponsor because he dropped a popular singer. If the Motivation Researchers are really successful, then they will fight themselves to a standoff as each advertising agency has access to the same questionable principles peddled to them by equally questionable authorities. For the most part such authorities are psychiatrists and psychoanalysts and not psychologists, and psychologists can hardly be blamed for their practices. Raymond Bauer (1958) in a review of three books on Motivation Research concluded: "It is my impression from talking to psychologists and from some of their printed statements, that they take quite seriously the possibility that Motivation Researchers are indeed wielding some magical influence over the buying behavior of the American public. If the reader's sole purpose in perusing this review is to find an answer to that question, the answer is simply that there is no basis for assuming such magical influence is indeed being wielded." People are not so easily pushed around and manipulated as manipulators think. Frequently they are in no position other than to accept the pushing, but if there has been truly no other than "psychological" pressure in a Motivation Researcher's sense, the behavior is not likely to be stable and predictable.

The weight of the evidence (see Erickson, 1958) at the present time negates the more extravagant claims made by some advertisers that their messages could be presented *subliminally* to our "unconscious minds." It appears that no reliable or valid evidence exists that anyone can be "conditioned" to act in some fashion to stimuli of which he was unaware. We are talking about stimuli related to effecting instrumental behavior, of course. It is quite possible to condition some *responses,* e.g., the PGR or psychogalvanic reflex of which the subject is unaware. Similarly, it is possible to develop various unconscious "sets" which will control some instrumental responses. In the latter case, the subject may know *what* he is doing and not be able to say why he is doing it. This is quite different from doing something we are opposed to doing, however; in such situations the effect is brought about by stimuli which are not subliminal but rather unanalyzed or unattended to. We need not fear the advertiser or propagandist who wants to guide our behavior by unseen messages on our television screens. Nor will we ever be taught to love Big Brother while we sleep.

We turn to more serious attempts at psychological control, the attempts at "brain washing." We have already discussed such "educational" and propaganda techniques and there is no question that by various measures (hypnosis, restriction of the environment, restriction of sources of information, repetition of a one-sided story) people can be made to accept various statements as correct and endorse them, come to believe them. We made the point previously that every country brain washes its own children. Every family co-operates in filling the heads of the youngsters with the local folklore and fairy tales. Children grow up with the superstitions and beliefs of their elders, with the loyalties of their parents toward political parties, economic beliefs, religious orientations. In many instances they retain some particular delusional beliefs until death, never learning other views. By suitable reinforcement anyone can be brought to believe almost anything. This is what horrifies Aldous Huxley and others who fear for the world's safety. But the *almost* is important. Some things can be believed forever with no particular harm resulting. A mirror is shattered. Seven years bad luck. Does it matter whether any individual subscribes to this belief? He has no way of proving or disproving the belief. In the next seven years, let us presume, he will probably break additional mirrors and he can regard his whole life as unlucky, but there is no record of anyone having resigned from the human race because he broke a mirror. Black cats cross our paths occasionally. If we believe this to be unlucky we might be wary for a moment or two, but probably no harm is done. We cannot prove that we have not been unlucky. If the cat had not crossed our path we might have found a million dollars in the street. But, again, we do not worry about the good fortune we might have had *if*. Some people react more violently to superstitious situations than do others. We must not forget about the power of "magic" on primitive savages. But here, again, the reinforcements may be powerful. Children believe in Santa Claus until they are seven or eight or so. Sooner or later the truth comes out because the child now has to play Santa Claus to someone else. It cannot be demonstrated that any child's life was ruined because he was taught to believe in Santa Claus and later found out that the whole world lied to him.

The moral of Santa Claus is very helpful for our present discussion. People cannot be made to believe anything of genuine importance in their lives if it is possible to show that it is not true. We might recall Abraham Lincoln's words: "You can fool all of the people some of the time and some of the people all the time, but you can't fool all of the people all of the time." If it is not possible to demonstrate the falsity of some statement, some people will believe it so long as it is reinforcing to them to believe it. Here we encounter the only saving grace which the psychology of learning provides: neither dog, nor rat, nor man will believe anything that is not true in the sense that it is not reinforced. If it is strongly reinforced, he will believe it strongly; if it is only occasionally reinforced, he will believe it less avidly.

We must take note of exceptions to these remarks. They apply only to healthy people. Schizophrenics and other "disturbed" people act as if they believed things that are obviously untrue, unrealistic to us. But even such beliefs, for the people who have them, might receive support or reinforcement of some unknown nature. The paranoid who believes "the whole world is against me" may be able to point, in fact, to some, perhaps many, instances of mistreatment or abuse. He may have learned to distrust a friendly greeting when such greetings were followed by unpleasant consequences. Similarly, we must account for the behavior of gamblers who (it is claimed) must lose "in the long run." Here we must reckon with the power of "partial reinforcement," which will maintain a long-run of unreinforced activity. The gambler wins occasionally, the "house" or the nature of the game sees to that. But even if he loses, we must not overlook other sources of reinforcement. Gambling gives him a chance to associate with people who may provide other reinforcements. From the way in which some gamblers spend their winnings, we can be reasonably sure that money is not always, and for everyone, the only or major reinforcement.

THE POWER OF EDUCATION

Let us apply the Santa Claus moral to education. Education, like science, is self-correcting. Children are taught to test, check, and prove. They come to believe in arithmetic because it works. Geography also works. Physics and chemistry work sometimes—the instructor sometimes is unable to carry off the demonstration and asks the students to take his word for it. Some of them do, if they have been reinforced for taking his word for it before. Others are skeptical because they have been taught (whether by teachers or experience is irrelevant) to be skeptical. An economic theory or social law does not always work and finds fewer ardent supporters.

Modern civilization requires more and more education of its citizens. With each advance in education students become equipped with more and more skepticism, with more doubt. They are taught to look for the truth because only the truth will work in science or in practical affairs. If a given philosophy or set of rules for living works, i.e., reinforces the population, the population believes. If it does not work, the population will cease to believe. The citizens of the United States look with alarm at the growing power of the Soviet Union and worry over the way in which young children there are being taught to believe in communism. We have good reason to believe that communism, certainly as described by Karl Marx, is a fallacious economic and social doctrine. If anything is working in the Soviet Union, it is not Marxism.[1] The official pronouncements may all be couched in communistic phraseology about capitalist exploiters and imperialistic warmongers, but we need not assume that anyone actually believes such slogans except perhaps the very young who also still believe in Santa Claus or his communist equivalent. The higher the level of education, the more the dependency upon proof and demonstration, the more the need for testing, for supporting claims and hypotheses by facts and the less support of dogmatic teaching. It is unlikely that any society can produce brilliant, intellectual slaves. The educational operation is like Frankenstein's monster which turned on its creator. If a society wishes to progress, it must educate. If it educates, it cannot feed the learners with lies. As the educational process continues, it will lead to distrust, dissatisfaction, and defections from the society unless the society changes. The process might be slow, but appears inevitable. It is possible that brilliant individuals can pursue certain kinds of study where empirical proof is irrelevant without ever doubting "rational" beliefs. But the lowliest peasant will not believe promises about next year's bread if last year's promises have not been kept. If the peasant is given "a little knowledge" he might believe a little longer as "a little knowledge is a dangerous thing" in the sense that it allows others to confuse you. The magician with his "palaver" may fool the adult but not the child, or the dog who watches the hand and not the mouth. When people have been only modestly educated, they can be confused by language more readily than when they do not know what is being said. But more education makes them specialists in the language, too, and then they cannot be fooled any longer.

The above remarks were not meant to be reassuring. They do not mean we have nothing to fear from a country where large populations are forced to work along particular lines. If the people of China and India, for whatever reason, started to march westward they would overrun the rest of the world through sheer numbers alone, without the aid of psychology. We have only taken the trouble to point out that there is little to fear from abuses of psychology, at least at present. Soviet Psychology, from what we are able to learn, is far more "idealistic"

[1] The student might be interested in a criticism of Yugoslavian communism by Milovan Djilas (1958); Polish communist thinking by Czeslaw Milosz (1953); and a philosophical critique of revolutionists, in general, by Albert Camus (1956).

than American Psychology (Razran, 1957, 1958). While Soviet psychologists ostentatiously glorify Pavlov, Lenin, and Marx, their psychology is far more subjective and certainly less "applied" than is our own. Their psychology is no more effective than was that of Hitler's psychologists who were constrained to work out a scientific proof for the Herrenvolk or Master Race concept. Hitler's psychologists spent the war years determining "types" of men. We have already found sufficient reason to dismiss such approaches.

Soviet psychologists today are largely concerned with "cognitive" problems. They object to Gestalt, psychoanalytic, and other "bourgeois" formulations and have no interest in what we regard as "social psychology." They show even less interest in mental tests or other kinds of aptitude measurement (psychometrics), perhaps because they are un-Marxist, i.e., reflect hereditary differences. The bulk of psychological work in the Soviet Union is done by "psychophysiologists" who, following in the tradition of Pavlov, are concerned with "higher nervous processes." According to Razran, they are very advanced in such work, perhaps well ahead of American physiological psychologists. Some of their work on verbal conditioning might be interpreted as bearing on some future possible "thought-control," but that day is not yet here, and considering the difficulties involved, an unlikely development. Soviet psychophysiology is comparable to American behavioristic psychology; their "psychology" is not comparable to anything we know as it is an attempt to fit Pavlov to Marx as well as to make "conscious" activity a dialectical "emergent" by which man's destiny can be controlled.

Learning and performance reconsidered

When we discussed learning, we drew a distinction between learning and performance. We found that having a habit, an association, a bit of knowledge did not necessarily result in its employment. For putting such information to use, some other kinds of situational variables (stimuli from inside or outside the body) were necessary. We can now expand this concept of a distinction between learning and performance in the present context. When discussing learning we ignored (because there is no adequate research support) a fact that is rather obvious, at least on a human level, that we are capable of learning many things about which we do nothing, and about which we may never do anything. In schools we might find some use for such information on examinations but, outside of the limited academic use, there may be no real way for practicing the knowledge. We learn, for example, that Columbus discovered America. We note that the teacher wears this or that garment on Tuesdays; that it is raining outside; or that Christmas will be on Monday in some year. Some of this information is potentially useful but may never be employed in any serious way. Similarly, we may hear a chance remark and remember it. We are all walking encyclopedias of useless facts which we never use and which do not necessarily guide our behavior. On the other hand, most of us are *forced* to behave in fashions that do not reflect any firm learned views about the worthiness of the effort. The parent is sometimes reduced, by his own imperfections, to threatening the child and saying "Do as I say, not as I do." The child may then learn what the parent says, and he may learn to behave in a certain manner that will escape punishment, but there never was nor will there necessarily ever be an integration between the behavior in question and some belief in the virtue of the parent's words. Most of us learn to obey traffic signals without necessarily endorsing their value for us.

The early behaviorists, like Watson, tended to ignore the internal behavior of people and depended for their predictions upon the external observable reactions. Thus if a person contributes to a community charity, his donation is all that counts. How he feels about giving the money is irrelevant even if he does not smile cheerfully as he hands over the check. We should have learned by now that internal behavior may be as important if not more so than external activity. If the donor gives only because he saves on his income tax or from some kind of pressure he may not be so charitable under different conditions. The children who do what teacher says may be "nice, obedient children" until conditions change. We need to emphasize as strongly as possible that superficial, official, public behavior may be learned, and practiced, without any wholehearted intoxication with the virtues involved. We can learn what someone says, we can mouth it with great verve, as does the actor on the stage, and believe not a word of it. While actions speak louder than words, we must not ignore the hidden, internal words that may lead to other and unexpected actions on some occasion.

Individual differences

Skinner promised to make everyone happy, creative, and productive. We have also learned, however, that not all people are born equal in the sense of physical equipment, sensitivities, brain health and structure. In whatever way we look at men, we find differences; differences in size, in health, in strength, in ability and agility, in problem solving, in adaptation readiness, in emotional stability, in whatever we can think of. Sticking for the moment to intellectual matters, we find that from 2 to 3 per cent of the people are doomed at birth to amount to very little as far as productive citizenship is concerned. We call this group "retarded." Earlier we learned that as we depart from this low level group, we get greater and greater percentages of more capable people until we reach the "average," then fewer and fewer bright people until we end up with another 2 or 3 per cent of people who might be labeled "very superior" or "genius." Such differences appear to be bound to some degree to inheritable factors and since we are unlikely to do anything about heredity, there is every likelihood that we will continue to have a range of capacities which will be maintained even if we raise the entire level of education and training. Putting it bluntly, somebody will always be smarter or "better" than somebody else. If this situation persists, will it be possible to achieve any genuine, real "improvement" in standards of living, in "happiness," in "creativity"? Will we not have the same situation of general dissatisfaction with us if someone else is more adjusted, more creative, happier, etc., in the new regime? It is characteristic of the American economy that when an individual's income rises, so do his expenses, and he finds himself, often enough, no better off in a relative sense. The new expenses he encounters may, in fact, make him work harder, worry more, and enjoy less than his previous lowly condition. We do not wish to press this point, but the fact of individual differences cannot be gainsaid. Such differences at present are part of the general dissatisfaction that leads reformers to suggest courses designed to "improve."

There is little doubt that the general level of education and many other aspects of life could be altered, changed, "improved." The question remains, however, whether anything can be done about individual differences, and if such differences are at the heart of any problems, whether the problems would not still remain.

Convergence and divergence

The facts of individual differences force us to take account of individuals and the lives of individuals, their own specific locales, habits, daily routines, their companions, in fact, their entire circumstances, when we wish to predict behavior. If psychology is to be a predictive science, it must decide whose behavior is to be predicted. Will it be the behavior of individuals or groups? Some group behavior is already reasonably well predicted. The most obvious example is the success of various "pollsters" who interview samples of the population to forecast voting behavior on election day. The margin of error in such predictions is relatively small and they can nowadays be relied on as fairly effective prognosticators. But pollsters never predict how an individual will vote. An individual in the election booth may, for any number of reasons, vote in a completely different fashion from that announced to his friends; still, the individual vote, in this context, does not matter. Enough people will vote according to whatever population sample they belong to to satisfy the pollsters. Restaurant owners too, if they are successful, predict group behavior. They know how much to buy of various kinds of foods and are rarely caught short with too little or with an oversupply that cannot be used again. No restaurateur would assume to predict any individual patron's order, yet he finds that, in the mass, his predictions are reasonably stable. If they are not, he goes into some other line of work. On holidays airlines and bus companies put on more help to handle the predicted crowd, and in general, businessmen predict well enough or they go out of business.

The basis of successful group prediction cannot be easily stated. We become aware, vaguely or otherwise, of characteristic repetitive patterns that are common to most of the population. Thus we recognize in a given culture that people eat three meals a day and we know the normal times of such activity. Most people go to sleep sometime after dark and get up sometime after sunup. Most people wear certain kinds of clothes for specific purposes and in specific seasons. The culture, we found, is the result of such conformity in the mass. Parents go to work to earn their families' livelihoods; children are sent to school; housewives do their marketing in fairly regular patterns. Rules are set up to facilitate business, traffic, and all activity. Nonconformists are relatively rare or we would have no culture pattern worth talking about. The arrangements for living become complicated and it becomes necessary to dovetail activities of the individuals to avoid conflict and disturbances. Children are in school when the parents are busy, for example, and not when parents are home as on weekends. When the majority of potential baseball fans are at work during the day, games are arranged at night. In many ways the dovetailing features of the culture force a regularity and predictability upon the populace. When the society needs more engineers it gets them at the expense of other kinds of specialists. Pressures of various kinds can be thought of as "converging" upon the population to enforce certain kinds of activities. If everyone else is sleeping, one can hardly get up a party. London (1946) has emphasized such "convergence" tendencies as accounting for the predictability of mass behavior. A given event occurs because everything necessary for its occurrence was at work toward that end. We may not be in position to know what all the specific factors are nor how they worked on any particular individual, but we can appreciate, after the event, and frequently enough before the event, why it must have happened in the way it did. When a Democratic Party landslide is observed in the country we look for explanations in terms of the weather, unhappiness among farmers because of prices, high taxes, desire for a change, or any of a great many possibilities which "converged" upon the situation and produced the result. Such "convergent" behavior is, in principle, predictable, says London, but, it applies to group activity for the most part, not to individuals. In our present discussion, we will use the terms "convergent" and "divergent" in somewhat different senses from London's usage. They are useful terms, however, for distinguishing between factors that tend to "average out" behavior and factors that make prediction difficult, if not impossible.

When we come to examine an individual's behavior, London argues that the psychologist must recognize "divergent" features. For any individual far too many factors are determining his behavior for anyone really to take into account. An individual is lost in a sea of other individuals and is buffeted about by any number of "chance" factors over which no one appears to have any specific control. Thus we might predict in a given city that there will be a number of accidents on Monday. Who will have them is unpredictable. Individual A gets up from bed, dresses, takes an extra cup of coffee (for no predictable reason, at least no reason anyone would bother taking into account), delays his departure by two minutes and eight seconds, gets into his car, cruises along in time to be stopped by a stop light at the fifth intersection he passes. He proceeds when the light changes and arrives at Corner X in time to be crushed by a truck just turning into the street. Had he not stopped for the light at the fifth intersection he would have been past the danger point and would have had no accident, at least, not with that truck. The extra cup of coffee did it. Another individual makes plans to observe his Golden Wedding anniversary, prepares the church, buys his wife a golden gift, and on the great day finds that the church burned down during the night, or his "best man" died. The best laid plans of men (mice do not make plans) "gang aft agley." Any individual is subject to so many possible sources of influence that it becomes impossible to take them all into account. A baby now being born may be the agency of some adult's future destruction. College professors, quietly minding their business, may be blissfully unaware that some ladies' club is now discussing the advisability of inviting them to address the annual installation meeting; or that officials in the nation's capital may be musing over their qualifications for some post in Karachi where a "good man is needed." In short, we have to study not only the individual in question but all the individuals who might have some potential influence on him in order to make any predictions. This is, *in principle,* impossible says London because we do not know who these others may be.

We might conclude this commentary with a reference to the old bit of wisdom: "Marriages are made in heaven." It should be readily appreciated that who marries whom is a most unpredictable matter. People meet by merest chance in airplanes or in dime stores, at dances, parties, in schools, on the street. A marriage may result, suitable or otherwise. For all anyone can predict, it might as well have been made in heaven. If marriage, which is certainly an event of no small significance, cannot be readily predicted, can one predict much of anything else of importance about an individual? One can recommend and encourage an individual to become a physician, for example. Most physicians do encourage their sons in that direction. Only 15 per cent of physicians' sons, however, enter that profession. What order of prediction is available here? In most cultures, as we pointed out in discussing personality, what a man does for his living is of paramount importance to many of his views, attitudes, behavior. Yet a man's occupation cannot be predicted even after he has embarked upon a training program or even after he has been actively engaged in it for some time, perhaps years. Ministers leave the ministry, teachers leave the classroom, West Pointers leave the army, a king abdicates "for the woman I love." The divergent variations of individual behavior suggest that prediction is quite out of the question on any significant level. Individuals do not behave in vacuums. Their behavior is like a chain reaction. One affects another, who affects a third, and so on. At this moment any number of events may be transpiring which will bring their fruits, sweet or sour, to our individual doorsteps. An undiplomatic word in some embassy may result in millions of individuals donning uniforms and manning the guns. Which individuals will don which uniforms and man which guns is a question that no one is going to try to answer.

The student might have become disturbed by London's predictable "convergence" and unpredictable "divergence," if he has been properly attentive to our earlier discussions of the nature of psychology. It is not the business of psychology to predict events. Rather is it the business of psychology to predict *behavior*. The difference between *behavior* and an *event* is not especially difficult to appreciate, even though both are difficult to define. An explosion is an event; pushing the plunger which sets off the explosion is behavior. An accident is an event; turning the wheel of a car so that a collision occurs is behavior. Psychologists do not predict future history. They predict responses of a very limited variety, responses related to specific stimulus conditions. Physicists could not predict a submarine passage under the North Pole. They could only talk about bouyancy, pressure, power, etc.

Psychology has never offered to predict Fourth-of-July activities on the basis of Christmas observations. All that we can ask of psychology is to explain why some behavior *could have been* predicted on the basis of the nature of the organism, its learning history, and the stimulus situation when the principles of psychology are taken into account. The predicted behavior in question is limited to the immediately present stimulus situation. If that situation changes, so must the prediction. Again we remind the student, no psychologist cares about predictions per se. Their only function is to test principles. These principles apply to *here* and *now* and not to *there* and *then.*

Prediction versus explanation

Throughout this text we were never concerned about predicting behavior. We were content to try to explain as much of it as possible. This is the real task of any science. It is not the burden of psychology as a science to improve the human race or ease its troubles any more than it is the burden of physics or biology. When the physicists build bombs that can blow up the earth we might become alarmed; some physicists regretted working on the first atom bombs, yet, under the circumstances, it was hardly their responsibility, in our culture, to do anything about it except make the best of all possible bombs. Actually the physicists were exploring the implications of atomic theory; the fact of the bomb was an *engineering* operation. Sometimes the culture may impose engineering obligations upon scientists as when chemists are asked to look into poison gases and biologists are asked to consider "biological warfare"; similarly psychologists have been asked to perform essentially engineering duties in times of social stress. But *as scientists,* neither physicists, biologists, nor psychologists, have any special obligations to society other than to investigate phenomena and try to explain them. Should someone find their explanations useful and attempt to apply them in building better refrigerators, bridges, can openers, or personalities, that is another problem, quite outside the scientist's domain. Many scientists are becoming concerned over the results of applications and are beginning to raise questions about "values." We cannot tell, yet, what the outcome of such questioning will be.

Psychologists are concerned about accounting for behavior, for explaining it, for relating it to conditions that prevail. They are interested in how man thinks, and not especially in what he thinks about except as this might be of interest in connection with the function of some other variable. Earlier in this text we made the point that psychologists are interested in man, not men. We still proclaim that interest. If, in the course of our considerations anything has been learned that might apply to men, the learner is welcome to it.

SUGGESTIONS FOR THE FUTURE STUDY OF PSYCHOLOGY

This text has been an introductory excursion into a vast territory. Only highlights have been observed and these frequently only superficially. We have taken a rapid tour over material that requires much additional study before really satisfactory appreciation can result. The tourist who "does" Notre Dame in one morning can hardly have caught more than a glimpse of its interest value. Similarly, reading a chapter on thinking or learning can hardly provide the basis for secure conclusions. The student who retains some interest in psychology or whose interest might have been sharpened by his studies is now ready for more detailed application. There are literally thousands of books and articles on psychological subjects that are inviting his attention. There are guides to psychological literature that the student might consult in looking into any special topic or problem. The *Psychological Abstracts,* for example, provide short summaries of all articles appearing in psychological journals. *The Annual Review of Psychology* summarizes the research reports on various topics every year. *Contemporary Psychology* is a monthly journal of book reviews. These three sources should provide starting points for further study.

There is no special or fixed curriculum for the student to follow but a stronger foundation is required than this book could provide by itself if the student is to prosper in his future investigations. A seemingly wise course to follow would be one of carefully perusing the references provided in each chapter and then embarking upon a serious study of some standard experimental and physiological psychology texts. There are excellent books available dealing with special topics like learning, thinking, and perception. The student might be ready to try some of these and would be well advised to do so before attempting what might appear more attractive subjects like "abnormal" and clinical studies. By gradual stages he might prepare himself for the more involved problems of personality and social psychology. In every case he will find that the literature is vast and the degree of specialized knowledge enormous. It is no longer possible for anyone to master the field of psychology as a whole, as it is no longer possible to master any field in a single lifetime. The day of the encyclopedist is over. One can no longer plan or hope to learn everything there is to know. We must constantly remind ourselves of the danger of a little knowledge and the corresponding necessity to know something of what is going on in other areas. The dangers of narrowness are equally punitive. The best that can be hoped for in psychology is some rough familiarity with the general field and then concentration in some relatively narrow interest area. One must reconcile himself to the breadth of the world's wisdom, little as we sometimes might think it is. Robert Oppenheimer (1958), in describing the current situation in science in general, actually spelled out the situation in psychology as well as anyone could state it. His remarks about science make an appropriate closing commentary for this text.

> To sum up the characteristics of scientific knowledge today, then, I would say that it is mostly new; it has not been digested; it is not part of man's common knowledge; it has become the property of specialized communities who may on occasion help one another but who, by and large, pursue their own way with growing intensity further and further from their roots in ordinary life.

References Cited

REFERENCES CITED

The date of each publication corresponds with the date given in the text. Where journal articles are cited, the practice of the American Psychological Association has been followed (see the Publication Manual).

ADLER, A. 1917. *Study of organ inferiority and its psychological compensation.* Washington: Nervous and Mental Disease Publishing Co.

ALBERTS, E., and D. EHRENFREUND. 1951. Transposition in children as a function of age. *J. exp. Psychol.* 41, 30–38.

ALEXANDER, F. 1950. *Psychosomatic Medicine.* New York: Norton.

ALLPORT, F. 1947. Institutional behavior. In T. Newcomb and E. Hartley (eds.), *Readings in Social Psychology.* New York: Holt.

ALLPORT, G. W. 1937. *Personality.* New York: Holt.

———. 1944. *A B C's of Scapegoating.* Chicago: Central YMCA College.

———. 1954. The historical background of modern social psychology. In G. Lindzey (ed.), *Handbook of Social Psychology.* Reading, Mass.: Addison-Wesley.

AMES, L. See GESELL, A. 1943, 1946.

ANTONITIS, J. J. See SCHOENFELD, W. N. 1950.

ASCH, S. 1955. Opinions and social pressure. *Sci. Amer.* 193, 31–35.

AX, A. F. 1953. The psychological differentiation between fear and anger in humans. *Psychosom. Med.* 15, 433–442.

BACK, K. See FESTINGER, L. 1950.

BARD, P. 1934. The neuro-humoural bases of emotional reactions. In C. Murchison (ed.), *Handbook of General Experimental Psychology.* Worcester, Mass.: Clark University Press.

BAUER, R. 1958. Motivation Research (Three reviews). *Contemp. Psychol.* 3, 292–294.

BEACH, F. 1951. Instinctive behavior. In S. S. Stevens (ed.), *Handbook of Experimental Psychology.* New York: Wiley.

BEARDSLEE, D. C. See DULANY, D. E. 1958.

BERGLUND, H. J., and H. L. NICHOLS. 1953. *It's Not All in Your Mind.* Greenwich, Conn.: North Castle.

BERGMANN, G. 1956. The contribution of John B. Watson. *Psychol. Rev.* 63, 265–276.

BERLIN, I. 1956. *The Age of Enlightenment.* New York: New American Library.

BERSH, P. J. See SCHOENFELD, W. 1950.

BIRCH, H. G. 1945. The relation of previous experience to insightful problem-solving. *J. comp. physiol. Psychol.* 38, 367–383.

BORING, E. G. 1933. *The Physical Dimensions of Consciousness.* New York: Appleton-Century-Crofts.

———. 1945. *Psychology for the Armed Services.* Washington: Infantry Journal.

———. 1950. *A History of Experimental Psychology* (2nd ed.). New York: Appleton-Century-Crofts.

———. 1957. When is human behavior predetermined. *Sci. Mon.* 84, 186–189.

BRADY, J. 1958. Ulcers in executive monkeys. *Sci. Amer.* 199, 95–100.

BRIDGES, K. M. B. 1932. Emotional development in early infancy. *Child Develpm.* 3, 324–354.

BROGDEN, W. J. See ROESSLER, R. L. 1943.

BROWN, H. O. See SMITH, S. M. 1947.

BROWN, J. F. 1936. *Psychology and the Social Order.* New York: McGraw-Hill.

BROWN, J. S. 1942. The generalization of approach responses as a function of stimulus intensity and strength of motivation. *J. comp. physiol. Psychol.* 33, 209–226.

———. 1953. Problems presented by the concept of acquired drives. In M. R. Jones (ed.), *Current Theory and Research in Motivation.* Lincoln: University of Nebraska Press.

BUGELSKI, B. R. See MILLER, N. E. 1948.

———. 1956. *The Psychology of Learning.* New York: Holt.

———, and T. C. CADWALLADER. 1956. A reappraisal of the "transfer and retroaction surface." *J. exp. Psychol.* 52, 360–366.

BŰHLER, C. 1933. The social behavior of children. In C. Murchison (ed.), *Handbook of Child Psychology.* Worcester, Mass.: Clark University Press.

BURTT, E. A. 1939. *The British Empiricists.* New York: Random House.

CADWALLADER, T. C. See BUGELSKI, B. R. 1956.

CAMUS, A. 1956. *The Rebel.* New York: Vintage Books.

CANNON, W. B. 1929. *Bodily Changes in Pain, Hunger, Fear, and Rage* (2nd ed.). New York: Appleton-Century-Crofts.

———. 1939. *The Wisdom of the Body* (rev. ed.). New York: Norton.

CARMICHAEL, L. 1954. The onset and early development of behavior. In L. Carmichael (ed.), *The Manual of Child Psychology.* New York: Wiley.

CARPENTER, C. R. 1934. A field study of the behavior and social relations of howling monkeys. *Comp. Psychol. Monogr.* 10, No. 2.

CHAPANIS, A., W. GARNER, and C. MORGAN. 1949. *Applied Experimental Psychology.* New York: Wiley.

CHOW, K. L. See NISSEN, H. W. 1951.

CLARKE, R. S., W. HERON, M. L. FETHERSTONEHAUGH, D. G. FORGAYS, and D. O. HEBB. 1951. Individual differences in dogs: Preliminary report on the effects of early experience. *Canad. J. Psychol.* 5, 150–156.

CONANT, J. B. 1953. *Modern Science and Modern Man.* New York: Anchor Books.

COURTS, F. A. 1939. Relations between experimentally induced muscular tension and memorization. *J. exp. Psychol.* 25, 235–256.

CRUTCHFIELD, R. S. See KRECH, D. 1948.

———. 1955. Conformity and character. *Amer. Psychologist.* 10, 191–198.

DALLENBACH, K. See JENKINS, J. G. 1924.

———. 1955. Phrenology versus psychoanalysis. *Amer. J. Psychol.* 68, 511–525.

DARWIN, C. 1955. *The Expression of Emotions in Man and Animals.* New York: Philosophical Library.

DENNIS, M. G. See DENNIS, W. 1940.

DENNIS, W., and M. G. DENNIS. 1940. The effect of cradling practices upon the onset of walking in Hopi children. *J. genet. Psychol.* 56, 77–86.

DEUTSCH, M., and H. B. GERARD. 1955. A Study of normative and informational social influences upon individual judgment. *J. abnorm. soc. Psychol.* 51, 629–636.

DE VALOIS, R. L. See DULANY, D. E. 1958.

DEWEY, J. 1910. *How We Think.* Boston: Heath.

———. 1938. *Logic.* New York: Holt.

DJILAS, M. 1958. *The New Class.* New York: Praeger.

DOANE, B. K. See HERON, W. 1954.

DOLLARD, J., L. W. DOOB, N. E. MILLER, O. H. MOWRER, and R. R. SEARS. 1939. *Frustration and Aggression.* New Haven: Yale University Press.

———. See MILLER, N. E. 1941.

———, and N. E. MILLER. 1950. *Personality and Psychotherapy.* New York: McGraw-Hill.

DOOB, L. W. 1935. *Propaganda: Its Psychology and Techniques.* New York: Holt.

———. See MAY, M. 1937.

———. See DOLLARD, J. 1939.

DUFFY, E. 1951. The concept of energy mobilization. *Psychol. Rev.* 58, 330–340.

DULANY, D. E., R. L. DE VALOIS, D. C. BEARDSLEE, and M. R. WINTERBOTTOM (eds.). 1958. *Contributions to Modern Psychology.* New York: Oxford University Press.

DUNBAR, H. F. 1943. *Emotions and Bodily Changes.* New York: Columbia University Press.

DUNNETTE, M. D. 1958. Use of the sugar pill by industrial psychologists. *Amer. Psychologist.* 12, 223–225.

ECCLES, J. C. 1953. *The Neurophysiological Basis of Mind.* New York: Oxford University Press.

EHRENFREUND, D. See ALBERTS, E. 1951.

EMMONS, W. H. See SIMON, C. W. 1956.

ERICKSON, C. W. 1958. Unconscious processes. In M. R. Jones (ed.), *Nebraska Symposium on Motivation.* Lincoln: University of Nebraska Press.

ESTES, W. K. 1944. Experimental studies of punishment. *Psychol. Monogr.* 57, No. 3.

EYSENCK, H. J. 1952. The effects of psychotherapy. *J. consult. Psychol.* 16, 319–324.

FAW, V. 1949. A psychotherapeutic method of teaching psychology. *Amer. Psychologist.* 4, 104–109.

FESTINGER, L., S. SCHACHTER, and K. BACK. 1950. *Social Pressures in Informal Groups.* New York: Harper.

FETHERSTONEHAUGH, M. L. See CLARKE, R. S. 1951.

FORGAYS, D. G. See CLARKE, R. S. 1951.

FREEMAN, F. 1934. *Individual Differences.* New York: Holt.

FRENCH, J. D. 1956. The reticular formation. *Sci. Amer.* 196, 55–60.

FREUD, A. 1937. *The Ego and the Mechanisms of Defense.* London: Hogarth Press.

FREUD, S. 1938. *A General Introduction to Psychoanalysis.* New York: Garden City.

———. 1938. *Totem and Taboo.* In A. Brill (ed.), *The Basic Writings of Sigmund Freud.* New York: Modern Library.

———. 1947. *Leonardo da Vinci.* New York: Random House.

GALAMBOS, R. 1959. Electrical correlates of conditioned learning. In M. A. B. Brazier (ed.), *The Central Nervous System and Behavior.* New York: Josiah Macy, Jr. Foundation.

GALTON, F. 1883. *Inquiries into the Human Faculty and Its Development.* London: Macmillan.

GARDNER, M. 1957. *Fads and Fallacies in the Name of Science.* New York: Dover.

GARNER, W. See CHAPANIS, A. 1949.

GARRETT, H. E. 1930. *Great Experiments in Psychology.* New York: Appleton-Century-Crofts.

GELDARD, F. 1953. *The Human Senses.* New York: Wiley.

GERARD, H. B. See DEUTSCH, M. 1955.

GESELL, A., and F. L. ILG. 1943. *The Infant and Child in the Culture of Today.* New York: Harper.

———, and ———. 1946. *The Child from Five to Ten.* New York: Harper.

———, ———, and L. AMES. 1956. *Youth.* New York: Harper.

———, and H. THOMPSON. 1941. Twins T and C from infancy to adolescence: A biogenetic study of individual differences by the method of co-twin control. *Genet. Psychol. Monogr.* 32, 575–580.

GIBB, C. 1954. Leadership. In G. Lindzey (ed.), *Handbook of Social Psychology.* Reading, Mass.: Addison-Wesley.

GOLDMAN, B. 1953. "The measurement of cohesiveness." Unpublished Ph.D. dissertation, The University of Buffalo.

GOODMAN, M. P. See SMITH, S. M. 1947.

GRAY, G. W. 1948. The great ravelled knot. *Sci. Amer.* 179, 26–39.

GREENSPOON, J. 1955. The reinforcing effect of two spoken sounds on the frequency of two responses. *Amer. J. Psychol.* 68, 409–416.

GUTHRIE, E. R. 1938. *The Psychology of Human Conflict.* New York: Harper.

———. 1944. Personality in terms of associated leaerning. In J. McV. Hunt (ed.), *Personality and the Behavior Disorders.* New York: Ronald.

———. 1952. *The psychology of learning* (rev. ed.). New York: Harper.

HALL, C. S. 1953. *The Meaning of Dreams.* New York: Harper.

———. 1954. *A Primer of Freudian Psychology.* New York: World.

HAMBURGER, V. 1957. The concept of development in biology. In D. B. Harris (ed.), *The Concept of Development.* Minneapolis: University of Minnesota Press.

HAMPSHIRE, S. 1956. *The Age of Reason.* New York: New American Library.

HARLOW, H. 1949. The formation of learning sets. *Psychol. Rev.* 56, 51–65.

HARSH, C. M. See HERBERT, M. J. 1944.

HARTSHORNE, H., and M. MAY. 1927. *Studies in Deceit.* New York: Macmillan.

HAVEMANN, E. 1957. *The Age of Psychology.* New York: Simon and Schuster.

HAYES, K. J. 1953. The backward curve: a method for the study of learning. *Psychol. Rev.* 60, 269–275.

HEBB, D. O. 1945. Man's frontal lobes. *Arch. Neurol. Psychiat.* 54, 10–24.

———. 1946. On the nature of fear. *Psychol. Rev.* 53, 259–276.

———. 1947. *The Organization of Behavior.* New York: Wiley.

———. See CLARKE, R. S. 1951.

———. 1951. The role of neurological ideas in psychology. *J. Pers.* 20, 39–55.

———. 1953. Heredity and environment in mammalian behavior. Reprinted in D. E. Dulany, *et al.* (eds.), *Contributions to Modern Psychology.* New York: Oxford University Press.

———. 1958. *A Textbook of Psychology.* Philadelphia: Saunders.

HEIDBREDER, E. 1946. The attainment of concepts. I. Terminology and methodology. II. The problem. *J. gen. Psychol.* 35, I: 173–189, II: 191–223.

HERBERT, M. T., and C. M. HARSH. 1944. Observational learning by cats. *J. comp. physiol. Psychol.* 37, 81–95.

HERNANDEZ-PEÓN, R., H. SHERRER, and M. JOUVET. 1956. Modification of brain activity during attention. *Science.* 123, 331–332.

HERON, W. See CLARKE, R. S. 1951.

———, B. K. DOANE, and T. H. SCOTT. 1954. Visual disturbances after prolonged perceptual isolation. *Canad. J. Psychol.* 8, 70–76.

HERSEY, J. *The Wall.* New York: Knopf.

HESS, E. H. See RAMSAY, A. 1954.

HOGBEN, L. 1938. *Science for the Citizen.* New York: Knopf.

HORNEY. K. 1939. *New Ways in Psychoanalysis.* New York: Norton.

HOVLAND, C. I. 1954. Effects of mass media of communication. In G. Lindzey (ed.), *Handbook of Social Psychology.* Reading, Mass.: Addison-Wesley.

———, and K. H. KURTZ. 1952. Experimental studies in rote learning: X. Pre-learning syllable familiarization and the length-difficulty relationship. *J. exp. Psychol.* 44, 31–39.

HULL, C. L. 1920. Quantitative aspects of the evolution of concepts. *Psychol. Monogr.* No. 123.

———. 1930. Knowledge and purpose as habit mechanisms. *Psychol. Rev.* 37, 511–525.

———. 1932. The goal-gradient hypothesis and maze learning. *Psychol. Rev.* 39, 25–43.

———. 1943. *The Principles of Behavior.* New York: Appleton-Century-Crofts.

HUXLEY, A. 1958. *Brave New World Revisited.* New York: Harper.

HYMOVITCH, B. 1952. The effects of experimental variation on problem solving in the rat. *J. comp. physiol. Psychol.* 45, 313–321.

ILG, F. L. See GESELL, A. 1943, 1946.

ISRAEL, H. E. See REES, H. J. 1935.

JACOBSEN, E. 1932. Electrophysiology of mental activities. *Amer. J. Psychol.* 44, 677–694.

JAMES, W. 1890. *The Principles of Psychology.* New York: Holt.

JENKINS, J. G. 1933. Instruction as a factor in incidental learning. *Amer. J. Psychol.* 45, 471–477.

———. 1948. Nominating technique as a method of evaluating air-group morale. *J. Aviat. Med.* 19, 12–19.

———, and K. DALLENBACH. 1924. Oblivescence during sleep and waking. *Amer. J. Psychol.* 35, 605–612.

JOHN, E. R. 1959. Comments on papers in M. A. B. Brazier (ed.), *The Central Nervous System and Behavior*. New York: Josiah Macy, Jr. Foundation.

JONES, E. 1947. *The Problem of Hamlet and the Oedipus Complex*. London: Vision Press.

———. 1953. *The Life and Work of Sigmund Freud*. Vols. 1–3. New York: Basic Books.

JONES, F. N. See WENGER, M. A. 1956.

JONES, M. C. 1924. The elimination of children's fears. *J. exp. Psychol.* 7, 382–390.

JONES, M. H. See WENGER, M. A. 1956.

JORDAN, A. M. 1933. Parental occupations and children's intelligence scores. *J. appl. Psychol.* 17, 103–119.

JOUVET, M. See HERNANDEZ-PEÓN, R. 1956.

KALLMAN, F. J., and B. ROTH. 1956. Genetic aspects of pre-adolescent schizophrenia. *Amer. J. Psychiat.* 112, 599–606.

KAMIN, L. J. See SOLOMON, R. L. 1953.

KATONA, G. 1940. *Organizing and Memorizing*. New York: Columbia University Press.

KATZ, B. 1952. The nerve impulse. *Sci. Amer.* 187, 55–62.

KETY, S. 1959. Biochemical theories of schizophrenia. *Science.* 129, Part I: 1528–1532; Part II: 1590–1596.

KINSEY, A. C., W. B. POMEROY, and C. E. MARTIN. 1948. *Sexual Behavior of the Human Male*. Philadelphia: Saunders.

KLEIN, M. 1956. *Mental Hygiene* (rev. ed.). New York: Holt.

KLEINBERG, O. 1938. Emotional expression in Chinese literature. *J. abnorm. soc. Psychol.* 33, 517–520.

KLUCKHOHN, C. 1958. *Mirror for Man*. New York: Premier Books.

KOFFKA, K. 1935. *Principles of Gestalt Psychology*. New York: Harcourt, Brace.

KOHLER, W. 1925. *The Mentality of Apes*. New York: Harcourt, Brace.

———. 1930. Grouping in visual perception. Abridged in D. E. Dulany, *et al.* (eds.), *Contributions to Modern Psychology*. New York: Oxford University Press.

———, and H. WALLACH. 1944. Figural aftereffects. *Proc. Amer. Phil. Soc.* 88, 269–357.

KONORSKI, J. 1949. Pavlov. *Sci. Amer.* 181, 44–47.

KRECH, D., and R. S. CRUTCHFIELD. 1948. *Theory and Problems of Social Psychology*. New York: McGraw-Hill.

KURTZ, K. H. See HOVLAND, C. I. 1952.

LAND, E. H. 1959. Experiments in color vision. *Sci. Amer.* 200, 84–99.

LANDIS, C. 1924. Studies of emotional reactions: General behavior and facial expression. *J. comp. Psychol.* 4, 447–501.

LASHLEY, K. 1929. *Brain Mechanisms and Intelligence.* Chicago: University of Chicago Press.

LEEPER, R. 1935. A study of a neglected portion of the field of learning—The development of sensory organization. *J. genet. Psychol.* 46, 61–73.

———. 1948. A motivational theory of emotion to replace emotion as disorganized response. *Psychol. Rev.* 55, 5–21.

LEONARD, I. N. 1953. *Flight into Space.* New York: Random House.

LEUBA, C. 1940. Images as conditioned sensations. *J. exp. Psychol.* 26, 345–351.

———, 1955. Toward some integration of learning theories: the concept of optimal stimulation. *Psychol. Rep.* 1, 27–33.

———. 1958. A new look at curiosity and creativity. *J. hi. Educ.* 29, 132–140.

LEWIN, K. 1935. *A Dynamic Theory of Personality.* New York: McGraw-Hill.

———. 1948. *Resolving Social Conflicts.* New York: Harper.

LIDDELL, H. S. 1944. Conditioned reflex method and experimental neurosis. In J. McV. Hunt (ed.), *Personality and the Behavior Disorders.* New York: Ronald.

LINDSLEY, D. B. 1951. Emotion. In S. S. Stevens (ed.), *Handbook of Experimental Psychology.* New York: Wiley.

LINDZEY, G. (ed.). 1954. *Handbook of Social Psychology.* Reading, Mass.: Addison-Wesley.

LIPPIT, R., and R. K. WHITE. 1943. The "social climate" of children's groups. In R. G. Barker, J. S. Kounin, and H. F. Wright (eds.), *Child Behavior and Development.* New York: McGraw-Hill.

LONDON, I. 1946. Some consequences for history and psychology of Langmuir's concept of divergence and convergence of phenomena. *Psychol. Rev.* 53, 170–188.

———. 1948. Free will as a function of divergence. *Psychol. Rev.* 55, 41–47.

LORENZ, K. Z. 1952. *King Solomon's Ring.* New York: Crowell.

LUCHINS, A. S. 1946. Classroom experiments on mental set. *Amer. J. Psychol.* 54, 295–298.

MAC CORQUODALE, K., and P. MEEHL. 1948. On a distinction between hypothetical constructs and intervening variables. *Psychol. Rev.* 55, 95–107.

MC CANDLESS, B. See SPIKER, C. 1954.

MC CORMICK, E. J. 1957. *Human Engineering.* New York: McGraw-Hill.

MC DOUGALL, W. 1915. *Social Psychology.* Boston: John W. Luce.

MC GEOCH, J. 1942. *The Psychology of Human Learning.* New York: Longmans, Green. Revised by A. L. Irion, 1952.

MC GRAW, M. 1935. *Growth: A Study of Johnny and Jimmy.* New York: Appleton-Century-Crofts.

MAHUT, H. 1958. Breed differences in the dog's behaviour. *Canad. J. Psychol.* 12, 35–44.

MAIER, N. 1933. An aspect of human reasoning. *Brit. J. Psychol.* 24, 144–155.

MARTIN, C. E. See KINSEY, A. C. 1948.

MASLOW, A. H. 1936. The role of dominance in the social and sexual behavior of infra-human primates. *J. genet. Psychol.* 48, 261–277.

———. 1956. Toward a humanistic society. *ECT,* 4, 10–22.

MAX, L. W. 1935. An experimental study of the motor theory of consciousness. III. Action current responses in deaf mutes during sleep, sensory stimulation, and dreams. *J. comp. Psychol.* 19, 469–486.

MAY, M. See HARTSHORNE, H. 1927.

———, and L. W. DOOB. 1937. *Competition and Co-operation.* Washington: Soc. Sc. Res. Counc. Bull. No. 25.

MEEHL, P. See MAC CORQUODALE, K. 1948.

———. 1958. See chapters in *What Then Is Man?* A symposium published by Concordia Publishing House, St. Louis, Mo.

MELZACK, R., and T. H. SCOTT. 1957. The effects of early experience on the response to pain. *J. comp. physiol. Psychol.* 50, 155–161.

MILLER, J. 1942. *Unconsciousness.* New York: Wiley.

MILLER, N. E. See DOLLARD, J. 1939.

———. 1944. Experimental studies of conflict. In J. McV. Hunt (ed.), *Personality and the Behavior Disorders.* New York: Ronald.

———. 1948. Studies of fear as an acquirable drive. I. Fear reduction as reinforcement in the learning of new responses. *J. exp. Psychol.* 38, 89–101.

———. See DOLLARD, J. 1950.

———, and B. R. BUGELSKI. 1948. Minor studies of aggression. II. The influence of frustration imposed by the in-group on attitudes expressed toward outgroups. *J. Psychol.* 25, 437–442.

———, and J. DOLLARD. 1941. *Social Learning and Imitation.* New Haven: Yale University Press.

MILOSZ, C. 1953. *The Captive Mind.* New York: Vintage Books.

MORENO, J. L. 1934. *Who Shall Survive?* Washington: Nervous and Mental Disease Publishing Co.

MORGAN, C. See CHAPANIS, A. 1949.

MORGANBESSER, S. 1958. Role and status of anthropological theories. *Science.* 128, 283–288.

MOWRER, O. H. See DOLLARD, J. 1939.

———. 1940. Anxiety reduction and learning. *J. exp. Psychol.* 27, 497–516.

NELSON, A. K. See PRATT, K. C. 1930.

NEWMAN, E. B. 1939. Forgetting of meaningful material during sleep and waking. *Amer. J. Psychol.* 52, 65–71.

NICHOLS, H. L. See BERGLUND, H. J. 1953.

NISSEN, H. W. 1954. The nature of drive as innate determinant of behavioral organization. In M. R. Jones (ed.), *Nebraska Symposium on Motivation.* Lincoln: University of Nebraska Press.

———, K. L. CHOW, and J. SEMMES. 1951. Effects of restricted opportunity for tactual, kinesthetic, and manipulative experience on the behavior of chimpanzee. *Amer. J. Psychol.* 64, 485–507.

NOBLE, C. E. 1952. An analysis of meaning. *Psychol. Rev.* 49, 403–418.

OGDEN, M. H. See TERMAN, L. M. 1957.

OLDS, J. 1956. Pleasure centers in the brain. *Sci. Amer.* 193, 105–116.

OPLER, M. 1957. Schizophrenia and culture. *Sci. Amer.* 197, 103–111.

OPPENHEIMER, R. The tree of knowledge. *Harper's.* 217, 55–60.

ORWELL, G. 1946. *Animal Farm.* New York: Harcourt, Brace.

OSGOOD, C. E. 1949. The similarity paradox in human learning: A resolution. *Psychol. Rev.* 56, 132–143.

———. 1953. *Method and Theory of Experimental Psychology.* New York: Oxford University Press.

———, G. J. SOUCI, and P. H. TANNENBAUM. 1957. *The Measurement of Meaning.* Urbana: University of Illinois Press.

PACKARD, V. 1957. *The Hidden Persuaders.* New York: McKay.

———. 1959. *The Status Seekers.* New York: McKay.

PATERSON, D. 1951. *Counseling and Psychotherapy.* Englewood-Cliffs, N.J.: Prentice-Hall.

PAVLOV, I. P. 1927. *Conditioned Reflexes* (trans. by G. V. Anrep). London: Oxford University Press.

PENFIELD, W., and T. RASMUSSEN. 1950. *The Cerebral Cortex of Man.* New York: Macmillan.

PETERS, C. C., and W. R. VAN VOORHIS. 1940. *Statistical Procedures and their Mathematical Bases.* New York: McGraw-Hill.

POMEROY, W. See KINSEY, A. C. 1948.

PRATT, C. C. 1937. *The Logic of Modern Psychology.* New York: Macmillan.

PRATT, K. C., A. K. NELSON, and K. H. SUN. 1930. *The Behavior of the Newborn Infant.* Columbus, Ohio: Ohio State University Studies in Psychology. No. 10, p. 237.

PRESTON, G. H. 1940. *Psychiatry for the Curious.* New York: Rinehart.

RAMSAY, A. O., and E. H. HESS. 1954. A laboratory approach to the study of imprinting. Wilson Bull. No. 66. 196–206. Reprinted in D. E. Dulany, *et al.* (eds.), *Contributions to Modern Psychology.* New York: Oxford University Press.

RASMUSSEN, T. See PENFIELD, W. 1950.

RAYNER, R. See WATSON, J. B. 1920.

RAZRAN, G. H. 1936. Salivating and thinking in different languages. *J. Psychol.* 1, 145–151.

———. 1957. Recent Russian psychology. *Contemp. Psychol.* 2, 93–100.

———. 1958. Materials on the conference on psychology. *Contemp. Psychol.* 3, 85–86.

REES, H. J., and H. E. ISRAEL. 1935. An investigation of the establishment of mental sets. *Psychol. Monogr.* 46, 1–26.

RIESEN, A. 1947. The development of visual perception in man and chimpanzee. *Science.* 106, 107–108.

———. 1950. Arrested vision. *Sci. Amer.* 183, 16–19.

RIGBY, W. K. 1954. Approach and avoidance gradients and conflict behavior in a predominantly temporal situation. *J. comp. physiol. Psychol.* 47, 83–89.

ROCK, I. 1957. The role of repetition in associative learning. *Amer. J. Psychol.* 70, 186–193.

ROESSLER, R. L., and W. J. BROGDEN. 1943. Conditioned differentiation of vasoconstriction to subvocal stimuli. *Amer. J. Psychol.* 56, 78–86.

ROGERS, C. 1951. *Client-centered Therapy.* Boston: Houghton Mifflin.

ROGERS, C. 1952. "Client-centered" psychotherapy. *Sci. Amer.* 187, 66–76.

———. 1956. Implications of recent advances in prediction and control of behavior. *Teachers College Record.* 316–322.

———, and B. F. SKINNER. 1956. Some issues concerning the control of human behavior. *Science.* 124, 1057–1065.

ROTH, B. See KALLMAN, F. J. 1956.

ROUSSEAU, J. J. 1762. *Emile* (any modern edition).

———. 1762. *The Social Contract* (any modern edition).

RUSSELL, W. A., and L. H. STORMS. 1955. Implicit verbal chaining in paired associate learning. *J. exp. Psychol.* 49, 287–293.

SALTZMAN, I. J. 1949. Maze learning in the absence of primary reinforcement: A study of secondary reinforcement. *J. comp. physiol. Psychol.* 42, 161–173.

SCARNES, J. 1956. *Amazing World of John Scarnes.* New York: Crown.

SCHACKTER, S. See FESTINGER, L. 1950.

SCHEINFELD, A. 1950. *The New You and Heredity.* Philadelphia: Lippincott.

SCHOENFELD, W. N., J. J. ANTONITIS, and P. J. BERSH. 1950. A preliminary study of training conditions necessary for secondary reinforcement. *J. exp. Psychol.* 40, 40–45.

SCHLOSBERG, H. 1953. Three dimensions of emotion. *Psychol. Rev.* 61, 81–88.

———. 1955. Three dimensions of emotion. In H. A. Abramson (ed.), *Problems of Consciousness.* Trans. Fifth. Conf. New York: Josiah Macy, Jr. Foundation.

SCHUTZ, W. C. 1958. *FIRO.* New York: Rinehart.

SCOTT, T. H. See HERON, W. 1954.

———. See MELZACK, R. 1957.

SEARS, R. R. 1936. Experimental studies of projection. I. Attribution of traits. *J. soc. Psychol.* 7, 151–163.

———. See DOLLARD, J. 1939.

———. 1943. Survey of objective studies of psychoanalytic concepts. *Soc. Sc. Research Counc. Bull.* 51.

SELYE, H. 1950. *The Physiology and Pathology of Exposure to Stress.* Montreal: ACTA Press.

SEMMES, J. See NISSEN, H. W. 1951.

SHEFFIELD, F. D. 1948. Avoidance training and the contiguity principle. *J. comp. physiol. Psychol.* 41, 165–177.

SHELDON, W. H. 1954. *Atlas of Men: A Guide for Somatotyping the Adult Male at All Ages.* New York: Harper.

SHERMAN, M. 1927. The differentiation of conditioned responses in infants. *J. comp. Psychol.* 1, 265–284.

SHERRER, H. See HERNANDEZ-PEÓN, R. 1956.

SHERRINGTON, C. 1950. *Man on his Nature.* New York: Anchor Books.

SHIRLEY, M. M. 1931. *The First Two Years: A Study of Twenty-five Babies.* Vol. I. *Postural and Locomotor Development.* Minneapolis: University of Minnesota Press.

SHLIEN, J. M. 1959. Mental testing and modern society. *The Humanist.* 19, 356–364.

SIIPOLA, E. M. 1935. A study of some effects of preparatory set. *Psychol. Monogr.* 46, 28–37.

SIMON, C. W., and W. H. EMMONS. 1956. EEG, "consciousness" and sleep. *Science.* 124, 1066–1069.

SKINNER, B. F. 1938. *The Behavior of Organisms.* New York: Appleton-Century-Crofts.

———. 1948. *Walden II.* New York: Macmillan.

———. 1951. How to teach animals. *Sci. Amer.* 185, 626–629.

———. 1953. *Science and Human Behavior.* New York: Macmillan.

———. 1955. Freedom and the control of men. *Amer. Schol.* (Winter), 1955–1956. Reprinted in B. F. Skinner, 1959. *Cumulative Record.* New York: Appleton-Century-Crofts.

———. 1956. A case history in scientific method. *Amer. Psychologist.* 11, 221–233.

———. See ROGERS, C. 1956.

SLATER, E. 1953. *Psychotic and Neurotic Illness in Twins.* Medical Research Council Special Report. No. 278. London: H.M. Stationery Office.

SMITH, R. P. 1957. *Where Did You Go? Out. What Did You Do? Nothing.* New York: Norton.

SMITH, S. M., H. O. BROWN, J. E. P. TOMAN, and M. P. GOODMAN. 1947. The lack of cerebral effects of d-Tubocurarine. *Anaesthesiology.* 8, 1–13.

SOLOMON, R. L. 1947. The role of effort in the performance of a distance discrimination by albino rats. *Amer. Psychologist.* 2, 301.

———, L. J. KAMIN, and L. C. WYNNE. 1953. Traumatic avoidance learning: The outcome of several extinction proceedings with dogs. *J. abnorm. soc. Psychol.* 48, 291–302.

SOUCI, G. J. See OSGOOD, C. E. 1957.

SPEARMAN, C. 1904. "General intelligence" objectively determined and measured. *Amer. J. Psychol.* 15, 201–293.

SPENCE, K. 1956. *Behavior Theory and Conditioning.* New Haven: Yale University Press.

SPIKER, C., and B. MC CANDLESS. 1954. The concept of intelligence and the philosophy of science. *Psychol. Rev.* 61, 255–265.

STAGNER, R. 1958. The gullibility of personnel managers. *Personel. Psychol.* 11, 347–357.

STORMS, L. H. See RUSSELL, W. A., 1955.

STREET, R. F. 1931. A gestalt completion test: A study of a cross-section of intellect. *Columbia University Teach. Coll. Contr. Educ.* No. 481.

STRONG, E. K. 1943. *Vocational Interests of Men and Women.* Stanford: Stanford University Press.

STRUGHOLD, H. 1953. See the report in LEONARD, I. N. 1953.

SUN, K. L. See PRATT, K. C. 1930.

TANNENBAUM, P. H. See OSGOOD, C. E. 1957.

TERMAN, L. 1954. Discovery and encouragement of exceptional talent. *Amer. Psychologist.* 9, 221–230.

———, and M. H. OGDEN. 1947. *The Gifted Child Grows Up.* Stanford: Stanford University Press.

THOMPSON, H. See GESELL, A. 1941.

THOREAU, H. 1854. *Walden.* New York: New American Library.

THORNDIKE, E. L. 1898. An experimental study of the association process in animals. *Psychol. Monogr.* 2, No. 8.

———. 1932. *The Fundamentals of Learning.* New York: Teachers College, Columbia University Press.

———, and R. S. WOODWORTH. 1901. The influence of improvement in one mental function upon the efficiency of other functions. *Psychol. Rev.* 8, 247–261.

THURSTONE, L. L. 1938. Primary mental abilities. *Psychometr. Monogr.* No. 1. Chicago: University of Chicago Press.

———. 1948. Psychophysical methods. In T. G. Andrews (ed.), *Methods of Psychology.* New York: Wiley.

———. 1959. *The Measurement of Values.* Chicago: University of Chicago Press.

TINKLEPAUGH, O. L. 1928. An experimental study of representative factors in monkeys. *J. comp. Psychol.* 8, 197–236.

TOLMAN, E. C. 1938. The determiners of behavior at a choice point. *Psychol. Rev.* 45, 1–41.

———. 1949. There is more than one kind of learning. *Psychol. Rev.* 56, 144–155.

TOMAN, J. E. P. See SMITH, S. M. 1947.

TRAGER, G. L. 1956. Language. *Encyclopedia Britannica.* XIII, 696–702.

TUFTS COLLEGE INSTITUTE OF APPLIED EXPERIMENTAL PSYCHOLOGY. 1952. *Handbook of Human Engineering Data.* Tufts College.

TYLER, L. E. 1956. *The Psychology of Human Differences* (2nd ed.). New York: Appleton-Century-Crofts.

UNDERWOOD, B. 1957. *Psychological Research.* New York: Appleton-Century-Crofts.

VAN VOORHIS, W. R. See PETERS, C. C. 1940.

VIERECK, P. 1958. The unadjusted man. *Sat. Rev.* 41, 13–15.

VOECKS, V. 1948. Postremity, recency, and frequency as bases for prediction in the maze situation. *J. exp. Psychol.* 38, 495–510.

VON FRISCH, K. 1955. *The Dancing Bees.* New York: Harcourt, Brace.

WALLACH, H. See KOHLER, W. 1944.

———. 1948. Brightness constancy and the nature of achromatic colors. *J. exp. Psychol.* 38, 310–324. Abridged in D. E. Dulany, *et al.* (eds.), *Contributions to Modern Psychology.* New York: Oxford University Press.

WALTER, W. G. 1953. *The Living Brain.* New York: Norton.

WATERS, R. H. 1958. Behavior: datum or abstraction. *Amer. Psychologist.* 13, 278–282.

WATSON, J. B. 1930. *Behaviorism* (rev. ed.). New York: Norton.

———, and R. RAYNER. 1920. Conditioning of emotional reactions. *J. exp. Psychol.* 3, 1–14.

WECHSLER, D. 1942. *Mental Health in Later Maturity.* Supplement No. 168 to Public Health Report, Federal Security Agency. U.S. Public Health Service. Washington: Government Printing Office. Pp. 43–52.

WEISS, F. 1950. Physical complaints of neurotic origin. In E. Hartley, H. Birch, and R. Hartley (eds.), *Outside Readings in Psychology* (rev. ed.). New York: Crowell.

WEITZENHOFFER, A. M. 1953. *Hypnotism.* New York: Wiley.

WENGER, M. A., F. N. JONES, and M. H. JONES. 1956. *Physiological Psychology.* New York: Holt.

WERTHAM, F. 1954. *The Seduction of the Innocent.* New York: Rinehart.

WEVER, E. G. 1949. *Theory of Hearing.* New York: Wiley.

WHITE, R. K. See LIPPIT, R. 1943.

WILLIAMS, R. J. 1958. *Biochemical Individuality.* New York: Wiley.

WINTERBOTTOM, M. R. 1958. See DULANY, D. E. 1958.

WOLFE, W. B. 1930. The Adlerian approach to personality. In *The Pattern of Life.* New York: Rinehart.

WOLPE, J. 1952. Primary stimulus generalization. *Psychol. Rev.* 59, 8–10.

———. 1954. Reciprocal inhibition as the main basis of psychotherapeutic effects. *Arch. Neurol. Psychiat.* 72, 205–226.

WOODWORTH, R. S. See THORNDIKE, E. L. 1901.

———. 1931. *Contemporary Schools of Psychology* (rev. ed.). New York: Ronald.

WYNNE, L. C. See SOLOMON, R. 1953.

Index to Names and Subjects

INDEX TO NAMES AND SUBJECTS

The page references given throughout this index indicate only the page on which the discussion begins.